Encyclopedia of
AFRICAN HISTORY AND CULTURE

Encyclopedia of
AFRICAN HISTORY
AND CULTURE

VOLUME II

AFRICAN KINGDOMS

(500 TO 1500)

Willie F. Page, Ph.D.

Emeritus Professor of Africana Studies,
Brooklyn College

A Learning Source Book

☑®
Facts On File, Inc.

Encyclopedia of African History and Culture,
Volume 2: African Kingdoms (500 to 1500)

Copyright © 2001 by The Learning Source, Ltd.

A Learning Source Book
Editorial: Brian Ableman, Edward C. Haggerty,
Bertram Knight, Christopher Roberts
Consultant: Emilyn Brown

Facts On File, Inc.
132 West 31st Street
New York NY 10001

Library of Congress Cataloging-in-Publication Data

Page, Willie F., 1929-
    The encyclopedia of African history and culture / Willie F. Page.
        p. cm.
    "A Learning Source Book"
    Includes bibliographical references and index.
    Contents: v. 1. Ancient Africa — v. 2. African kingdoms — v. 3. From conquest to colonization.
    ISBN 0-8160-4472-4 (alk. paper)
    1. Africa — Encyclopedias. I. Facts on File, Inc. II. Title

DT3 .P27 2001
960'.03--dc21

00-063613

Facts On File books are available at special discounts when purchased in bulk quantities for businesses, associations, institutions or sales promotions. Please call our
Special Sales Department in New York at (212) 967-8800 or (800) 322-8755.

You can find Facts On File on the World Wide Web at
http://www.factsonfile.com

Design: Joan Toro, Joseph Mauro III
Illustrations: Pam Faessler
Maps: Dale Williams

Printed in the United States of America

V B 10 9 8 7 6 5 4 3 2 1

This book is printed on acid-free paper.

For my wife, Grace,
and my sons, Ed & Chris

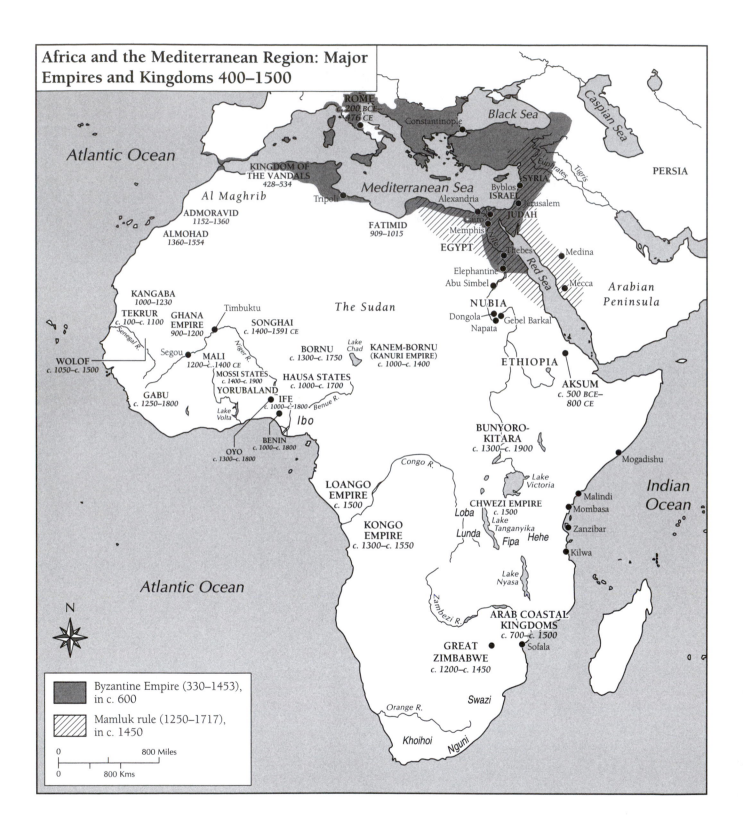

Africa and the Mediterranean Region: Major Empires and Kingdoms 400–1500

Atlantic Ocean

ROME
200 BCE–
476 CE

Constantinople

Black Sea

Caspian Sea

KINGDOM OF
THE VANDALS
428–534

Mediterranean Sea

Byblos
Alexandria
SYRIA
ISRAEL
Jerusalem
JUDAH

Euphrates

Tigris

PERSIA

Al Maghrib

Tripoli

FATIMID
909–1015

Cairo
Memphis

EGYPT

Thebes

Medina

Elephantine
Abu Simbel

Red Sea

Nile R.

Mecca

*Arabian
Peninsula*

ADMORAVID
1152–1360

ALMOHAD
1360–1554

KANGABA
1000–1230

The Sudan

NUBIA

Dongola
Gebel Barkal
Napata

TEKRUR
c. 100–c. 1100

GHANA
EMPIRE
900–1200

Timbuktu

SONGHAI
c. 1400–1591 CE

Senegal R.

Niger R.

Segou

MALI
1200–c. 1400 CE

BORNU
c. 1300–c. 1750

*Lake
Chad*

KANEM-BORNU
(KANURI EMPIRE)
c. 1000–c. 1400

ETHIOPIA

WOLOF
c. 1050–c. 1500

MOSSI STATES
c. 1400–c. 1900
YORUBALAND

HAUSA STATES
c. 1000–c. 1700

AKSUM
c. 500 BCE–
800 CE

GABU
c. 1250–1800

IFE
c. 1000–c. 1800

*Lake
Volta*

Benue R.

Ibo

BUNYORO-
KITARA
c. 1300–c. 1900

OYO
c. 1300–c. 1800

BENIN
1000–c. 1800

Congo R.

Mogadishu

LOANGO
EMPIRE
c. 1500

*Lake
Victoria*

Loba

CHWEZI EMPIRE
c. 1500
*Lake
Tanganyika*

*Indian
Ocean*

Malindi
Mombasa

Zanzibar

KONGO
EMPIRE
c. 1300–c. 1550

Lunda

Fipa

Hehe

Kilwa

*Lake
Nyasa*

Atlantic Ocean

N

Zambezi R.

ARAB COASTAL
KINGDOMS
c. 700–c. 1500

Sofala

GREAT
ZIMBABWE
c. 1200–c. 1450

Swazi

Orange R.

Byzantine Empire (330–1453),
in c. 600

Mamluk rule (1250–1717),
in c. 1450

Khoihoi

Nguni

0   800 Miles

0   800 Kms

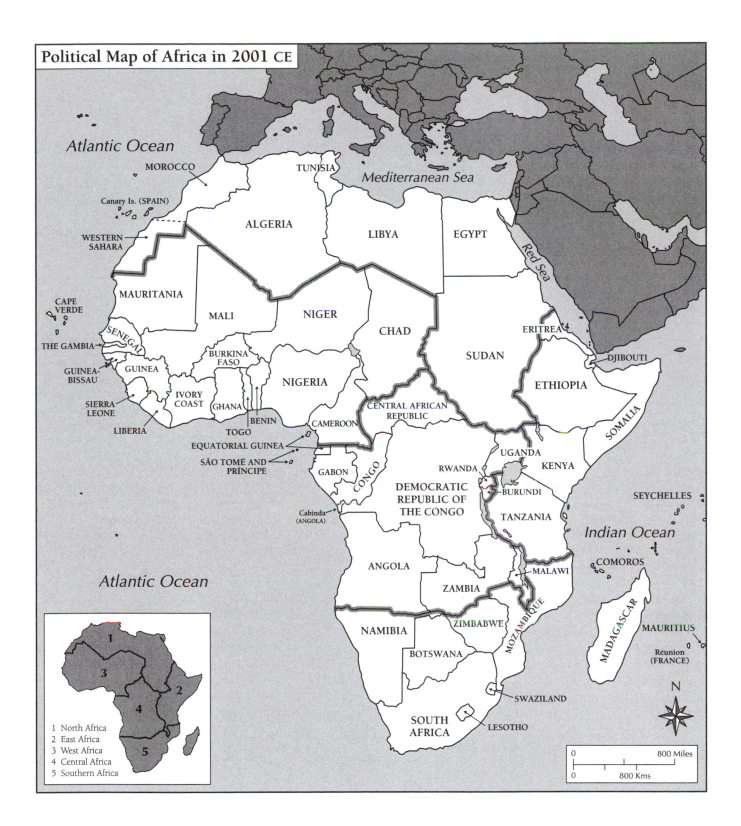

Political Map of Africa in 2001 CE

Atlantic Ocean

MOROCCO
TUNISIA
Mediterranean Sea

Canary Is. (SPAIN)

ALGERIA
LIBYA
EGYPT

WESTERN SAHARA

Red Sea

MAURITANIA

CAPE VERDE

MALI
NIGER
CHAD
ERITREA

SENEGAL

THE GAMBIA

SUDAN
DJIBOUTI

GUINEA-BISSAU
GUINEA
BURKINA FASO

SIERRA LEONE
IVORY COAST
NIGERIA
ETHIOPIA

GHANA
CENTRAL AFRICAN REPUBLIC
SOMALIA

LIBERIA
TOGO
BENIN

CAMEROON

EQUATORIAL GUINEA

UGANDA
KENYA

SÃO TOMÉ AND PRÍNCIPE

GABON
CONGO
RWANDA

Cabinda (ANGOLA)

DEMOCRATIC REPUBLIC OF THE CONGO
BURUNDI

SEYCHELLES

TANZANIA

Indian Ocean

Atlantic Ocean

ANGOLA
MALAWI
COMOROS

ZAMBIA

ZIMBABWE
MOZAMBIQUE
MADAGASCAR
MAURITIUS

NAMIBIA

Réunion (FRANCE)

BOTSWANA

N

SWAZILAND

SOUTH AFRICA
LESOTHO

1 North Africa
2 East Africa
3 West Africa
4 Central Africa
5 Southern Africa

0   800 Miles

0   800 Kms

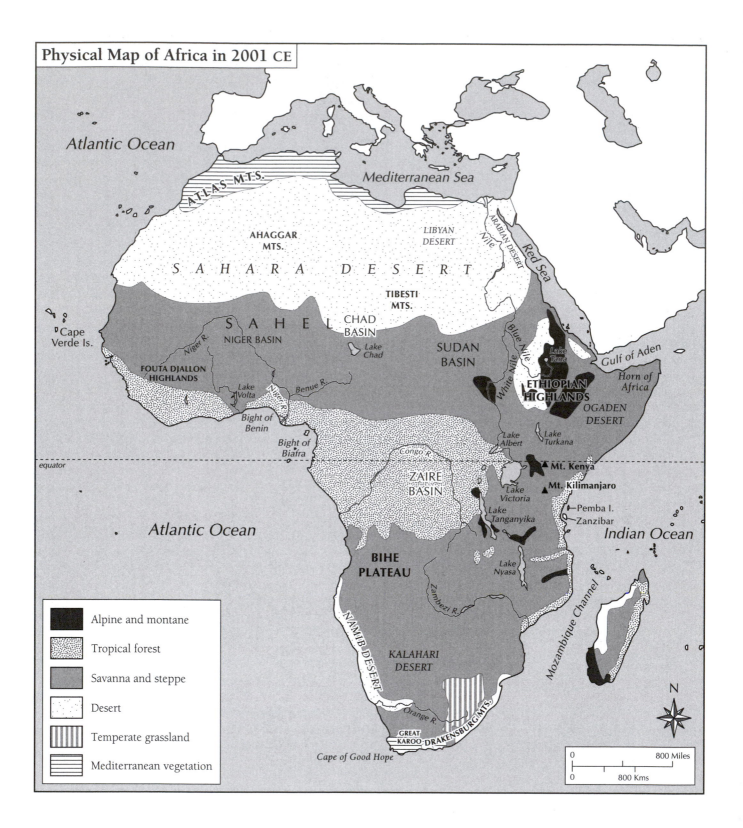

Physical Map of Africa in 2001 CE

Atlantic Ocean

Mediterranean Sea

ATLAS MTS.

AHAGGAR MTS.

LIBYAN DESERT

Nile

Arabian Desert

Red Sea

S A H A R A   D E S E R T

TIBESTI MTS.

Cape Verde Is.

S A H E L

NIGER BASIN

Niger R.

FOUTA DJALLON HIGHLANDS

Lake Volta

Niger R.

Benue R.

CHAD BASIN

Lake Chad

SUDAN BASIN

Blue Nile

White Nile

Lake Tana

ETHIOPIAN HIGHLANDS

Gulf of Aden

Horn of Africa

OGADEN DESERT

Bight of Benin

Bight of Biafra

equator

Congo R.

ZAIRE BASIN

Lake Albert

Lake Turkana

▲ Mt. Kenya

Lake Victoria

▲ Mt. Kilimanjaro

Pemba I.

Zanzibar

Atlantic Ocean

Lake Tanganyika

Indian Ocean

BIHE PLATEAU

Lake Nyasa

Zambezi R.

Mozambique Channel

NAMIB DESERT

KALAHARI DESERT

Orange R.

GREAT KAROO

DRAKENSBURG MTS.

Cape of Good Hope

N

Alpine and montane

Tropical forest

Savanna and steppe

Desert

Temperate grassland

Mediterranean vegetation

0   800 Miles

0   800 Kms

Contents

List of Entries

List of Images

Maps

Introduction

There is no era in Africa's history that exemplifies its greatness and grandeur more than the medieval, or middle, period, from 450 to 1500 CE. This period is, on the one hand, replete with activity, from the great Bantu Migration—the largest movement of peoples in human history—to the development of centralized states. It is also an era that saw the rise of many of Africa's most noteworthy kingdoms. Some, like Great Zimbabwe, Ghana, and Mali, are well known. Others, however, are less familiar but equally fascinating. There is, for example, Mapungubwe, the kingdom that preceded Great Zimbabwe, which, well before the twelfth century, grew into an urban center with a population of more than 10,000. There also is the Kongo Kingdom of the fourteenth century, with its complex system of royal rule that lasted for almost 200 years, and the Wolof Empire, which maintain a rigid, autocratic caste system and a military so powerful that, by the sixteenth century, it could assemble an army of 10,000 cavalry and more than 100,000 foot soldiers. Even more remarkable was the Songhai Empire, which by the fifteenth and sixteenth centuries became the most extensive empire in West Africa, controlling even the once-dominant empires of Ghana and Mali.

This period is also of great interest because of the links that were established with the world outside of Africa. It was during these years, for example, that Islam spread through Africa, creating a bond between the continent and realms as far away as Spain, Turkey, and Persia. It was also during this medieval period that the great trans-African trade routes developed, carrying African products to the world at large but also bringing to Africa goods from lands as far away as China. The rise of these trade routes also caused the growth of the fabled cities of Gao, Timbuktu, and Kano, which contributed to the mystique that came to surround much of Africa. North-south trade and Indian Ocean trade brought gold, and ivory and other trade goods from Africa to markets along the Mediterranean Sea and across vast oceans.

Prior to the end of the fifteenth century, the major item of trade was gold. Indeed, the presence of gold in Africa was a magnet that drew European explorers to the continent, an event that would change Africa forever. The fourteenth century pilgrimage to Mecca by Mali's Mansa Musa I attracted the attention of people throughout the old world. It has been estimated that Mansa Musa assembled between 24,000 and 30,000 pounds of gold dust for his *hajj*, during which he dispersed so much gold that he almost ruined the gold market in Cairo. Tales about the wealth of Mansa Musa I circulated around Europe for more than a century before Prince Henry the Navigator of Portugal commissioned explorers to find a route to West Africa's coast, and the quest for African gold clearly was one of the primary motives behind this Portuguese exploration. The sheer volume of the gold acquired in this effort is staggering, with estimates running to as much as one hundred and forty-three tons between the years 1472 and 1696—and that is for Portugal alone!

Gold, of course, was not the only magnet that drew Europeans to Africa. Another one—and the one that scarred the continent, its people, and his history more than any other—was the traffic in human beings. The domestic slave trade in Africa was almost totally overshadowed by the gold trade during the middle period. And while a thorough discussion of slavery in Africa during the middle period is not feasible in this introduction, a few words are necessary to clear up some misconceptions. The vastness of Africa and the diversity of its peoples make it impossible to list all the various forms of bondage that existed. However, scholars of African culture have isolated a few universal factors, most of which differed significantly from the brutal form of slavery practiced in the Americas from the sixteenth to the nineteenth century.

In Africa, slaves traditionally were not chattel, or property, and they enjoyed certain rights. (Among the most important of these rights was the right not to be separated from their families.) In general, slaves had been captured in war, convicted of a serious crime, or had been found guilty of defying or violating traditional mores such as disrespecting the ancestors. As Basil Davidson, the eminent scholar of African history, has noted, the bondage that was traditionally found in African societies involved a kind of enforced service, often by men captured in war or even by certain lawbreakers—something far different from the "plantation slavery" that was put into practice in the Americas. There even were individuals held in a kind of debt bondage, bound for a specified period of time in order to settle an outstanding debt of some kind. As a result, as Suzanne Miers and Igor Kopytoff have found, in many African societies, the distinction between enslaved and free individuals was so fluid that, in some cases, people considered to be "slaves" owned slaves themselves, while some individuals considered to be "free" were able to be bought or sold.

Unfortunately, European observers—and even scholars—often did not see or even ignored these complex levels of social stratification. As a result, they lumped all traditional African forms of bondage under the convenient title of "slavery," a misstatement as severe as a commentator on European medieval or Renaissance history overlooking Europe's complex social strata of serfs, peons, vassals, helots, and villeins and simply calling all of these individuals "slaves." Also ignored (or at least not widely acknowledged) is the fact that, because slavery was, in various forms, practiced throughout the world during this period, there actually was a slave trade bringing European and Asian slaves *into* both North and West Africa at this time.

While the topic of slavery is crucial to this era—and is virtually inexhaustible— it is not the focus of this volume. Instead, we have tried to present the full scope of African history and culture during this period. And it is our hope that in doing so we can help readers understand and appreciate the grandeur of the continent, its people, and its history.

How to Use This Book

Throughout, the attempt has been made to make this encyclopedia as accessible and easy to use as possible. Entries are arranged alphabetically letter-by-letter, usually according to the most commonly found spelling or representation of that spelling.

The question of spelling, of course, is always a major question when dealing with languages that, for thousands of years, have been oral rather than written. In general, we have tried to give as many common variants as possible, but only within the entries themselves. For easy access to variant and alternate spellings, readers should consult the index, which lists and cross-references all of the alternate spellings that appear in the text. There is a glossary that will help with this as well.

In general, the entries are written to provide the reader with the basic information needed. To help those who wish to go further, we have linked the contents of each entry with other entries via cross-references. (Cross-references always are shown in SMALL CAPITALS.) Many of these cross-references are embedded within the text of the entries. But many entries also conclude with **See also** references that direct readers to other entries in one of the volumes of the encyclopedia. When using these cross-references, readers should simply be aware that cross-references embedded in the text and in the See also section use only word forms that agree with the entry word itself.

Many entries also include suggestions for further reading that guide readers as they search for more in-depth knowledge of a particular area. On the whole, we have included among these works those that are most likely to be easily obtained in libraries, which means that, for the most part, they have been published fairly recently and by publishers whose products are readily available for the general reader.

The volume also contains several appendices of timelines, maps, and a glossary. At the end of Volume 3 there also is a cumulative index and a bibliographic section of further readings. These should provide handy tools for readers of all kinds and interests.

Time Line

c. 100–600	Aksum flourishes.
400–1400	Ga people inhabit southeastern area of present-day Ghana.
	Hutu begin to migrate into area occupied by the Twa, around Lake Kivu.
450	Jenne-Jeno becomes a major settlement.
c. 500	Taghaza, in central Sahara, becomes major point on gold and salt trade routes.
500–1000	Bantu speakers displace indigenous Twa people in Rwanda.
500	Byzantine emperor Justinian takes control of northern Africa.
	Migrations of Bantu-speaking peoples continues through much of central Africa.
541	Christian era begins in Nubia.
c. 600	Aksumites relocate to Amhara and Shoa.
	Takedda becomes the major trading center in western Sudan.
622	The prophet Muhammad flees from Mecca to Medina; the Hejira (Hijra) marks the start of the Muslim calendar.
c. 650	Muslims conquer northern Africa.
c. 700	Soninke people found al-Ghaba.
	Arabs conquer North Africa. After much resistance, the Berber people accept Islam.
	Kaniaga Kingdom flourishes in the area of present-day Mali.

c. 800	City of Zeila serves as a trading nexus between Ethiopia and Arabia.
	Songhai people found the city of Gao.
	Beja people begin to take control of Eritrea from Aksumites.
c. 800–c. 1846	Sefuwa dynasty rules in Kanem-Bornu.
850	Bornu is founded in the area of present-day Nigeria.
	Ile-Ife is established in the southwestern region of modern-day Nigeria.
900–1100	Audaghost flourishes as the terminus of trans-Saharan trade route.
900–1240	Ghana Empire flourishes.
900–1300	City of Sijilmasa flourishes as a trading center in Morocco.
c. 900–c. 1700	Tekrur Kingdom flourishes in western Africa.
915	The Indian Ocean city of Sofala, the oldest port in southern Africa, is founded.
950	Karanga people establish their kingdom in eastern Zimbabwe.
969	Fatimids take power in Egypt.
	Cairo is founded.
970	Mosque of al-Azhar is built in Cairo.
c. 1000	Akan peoples migrate to the Guinea coast.
	Bagauda founds the Hausa state of Kano.

c. 1000	Barmandana brings Islam to Mali.
	Legendary founding of Old Oyo by Prince Oranmiyan.
	Four trans-Saharan trade routes carry goods across Africa.
	Kangaba Kingdom established in western Sudan; it becomes the foundation of the Mali Empire.
1000–1200	Hausa states are established.
	Mombasa founded by Arab merchants.
	Mining of salt begins at Idjil in modern-day Mauritania.
c. 1050	The Sanhaja Berbers found the Almoravid Empire; by 1150 it controlled the Maghrib and Muslim Spain.
c. 1063	Tunka Manin rules in the Ghana Empire.
c. 1075	Mapungubwe is founded in southern Africa.
1085–1097	Mai Umme converts Kanem-Bornu to Islam.
c. 1100	Tuaregs found a seasonal camp at Timbuktu.
	Agaw people take control of Ethiopia.
	Bamaka, in Mali, becomes an important center of Islamic learning.
	The city-state of Kilwa is founded along the Indian Ocean.
1100–1200	Golden age of Gedi as a trading city begins.
	Zagwe dynasty rules in Ethiopia.
c. 1133	Tuaregs under Chief Akil rule Timbuktu.
1147	The Berber Almohad Empire, inspired by Ibn Tumart and led by al-Mumin, supplants the Almoravid Empire in the Maghrib and Spain.
c. 1150–1270	Jenne is founded near Jenne-Jeno.
	Zagwe dynasty rules in Ethiopia.
	Kilwa becomes a major trading port on the East African coast.
	Sumanguru establishes the Kaniaga Kingdom.
c. 1200	Zagwe emperor Lalibela begins construction of the rock churches.
1200–1500	Tutsi people migrate, possibly from the upper Nile Valley, into Hutu lands in present-day Burundi and Rwanda.
1250–1800	Gabu Kingdom flourishes in West Africa.
1221–1259	Dibbalemi rules as *mai*, or king, of Kanem-Bornu in West Africa.
1230–1255	Sundiata rules in Mali.
c. 1235–1250	Sundiata conquers Ghana Empire and founds Mali Empire.
1235–1400	Mandinka Empire of Mali flourishes.
c. 1250	Great Zimbabwe is established in southern Africa; the Hill Complex and the Great Enclosure are built.
1270	Yekuno Amiak overthrows the Zagwe dynasty in Ethiopia.
1270–1700	Solomonic dynasty rules Ethiopia.
1275–1400	Sabbatarians are in conflict with the state in Ethiopia.
1285–1300	Mansa Sakura restores lost glory to Mali.
c. 1300	Husuni Kubwa Palace is built in present-day Tanzania; it is the largest building in sub-Saharan Africa at the time.
	Tanga is established by Persian merchants as a trading port linking the interior of East Africa with lands as far away as China.
	Wolof people migrate into the area of present-day Senegal and Gambia and establish the Wolof Empire.
	Timbuktu in Mali flourishes as a center of the trans-Saharan gold and salt trade and as a Muslim center of learning.

1307–1337	Mansa Musa I reigns in Mali.
	Kongo Kingdom is formed.
1314–1344	Emperor Siyon expands Christian Ethiopia.
1324	Emperor Mansa Musa of Mali begins his hajj to Mecca.
1341-1360	Mansa Sulayman rules during height of Mali Empire's political and economic power.
1349–1385	Sarki Yaji becomes the first Muslim Hausa king.
c. 1350–1400	Bachwezi rule in Kitara in East Africa.
	Buganda founded; it eventually becomes the most powerful kingdom in East Africa.
	Chwezi Kingdom rises.
	Kanem-Bornu enters a period of decline.
c. 1400	Akan begin to develop organized states along the Guinea coast.
	Bonny becomes an important Atlantic coast trading center.
c. 1400–1590	Songhai Empire flourishes in eastern Mali and western Niger.
	Jenne-Jeno is no longer a functioning city.
	The mines at Taghaza in the Sahara near Morocco become the main source of salt in West Africa.
1404, 1433	Chinese admiral Cheng-Ho voyages to Africa.
1434	The first Portuguese explorers sail past Cape Bojador in West Africa and began to exploit the region, especially for African captives.
1441	Portuguese begin to enslave black Africans.
1443–1468	Tuaregs regain control of Timbuktu.
1448	Portuguese build the Arguin trading fort off the western coast of Africa.

1448–1450	Bornu becomes a major gold-producing state.
	Mutota Mwenematapa founds the Mutapa state in southern Africa.
1450-1600	Lunda Kingdom established in central Africa.
1465	Muhammad Rumfa makes Islam the official religion of Kano.
1468	Sunni Ali captures Timbuktu for the Songhai Empire.
c. 1475–1490	Sunni Ali expands the Sonhghai Empire.
	Wagadugu becomes the capital of the Mossi states.
1473–1480	Ewuare the Great rules in Benin.
c. 1480	Portugese explorers land on the coast of the Kongo Kingdom.
c. 1490	The Changamire Empire, later the most powerful central African kingdom until its fall c. 1830, is established.
	Nzinga Mbumba, ruler of the Kongo Kingdom, converts to Christianity and takes the name of Afonso I.
1497–1498	Vasco da Gama of Portugal sails around Africa to India.
1500	Queen Eleni dominates Ethiopian political and religious affairs.
	Bunyoro-Kitara Kingdom is formed in East Africa.
1502	Vasco da Gama establishes Portuguese presence in Mozambique and Sofala.
c. 1505	Portugese take over Kilwa, the preeminent East Coast trading city for more than 300 years.
1513	Askia Muhammad Touré of Songhai captures all the Hausa States except Kano. The Songhai Empire reaches its fullest territorial extent.

A

Aba A branch of the IBIBIO people and the city in present-day Nigeria named after them. The Ibibio are the ninth-largest ethnic minority in Nigeria, and the members of the Aba branch share similar customs with the IBO, one of Nigeria's ethnic majorities. The Aba are an agrarian people, but they are also known for their mastery of woodcarving. Their villages are organized around paternal lineages and individual spirits. Councils, made up of the heads of each household, dominate village life.

The city of Aba is located on the Aba River and was once a market town for the Ibo people. Excavations have suggested that the Ibo had settled in the area as early as the ninth century and remained active traders until the arrival of European explorers toward the end of the fifteenth century.

Abba Libanos One of eleven thirteenth-century monolithic churches at the city of al-ROHA (later Lalibela) in the highlands of northern ETHIOPIA.

The churches are clustered into two groups and are connected by elaborate underground tunnels and mazes. Along with Amanu'el (House of Emmanuel), Marqorewos (House of Mercurios), and Gabr'el-Rufa'el (House of Gabriel), Abba Libanos is encircled by a 36-foot (11-m) trench and is partially detached from the volcanic tuff that surrounds it. Its four walls are freestanding and its roof is connected to a rock cliff.

King LALIBELA of the ZAGWE DYNASTY, for whom the city of al-Roha was renamed, is credited with commissioning these churches, which remain an archaeological wonder to this day. Tradition claims that it took Lalibela twenty-four years to build the eleven churches, although most archaeologists agree that, on the basis of the immensity of the buildings and the meticulous nature of the workmanship, it had to have taken much longer.

Abba Libanos is believed to have been built by Lalibela's wife, Maskal Kabra, as a monument to him after his death. According to the Ethiopian legend, the queen, assisted by angels, completed the church in only one night.

Abd Alla ibn Yasin (Abdallah ibn Yasin) (d. c. 1059) *Founder of Almoravid reform movement of Islam.*

Abd Alla ibn Yasin, a Muslim scholar from the SANHAJA BERBERS of MOROCCO, was sent by a religious leader to bring ISLAM to the BERBERS of northern Africa. There, he met resistance to his insistence on strict observance of Islamic law, and, about 1042, he ended up waging an unsuccessful attack on the Berbers. By about 1050, Abd Alla ibn Yasin retreated to a *ribat*, or "fortified place of seclusion," that lay to the south. Followers who learned of the *ribat* and followed him to it came to be known as *al-murabitin*, meaning "the people of the fortress," or more commonly, ALMORAVIDS. Gaining strength as time passed, the Almoravids invaded Morocco around 1056.

Considered extreme by the Juddala Berbers, Abd Alla ibn Yasin later united these groups and others under Islam through a JIHAD, or holy war, against both the non-Muslim SONINKE of the GHANA EMPIRE and a group of Berber Muslims whom the Almoravids considered to be heretics. By the time he died, around 1059, Abd Alla ibn Yasin had founded the dynasty that would unify the MAGHRIB area under Berber Islamic rule for the first time.

See also: ISLAM, INFLUENCE OF (Vol. II).

Abd al-Mumin (Abd al-Mu'min Ibn 'Ali)

(c. 1094–1163) *Berber caliph and warrior who was perhaps the greatest Almohad leader of North Africa.*

In 1117, the young Abd al-Mumin heard the founder of the ALMOHAD movement, MUHAMMAD IBN TUMART, preach at Mellala. In keeping with Almohad doctrine, Tumart urged his followers to adhere to strict Islamic law and to profess their allegiance to the doctrine of the oneness of Allah. Al-Mumin was so taken with the Almohad faith that he joined Tumart on his journey to MARRAKECH. Al-Mumin continued to follow Tumart when, sometime later, Tumart declared himself the MAHDI (the divinely guided one) and asserted his opposition to the ALMORAVIDS. So loyal a follower was al-Mumin that he became Tumart's second in command after the death of Al-Bashir, Tumart's designated successor. Upon Tumart's death in 1130, al-Mumin became the Almohad leader and assumed the title of caliph.

As the new mahdi, al-Mumin gathered an army and attacked the Almoravids and the Christian knights who served them. Al-Mumin's forces gradually extended the areas under Almohad control until they finally won a major victory, in 1145, near TLEMCEN, a town on the eastern edge of the Moroccan kingdom.

By 1147, al-Mumin had conquered Marrakech, slaughtering the Almoravid citizens. Rather than abandon the city, which had become a symbol of Almoravid power and theology, al-Mumin destroyed its palaces and mosques, transforming it into the capital and center of his new BERBER empire.

For the next few years, al-Mumin continued conquests across North Africa, capturing the city of Constantine and surrounding areas in 1151. Seven years later, al-Mumin conquered Tunisia and Tripolitania. This feat made him one of the most powerful rulers in North Africa and brought Berber power in the Muslim world to its peak.

Al-Mumin restructured the governments of his conquests, replacing the traditional Berber clan system with a *makhzan* (central administration) modeled after similar Muslim governments in al-ANDALUS (Spain). To supplement government revenue, al-Mumin established a land registry. Until his death in 1163, al-Mumin used this income to rebuild mosques in his newly conquered cities. Abd al-Mumin was succeeded by his son, ABU YAQUB YUSUF.

See also: ISLAM, INFLUENCE OF (Vol. II).

Abdullahi Burja (r. 1438–1452) *Ruler of the Hausa kingdom of Kano.*

Abdullahi Burja ruled the Muslim kingdom of KANO, in what is now Nigeria, and was known for establishing trade relations with BORNU, a KANURI kingdom south and west of Lake CHAD. Kano had become a tributary state of Bornu during the reign of Abdullahi Burja's predecessor, Sarki DAUDA (1421–1438).

See also: HAUSA STATES (Vol. II); KANEM-BORNU (Vol. II); KANO (Vol. III).

Abo (Toposa)

Nomadic people of West Africa. The Abo speak central and East African NILOTIC languages. Much of what is known about the early history of the Abo has been handed down orally. The Abo believe their founder was a ruler named Esumaiukwu. Esumaiukwu's father, Oba Ozolua, ruled Benin City in the mid-fifteenth century. Ozolua was a cruel leader who oppressed his people in order to build a powerful empire. He levied heavy taxes and executed those who rebelled against him. The resulting turmoil sparked the migration of a large group of Abo people.

Esumaiukwu led a group of followers to find a new, more peaceful home. His brothers Oputa, Exoma, Akilini, Osimili, Etim, and Chima Ukwu accompanied him. The followers split into two groups at AGBOR, in the southeastern part of what is now Nigeria. The first group, led by Chima Ukwu, settled throughout the Agbor-Assaba region. Esumaiukwu led the second group toward Ukwuani to Ologwu. After many months, Esumaiukwu and his siblings moved on, his brothers eventually settling and forming the kingdoms of Usoro, Ashaka, Afor, and Osissa.

Esumaiukwu and his remaining followers finally settled at Ugboko Ukwa, an area inhabited by the Akiri people. The Akiri were unwilling to integrate peacefully with the Abo, so Esumaiukwu and his people defeated them. A kingdom was established, and Esumaiukwu became the ruler, or *obi*, of the Abo people. His children inherited the throne upon his death, and, throughout the sixteenth and seventeenth centuries, the Abo gradually gained control over much of the lower Niger region.

Abu al-Hasan Ali (Ali al-Hasan) (1297–1351)

Sultan of Morocco, noted for increasing the territories of his Marinid dynasty and creating a united North African empire.

Abu al-Hasan 'Ali became king of MOROCCO after the death of this father, Abu Sa'id. He then led armies into battle in al-ANDALUS (Spain) and ALGERIA, winning important victories at Algeciras and Gibraltar in 1333, and at TLEMCEN in 1337. Ultimately, however, he was forced to retreat from al-Andalus, at which time he turned his attention to Tunisia, where he extended his control by marrying the daughter of an important Tunisian ruler, ABU BAKR. Abu al-Hasan managed to take more lands in Tunisia, including the city of TUNIS in 1347. But he soon suffered a major defeat at Kairouan at the hands of Tunisian groups. After this, Abu al-Hasan returned to Algeria, trying to maintain his rule. In 1351, however, he was forced to abdicate the throne in favor of his son, Abu 'Inan, and died soon thereafter.

See also: TUNISIA (Vol. I); MARINIDS (Vol. II).

Abu Bakr   (r. 1274–1285) *Grandson of Sundiata and ruler of the Mali Empire.*

The great ruler of Mali SUNDIATA was succeeded by his son, Mansa Uli, who died in 1270. A dynastic struggle ensued, with the primary candidates for the throne being Sundiata's sons, Wati and Khalifa, and his grandson, Abu Bakr. Eventually, both Wati and Khalifa came to the throne, but neither proved to be either an effective or a long-term ruler. Ultimately, Abu Bakr assumed power, ruling until the throne was seized by Sakura. One of Sundiata's generals, Sakura went on to restore the empire to strength and prosperity.

Abu Salih (I) (eighth century) *Turkish-born governor of Egypt.*

Appointed governor of Egypt during the Abbassid period of Muslim rulers (c. 750–945), Abu Salih reported back to the caliphate in Baghdad. While the Abbassid caliphs turned their attention to the east and began incorporating many non-Arab elements into the Islamic empire, Abu Salih and other Abbassid governors of Egypt set about emphasizing both law and order and commercial and intellectual progress. Individual freedoms were restricted by new laws dictating ways of living, behaving, and dressing. (Doors were left open, for example, since people caught stealing were summarily executed.) At the same time, the Egyptian rulers of the Abbassid period, like those elsewhere, encouraged learning in medicine, mathematics, and astronomy. Eventually, however, the introduction of non-Arab and even non-Muslim elements into the empire's armies led to a general weakening of the authority of the caliphate. In Egypt, this led to the rise of the MAMLUKS, who ultimately were able to seize power.

Abu Salih (II) (Abu el Marakim)   (thirteenth century) *Armenian author and historian who provided important historical writings on North Africa.*

Although he was not a firsthand witness of the events he recorded, Abu Salih used existing documents to compile one of the few comprehensive histories of North Africa during this time. His writings on Nubia, ETHIOPIA, and the ZAGWE DYNASTY provided the foundation for much of our present-day understanding of these regions.

Abu Yaqub Yusuf (Yusuf I)   (r. 1163–1184) *Berber caliph of the Almohad dynasty and son of Almohad founder Abd al-Mumin.*

In 1147, the ALMOHADS, who held a belief in the unity of God, succeeded the ALMORAVID dynasty, which controlled most of the MAGHRIB (northwestern Africa) and al-ANDALUS (southern Spain). Yusuf was appointed governor of al-Andalus in 1156 and succeeded his father as the Almohad caliph in 1163. By 1172, he had crushed the few Almoravid strongholds in al-Andalus that had managed to survive al-Mumin's reign. The Almohad conquest of the rest of Muslim Spain soon followed.

Intellectual activities thrived under Yusuf's leadership, and he supported the study of arts and science. The renowned Muslim philosopher Ibn Tufail introduced Yusuf to his student Averroes (Ibn Rushd) and the two became fast friends. So impressed was Yusuf with Averroes, that he elected him chief judge and physician. With Yusuf's help, Averroes completed his celebrated commentaries on Aristotle.

Despite Yusuf's military achievements, he often had to deal with the sometimes violent opposition of the MASMUDA chiefs, who resented the fact that al-Mumin had selected his son and not their choice, Abu Hafs 'Umar, to be the next caliph. Yusuf's son, Abu Yusuf YAQUB AL-MANSUR assumed the caliphate upon his father's death in 1184.

See also: ABD AL-MUMIN (Vol. II); BERBERS (Vol. II).

Accra   Atlantic coast city on the Gulf of Guinea built on the site of villages once inhabited by the GA people. Accra has become the largest city and capital of the modern country of Ghana. Accra is built on a high plateau rising approximately 40 feet (12 m) above sea level. The largest of the villages was Ayawaso, located approximately 15 miles (24 km) north of present-day Accra.

Some sources indicate that internal warfare among the Ga led to the destruction of Ayawaso. The region had also begun to attract other groups, such as the neighboring DANGME, who reportedly traveled down the VOLTA RIVER, reaching Accra sometime in the early thirteenth century and possibly contributing to the city's demise.

After the Portuguese settled in the region c. 1482, both they and the Dangme appear to have moved closer to the coast, where they participated in trading and related activities.

See also: ACCRA (Vol. III).

Acholi (Shuli, Gang)   People of UGANDA and the region named after them; the Acholi also occupied parts of the modern-day Republic of the Sudan. Located on a plateau, Acholi comprises nearly 11,000 square miles (28,490 sq km) of lightly wooded grasslands. The numerous rivers that divide the grasslands provide essential water in an otherwise dry climate. The Acholi peoples speak a language of the NILO-SAHARAN family.

Information about the Acholi people prior to the seventeenth century is sparse. Their ancestors may have arrived as early as the eleventh century when the historically wet climate became dry enough to support agriculture. The riverbanks were natural settlement sites because they offered fish, rich farmland, a variety of native trees, and protection from invaders. The early Acholi probably faced devastating periods of famine due to the inconsistent rainfall in the area. Their region receives most of its rain from April to October, followed by a harsh dry season.

The ancestors of the modern Acholi were a mix of central Sudanic, eastern Nilotic, and western Nilotic LUO peoples. Each group retained its own language and established separate communities throughout the Acholi region. Evidence of early farming throughout eastern and central Sudan indicates that the central Sudanic speakers, some of the earliest eastern farmers, probably settled in Acholi around the second or first century BCE. Eastern Nilotic speakers migrated to Acholi between 1000 and 1600, pushing the central Sudanic people further west. A limited number of Luo-speaking people probably arrived in Acholi in the early fifteenth century, settling on the outskirts of the region. These three groups of people settled into small communities throughout Acholi. While these peoples were politically and geographically independent of one another, the communities shared many economic and social practices. Collectively they became known as the Acholi people.

The early Acholi settlers lived off the land, growing eleusine millet, sesame, sorghum, bulrush millet, and vegetables.

The crops cultivated by the early Acholi, particularly eleusine millet (used for food and for making beer), are still staples for the many Acholi who live in the region today.

The Acholi relied on two types of IRON hoes to work the land, a straight stake and an angled stick for digging. The central Sudanic speakers, who were known as early ironworkers, probably introduced iron tools to the region. Without these implements, farming the savanna would have been nearly impossible for the early Acholi. Cultivation required intensive labor, and Acholi men did most of the farming, forming small groups to work large plots of land. The men would also do the fishing and hunting, relying on local wild game. Women gathered firewood, picked wild fruits and vegetables, prepared food, made beer, and cared for the children.

Early Acholi villages were small, lineage-based communities dominated by the senior paternal male.

However, marriages were always conducted outside the lineage. Dowries given to the bride's family reinforced the paternal structure of the village. Evidence suggests that the Acholi had no formal political structure until the seventeenth century, when chiefdoms were introduced.

See also: LINEAGE (Vol. I).

Adal Eastern lowlands of ETHIOPIA bordered by Shewa, ZEILA, the Awash Basin, and Ifat on the Harer Plateau. Recognized as an important trade center, the region was originally populated by agriculturists and nomadic cattle herders. Later, during the second millennium, it grew to statehood as a result of Muslim traders who controlled trade routes leading from the port of Zeila to Ethiopia's central regions. By the early fourteenth century, it had become an independent kingdom led by members of the Walasma dynasty who had rebelled against the leaders of HARER.

Ethiopian rulers had never been able to resurrect the level of trade experienced during the rule of AKSUM. However, it appears that resumption of trade was a critical task for successive generations of Solomonic rulers who were aligned with the Orthodox Church. Their lack of success has been attributed to their decision to exercise indirect control rather than permanent occupation of rebellious Muslim-held territories. Therefore, the Walasma, the founding members of the Islamic dynasty created in the twelfth to thirteenth centuries, continued to grow, moving from Damot to Shoa, then to Ifat, and ultimately to Adal. This resulted in a succession of battles, raids, and border skirmishes that lasted from the fourteenth until the sixteenth centuries.

By the fifteenth century, Adal leadership had won many religious converts, which led to the establishment of a standing army made up of both Somali troops and Afar cavalrymen. Under the leadership of Sultan Ahmad Badlay ibn Sa'ad-Din, whose militant strategies were sanctioned by his belief in ISLAM, these troops engaged in a series of battles with the forces of the Christian Ethiopian Empire. These conflicts lasted until 1445, when they were routed by Ethiopia's noted emperor and military leader ZARA YAKOB (r. 1434–1468). Despite the fact that Zara Yakob pursued Adal's forces as far as the Awash River, Adal continued to cause problems for Ethiopia for several more decades. As late as the time of the Ethiopian ruler Baeda Maryam (r. 1468–1478), for example, two of that leader's trusted generals were reportedly killed in Adal when they attempted to discourage a planned attack against Christian regions.

The matter was left unresolved by Maryam's death, and rulers of Adal attempted to create a new capital city near Däkär in the Ethiopian Lowlands. An ill-advised raid by Emperor Eskender (r. 1478–1494), the son and royal heir of Baeda Maryam, led to the destruction of this capital city in 1478. A counter raid led by Sultan Shams al-Din ibn Muhammad (r. 1472–1487) immediately followed, resulting in the death or imprisonment of most of Eskender's army. Chronicles written about the young emperor's miraculous escape credited holy intervention and led to his building a church known as Debra Meshwa'e to commemorate the sacrifice of his men.

See also: ADAL (Vol. III); ADEN, GULF OF (Vol. II); CHRISTIANITY, INFLUENCE OF (Vol. II).

Further reading: Richard Pankhurst, *The Ethiopian Borderlands* (Lawrenceville N.J.: The Red Sea Press, 1997); Philip Curtin, Steven Feierman, Leonard Thompson, and Jan Vansina, *African History from Earliest Times to Independence,* 2nd ed. (London: Longman Group Limited, 1995); Harold G. Marcus, *A History of Ethiopia* (Berkeley: University of California Press, 1994).

Adefa (Adafa, Edessa, al-Roha, Lalibela)

Capital city of the kings of the Christian ZAGWE DYNASTY of ETHIOPIA during the twelfth and thirteenth centuries. Ruling from Adefa, the Zagwe king LALIBELA (c. 1185–1225) directed the construction of eleven stone churches in the nearby Lasta Mountains. The area in which the churches were built, known to the Arabic-speaking people of Ethiopia as Roha, later was renamed Lalibela, after the king. The Zagwe ruled from Adefa until 1270, when the Amharan king YEKUNO AMLAK (r. 1270–1285) established his reign.

Aden, Gulf of

Body of water located between the Arabian coast and the Horn of Africa. The coastal region of the Gulf of Aden is known to be one of the earliest areas of Arab settlement in northeastern Africa. Even though the coastal peoples continued to follow their traditional religions into the tenth century, it is likely that ISLAM was established in the gulf region as early as the start of the eighth century. Little is known about the African peoples who migrated to the coast of the Gulf of Aden before Arab settlement occurred, but it is thought that they spoke various dialects of the eastern Kushitic languages. They may have been ancestors of the SOMALI peoples.

The most important port on the Gulf of Aden was the city of ZEILA (modern Seylac), located in the far northwestern area of present-day Somalia. By the ninth century, Zeila had become an important Arab trading community and the middleman between ETHIOPIA and Arabia. CARAVAN routes linked Zeila with the Ethiopian kingdoms of the region, including the Shuwa and the Amhara.

Arab traders exchanged IVORY, hides, incense, and captives from Ethiopia and its trading partners in the interior for metal products and CLOTH from the Arabian Peninsula.

See also: AMHARA (Vol. I); ARAB COASTAL TRADE (Vol. II); RED SEA TRADE (Vol. II); SLAVERY (Vols. II, III).

Adulis

Important port city of the kingdom of AKSUM. The Aksumite kingdom reached the height of its influence from the fourth to the sixth centuries, but Adulis remained an important trade center well into the eighth century. Strategically located in the northeastern region of the Ethiopian Highlands, Adulis became the center of a network of trade routes emerging from the interior regions of the continent.

The fertile land in Adulis and the surrounding Aksumite kingdom was well-suited for an agrarian economy. Its location, agricultural success, and a diverse population that included Semitic immigrants from southern Arabia enabled the kingdom to grow rapidly after it was founded in the first century CE. A complex social system soon emerged that centered on a monarchy supported by three classes of citizens: the elite, the middle class, and the peasant class.

As a result of the thriving commercial activity in trading centers like Adulis, Aksum became the first African kingdom to mint coins of GOLD, silver, and COPPER.

Adulis's trade contacts extended from Rome to South Arabia, and into SOMALI territory, Meroë, and India. IVORY, gold, emeralds, hippopotamus teeth, rhinoceros horn, animal hides, tortoise shells, obsidian, and live animals were the chief exports. Imported goods consisted of metal, glass, and ceramic wares, cloth, wine, sugar cane, vegetable oils, and spices. The trade in human captives also was a significant element in Adulis's prosperity, with captives arriving from the Nile Valley, Mediterranean countries, the Horn of Africa, and the East African coast. Put up for sale in a carefully supervised market, the captives were shipped across the Red Sea to the Arabian Peninsula. Late in the sixth century, the military activities of Sassinian Persians disrupted Adulis's RED SEA TRADE, leading to the decline of Aksumite influence—and, therefore, Adulis's importance as a trading center—in the region.

See also: AKSUM (Vol. I); ARAB COASTAL TRADE (Vol. II).

Afar (Denkel, Danakil, Adalis)

Ethnic group primarily inhabiting the arid coast of the eastern Danakil province in ETHIOPIA, Massawa in the north, and the southern region of ERITREA; also the language these people speak. The Afar have been described as sedentary pastoralists, and their history dates back to the prehistoric era. Their early settlements were established in close proximity to the region's limited water sources. Over time, as their numbers increased from small, segmented groups to chiefdoms, diminishing water supplies led the Afar to repeatedly clash with neighboring SOMALI clans.

For much of the history of Ethiopia, the Afar remained beyond the sphere of Christian culture and influence. This was due to the independence they attained as suppliers of rock salt shaped into bars known as *amoles*. This rock salt was so valuable a commodity that it was often used as currency and in exchange for GOLD. Another important factor in the Afar's independence was their geographical distance from Ethiopia's seat of government.

The Afar eventually became embroiled in Christian-Muslim conflicts during the fourteenth century. At that time, large segments of the population were organized under the central rule of Islamic sultans based in ADAL. Afar men, however, became a crucial part of the cavalry recruited by the Christian Ethiopian emperor AMDA SIYON (r. 1314–1344). In 1329, under the direction of Muslim Sultan ad-Din II, a combined army of Afar and Somali troops launched three successive assaults on Amda Siyon's forces, all of which failed. The Afar-Somali troops subsequently retreated to their region, where they were pursued and eventually conquered by Amda Siyon and his army.

See also: AFAR (Vol. III); SALT TRADE (Vol. II).

Further reading: Harold G. Marcus, *A History of Ethiopia* (Berkeley: University of California Press, 1994).

Afro-Asiatic languages One of the four major language families of the African continent. The Afro-Asiatic languages include Semitic, Berber, Kushitic, Chadic, and Egyptian branches.

See also: LANGUAGES (Vol. I).

Agaw (Agau, Agew) An early Kushitic-speaking people who lived in parts of present-day ETHIOPIA and ERITREA. As the original inhabitants of the region, the Agaw are considered the ancestors of modern Ethiopians, along with the Amhara and TIGRAY. Their language, also called Agaw, contributed to the development of the Amharic language. Historically, the Agaw were a distinct group of people living in the Amhara, Gojjam, and Shewa regions. After centuries of intermarrying with local people, the true Agaw largely disappeared (although a small group still lives in Ethiopia today). Groups that trace their heritage to the Agaw people include the Aweya, Kemant, Kayla, Quarra, Kamta, Kharmir, and Bogos.

The Agaw ancestors were native Kushitic, non-Semitic people. They were small-scale agriculturalists who had little political influence over ancient Ethiopia

until the early twelfth century. Previously, the ancient Ethiopian kingdom of AKSUM had dominated RED SEA TRADE, but by the early ninth century, the Aksumites were forced to migrate south into Agaw territory because they had lost their power. These Orthodox Christians subdued the Kushites, established military settlements, and implemented a feudal social order that utilized Kushite agricultural resources. The Aksum kingdom then supported itself by exploiting these Kushite farmlands. Many of the resident soldiers married local women, and their children became the early Agaw, a mix of Aksumite and Kushitic peoples. The Agaw never fully integrated with the Aksumites, and they even rebelled in the early eleventh century against the weak Aksum kingdom. In the early twelfth century, Aksum fell, and the Agaw people emerged as the rulers of Ethiopia. Many of them converted to a nonorthodox version of CHRISTIANITY, and a new line of non-Semitic power emerged. The Christian Agaws are known for their insistence that they are direct descendants of Moses, and thus "the chosen people."

Around 1137, the founding chief of the new Agaw dynasty, Marara of the ZAGWE DYNASTY of kings, established the capital at ADEFA. With the decline of Red Sea trade, Ethiopia became isolated from coastal Arabs as well as from inland trading groups. Ties with Egyptians, to the north, were also largely severed.

The Agaw did maintain ties with the Egyptian Church, though. Following the death of Emperor LALIBELA (c. 1225), often considered the greatest of the Agaw rulers, the Zagwe dynasty faced a period of gradual decline. Lalibela's nephew, Naakweto Laab, had to abdicate the throne when Lalibela's descendant, YITBAREK, defeated him. This shift in power weakened the Zagwe dynasty, as did regional opposition from the areas of TIGRAY, Amhara, and Shewa; opposition within the Christian Church caused further turmoil. In 1270, the Agaws were finally overthrown by YEKUNO AMLAK, a claimant to the SOLOMONIC DYNASTY of Ethiopian rulers.

According to one legend, Yekuno Amlak murdered Yitbarek in the church in which Yitbarek sought refuge. Yekuno Amlak then proclaimed himself the emperor of Ethiopia, and, as a descendant of Solomon, the restorer of the "rightful" Solomonic rule. The Solomonic Dynasty maintained the throne from 1270 until the country became a republic in 1974.

See also: AGAW (Vol. I); AMHARA (Vol. I); ETHIOPIA (Vols. I, III); GOJJAM (Vol. III); SHEWA (Vol. III).

Further reading: Harold G. Marcus, *A History of Ethiopia* (Berkeley: University of California Press, 1994).

Agbor IBO settlement located in southeastern Nigeria. Little is known about the history of Agbor, although it is thought that their earliest ancestors may have come from EDO territory to the west and settled in the region between 4,000 and 5,000 years ago. By the end of the thirteenth century, Agbor was a collection of about twenty clans that were led by a chief and subsisted mostly through agriculture. By the beginning of the sixteenth century, Agbor was part of a complex marketplace economy that traded handcrafts, CLOTH, and beads with other Ibo villages.

See also: AGBOR (Vol. I); IBO (Vols. I, III); NIGERIA (Vol. III).

Age of Discovery Period during which European nations launched expeditions in search of riches and territories beyond their immediate boundaries in continental Europe.

During the fifteenth and sixteenth centuries, many European nations, begining with Portugal, took part in these voyages, some of which were aimed at securing trade routes to the riches of either the Far East or Africa and some of which sought to explore the newly found lands of the Americas.

The initial phases of the Age of Discovery were fueled by the rich trade in spices and other goods that had developed between Europe and the Far East during the Renaissance. For many years, this trade was dominated by such powerful, seagoing Italian city-states as Venice and Genoa. By the early years of the fifteenth century, however, other nations, most notably Portugal, began to look for ways to share in the riches offered by this lucrative trade. Also providing motivation to the Portuguese was their military victory at Ceuta, in MOROCCO, which, by 1414, had made Portugal's leaders aware of the profits to be made in African trade. As a result, the Portuguese, under the leadership of Prince HENRY THE NAVIGATOR (1394–1460), initiated a number of important voyages that greatly extended European knowledge of the world at large.

These Portuguese explorations began as relatively short voyages that grew in size and scope until they ultimately disproved most of the misconceptions Europeans had about everything from the distance to the Far East to the supposedly boiling temperature of the sea to the south. By 1418, the Portuguese had established forts, including the well-known Elmina, along the African coast, and by the 1440s, they had initiated what became the trade in African captives.

Early Portuguese Voyages of Discovery

1433 Gil Eannes sails around Cape Bojador, the "point of no return" for many early sailors.

1435 Gil Eannes finds evidence of human habitation in an area located 50 leagues (150 miles/241 km) south of Cape Bojador.
1436 Portuguese reach Río de Oro.
1441 Portuguese reach Cape Blanco, bringing two indigenous Africans back to Europe.
1445 Dinis Dias sails around Cape Verde.

These voyages—which continued even after the death of Prince Henry—culminated, in 1484, in Bartolomeu Dias's expedition around the Cape of Good Hope and the successful journey of Vasco Da GAMA to Calcutta and back. These fifteenth-century voyages set the stage for the more extensive Portuguese explorations and settlements that followed in the next century.

For many years, European sailors were faced with a major obstacle to any long-range journeys. Their ships, which were equipped with square sails, performed well in fair weather. They sailed poorly, however, in bad weather and northward winds—precisely the kind of weather they would encounter when traveling back to Europe from a long voyage to the Far East.

The Portuguese eventually solved the problem with a new type of ship, called the caravel, created especially for these long-distance voyages. Small in size and light in weight, the caravel was fast. It also had three masts, each carrying a triangular, or lateen, sail. These sails, although not as effective in fair weather, were ideal for the winds and conditions that prevailed on the voyages home to Europe. So, by sacrificing some speed on the outbound journey, the caravels made it possible for Portuguese sailors to return home safely.

Although Spanish leaders were committed to their efforts to drive the last remnants of Moorish power from their country, they too saw the value in seeking direct trade routes to the East. Unable to afford the more extensive explorations of the Portuguese, however, in 1492, Spain ultimately dispatched Christopher Columbus in quest of a shorter, western route to the Far East. Of course, Columbus did not find that route, but he did open the way to the Americas. With Columbus's voyages, Spain joined in the hunt for new routes and new lands to exploit, and, by the early sixteenth century, the English, French, and Dutch followed suit.

See also: PORTUGAL AND AFRICA (Vol. III); SHIPBUILDING (Vol. II); SPAIN AND AFRICA (Vol. III).

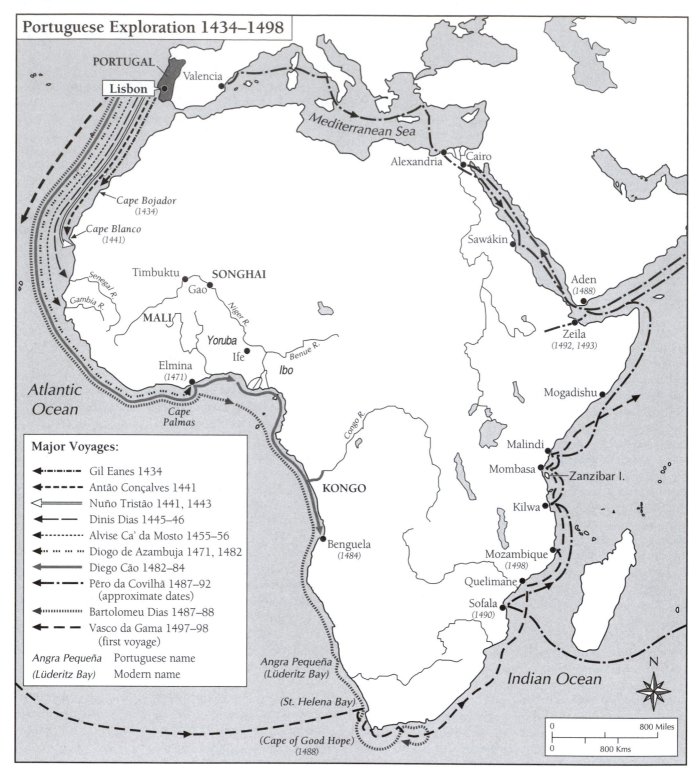

Portuguese Exploration 1434–1498

PORTUGAL
Lisbon · Valencia

Mediterranean Sea

Alexandria · Cairo

Sawákin

Aden
(1488)

Zeila
(1492, 1493)

Cape Bojador
(1434)

Cape Blanco
(1441)

Senegal R.
Timbuktu   **SONGHAI**
Gao

Gambia R.
MALI   *Niger R.*

Yoruba
Ife   *Benue R.*
Ibo

Elmina
(1471)

Mogadishu

*Atlantic
Ocean*

*Cape
Palmas*

Congo R.

Malindi

Mombasa —— Zanzibar I.

KONGO

Kilwa

Major Voyages:

◄—·—·— Gil Eanes 1434
◄— — — Antão Conçalves 1441
◄═══ Nuño Tristão 1441, 1443
◄— — Dinis Dias 1445–46
◄········ Alvise Ca' da Mosto 1455–56
◄··— ··— Diogo de Azambuja 1471, 1482
◄═══ Diego Cão 1482–84
◄—·—·— Pêro da Covilhã 1487–92
        (approximate dates)
◄·········· Bartolomeu Dias 1487–88
◄— — — Vasco da Gama 1497–98
        (first voyage)

Angra Pequeña   Portuguese name
(Lüderitz Bay)   Modern name

Benguela
(1484)

Mozambique
(1498)

Quelimane

Sofala
(1490)

*Angra Pequeña
(Lüderitz Bay)*

(St. Helena Bay)

N

Indian Ocean

*(Cape of Good Hope)
(1488)*

0   800 Miles
0   800 Kms

Aïr Massif Mountain range located in modern-day Niger, long associated with the TUAREG ethnic group. With its tallest peak reaching 6,628 feet (2,020 m), the mountains of the Aïr Massif rise up in central Niger and stretch northwest toward present-day ALGERIA.

The French word *massif* translates as "massive" or "solid."

The mountains, oases, valleys (known as *koris*), and surrounding areas that make up the Aïr Massif region were inhabited mostly by the pastoral Tuareg peoples from around the fourteenth century onwards. With their original kingdom of TAKEDDA located to the west of the Aïr, the Tuaregs dominated the region by controlling the local TRANS-SAHARAN TRADE ROUTES and COPPER mines. Copper was an especially lucrative business during this time as it was a common medium of exchange used throughout western Africa.

During the fifteenth century, the Tuaregs conquered the trading city of Agades, located on the southern end of the Aïr Massif, and made the city the seat of their new kingdom. From Agades the Tuaregs held sway over CARAVAN routes, which carried commodities such as salt and GOLD.

In 1496, the SONGHAI leader ASKIA MUHAMMAD TOURÉ (r. 1493–1528) displaced Tuaregs living around a large Aïr oasis and established a Songhai settlement. Even though the Songhai Empire later conquered regions around the Aïr Massif, including the city of Agades, the Tuareg peoples continued to lay claim to the mountainous region and still remain in the area to the present day.

See also: AGADES (Vol. III); AÏR MASSIF (Vol.III); SONGHAI (Vol. III).

Aja (Adja) Subgroup of the EWE group that established several powerful kingdoms, including DAHOMEY, which would become influential in the seventeenth century. Known for their expert ironwork, they also engaged extensively in trade with the HAUSA STATES and the SONGHAI of the Niger River valley.

See also: AJA (Vol. III); DAHOMEY (Vol. III).

Akan People, region, and language of West Africa. The Akan speak numerous Akan languages, all of which are a subset of the NIGER-CONGO language family. The early Akan were agriculturalists. They lived in villages dominated by matrilineal clans headed by a senior male. The members of each clan traced their lineage to a common female ancestor. The head of each clan was responsible for maintaining peace in his clan and connecting the spiritual world with the earthly realm.

The Akan migrated to the Guinea coast over a period of several hundred years, beginning in the eleventh century.

Oral tradition says that the progenitors of the Akan were called the Nta or Ntafo. These ancestors probably came from the north, but the various subgroups of the Akan do not agree on the exact location. Some groups, like the Akan residents of the modern city of Hani, have origin myths that say that their descendants fell from heaven or emerged from a crack in the earth near Asantemansano.

Why the Akan came to the Guinea coast is largely unknown. Most groups believe that they were forced to leave their homeland after an invasion by either the FULANI or BANTU people. Another theory speculates that the Akan may have originally inhabited the area near the GHANA EMPIRE but left when ISLAM began to spread through the region in the eleventh century. A refusal to accept the new religion would have reduced the Akan to a position of inferiority in the region.

The majority of the early Akan, or Ntafo, peoples probably migrated in three phases. The first wave consisted of the Guan, followed by ancestors of the FANTE, and then by Twi-speaking people. The early Akan states founded by these peoples were established by the end of the fifteenth century.

The Akan groups established trade routes between neighboring villages and eventually became a conglomerate of powerful states. Their kings pushed the Akan to the forefront of the GOLD trade. Indeed, when Europeans landed on the Guinea coast in the fifteenth century, the Akan were already established as successful traders.

Traditional Akan religion centered on the worship of one god, Onyame, who created the earth and heavens, but each lineage also recognized lesser gods and ancestral spirits.

See also: AKAN (Vols. I, III); AKAN GOLD WEIGHTS (Vol. I); AKOFENA (Vol. II); ASHANTI (Vol. II); ASHANTI EMPIRE (Vol. III); BANDA (Vol. II); BONO (Vol. II).

Akil, Chief (r. 1433–1468) *Tuareg ruler of Timbuktu in the fifteenth century.*

The TUAREG were pastoralists of BERBER descent who lived in the region between the trading city of Walata and the Niger bend in the western SUDAN. Around 1100, they founded Timbuktu as a seasonal camp.

> According to tradition, Timbuktu was named after an old woman who looked after the camp while the Tuareg were traveling in the SAHARA. Her name was Tomboutou, Timbuktu, or Buctoo, meaning "mother with a large navel."

In 1433, under the direction of Akil, the Tuareg recaptured Timbuktu. Chief Akil ruled over the city from the desert and although the resident Muslims paid yearly tribute, he still would frequently raid the city for its resources. Timbuktu became the center of Muslim culture for the MALI EMPIRE and the center of the trans-Saharan GOLD and salt trade. However, the Tuaregs' conquest over the city resulted in the Mali Empire's loss of control over important TRANS-SAHARAN TRADING ROUTES and began the century-long period of its decline.

According to tradition, toward the end of the fifteenth century the Muslim people of Timbuktu asked their SONGHAI neighbors to help them overthrow Akil and his oppressive reign. Helped by strategic information provided by the Muslim people of Timbuktu, the superior Songhai army, led by SUNNI ALI, conquered the city without a struggle around 1468. To the dismay of the people of Timbuktu, Sunni Ali proved to be even more ruthless than Chief Akil, but they were unable to overthrow the powerful ruler.

akofena   A short sword used by AKAN peoples during ritual and political ceremonies. The Akan began to develop organized states along the Guinea coast as early as 1400, and the *akofena* became the symbol associated with state authority.

The *akofena* was used in the oath-taking ceremonies of Akan kings and their subjects as well as on diplomatic missions. The purpose of the mission was designated by a symbol emblazoned on the knife's sheath. The *akofena* appears often as a symbol in Akan culture. Represented by a pair of crossed swords, it signifies state authority and the legitimacy of a ruler.

Aksum   Kingdom and capital city in ancient ETHIOPIA that dominated RED SEA TRADE from the third to seventh centuries.

The Aksumite kingdom reached the height of its power in the middle of the fourth century, under King Ezana. Ezana is remembered as the first Aksumite king to be converted to Christianity. He later declared Christianity the official religion of Aksum, in part to solidify relations with Constantine, the Christian emperor of Rome who controlled trade throughout the Hellenic Empire. Several centuries after Ezana, Aksum aligned itself with the Egyptian Christian Church, but this alliance did not spare the kingdom from a decline in power that began when the Roman Empire began to crumble in the fifth century.

In the seventh century, Muslim conquests of EGYPT and North Africa cut off Aksum from its trading partners. When the important trade center of ADULIS fell, the Aksumites were forced to abandon their trading lifestyle and migrated south. They settled in the Amhara and Shewa regions. Some of the Aksumites intermarried with the local Kushite people, thus establishing a mixed people who became the AGAW. The remaining Aksumites gradually lost their power, and the Agaw became the new rulers of Ethiopia in the twelfth century.

See also: AKSUM (Vol. I).

Further reading: Harold G. Marcus, *A History of Ethiopia* (Berkeley: University of California Press, 1994).

Akure   Major city in the Ondo state of the YORUBA kingdom.

Although several versions exist, the most common account of Akure's early history traces its origins to ILE-IFE, a city founded most likely during the eleventh century (although perhaps as early as the ninth century). The first Ife king, Asodeboyede, was given the title of Ajapada ("one who kills a rat with a rattle"), and it was by this line of rulers that Akure was established. During a journey to BENIN, the seventh Ajapada, Owa Atakunmasa, stopped in Akure and fathered a child. This boy, Ogunja, would become the first ruler of Akure. Upon taking the throne, Ogunja was renamed Deji, which became the honorary title taken by all subsequent Akure kings.

Akure soon developed into the primary center for Benin trade. IRON casting, particularly of weaponry and tools, was an important aspect of Akure life. An annual festival in honor of Ogun, the iron god, is still held in the city today. Aside from trade, agriculture was an important means of subsistence for the people, and products included yams, cassava, corn, BANANAS, palm oil, okra, and pumpkins.

Akyem   AKAN people who are concentrated along the Guinea coast, particularly in present-day Ghana and Togo. The Akyem speak Twi, a language of the NIGER-CONGO family. The Abuakwa, Bosume, and Kotoku are all members of the Akyem group. With their Akan relatives, the Akyem migrated to their present location beginning in the eleventh century. By the fifteenth century, they had established several cohesive, powerful states that thrived on agriculture and trade.

Akyem elders were elected to village councils and served as custodians of the sacred lineage stools. These stools were an important part of Akyem society, representing a symbolic link between the human and spiritual realms.

Akyem social order was established by hierarchical clans that were organized into compact villages ruled by a chief. The importance of clan ties was underscored by the traditional religious beliefs of the Akyem, which centered on ancestor worship.

See also: AKAN (Vol. III); AKYEM (Vol. III); CLANS (Vol. I); LINEAGE (Vol. I); STOOL, ROYAL (Vol. II).

alafin Traditional title of the ruler of the OYO KINGDOM. According to YORUBA mythology, the first *alafin* was Oranmiyan, who supposedly was the grandson of Oyo's founder, ODUDUWA. Traditionally, the *alafin* was selected with the assistance of the OYO MESI, or ruling council.

The *alafin's* power, though great, was not absolute, and he could be deposed by the people. The exact mechanism for this is unclear, with some traditions stating that an *alafin* was informed of his fate by the delivery of an empty calabash or parrot's eggs, and others claiming that the prime minister, or *basorum*, of the Oyo mesi informed the deposed *alafin* with the words, "The gods reject you, the people reject you, the earth rejects you." At this point, the rejected leader was supposed to commit suicide.

The mechanism for succession to the throne is equally unclear. According to some traditions, when an *alafin* died, his eldest son, known as the *aremo*, had to commit suicide. The Oyo mesi then chose a new *alafin* from a group of royal candidates. Other traditions assert that it was a member of the Oyo mesi, not the king's son, who committed suicide as a way to encourage the Oyo mesi to hesitate before making a decision to condemn an *alafin*.

See also: OYO EMPIRE (Vol. III).

Algeria Country in North Africa, bordering the MEDITERRANEAN SEA to the north, the modern countries of Niger and Mali to the south, MAURITANIA and Western Sahara to the west, Tunisia and LIBYA to the east, and MOROCCO to the northwest. Over the course of its long and storied history, Algeria has belonged to many empires, from the Phoenicians to the Romans to the Arabs.

From around the first century BCE to the fifth century CE, Algeria was controlled by the Roman Empire. With the decline of Rome, though, Algeria fell into the hands of the Vandals, a Germanic peoples. They, in turn, were overthrown in the sixth century by the Byzantine emperor Justinian, who sought to restore the Roman Empire to its past glory. Justinian's dreams of a restored and revitalized Roman Empire, however, foundered not long after the establishment of ISLAM, as Muslim ARABS conquered Algeria in the seventh century. The Arabs had a profound influence on Algeria and its native BERBERS, with many Berbers intermarrying with Arabs. Many Berbers also adopted Islam as their religion and Arabic as their language.

Some Berbers, like Queen DAHIA AL-KAHINA, a high priestess of the Jawara Berbers, tried to resist the Arab invasion. But such efforts proved largely unsuccessful, and Algeria soon became an Arab-ruled province of the Umayyad caliphate. By the eighth century, the Berbers of North Africa had formed Islamic governments in a number of kingdoms. These included both the Rustamids, who flourished at Tahert in central Algeria in the eighth and ninth centuries, and the FATIMIDS, who rose to power during the early tenth century in northeastern Algeria.

From the eleventh to the thirteenth centuries, the ALMORAVIDS and the ALMOHADS came to power. These Berber dynasties, which were centered around Morocco, controlled northwestern Africa and al-ANDALUS (Muslim Spain). The Almohad capital of TLEMCEN became the religious and academic center of the dynasty, while the Algerian seaports of Annaba and Algiers conducted trade with European cities. The main Algerian exports at this time included fine leather, fabrics, and the famous Barbary horses.

See also: ALGERIA (Vol. I).

Allada (Alladah, Ardres, Andrah, Great Ardrah) Ancient kingdom in present-day DAHOMEY. Allada was ruled by the Agassuvi ("Children of the Agassu") ethnic group. They migrated from present-day Togo and western Dahomey to the Allada region in the fifteenth century.

Oral tradition traces Allada's origin to the kingdom of Tado. Supposedly, the founder of the universe divided Tado into separate kingdoms, giving each to one of two brothers. The first established the kingdom of Ife, the home of the YORUBA people, while the second founded Tado. According to legend, the King of Tado had several daughters, one of whom was seduced by a wild panther and had an exceptionally strong son. His children tried to take control of the Tado throne but failed, so they migrated eastward and established Allada.

Allada became an important trading post and was eventually integrated into the kingdom of Dahomey.

See also: DAHOMEY (Vol. III).

Almohads BERBER Muslim dynasty that controlled North Africa and al-ANDALUS (Spain) during the twelfth and thirteenth centuries. The Almohad dynasty began as a movement of religious and social reform led by MUHAMMAD IBN TUMART (c. 1080–1130). Under the leadership of Tumart's successor, ABD AL-MUMIN (c. 1094–1163), the Almohads dismantled the preceding ALMORAVID dynasty. Tumart's followers were known as Almohads (al-muwahhidun), meaning "unitarians," or "those who believe in the unity of God."

Tumart was a member of the MASMUDA Berbers of the Atlas Mountain region in southern MOROCCO. After studying Islamic thought, Muhammad ibn Tumart came to the conclusion that the reigning Almoravid dynasty had strayed too far from traditional Islamic law. When he failed to win support in the important city of MARRAKECH, he returned to the Atlas Mountains in 1120 and began to gain a following among Arabs and Berbers. He proclaimed himself MAHDI, or "righteous leader," and created an advisory council consisting of his ten oldest disciples. Later, ibn Tumart formed an assembly of fifty leaders from various North African groups. In 1125, under his leadership, the Almohads began to attack the Almoravid dynasty in such major Morrocan cities as Marrakech and Sus.

After Muhammad Ibn Tumart's death in 1130, his successor, Abd al Mumin, named himself caliph of the Almohads. Tumart had appointed many of his relatives to powerful positions and established the Almohad dynasty as a traditional monarchy. By 1147, Abd al Mumin had successfully defeated the Almoravids, capturing the MAGHRIB, including Marrakech, the future capital of the Almohads. By the end of Mumin's reign, the Almohads gained control of the entire Maghrib in addition to conquering much of Muslim Spain and parts of Portugal.

Following Mumin's death in 1163, his son ABU YAQUB YUSUF (r. 1163–1184) and grandson, Abu Yusuf YAQUB AL-MANSUR (r. 1184–1199), controlled the Almohad dynasty during the height of its power. Under al-Mansur, the Almohads captured Seville and the rest of Muslim Spain. Then, during Yaqub's reign, the Almohads fought off Christian Crusaders in Spain and put down rebellions in their eastern Arab provinces. In contradiction of the puritanical Tumart, Yaqub built a number of richly ornamented monuments. Eventually, the Almohads put aside Tumart's teachings altogether.

By the early thirteenth century, the strain of fighting both Christian Crusaders abroad and Arab rebels at home proved too much for the Almohads. In 1212, the united forces of the kings of Castile, Aragón, and Navarre defeated the Almohad army in the Battle of Las Navas de Tolosa. By 1232, the Almohads had lost control of Spain. Another group of Berbers, the MARINIDS, succeeded the Almohads in North Africa. The Marinids conquered the last Almohad stronghold, Marrakech, about 1271.

See also: ATLAS MOUNTAINS (Vol. I); CRUSADES (Vol. II); ISLAM (Vol. II); ISLAM, INFLUENCE OF (Vol. II); MOORS (Vol. III).

Further reading: Michael Brett and Elizabeth Fentress, *The Berbers* (Malden, Mass.: Blackwell Publishing, 1997).

Almoravids BERBER Muslim dynasty that ruled MOROCCO and al-ANDALUS (Muslim Spain) in the eleventh and twelfth centuries; the term *Almoravid* is Spanish for the Arabic *al-murabitun*, meaning "monks" or "the people of the fortress."

The Almoravid movement developed early in the eleventh century among the SANHAJA BERBERS of the western SAHARA, a confederation of the Lamtuna, Gudalah, and Massufah peoples. The Lamtuna made up the ruling class within the clan and held all important administrative and military positions. During the eleventh century, Sanhajan control over TRANS-SAHARAN TRADE was threatened from the south by the GHANA EMPIRE and from the north by the infiltration of Zanatah Berbers into southern Morocco. About 1048, Yahya ibn Ibrahim al Jaddali, a leader of the Lamtuna people, returned from his HAJJ. Accompanying him back from this pilgrimage to the holy city of MECCA was a Moroccan scholar, ABD ALLAH IBN YASIN, who, he hoped, would institute religious reforms that would increase the unity and power of the Sanhaja people.

At first, Ibn Yasin focused on increasing the level of Islamic knowledge and practice among his followers. By 1054, however, the Almoravid movement shifted from religious reform to military conquest. After consolidating their control over SIJILMASA in 1056, the Almoravids invaded Morocco. A few years later, Ibn Yasin was killed during an attack on the Barghawata tribal confederation on the Moroccan coast, and Abu Bakr ibn 'Umar, the chief of the Lamtunah people, became the new leader of the Almoravids. Military expansion continued, and, by 1082, Almoravid rule extended as far east as ALGERIA.

Soon, the Spanish Muslims appealed to the Almoravids for help in fighting off military advances by Christian forces. The efforts of the Almoravids were successful, and the Almoravids became masters of the whole of Muslim Spain up to the Ebro River. They also conquered Morocco and the MAGHRIB as far east as Algiers. They had religious influence over their territories and controlled the region's lucrative GOLD trade. The capital of their expanded empire was Marrakech.

Although it was not an entirely peaceful time, North Africa thrived both economically and culturally during the Almoravid period, which lasted until 1147. The Lamtuna ruled forcefully, and as the empire grew, so did abuses of

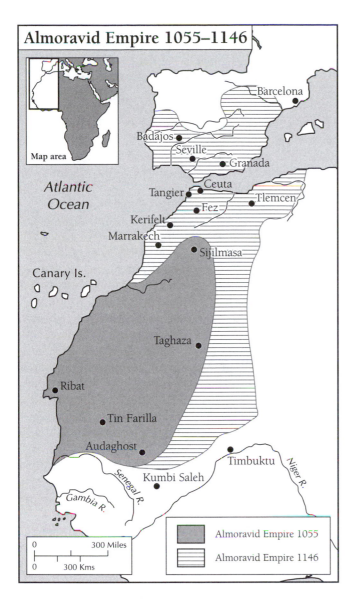

Almoravid Empire 1055–1146

Atlantic Ocean

Barcelona
Badajos
Seville
Granada
Ceuta
Tangier
Tlemcen
Fez
Kerifelt
Marrakech
Sijilmasa
Canary Is.
Taghaza
Ribat
Tin Farilla
Audaghost
Timbuktu
Niger R.
Kumbi Saleh
Senegal R.
Gambia R.

| | Almoravid Empire 1055 |
| | Almoravid Empire 1146 |

0   300 Miles
0   300 Kms

power, and many Berber groups resented the often oppressive dynasty. One of these, the Zenata Berbers of North Africa, unified and, calling themselves the ALMOHADS, declared a JIHAD against the Almoravids. In 1147, the Almohads took Marrakech, bringing an end to the Almoravid Empire, and by 1172 they controlled all of Muslim Spain.

See also: ISLAM, INFLUENCE OF (Vol. II).

Further reading: Michael Brett and Elizabeth Fentress, *The Berbers* (Malden, Mass.: Blackwell Publishing, 1997).

Alur NILOTIC-speaking people related to the LUO people of KENYA. The Alur primarily inhabited regions in the northwestern part of present-day UGANDA and northeastern region of the modern Democratic Republic of Congo. Historians suggest that the Alur originally inhabited pre-

sent-day Republic of Sudan. Then, during the fifteenth century, they migrated south to Uganda, supplanting the CHWEZI KINGDOM of the Lake Albert region. The Alur considered each individual household to be a self-sustaining economic unit. And, though they were considered agriculturalists, the Alur relied more on raising cattle, bananas, and root crops than on seed agriculture.

Amda Siyon (Amda Tsyon) (r. 1314–1344) *Christian emperor of Ethiopia.*

Emperor Siyon was a celebrated Christian ruler whose reign in ETHIOPIA resulted in the expansion of the kingdom into the southern highlands and former AGAW strongholds near Lake Tana. He was also noted for having used military force to subdue a number of rebellions that took place in the Muslim states of Ada, Ifat, and Dawaro during the fourteenth century. These rebellions stemmed from Emperor Siyon's demands for tribute from those Muslim states, in return for which he offered them a degree of autonomy.

Siyon's policy toward these Muslim states often had disastrous results, however. One example involved an alliance that developed between Sultan Ad-Din II of Ifat and a government official named Haydara, who had been appointed by Siyon and stationed in Dawaro during the latter part of the fourteenth century. The two plotted to topple Siyon's rule, going so far as to murder the emperor's servants and seize the expensive goods they were carrying. In retaliation, King Siyon torched Dawaro, killing the men and taking women and children as prisoners.

See also: SOLOMONIC DYNASTY (Vol. II).

Further reading: Richard Pankhurst, *The Ethiopians* (Malden, Mass.: Blackwell Publishers, 2001).

Amharic An AFRO-ASIATIC language of the southern Semitic branch. Amharic is related to the Kushitic languages and is the national language of ETHIOPIA. The predecessor to Amharic was GE'EZ, the original language of the Ethiopian Christian Church. Early Amharic, known as AGAW, emerged around the ninth century as the distinct language of the Agaw people. Both the Agaw and their language were a combination of Semitic and Kushite ancestral roots. Songs and poems, the first written records of the Amharic language, did not surface until the fourteenth century.

See also: AMHARIC (Vol. I); GE'EZ (Vol. I).

al-Andalus (bilad al-Andalus) The region of the Iberian Peninsula also known as Muslim Spain. Although the origin of the word *Andalus* is unknown, the name first appeared around 716. In the early years of that century, Spain was a Visigoth kingdom, having been unified during the late sixth century when the Visigoths took control over the various native Ibero-Celtic and invading Germanic peoples. This Visigoth kingdom was torn apart by constant feuds between the nobles and serfs and was ripe for conquest when Musa ibn Nusayr, an ARAB leader who had just captured parts of northern Africa, sent one of his military commanders to invade the coastal kingdom. Beginning c. 711, Musa was able to conquer most of the peninsula with little effort, securing Arab access to Spain. Within a few years, he had penetrated the Pyrenees Mountains, capturing Avignon, Arles, Lyons, and Narbonne, thus founding al-Andalus.

The eighth-century boundaries of al-Andalus ran all the way to Galicia in the northwestern part of the peninsula. Within the Arab army, made up of both Arabs and their African BERBER allies, tensions began to arise. As more non-Arab Berbers migrated to al-Andalus, the Arab position weakened. Internal conflict among rival Arab clans exacerbated the problem. Nonetheless, the Arabs managed to convert many of the native Andalusians to ISLAM, although the Arabs considered these new converts (*muwalladun*) inferior in social rank.

For thirty years, the Arabs controlled al-Andalus under the authority of thirty short-lived emirs. In 755, the UMAYYADS, under the leadership of Abd al-Rahman ibn Mu'awiya (The Immigrant), overthrew the Arabs and established the Umayyad dynasty at Córdoba. The Umayyads would rule for the next 300 years. The only great leaders during this period were the founder of the dynasty, Abd al-Rahman (756–788), Abd al Rahman III (961–978), and al-Mansur (?–1002). Arab, Berber, and peasant rebellions plagued the remainder of Umayyad rule. At the same time, the Christians (Mozarabs) who inhabited al-Andalus and neighboring areas offered minimal resistance to Umayyad rule.

In the tenth century, the Umayyads had to confront the FATIMIDS, religious reformers who were advancing along the coast of Morocco. Despite internal conflict, the Berbers and Christians rallied to keep the radical reformers out of their country.

In 1031, the Umayyad reign ended with the death of Hisham III. Ruling regents divided al-Andalus into numerous city-states that remained intact for sixty years, albeit in a state of constant disarray. By 1085, the Spanish king Alfonso VI had taken advantage of al-Andalus's weakened political position and began to reconquer parts of the country. At the same time, the ALMORAVIDS penetrated the area and recruited Berbers to join their cause. Under the leadership of YUSUF IBN TASHBIN, they defeated King Alfonso, but the remaining Andalusians were slow to accept their new leaders. Then, after ten years of battle, the Almoravids finally conquered Muslim Spain.

Fifty years later, another Muslim reformist group, the ALMOHADS, conquered al-Andalus. The Almohads would control al-Andalus until 1212, when the army of Pope Innocent III defeated them at the Battle of Las Navas de Tolosa. By end of the thirteenth century, Muslim Spain was confined to the southern kingdom of Granada, and the powerful Christian kingdoms of Aragón and Castile forced al-Andalus's Islamic inhabitants to convert or be persecuted.

Angola Wooded region in southwest Africa; the present-day country is bordered on the west by the Atlantic Ocean, to the north and east by the Democratic Republic of the Congo (Kinshasha), to the south by Namibia, and to the southeast by Zambia.

Archaeological discoveries in the Angolan region have been limited, but the existing evidence suggests that people may have inhabited the area since the Late Stone Age (40,000 to 3200 BCE). Between 1000 BCE and 500 CE, BANTU-speaking peoples moved into the region. Historically, the Bantu were fishermen and farmers, using IRON tools to clear forests and plant their traditional crops of yams and cocoyams. Limited livestock herding and POTTERY manufacturing soon spread throughout the region.

Until the fifteenth century, the Bantu inhabitants of Angola were isolated from the rest of world. One group of Bantu, the MBUNDU, played a central role in the commercial development of the Angola region, building the kingdom of Angola on the southern edge of the KONGO KINGDOM. Prior to the fifteenth century, the Mbundu were salt traders, but, during the late fifteenth century, they developed extensive commercial ties with the Portuguese, who had landed on the coast of Angola. Partly due to their early contact with the Portuguese, Angola became an important trading center in the sixteenth century.

See also: ANGOLA (Vol. III); SALT TRADE (Vol. II); SLAVERY (Vols. II, III).

Arab coastal trade Trade conducted by seafaring ARABS and coastal peoples of eastern Africa, especially across the Red Sea. Trade between Arabs and coastal Africa can be traced to as early as the first century BCE. At first extensive, it declined from the third to seventh centuries with the Fall of Rome, warfare in ETHIOPIA, and internal conflict among African groups.

In the seventh century, Arab trade along coastal Africa increased dramatically with the rise of ISLAM. The decline of AKSUM as a trading center provided an open market for the renewed flood of Arab immigrants who settled in Ethiopia under the direction of the Muslim prophet MUHAMMAD. Muhammad encouraged his followers to migrate to Ethiopia to avoid discrimination in MECCA. Many settled along the coastal regions and revived RED SEA and INDIAN OCEAN TRADES. Between 639 and 705, Muslim Arabs captured EGYPT, LIBYA, Tunisia, and much of the African coastline along the MEDITERRANEAN SEA. During this period of increasing Arab dominance, trade between eastern Africa, Arabia, and the

As Arab trade increased, knowledge of Africa's treasures expanded overseas, ultimately sparking interest from other countries. By the fifteenth century, increasing competition from Portuguese traders ultimately led to the decline of Arab coastal trade.

See also: ADEN, GULF OF (Vol. II); ARAB COASTAL TRADE (Vol. I); ERITREA (Vols. II, III); PERSIAN TRADERS (Vol. II).

Arabic Semitic language spoken in much of North Africa and the Middle East. As the sacred language of ISLAM, it is a major unifying characteristic of the Arab people. Semitic languages have existed for thousands of years, but the widespread use of Arabic did not occur until the seventh century with the rise of Islam.

Spoken Arabic sounds much more guttural than Western languages because many of the words are formed at the back of the mouth and throat. Like Hebrew, another Semitic language, Arabic is written from right to left. The basic sentence structure of Arabic is composed of a verb followed by its subject and object. The standard Arabic alphabet has twenty-eight consonants and three vowels. Each consonant and vowel is written by placing dots above or below one of eight shapes that form the Arabic script. Simple nouns and verbs are typically composed of three-consonant roots attached to various vowels. Word meaning is derived from the combination of vowels attached to any standard root. Prefixes or suffixes are attached to these basic root and vowel combinations to make more complicated nouns or verbs. Nouns and adjectives have multiple plural patterns with many irregular formations. Verbs are more standard, with simple alterations in stems used to conjugate and change their meaning.

As the holy language of all Muslims, Arabic is spoken extensively in Islam-dominated regions like North Africa and the Middle East. According to Islamic doctrine, the KORAN was revealed to the prophet Muhammad in Arabic. Prior to the Koran, Arabic had not yet developed into a standardized written form. Those who spoke the Semitic precursor to the Arabic language had not established a universal language, so several varieties of early Arabic developed simultaneously. As the Arabian Empire expanded, the need to standardize the Arabic language became imperative, and, after the Arab conquest of North Africa in the seventh and eighth centuries, much of the region adopted classical Arabic as the dominant language.

This illustration from a thirteenth-century manuscript owned by the sultan of Oman shows the kind of dhow, or ship, that Arab coastal traders used to sail up and down the Indian Ocean coast of Africa. © Arne Hodalic/CORBIS

Persian Gulf increased. Some of the Arabs settled near the Mozambique Channel, where they founded the powerful ZANZIBAR Empire, an important center for Middle Eastern trade.

By the eleventh century, Islam had spread inland across the SAHARA along the Arab trade routes. These CARAVAN routes transported GOLD, salt, honey, CLOTH, BEADS AND JEWELRY, and other goods from the African interior to the Arab-dominated coastal ports. Along the way, Islam spread to the HAUSA STATES, KANEM-BORNU, and neighboring kingdoms. Over the next few hundred years, many coastal African kingdoms incorporated the Arabic language and Arab customs into their own cultures.

In the twelfth century, SHIRAZI ARABS, merchants from Iran, began mixing with indigenous BANTU-speaking peoples along Africa's eastern coast, thereby starting the SWAHILI culture. KISWAHILI, the language they spoke, incorporated many words from Arabic.

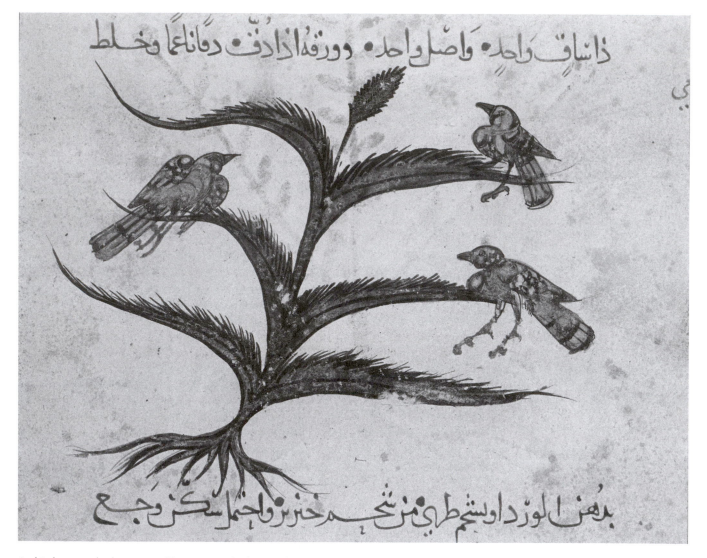

Arabic became the language of business and religion wherever in Africa Islam gained a foothold. This illuminated manuscript, *Plant with Birds*, by Abdullah ibn al-Fadl, was created in 1222. © *Burstein Collection/CORBIS*

During the first few centuries after the introduction of Islam, many non-Arabic languages in Muslim territories virtually disappeared. Arabic became the language of religious, political, and scholarly discourse. In EGYPT, Arabic had begun to replace the native Coptic language as early as the tenth century, and by the fourteenth century, the only surviving Coptic speakers were limited to rural areas.

As the spread of Arabic passed along the Nile from northern Egypt to the western SUDAN and CHAD, four distinct Egyptian dialects emerged: Upper Egyptian, Middle Eastern, Cairo, and Delta Arabic.

Arabic spread through West and central Africa along with the migration of Arab peoples. In many places, Arabic coexisted with native languages, while in other regions they intermixed to form new dialects. The Sulaym, Eastern Hilal, Central Hilal, and Ma'qil dialects emerged during this time. The KISWAHILI language, spoken by traders along Africa's east coast beginning in the twelfth or thirteenth century, is a language that has a BANTU structure but borrows many words from Arabic.

See also: ARABIC (Vol. I); ISLAM, INFLUENCE OF (Vol. II).

Arabs The ancient and modern peoples who inhabit the Arabian Peninsula; the name *Arab*, in ARABIC, means "speaker of Arabic," underlining the common bond and symbol of cultural unity Arab peoples share.

Before the rise of ISLAM, the early Arabs were nomadic, Semitic pastoralists who herded sheep, goats, and camels in the harsh environment of the Arabian Peninsula. Islam brought together the desert-dwelling, nomadic Bedouins with the town dwellers and farmers

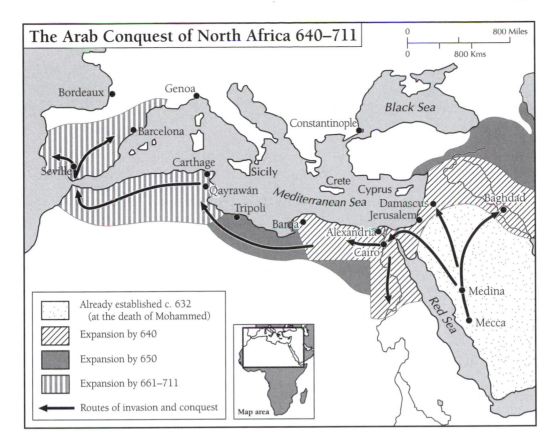

The Arab Conquest of North Africa 640–711

0   800 Miles
0   800 Kms

Bordeaux
Genoa
Barcelona
Seville
Carthage
Qayrawán
Tripoli
Barqa
Alexandria
Cairo
Constantinople
Black Sea
Sicily
Crete
Cyprus
Mediterranean Sea
Damascus
Jerusalem
Baghdad
Medina
Mecca
Red Sea

☐ Already established c. 632
    (at the death of Mohammed)
▨ Expansion by 640
■ Expansion by 650
▥ Expansion by 661–711
← Routes of invasion and conquest

Map area

who lived at the oases to form a missionary force of great fervor and purpose. These oases served as centers of commerce and trade. The caravan routes that brought GOLD and spices from Arabia to lands north and south in Africa became conduits to spread Islam. Today, the word *Arab* may name any number of people from North Africa, EGYPT, the Republic of the Sudan, the Arabian Peninsula, Syria, and Iraq who speak a common language and often but not always share a common religion, culture, and customs. Not all Arabs are Muslims; about 5 percent are Christian, Jewish, animist, or Druze, an eleventh century offshoot of Islam.

Arabs, influence of Arabs came to the continent of Africa as early as the first century BCE. They crossed the Red Sea and established trading kingdoms along the eastern coast and Horn of Africa. These early trading kingdoms exported GOLD, IVORY, honey, and captives. In ETHIOPIA, Arab traders intermarried with the local inhabitants and a new race, the Aksumites, emerged to establish a powerful trading empire at AKSUM. Around the same time, other Arabs crossed the Red Sea at the Strait of Mandeb, where they settled farther south along the coast. The sub-Saharan coastal region was an ideal location to establish trade routes to the African interior. Despite substantial early Arab settlement along the east coast, few Arabs immigrated to the western coast, perhaps because BERBERS already dominated the region.

Like the Greeks and Romans before them, early Arab immigrants were actively involved in the slave trade. Nubian and Abyssinian captives were the most common, but various other captives were also sold abroad.

The impact of these early Arab traders on Africa was more than economic. Their native Semitic language and Sabaean Religion were gradually integrated into the local languages and religions. In many places, they introduced basic writing and building techniques. Most early Arabs were nomadic pastoralists. This lifestyle, combined with a trade economy, hastened the penetration of the Arab culture to new areas of Africa.

Ties between Africa and Arabia increased in the sixth century when Aksum conquered the Christian Arab state of Yemen. By the end of the century, a new wave of Arabs began to migrate to Africa at the recommendation of the prophet MUHAMMAD. Early in his career, around 615, Muhammad encouraged his followers, facing persecution in MECCA, to migrate to Ethiopia. Despite the domination of CHRISTIANITY in Ethiopia at this time, the Ethiopian king Ella Saham (r. c. early 600s) was receptive to the new immigrants, and the two religions were able to coexist for many centuries. For the most part, the Christians remained in the central highlands, and the nomadic Muslims resided in the northern and western lowlands.

The seventh century brought a renewed influx of Muslim Arabs to Africa. They conquered Egypt at the end of the century and incorporated high-ranking officials from the Egyptian court into their political system. Arabs entered the continent through Egypt and dispersed throughout the northern parts of Africa. By 705, they had overtaken LIBYA, Nubia, Northwest Africa, Byzantine North Africa, Tunisia, the coast from the Gulf of Sirte to the Atlantic, and parts of the interior. The renewed interest in Africa also meant an increase in the number of African slaves shipped abroad. Prior to the spread of Islam, the Arab slave trade was small. As Muslim power grew, the need for slaves increased, both on the African continent and abroad. Slaves were used for manual labor, domestic work, military conquests, and as concubines.

With control of Nubia (modern-day Republic of the Sudan), Arabs were able to penetrate the African interior for the first time. The Baqt, a treaty signed in 651, established trade relations between Arabs and Nubians and ensured continued peace between the Muslims and Christians in the region. ARAB COASTAL TRADE continued to flourish, and by the thirteenth century, many nomadic Arabs had penetrated inland to the Middle Nile Valley. By the fifteenth century, powerful Muslim kingdoms emerged in the region, including Funj, Tagali, and Darfur. As in other regions, a diverse culture developed as Arabs and Nubians intermarried.

Like the Nubians, the North Africans largely accepted their Arab conquerors. Ironically, Arabia had enlisted thousands of Africans to conquer North Africa. The Banu Hilal and Banu Salim, two of the larger Arab groups, ruled over the native Berber people by the eighth century and established the Muslim kingdoms of Idrisis, Murabitin, and Muahadin.

In West Africa, seventh-century Arab migrations also led to the formation of several powerful Muslim communities. Islam was first accepted by the upper class in this area, thus facilitating the spread of Islam to the remainder of the population. Through the TRANS-SAHARAN TRADE ROUTES leading to the western SUDAN, Arab traders had exposed the Upper Niger, the HAUSA STATES, and KANEM-BORNU regions in the African interior to Islam by the eleventh century. Between the thirteenth and sixteenth centuries, the West African kingdoms of MALI and SONG-HAI also emerged as Muslim states. Arab influence was increasingly evident in native literature and poetry. The first written forms of such languages as HAUSA were in the Arabic alphabet, and Islamic doctrine was integrated into traditional religious customs.

Despite this widespread integration of Islam into African culture, native populations did not simply become Arab. Rather, they adopted the Arab religion, language, and trade practices while retaining the core of their traditional system. In many areas, Islam did not spread as quickly among people in the countryside, who held on to traditional beliefs long after town dwellers embraced Islam.

The dominance of Arabs in the overseas trade markets soon sparked international interest in Africa. European traders would arrive in the late fifteenth and early sixteenth centuries and take over much of the Arab territories in Africa.

See also: ARAB COASTAL TRADE (Vols. I, II).

archaeology Many of the most important African archaeological sites related to the medieval period are associated with the rise of African state systems. As a result of conquest, trade, and migration, many powerful states were organized during this period. In the YORUBA states of West Africa, where populations were most dense, some of the richest archaeological deposits of the continent have been found. For example, ILE-IFE in southwest NIGERIA was one of the most formidable city-states in the region. It is thought that approximately twenty early city-states were organized and ruled by dynasties that traced their descent from Ife's founding hero, ODUDUWA.

Artifacts recovered from the Ife site suggest the extent of its role as both a governmental force and a center of industry and trade. As a center of government, for example, Ife controlled surrounding farming settlements, which provided the city with food and other goods in return for governmental and military protection. Similarly, the city was an important location for the production of IRON and glass, examples of which have been found in abundance. Archaeological discoveries have also borne out traditional views that Ife was involved in the creation of brass and BRONZE, the most notable examples of which were produced at the important brass works during the eleventh and twelfth centuries.

Another important medieval site was Igbo Ukwu in modern-day Nigeria. Items found there date back as far as the ninth century and have done much to add to the archaeological record. The excavation at Igbo Ukwu, which took place about 1960, was conducted at several compounds and led to the recovery of a royal burial site, the origins of which have largely remained shrouded in mystery. The individual recovered in a wood-lined chamber was seated and wearing a crown and beaded necklaces. Archaeologists have indicated that other items surrounding the figure—including a ceremonial staff—could be considered royal regalia.

Beginning in 1977, major fieldwork was carried out at the one-time trading center of JENNE, which is situated within the INLAND NIGER DELTA in modern-day Mali. This site has yielded innumerable artifacts—especially remnants of POTTERY and beads—and has the unusual distinction of having been built on a preexisting town, which is also known as Jenne or JENNE-JENO ("Old

Jenne"). Although Jenne was abandoned in the fifteenth century, it is known to have been an important trading center at which kola nuts and GOLD were frequently exchanged. Although work continues at the site, progress is made difficult by annual flooding, which erodes the soil and washes away artifacts.

The recovery of *crucibles* (vessels used for melting materials at high temperatures) indicates that iron making was important to Ife even in the city's early days. Likewise, the discovery of molded glass beads, at the deepest levels of the archaeological digs as well as in burial sites, suggests the extent to which glass-making was a major activity of the city. Archaeologists have found evidence that these beads were traded both locally and in long-distance transactions.

Archaeological sites have also been explored in East Africa, where artifacts dating back to the ninth and tenth centuries confirm the rise of the city-states along the SWAHILI COAST, including the town of Manda in the LAMU archipelago. Consisting of nearly fifty acres, Manda flourished between the ninth and eleventh centuries. Its population of approximately 5,000 reportedly lived in houses made of blocks of coral solidified by lime mortar. Evidence of a surrounding wall and the recovery of glazed pottery give some indication of its wealth, derived from the INDIAN OCEAN TRADE.

One of the most prosperous of the Swahili city-states was KILWA, where archaeological excavations have unearthed evidence that COPPER coins were being minted there by at least the thirteenth century. Here, as in the Lamu archipelago, prosperity apparently was linked to merchant traders. Small CARAVANS carried trade goods— including cotton CLOTH, glass beads, and luxury items— to the interior regions of East Africa. The trade caravans apparently returned with, among other goods, gold dust and copper ingots. By the end of the thirteenth century, Kilwa's ruling Hasan dynasty was replaced by the Mahdali dynasty, founded by al-Hasan ibn Tulut. This dynasty remained in power until the arrival of Portuguese traders late in the fifteenth century. Archaeologists have identified the Mahdali rulers' cliff-top residence, the HUSUNI KUBWA PALACE, that included a bathing pool, reception court, apartments, and a warehouse.

See also: ARCHAEOLOGY (Vols. I, III); ARCHITECTURE (Vol. II).

Further reading: Brian M. Fagan and Roland Oliver, *Africa in the Iron Age, C. 500 BC to AD 1400* (Cambridge, Eng.: Cambridge University Press, 1975).

architecture Precolonial Africa's traditional housing structures have been called the most complex in the world. Contributing to this complexity are the wide range of styles that were in common use and the various building materials that were employed by the hundreds of ethnic groups that populate the continent. Traditional building methods took into account a people's cultural and religious beliefs and needs. Other building styles developed as a result of migratory patterns or were influenced by interaction with other peoples through trade.

The earliest homesteads were often constructed in response to the environment. The materials used reflected harmony with nature rather than a depletion of natural resources. In CAMEROON, for example, the Mousgoum (Mouloui) people living on the floodplains near the Shari River traditionally constructed houses with incised decoration, that resembled overturned mud pots. It is believed that this style and its design helped prevent erosion of the house. Similarly, in the grass valleys of Cameroon, the traditional homesteads of the Bamileke were made of square rooms with a peaked roof made of thatch or local grasses. Such houses were frequently built and rebuilt as needed and reflected the permanence of community among new generations.

Since the family unit was responsible for building the homestead, houses could be custom-built to place emphasis on cultural, social, and economic identity. A homestead, therefore, typically consisted of many buildings, with each building functioning as a kitchen, bedroom, storage hut, or granary. A fence or wall often surrounded the compound. Stylistically, however, homesteads varied greatly across regions, and at least twenty or more regional styles or categories have been identified. Noted differences included size and use of building materials. For example, the Nuba, who inhabit the hills of the Kordofan region of what is now Sudan, once built traditional homesteads made of red clay and gravel with thatched roofs. Several buildings served as sleeping rooms, a storeroom with grinding stones, and enclosures for animals.

Similarly, the traditional cliff dwellings of the DOGON, a people living in isolation on the Bandiagara Escarpment in present-day Mali, reflected the people's religious beliefs. Ancient and medieval Dogon villages were laid out in the form of a *nommo*, the ancestral first humans made by their creator god. The smithy and men's house formed the head; the houses of clan leaders were the chest; the women's houses were its hands; its genitals were an altar and a heavy grinding bowl; and the feet were shrines to the gods. The elaborately carved doors on their buildings ritually protected community food supplies and sacred objects.

Cultural identity was also important to the Batammaliba of Togo, whose name literally means "people who are the architects." They decorated their houses

1. Nuba-style house

The Nuba of what is now Sudan traditionally built dwellings made of a number of buildings set in a ring pattern, with walls connecting the individual structures. The buildings provided living and storage space and sometimes pens for domesticated animals.

2. Yoruba-style house

The Yoruba people of what is now Nigeria traditionally built dwellings along one large courtyard and sometimes secondary courtyards. These courtyards let in light and helped to collect rainwater. Elaborately carved pillars served as roof posts. Rooms were used for living, storage, and cooking space.

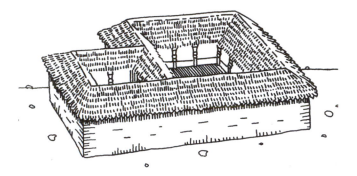

3. Somolo-style house

The Somolo of Upper Volta traditionally built multistory houses with mud brick walls and roofs thatched with palm leaves. These dwellings consisted of as many as twenty rooms, used as living quarters, storage rooms, kitchens, and grinding rooms.

with the same scarification patterns worn by Batammaliba women. The Pende people of the lower Congo River region placed carved figures called *tungunlungu*, representing the female ancestry of the clan, in front of the house of the chief, who succeeds to the throne by matrilineal descent.

Prominent among the housing styles of Africa were circular designs, such as the ones used by the Somolo of the Upper VOLTA RIVER. Their circular homesteads varied, but some were multilevel structures of mud, with a palm frond roof supported by posts. Each household had its own courtyard and a house or room for members of the extended family, as well as kitchens, storerooms, and grinding rooms. Other circular styles included the *domical*, or beehive, a cylinder-shaped house topped by a thatched cone roof, which, if wide, might be supported by surrounding poles. There were also long gable-roofed houses with adjoining portions found most often in central Africa.

The rectangular building was present in Africa from an early period and often reflected the wealth or the high social status associated with urbanized areas. In the forests of Ghana and western NIGERIA, various groups that include the AKAN, YORUBA, and EDO constructed their houses as a type of rectangular compound. Houses with open doors faced a large courtyard with a number of other smaller intersecting yards to let in air and light.

A distinctive feature of these homesteads was the sunken courtyard known as an *impluvium*. This feature was also found in the excavation of ancient houses in Egypt and Kush.

Quadrangular-style buildings made of mud housed the large extended family of the king or local chief and included rooms for wives and children and workrooms for making craft items. These buildings were surrounded by a continuous wall, important in the protection of the city. Islamic influences also accounted for the rectangular homes of fourteenth-century Mali. When Mansa MUSA (c. 1313–1337) returned from MECCA with Abu Ishaq al-SAHILI, a poet-architect from Grenada in al-ANDALUS (Muslim Spain), he reportedly introduced the use of sun-dried or baked mud brick. These bricks made it easier to create and maintain rectangular buildings of several stories. Other rectangular housing styles influenced by Islamic techniques included the clay box with a dome structure found throughout the SUDAN. In the fifteenth century, in KANO, a city in northern Nigeria, the HAUSA created many high-domed structures. Built without blueprints and with simple tools, such buildings used imported timber arches to buttress the high interior ceilings. Four distinctive spires marked the exterior.

See also: GREAT ZIMBABWE (Vol. II); HUSUNI KUBWA PALACE (Vol. II); LALIBELA, CHURCHES OF (Vol. II).

Further reading: Nnamdi Elleh, *African Architecture: Evolution and Transformation* (New York: McGraw-Hill, 1996).

Arguin, trading fort of Fifteenth-century trading post built by the Portuguese off the Saharan west coast (modern Mauritania). The Portuguese had been active in the area as early as the 1440s, and built the Arguin Island fort in 1448, hoping to capitalize on the West African coastal trade. The island was located in rich fishing waters, which helped to support a large seal population. The Portuguese sent fish, sealskins, and oils back to Europe and simultaneously began to establish trade contacts with various ARAB and nomadic peoples from the African continent.

A further reason for the choice of Arguin as the location for the trading fort was so that the Portuguese might intercept some of the goods carried by the GOLD caravans on their way to MOROCCO.

Gold, however, was not the only reason for Arguin's prosperity. From the time they first arrived, the Portuguese raided coastal communities in order to secure African captives for the slave trade. By the end of the fifteenth century, Arguin was a flourishing trading center in which the Portuguese exchanged cloth, luxury goods, and horses for gold and other items.

See also: AGE OF DISCOVERY (Vol. II); PORTUGAL AND AFRICA (Vol. III).

Arochuku Oracle The authority through whom Chuku, the supreme god of the Aro people, spoke. Well before the arrival of Europeans in the sixteenth century, Arochuku was an Aro trading settlement, located about 60 miles (96.5 km) from the coast in what is now southern Nigeria. The Oracle at Arochuku was established as the final judge in all disputes among the Aro. The Oracle of Arochuku was widely feared and respected by the IBO, of whom the Aro are a subgroup. The Oracle, therefore, provided the Aro with tremendous power, which they used to organize a lucrative trade network. Through their successful trading efforts, the Aro became the primary merchant class of Iboland, helping them to accrue wealth and power that continued to increase even after the arrival of Europeans. This continued well into the sixteenth century.

art During much of Africa's history, art, especially in the regions south of the SAHARA, was designed to reflect all aspects of life. Many of these works were highly functional, including such items as BEADS AND JEWELRY, POTTERY, household furnishings, cups and spoons, CLOTH, and even certain types of weaponry.

Other works gained importance or value because they were created with certain methods of production or in accordance with particular religious beliefs, cultural practices, or inspiration. Products like these frequently are based upon societal myths as well as on both family and regional history. One of the best-known forms of such art is the various masks used for initiation rites and festivals, as well as for the ceremonies and activities of secret societies. Other such art forms include sculptured figures linked to ancestor veneration, ritual objects, shrines, and burial displays.

The LUBA people of CONGO traditionally made wooden memory boards, known as *lukasa*, whose shape, beadwork, and engravings were codes that expressed ancient myths, clan lineage, and medicinal formulas.

One of the most fascinating examples of this traditional art is produced by the Bobo people of BURKINA FASO, who still make traditional leaf masks based on ancestral practices and beliefs that regard leaves as a revelation of the creator god, Wuro. Similarly, BAKONGO groups like the Bapende traditionally make small IVORY faces, which are worn as pendants and which represent venerated figures.

Wood, stylized with seashells, beads, or feathers, was by far the most widely used material for these works made in accordance with long-standing traditions. Styles varied widely from region to region and were influenced by their intended use. Those objects associated with the DOGON of Mali, for instance, have always been invested with symbols that convey the people's spiritual beliefs. These beliefs are extended to the Grand Mask worn at celebrations of renewal every sixty years. The making of this mask required appropriate prayers and offerings to the tree that was used, as well as protective measures taken by the individual who chopped it down. Another traditional art form of the Dogon involved the ancestor figure with raised arms. Preserved in the caves of the Bandiagra Escarpment, these figures have been dated by radiocarbon methods to the fifteenth century. The upraised arms on these figures have been interpreted by some to be either a symbolic appeal for rain or a gesture associated with rites of harvest.

Other artworks, and ones that are perhaps even more widely associated with the middle centuries, make up the body of art created to acknowledge the formality and rank associated with divine kingship. With the advent of the Iron Age, artists appear to have been supported and commissioned by the rulers of the state. These artists increasingly turned to IRON, BRONZE, and COPPER for their durability. These metals also were desirable because they potentially offered a number of different results, depending upon which methods were used. Bronze, copper, and brass were often melted and shaped in casts, in open molds, or through the LOST-WAX PROCESS, also known as *cireperdue.*

In addition, steel and iron were forged and hammered. As a result, in some regions metalwork was placed within a ritual context, largely under the domain of local blacksmiths. BAMBARA blacksmiths, or NYA-MAKALAW, for example, were organized into special clans responsible for making iron sculpture. Their power, known as *nyama,* was associated with the gods. In order to harness *nyama,* the *nyamakalaw* fashioned small protective iron amulets, the creation of which became one of their specialities.

Archaeological excavations at Igbo Ukwu have unearthed a wealth of artwork associated with a former palace and adjoining temples. Of the nearly 800 bronze sculptures recovered at that site, many were naturalistic and stylized images of deities, ancestor figures, and totem animals. Others involved forms, symbols, and styles linked to the rituals of reigning kings and their lineage clans. Radiocarbon dating methods have dated some of this recovered art to the ninth century.

The YORUBA, considered by many to have been the most prolific producers of sculptured art in Africa, created works that honored their kings as well as the deities that were known as orishas. At ILE-IFE, the city-state associated with the beginnings of Yoruba culture, naturalistic sculptures in terra-cotta and bronze have been recovered that appear to have been made at some time between the twelfth and fifteenth centuries. This Yoruba art influenced the neighboring kingdom of BENIN at some point during or shortly after the fifteenth century, leading to the production of a brilliant range of commemorative artwork in that state as well. Although numerous detailed plaques and naturalistic busts of human figures have been recovered from this former kingdom, little is known of their original context except that busts created by the artists most likely represented former reigning kings, or *obas.*

See also: AKAN (Vol. I); ART (Vols. I, III); FESTIVALS (Vol. I); INITIATION RITES (Vol. I); MASKS (Vol. I); SECRET SOCIETIES (Vol. I).

Further reading: Rosalind J. Hackett, *Art and Religion in Africa* (London: Cassell, 1996); Laure Meyer, *Art and Craft in Africa* (Paris: Terrail, 1995); Jocelyn Murray, ed., *Cultural Atlas of Africa* (New York: Checkmark Books, 1998).

Ashanti (Asante) Subgroup of the AKAN people who have long lived in regions of present-day Ghana, Togo, and the Ivory Coast. The Kumasi, Mampong, Bekwai, Kokofu, Nsuta, Dwaben, Effiduase, Asokore, Ejisu, Bonwire, Assumigya, and Senfi are all Ashanti peoples. They speak a Twi subset of the NIGER-CONGO language family.

Ashanti life prior to the sixteenth century is known only through oral history. Several versions of their beginnings exist, but they all concur that the Ashanti were originally part of a unified Akan clan that included the FANTE, Wassaw, and other Twi-speaking peoples. It is likely that an invading group forced the Akan people to flee south toward the forest. They eventually migrated to the coast and settled in small villages.

Sometime along their journey to the coast, the Akan split into two groups, the Ashanti and the Fante. According to one legend, FULANI invaders destroyed their crop fields, forcing the Akan to forage for food. They collected *fan* and *shan,* two types of edible wild plants. The

These Ashanti fertility statuettes now in the Musée Nationale des Arts Africains et Océaniens in Paris, France, were created in a traditional Ashanti style. To enhance her fertility, a woman wishing a child would carry one of these statuettes with her on her back, nurturing it and bathing it as if it were a real child. © *Archivo Iconografico, S.A./CORBIS*

two groups then separated and were henceforth called the *Fan-dti* and *Shan-dti* (*dti* means "to eat").

Another oral history attributes the splitting and naming of the Akan people to a dispute with the ruling king. According to this version, a group of loyal subjects offered the king some *fan* out of tribute, while a group of rebellious subjects attempted to poison the king with the deadly herb *asun*. The groups derived their names from their offerings to the king, *Fan-ti* and *Asun-ti*.

Still another version attributes the split to a dispute between two factions of the Akan. In this version, one group left the kingdom and became known as the *Fa-tsiw-fu* ("people who cut themselves from the main body"). The Akan who remained rejected a request by the king to restore peace among the two groups. As a result, the latter became known as the *Asua-tsiw-fu* ("people who refused to listen").

The Ashanti traditionally organized themselves into matrilineal clans. Their primary means of subsistence was farming, but they were also known as master weavers, potters, and metalworkers. They practiced ancestor worship, but the traditional religion centered on the worship of a single deity known as Onyame.

See also: AKAN (Vol. I); ANCESTOR WORSHIP (Vol. I); ASHANTI EMPIRE (Vol. III); GOLDEN STOOL (Vol. III); WASSAW (Vol. III).

Askia Muhammad Touré (Muhammad ibn Bakr Ture; Muhammad I) (r. c. 1493–1528)
Powerful caliph of the Songhai Empire.

Askia Muhammad Touré assumed the throne of the SONGHAI Empire in 1493 after the death of SUNNI ALI (1464–1492), the leader of the Sunni dynasty. He established Islam as the official state religion and consolidated the region of the central western Sudan into one political unit.

Muhammad controlled a vast area, with lands, according to some sources, extending to the Atlantic Ocean to the west, the salt mines of TAGHAZA to the northwest, to Bendugu in the southwest, and to Bussa in the southeast. He also gained control of trade routes that stretched to Tripoli and EGYPT. In time, Muhammad subdued the MOSSI STATE of YATENGA, and his army established a colony in the TUAREG sultanate on the AÏR MASSIF, giving him access to the caravan markets to the north.

Muhammad spent much of his time in the capital of GAO, organizing the state. He created a complex system of tithes and taxes, initiated regulations for agriculture, and arranged for the selection and training of governors. He also established Islam as the official religion of the Songhai nobility. Among his other acts was to create for his brother Umar (fl. c. 1518) a powerful position and title—*kurmina fari*—allowing Umar to govern the western provinces and to act for Muhammad in the ruler's absence.

Muhammad's reign ended in 1528 when his son Musa (r. 1528–1531) took power by means of a series of successful plots. Ultimately, Muhammad was banished to an island, remaining there until 1537, when his son Askia Ismail (r. 1537–1539) came to power and recalled his father to the capital. Muhammad died in 1538.

Oral tradition has it that Muhammad was able to communicate with the *jinni*, spirits that have such supernatural powers, such as the ability to change shapes. Indeed, some sources claimed that the *jinni* were responsible for the appointment of Muhammad to the caliphate. Oral traditions from a later period assert that Muhammad even became a *jinni* himself.

See also: KINGDOMS AND EMPIRES OF THE WEST AFRICAN SAVANNA (Vol. II)

Asmära (Asmera)
City established as the capital of ERITREA during the fourteenth century. According to traditional folklore, the name *Asmära* symbolizes unity, a testimony to the efforts of local women who worked together to bring to an end the bloodshed among their warring villages.

Historically, Asmära functioned as an important trading port during the time when it was part of the former kingdom of AKSUM. After that, Asmära may have declined for a brief period. It was later restored through the efforts of Emperor ZARA YAKOB (1434–1468), becoming a vibrant, cosmopolitan city that attracted traders from Arabia, Europe, and India.

See also: RED SEA TRADE (Vol. II).

Audaghost (Awdaghost, Awdaghust, Aoudaghast)
Important Saharan commercial center during the ninth through eleventh centuries.

Audaghost was a town in the southwestern SAHARA Desert located within the GHANA EMPIRE and was the terminus of one of the main TRANS-SAHARAN TRADE ROUTES. As the primary desert town of Ghana, it attracted North African traders who took advantage of the lucrative GOLD trade controlled by Ghana's kings.

Despite its desert location, Audaghost had an abundant supply of water. This allowed for widespread agriculture and animal husbandry, enhancing its role as an important trade center. As a result, Audaghost was a wealthy town whose residents lived in relative luxury.

In 1055, Audaghost was captured by the ALMORAVID movement of SANHAJA BERBERS and fell into decline. Archaeological evidence suggests that Audaghost occupied the site of what is now the Mauritanian desert town of Tegdaoust.

Augila (Aujila, Aoudjila) North African commercial trading center that flourished during the height of ARAB COASTAL TRADE. Located near ancient Cyrenaica in LIBYA, Augila was a BERBER settlement, largely shaped by the extensive Arab trade routes that passed through it over the centuries. Before the arrival of the Arabs in the seventh century, Augila supported traditional patrilineal clans (*qabila*). Clan leaders (*shaykh*) served as the political heads of the villages. Although exposed to Christianity in the sixth century, Augila was more extensively influenced by ISLAM. The first contact with Muslims probably occurred in 641 when Arab invaders conquered the North African coast. Islam quickly took root in places like Augila, thus facilitating Arab trade in these areas.

Augila was an important stop along the Mediterranean-Chad trade route, connecting trade cities near Lake CHAD to CAIRO, a central FATIMID commercial center. This same trade route also served as a Muslim pilgrimage road, which helped to spread Islam throughout North Africa. Slaves were the primary trade commodity, although CLOTH and leather were also sought from the SAHARA interior.

See also: CYRENE (Vol. I); MEDITERRANEAN SEA (Vol. II); TRANS-SAHARAN TRADE ROUTES (Vol. II).

al-Azhar Mosque and university in EGYPT and an ancient center of Islamic and Arabic studies. The mosque of al-Azhar was built in central CAIRO in 970, shortly after the FATIMIDS came to power in 969. Although the origin of the mosque's name is uncertain, it is believed to be linked to Fatima al-Zahra, the daughter of the Prophet MUHAMMAD, the founder of ISLAM.

Al-Azhar was originally used as a place for religious worship and Islamic celebrations of the Ismaili-Shiite sect. Soon after its construction, however, the Fatimid caliph established a *halaqa*, or tutoring circle, which quickly became the basis for Azharite education at al-Azhar. Under Fatimid rule, the university became a focal point for the teaching of Islamic law and theology, as well as of the Arabic language. Al-Azhar was financially supported by the Fatimid caliphs, who were interested in spreading Ismaili-Shiite doctrine throughout Egypt. When the Ayyubids took hold of Egypt, during the twelfth century, al-Azhar's teachings were changed over to Sunni teachings, and it lost its importance as a place of learning in the Islamic world. After 1250, under the leadership of MAMLUK vice-sultan Izz al-Din Aydmer, al-Azhar's importance was revived, and it attracted a large number of scholars, making it a center of teaching for the Islamic world once again.

See also: ISLAMIC CENTERS OF LEARNING (Vol. II); MALIKI SUNNI DOCTRINE (Vol. II).

B

babalawo The highest ranking of the YORUBA priests. *Babalawo*, who are known as "the fathers of the mysteries," are priests of the oracle divinity Orunmila in the Yoruba faith, which developed its recognizable forms by the end of the BANTU MIGRATIONS, c. 1000 BCE to 500 CE.

The Yoruba practice Ifa, a divination system that utilizes priests like the *babalawo* to connect with different gods. As one of those gods, Orunmila is an important part of Yoruba daily life. He is consulted before an individual starts any major project. The Yoruba believe that only the *babalawo* can connect spiritually with Orunmila. Through the *babalawo*, the Yoruba can ascertain Orunmila's wishes and act accordingly.

To become a *babalawo*, a Yoruba man must spend several years studying Ifa divination. During his apprenticeship, he learns the sacred chants and recitations that will be used to summon Orunmila and the other gods. A *babalawo* apprentice abstains from certain foods and lives an ascetic life to prepare for his role as priest. The Yoruba believe that purity allows the *babalawo* to connect with the divine through prayer. If the *babalawo* succumbs to evil, Orunmila may become angry and call for his death.

Once initiated, the *babalawo* traditionally dresses in white to symbolize his purity. He wears a palm fiber charm and carries a fly whisk. For ritualistic ceremonies, he will also shave his head. At the beginning of a ceremony for a client, the *babalawo* sits on a mat in front of a traditional divining board. He then scatters a thin layer of special dust, *iyerosun*, on the board and invokes Orunmila by tapping on the tray and chanting. When the spirit has been summoned, the *babalawo* takes sixteen sacred palm nuts (Ikin) in his left hand and passes as many as he can into his right. Depending on the number of nuts remaining in his left hand, he will make a mark in the dusted board. The process is repeated eight times, until a pattern emerges in the dust. By reading the pattern, the *babalawo* interprets Orunmila's wishes and passes the message to his client. After he has interpreted Orunmila's message, the *babalawo* recommends the appropriate ritualistic sacrifice that will please the gods and solve his client's problem.

See also: BANTU (Vols. I, II).

Bachwezi (Chwezi, Cwezi) People who ruled over the KITARA Kingdom of eastern Africa during the fourteenth century. The BANTU-speaking inhabitants of the early BUGANGAIZI Kingdom were the predecessors of the Bachwezi. They probably emerged during the TUTSI migration to the Kitara region during the thirteenth and fourteenth centuries, when Tutsi pastoralists from the northeast mixed with local Bantu people. However, some historians believe the Bachwezi were simply members of existing Bantu people who gained political power and became known as a separate people.

The Bachwezi leader NDAHURA founded the Kitara Kingdom in 1344. Legend holds that Ndahura was the grandson of a great Kinyoro officer and founder of the clan, Bukuku. During his reign, Ndahura conquered parts of present-day Bunyoro, Buganda, Toro, northern Kigezi, northeast RWANDA, and western KENYA. Although Ndahura was unable to establish a centralized political system to govern his territory, he achieved some success by appointing subrulers to represent him in these areas. In 1371, he was captured while invading a neighboring territory. Upon his release, he migrated far from the kingdom to avoid disgrace.

WAMARA (c. 1371–1398) was the second ruler of the Bachwezi. Although Bachwezi authority was still new in the Kitara region during this period, Bachwezi power was already on the wane during Wamara's rule. Wamara attempted to integrate several new migrating ethnic groups into Bachwezi society by giving their leaders positions of authority within the existing government. But, despite his efforts, these groups, including the Tutsi, Bashambo, LUO, and some new Bantu immigrants, never fully accepted Bachwezi authority. Political unrest was exacerbated by a severe famine and disease among the local livestock, which eventually sparked a military coup among conflicting cultural groups. The Luo and Bahima peoples overthrew the Bachwezi in 1398 and formed two new states, BUNYORO-KITARA to the north and Bahima in the south, thus ending the Bachwezi dynasty.

See also: BANTU (Vol. I); BANTU MIGRATIONS (Vol. II); PASTORALISM (Vol. I).

Bagauda (c.1000) *Founder of the Kano Kingdom.*

Bagauda was the first in a long line of *sarkis*, or kings, who ruled the KANO kingdom and served as both political and spiritual leaders. Bagauda's grandfather Bayajida (or Bayajidda) is said to have been the ancestor of the HAUSA people. According to legend, Bawo, Bagauda's father, was the ancestor of the seven Hausa states. The traditional "Song of Bagauda" gives some insight into the history of the Kano kingdom, but most of what is known about Bagauda comes from the KANO CHRONICLE, written by native Hausa about 1890.

Baggara (Bakara, Kara) Pastoral group of people

who have long inhabited the region from Lake CHAD to the Nile River, an area that comprises modern Chad, the Central African Republic, and the Republic of the Sudan. Baggara—from the Arabic *baqqara*, meaning cow—is a collective term which describes the cattle-raising peoples who began migrating from the area near the Red Sea during the twelfth and thirteenth centuries, bringing ISLAM to the region. As they migrated, the Baggara maintained their traditional nomadic way of life. Baggara peoples traditionally identified themselves as members of their subgroups before the collective group. Those subgroups include the Shuwa Arabs, the Hawazma, the Ta'isha, and the Habbania, among others.

See also: CHAD, LAKE (Vol. I); NILE RIVER (Vol. I); PASTORALISM (Vol. I).

Bagisu (Bugisu, Abagisu, Bamasaba, Gisu, Masaba) BANTU-speaking people of present-day UGANDA and KENYA; descended from the Luhya family of people, they speak a Western-Bantu language called Luluyia.

From the time of the great BANTU MIGRATIONS, the Bagisu have lived primarily around Mount Elgon along the Uganda-Kenya border. While their society traditionally has been organized through paternal lineages, they generally have been less cohesive than the neighboring KARAMOJONG, Teso, and Sogo peoples. Their political structure is based on clans, with each clan having an elder known as *umwami we sikoka*, or "chief of the clan." These leaders, whose job it was to protect the clan's future and maintain law and order within it, generally were selected from among the leading and richest members of the group. In spite of their fairly long history, the Bagisu remained divided, with no clan or clan leader gaining any long-standing ascendancy over the others.

Within Bagisu culture, the circumcision of young men remains one of the most basic rituals. Generally performed as part of an initiation into adulthood, the circumcision ritual also represents the young man's availability for marriage.

See also: BANTU (Vol. I); BANTU MIGRATIONS (Vol. I); LUHYA (Vol. III).

Bahinda (Bahima) Southern Kushitic people who

inhabited eastern Africa in the thirteenth through the fifteenth centuries. The origin of the Bahinda people is widely disputed. Some historians believe they were NILOTIC-speaking members of the LUO people, while others argue that they were Bagyesera people. According to Bahinda oral tradition, however, they were direct descendants of the fourteenth-century BACHWEZI ruler WAMARA.

If the Nilotic-Luo theory is correct, the Bahinda migrated to the KITARA region early in the fifteenth century. These pastoral people from the northeast integrated with BANTU agriculturalists living in the area. Most historians believe the Bahinda acquired control of the local government and a new people emerged: the BACHWEZI. The first Bachwezi ruler was NDAHURA (1344-1371), a warrior king who founded the Kitara Empire. When Kitara fell fifty-four years later, it was divided into two states by the Luo-Babito and the Bahinda. The Bahinda states were located in the southern region of the old empire and included Karagwe, Nkore, Kyamutwara, and Ihangiro.

For many years to come, the Bahinda and the Luo-Babito states vied for political control of the Kitara region. The diverse ethnicities of the people living in the area exacerbated the instability, and not until 1500 did the internal unrest diminish, with the advance of the more powerful Luo-Babito state of BUNYORO-KITARA.

See also: BANTU (Vols. I, II); BANTU MIGRATIONS (Vol. II).

Bahutu (Hutu) BANTU-speaking people who make up

the majority of the population of RWANDA and Burundi.

The Bahutu are also concentrated in the present-day countries of Democratic Republic of the Congo and Tanzania.

Although little is known about the origin of the Bahutu, they apparently migrated to present-day Rwanda and Burundi around the second century CE from the present-day Chad and Niger regions of northwestern central Africa. By the fifteenth century, their presence had been well established in east central Africa.

The Bahutu traditionally have been small-scale agriculturalists organized into local clans ruled by a petty king. By the end of the fifteenth century, the TUTSI people conquered the Bahutu and subjugated them under a feudal relationship. Since then, the Bahutu and Tutsi cultures have been largely integrated, but tense political relations frequently continued to exist between the two peoples.

Bakongo (Koongo, Badondo, Bandibu) BANTU-speaking people of ANGOLA, Congo, and modern Democratic Republic of Congo. The Bakongo are part of the Kasai clan of west central Africa. Several groups, including the Bashikongo, SUSU, Pombo, Solango, and Ashiluanda make up the Bakongo. They all speak the Bantu language of Kikongo.

The Bakongo's lineage can be traced to the last millennium BCE when their ancestors lived in the forest region of the lower Zaïre River. In the fourteenth and fifteenth centuries, they developed a loose confederation of local states that would become the kingdom of Kongo. The coastal zone of the Kongo was a sparsely populated area due to the lack of rainfall, but the central area was lush with rich soil and densely populated. Agriculture became the predominant subsistence activity of these early Bakongo.

See also: BAKONGO (Vol. III); KONGO KINGDOM (Vols. II, III).

al-Bakri (1094–?) *Arab scholar.*

Al-Bakri was noted for his work in the fields of geography, religion, philosophy, and botany. Best known for the work *Book of the Roads and Kingdoms*, which discussed the political, social, economic, and cultural environment of al-ANDALUS (Muslim Spain) and North Africa through the middle of the eleventh century. Although he never traveled abroad, al-Bakri meticulously gathered information from the personal accounts of those familiar with the region. The result was an amazingly accurate and detailed historical study.

Bali Southern Ethiopian state bordered by the Shabelle and Ganale Doria Rivers. Originally inhabited by the SIDAMO people, who followed a traditional, animistic religion, the area had been extensively penetrated by ISLAM by

the fifteenth century. At that time, the Muslim Walashma dynasty, which became a dominant force in the region, rebelled against the tributary rule imposed by Ethiopian emperor ZARA YAKOB. Many smaller traditional societies followed suit, as did the Muslim chieftain Mahiko of neighboring Hadeya. The combined forces of these various groups attacked the indigenous Christians of the region. Conflict continued during the reign of Yakob's son, Baeda Maryam, who ruled from 1468 to 1478.

Bali is also noted for its holy mountain, Abu'l Qasim, to which people made pilgrimages to pay homage to Muslim sheikh Hussein for the miracles he reportedly performed there.

Further reading: Richard Pankhurst, *The Ethiopian Borderlands* (Lawrenceville, N.J.: The Red Sea Press, 1997).

Bamako Capital and largest city of present-day Mali, located on the Niger River. From the eleventh to the fifteenth centuries, Bamako was an important ISLAMIC CENTER OF LEARNING under the powerful MALI EMPIRE. When the Mali Empire fell in the sixteenth century, the town became a center of trade for the BAMBARA.

Bambara (Bamana) MANDE-culture people who settled in regions of the present-day Republic of Mali. The people who make up the Bambara were a part of the powerful MANDINKA Empire of MALI, which flourished from 1235 to 1400. The language they speak is Bamana, a member of the NIGER-CONGO family of languages. The Bambara rose to political prominence after 1600 when they established independent kingdoms at Segou and Kaarta.

The people who make up the Bambara did not refer to themselves as such. The name *Bambara* means "infidel" or "unbeliever," reflecting the fact that they staunchly resisted ISLAM after the Muslim SUNDIATA came to power in the thirteenth century. Though many were nominally converted to Islam, most Bambara continued to practice their traditional religion based on ancestor worship. They also worshiped a creator god, Ngala (sometimes called Bemba), and several lesser gods related to air, fire, water, and earth.

Early Bambara society centered on agriculture, animal husbandry, and trade. The Bambara are recognized as one of the first groups to develop advanced plowing techniques. Their staple crops included rice, millet, and sorghum.

Fashioned in the form of a woman, this twentieth-century Bambara wood-and-metal door lock from Mali is 19 3/4 inches high and 15 1/8 inches wide (47.7 cm high and 38.5 cm wide). It utilizes methods, materials, and designs that are hundreds of years old. © *North Carolina Museum of Art/CORBIS*

See also: ANCESTOR WORSHIP (Vol. I); BAMAKO (Vol. II); BAMANA (Vol. I); BAMBARA (Vol. III); CHIWARA (Vol. I); KAARTA (Vol. III); NUMUW (Vol. II); NYAMA (Vol. II); NYAMAKALAW (Vol. II); SEGU (Vol. III).

banana Vitamin-rich, seedless fruit and staple crop grown in present-day ETHIOPIA, CAMEROON, GUINEA, and Nigeria. It is from the genus *Musa* and the family Musaceae. Native to India and China, the banana was introduced to Africa by East Coast traders—either by Indonesian merchants, or Arab merchants who had obtained it from the Indonesians—during the second half of the first millennium. By the tenth century, it had spread to the African interior and replaced the yam in many areas as the staple FOOD. Knowledge of the banana presumably spread from the Pare Mountains to the eastern interior. In the West, it spread from Malawi and the Zambezi River basin through the CONGO BASIN and West Africa.

Simultaneous with the spread of the banana, revolutionary agricultural techniques emerged to accommodate its production. Highland planting, used in places like eastern Tanzania, was a system of regulated irrigation and manure fertilization that produced a superior banana crop. In other regions of Africa, agricultural techniques similar to highland planting were developed independently of the Tanzanian methods.

Several types of bananas have been cultivated in Africa since their introduction more than 1,000 years ago. The Cavendish, or dwarf, banana is found in southern Africa; the plantain is grown in warm coastal regions; and the common banana (*M. sapientum*) is found throughout the continent. The banana plant flourishes in loose, well-drained soil and humid climates like those of tropical Africa.

Growing up to 30 feet (9 m) high, the banana plant is a giant shrub with an underground stem called a rhizome. Above ground, the stem forms a false trunk of leaf-stalk bases and resembles a tree trunk. Towering 10 to 20 feet (3 to 6 m) tall, the trunk is topped by many large leaves measuring 10 to 11 feet long (3 to 3.5 m). A flower emerges from the top of the plant that bends to the ground, heavy with clusters of fruit. Each cluster, known as a hand, has fifty to 150 individual bananas.

The banana plant does not require pollination to bear fruit. Therefore, fruit production is essentially continuous after the first harvest. When the first crop matures, in ten to fifteen months, the plant is cut to the ground to regrow. The stem sprouts several new growths, some of which are pruned, while others are allowed to grow into mature plants. Within six months a new banana crop will be ready to harvest, and the cultivation process is repeated throughout the life of the plant.

When ripe, bananas are an excellent source of potassium, carbohydrates, and vitamins C and A. For this reason they were an important addition to the early African diet. Most varieties are eaten raw, except the plantain, which must be cooked. A plantain has the highest starch content of banana fruits because it does not become sweet when it ripens like other varieties. Today, most bananas are picked when green and sent to distribution centers for final ripening to insure freshness for shipping throughout Africa and abroad. Although it has been grown in Africa for hundreds of years, the banana remains an important staple of African food production.

Banda AKAN trading state located on the Guinea coast. Banda reached its height of influence in the fourteenth and fifteenth centuries.

Banda was probably founded by MANDE peoples before 1000, around the same time as the founding of the neighboring Akan state of BONO. Though little is known about the Banda Kingdom before the seventeenth century, it is referred to in Arabic texts from the fourteenth century, and it is likely that the kingdom emerged in the thirteenth century, along with development of the West African GOLD trade.

Banda was ruled from the city of Begho, a forest trade center located in the southern region of the kingdom. By the fifteenth century, DYULA traders had established settlements in Begho to take advantage of the important trade routes between the Akan states and the MALI EMPIRE. During the sixteenth century, the gold trade in the area was curtailed considerably and, though Begho would remain an active commercial center, the Banda kingdom no longer wielded influence in the area.

See also: BANDA (Vol. III); WANGARA GOLD FIELDS (Vol. II).

Banjul Capital city of modern GAMBIA, located at the mouth of the GAMBIA RIVER. Archaeological evidence suggests that the coastal area around Banjul was inhabited as early as 750. Portuguese explorers visited the area in the fifteenth century, and British traders followed soon after.

See also: PORTUGAL AND AFRICA (Vol. III).

Bantu Language and people who dominate the southern half of the African continent. The Bantu are concentrated in equatorial Africa and extend as far south as Cape Province.

The diverse, nomadic Bantu peoples are connected linguistically. The term *Bantu* (literally "people") describes the large number of people who speak dialects of the Benue-Congo branch of the NIGER-CONGO family of languages. All Bantu languages stem from the same ancestral language: proto-Bantu. It may have been a fusion between proto-Hamitic and proto-Sudanic languages, although the exact root is not certain.

The Bantu family of languages is composed of more than 200 distinct languages that are spoken by approximately one-third of the African population. Over the years, *linguae francae*, or common languages, have arisen, as have mixed languages derived from early Bantu. Major Bantu languages include KISWAHILI, Rwanda, Makua, XHOSA, and Zulu.

Bantu origins can be traced back 4,000 years to when Hamite and black African people from present-day CAMEROON and Niger intermixed. Known as the Bantu, these mixed people were probably concentrated in the Great Lakes region of eastern Africa. Over a period of several thousand years, they migrated west and south, dividing into hundreds of groups, the two principal of which are the Eastern and Western Bantu. The Eastern Bantu live primarily in UGANDA, KENYA, RWANDA, Burundi, Tanganyika, Malawi, and MOZAMBIQUE. The Western Bantu make their home in Cameroon, Congo, ZAMBIA, and ANGOLA. Bantu-speaking people from both the Eastern and Western groups migrated as far south as ZIMBABWE and SOUTH AFRICA.

The early Bantu were forest dwellers. Those who migrated west became farmers, developing advanced techniques for growing root crops, foraging, and fishing. Those who settled to the east focused on grain agriculture and pastoralism. Each group's success at maintaining their food supply enabled the populations to grow quickly.

Bantu men tended the cattle, while the women tilled the fields, gathered wood, and prepared meals. Among the various Bantu groups, corn, millet, sugarcane, cowpeas, and melons were among the first crops cultivated. Tilling could not commence until the chief granted approval and an offering of seed was made to him, and cultivation could not begin until the chief blessed the fields to ensure a good crop.

Individual Bantu groups were traditionally organized into small villages linked by their clans. Their houses were usually single-room *rondavel,* or dome-shaped structures. Materials used to build them varied depending on location, although poles, grass, clay, and stone were the most common. Clay POTTERY was used by most Bantu, as were wicker objects like baskets and mats. Four to five villages, totaling around 500 people, worked in collaboration to grow food, conduct religious ceremonies, and defend their territory. These collaborations may have been the key to early Bantu success and rapid population growth.

Traditional Bantu social structure, which is still in effect in many groups today, varies. Some observe patrilineal descent, while others trace their clan lineages to the mother. The lineage determines hereditary rights, rights to children, and political power. Marriage is usually conducted outside the descent line.

Bantu political structure is based on hereditary leadership. Headmen may serve as subchiefs over individual villages, but a chief is the leader of the village groupings. Spiritually, most Bantu practice ancestor worship, although religious observances vary from group to group. They generally believe in a supreme being and in supernatural magical powers. Villages have healers who often practice divination, a process of connecting with otherworldly spirits, and exorcise evil spirits with charms, potions, or ceremonies.

See also: BANTU (Vol. I); BANTU MIGRATIONS (Vol. II); CLAN (Vol. I); DIVINATION (Vol. I); LINEAGE (Vol. I).

Bantu migrations Massive movement of the BANTU people across subequatorial Africa. The origins of Bantu-speaking people can be traced linguistically to present-day Nigeria and CAMEROON during the Early Iron Age. Over a period of several thousand years, they spread across central, southern, and eastern Africa. Around 1000 BCE, they began to migrate to the surrounding savanna regions and tropical rain forests. They settled along the GABON coast, where they initially split into two distinct groups, the Western and Eastern Bantu.

The reasons for the split and subsequent migrations are unclear. Early historians speculated that they coincided with advances in IRON technology, but new theories place more emphasis on the introduction of new CROPS. Other theorists believe that the Bantu migrations were driven by pressure from encroaching neighbors, or that they were forced to migrate in response to changing climatic conditions in the SAHARA. The Western Bantu moved toward ANGOLA, while the Eastern Bantu headed southeast toward the Great Lakes region. The bulk of Bantu migrations occurred during the first millennium CE.

The Bantu prospered in their new territories, adapting to the region and local customs. Although most of the Bantu dispersion had occurred by the eleventh century, they continued to merge with native groups. Organized Bantu towns and kingdoms began to emerge, replacing the early loose associations. In coastal areas, Bantu-speakers developed more complex societies as they came in contact with ARAB traders. Shungwaya, an extinct Bantu kingdom along the East African coast, reached its height during the twelfth to fifteenth centuries. The success of Shungwaya indicates that the Eastern Bantu were prospering by the twelfth century.

At the same time, three distinct Bantu groups emerged along the eastern coast: the Sabaki, Waseuta, and Ruvu. These groups, particularly the Sabaki, intermixed with and influenced the local hunters and gatherers. Farther to the south, the Waseuta were known for integrating Indonesian crops into their traditional planting techniques. The Ruvu split into two groups, the East Ruvu and the West Ruvu. The East Ruvu inhabited the lush lowlands, enabling them to grow the same Indonesian crops as their Waseuta neighbors. In contrast, the West Ruvu subsisted on grains and livestock due to the drier climate. At the same time several Bantu groups settled along the southern edge of the eastern coast near Lake Nyasa. Between 1100 and 1600, the Kilapwa and Songea Bantu migrated throughout the region, absorbing local populations along the way. In the area around Lake VICTORIA, Bantu people settled between Mara and the Kavirondo Gulf. A second group settled further to the south, near Mount Elgon.

Farther inland, in KENYA and Tanzania, scattered Bantu groups had settled among the NILOTIC and Southern Kushitic people by the twelfth century. Their willingness to shift crop production from traditional root crops to the millet and sorghum of the native inhabitants allowed the Bantu population to increase rapidly. By the sixteenth century, major expansions and diversification in these areas occurred among the Takama Bantu. The Bantu in the mountain regions of Kilimanjaro and Kenya were responsible for the development of highland agriculture that could support an essential new crop, the BANANA. Closer to the Great Lakes, the Bantu intermixed with pastoralists.

The number of Bantu subgroups is too numerous to chart in detail. Each developed its own customs and tra-

ditions as it intermixed with local people. Thus, the Bantu should be considered a people connected by the language they speak, and not by social, economic, or religious customs.

See also: BANTU (Vols. I, III); BANTU LANGUAGES (Vol. I).

Banu Marin See MARINIDS.

Banyaruanda (Nyaruanda) People of central and East Africa largely confined to the Bifumbira region of UGANDA. The Banyaruanda group consists of many peoples who were originally indigenous to RWANDA, most notably the HUTU and TUTSI.

Barea (Bareya) Ethnic group populating the region near Juba, in ETHIOPIA, and the southern region of the present-day Republic of the Sudan. From an ancient period, the Barea have functioned as farmers within a patrilineal society, tracing their origins to a common male ancestor. Their language is part of the NILO-SAHARAN language families that include thousands of NILOTIC and Nubian dialects and languages.

Part of a stateless society, the Barea were divided and regulated by a caste system that held that the practitioners of certain crafts, such as IRONWORKING and other trades, were inferior. In contrast, those who belonged to recognizable familial clans attained initiation, which included scarification and tooth modification for men and women. Male initiates subsequently entered age sets.

In the thirteenth and fourteenth centuries, the Barea were also noted as skilled archers. They were mentioned prominently in the chronicles of AMDA SIYON (r. 1314–1344) as a crucial part of his military force.

See also: CLANS (Vol. I); LINEAGE (Vol. I); SCARIFICATION (Vol. I).

Further reading: Richard Pankhurst, *The Ethiopian Borderlands* (Lawrenceville, N.J.: The Red Sea Press, Inc., 1997).

Bariba (Borgawa) Ethnic group of the Borgu region in West Africa that, in precolonial times, was best known for its IRONWORKING. The Bariba are one of the three sugroups of the Bargu (the Borgo and Borgenci being the other two) that speak a Voltaic dialect of the NIGER-CONGO language family. Early Bariba people may have been Wasangari, precolonial raiders of mixed Batonum, Mokole, Boko, and FULANI descent. Other theories attribute Bariba ancestry solely to the Batonum.

Traditional Bariba dwellings were mud-brick structures organized around a courtyard that served as the kitchen. The Bariba were accomplished CRAFTSPEOPLE, sometimes recognizable by their unique woven hats (which some older Bariba still wear today), but they were mostly known for their work with metal.

The Bariba ethnic group still has a presence in regions of Nigeria and BENIN and also in parts of BURKINA FASO and Togo.

See also: BARIBA METALLURGY (Vol. II).

Bariba metallurgy

Bariba metallurgy Metalworking techniques of the BARIBA, an ethnic group that inhabited the Borgu region in Nigeria and BENIN. Due to the abundance of IRON ores found just beneath the earth's surface in Borgu, ironworking was common in traditional Bariba societies. For the Bariba, ironworking involved mining, ore preparation, fuel collection, furnace building, smelting, refining, and smithing.

Mining was a family affair that occurred over a period of several months in order to build a reserve large enough for smelting. The most common fuels used by the Bariba were slow-burning hardwoods, which were placed in termite clay furnaces where smelting techniques were used to separate the iron from slag. The iron was then worked by a smith, who was held in high esteem in Bariba culture.

Like other groups, the Bariba considered metalworking a sacred rite, so elaborate ceremonies accompanied the smithing process. They believed that knowledge of iron working was passed to smiths directly from God through an earthly intermediary. This intermediary existed in the form of a sea crab, which the Bariba believed lived in the anvil of the smith's forge. The Bariba often sacrificed goats out of respect for the crab, and they believed that anyone who touched the smithing tools would be cursed with illness.

See also: IRONWORKING (Vol. II).

bark fiber

bark fiber The soft inside layer of the protective outer covering of trees. For centuries, it has been woven into a light, versatile CLOTH throughout Africa.

The history of bark fiber production is not clear. Archaeological evidence suggests that it originated in central Africa and moved east into KENYA, Tanzania, MOZAMBIQUE, and Malawi. While it is unknown when bark fiber production began, the most prolific periods of bark cloth production on record occurred in the eighteenth and nineteenth centuries, before Europeans brought substantial amounts of Western cloth to Africa. By the mid-twentieth century, bark fiber production had virtually disappeared in favor of more durable and easily obtainable European cloth.

Bark cloth was typically produced by harvesting the inner bark of *Ficus* and *Brachystegia* trees. Both of these trees could survive only in the wet regions of Africa, so bark cloth was not made in the desert regions. The trees were easy to cultivate and matured quickly. They were ready to harvest only three years after planting. The first harvest always yielded poor quality fiber, but by its fourth harvest, the tree reached its prime. Trees could be harvested for twenty to thirty years if the bark was stripped annually to prevent the healing skin from becoming too stiff.

Many African peoples practiced a bark harvesting ritual. Those who participated in the harvest had to abide by strict rules. For instance, the cutter was not allowed to drink anything or have any oil on his body before cutting. It was considered bad luck if he perspired on the bark, and he had to wash the bark in cold water if the tree had an unusually large amount of sap. To prevent the trunk from drying, the cutter worked in the early morning or late afternoon. He would cut a horizontal slash around the base and top of the trunk and then make a vertical cut down the length of the tree. He could then peel off the bark in large rectangular sections. In Uganda, a harvester covered the tree trunk with animal dung and wrapped it in banana leaves to accelerate the healing process.

The harvested bark was soaked in water for several days until it was soft enough to remove the inner bark fibers. A wood mallet was then used to beat the bark pulp, which caused the fibers to intertwine. After folding and pounding the cloth numerous times, the cloth maker would wring out the excess water and set the cloth out to dry. The cloth would then be stretched and kneaded by hand for several hours, making it soft and pliable. The best cloths were thin, yet strong, and relatively free from holes or patches.

By the time the cloth was finished, the bark fibers had become tightly intertwined into the fabric. Although it was not particularly strong, good bark cloth could be used for a variety of purposes. Many peoples used it as clothing, particularly for cloaks. It was also used to make burial shrouds. For instance, the bodies of dignitaries in southern Uganda would be wrapped in fifty or sixty of the cloths in preparation for burial. It could also be sewn into sacks to store grain, salt, or personal belongings. Many groups made lightweight bedding or floor mats from the cloth. The European settlers used it to make cushion covers and roofs for temporary shelters. Today, with modern technology, the arduous process of turning bark fiber into cloth is a dying African art.

Barmandana (Baramendena)

Barmandana (Baramendena) (fl. c. 1050) *Muslim ruler who brought Islam to the Mali Empire during the eleventh century.*

Barmandana, a MANDINKA king, governed the MANDE-speaking peoples of the MALI EMPIRE as a *mansa*, or appointed caste leader. His position eventually evolved into that of a king.

During Barmandana's rule, Mali suffered a debilitating drought. According to legend, a visitor to the Mandinka court advised Barmandana that his conversion to ISLAM would bring rain. So the mansa adopted the faith and, so the story goes, the rains fell, thus encouraging several of Barmandana's subjects to convert also. The mansa didn't force any of his subjects to accept Islam, however. Instead, many Mandinkans maintained their old beliefs, enjoying a religious freedom that was maintained for hundreds of years.

Mali, which during Barmandana's rule was a subordinate kingdom to the powerful GHANA EMPIRE, was served well by his conversion to Islam (even though most of the people of his kingdom continued to practice their traditional, non-Muslim religion). Mali's status as a Muslim kingdom helped it to become incorporated into the developing Sudanic and TRANS-SAHARAN TRADE ROUTES, which were controlled by Islamic interests. Within a few centuries after Barmandana's rule, Mali would be the most powerful empire in West Africa.

See also: ISLAM, INFLUENCE OF (Vol. II)

beads and jewelry   Items often used in Africa for trade and body ornamentation. Although many African groups used them differently, beads and jewelry were an important part of both special rituals and daily life. Beads often decorated clothing, jewelry, sheaths for staffs, masks, and various religious objects. Depending on custom, jewelry was made in a variety of styles and materials. Items made of GOLD, silver, COPPER, cowry shells, IVORY, beads, and clay have been found in different parts of Africa. To gain a broader understanding of practices throughout Africa, the individual groups must be explored.

A rich display of bone, bronze, ivory, and gold jewelry as well as glass beads was found at archaeological sites of the IBO culture in present-day Nigeria in West Africa. These materials were most likely imported from the ancient GHANA EMPIRE by early BERBER traders in the eighth century. The Ghana Empire, located in the western SUDAN, was a powerful and wealthy kingdom, with vast supplies of gold, ivory, and silver. Intricate bracelets, necklaces, and pendants have been found at early sites in the region. Stylistic similarities between early Ghanaian jewelry and that of neighboring kingdoms indicate extensive contact between early Sudanese civilizations.

The SAO people of the Chari Delta near Lake CHAD got their inspiration from Mediterranean and NILOTIC traders. Their copper, silver, and clay jewelry has an international flair that emerged sometime in the tenth century. In the region of present-day Democratic Republic of the Congo, BANTU speakers made copper wire bracelets, copper beads, and ivory necklaces as early as the eighth and ninth centuries. For many of the semi-nomadic people of the African interior, jewelry was made from materials more easily obtainable like shells and beads. Although contact with coastal traders influenced the jewelry stylistically, it was not until ARABS penetrated the African interior in the ninth century that jewelry began to reflect external influences.

Around the same time, the ASHANTI, along the Gold Coast, prospered as gold traders. Masks, pendants, and jewelry were produced in large quantities. They were primarily used in religious ceremonies and worn by royalty. Gold rings on chains were popular among aristocrats. Beads, prevalent in Ashanti society, decorated ceremonial items like masks and were even used as currency in the early SALT TRADE and other transactions.

Some African peoples like the FULANI of West Africa used decorative body painting as a form of jewelry. They also braided cowrie shells, silver, or beads in their hair and decorated their garments with chains. Copper anklets were worn to indicate the age and status of the wearer.

See also: COWRIE SHELLS (Vol. I); CRAFTSPEOPLE (Vol. II); IBO (Vol. I); MASKS (Vol. I); MONEY (Vol. I).

Beja   Ethnic group, also known as Hedareb nomads, located in the eastern SUDAN, including parts of ERITREA, ETHIOPIA, and EGYPT. For much of their history, the Beja were considered "pagans," and they were one of the few groups to have resisted both CHRISTIANITY and ISLAM. Some Beja did become Christians as early as the sixth century, though, when they inhabited regions of Ethiopia and Eritrea that comprised the Christian kingdom of AKSUM.

During the seventh century, once it was discovered that Beja territories held many GOLD mines, Islamic rulers in Baghdad dispatched troops to the region. After a few skirmishes, these troops subdued the Beja and forced them to pay annual tribute in gold. By the fourteenth century, most Beja had been converted to ISLAM, primarily as a result of frequent intermarriage with the ARABS who settled in the region. Despite their embrace of Islam, however, many Beja groups continued to practice their traditional beliefs.

See also: BEJA (Vol. I).
Further reading: Harold G. Marcus, *The History of Ethiopia* (Berkeley: University of California, 1995).

Benin   Ancient EDO state located in present-day southern Nigeria. (This kingdom should not be confused with the modern country of the same name.) For nearly 3,000 years, Edo peoples have inhabited a large area west of the Niger River in what is now the Benin province of southern Nigeria. Originally, single-family settlements dominated the area; however, around the fifth century, village communities formed to provide families with greater defense and allow them more efficient use of natural resources.

While these communities developed a network of trade routes, successful villages grew into towns. One such town, Benin, evolved into a hereditary monarchy ruled by a king, or *oba*, and a court of hereditary chiefs, called UZAMAS. Benin remained a small Edo state until the fifteenth century, when, sometime after 1480, it was conquered by EWUARE (c. 1440–1480), a great warrior chief. Ewuare rebuilt the destroyed city around a centrally located grand royal palace. In the palace, he housed the skilled artisans who created the art for which Benin is known today.

This bronze head of an unnamed princess was made in Benin c. 1360 to 1500. It is on display at the Fogg Art Museum in Cambridge, Massachusetts. © *Burstein Collection/CORBIS*

Benin ART from the fourteenth, fifteenth, and sixteenth centuries is widely regarded as some of the best African art from that period. Artisans and CRAFTSPEOPLE were commissioned by the obas to create detailed BRONZE castings in the likenesses of celebrated royal family members. These bronze sculptures also had distinctive markings that helped the royal family to record its history. Other interesting items made by Benin's artists included IVORY carvings, BRONZE bells, and special hip or belt masks, which were worn by the obas during special ceremonies.

During his reign, Ewuare instituted the law of primogeniture, by which the son's reign would follow that of his father. Ewuare also expanded Benin into a sprawling kingdom by conquering neighboring peoples. There is some debate as to whether Ewuare was still oba when Portuguese merchants arrived late in the fifteenth century, but, in any case, Benin was powerful enough to maintain peaceful and cooperative trade with the Europeans.

See also: BENIN (Vol. III); BENIN, BIGHT OF (Vol. III); BENIN, CITY OF (Vol. III); EDO (Vol. I); NIGER DELTA (Vol. I); NIGER RIVER (Vol. I); NIGERIA (Vol. III).

Benue River West African river and the longest tributary of the Niger River. During the medieval period, the Benue was an important water highway for the transportation of trade goods and people. The Benue originates in the highlands of northern CAMEROON and flows into central Nigeria. The fertile triangular region around the confluence of the two rivers has been home to various peoples, including the Nupe and Kwararafa (who established two of the minor HAUSA STATES), IGALA, Igbira, and Jukun. During the fourteenth and fifteenth centuries, these peoples were able to take advantage of the ideal farming conditions to carry on trade with the YORUBA states downstream and with the land CARAVANS that brought goods to and from the SUDAN to the north.

See also: HAUSA STATES (Vols. II, III); JUKUN (Vol. III); KWARARAFA (Vol. III); NUPE (Vol. III).

Berbers Ethnic group of Northwest Africa and the SAHARA who established ruling dynasties that controlled much of North Africa and southern Spain from the eleventh century to the thirteenth century.

In the fifth century, the Berber clan was made up of two distinct groups: agriculturalists who settled along the southern coast of the MEDITERRANEAN SEA, and nomadic pastoralists who lived in the mountain passes and on the steppes of northern Africa. As early as the fifth century, some of the Berbers who lived along the coast had become merchants and traded their agricultural goods and foodstuffs for manufactured Mediterranean goods.

The Berbers of the interior, or MAGHRIB, were assimilated by invading Arab Muslims beginning in the seventh century. By the tenth century, FATIMID Berbers controlled much of EGYPT and the Red Sea coast, and the SANHAJA Berbers controlled vast areas of the Sahara. By the eleventh century, practically all of the Berbers of North Africa had converted to ISLAM.

From the eleventh to the thirteenth centuries, Islamic Berber clans dominated North Africa. Their most powerful ruling dynasties were the FATIMIDS, ALMORAVIDS, ALMOHADS, MARINIDS, Zayyanids, and Hafsids.

At the height of its power, the Berber empire included the African regions of MOROCCO, ALGERIA, LIBYA, EGYPT, and northern Niger. (They also controlled most of southern Spain, an area they called al-ANDALUS.) Important Berber cities in Africa included TUNIS, MARRAKECH, TLEMCEN, and al-Qahira (CAIRO) in the north, and TIMBUKTU and AUDAGHOST, trans-Saharan trade centers of the western SUDAN. By the end of the thirteenth century, Berber dynasties no longer held sway in the western Sahara, but the Berber people did assimilate into the Islamic Arab culture that assumed power in the region.

During the fourteenth and fifteenth centuries, many of the trading routes in the Sudan were run by a semi-nomadic people called TUAREGS, who claim descent from the original Berber clans of North Africa.

See also: BERBERS (Vols. I, III); NOMADS (Vol. I).

Beta Israel (Falasha)

Ethiopian agriculturalists who long maintained a faith in the Jewish religion. The origins of the Beta Israel are unclear, and the many legends about their beginnings often conflict. However, it is clear that they were practicing their faith within various parts of Ethiopia well before the beginning of the common era.

The Beta Israel subscribe to religious and cultural practices similar to Judaism; their name, Beta Israel, means "House of Israel." They practice an ancient biblical form of Judiasm, guided by the Orit (the Pentateuch, or first five books of the bible, translated into Ge'ez), but possess none of the post-biblical laws and interpretations collected in the Talmud. However, unlike conventional Jewish practice, they pray in Ge'ez, the ancient Ethiopian vernacular and liturgical language, and practice both male and female circumcision.

Various traditions explain the origins of the Beta Israel. One holds that they are an AGAW people who were converted to Judaism before the ancient Ethiopian kingdom of AKSUM was Christianized in the fourth century. The contrary tradition holds that they are Jewish migrants from Egypt, possibly connected to the house of Dan (the fifth of the Twelve Tribes of Israel descended from the twelve sons of Jacob) who entered Ethiopia early in the common era. The word *falasha* means "stranger," "exile," or "immigrant" in Ge'ez and characterizes the distinctiveness of the Beta Israel within Ethiopian culture.

In the second half of the twelfth century, the legend of Prester John—a Christian priest who ruled over a vast empire in the East—began to circulate in Europe. In some versions of this legend, Prester John's kingdom is identified with Ethiopia. Rumors based on these legends claimed that the Beta Israel were at constant war with Prester John and that their armies were advancing on Rome.

Although there is evidence that the Beta Israel were persecuted for assisting the Agaw, whose rejection of Christianity led to the destruction of AKSUM (c. 900–1000) and fueled numerous other rebellions, little of fact is known about the Beta Israel until the Christian emperors of the SOLOMONIC DYNASTY began persecuting them in the fourteenth and fifteenth centuries. They had begun to be regarded as an identifiable group during Ethiopia's Heroic Age that began c. 1270, when many legends about Ethiopia's past began to take form. In the following century, they had grown into a populous and prosperous community numbering in the many thousands.

By the fifteenth century, ruling monarchs such as ZARA YAKOB (r. 1434–1468) and his son Baeda Maryam (r. 1468–1478) were actively engaged in warfare against the Beta Israel. These organized massacres led to heavy losses among the Beta Israel, who still managed, however, to collaborate with the Agaw again in a major rebellion during the seventeenth century. In retaliation, the emperor Susneyos (r. c. 1607–1632) launched a crippling attack that led to the loss of the Beta Israel's independence, the burning of their holy books and texts, and their forced conversion to Christianity. Those who refused to convert were killed, taken captive, or forced off their lands. It was not until Susneyos's son Fasiladas (r. 1632–1667) ascended the throne that the warfare against the Beta Israel abated. Eventually the Beta Israel were allowed to resume their religious practices, but they continued to face severe economic deprivation for centuries.

See also: BETA ISRAEL (Vols. I, II).

Betsimisaraka Ethnic group of the island of MADA-GASCAR, located off East Africa. Primarily farmers, the Betsimiseraka lived along a narrow section of the eastern Madagascar coast. Their ancestors were a mix of African, Malayo-Indonesian, and ARAB peoples who spoke the West Austronesian language of MALAGASY. This diverse group of people became known as the *Betsimisaraka*, which translates literally as "the inseparable multitude." Before establishing their own kingdom in the early eighteenth century, the Betsimisaraka were pirates, sailors, whalers, and fishermen.

See also: BETSIMISARAKA (Vol. III); INDONESIAN COLONISTS (Vol. II).

Bigo (Bigo bya Mugenyi) Kingdom located, during the fourteenth to fifteenth centuries, in present-day UGANDA; known for its massive earthworks.

Located on the Katonga River, Bigo was an ancient BACHWEZI kingdom. Archaeological evidence indicates that the BAHINDA, a BANTU-speaking Bachwezi people of western Uganda, established Bigo around the mid-four-teenth century. Excavations revealed that these semi-nomadic pastoralists raised a substantial number of cattle and abandoned the area in the mid-sixteenth century when the NILOTIC-speaking LUO people encroached on their territory.

Bigo is best known as the site of large earthworks built and occupied during the height of Bigo power (1350–1550). These vast ditches run 6.5 miles (10.5 km) around the ancient kingdom. In many places carved from solid rock, the earthworks are up to 20 feet (6.1 m) deep and 30 feet (9.1 m) wide. The purpose for these earth-works is not fully understood.

Bilad al-Sudan Arabic expression meaning "Land of the Blacks." Bilad-al Sudan was the term generally used by ARABS to describe the area south of the SAHARA in west-ern Africa.

ISLAM came to Africa in the seventh and eighth cen-turies. The Dya' go dynasty of the kingdom of TEKRUR on the banks of the SENEGAL RIVER, who converted to Islam in 850, were the first black people to become Muslims. Their territory was given the name Bilad-al Sudan by Islamic geographers and historians.

As a geographical term, *sudan* refers to the strip of semiarid land between the lower edge of the Sahara and the equatorial rain forests, as well as the region south of the Sahara in the modern-day country of the Republic of the Sudan.

The introduction of Islam led to increased trade, wealth, and literacy in western Africa. Because of the Muslim scholars of the time, a great deal is known about the history of Bilad-al Sudan prior to the era of European colonization that occurred after 1500.

See also: ISLAM, INFLUENCE OF (Vol. II).

Biram One of the seven independent kingdoms of HAUSA STATES located between the NIGER RIVER and Lake CHAD. The HAUSA STATES, established between the tenth and the thirteenth centuries by the KANEM-BORNU Empire, included Biram, DAURA, KATSINA, ZARIA, KANO, RANO, and GOBIR.

The eponymous Biram was founded and ruled by Biram, the son of Bayajida and the princess Magira of Bornu. As with the other Hausa states, Biram was an important trading center. It was also the original seat of the Hausa government.

See also: HAUSA STATES (Vol. III).

Bissau Important port city of the MALI EMPIRE from the thirteenth to the fifteenth centuries.

Located at the mouth of the GEBA RIVER on the Atlantic Ocean, Bissau, also spelled Bissao, was populated primarily by the Balanta, Fula, and Manjaca peoples. Bissau's economy was based on agriculture because of its warm, rainy climate. Local CROPS included yams, beans, kola nuts, millet, rice, and other grains.

See also: BISSAU (Vol. III); GUINEA-BISSAU (Vol. III); PORTUGAL AND AFRICA (Vol. III).

Bito (Babito) NILOTIC people who established the influential Bunyoro Kingdom. These East African people speak Luo, a NILO-SAHARAN language of the Chari-Nile branch. Prior to the fourteenth century, they lived peace-fully along the Bahr al-Ghazal tributary of the White Nile, where they grew millet and raised cattle.

The ancestors of the Bito, the LUO people, originally inhabited the southern areas of present-day SUDAN. During a period that extended from the seventh to the eleventh centuries, some of the Luo migrated towards the Agoro Mountains, where they intermarried with the local people and lived as hunters and farmers. After a devastating outbreak of a livestock disease, many of the mountain people migrated across the Nile.

These Luo people headed south to the KITARA region of eastern Africa sometime during the reign of that region's BACHWEZI ruler WAMARA (c. 1371–1398). Although the Bachwezi had only recently established their authority over the native BANTU-speaking peoples, their power was already at risk. Despite attempts by Wamara to integrate the Luo immigrants into Bachwezi society, they never fully assimilated. Political unrest between the people living in Kitara was exacerbated by a severe famine, which eventually sparked a military coup. As a result, the Bachwezi lost control of Kitara to the Luo and the TUTSI people. The new rulers divided Kitara and formed their own states, BUNYORO-KITARA to the north and Bahima in the south.

Kagoro, a Luo military commander appointed to office during Wamara's reign, ruled the new Bunyoro-Kitara Kingdom. He was followed by Owiny I, who ruled during the early fifteenth century and then by Prince Rukidi. Rukidi's followers were the first Luo to be officially recognized as Bito people (Bito-Luo). Rukidi's ascent to power can be traced back to the Luo who stayed in the Agoro Mountains after the outbreak of livestock disease. The Bito-Luo people encountered much hostility within their new kingdom and were eventually forced to move their capital from Bwera to BUGANGAIZI. As their power increased, they expanded their territory into the Bahinda states and RWANDA.

In their new kingdom, the Bito continued to practice agriculture and raise livestock. They were open to various forms of religion and emphasized loyalty to the king above all else. At first, kings (*kabaka*) were given almost divine status and were freed from such traditional practices as appointing tribal chiefs according to heredity. Instead, the kings were able to make autonomous decisions regarding the kingdom. However, before long, the Bito returned to their traditional government structures, relying more on hereditary rights and clan lineage than on a centralized political power.

See also: CLAN (Vol. I); LINEAGE (Vol. I).

blacksmiths See CRAFTSPEOPLE (Vol. II); IRON (Vol. II); IRONWORKING (Vol. II); *NUMUW* (Vol. II); *NYAMAKALAW* (Vol. II).

Bobo (Bwa) Ethnic group of the Volta River basin in West Africa. The Bobo are a subgroup of the MOSSI peoples who settled in areas of modern BURKINA FASO and IVORY COAST. Prior to the fifteenth century, the DYULA established a trade settlement in Bobo territory, south of JENNE. Called Bobo-Dioulasso, it was part of a network of

trade routes that connected it with WAGADUGU, the capital of the GHANA EMPIRE and the center of the West African GOLD trade.

> The Bobo are known as excellent CRAFTSPEOPLE and artists. Their traditional masks, some of which measure six feet high, are popular items on the modern African art market.

Like other Mossi people, the Bobo lived in autonomous village communities dominated by paternal lineages and maintained a caste system.

Bonny An Atlantic port city located in Nigeria. Bonny served as the capital of the kingdom of Bonny beginning in the 1400s, and it was the primary trading center of the IJO people. In 1505, the Portuguese captain Pacheco Pereira reported a "large village of some 2,000 dwellings," which has been identified as Bonny. The name of the city is derived from *Ibani*, the local name of the area.

See also: BONNY (Vol. III).

Bono People and state located west of the VOLTA RIVER in what is now modern Ghana. Bono was founded in the first half of the fifteenth century by the FANTE, a subgroup of the AKAN people, who occupied the forests of coastal Ghana. Bono contained numerous GOLD fields, and quickly developed into a major supplier in the trans-Saharan gold trade. Bono's capital, Bono-Mansu, was an active stop on the trade route from the northern city of JENNE.

> The kings of Bono, and especially Obunumankoma, who reigned from 1450 to 1475, are thought to have increased Bono's gold production by introducing advanced mining technology to the Akan fields.

The original Fante founders of Bono were not converts to ISLAM, but Muslim DYULA traders in Bono and the neighboring kingdoms of BANDA and Begho were instrumental to the prosperity of the region. During the late fifteenth and sixteenth century, some rulers of Bono were Muslims.

See also: BONO (Vol. III).

Borkou (Borku) Southeastern SAHARA desert region located in CHAD, between the Tibesti Massif and the Ennedi Plateau. The most important settlement in the region is the oasis town of Faya.

Although the harsh climate made life difficult, a small number of nomadic ARABS, BERBERS and TEDA people populated the area, perhaps as early as the seventh century. By the thirteenth century, Borkou was crossed by TRANS-SAHARAN TRADE ROUTES that linked West Africa with Cyrenaica, in LIBYA. Muslim pilgrims en route to MECCA from West Africa also passed through the region.

See also: CYRENE (Vol. I); HAJJ (Vol. II); TIBESTI (Vol. III).

Bornu Early state of present-day Nigeria active between the ninth and nineteenth centuries. Founded on the southern and western shores of Lake CHAD in 850, Bornu was originally inhabited by the SAO, Sudanic-speaking trans-Saharan traders who claimed their descent from the Dugu. These Hamito-Semitic people organized the early state of Bornu under traditional divine kingship rule. Saif, their first king, established NJIMI as the capital of the kingdom. In 1068, a Muslim member of the Duguwa royal family, MAI UMME, ascended to the Bornu throne. He founded the SEFUWA dynasty and set out to destroy the Duguwa traditional religion.

The early Sefuwa kings expanded Bornu territory from KANO in present-day Nigeria to parts of the SUDAN. By the late twelfth century, the powerful neighboring Muslim kingdom of Kanem began to encroach on Bornu territory. In 1242, the Duguwa regained control of Bornu from the Saifawa, but conflict with the Kanem continued.

The early Bornu state finally collapsed around 1260. At that time, Kanem took control of the region and established the KANEM-BORNU Empire. Dunama DIBBALEMI served as the first king of the new empire, which included Kano, Wadai, Adamawa, and Bornu. By 1400, the BULALA had seized Kanem-Bornu, converting it once again to the Bornu empire. The Bulala captured Njimi and reestablished the old Bornu dynasty until they were overthrown in the early 1500s.

See also: KANEM-BORNU (Vol. III)

Botswana (Bechuanaland) Modern landlocked country in southern Africa that is located on the African Plateau. Botswsana is bordered by present-day Zambia, ZIMBABWE, NAMIBIA, and SOUTH AFRICA.

Formerly known as Bechuanaland, Botswana consists mainly of semiarid desert and sparse savanna. The terrain is dominated by the Okavango Swamp to the northwest, rocky hill ranges to the east, and the KALAHARI DESERT to the south. Other than the Chobe, Okavango, and LIMPOPO Rivers, no other dependable water sources exist in Botswana. Thus, the country is sparsely inhabited, albeit by diverse groups of people. Approximately half of the population is ethnic Tswana, while the remainder is composed of Kgalagadi, Nwato, Tswapong, Birwa, and Kalanga peoples.

The early inhabitants of Botswana were the nomadic SAN and KHOIKHOI peoples, pastoralists whose ancestors lived there thousands of years ago. BANTU-speaking people migrated to the area around the first century CE. Settling throughout Botswana, the Bantu migrated as far east as the Kgalalgadi region by the eighth century. By the thirteenth century, new kingdoms had been established at Gabane to the south and in the Tsodilo Hills to the north.

The most numerous people in Botswana, the Tswana, migrated to present-day Transvaal in the eleventh to twelfth centuries. They established dynasties near the Vaal River, where they farmed and raised cattle. These nomadic people did not establish extensive permanent settlements in Botswana until the eighteenth century.

See also: BANTU (Vol. I); BOTSWANA (Vols. I, III); PASTORALISM (Vol. I); SAN (Vols. I, III); TRANSVAAL (Vol. III).

Brass Kingdom or chiefdom located in present-day Nigeria at the convergence of the NIGER RIVER and the Brass River in the Niger Delta. It was founded c. 1450 by Kala-Ekule, most likely as an early settlement of people migrating from BENIN.

Brong West African ethnic group and the region that they occupy in present-day Ghana. A subgroup of the AKAN people, the Brong traditionally have lived in regions of present-day IVORY COAST and the Brong region of Ghana. Their language, TWI, comes from the Kwa branch of the NIGER-CONGO family. Archaeological evidence suggests that the early inhabitants of the Brong region were pastoralists who also engaged in a limited amount of farming. The chief components of Brong civilization, which emerged from the sixth to eleventh centuries, included metallurgy, urban development, long-distance trade, and the formation of a state-based political system.

See also: AHAFO (Vol. III); BRONG (Vol. III); PASTORALISM (Vol. I).

bronze Alloy of COPPER and tin used in metalworking throughout Africa. The use of copper alloys developed in the northern regions of the continent, but by the fifth century, coppersmithing technology had spread into sub-Saharan Africa via TRANS-SAHARAN TRADE ROUTES.

Due to its softness and scarcity, copper was primarily used for decorative objects. Bronze, on the other hand, was a much harder metal, so it was often used to make weapons and tools. Bronze was not used exclusively for practical purposes, though. Archaeological evidence indicates that as early as the ninth century, peoples of Guinea and CAMEROON were casting bronze ornaments using the LOST-WAX PROCESS.

See also: BRONZE AGE (Vol. I).

Buganda Early East African kingdom in present-day UGANDA established by the GANDA (or Baganda) people. Founded at the end of the fourteenth century by BANTU-speaking people, Buganda became the most powerful kingdom in East Africa in the nineteenth century.

Oral tradition traces the origin of Buganda to a mystical figure named Kintu, or "First Man." The Ganda believed that Kintu and his wife, Nambi, not only founded Buganda along the shores of Lake VICTORIA, but also made the first cattle and BANANA plants in the region.

Modern archaeologists refer to the people who settled in Buganda from the thirteenth to sixteenth century as the Kintu complex of clans. These people established Buganda along with several other small principalities as they migrated southward from their homelands in what is now northwestern Uganda. The people of Buganda were united together under a single king (*kabaka*) who may well have been called SEKABAKA KINTU, as the oral tradition dictates.

Other historians believe that the first Buganda king was really Prince Kimera, a fifteenth-century rebel. NILOTIC-speaking people from the north also settled in Buganda around the same time. Together, these early inhabitants were known as *banansagwa*, meaning "people found in the place."

The Buganda social structure was based on paternal lineages. Regional chiefs served beneath the king, who acquired his wealth and power largely by raiding weak neighboring kingdoms. The inhabitants of Buganda relied primarily on agriculture for their livelihood, particularly on BANANAS, which were a major source of nourishment and were used to make beer. Buganda reached the height of its power in the nineteenth century.

See also: BUGANDA (Vols. I, III); BUNYORO (Vol. III).

Bugangaizi Early kingdom of the Great Lakes region of East Africa that was active between c. 1200 and 1500. BANTU-speaking people migrated to the Kitara region as

well as into present-day Bunyoro and Toto about the tenth and eleventh centuries. There, these agriculturalists formed several small kingdoms, including Bugangaizi.

Bugangaizi was founded by Hangi, a member of the Bagabu clan. By 1250, though, several other small Bantu kingdoms had emerged as offshoots of Bugangaizi. During the next 200 years, these small pastoral kingdoms joined together to become part of the BACHWEZI kingdom of Kitara, the predecessor of the BUNYORO-KITARA and BAHINDA states. Exactly how this evolution took place, however, is not altogether clear, as information from the period is limited to clan histories and oral tradition.

According to one theory, Bugangaizi and the surrounding Bantu kingdoms integrated with the HIMBA, who originally came from the northeast. These pastoralists apparently arrived peacefully during the thirteenth and fourteenth centuries and slowly gained political control of the Bantu kingdoms. Eventually they came to be known as a distinct people, the Bachwezi.

Other scholars believe that the Bachwezi emerged from established local rulers who gained control over Bugangaizi. Bugangaizi became part of the new empire of Kitara, which was founded by NDAHURA (c. 1344–1371), who conquered present-day Bunyoro, Buganda, Toro, northern Kigezi, northeast RWANDA, and western KENYA. Although Ndahura was unable to establish a centralized political system throughout his territory, he enjoyed a limited amount of success by appointing subrulers to represent him in these areas.

See also: BANTU (Vol. I); BUNYORO (Vol. I).

Bulala Nomadic people from the area around Lake Fitri who invaded Kanem in the fourteenth century. The Bulala took advantage of the disorganization of the SEFUWA (also known as Sayf or Sayfawa) dynasty that had ruled the KANEM-BORNU trading empire since the ninth century. Several related Sef *mais*, or kings, were fighting each other for control of the empire. Without a strong unified military force defending them, the kingdom was especially vulnerable. The Bulala took advantage of this opportunity and attacked Kanem around 1380, killing most of the *mais*. Some time around 1396 the Bulala drove Mai Umar Idrismi out of NJIMI, pushing him and the Kanembu people to the new Sefuwa capital at Bornu, on the west shore of Lake CHAD.

Bunyora-Kitara BANTU and NILOTIC kingdom that developed during the twelfth to fifteenth centuries in present-day UGANDA; it was once part of the Kitara complex.

The first settlers in the area, thought to be central Sudanic peoples, appear to have arrived in the Kitara complex as early as c. 700. Once there, they mixed with Bantu-speaking people who arrived from the west at about the

The Byzantine basilica called Hagia Sophia in Constantinople was once one of the premier churches in Christendom and the administrative headquarters of the church in Africa. The building, which dates to c. 535, became a mosque after the fall of Byzantium to the Turks. It is shown here in a lithograph by Louis Haghe (1826–1885), as based on a drawing by Chevalier Caspar Fussati. © *Historical Picture Archive/CORBIS*

same time. Forming small, agriculturally based villages, this new group primarily grew sorghum and other grains.

Eventually, the villages grew into small states that came under the control of BACHWEZI rulers. The warrior king NDAHURA (1344–1371) ultimately created and ruled over the Kitara complex, including the Bunyoro region. His successor, WAMARA (1371–1398), however, was overthrown by various invaders from the south and north.

Bachwezi's loss of control over Kitara resulted in a struggle for power between the people of Bunyoro-Kitara and the TUTSI states to the south. Finally, in 1500, Bunyoro-Kitara was victorious and began to expand toward the BAHINDA. It continued to flourish, becoming the most powerful state in the region until it was overshadowed by BUGANDA in the early nineteenth century.

See also: BUNYORO (Vols. I, III); BUGANDA (Vol. III).

Burkina Faso Landlocked West African country bordered by present-day Benin, IVORY COAST, Ghana, Mali, and Togo. Lying on a sloping plateau, Burkina Faso contains extensive plains, low hills, and high savannas, as well as a northern desert. Apart from Stone Age axes that have been found in the north, the region's first inhabitants left few clues as to who they were and how they lived. The most widely accepted theory is that they were agriculturalists who settled the savanna west of the Mouhoun (Black Volta) River, perhaps around 1100.

By the thirteenth century, the ancestors of the MOSSI people began migrating into the area from the east. By 1500, they were joined by horsemen from the north who subjugated the peoples they found in the region. From these groups eventually arose the Mossi states.

See also: KINGDOMS AND EMPIRES (Vol. II).

Bushmen See SAN.

Byzantine Africa   Area of North Africa, including EGYPT and part of LIBYA, that belonged to the Byzantine Empire from the third century CE until the rise of ISLAM in the seventh century.

Africa held an important place in the Byzantine emperor Justinian's scheme for reuniting the Roman Empire and destroying the Germanic Vandals who had invaded Africa toward the end of the fourth century. While his own invasion attempt was unsuccessful, his general Belisarius succeeded. In 533, Belisarius landed in North Africa, and within a year destroyed the Vandal kingdom.

Justinian (483–565) and his wife, Theodora (c. 502–548), were instrumental in the building, and particularly the decoration, of churches in Byzantine Africa and in the reestablishment of Christian orthodoxy. Little is known of Byzantine Africa after the death of Justinian. The power of the military in the provinces grew, and between 585 and 591 a new official, the *exarch*, was placed in charge. The court of Constantinople tended to neglect Africa because of the more immediate dangers on the eastern and Balkan borders, and the exarch functioned as the court's deputy in Africa. In 610, Heraclius, son of the ruling exarch, sailed from Carthage to Greece in a revolt against the unpopular emperor Phocas and succeeded him the same year.

Africa still had some importance to the empire in 619; the Persians had overrun much of the East, including Egypt, and at one point reached even the walls of Constantinople. Only Africa appeared able to provide money and recruits to keep the empire secure. Heraclius even briefly entertained leaving Constantinople to return to Carthage but changed his mind due to popular sentiment in the capital.

The rise of Islam, however, ended the Persian threat and also removed Egypt from Byzantine rule. Muslim ARAB armies invaded Persia and defeated the Persian army in 637. In 639, Arab Muslims invaded Egypt; by 642 they had captured Alexandria, the capital, and the Eastern Roman Empire was no longer a force in Africa.

See also: BYZANTINE AFRICA (Vol. I); CAESAR, OCTAVIAN (Vol. I); CHRISTIANITY (Vol. II).

C

Cairo Capital of EGYPT and largest city in Africa. Cairo was officially founded in 969. Prior to this, the city had a variety of names—Memphis, Heliopolis, Babylon, al-Fustat, al-Qataei, and al-Askar being just a few of them. During its history, it has been governed by an equally long list of rulers, from the ancient Egyptians, Greeks, and Romans to the ARABS, Turks, French, and British.

About 5,000 years ago, Menes, the legendary pharaoh who united the kingdoms of Upper and Lower Egypt, supposedly founded the city of Memphis, approximately 15 miles (24 km) south of modern-day Cairo. In 525 BCE, invading Persians established a fort, called Babylon, north of Memphis, from which they controlled Egypt. Babylonian domination continued until the arrival of Alexander the Great in 332 BCE. The region later fell under the rule of the Romans. The arrival of Islamic Arabs, around 640 CE, led to the founding of the town of al-Fustat, the seed from which contemporary Cairo sprang.

In 969, the FATIMIDS invaded Egypt from what is now Tunisia. A new walled city called al-Mansuriyah was established northeast of the existing settlements. In 973, the Fatimid caliph al-Mu'izz renamed the city al-Qahirah, or Cairo, making it the capital of a dynasty that lasted for 200 years. Al-Qahirah and al-Fustat coexisted until 1168, when al-Fustat was set on fire during the Christian CRUSADES. Eventually the Crusaders were defeated by an Islamic army from Syria. Their commander, the famous SALADIN (1137–1193), founded the Ayyubid dynasty, which claimed Cairo for the seat of its rule.

Under Saladin, Cairo became a thriving metropolis. Saladin constructed mosques, palaces, colleges, hospitals, and a fortress, called the Citadel, which has remained one of Cairo's most important landmarks ever since. After his death in 1193, Saladin was succeeded by male family members until the rule of Shagaret-el-Dorr, a MAMLUK who was the wife of the last Ayyubid sultan, al-Saleh. One of three women ever to rule Egypt, Shagaret-el-Dorr had a great influence on Cairo. After her murder, in 1260, Cairo became the capital of the Mamluk empire with Baybars I as its sultan.

By 1340, Cairo was at its height, with nearly 500,000 people living in an area five times larger than the original Fatimid walled city. Under the Mamluks, Cairo became the greatest city of Africa, Europe, and Asia Minor. The city's AL-AZHAR University was the undisputed center of Islamic scholarship. Cairo also was an important link in the lucrative East-West spice trade. This was also the period during which many of Cairo's architectural masterpieces were built.

In 1348, Cairo's population was decimated by plagues, including the infamous Black Death that swept across Europe. Decline set in soon after. Another blow came in 1497, when Vasco de GAMA's voyage from Portugal to India broke Cairo's spice-trade monopoly. Then, in 1517, the Turks conquered Cairo.

See also: CAIRO (Vols. I, III); MEMPHIS (Vol. I).

Cameroon Modern country in West-central Africa. The region that became Cameroon was occupied by various peoples, including the Sudanic-speaking SAO and FULANI, and the BANTU-speaking DYULA, FANG, and Bamileke, during the fifth through the fifteenth centuries.

Between the ninth and fifteenth centuries, the Sao established a kingdom that covered large parts of northern Cameroon and Nigeria. The Fulani, a Muslim people who first came to Cameroon in the eleventh century, lived on the Adamawa Massif. They dominated the peoples inhabiting the valleys of the Logone, Kebbi, and Faro Rivers valleys, converting many of them to ISLAM.

The Bamileke lived in the area that is now western and southern Cameroon. They were mainly farmers whose staple crops include corn and taro. Like other Bantu-related tribes, they migrated to Cameroon from equatorial Africa.

See also: BAMENDA GRASSFIELDS (Vol. III); BANTU MIGRATIONS (Vol. II); CAMEROON (Vol. III).

Cape Verde Islands Archipelago located in the central Atlantic Ocean, 385 miles (620 km) from the coast of present-day SENEGAL. Consisting of ten islands and five islets, Cape Verde is historically associated with the Portuguese olive trade to the Americas.

Cape Verde was discovered, in 1460, by the Portuguese navigators Diogo Gomes and António de Noli. There is little evidence to support the assertion that the islands were inhabited before the European arrival, although it is believed that the Moors may have sought salt here in previous centuries. In 1462, the first settlers arrived and founded the oldest European city in the tropics, Ribeira Grande. A governor and bishop were installed on the island of Santiago to administer to political and spiritual affairs.

Under the Charter of 1466, Portuguese settlers were allowed to trade freely with the Upper Guinea coastal cities, from Senegal to Sierra Leone. After securing trading posts on the islands, settlers began to establish trading settlements on the African mainland. As a result, the settlers merged with the African societies with whom they traded, taking African wives and establishing trading alliances with the leaders and local traders. These alliances gave rise to a new society called *lancados*, European or half-caste traders, who became acculturated in the African communities.

Although fishing and cane farming were established as principle industries early on, Cape Verde's limited rainfall, frequent droughts, and significant soil erosion were—and remain—incompatible with large-scale crop cultivation. Instead, grazing, subsistence farming, and fishing supplemented a limited salt and BANANA trade. Much more significant to the islands' economy was their location, which made Cape Verde a logical point of departure for trade between Africa and the Americas.

See also: CAPE VERDE (Vol. III); PORTUGAL AND AFRICA (Vol. III).

caravans Traders and others traveling together for mutual safety with their baggage and other goods through difficult or dangerous terrain. In Africa, the caravan is most often associated with trans-Saharan trade, although caravans were used on trade routes throughout Africa. Muslim pilgrims also traveled to MECCA in caravans.

The earliest animals possibly used to cross the desert were pack oxen, as depicted in Saharan rock art dating from before 4000 BCE found at Tassili in Algeria. The record here is unclear, however, because many scholars question the validity of using those paintings to establish historical fact. Reliable sources indicate that the Arabian camel, introduced into North Africa in the first century CE, became, by the fifth century, the pack animal of choice among the BERBER nomads. Although it could not carry much more than a pack ox, the camel could maintain a steady pace over longer distances and travel without water for up to ten days. The camel's broad, splayed feet gave it secure footing when walking on shifting sand, and it was equally able to endure the extreme heat of the desert day and the chilling cold of the desert night.

Loads of 350 pounds (160 kg) or more were equally divided and loaded onto the camel's back. Strings of forty or more camels were tethered together by a rope from each camel's nose ring to the saddle of the camel in front. Commonly, three or four strings of camels traveled abreast, moving at a speed of 2 to 3 miles (3 to 5 km) per hour for ten to fourteen hours daily, often at night for protection from the heat. It was a two-month journey, under the direction of a caravan chief with the assistance of local guides, to travel the TRANS-SAHARAN TRADE ROUTE from Sijilmasa in North Africa to Walata in the trading empire of Mali. Caravans taking this route often made a stopover at the Taghaza salt mines in the desert. Many caravans were lost to raiders or the elements. Gaining or keeping control of the staging areas were important goals of all the trading empires of West Africa.

The size of the trans-Saharan caravans was significant. Caravans averaged 1,000 camels with their loads. The Tunis-born Arab historian Ibn Khaldun (1332–1406), who wrote a definitive history of Muslim North Africa, records caravans of 12,000 camels between West Africa and Egypt. The largest caravans were usually involved in the all-important salt trade or in taking Muslim pilgrims on pilgrimage to Mecca in Saudi Arabia, one of the most important spiritual duties of the observant Muslim. These pilgrim caravans had to arrive in Mecca on the prescribed eighth day of Dhu al Hijjah, the last month of the Muslim year.

See also: TRANSPORTATION (Vol. II).

Casamance River River located in the coastal floodplain region of West Africa between present-day GAMBIA and Guinea-Bissau. The river is 160 miles (257 km) long and flows to the west, emptying into the Atlantic Ocean. During the period prior to European colonization, the land on either side of the river was populated by the Blante, the DYULA, and the Felupe peoples. During the

1500s, Portuguese explorers sailed through the estuaries and inlets of the river to penetrate inland, thereby transforming the Casamance River into a thoroughfare for the exchange of goods and ideas between the two civilizations.

See also: GUINEA-BISSAU (Vol. III); PORTUGAL AND AFRICA (Vol. III); SLAVERY (Vol. III).

cassava Edible starchy tuber that is also called manioc, mandioc, and yuca. Cassava is cultivated throughout sub-Saharan Africa and is used to make flour, breads, and *fufu*, a gelatinous food common in West Africa. Cassava, which also is cultivated on the east coast of Africa, has been a staple in the diet of native African peoples. It is believed that cassava was introduced to East Africa sometime between the fourth and eighth centuries by INDONESIAN COLONISTS and that cultivation spread rapidly.

Cassava, unlike millet and other grain CROPS, is easy to cultivate, which usually leads to a successful harvest. The plant itself is perennial and has palm-shaped leaves. It can thrive in dry areas and can grow in alkaline soil or in acidic mud banks along rivers. It is an extremely adaptable species and comprises many different varieties. Certain species produce a sugar derivative that contains cyanide (hydrocyanic acid). The poison, which is manufactured by a system of grating, pressing, and heating the roots, is used as the toxin on poison darts and arrows.

cavalry Horse-mounted branch of the military. In Africa, horses were traded via the TRANS-SAHARAN TRADE ROUTES from North Africa and the Middle East to the western SUDAN, where the region's empires and kingdoms used horses in their military conquests.

African cavalry units often came from the highest levels of society. The cavalry of the empire of MALI, for example, was an elite corps of the military, and membership was reserved for the aristocracy. The members of the cavalry were called the *ton-tigi*, or "quiver and bow bearers."

The powerful SONGHAI Empire of the fifteenth century also possessed an impressive cavalry, with as many as 10,000 horse-mounted soldiers. Because of the high cost of the horses (each horse was equivalent in cost to ten captives), the Songhai cavalry, too, was composed only of members of the aristocracy.

At the start of the twelfth century, horses were brought from areas north of the SAHARA and traded for GOLD and IVORY. By the end of the century, however, they were being bred in the Niger River valley.

In Kanem, the capital of the kingdom OF KANEM-BORNU, North African merchants traveled to the city to trade for horses during the fifteenth century. These horses were referred to as "war horses" since they were larger and stronger than the ones owned and bred within the empire. It is reported that the king of Kanem had a cavalry of more than 40,000 horses, which illustrates the enormous impact of trade upon Kanem-Bornu's prosperity.

See also: HORSES (Vol. I); WARFARE AND WEAPONS (Vol. II).

Chad Region of Africa marked by the Tibesti Massif to the north, Lake CHAD to the west, and the savannas of the Sahel to the south, and separated into two distinct northern and southern regions by the Chari River. It is bordered by the modern country of LIBYA to the north, Niger to the West, Equatorial Guinea to the southwest, the Central African Republic to the south, and SUDAN to the east.

Because of its strategic location on Lake Chad, the region saw many kingdoms and conquests during its history. In the eighth century, BERBERS migrated into the area in order to escape the droughts of the Saharan borderlands. By the eleventh century, Muslim ARABS from the north had begun regularly raiding the area for captives, establishing their religion as they came and went. As a result, Arab culture gradually superseded the native African ones and undermined the autonomy of the local kingdoms.

The KANEM-BORNU Empire, located to the northeast of Lake Chad, was an amalgamation of nomadic peoples who spoke Teda-Daza languages and were dominated by the ZAGHAWA people. (The names *Zaghawa* referred to the people who lived in the region and *Kanem* referred to the configuration of states that bordered the lake.) Local oral traditions speculate that the Arab Sayf ibn Dhu Yazan united these people and began the SEFUWA dynasty, which ruled Kanem from the ninth century to the nineteenth century.

See also: CHAD (Vol. III); KANEM-BORNU (Vol. III).

Chad, Lake Large lake located in West-central Africa. The fourth-largest lake in Africa, Lake Chad is what remains of a much larger and more ancient inland sea. A shallow lake with two basins, one at the north and one at the south, its main tributaries are the Chari and Logone Rivers.

During the ninth century, the empire of KANEM-BORNU was established to the northeast of Lake Chad. The state was a melding of several nomadic people who spoke languages of the Teda-Daza (Toubou) group. The leaders were ancestors of the Kanembu people and were given the title *mai,* or king. SEFUWA lineage was established as the ruling dynasty of Kanem.

During the tenth century, Arabs migrated from the north and east, bringing their Islamic religion to the area. Around the end of the eleventh century, the Sefuwa king Mai Humai Dunamab Ifummay converted to Islam.

Kanem expanded, and by the thirteenth century a capital was established at NJIMI, northeast of Lake Chad. The expansion of Kanem was at its height under the reign of Mai Dunama Dibbalemi (c. 1221–1259).

Chadic languages Major subgroup of the family of AFRO-ASIATIC LANGUAGES. The Chadic group is comprised of many languages, the most important of which is HAUSA. During the thirteenth century, some of the Chadic languages changed substantially as North African Muslim traders integrated with the native Chadic-speaking groups, introducing many of their their ARABIC words to the language.

See also: LANGUAGES (Vol. I); LANGUAGES, MAJOR (Vol. II).

Changamire (fifteenth century) *Ruler of Matapa state in modern-day Zimbabwe.*

During the middle of the fifteenth century, the BANTU-speaking Karanga peoples created a powerful kingdom that eventually came to include the majority of the southern part of modern-day ZIMBABWE. The kingdom's ruling dynasty, the founding of which is variously ascribed to the warrior kings Mutapa or Nyatsimba, successfully dominated the region for a number of years. In the late fifteenth century, King Matope expanded the kingdom significantly. By the time Matope's son Mokombo came to the throne in 1480, however, the *mwene matapa,* as the ruler was known, faced increasing unrest among the kingdom's various provincial governors and other vassals.

The title used by Changamire's rulers—*mwene matapa*—means "master pillager." Instead of being considered an insult, the term was thought of as a title of respect.

Ultimately, in about 1490, one of Mokombo's governors, Changamire, led a full-scale insurrection. According to various tales, Changamire believed that Mokombo wanted to kill him, and, in response, led a group of soldiers to Mokombo's capital, GREAT ZIMBABWE. There, the majority of Mokombo's soldiers deserted him, leaving only a handful of guards and courtiers to defend him. Entering the royal quarters, Changamire quickly beheaded Mokombo with a single blow of his sword and proclaimed himself king.

Changamire then attempted to make his position on the throne more secure by trying to have all twenty-two of Mokombo's children killed. One of the princes escaped, however, and, four years later, led an army against Changamire. The battle that resulted apparently lasted for several days until Changamire finally was killed by the young prince himself.

Mokombo's son then became the *mwene matapa.* While much of the country recognized Mokombo's authority, a number of Changamire's supports resisted. Strife between the two factions continued for a number of years, with Changamire's allies eventually establishing a small, independent kingdom centered around the remnants of the city of Great Zimbabwe. During this period, both mining and the GOLD trade suffered significantly, which apparently led the Portuguese to take more direct control of the region. By the beginning of the sixteenth century, power had begun to pass to the Portuguese, and even the *mwene matapa* was under Portuguese domination.

See also: CHANGAMIRE DYNASTY (Vol. III); INDIAN OCEAN TRADE (Vol. II); MWENE MATAPA (Vol. III); ROZWI (Vol. III).

Chemama Region and river valley on the northern bank of the Senegal River in present-day Mauritania. It was part of the MALI EMPIRE during the fourteenth century, and later, in the sixteenth century, became part of the HAUSA STATES. A biologically diverse region, Chemama has a complex ecosystem created by the annual flooding of the SENEGAL RIVER. Its land has rich alluvial soils that have long supported farming and herding.

Chinese trade Despite reports of the presence of Chinese traders in Africa as early as the seventh century BCE, Chinese trade did not begin in earnest until the expeditions of Cheng-Ho, which took place between 1405 and 1433. Cheng-Ho, a grand admiral of the Chinese navy, commanded a large squadron of ships that landed on the SWAHILI COAST at the port of KILWA in East Africa.

The relatively late arrival of the Chinese to Africa is explained by the fact that it was not until after the eleventh century that Chinese vessels sailed south or west of the

Indonesian island of Java. Then, in 1402, a Korean map was published that included an outline of southern Africa.

The ships in Cheng-Ho's fleet were up to 500 feet long (152.4 m), making them five times larger than any of the Portuguese-made vessels that arrived at the same East African port in the early sixteenth century. The squadron was equally large in number. On previous voyages, which had gone to ports in Southeast Asia and the Red Sea, Cheng-Ho had commanded fleets of up to sixty-two ships, carrying as many as 27,800 men.

The African products that Cheng-Ho brought back—including GOLD, amber, IVORY, and captives—were highly valued in China. It is reported that in 1417 he returned with a delegation from Malindi who presented the royal court at Beijing with a giraffe.

Chinese trade was dominated by the import of porcelain in East Africa. Pieces created during the rule of China's Song dynasty have been documented through excavation in several homes of wealthy Swahili traders during the period. Bluish-white Ming porcelain arrived in the fifteenth century at the port of GEDI. Chinese trade—along with Persian, Arab, and Indian trade—contributed both to the cultural and economic development of Swahili civilization in the fifteenth century. By the end of the fifteenth century, however, China returned to a policy of isolation. From that time on, trade with Africa was curtailed.

Chokwe (Cokwe, Ciokwe, Bajokwe, Badjok)

Central African people who trace their origins to the Mbuti. Around 1500, the Chokwe came under the rule of the LUNDA KINGDOM when a disinherited Lunda prince moved westward into the area straddling present-day ANGOLA, Democratic Republic of Congo, and Zambia. Conquering the people in his path, the prince created a kingdom for the Chokwe people.

See also: CHOKWE (Vol. III); LUNDA EMPIRE (Vol. III).

Christianity

The religion based on the teachings of Jesus Christ; JUDAISM, Christianity, and ISLAM, are the world's three great monotheistic religions.

Chapter 2 of the Gospel of St. Matthew, the first book of the New Testament of the Christian Bible, records the flight of the holy family from Judea in Palestine into Egypt to keep the infant Christ from falling into King Herod's hands. Although this visit, otherwise undocumented, antedated Christian missionary activity by several hundred years, it points to the long-term connection between Africa and Christianity.

Doctrinal disputes were frequent in the early days of the Christian Church. Some, like Arianism, originated in Africa. Others arose elswehere but soon engulfed the universal church. The patriarch of Rome, the pope, was beginning to emerge as the central authority of the church in the West, but patriarchates also existed in Constantinople, Jerusalem, Antioch, and Alexandria, and each *patriarch*, or bishop of the highest rank, jealously guarded his prerogatives. Dogma and doctrine were shaped and refined as church leaders convened in ecumenical councils, including the Council of Nicea in 325 (at which the Nicene Creed, or statement of beliefs, was developed), the Council of Constantinople in 381, and the Council of Chaccedon in 451. These ecumentical councils, attended by the bishop from every local church, determined the official position of the universal church on the major theological disputes of the period.

Donatism and Pelagianism The church in North Africa in the fifth century continued to be embroiled in its own internal disputes, some stemming from issues in speculative theology and others from juridical concerns that had originated in earlier centuries. Donatism and Pelagianism remained issues in the North African Church and in the church at large. The Donatist schism between Rome and large segments of the church in North Africa persisted until the rise of Islam in the seventh century effectively ended a meaningful Christian presence in the region. Many historians believe that these internal theological and political disputes turned the church's energies inward, not just in Africa but across the whole Byzantine Empire, and left the empire in a diminished position to face the onslaughts of Islam in the seventh century.

Donatism, which had persisted since the third century, was based on disagreement on the question of whether an unworthy minister may worthily administer the sacraments. The African Church took the position, condemned by the church at large, that the minister himself had to be holy. Rome's position was that the validity of the sacraments came from God, not man.

The Pelagian heresy, prompted by the teachings of the early fifth-century British monk Pelagius, centered on the more speculative matters of free will, predestination, original sin, and divine grace.

Arianism The Arian heresy, which arose in Egypt in the third century, dominated the Greek-speaking Eastern

Church in the fourth century, and then spread through the Western Church, remaining a force in Europe until the eighth century. The Vandals that invaded North Africa from Europe in the fourth century and captured Carthage were Arian Christians. The Visigoths, who established a large empire in what is now Spain and France, were also Arian Christians, as were the Germanic groups that sacked Rome in the late fifth century. Their cause was both political and theological.

Arius (c. 250–336), a priest from Alexandria in Egypt, preached a doctrine that said that Christ, who died on the cross, could not be one with God the Father, the transcendent Creator. The Council of Nicea, a meeting of church leaders in 325, condemned Arian beliefs as heretical.

Monophysitism The Council of Chalcedon of 451, which affirmed traditional beliefs in the dual nature of Christ as god and man, alienated Monophysite believers in Egypt and Syria, who held that Christ had a single, divine nature. During the next 250 years, the Byzantine emperors and patriarchs sought to reconcile the Monophysites but in vain. The Armenian Apostolic Church, Coptic Orthodox Church, Ethiopian Orthodox Church, and Syrian Orthodox Church were formed in schism with Constantinople, the city that was the center of the church in the Eastern Roman Empire, and were outside the mainstream of Christian thought.

In the seventh century and later, many, but not all, members of the Coptic Church converted rather than suffer the periodic bouts of persecution waged by Islamic rulers. Nevertheless, the Coptic Church has remained intact to modern times. Similarly, in Nubia, adherents of Christianity underwent pressure to adopt Islam but after a brief stand-off, they retained their right to Christian worship.

The Ethiopian Orthodox Church The church in Ethiopia, though sometimes beset by its Muslim neighbors, kept its independence but became a church turned in on itself, with few influences from the outside world. Although its bishops were named by the Coptic Church of Egypt (a practice that ended in the twentieth century), neither church was in communion with the main centers of Christianity in Rome or Constantinople because of their adherence to Monophysite beliefs. The Ethiopian Church's main contact with the outside Christian world was through the Ethiopian monastery in the holy city of Jerusalem. Since the late 1100s, this group has maintained control of a chapel in Jerusalem's Church of the Holy Sepulchre, thought by believers to be the burial place of Jesus Christ.

The kingdom of AKSUM established Christianity as its state religion in the fourth century. Surrounded by regions in which traditional African religion flourished, the Ethiopian Orthodox Church remained highly conservative. Christian beliefs won converts through interaction with local populations, and its rites and religious practices were infused with traditional African elements. For instance, many of Ethiopia's monasteries attracted priests who were highly politicized and outspoken advocates on behalf of the poor. The church celebrated the Virgin Mary in keeping with its belief in the divine nature of Christ but also recognized many martyred saints. Church officials were known for performing exorcisms to rid the population of evil spirits. A widespread belief held that these spirits were kept at bay by amulets containing prayers and formulas carried in little books or leather cases. These were worn around the neck or arms by local populations as well as by visiting Islamic merchants, who held similar beliefs. The observance of fasts, feasts, and Jewish practices related to diet were also among the Christian practices of Ethiopia. Ethiopia's imperial leadership resisted the advance of Islam through its powerful alliance and support by the church. After Aksum declined in the seventh and eighth centuries, subsequent leadership maintained Christian traditions in the face of repeated clashes involving the establishment of powerful Muslim states within its interior.

Christianity began to spread southward from Ethiopia in the twelfth and thirteenth centuries, but only slowly, because of Arab naval supremacy in the Indian Ocean. It remained for missionaries from Europe to return Christianity to a greater level of importance, but that did not occur until the colonial era.

See also: CHRISTIANITY (Vol. I); DEBRE DAMO (Vol. II); GUDIT (JUDITH), QUEEN (Vol. II); KINGDOMS AND EMPIRES (Vol. II); KONGO KINGDOM (Vol. III); LALIBELA (Vol. II); MONOPHYSITE (Vol. I); NINE SAINTS (Vol. II); NUBIA, CHRISTIAN (Vol. II); SABBATARIANS (Vol. II); ZAGWE DYNASTY (Vol. II).

Further reading: Elizabeth Isichei, *A History of Christianity in Africa: From Antiquity to the Present* (Grand Rapids, Mich.: Eerdmans Publishing, 1996); John S. Mbiti, *African Religions and Philosophy*, 2nd ed. (Oxford, Eng.: Heinemann Educational Publishers, 1989).

Christianity, influence of Between the fifth and fifteenth centuries, the influence of CHRISTIANITY was strong in North Africa, EGYPT, Nubia, and ETHIOPIA until the rise of ISLAM and all but nonexistent in SUB-SAHARAN AFRICA. Despite the decline of Christian influence during this period, many events that happened in the early centuries of the church in Africa had long-term repercussions for the Christian Church outside Africa.

Christian culture in the fifth century kept Africa in contact with the broader world of Mediterranean culture

This tenth-century fresco of Adam and Eve from the Old Testament is in the Coptic Museum in Cairo, Egypt. © *Gianni Dagli Orti/CORBIS*

in the same way that Islam in the eighth century placed Africa in the cultural orbit of Muslim Baghdad and Damascus in the Middle East. In the fifth century, however, Rome and Constantinople were the dominant cultural and religious influences in the region. The major figures of the church in Africa in previous centuries, notably St. Augustine, the late fourth-century bishop of Hippo Regius, near Carthage, influenced religious thought throughout the Christian world. As the fifth century began, the church in Africa faced the same questions about its core beliefs that challenged the church at large.

The Church in Sub-Saharan Africa Until Portugal's attempt to introduce Christianity into sub-Saharan Africa during the reign of Prince HENRY THE NAVI-GATOR (1394–1460), indigenous Christianity existed primarily in North Africa and along the eastern regions of the continent—in Egypt, Nubia, and Ethiopia. Besides being motivated by religious zeal to Christianize the lands south of the Sahara, Prince Henry, some authorities conclude, may have been attempting to outflank ISLAM, Europe's main rival, from the rear as well as gain a political and commercial foothold in the region. These attempts at conversion, though successful in such places as the KONGO KINGDOM in 1491, had no long-term results, and Christianity vanished almost without a trace in these regions until missionaries returned in the 1800s.

The Church in North Africa From the end of the second century, Carthage had its own bishop, and North African Christianity was in the mainstream of the Western Church centered in Rome.

Throughout the fourth and fifth centuries, the North African Church was beset by Pelagianism and the schism caused in 311 by the Donatists, which was to last until Roman Africa fell to Islam in the mid-seventh century. Pelagianism, the doctrine preached by the early fifth-century British monk Pelagius, denied the orthodox doctrine of original sin and the need for God's grace. St. Augustine (c. 354–430), bishop of Hippo (modern Annaba, Algeria), was its fiercest opponent. Pelagianism was condemned by the Council of Carthage in 418 and finally disappeared by 529.

At its height, Donatism, a separatist movement led by a North African bishop named Donatus (d. 355), held the allegiance of 500 bishops in North Africa; the Donatists successfully exploited the differences between the wealthy Latin-speaking peoples in the coastal cities and the poor Punic-speaking people in the hinterlands by, among other ways, celebrating the liturgy in Punic rather than in Latin. The Donatist schism survived into the seventh century and the arrival of Islam.

The Arab invasions of North Africa (640–711) effectively ended the presence of Christianity in North Africa. Christianity had never taken root among the BERBER peoples, and Islam had no greater success at this time. Early Arab rulers in North Africa made few efforts to convert the hinterlands; it took more than a century for Islam to spread beyond the coastal towns. As long as they paid tribute to local Arab rulers, the Berbers were left alone.

The Church in Egypt COPTIC CHRISTIANITY was strongly influenced by the Monophysite belief in the single divine nature of Jesus Christ. In 451, the Council of Chalcedon, a meeting of important church leaders, declared Monophysitism a heresy, leading the Coptic Church to break with Rome and establish the Coptic Orthodox Church, with the patriarch of Alexandria as its head. Popular feelings ran high. In Alexandria, a band of Monophysite monks was boiled in oil in front of the cathedral. There were bloody uprisings among the people, and the dispute about the single or dual nature of Jesus Christ raged on for years. These internal conflicts very likely weakened Egypt and the empire and left both less able to resist the single-minded threat of Islam. By the sixth century, three distinct Monophysite churches had developed, the Jacobite Church of Syria, the Orthodox Church in Armenia, and the Coptic Church in Egypt and Ethiopia.

After the Muslims invaded Egypt in 639, the Coptic Church used the opportunity to assert its independence from Constantinople, its rival, and set up an autonomous Monophysite Church under the patriarch of Alexandria. The Coptic Church, however, moved to the periphery of Egyptian life because the majority of Egyptians converted to Islam.

The Church in Ethiopia Ethiopia was converted in the fourth through sixth centuries by Monophysite missionaries from the Coptic Church of Egypt.

When the power of AKSUM waned, other Ethiopian states arose in the highlands; of their history, little is known. Through their influence, some of the characteristic features of Ethiopian Christianity began to emerge, including its emphasis on its alleged Old Testament roots and its strong identification with Zion. Like the Ethiopian Coptic Church, from which it received most of its metropolitans, or heads of church, the Ethiopian Church had a strong monastic tradition, and its monasteries were centers of learning. Ethiopia's isolation at this point in its history—and not the traditionally held descent from a lost tribe of Israel—may be the factor that led the church to link itself so closely in life and worship to the Old Testament.

The kings of the eleventh- and twelfth-century ZAGWE DYNASTY built many churches in honor of the Christian religion, the most famous of which are the underground stone churches at the capital city of al-ROHA, renamed LALIBELA after the builder-king. The Zagwe kings trace their ancestry to the daughter of the last Aksumite kings, from whom the Zagwe rulers usurped the throne. The church legitimized their seizure of power, it is thought, in return for sizable donations. Yehrahana Krestos (r. 1133–1172), Lalibela (r. 1172–1212), and Ka'akweto La'ab (r. 1212–1260), three renowned church-builders who were members of this dynasty, were canonized by the Ethiopian Church.

The Ethiopian church traces its stewardship of one of the chapels in the Church of the Holy Sepulchre, the reputed burial site of Jesus Christ, in Jerusalem, to a gift from the Egyptian sultan SALADIN (c. 1137–1193) to King Yehrahana Krestos and the Christians of Ethiopia.

The successor of Yehrahana Krestos, his cousin Harbe, attempted to break the dependence of the Ethiopian Church on the Coptic Church by demanding that the Ethiopian bishop Abba Mika'el ordain more bishops, a privilege Abba Mika'el said was restricted to the patriarch of Alexandria. With more bishops, Harbe thought, the Ethiopian Church could consecrate an archbishop and free itself from Egypt. Although Muslim authorities in Egypt supported Harbe's move, the patriarch did not, warning that the move could cause hostility between Muslims and Christians. The issue was dropped, and Egypt continued to name the head of the Ethiopian Church until 1959, when Emperor Haile Selassie (1892–1975) finally made the break.

The Church and the Byzantine Empire The Byzantine emperor Justinian I (r. 527–565), a strong defender of religious orthodoxy, attempted to unite the Church across the empire. Under his absolute power, the Church was to achieve its greatest influence in the East. Among his accomplishments in religious matters, he made sure that the bishops of all the major centers of Christianity—Rome in Italy, the empire's capital at Constantinople, Antioch in southern Turkey, Alexandria in Egypt, and Jerusalem in Palestine—were officially given the title of patriarch, with extensive privileges and an official income.

The rise of Islam in the following century, however, drastically lessened the authority of Alexandria, Antioch, and Jerusalem as centers of Christianity. With the loss to the Arabs of these patriarchates and the marginalization of their influence in the Christian world, religious power became more concentrated in the hands of their ancient rivals, Rome and Constantinople. Eastern Christianity centered ever more strongly on Constantinople as the church in the East and West drifted culturally and politically apart. As Europe drifted more deeply into its Dark Ages (400–1000), learning and culture, at an ebb in Europe, centered on and flourished in Constantinople, which finally broke with Rome in 1054. The eastern portion became known as the Orthodox Church; the western branch, the Catholic Church.

The Church in Nubia Christian missionaries converted NUBIA in the sixth century. Theodora (497–548), the wife of the Byzantine emperor Justinian I, was an outspoken defender of Monophysite doctrines, although the emperor himself was orthodox in his beliefs. In 543, at Theodora's request and at the request of the Egyptian Coptic Church, the monk Julian traveled to Nobatia, one of the three kingdoms that made up the Nubia of the day. By 580, the last of the three kingdoms of Nubia were converted. Christian Nubia left the world a substantial legacy of religious art and architecture from this period. The Nubian Church, however, had little effect on the church at large.

By 652, a Muslim army captured the citystate of Dongola, the last Christian stronghold in Nubia, and forced it to pay tribute to Egypt. In a highly unusual move for its time, the Muslim conquerors and the Nubian Christians lived under a treaty, called a *bakt*, that guaranteed a strong measure of autonomy and religious freedom to Nubia. Dongola remained Christian until the fourteenth century, and another Nubian city, Alwah, remained Christian until the sixteenth century, when each fell to Turkish or Muslim invaders.

See also: CHRISTIANITY (Vol. I); CHRISTIANITY, INFLUENCE OF (Vol. III); BYZANTINE AFRICA (Vol. II); LALIBELA, ROCK CHURCHES OF (Vol. II); NUBIA, CHRISTIAN (Vol. II).

Further reading: Elizabeth Isichei *A History of Christianity in Africa: From Antiquity to the Present* (Grand Rapids, Mich.: Eerdmans Publishing, 1996).

Chwezi (Cwezi) kingdom One of the most important kingdoms of the interior of eastern Africa by the fourteenth century. The Chwezi kingdom was located in the region of modern UGANDA. It existed only for a relatively short period and was characterized by a small population ruled by a sophisticated system of government. Its elite class and its common people were subject to different laws, with the burden of taxation heavier on the common people.

The BACHWEZI, as the people of the Chwezi kingdom are known, ruled over several districts between the Somerset, Nile and Katonga Rivers, the foothills of Mount Rwenzori, and the plains of central BUGANDA. These districts included Bunyara, Buruli, Bugaya, Bugoma, Mwenge, Kyaka, TORO, Busongora, and Bwera.

Unlike the vast lands ruled by the kingdoms of the SUDAN, ETHIOPIA, GREAT ZIMBABWE, or the other kingdoms of the period, the territory ruled by the Chwezi kingdom was small and surrounded by hundreds of tiny chiefdoms which were located throughout the area of present-day Buganda, eastern RWANDA, and northwestern Tanzania. These populations had little contact with each other despite their proximity. It was not until the post-Chwezi period that these populations combined to create the first precolonial states of the region.

See also: CHWEZI DYNASTY (Vol. III).

city-state Political, social, and territorial system in Africa in which a city governs its surrounding regions; city-states generally are the smallest system of organization as compared to kingdoms and empires. In Africa, the populations of such cities and their neighboring regions usually were of a common culture and were united under the leadership of a sovereign king.

The HAUSA city-states of Nigeria and the city-states of the YORUBA are among the most notable examples of this system. In each case the city-state was run by a sophisticated system of cultural and political codes. A mother city, DAURA for the Hausa city-states and ILE-IFE for the Yoruba, served as the locus for all activities.

Historically, city-states often evolved into larger kingdoms or empires by means of the acquisition of new territories. (This usually was accomplished through conquest.) KANEM-BORNU in Chad, for example, emerged from two independent city-states, Kanem and Bornu. The thirteenth-century city-state of GREAT ZIMBABWE in southern Africa is another example of a powerful city-state, although it was abandoned by 1450 and did not evolve into a larger political and social structure.

See also: KINGDOMS AND EMPIRES (Vol. II).

A weaver in the Royal Weavers Village of Bonwire, near Kumasi in modern Ghana, demonstrates how cloth was woven on the traditional heddle loom. The long threads are the warp. © *Owen Franken/CORBIS*

cloth Domestic and trade textiles, usually made by loom. Such cloth was used for clothing and ceremonial purposes. Some cloth was exchanged in internal trade with other African peoples; most was kept to satisfy domestic needs. Fine cloth, including silk, however, was often imported from China by Arab traders and sold to inland peoples. In some cases, the silk was unraveled and the threads used to make local cloth, often destined for the garments of an important ruler. Because of the climate and the fragility of cloth, few African textiles of any antiquity have been preserved. The earliest fragments of loom-woven cloth date from the eleventh century and were found in burial caves along the Bandiagara cliffs in the area of modern Mali inhabited by the DOGON people.

All cloth, no matter its origins, is woven on a loom in similar ways. The long parallel threads that run lengthwise in a piece of cloth are called the *warp*. The warp threads are attached to the base and at the top of the loom. The warp usually consists of two separate sets of alternating threads, which are moved apart to allow a cross thread to be passed between them by means of a device called a *shuttle*. The cross threads are called the *weft* or the *woof*. Using different colors of thread in the weft creates a design. The development of the heddle, not original to Africa but used throughout the continent, is considered to be the most important single advance in loom technology. Its origin is not known. A heddle is a device that separates the warp threads so that the shuttle can be inserted and passed between them. The width of the cloth is determined by the width of the loom; narrow strips of cloth can be sewn together to produce wider sheets of fabric.

Of the two main types of looms used in Africa, the earliest is the pit loom, which may have been used originally in Arabia. A pit loom utilizes a frame built over a pit, into which extend the treadles used to separate the warp threads. The weaver's hands are thus left free to operate the shuttles. The other common loom is called a heddle loom, which, in its earliest forms, used movable rods to separate the warp threads to either side of the main sheet of cloth. The eleventh-century Arab traveler al-BAKRI recorded seeing what is thought to have been a double heddle narrow strip loom in 1068 in the town of SILLA, in present-day MAURITANIA. Remnants of c. ninth-century fabric from a single heddle loom were found at Igbo Ukwu in Nigeria. Vertically mounted single heddle looms are known to have been in use among the IBO and the YORUBA peoples. Vertical looms were used in what is now eastern Nigeria and the Democratic Republic of Congo to produce raffia cloth from grass fibers. Simple ground looms were widely used in parts of CAMEROON and throughout East Africa. Both the narrow strip loom and the vertically mounted single heddle loom were very likely developed in Africa.

Kinds of Cloth Embroidered raffia cloth, made from the leafstalks of various varieties of palm trees, was once produced across central Africa. For example, the BANTU-speaking Kuba people, whose kingdom emerged c. 1600 from a cluster of Bantu-speaking groups who lived between the Kasai and Sankuru Rivers in what is now the Democratic Republic of Congo, produced long raffia dance skirts and embroidered cloth panels for court ceremonies and rituals. Looms for raffia cloth were generally operated only by men. The cloth fragments found at Igbo Ukwu were made of raffia fiber. Throughout Africa, grass cloth was handwoven into bold geometric patterns and used to make baskets, headdresses, and other objects.

Gender roles often defined weaving and other occupations. In SUB-SAHARAN AFRICA, sculptors and blacksmiths were most often men, but potters were women. The weavers who used the double heddle narrow strip looms and central African rafia looms were men, whereas it is thought that female weavers, especially among the Yoruba and the Ibo peoples, most often used single heddle looms, which were propped vertically against a house wall. The single heddle loom was used to produce wider cloths. Among the Yoruba and the SONINKE, indigo dying was women's work, yet among the HAUSA, males did the dyeing. There are also religious overtones to the work. Among the Yoruba, cloth was taken to a dyer called an *aloro* who was believed to work under the protection of the orisha, or minor divinity, Iya mapo.

Besides raffia, cloth was made from a variety of fibers. Antedating woven textiles is cloth made of tree bark, which, for example, the GANDA people, now of Uganda, traditionally wore as part of ritual garb on ceremonial occasions when ancestors were worshiped. Throughout Africa locally grown cotton was spun into thread for weaving. In North Africa and the Sahel, women also spun thread and made cloth from camel hair and sheep hair. Jute and flax were also used in West Africa.

African weavers wove both patterned fabrics and plain cloth, the latter often used for daily wear or deco-

rated in a variety of ways, commonly by dyeing, embroidering, and sewing on contrasting fabrics. Vegetable dyes were commonly used as coloring agents. Indigo plants produced a deep blue color; kola nuts and the bark of camwood and redwood trees produced reddish brown colors. A variety of other plants and tree barks were used to produce greens, yellows, and blacks. Cloth was sometimes dyed by using a dye-resistant substance such as CASSAVA paste or wax with which to draw a pattern on the cloth. When dipped into the dye, the treated portions do not accept the color and the pattern emerges. Soninke women applied the paste with a comb to produce wave-like designs. The BAMBARA applied the paste to produce a speckled pattern. Other fabrics were colored by tie-dying, in which raffia thread was used to tie off patterned bundles of the fabric, keeping the dye from penetrating them.

In North Africa, Arab and BERBER patterns appear in textile designs; SUB-SAHARAN AFRICA has its own indigenous designs, the most famous of which is the richly textured *kente* cloth, which dates back to the twelfth century and was first worn at the court of the king of ancient Ghana. The name of this cloth comes from an ASHANTI word that means "basket," after its resemblance to the texture of a woven basket. Kente cloth was traditionally made of silk obtained in trans-Saharan trade and, later, in Indian Ocean coastal trade. The traditional *bogolonfini*, or mud cloth, fabric made by Bambara women of ancient Mali uses colors and designs seen also in TIMBUKTU and other cities of the MALI EMPIRE. Garments of this cloth were worn in ceremonies marking birth, coming of age, marriage, and death. The first indigenous printed fabric, the *andinkra* cloth made by the Ashanti people, was not produced until the early 1800s.

The Cloth Trade Commercial cloth production was important in some parts of precolonial Africa. Guilds of weavers and dyers were formed in Tunisia as early as the tenth century. Cloth was often used as currency in West Africa.

Cloth from sub-Saharan Africa was frequently transported along the TRANS-SAHARAN TRADE ROUTES. The distinctive blue veil that TUAREG men traditionally wore around their heads was made from cloth purchased from Hausa traders. By the fifteenth century, the Kofar Mata dye pits in the HAUSA STATE of KANO, the oldest in Africa, were known to traders even along the Mediterranean coast. It is thought by some that the need to supply West African converts to ISLAM with appropriate religious attire helped spread weaving technologies throughout the region.

Raffia cloth made by the Kuba people of central Africa often appeared in sixteenth-century European markets, brought there by Portuguese traders. In southern Africa, the presence of imported cloth, very likely the result of contact with Arab traders along the Indian Ocean, has been noted at MAPUNGUBWE and GREAT ZIM-

BABWE before 1450. A local cloth-making tradition is likely but few details exist. It is known that by the 1530s the Portuguese controlled all the trade exits to the coast at the mouth of the Zambezi River, Africa's fourth-largest river system, which rises in the central African plateau and empties into the Indian Ocean at the Mozambique Channel. IVORY and GOLD from the interior were bartered for beads and cloth at trade fairs run by the Portuguese. By 1550, they had established forts to protect their commercial interests n the region.

See also: CARAVANS (Vol. II); CLOTH (Vol. III); INDIAN OCEAN TRADE (Vol. II); TEXTILE PRODUCTION (Vol. I).

coffee   Beverage brewed from the roasted and ground seeds of a tropical evergreen plant. Coffee is valued for, among other things, its stimulating properties, which are derived from caffeine, an alkaloid that is present in green coffee.

According to a popular legend, the stimulating effects of coffee were first discovered in ETHIOPIA when a goatherd observed the effects the plant's berries had on his goats. Although exactly when the plant and its effects were discovered is unknown, its origins are believed to lie in Africa, possibly in KAFFA, Ethiopia. From there the plants apparently were brought to southern Arabia, where they were cultivated as early as 1200. In the years that followed, coffee was used as everything from a food to a medicine before it finally became a popular beverage.

Congo basin   Area in tropical West-central Africa that is drained by the Congo River. The basin covers 1,600,000 square miles (4,100,000 square kilometers) and occupies most of the Congo (formerly known as ZAÏRE) and the Congo Republic, as well as parts of northern ANGOLA, western ZAMBIA, Tanzania, and southern Central African Republic. The basin consists of an intricate system of tributaries and channels, which are surrounded by dense tropical rain forest. In ancient times, the area was inhabited by Mbuti people. Between 500 and 150 BCE, BANTU-speaking peoples brought IRON technology to the region and established fishing and farming communities along the river.

In the period prior to European colonization, the region was dominated by various empires, which often traded in goods such as COPPER and IVORY. The KONGO KINGDOM (after which the river is named) was founded in the fourteenth century, with boundaries extending over modern Angola, between the Congo and Loge Rivers and from the Cuango River to the Atlantic. This kingdom was led by a king elected from the descendents of Wene, the founding ruler.

See also: CONGO (Vol. III); CONGO BASIN (Vol. I); CONGO RIVER (Vol. I); MBUTI (Vol. I).

Conical Tower   Stone structure located in the Great Enclosure of the GREAT ZIMBABWE ruins. Great Zimbabwe is a stone ruin located in the southeastern region of present-day ZIMBABWE on the Zimbabwe plateau.

Lying to the south of the Hill Complex, the Great Enclosure is the largest single structure in ancient SUB-SAHARAN AFRICA. Construction of the Great Enclosure and the Conical Tower began in the twelfth century and took more than a century to finish. Both were built with mortarless stone construction. The Conical Tower is 33 feet (10 m) high and 16 feet (5 m) in diameter. Its purpose is unknown, but many experts have theorized that it was a symbolic grain bin or a phallus symbol. The Great Enclosure is made of an outer wall that is 820 feet (250 m) in circumference with a height reaching as much as 80 feet (25 m). An inner wall runs beside the outer wall, forming the narrow, long passage that leads to the Conical Tower.

See also: ARCHITECTURE (Vol. II).

copper   A reddish mineral that, when processed, is an extremely ductile, or easily shaped, metal. Copper is readily found in its free metallic state in nature and has a long history as a precious metal in Africa.

Copper was mined throughout SUB-SAHARAN AFRICA in the medieval period in the kingdoms of the western Sudan, the HAUSA kingdoms of present-day Nigeria, the kingdom of GREAT ZIMBABWE in southern Africa, and the copper belt of present-day ANGOLA and Zambia.

Copper was used throughout Africa for making BEADS AND JEWELRY for the various political authorities of a society, and as money in the form of small bars, or ingots. Around the year 1000, the copper belt was the first place in Africa that circulated copper ingots as a form of money. Smaller pieces of copper served as everyday currency. In the fourteenth century, Mansa MUSA I (c. 1307–1337) of Mali mined red copper at TAKEDDA and then exported it to the south, where it was exchanged weight-for-weight for GOLD. Throughout Africa, copper was traded and exchanged for other goods, including salt and cotton.

See also: AGE OF METALS (Vol. I); COPPER (Vol. I); COPPER MINES (Vol. II).

copper mines   During the period prior to European colonization, copper was mined throughout Africa, from the MAGHRIB in the north to the northeastern Transvaal in southern Africa. In southern Africa there is evidence of copper mining from the eighth century at the site of Phalaborwa in the northeastern Transvaal. TAKEDDA was the main center of copper mining in the eastern Maghrib; its copper was exported to the MALI EMPIRE, HAUSA STATES, KANEM-BORNU, and the central SUDAN. By the fourteenth century, Takedda was a thriving mining center for copper.

In southern central Africa, the main mining center in the fifteenth century was Chedzurgwe, a site at the heart of the copper belt in present-day ZAMBIA. Another major copper mine of the region was Urungwe, which was worked by the people of Ingombe Ilede. Their copper was sold to people throughout the region from north of the Zambezi River to the peoples of the lower valley.

See also: COPPER (Vol. I); INGOMBE ILEDE (Vol. III); MINING (Vol. III).

Coptic Christianity The Christian Church in Egypt before and after the ARAB conquest of the seventh century. Tradition has it that Mark, one of the four Evangelists, brought CHRISTIANITY TO EGYPT in the first century during the reign of the Roman Emperor Nero (37–68 CE) and established the Patriarchate of Alexandria in 61. The Coptic Church (from the Arabic word qubt, "Egyptian") expanded over the next three centuries, despite Roman persecution of Christian converts throughout the empire. The year 202 started almost a century of Roman persecution of Coptic Christians, culminating in a bloody massacre in 284 at the start of the reign of the emperor Diocletian (245–305). In 313, the emperor Constantine the Great (c. 288–337) granted freedom of worship to all religions in the Roman Empire. By the late 300s, Christianity had become the official religion of the empire. Among the Coptic Church's contribution to the church at large was the work of the theologians St. Athanasius (293–373) and St. Cyril the Great, who was patriarch of Alexandria from 412 to 444.

Monasticism Christian monks such as the Benedictines are credited with preserving Western civilization during the Dark Ages in Europe. The monastic movement got its start in Egypt in about 291 when St. Anthony of Thebes (251–356) went into the desert to live a life of prayer and fasting as a hermit. In 320, a Coptic monk named St. Pachomius organized the first monastery, eventually establishing nine monasteries for men and two for women. Among the most important are the monasteries of St. Catherine, St. Paul, and St. Anthony and those at Wadi Natrun and Sohaag. Pachomius's monastic regulations became the model on which all other monastic rules, especially St. Benedict's and St. Basil's, were modeled.

The Coptic Break with Rome Before the fifth century, a single Christian Church existed, with Rome as its head but with many local differences in language, liturgy, and sometimes theology. Beginning in the fifth century, the churches in the Eastern Roman Empire began to drift away from the authority of Rome and the church in the West. The MONOPHYSITE beliefs of the Coptic Church led to the first schism between East and West.

Coptic Christianity emphasized belief in the single divine nature of Christ, as opposed to the more widely accepted belief that Christ had both human and divine natures. Adherence to this belief led to the persecution of the Copts by Roman authorities and eventually to the condemnation of Monophysite beliefs in 451 by the Council of Chalcedon, the fourth ecumenical council of the Christian Church. The Coptic Church broke with the authority of the Roman Church and established the Coptic Orthodox Church, its head the patriarch of Alexandria. The church in Ethiopia also adhered to Monophysite beliefs and split with Rome to form the Ethiopian Orthodox Church. Apart from these differences, however, the Byzantine Empire's rule over Egypt remained relatively stable until the coming of ISLAM. In 639, Arab Muslims invaded; by 642 they had captured Alexandria, the capital. Islam transformed Egypt, which gradually adopted the Arabic language and converted from Coptic Christianity to Islam.

See also: BYZANTINE AFRICA (Vol. II); CHRISTIANITY, INFLUENCE OF (Vol. II).

cotton Important crop and trading commodity. In Africa, cotton has long been cultivated, primarily for making CLOTH. Cotton also was an important commodity that was traded among different populations, similar to the trading of COPPER or GOLD. In the MOSSI kingdom (c. 1450–1500) of the Niger bend in West Africa, weaving was an important economic activity that led directly to the development of trade with its neighboring kingdoms. In this case, cotton strips were used as freight merchandise between traders. Cubits of cotton also served as a standard of currency in trade between northern Africa, which supplied salt from the SAHARA, and lands to the south, which supplied kola nuts and gold. The SONGHAI Empire (c. 1400–1591) also cultivated cotton, and, because of the abundance of indigo in the savanna region, was known for its dyeing techniques. The HAUSA states (c. 1200) in what is now Nigeria also used indigo dyeing techniques on the cotton fabrics they produced.

See also: COTTON (Vol. I); TEXTILE PRODUCTION (Vol. I).

craftspeople It is difficult to define a segment of African society as "craftspeople," because more often than not, the individuals who created handicrafts functioned also as artists, priests, historians, and storytellers. They created goods ranging from useful but unremarkable baskets and wooden cups to the sacred and mysterious masks and musical instruments that were used in elaborate ceremonies.

For many African peoples, like the ASHANTI, BAMBARA, and DOGON of West Africa, arts and crafts were considered a sacred means by which to express mystical power or religious belief, and craftspeople and their objects were seen as mediums for the messages of the gods and spirits. In these cultures, skilled artisans were highly regarded members of society.

In BENIN, the *igbesanmwan*, a hereditary guild of IVORY carvers, were given special quarters in the royal palace compound of King EWUARE. Some groups, like the GANDA of BUGANDA, rewarded their craftspeople with government positions and large expanses of land.

Some African societies did not hold their artisans in such high esteem, however. In parts of ETHIOPIA and among certain ethnic groups in West Africa, the highly stratified WOLOF society, for instance, craftspeople were relegated to the lower strata of society and were not allowed to marry outside of their castes. The AMHARA of Ethiopia associate leather workers, weavers, and iron workers with the evil eye.

See also: ART (Vols. I, II, III); BARIBA METALLURGY (Vol. II); BARK FIBERS (Vol. II); BLACKSMITHS (Vol. I); CASTE SYSTEMS (Vol. I); IRON WORKING (Vol. II); LOST-WAX PROCESS (Vol. II); MASKS (Vol. I); NYAMAKALAW (Vol. II); SCULPTURE (Vol. I); TEXTILE PRODUCTION (Vol. I).

crops Crops that were commonly grown in Africa during the fifth through fifteenth centuries—many of which are still widely cultivated today—include BANANA, CASSAVA, COFFEE, corn, cowpeas, rice, yams, sorghum, millet, and COTTON.

Regions within GUINEA, Guinea-Bissau, Liberia, SIERRA LEONE, and the western IVORY COAST have cultivated rice from an ancient period. In fact, it is now known that rice was domesticated in Africa approximately 3,000 years ago, prior to contact with Asian traders. Arabic, Portuguese, and European travelers from the eighth to sixteenth centuries commented on rice cultivation in the INLAND NIGER DELTA.

Various techniques traditionally were used to produce a rich enough soil to support cereal grains as a primary crop. In the eastern and central regions of Africa, many small farmers with simple handheld hoes used the technique known as *citemene*, or "shifting culture." This entailed clearing an area in a wooded region and building a fire from the branches of large trees. Smaller trees were usually reduced in size to a stump and became focal points for new crops. This method, usually carried out by men, occurred near the end of a dry season and before the start of the rainy season. Farmers learned whether or not the soil of a particular area was conducive to growing grain crops by observing the quality of surrounding grasses or even noting the presence or absence of certain types of insects and animals.

Burning dead grass and undergrowth enriched the soil with minerals and nutrients that were useful for planting new crops. After two to three years of crop pro-duction, the ground was often allowed to lie fallow in order to recover its strength. During that time, a new crop of cereal grains was planted elsewhere or in combination with secondary crops such as pumpkins, beans, or cowpeas. These secondary crops helped ensure proper drainage and supplied other types of nutrients.

The effectiveness of these techniques varied from region to region. In addition, the populations of some regions planted grain randomly. Generally, however, the entire family had specific tasks in relation to the planting and harvesting of grain. Families sometimes were assisted by the community's age sets during harvest time, when extra labor was critical. Harvesting grain required that the seeds be dried in the sun, threshed, and then transported to large granaries. In traditional societies the first harvested grain was given as a symbolic gift to wives or other members of the family. Over the centuries, family farmers formed societies that managed to create a surplus that could be traded for needed items or stored against hard times. This surplus also left the people time for raising other foodstuffs and for the development of society as a whole.

See also: AGRICULTURE (Vol. III); COTTON (Vol. I); FARMING TECHNIQUES (Vol. I); FOOD (Vol. II); MILLET (Vol. 1); SORGHUM (Vol. I); TOBACCO (Vol. III).

Further reading: Ralph A, Austen, *Africa in Economic History* (London: James Currey, 1996); James L. Newman, *The Peopling of Africa: A Geographic Interpretation* (New Haven, Conn.: Yale University Press, 1995).

Crusades, the Christian religious and military movement initiated against Muslim rulers of the Holy Land between 1095 and 1291; this series of military expeditions sought to restore Christian control to lands important in the life of Jesus Christ (c. 6 BCE–c. 30 CE).

Although the Crusades, which occurred in eight successive phases, were a major preoccupation of the European monarchs and affected many parts of the Muslim world, they spent very little time on African soil. It was not until 1146, during the Second Crusade, that the Muslim city of Tripoli in North Africa was seized by a force of Sicilian Normans. (A crusader state called the County of Tripoli was established during this time period, but it was located in the Middle East and not in North Africa—between the crusader Kingdom of Jerusalem to the south and the crusader Principality of Antioch and the County of Edessa to the north.) The occupation of Tripoli in North Africa lasted only until 1158.

Africa's major contribution to the Crusades was in the person of SALADIN (c. 1137–1193), the Muslim sultan of EGYPT before and during the Third Crusade (1191). His armies, fighting in the Middle East, captured Jerusalem in Palestine in October 1187, breaking the Christian Franks' eighty-eight-year occupation of the Holy City.

See also: CHRISTIANITY (Vol. II).

D

Daboya Important source of salt on the White Volta River in the region that is modern coastal Ghana. Near the end of the fifteenth century, Daboya fell into the hands of the growing kingdom of DAGOMBA, whose rulers were eager to take control of the SALT TRADE from the DYULA, whose hold on trade from the area was weakening. In 1464, invasions by the SONGHAI Empire forced Dagomba to move its capital from near Daboya to a site further east.

See also: SALT TRADE (Vol. I).

da Gama, Vasco See GAMA, VASCO DA.

Dagomba Gur-speaking people of Dagbon, a kingdom that flourished in the northern part of modern coastal Ghana. The Dagomba people emerged after native Gur people were conquered by horse-mounted invaders in the middle of the fourteenth century.

According to tradition, a warrior named Nyagse conquered the indigenous people and executed their earth priests (*tindamba*), the religious leaders who had extensive authority. The new rulers adopted the native language, Dagbane, and called the kingdom Dagbon. Inheritance was patrilineal. Nyagse established an aristocratic caste system in which social status was acquired through competition, although children could not gain status higher than their father's. For the royal class, descent from a certain grandfather was most important. Thus, the royal lineage of the Ya-Na, or chief, was preserved in Dagomba society. The Dagomba royal line still hails only from the Ya-Na.

The Dagomba retained much of the native Gur culture. Like the Gur, their primary means of subsistence was farming, with sorghum, millet, corn, yams, and peanuts their crops of primary importance.

See also: DAGOMBA (Vol. III).

Dahia al-Kahina (Queen Dahia, al-Kahinah) (?–c. 705) *Seventh-century Algerian queen of the Jawara Berbers remembered for her strong resistance to invading Islamic Arabs.*

Known by her Arabic name *al-Kahina* ("the priestess"), Queen Dahia ruled a Jawara kingdom that was located in the eastern regions of the Aurés Mountains of ALGERIA. Legend says that Dahia and her people had been converted to the Jewish faith, and it was due in part to this adherence to JUDAISM that she so intensely resisted the Muslim ARABS who invaded North Africa in the mid-seventh century.

Al-Kahina inherited the battle against Islamic rule from Kuseila, or Kuysayla, the chief of the Awraba peoples, who was himself a leader of the SANHAJA BERBERS in the central MAGHRIB. The battle for control of the region began as early as 670 when advancing Arab armies invaded the northern region of the continent, then known as IFRIQIYA. Initially, Kuseila, like thousands of other BERBERS, embraced the Islamic faith, even assisting Muslim armies in their conquest of many local towns formerly governed by Berber chieftains. After the Arabic governor Ukba invaded and plundered Kuseila's homeland of TLEMCEN, however, Kuseila sought revenge. Taking the title of governor, he organized armed resistance against any further absorption into the growing Islamic Empire.

By about 687, the Berber kingdom established by Kuseila bordered Queen Dahia al-Kahina's territory. Upon his death, about 690, she joined the battle, and by 698 she had become a formidable force, successful at driving Arab armies from the region. After suffering a stunning defeat in 701, Arab forces regrouped, adding converted Berbers to their ranks. The Arab army, led by Hassan ibn an-Nu'man, advanced on northern Africa again. In 705, a major battle took place near Carthage, in modern-day Tunisia, during which al-Kahina was killed.

Queen Dahia al-Kahina supposedly used a "scorched-earth" policy in her efforts to resist the Muslim invaders. She ordered her capital, Baghaya, to be burned to the ground rather than let it be taken by Hassan and his forces.

See also: ISLAM (Vol. II); CARTHAGE (Vol. I); QUEENS AND QUEEN MOTHERS (Vol. II).

Further reading: Ivan Van Sertima, ed., *Black Women in Antiquity* (New Brunswick, N.J.: Transaction Publishers, 1997).

Dahlak Archipelago The largest of several islands situated off the Red Sea coast of MASSAWA in today's eastern ERITREA. Approximately 32 miles (51.2 km) long and 18 miles (28.8 km) wide, Dahlak's history as a commercial trading center extends back to the time of Roman occupation in Northeast Africa. The Dahlak Islands have also been cited as one of several trade routes that introduced Islam into the Horn of Africa. During the eighth century, Arabian merchants dominated the markets of Dahlak, using religious ties to exclude Greeks and other traders. During this same period, AKSUM's primary port of ADULIS was destroyed by ARABS in retaliation for raids that Aksumite rulers orchestrated in southern Arabia.

Noted for their pearl fisheries and exotic tortoiseshell, the Dahlak Islands had grown to such a commercial center by the ninth century that the noted Arabian geographer al-Yaqubi described it as the primary trading port of ETHIOPIA and detailed its many links to lucrative foreign markets. However, by the sixteenth century, intermittent skirmishes over the control of trade at Dahlak and other Ethiopian ports escalated between Muslims and the Amhara nobles of the SOLOMONIC DYNASTY.

See also: ARAB COASTAL TRADE (Vol. II); RED SEA TRADE (Vol. II).

Dahomey (Danxome, Danhome) Kingdom of West Africa located between the Niger River and the Atlantic Ocean, in the southern part of modern Benin. Little is known of Dahomey prior to the seventeenth century, but evidence suggests that the region was inhabited by the AJA people, agrarian EWE-speakers who migrated there during the fifteenth and sixteenth centuries.

See also: AGAJA (Vol. III); AHANGBE, QUEEN (Vol. III); ALLADA, KINGDOM OF (Vol. III); DAHOMEY (Vol. III); PORTO NOVO (Vol. III).

Dala Hill Early capital of the KANO kingdom of Nigeria.

Dala Hill was the home of the Dala people, members of the Medi subgroup of the Kuri people. Although the date of the founding of Kano is unknown, Dala Hill served as its capital until about 998. Kano was captured by the Habe people at the end of the tenth century and became one of the true HAUSA states. For a brief period, the name Dala Hill was changed to Sheme, but by 1100, it had changed again to Kano City.

Damot Kingdom originally located south of the Blue Nile River; until the late thirteenth century, the territory included Wolamo and the entire Shewan plateau. Damot's most famous king was Motolomi., who, in the thirteenth century, converted to CHRISTIANITY under the influence of St. Tekla Haymonot.

Several oral traditions recount the story of King Motolomi's baptism. According to one, Tekla Haymonot was taken prisoner during an invasion of his homeland by Motolomi's forces. Transported to Damot, the saint preached to Damot's king, eventually converting the ruler to Christianity. In other versions, however, Tekla Haymonot made the trip to Damot of his own free will.

The Damot monarchy was very similar to the kingdom of KAFFA. Its hierarchical structure included subordinate kings and other members of the royalty, as well as various palace officials and governors, all of whom answered to a king whose rule was supreme.

Between 1316 and 1317, Damot was conquered by AMDA SIYON (c. 1314-1344) of the Christian kingdom to the north. As a result, for the next two centuries Damot was part of the Christian kingdom, although it managed to retain many of its roots in traditional religion. The Damot kingdom fell into further decline towards the end of the sixteenth century when the OROMO forced the people of Damot across the Blue Nile. By the seventeenth century the kingdom was completely absorbed and became a subdistrict of the region of Gojjam.

See also: DAMOT (Vol. III); GOJJAM (Vol. III).

Dangme (Adangme, Adampa) Ethnic group that lived in areas that are now modern coastal Ghana and Togo; also the Kwa language they spoke. The Dangme have long occupied the ACCRA plains along the Gold Coast. Prior to the seventh century, Dangme speakers were living in small villages, subsisting mainly through hunting and foraging, although evidence of early farming is found in some areas.

Between the eleventh and fourteenth centuries, the Dangme developed IRON technology, which helped them increase their crop yield. Villages subsequently became bigger and, by the fifteenth century, they had developed complex social structures under a political monarch.

Darfur Mountainous region in the modern Republic of the Sudan situated between Wadai (to the west) and Kordofan (to the east). Darfur is populated by sedentary peoples and nomads of Arabian origin, including the BAGGARA.

Prior to 1200, Darfur was fairly isolated from its neighbors, and there was an absence of trade. The region was governed by the Daju, who lived in the central Jebel Marra massif and established the first known dynasty in the area after dominating the local peoples. Though the Daju rulers had ARABIC names and claimed to have come from the east, their tradition holds that they were not of Arab origin.

A visitor to the eastern SUDAN around 1500 wrote an account of the founding of a kingdom by a runaway slave that may be the story of Dali, the founder of the Kayra dynasty, or of his father. The account reports that in Gaoga, which some historians believe to be Darfur, a servant murdered his master, stole the master's goods and weapons, and ran away to be protected by his nearby relatives. The servant later acquired wealth through raiding and became a powerful ruler.

Migrations from the east began around 1350, along the Darb al-Arb'in, or Forty-Days Road. There is evidence that some trading took place at this time between Darfur and EGYPT. During the migrations, incoming Arab nomads brought new breeds of cattle and new pastoral practices. One group of people, the Tunjur, arrived in Darfur and pushed the Daju southward. The Tunjur assumed power in Darfur in a peaceful fashion. They may have come from Nubia and been aided and influenced by Arab nomads, whose language the Tunjur adopted. Some historians believe that the Tunjur had come from Tunisia.

Around 1450, the Tunjur ruler, Shau, was deposed by his half-brother, Dali, who made many political changes in Darfur. He instituted a new legal system, which was later recorded in the *Kitab Dali*, or "Book of Dali," and he divided Darfur into five provinces.

See also: DARFUR (Vol. III); NUBIA (Vol. I).

Dauda, Sarki (r. 1421–1438) *Islamic ruler of Hausaland who continued the sarki rule established by Sarki Yaji, c. 1350.*

During Dauda's reign, KANO became a tributary state of the BORNU kingdom. Unlike previous periods of Kano's history, Dauda's reign was characterized by an increase in commercial activities and trade. A newly established TRANS-SAHARAN TRADE ROUTE brought prosperity to the area, along with its CARAVANS of salt and agricultural products. This peaceful prosperity and the flourishing of Muslim culture contributed to the increasingly cosmopolitan population of HAUSALAND.

See also: YAJI, SARKI (Vol. II).

Daura Ancient settlement in northern Nigeria, ruled by queens during the ninth and tenth centuries; became a CITY-STATE and the first of the seven original states of HAUSALAND.

According to legend, Abuyazid, a prince of Baghdad, became famous for aiding the sultan of BORNU and was given the name Bayajida by the people of Bornu. When the sultan became jealous and plotted against Bayajida, the prince fled and eventually came to the town of Daura. There he gained renown by slaying a snake that had prevented the townspeople from drawing water from the well. As a reward, he married Daurama, the queen of Daura, and ruled with her. Their son, Bawo, had six sons, who went on to found the Hausa race. These sons also founded the remaining six of the seven original Hausa states, which became emirates named BIRAM, GOBIR, KANO, KATSINA, RANO, and ZARIA.

Daura, whose name means "blacksmith," was peopled primarily with farmers and artisans. In addition, it was located on the savanna at the intersection of roads leading to Katsina, Kano, Zango, and Niger. As a result, it became an important center for trade, with salt and potash arriving from the SAHARA Desert, and slaves, leather, and CLOTH entering from the south.

Daza Saharan ARAB nomads who settled in the northwestern areas of present-day CHAD. These central African people are part of the Dazaga clan of the TEDA ethnic group. Due to the arid climate and sandy terrain of their homelands, the Daza are primarily nomadic cattle herders. Historically, they relied on limited amounts of trade as well as village raids to supplement their nomadic lifestyle. In the sixteenth century, they were forced by

Ottoman rulers to give up much of their nomadic lifestyle, long before the arrival of the French and Italian colonists in the nineteenth century.

See also: OTTOMAN EMPIRE (Vol. III); TIBESTI (Vol. III); TRANS-SAHARAN TRADE ROUTES (Vol. II).

Debo, Lake Body of water located in the central region of modern Mali on the Niger River between Mopti, to the south, and TIMBUKTU, to the northeast. Lake Debo is part of the network of lakes, creeks, and backwaters that join the Niger River. Lake Debo was one of the boundaries of the SONGHAI Empire, which prospered from the fourteenth to the sixteenth century. The empire was established in the area of the great bend in the Niger River from Lake Debo to the mouth of the Sokoto River in present-day Nigeria.

Debre Birhan (Mountain of Light) Former kingdom in northeast ETHIOPIA associated with the medieval rule of ZARA YAKOB (r. 1434–1468). The kingdom reportedly gained its name from bright stars visible from its high perch on the Ethiopian plateau.

During the fourteen years Emperor Yakob lived at Debre Birhan, he transformed the isolated region into a renowned center of cultural and literary achievement. Much of this cultural renaissance has been attributed to Yakob, who wrote many religious texts during his rule. Historians also cite the infusion of culture generated by the building of the king's palace and surrounding structures. Many artisans, both from within and outside Ethiopia, were attracted to the region, including at least one Italian painter. After Zara Yakob's death, in 1468, the site fell into disuse but was eventually reclaimed and restored by later successors of the SOLOMONIC DYNASTY.

Debre Damo Monastic region of ETHIOPIA situated east of Adowa (Adua) in the TIGRAY highlands. Founded during the fifth century by Abba Aregawi, one of the NINE SAINTS, Debre Damo still remains an active place of worship. Access to the site is the same as in ancient times: monks and visitors use a rope to scale the steep cliff on which the original monastery was founded. Despite these limitations, over several centuries, the good works of the monks attracted devout Christians who worked to establish a self-sustaining refuge by creating adjoining buildings and cultivating the grounds.

Debre Damo's remarkable architecture also provides an important glimpse of the distinctive style of the ancient kingdom of Aksum. One of the earliest churches built in the region by King Gebra-Masqal during the sixth century was constructed of stone and wood with an interior ceiling pattern of cross-beams. The interior of this church and other churches in the region characteristically have small recessed areas, archways, and carvings of animals, plants, and abstract forms. Large crucifixes, complemented by intricate borders, dominate the church.

A feature of the old Aksumite churches is their patterned windows and doors, many of which recall the towering stelae of the region. This corroborates a general belief that Aksum's stelae were tombs or "spiritual houses" built for deceased kings.

See also: CHRISTIANITY, INFLUENCES OF (Vol. II); ETHIOPIA (Vol. I); GIYORGIS, ST. (Vol. II); ZAGWE DYNASTY (Vol. II).

Further reading: Donald Crummey, *Land and Society in the Christian Kingdom of Ethiopia: From the Thirteenth to the Twentieth Century* (Champaign, Ill.: University of Illinois Press, 2000); Harold G. Marcus, *A History of Ethiopia* (Berkeley: University of California Press, 1994).

Dendi Region in the northwestern part of present-day Nigeria; original home of the SONGHAI people. Dendi also refers to the name of these people, a subgroup of the Bariba people, and the language they speak.

The Songhai people, who emerged from the Dendi region of Nigeria near the Niger River, are thought to have descended from the ZA kingdom of the eighth century. By about 800, and possibly earlier, the Songhai had moved north, establishing the prosperous trading city of GAO. Eventually, the MALI EMPIRE took control of both Gao and the Dendi region. When SUNNI ALI began the great expansion of the Songhai Empire, c.1465, he regained control of the Dendi region, and the Songhai people once again inhabited their homeland.

The SORKO people, who also speak a Songhai language, were also known to have lived, fished, and traded in the Dendi region. The FULANI lived in the Dendi region during the time when Sunni Ali reconquered it for the Songhai Empire.

Dhlo-Dhlo (Dhlodhlo) Stone structures located in ZIMBABWE. Situated near Bulawayo, the Dhlo-Dhlo ruins are small structures known for their intricately patterned walls covered in various herringbone, cord, and checkered patterns. Archaeological evidence indicates that Dhlo-Dhlo may have served as an early ARAB, Chinese, or Dutch trading site. Local inhabitants probably traded POTTERY, GOLD, and other precious goods in exchange for rare items like Arab CLOTH and glass.

See also: GREAT ZIMBABWE (Vol. II).

Diara (Zara) SONINKE kingdom of the ancient GHANA EMPIRE of West Africa. Diara was influenced by the DYULA, Muslim traders, as early as the eighth century, when it appears that many of the MANDE-speaking Soninke natives converted to ISLAM. In the eleventh century, the ALMORAVIDS gained control of Diara, AUDAGHOST, a Saharan trade center to the north of Diara, and most of the Ghana Empire. Toward the end of the fifteenth century, Diara fell to SONGHAI invaders.

See also: SUDAN, THE (Vol. II); SONGHAI (Vol. III).

Dias (Diaz), Bartolomeu (c. 1450–1500) *Portuguese navigator and explorer.*

Dias is considered by many historians to be the most important of the Portuguese explorers who explored the Atlantic Ocean during the fifteenth century. His voyages took him along the coast of Africa and across the Atlantic to the coast of Brazil. In 1488, by rounding the Cape of Good Hope at the southern tip of Africa, he helped to open India to Portugal's commercial ventures by showing his king, John II (1455–1495), that a sea route to India was possible. Portugal then had the opportunity to control the shipment of trade goods from the East. These goods had previously been transported overland by caravan to Europe through Muslim-held lands.

See also: PORTUGAL AND AFRICA (Vol. III)

Dibbalemi (Dunama Dibbalemi, Dabbalemi) (r. c. 1210–1248) *King of the Kanem Empire.*

Mai (or King) Dibbalemi was the ruler of the KANURI, a nomadic people of the SEFUWA confederation who had migrated into Kanem, northeast of Lake CHAD, around 1100. Born into Kanem's ruling dynasty, Dibbalemi, like other Kanuri kings, was considered divine.

Kanem means "south" in the TEDA language spoken by the Kanuri.

Dibbalemi mobilized Kanem's considerable military forces, including more than 40,000 horses, in his efforts to establish the Kanuri Empire. Declaring a JIHAD, or holy war, against Kanem's neighboring states, he successfully conquered the surrounding areas and gained control of the lucrative TRANS-SAHARAN TRADE ROUTES north of Lake Chad. As a result, CARAVANS traveling through North Africa had to pass through Kanuri territory. The commercial activity that developed from this transformed the lifestyle of the previously nomadic Kanuri. Becoming more sedentary, the Kanuri began to focus on trade.

These conquests also encouraged Dibbalemi to further increase his empire's territory through military action. Dibbalemi expanded the Kanem Empire from east of Lake Chad to the north, adding Kawar and the FEZZAN region. He also expanded the empire eastward to Wadai, westward to KANO—where he annexed Bornu—and south to the Adamawa grasslands (in present-day CAMEROON). At its height, Dibbalemi's empire extended from LIBYA to Lake Chad to HAUSALAND.

Dibbalemi's reign was both long and effective. In addition to his military successes, he established diplomatic relationships with sultans in North Africa. A devout Muslim, he was concerned with promoting religious observances among his people. As part of this he established a special hostel in CAIRO for those making the pilgrimage to MECCA.

To encourage and reward his military leaders, Dibbalemi gave commanders authority over the people they conquered. This system of power-sharing, which helped motivate his armed forces, ultimately proved problematic because commanders attempted to pass their positions on to their sons. As a result, these posts evolved into a new hereditary ruling class. Dibbalemi was able to control this during his lifetime, but after his death, dynastic feuds developed. These soon degenerated into civil war. People in the outlying districts stopped paying tribute, and the great empire of Kanem buily by Dibbalemi began to break apart.

Dinka Pastoralist people, closely related to the Nuer, who, since the tenth century, have inhabited an area on both sides of the White Nile in what is now the Republic of the Sudan. The Dinka speak a language of the NILOTIC subgroup of the NILO-SAHARAN family; they are subdivided into independent peoples, including the Agar, Aliab, Bor, Rek, and Malual, each of which is segmented into smaller political patrilineal clans with great autonomy. They are an intensely religious people whose rituals and practices permeate everyday life.

Dinka Religion The Dinka religious system is based on the pervasive relationship between the deity and humans, one that influences every facet of Dinka life. Among the Dinka, the deity is recognized as Nhialic or Nhial, which has been translated as "the sky." Access to Nhialic is accomplished through spirit possession.

Three primary ancestor figures also represent an important aspect of the Dinka belief system. One, known as Deng, is the founder of the Dinka nation. As in other religions that assign qualities of the natural world to specific deities, Deng is associated with thunder and lightning. He is also worshiped at a large shrine known as Luak Deng. Other important deities are Garang, who represents men, and Abuk, a female deity who oversees the work of women. These latter deities have often been compared to the myth of Adam and Eve associated with the Judeo-Christian tradition. In the origin stories of the Dinka, which were created centuries before the birth of Jesus, Nhialic warns the people about forbidden fruit and its consequences.

Many lesser deities are recognized by the Dinka and are divided into warrior or priestly clans. Described as totemic spirits, they included *ring*, or "flesh," the spirits that give voice to members of the priestly clans. These priests, known as Masters of the Fishing Spear, derive their powers from Aiwel, or Ayuel, or Longar, who was the heroic figure of Dinka myths. The priests are recognized by their symbolic fishing spears, which are considered the sacred tool of Longar, who, their myths explain, was conceived in the river. He was also credited with leading the Dinka to the site of their present nation.

According to Dinka origin myths, Longar, following a long period of drought, attempted to persuade the Dinka elders to relocate to new lands. Unfortunately, he failed. In retaliation, he refused to find sought after water sources and simply traveled away from the region. At some point the Dinka attempted to follow him, and, when they encountered obstacles such as mountains and rivers, they began to seek out his assistance. Longar apparently refused at first, even going so far as to kill several Dinka as they attempted to cross the river. Finally, however, a member of the priest clan wrestled his spear away. It was at this point that Longar began to stop fighting and started to help them across, giving his fishing spears to the first men to cross the river. These men formed the first members of the priest clan.

One of the most important elements of worship among the Dinka is the large number of animal sacrifices they dedicate to their gods. The Dinka view bulls or oxen as signficant gifts from Nhialic, which are returned to him through the act of sacrifice. It has been said that each of their cattle receives a name and its memory is preserved in the naming process of newborn calves. Spear master priests are responsible for maintaining traditional acts of worship and prayer. They voluntarily relinquish their hold of the title when they grow too old to reign. Dinka traditions called for them to give a final consultation before being buried alive.

See also: PASTORALISM (Vol. 1); RELIGION (Vol. I).

Further reading: John S. Mbiti, *African Religions and Philosophy*, 2nd ed. (Oxford, Eng.: Heinemann Educational Publishers, 1999); Benjamin C. Ray, *African Religions: Symbol, Ritual, and Community* (Upper Saddle River, N.J.: Prentice Hall, 2000).

disease in medieval Africa In ancient Africa, where the majority of peoples lived at a distance from each other and were connected by trade only sporadically, disease tended to be local and seasonal. Parasitical infections caused by *Echinococcus* larvae in the feces of domestic ani-

mals, schistosomes from infected lakes, and *Leishmania* from sand flies were common; the sickness they caused very likely lessened during the dry season and during times of drought. However, as Africa became less local through trade contacts with other regions and the world outside, the migration of peoples inside Africa, and the development of larger communities, the diseases that people faced also changed.

North Africa In the sixth century, bubonic plague, which existed in northern Africa as early as the fourth century BCE, swept from EGYPT through Syria and Asia Minor all the way to Italy. Records do not show if the plague penetrated SUB-SAHARAN AFRICA at this time. However, the sixth-century epidemic is the same highly contagious disease of the lymph glands, known as the Black Death, that originated in Mesopotamia and proved fatal to roughly 25 million people in Europe in the fourteenth century.

Sub-Saharan Africa Beginning in the third century BCE and continuing through colonial times, migrations across the African interior broadened the scope of previously isolated diseases. BANTU MIGRATIONS in the third century BCE facilitated the spread of diseases to the susceptible inhabitants of central Africa. Some of these early African people acquired disease through contact with animals. Called zoonoses, diseases spread by animals have been prevalent throughout the history of Africa. Rabies, trypanosomiasis, leishmaniasis, yellow fever, trichinosis, and anthrax are all spread via infected animals.

One of the most common parasites in Africa is trypanosomiasis, or sleeping sickness, an infection transported by the blood-sucking TSETSE FLY. This large fly thrives only in sub-Saharan Africa, where it feeds on wild animals, cattle, and humans. Living in the blood, lymph nodes, or cerebrospinal fluid, trypanosomiasis infects the host and usually causes death within a few days. For centuries, sleeping sickness has limited the amount of animal husbandry in sub-Saharan Africa, thus inhibiting the growth of both precolonial and colonial settlements in the area.

Changes in Lifestyle As peoples abandoned their nomadic lifestyle to live in settled, agrarian societies, disease became more prevalent. Prior to the emergence of agriculture, small nomadic groups of people helped keep disease at bay because a pathogen had fewer hosts to infect; an outbreak of a deadly virus was essentially restricted to the handful of nomads or animals it infected, and once the last surviving host died, so did the disease.

As people became more settled, infectious parasites and microbes were able to reproduce at rapid speeds before killing their hosts and moving on to new, healthy victims. Thus, the natural balance between life and death was disrupted, and pathogens often emerged as the victors.

Disease thrived in these close-knit communities, where viruses like smallpox were spread by daily contact between tribal members. The increased population density had disrupted the natural cycle of life and death between humans and diseases. Disease-carrying hosts like mosquitoes multiplied as forests were cleared for crops. Outbreaks shortened the immediate labor supply, making simple but crucial tasks like clearing fields or harvesting the crops difficult. Adding to the devastation, a poor crop yield could cause food shortages, which in turn led to malnutrition and an increased susceptibility to new diseases.

Finally, the development of Arab and European trade provided mass transport for old and new diseases. Coastal people, who had the most contact with foreigners, quickly developed a tolerance for many of the new diseases, but those who lived further inland were devastated by unfamiliar pathogens. Foreign traders brought home with them diseases previously limited to the African continent, such as malaria.

Malaria is a parasitic disease transmitted by female mosquitoes that has been common to Africa since precolonial times. It often results in kidney failure, coma, and death.

The malaria parasite (*Plasmodium*) has existed for millions of years. With the advent of agricultural societies, malaria was able to pass quickly throughout densely populated communities. In tropical Africa, the long history of the disease enabled the native populations to develop a genetic mutation to combat the parasite. The sickle-cell gene, which emerged by the seventh century, provided protection against malaria, but was itself deadly. If inherited from both parents, the gene usually caused death from severe anemia. Those who have only one parent with the gene can survive with increased immunity to malaria. Thus, the sickle-cell trait emerged only in those parts of Africa where malaria was common, particularly the eastern parts of the continent.

A similar case of immunity among Africans can be found in a separate malaria strain that kills only children. Evolution has made adults resistant to the disease, but young children are very susceptible. However, after a prolonged period away from the infected regions, adults lose their immunity. These types of genetic evolution have been very important in shaping African civilization. Without immunity, Africans would not have survived in the areas where diseases were most common.

See also: DISEASE IN ANCIENT AFRICA (Vol. I) DISEASE IN THE COLONIAL PERIOD (Vol. III).

divine rule Practice of worshiping monarchs as gods. The concept of divine kingship, which can be traced to the pharaohs of ancient Egypt, was a popular form of government throughout Africa from the fifth through the fifteenth centuries

The ZANJ of Southeast Africa called their king WAQLI-MI, which meant "son of the great god." Among the pastoral Shilluk of Malakal, located near the White Nile, the practice of electing kings who claimed divine rule was based on the moral order established by their mythic founder, Nyikang. It was believed that the spirit of Nyikang passed down from king to king. The YORUBA chose kings through Ifa divination because it represented the voice of their ancestors. Their kings were considered an essential link between the people, their ancestors, and their spiritual deities.

By the ninth century, the practice of divine kingship was common among other African societies as well. The SEFUWA dynasty of KANEM-BORNU established the royal *mai* line of divine kings. To maintain their divine image, the *mais* always spoke from behind a screen to keep themselves from having direct contact with their people.

In the West African forest, the WOLOF and SERER people elected their kings to positions of divinity. Once they gained power, the kings were protected by tribal taboos. Similarly, the Shona people of ZIMBABWE worshiped their kings like gods, bestowing elaborate gifts upon them. Among the BANTU, divine kingship was closely intertwined with social and religious customs like fertility and ancestor worship.

See also: DIVINE RULE (Vol. I); GOVERNMENT, SYSTEMS OF (Vol. II).

diwan (divan, dewen) Islamic fiscal administrative system first used in the seventh century during the Arab conquest by 'Umar I (r. 634–644), the second caliph to succeed the prophet MUHAMMAD after ABU BAKR.

Members of the diwan, mostly Arab rulers (including Muhammad's descendants) and warriors, were paid a share of the state's plunder and taxes (called *jizya*), in the form of a pension. The income was separated into two categories: movable and immovable. Movable funds were those distributed after setting aside 20 percent for the state's immovable reserve.

The diwan took on a bureaucratic significance in later years. By the end of the seventh century its meaning encompassed all levels of government infrastructure. The term was used similarly by Iranians, and in the sixteenth century, by Mughal Indians and the Ottoman Empire.

djallaba Arabic word meaning "traders;" often used to describe merchants from eastern savanna regions of the SUDAN. The djallaba were instrumental in the development of trade with the Sultanate of Fur, one of the Islamic kingdoms of the Sudan.

See also: TRANS-SAHARAN TRADE ROUTES (Vol. II); FUR SULTANATE (Vol. III).

Djibouti Modern East African coastal country on the Strait of Mandeb. Djibouti was an important Arab trade state until the sixteenth century. Bounded by ERITREA, ETHIOPIA, Somaliland, and the Gulf of Aden, Djibouti is a small country populated by a diverse group of people. The majority of the native people were AFAR, or SOMALI of the Issa clan. The Afars, concentrated in the north and western parts of Djibouti, traditionally were nomadic people, as were the Somalis to the south.

The livelihood of Djibouti's inhabitants has been dictated by the dry climate and barren terrain. Saltwater basins are found amid the arid, volcanic plateaus in southern and central Djibouti, lightly wooded mountains dominate the northern landscape, and coastal plains line the eastern shore. Temperatures rise to 106° F (41° C) in the summer, with lows of only 84° F (29° C) in the winter. Combined with a scant 5 inches (12.7 cm) of rainfall each year, the climate is largely unsuitable for agriculture or animal husbandry. Less than 1 percent of Djibouti is arable, and only 9 percent can sustain livestock. Native flora is limited to thorn scrub and hearty grasses in the desert regions, although the mountains do support some date palms, castor-oil palms, tamarind, and euphoria. Fauna includes jackals, antelopes, hyenas, gazelles, and ostriches.

Strategically located at the junction of the Red Sea and the Indian Ocean, Djibouti has been an important link between Africa and the Middle East for thousands of years. The earliest SEMITIC speakers migrated from the Middle East to Ethiopia via Djibouti in prehistoric times. Even the primary occupation of the Afar and Somali people, nomadic pastoralism, was introduced to Djibouti via the Strait of Mandeb.

As an important access point to the Middle East, the Djibouti region was enticing to many early settlers. The Afar people first settled in the countryside around the third century BCE, although Somali Issa settlements would push them to the north in the ninth century CE. Prior to the arrival of Muslim missionaries in 825, an Arab and Persian trade town bordering present-day Djibouti was established. Called ZEILA, the town became a successful silver and slave exporter. Its success gave rise to the extended Abyssinian kingdom of ADAL, which encompassed much of present-day Djibouti. Zeila was named the capital of Adal.

By the ninth century, ISLAM had penetrated the African coast via Zeila. Muslim Adal eventually gained its independence from Christian Abyssinia, but it would face ongoing battles with the Christians for many years to come. From the thirteenth to the sixteenth centuries, this religious struggle weakened Adal and allowed western invaders to conquer the kingdom late in the sixteenth century.

See also: ARAB COASTAL TRADE (Vol. II); DJIBOUTI (Vol. III); RED SEA TRADE (Vol. II).

Dogon West African people concentrated in southern Mali and northern Burkina Faso; they speak Dogon, a Gur dialect belonging to the NIGER-CONGO family of languages.

Oral history suggests that the Dogon were members of the Keita clan who fled their homeland between the tenth and thirteenth centuries because they refused to convert to ISLAM. However, archaeological evidence, coupled with the fact that they speak the Gur language, indicates that the Dogon had a much earlier presence in their current home.

Even today, the Dogon are primarily farmers and hunters. They settle in secluded areas and grow millet as

The cliffside village of Irel in the Bandiagara region of Mali shows the traditional dwellings of the Dogon people. The Dogon fled to the Bandiagara escarpment in 1490 to escape an invading army from the Mossi state of Yatenga. © *Charles & Josette Lenars/CORBIS*

a subsistence crop. These areas have historically been shared with FULANI pastoralists who exchange dairy products for Dogon grains and produce.

Dogon society centers around extended patrilineal families, with an occupational class structure that places farmers at the top of the hierarchy. In the absence of centralized authority, a *hogon*, or headman, provides religious and judicial leadership for the village. His authority is weak, however, as all decision-making power rests with a council of elders.

Traditional Dogon religion focuses on the belief in one creator, Amma. Ancestor worship also plays an important role in the Dogon faith. A comprehensive mythology dictates the order of the universe and the Dogon's place in that order.

While today nearly 35 percent of the Dogon people consider themselves Muslim, their isolated location has left them relatively untouched by outside influences. Therefore, their cultural and religious traditions have remained intact.

See also: DOGON (Vol. III); ORAL HISTORY (Vol. 1).

domestic animals Animals that are integrated into human society as objects of ownership. The existence of domesticated animals in Africa can be traced to early Iron Age civilizations when the natural supply of wild animals became insufficient to feed local populations. Wild animals were subsequently bred in captivity to increase the food supply. The only animals actually domesticated on the African continent were the guinea fowl, cat, donkey, and shorthorn cattle. Other species, like the domestic dog, pig, and chicken, arrived in Africa from other countries.

In many areas diseases limited the spread of domestic animals. Trypanosomiasis, a deadly disease spread by the TSETSE FLY, limited the sustainability of domestic animals in much of southern Africa.

In order for an animal to be domesticated, it must submit to human ownership, and some animals adapt to captivity more easily than others. Thus, animals like antelope are difficult to domesticate, whereas fowl, cats and dogs, pigs, goats, donkeys, horses and cattle have a high tolerance for humans.

Fowl Archaeological evidence indicates that domestic chickens from India and Asia were in Africa by 800 CE. They were probably bred from the red jungle fowl. Early Malaysian traders may have introduced the chicken to coastal Africa, where it was able to spread quickly throughout the continent. Although sixteenth-century Portuguese explorers named the guinea fowl, native peoples had domesticated them long before. In the western parts of the continent, the helmeted guinea fowl was bred in captivity, and peoples of eastern Africa raised a breed of guinea fowl as well.

Cats and Dogs Domestic cats were bred from the common wildcat that thrived throughout much of the continent. Even after domestication, the housecat would breed with the wildcat, making the separation of the species difficult. Dogs arrived on the African continent several thousand years ago from western Asia and Europe, where they were bred from small wolves. Dogs had many uses in traditional African societies. Although some dogs were human companions, others were eaten or used in ritualistic ceremonies. They were also raised for their hides or bred as hunters.

Goats Goats were also brought to North Africa from Asia and had dispersed throughout the southern parts of the continent by the fourth century CE. Dwarf goats, raised for their meat and hides, evolved in western Africa and the SUDAN, while short-eared varieties multiplied in semiarid parts of the continent. Other prominent domestic goat varieties include the red Sokoto, whose valuable hide is used to make Moroccan leather, and the small East African goat.

Pigs Descendents of the wild boar, pigs were popular in ancient Egypt but never became major factors in the African economy. Although European settlers brought new varieties in the fifteenth century, African pig populations were kept in check because they were vulnerable to disease.

Donkeys, Horses, and Camels The domestic donkey was probably first bred by the Egyptians from its wild counterpart native to North Africa and Arabia, possibly as early as 4000 BCE.

Domestic horses have long been present in Africa, but their numbers have been limited because—in contrast to camels—they do not adapt especially well to the arid Saharan climate, and they are susceptible to many diseases in SUB-SAHARAN AFRICA.

The lineage of camels is unknown because wild species have long been extinct. Domestic camels played an important role in making the previously uninhabitable desert regions suitable for limited agriculture and trade. The one-humped camel was probably brought to northern Africa from Arabia more than 5,000 years ago. With its tolerance for desert conditions, the camel thrived in the Sahel and northern KENYA. But due to the camel's susceptibility to trypanosomiasis, it was not able to survive in rainy climates where the tsetse fly thrived. Nonetheless, more camels are found in Africa than anywhere else in the world, and they have long been raised for milk, meat, and TRANSPORTATION.

Cattle Among domesticated animals, cattle, prized for their hides, meat, milk, and manure, have had the greatest social and economic impact on Africa. Domestic cattle in the arid North African regions include long- and shorthorn varieties as well as the Asian zebu, mostly found in ETHIOPIA. The Asian zebu interbred with local varieties to create the common sanga variety. Despite the presence of several deadly diseases in this region, more cattle are raised here than anywhere else on the continent. Several regional tribes, including the Dinka, Nuer, and Shilluk, virtually worship their cattle.

In western Africa, the large number of trypanosomiasis-carrying flies makes the area uninhabitable to many cattle breeds. Those that were able to cope with the disease, like the N'Dama and West African shorthair, monopolized the cattle population. Pastoral and agricultural natives raised these and a limited number of dwarf cattle.

Cattle populations in the Sahel and central Africa are smaller in number. In the Sahel, a region including parts of the modern countries of Burkina Faso, CHAD, Mali, MAURITANIA, Niger, and SENEGAL, the arid climate and frequent drought make the region unsuitable to many types of cattle. Zebu cattle are found in limited numbers, but camels are much more common. In central Africa, some zebu and sanga varieties were native to the area, but most cattle arrived much later with European settlers. A similar phenomenon occurred in the southern regions of Africa where precolonial breeds were limited to sanga cattle. With the arrival of European coastal explorers in the late fifteenth century, new breeds were introduced and intermixed with native herds.

Sheep Domestic sheep from Asia were abundant in ancient Egypt and early North African kingdoms. Next to cattle, they are the most important domesticated animals in Africa, although their lifespan is often abbreviated due to their susceptibility to disease. The three principal African sheep varieties are the thin-tail, fat-tail, and fat-rump. Thin-tailed sheep have been present on the continent for several thousand years. In the savanna regions dominated by cattle-herders, species of sheep called the Sudanese desert, the Fulani, and the Tuareg prevail. To the west, where agriculture is the primary economic activity, West African dwarf and Nilotic sheep are common. In the Sahel region, thin-tailed sheep thrive in the semiarid desert. This thin-tailed variety is not only revered for its coarse wool coat, but it provides an abundant supply of milk and meat to native pastoralists. The related fat-tailed variety has also inhabited the African continent for several millennia. They are used primarily as milk sheep, although their heavy tail has long been coveted as a source of thick, oil-like fat used in traditional cooking. The most common fat-tailed varieties are found in present-day Ethiopia and parts of East, central, and southern Africa. Fat-rumped sheep, prized for their fatty meat, as well as their hides and milk, are more prevalent in arid parts of the continent. They are also excellent sources of wool.

See also: CAMEL (Vol. I); CARAVANS (Vol. II); CATTLE (Vol. I); CAVALRY (Vol. II); DOG (Vol. I); GOAT (Vol. I); HORSES (Vol. I); PASTORALISM (Vol. I).

Dyula BANTU-speaking traders from the SUDAN who prospered in West Africa from the fourteenth through the sixteenth centuries. The Dyula's origins are thought to go back as far as the GHANA EMPIRE (as early as the eighth century CE). The MANDINKA called them Dyula, which means "Muslim trader," but West African ARABS knew them as Wangara.

The Dyula held prosperous commercial trade routes from SENEGAL to Nigeria and from TIMBUKTU to the northern IVORY COAST. Eventually they became agents, brokers, and financiers.

They primarily traded in GOLD, salt, and kola nuts, but, as their empire grew, they moved into goods such as livestock, CLOTH, COPPER, silver, IVORY, beads, glass, and other manufactured products. They also played a significant role in the trade from the Sudan to northern Africa, and their commercial expertise allowed them to trade with the European MERCHANTS, who arrived in the sixteenth century. Besides being excellent merchants, they excelled in the arts and other intellectual pursuits. In their communities, the Dyula formed the upper class, separating themselves from their peasant neighbors.

As converts to ISLAM, the Dyula spread their religion to the various communities in which they settled, such as the SONGHAI centers of Timbuktu, JENNE and GAO, and to many BARIBA and HAUSA towns. As a result they contributed enormously to the expansion of Islam in West Africa.

See also: DYULA (Vols. I, III); GHANA, ANCIENT (Vol. I); MALI EMPIRE (Vol. II).

Edessa See al-ROHA.

Edo People of the southern part of Nigeria who once ruled the historic city of BENIN from c. 1400 to c. 1800.

Prior to the colonial era, the Edo, also called the Bini, made their living from farming, hunting, and trading their wares, eventually becoming one of the first African groups to trade with the Portuguese. They were also known for their intricate IVORY and BRONZE sculptures and plaques, which adorned, among other places, the palace of the *oba*, or king, and portrayed Benin's distinguished history.

Other traditional skills have been passed down through the generations, such as woodworking, metal arts, and the weaving of CLOTH for ceremonies and other ritual customs.

The Edo speak the Kwa language of the NIGER-CONGO LANGUAGE family and have historically been ruled both religiously and politically by their oba. The first oba, Eweka, was the son of Prince Oranmiyan of ILE-IFE, who arrived during the thirteenth century to govern the Edo people. It is traditionally believed that the Edo became discontented with the ruling dynasty of the semimythical kings known as the *ogisos*. The most celebrated oba, however, was EWUARE (c. 1440–1480), who extended the power and size of the kingdom of Benin and introduced the idea of a hereditary line of succession to the throne.

While today many of the Edo practice either ISLAM or CHRISTIANITY, there are many who still practice the ancient religion, which is based on allegiance to their gods, heroes, *ogisos,* and spirits of the afterlife.

Egypt Nation in the northeastern part of the African continent. Egypt is bordered by the MEDITERRANEAN SEA, the Red Sea, and the modern countries of Israel, the Republic of Sudan, and LIBYA. The character of Egypt changed radically with the rise of ISLAM in the Arabian Peninsula. Before the year 1000, Egypt had been both Arabized and Islamized.

For thousands of years, Egypt has been an influential force on the African continent, as its ancient history attests. With the division of the Roman Empire in the late fourth century, Egypt became part of the Byzantine Empire, and by the fifth century, Egypt had been subdivided into numerous provinces under local authority. However, political unrest soon led to a more centralized, authoritarian government. At the same time, the rapid spread of Christianity led to conflict with adherents of the traditional religion.

The tenuous Byzantine grip on power ended around 639 when ARAB Muslims invaded Egypt, forcing Byzantine rulers to retreat to Anatolia (present-day Turkey). The Muslim conqueror, Amr ibn al-As (fl. 1640s), established the new Egyptian capital at al-Fustat. In general, non-Muslims were tolerated, although they were required to pay special taxes. Around 668 a new Muslim dynasty, the Umayyads, took the throne. During their reign, Muslim Arab immigrants arrived in large numbers.

Around 750, power in the region shifted to the SUNNI Muslim Abbasid dynasty. From their capital in Baghdad, the Abbasids ruled Muslim North Africa for more than 150 years. In 868, Turkish slaves united under Ahmad ibn Tulun (868–884) and overthrew the Abbasids. Tulun's reign was short-lived, as power shifted back to the

Abbasids by 905. The FATIMIDS, a Shiite Muslim sect, captured Egypt in 969. They established their capital at CAIRO and conquered much of the Arabian Peninsula and North Africa.

Although the rulers of the Fatimid dynasty (969–1141) espoused an esoteric branch of Islam called Isma'ili Shiism, the majority of Egyptians adhered to the orthodox Sunni branch and were generally tolerant of the dwindling number of Coptic Christians and Jews in the population. Isma'ili Shiism was a religious and political movement that stressed esoteric knowledge and distinguished between the ordinary believer and the initiate. The Fatimid desire to propagate these beliefs and the development of al-Azhar mosque and university made Egypt a center of Islamic scholarship and missionary activity during this period.

Fatimid power in Egypt lasted more than 200 years until a Syrian army commander, SALADIN (c. 1137–1193), overthrew the dynasty in 1171. Saladin reestablished an Abbasid allegiance and formed the Ayyubid dynasty (1171–1250).

The Rise of the Mamluks The Ayyubid dynasty returned Egypt to Sunni Islam. Determined to build up Egypt's independent military strength, they took into their military service large numbers of Turkish slaves called MAMLUKS (from the Turkish word for "slave."). The Mamluks exploited a palace feud to put one of their own into power, and in 1250 began the Mamluk period, which lasted until 1517. The non-Arab, non-Muslim Mamluks saved Egypt from Mongol attacks, defeating the invaders in 1260 at Ayn Jalut, near Nazareth in modern-day Israel. Mamluk strength made Egypt a stable country and an important center of the Arabic-speaking world. Accompanying this growth, however, was a diminution of the rights of Coptic Christians, who were openly persecuted. Some historians believe that the Mongols' use of Christian auxiliaries in battle may have turned the Mamluks against Christianity,

Mamluk power began to decline after the plague, known in Europe as the Black Death, beset Egypt in 1348 and often thereafter. Egypt's commercial rivals, the Portuguese, began to dominate trade with India in the early 1500s after a sea route around Africa to the Far East was discovered in 1498. Even the strong Mamluk sultan Qa'it Bay (r. 1468–1496), who built a fort at Alexandria from the stones of the ancient lighthouse of Pharos at Alexandria, could not preserve Egypt's freedom. The land was beset by Turkish attacks from Anatolia and Azerbaijan near the Black and Caspian Seas and other pressure from the OTTOMAN EMPIRE.

By the end of the fifteenth century, the Portuguese had displaced Egyptians as the dominant sea traders in the region. And, as internal conflict among the Mamluks increased, Turkish Ottomans easily conquered Egypt in 1517. Although the Ottomans retained ultimate authority over the Egyptian people, the Mamluks continued their administrative authority for the next 200 years.

See also: EGYPT (Vols. I, III).

Ekiti Ethnic group related to the YORUBA located in present-day southwestern Nigeria and known for their frequent conflicts with the kingdom of BENIN. The Ekiti were an agrarian group who lived in a patrilineal society based on the *ilu*, or town, which was headed by various chiefs from each village. The kingdom was ruled by the oba, or king, who held powers such as the ability to administer punishment and give out honors to his people. The oba was kept in check, however, by a council of chiefs who acted as advisers on both palace and village matters.

The Ekiti trace their origins to ODUDUWA, the founder of the first Yoruba city of Ife. They believe that one of Oduduwa's sons migrated from Benin and established their capital and first kingdom of Ado. In the fifteenth century, the kingdoms of Oye, Ikole, Ido, Ise, Ijero, Otun, Emure, Obo, Itaji, Effon, Ikere, Okemesi, Ogotun, Ise, Ara, and Isan developed when competing ruling factions broke away to form their own settlements.

The Ekiti people and kingdoms began their long history with the empire of Benin when they were forced to become tributaries during the reign of EWUARE (r. c. 1440–1480). The kingdoms of Ekiti periodically went back and forth from being ruled by Benin and regaining their independence until the colonial era in the nineteenth century.

See also: NIGERIA (Vol. III).

Eleni (Elleni, Illeni, Ileni) (c. 1468–c. 1522) *Empress and queen mother of Ethiopia who was an important political and religious figure from 1468 until her death in 1522.*

Born a Muslim princess in the Ethiopian town of Hadya, Eleni married Baeda Maryam (r. 1468–1478) and began to have an impact on ETHIOPIA when her husband came to power.

During her time as Baeda Maryam's *itege* (chief wife), she converted to Christianity and wrote two works on the subject, all the while managing to continue good relations with the Muslim world.

Known for her gentleness and intelligence, Eleni continued to be influential after the death of her husband in 1478 and acted as either a respected adviser or a regent for the subsequent four young rulers of Ethiopia.

During the reign of Eksender (1478–1494), another Ethiopian faction under the rule of Amda Michael attempted to gain control of the country but was overthrown by Empress Eleni and some of her aristocratic allies. Eksender's son and successor, Amda Siyon, was a young boy when he came to power and died after a reign of only six months.

After Siyon's death, another of Baeda Maryam's sons, Naod (r. 1494–1508), came to power. When Naod died, Eleni was instrumental in securing the throne for her grandson, Lebna Dengel (r. 1508–1540), for whom she served as regent for about the first half of his reign.

Eleni was also initially a powerful force in the relations between Ethiopia and Portugal, sending envoys c. 1509 to King Manuel, laden with gifts and expressing her country's desire to form an alliance with Portugal to defeat the Moors. The party sent in return by King Manuel did not arrive until 1520, though, and by then Eleni's influence was fading. By this time, Lebna Dengel had become known as a greedy and despotic ruler and, disregarding Eleni's prior call to action, he did nothing to ensure the alliance with Portugal, thereby diminishing the authority of Ethiopia's SOLOMONIC DYNASTY in the region.

See also: CHRISTIANITY, INFLUENCES OF (Vol. II); LEBNA DENGEL (Vol. III); PORTUGAL AND AFRICA (Vol. III).

Engaruka

Engaruka City in the northern part of present-day Tanzania that possessed one of the most important examples of effective irrigation systems in use from the fourteenth to the seventeenth centuries. Engaruka was originally inhabited by farmers who built stone houses and devised an intricate irrigation system. Using gravitational force, it directed the water of the Engaruka River into inland waterways. This irrigation system, the earliest of its kind so far discovered in Africa, was enhanced by highly advanced aqueducts, sluices, and trenches, some with slopes of 1 degree or less, which were used to help channel the water flow.

The builders of the irrigation system also constructed stone terraces to aid in the cultivation of their land. These terraces were used to prevent erosion by acting as a break on the steep slopes, which lowered the amount of sediment the water would carry down to the farmland.

Little is known about the people of Engaruka, who most likely spoke a Kushitic language. In time, a decrease in the annual rainfall led to deforestation and overgrazing, which changed the area in significant ways. As a result, the land was no longer easily cultivated, and the inhabitants migrated from the area.

See also: FARMING TECHNIQUES (Vol. I); IRRIGATION (Vol. I); TANZANIA (Vol. III).

Ennedi Region in the northeastern part of present-day CHAD, known for its ancient rock art. Stone, cave, and cliff paintings dating back to as early as 6000 BCE have been found on the massif of the Ennedi region. The types of rock art have changed considerably over time, with different colors and styles in their representation of the animal species, dress, and weaponry, but they are generally classified into three periods: Archaic, Bovine, and Dromedary or Equine.

The art of the Archaic Period, which ended around 2000 BCE, consists mainly of depictions of animals and human figures, wearing loincloths and jewelry, carrying clubs and sticks. Art from later in the Archaic Period also shows life scenes, including dancing, running, and women carrying baskets on top of their heads.

The Bovine Period, extending from 2000 BCE to 1000 CE, represents a significant change in the rock art of Ennedi. To a great extent this is due to the domestication of cattle and sheep as well as to the emergence of dogs as companions. Since these animals are consistently depicted as being healthy-looking and plentiful in number, it has been suggested by some scholars that the appearance of these domestic animals during this period is linked to climatic changes that brought about a general increase in prosperity in the area.

Human figures from the Bovine Period are shown as wearing more elaborate jewelry than the figures from the earlier Archaic Period. This ornamentation includes adornments for the ears and head as well as more extensive garments, such as headdresses, robes, and long, full skirts. Their weaponry also was more sophisticated, with spears, shields, and curved clubs all being depicted. The life scenes increased in scope as well, with depictions of containers filled from grain harvests, women in conversation or dancing, and musicians playing instruments.

The third period of Ennedi rock art ranges from 1000 to about 1700 and is called the Dromedary, or Equine, Period because camels, and later, horses, are widely represented. During this era, art initially was abundant, only beginning to decline with the introduction of ISLAM about the eleventh century. The human figures from the Dromedary Period are less like hunters and more like warriors, using shorter spears and adding spikes to the bridles and tails of their horses. As the period went on, the art became increasingly stylized, losing the realism of the previous eras.

It has been estimated that, over the centuries, there have been fifteen or more styles of rock art in the Ennedi region, each differing in its depiction of humans, animals, and daily life.

See also: ROCK ART (Vol. I).

Eritrea Trading kingdom located north of ETHIOPIA on the Red Sea in East Africa. Southern Eritrea was the site of part of the Aksumite kingdom, which flourished from the last millennium BCE to the first millennium of the common era. The most important Aksumite port, ADULIS (modern Zula), was located in Eritrea.

In the eighth century, Muslim traders began to settle in Eritrea, converting the AFAR and other native coastal peoples to ISLAM. From the ninth through the thirteenth centuries, Eritrea was controlled by the BEJA, a nomadic group also known as the Hedareb. During this time,

Aksum, a Christian kingdom, diminished in power and became more closely associated with Ethiopia under the ZAGWE and SOLOMONIC dynasties.

See also: AKSUM (Vol. I); ARAB COASTAL TRADE (Vol. II); ASMÄRA (VOL. II); BEJA (Vol. I); ERITREA (Vols. I, III); GE'EZ (Vols. I, II); RED SEA TRADE (Vol. II); TIGRAY (Vol. II).

Ethiopia Country in northeastern Africa bordered by present-day ERITREA, Somalia, DJIBOUTI, KENYA, and the Republic of the Sudan. Following the expansion of ISLAM in the seventh century, the Christian kingdom of AKSUM went into a decline. By the middle of the ninth century, Red Sea and INDIAN OCEAN TRADE had been taken over initially by the Persians and later by Arabic Muslims. At that time, remnants of the kingdom regrouped in the northern interior, where a semblance of Christian rule continued until the tenth century. The kingdom was then destroyed by an alliance of Muslim, Bejan, and AGAW rebels led by the Agaw Queen GUDIT. Her open defiance of Christian rule was rumored to have culminated in the death of the last reigning king of Aksum.

Rise of the Zagwe Dynasty Few records are available to give a complete view of the disarray that followed. However, it is clear that a new ruling class, composed primarily of Agaw-speakers who professed Christian beliefs, became known as the ZAGWE DYNASTY. The rise of this powerful ruling class has been attributed to the value of the land they held and to their ability to create a food surplus. Arranged marriages and tributary taxes added to the kingdom's wealth, which remained within the hands of the ruling elite. In power from approximately 1170 to 1270, the Zagwe kings eventually established a capital city at ADEFA, also known as al-ROHA. Located to the south, less than 240 miles (400 km) from the former kingdom of Aksum, this capital city was later renamed Lalibela in honor of one its most noted rulers, King LALIBELA (1185–1225).

The Zagwean kings openly traded with Muslim MERCHANTS, but they reportedly set strict guidelines for those merchants' attempts to win converts to the Islamic faith. The groups most critical of the Zagwe were concentrated among the AMHARA, as well as in TIGRAY and the northern highlands of Eritrea. These groups were also the most resistant to Islamic conversion. The elite class that developed among these groups was extremely vocal in their condemnation of the Zagwe kings, whom they considered usurpers of the throne that they believed belonged to the SOLOMONIC DYNASTY traditionally thought to have been founded by Menilik I, supposedly the son of King Solomon and the queen of Sheba.

Supported by the Ethiopian Christian Church, a powerful group of Amharic nobles seized the Zagwe throne in 1270. This restored the Solomonic Dynasty, bringing to power King YEKUNO AMLAK (r. 1270–1285) and helping the Ethiopian Church to amass both land and wealth. Considered a legitimate heir to the throne, Amlak reasserted the original Christian character of Ethiopia, ushering in a period that many historians describe as a heroic or chivalrous age of warrior kings that included AMDA SIYON (r. 1313–1344), Dawit I (r. 1380–1409), and ZARA YAKOB (r. 1434–1468).

Centered in the Amhara region in the central highlands, this imperial kingdom was ruled by the Ethiopian Church and men whose exploits were chronicled by their closest advisers and royal scribes. In many instances, references are made to their royal queens or consorts—for example Queen ELENI (r. c. 1468–c. 1522)—who not only participated in warfare but also had highly visible roles as state diplomats and administrators, mediators, and writers. Many of these queens also were Christian devotees known for their piety and good works.

However, the Solomonic dynasty was not without internal problems. After Amlak's death in 1285, his royal descendants engaged in their own battles for control well into the sixteenth century. To strictly control succession rights, all but duly appointed sons were permanently imprisoned within a royal prison situated on an inaccessible mountain. By some reports, this prison fortress also supplied potential candidates for the throne when an unexpected death occurred. Other problems of the dynasty included centuries of Christian and Muslim conflicts.

Christian-Muslim Conflicts As the first of the Solomonic rulers, Amlak was able to extend his direct control over the northern highlands and the outlying Muslim states and traditional societies to the south and east by using what historians describe as a "mobile kingdom," or tent city. In each region he settled, Amlak was supported by tribute. This led to grievances among the growing number of Muslim settlements. As Muslim trading sites expanded into city-states, Islamic conversion grew stronger among the SEMITIC and Kushitic speakers. By the ninth century, Islam had gained a solid foothold along the southern coast of ADEN, the East African coast, and neighboring societies. This was accomplished largely through the efforts of Arab merchants.

One of the most persistent problems faced by Ethiopian monarchs was the Kingdom of Ifat, also known as Wifat or Awfat, which was reportedly ruled by descendants of the prophet MUHAMMAD. Established in the twelfth century, Ifat became one of the richest Islamic city-states because of its close proximity to the trade between the port city and the country's central regions. This position also allowed Ifat's rulers to incorporate many traditional societies, including pastoralists and nomadic herders. Ironically, the first sultan of Ifat was Umar Ibn Dunya-Huz (d. 1275), appointed by King Amlak.

Other Muslim strongholds included Dawaro west of Harer, Sharka in Arusi, as well as BALI and Hadeya. The conflicts which arose from these established sultanates, or Muslim kingdoms, was based in part on their objections to demands for tribute. However, because they generally had been allowed to maintain their local chieftancies and to assert their religious practices, they inevitably attempted to organize rebellions against their Amharic overlords.

See also: ERITREA (Vols. I, III); ETHIOPIA (Vols. I, III); HARER (Vol. III).

Etosha Pan Extensive salt pan of approximately 1,900 square miles (4,920 sq. km.) located in northern NAMIBIA. By 1500, Etosha was inhabited by the HERERO and OVAMBO ethnic groups. The Herero were generally pastoralists, and the Ovambo were farmers and hunters. Bands of nomadic hunter-gatherers also roamed the area.

It is from the dry season that Etosha, meaning "place of mirages," gets its name. The intense heat reflects off the greenish white expanse of flat land and mirages make it seem as if the animals searching for water are iridescent and walking on air.

Consisting of both salt and clay that is hard but rich in minerals, the Etosha Pan harbors an abundance of fauna during both the dry and wet seasons, as well as relatively seasonal and area-specific vegetation. The animals, including roan antelopes, zebras, elephants, leopards and black rhinoceroses, use the outcroppings of mineral-laden clay as a salt lick to nourish themselves during the demanding heat of the dry season. During the wet season, however, the vegetation flourishes and a wealth of bird species, including the pink flamingo, flock to the Pan and add color to the extensive landscape.

See also: GEOGRAPHY (Vol. I); PASTORALISM (Vol. I); HERERO (Vol. III).

Ewe Ethnic group located on the Guinea Coast in West Africa. The ancestors of the Ewe probably migrated from the OYO area of Nigeria during the fifteenth century and set up villages in areas of modern Ghana, Togo, and Benin. These villages were based on the principle of *frome* (lineage), in which the eldest male in the family acted as a judge, administrator, family representative to the village, and even the religious connection to the spirits of the dead. The power surrounding these communities remained decentralized, however, and the villages tended to band together only during a war or other intense strife.

While some of the Ewe who lived along the rivers and coastline were strictly farmers, historically many were known to use their crops for trade as well as for sustenance. The Ewe were also known to be skilled potters, blacksmiths, and weavers.

The Ewe traditionally have spoken variations of the Ewe language, which is a dialect of the Kwa language branch of the NIGER-CONGO LANGUAGE family. Their religion is based on allegiance to Mawa, their god of creation, and Trowo, a series of minor gods whom the Ewe worship and from whom they gain direction for their daily lives.

See also: ANLO (Vol. III); AJA (Vols. II, III); CLAN (Vol. I); DAHOMEY (Vol. II, III); EWE (Vol. III); LANGUAGES (Vol. I); LINEAGE (Vol. I).

Ewuare (Ewuare Ne Ogidigan, Ewuare the Great) (c. 1440–1480) *Oba, or king, of the West African kingdom of Benin.*

Generally regarded as the most powerful and influential ruler of BENIN, Ewuare the Great was known as the oba who successfully expanded his kingdom's territory and created a hereditary line of succession to the throne.

Ruling from c. 1473 to c. 1480, Ewuare built many roads and surrounded EDO, his capital, with an extensive arrangement of protective moats and walls. He also is credited with changing the political structure from that of the UZAMAS, a powerful group of chiefs based on heredity, to that of selected chiefs known as the "town" chiefs and the "palace" chiefs. Through their taxation of the towns within the kingdom, these two groups of chiefs supplied the oba with his income, which usually consisted of such provisions as yams and palm oil. Under Ewuare's new political structure, any free man could vie for titles of power and seniority.

In Benin oral tradition, Ewuare is a larger-than-life figure. He is associated with the leopard and the viper, two animals that he believed foretold his destiny as a powerful and opportunistic ruler of his people.

Beyond his political stature, Ewuare was also known as one of the greatest warrior kings of Benin. According to legend, he won more than 200 battles and assumed control of each town he captured. His stature was made even greater by his reputation as an innovator—or even a magician—in the use of herbs for medicinal purposes.

Ewuare was eventually succeeded by a long line of powerful obas including his son Ozolua and his grandson Esigie, both of whom continued Ewuare's tradition of strong central authority in matters of religion, politics, and economics.

See also: BENIN (Vol. I, III); DIVINE RULE (Vol. II); OZOLUA (Vol. III).

F

Fang BANTU-speaking people living in parts of West Africa. The Fang inhabit the areas of CAMEROON south of the Sanaga River, mainland Equatorial Guinea, and the forests of the northern half of GABON south to the Ogooué River estuary. The earliest Fang groups migrated to the area before the arrival of the Portuguese in the fifteenth century, but their history prior to that is unclear.

The Fang belong to the Bantu subgroup of the NIGER-CONGO LANGUAGE family. Among the various Fang groups, there are three main linguistic divisions. The first, the Beti, is found in the north of the area inhabited by the Fang, and is spoken by the Yaunde, or Ewondo, and Bene. The second is Bulu, which is spoken by the Bulu, Fong, Zaman, and Yelinda. The third group is known as the Fang, which is spoken in the south by the Fang, Ntumu, and Mvae.

Some groups of the Fang, including the Balu, have traditionally been nomadic farmers, rotating their crops and moving on an annual basis in order to avoid soil erosion. Their traditional farming implement is the hoe, and their staple CROPS have included CASSAVA and corn.

The Fang traditionally have lived in bark houses arranged in a pattern along a straight street. The various Fang subgroups belong to strongly patriarchal clans and share similar political systems. Each village has a leader who is a descendant of the founding family of that village. The leader often serves as a judge in disputes and leads religious rituals.

Traditional Fang religion involves the worship of ancestors, who are believed to wield powers in the afterlife. Even the skulls and bones of deceased leaders are believed to influence the fortunes of the family.

Fang artwork consists of simple masks and figures. Typical of this is a *bieri*, a carved box containing the skeletal remains of ancestors. Some authorities believe the figures to be abstract portraits of the deceased ancestors, while others suggest that they are meant to protect the ancestral spirit from evil. Fang masks are worn by entertainers, as well as by sorcerers involved in hunting and meting out punishment. The masks are painted white and are detailed with black outlines.

See also: ANCESTOR WORSHIP (Vol. I); FERNANDO PO (Vol. III); MASKS (Vol. I).

Fante (Fanti) West African ethnic group located along the coastal regions of modern coastal Ghana. The Fante and the ASHANTI are the major subgroups of the AKAN ethnic group, and both speak a NIGER-CONGO LANGUAGE called Akan. It is thought that the ancestors of most of the coastal peoples, including the Fante, migrated west from regions around Lake CHAD and the BENUE RIVER. They first crossed the lower Niger and the VOLTA RIVER, then moved through the forest into what is modern-day Benin and Togo before reaching the coast. The Fante migration through the forest is supported by the connection between Akan and the Twi language of the forest peoples. The final leg of Fante migration to the coast was probably from the north, near Tekyiman, in central Ghana. When the Portuguese arrived in the 1470s, the Fante were one of the established Akan kingdoms along the Guinea Coast, with their capital at Mankessim.

Like other coastal peoples, the Fante lived in an autonomous kinship society. Their kings and queen held centralized power with the help of a priest who oversaw clan rituals and ceremonies. In the fifteenth century,

Fante society was largely organized around the production and trading of GOLD, which was mined in the region. They also traded captives with the MANDE and HAUSA peoples to the north and east.

All able-bodied Fante men were expected to be members of their kingdom's *asafo*, a military group that defended against invasion. Organized by patrilineage, the *asafo* was a common feature of Akan societies. Fante women could also be members of the asafo, and some even were respected war captains.

See also: AKAN (Vol. III); ASHANTI EMPIRE (Vol. III); FANTE (Vol. III).

farim Titled leaders of the MALI EMPIRE, which flourished from the thirteenth through the fifteenth centuries. *Farim* means "ruler" and refers to the representatives of the ruling power in the small states throughout the Mali Empire. *Farim* is equivalent to the title *farma* given to the leaders dispatched by the *mansa*, or emperor, to represent his power in the various outposts of the empire. The *farim* had power over the local chiefs in the states where they ruled. The decline of the empire in the sixteenth century increased the *farim*'s autonomy, and they ruled their states without allegiance to the *mansa*.

Fatimids Ruling dynasty of EGYPT from 969–1171. The Fatimids were Shiites who came to the eastern MAGHRIB region of North Africa from Arabia early in the tenth century. Claiming to be descended from Fatima, the daughter of the prophet MUHAMMAD, they believed that they were the legitimate spiritual leaders of SHIISM, a Muslim sect that broke with the SUNNI-led Abbasid caliphs of Baghdad. The Fatimids converted many BERBERS during their conquests of North Africa and soon controlled most of Tunisia and ALGERIA and had wrested Egypt from the rule of Baghdad. Under Caliph al-Mu'izz, they established their capital at al-Qahira (CAIRO) in 969.

Initially, the Fatimids enjoyed great prosperity in Egypt, especially as the country's ruling class. They controlled Egyptian agriculture and collected heavy taxes generated by Mediterranean trade and RED SEA TRADE. A major part of their success depended on a thriving textile industry that developed under the direct control of the caliphs. Through the extensive trade of COTTON and linen, MERCHANTS and caliphs alike grew wealthy.

Taxation was the main source of government income, but the Fatimid tax system was rife with corruption and contributed to the dynasty's downfall. By paying a certain sum to the caliph, for example, Fatimid Berbers were allowed to become "landlords" of the Nile Valley, with the right to institute unlimited taxes of their own. The Berbers frequently failed to pay the caliph, however, leaving him unable to pay for even the upkeep of his army. By the mid-twelfth century, the situation had deteriorated to the point that soldiers were looting the countryside. At the same time, violence among MAMLUKS, Berbers, and Sudanese disrupted trade and farming, leading to further weakening of Fatimid power. In the 1160s, Christian crusaders from western Europe were on the verge of overrunning the Fatimids but were thwarted by SALADIN, an army leader from Kurdistan. When the last Fatimid caliph, al-Adid, died in 1171, the vizier Saladin became ruler of Egypt and founded the Ayyubid dynasty.

Though devout Muslims, the Fatimids maintained peaceful relations with Christian and Jewish traders early in their rule. This contributed to their prosperity, as the riches that would be spent waging wars were used instead to glorify ISLAM. The situation changed, though, toward the end of the eleventh century, when European Christians launched the first of several CRUSADES to reclaim the Holy Land.

See also: ISLAM, INFLUENCE OF (Vol. II); MAHDI (Vol. II).

festivals Festivals are a long-standing tradition in Africa, and they often have been used to reinforce cultural values and to unify a community around common goals. Festivals have also served as traditional markers for significant rites of passage.

The earliest festivals may have been initiated to mark the advent of agricultural seasons, including the success of a harvest or, as in ancient Egypt, to acknowledge the annual inundation of nourishing silt from the Nile River. In farming communities south of the SAHARA, seasonal harvest celebrations like the new yam festivals, were held by many societies with widespread variation. These festivals frequently were marked by the wearing of specific colors and masks as well as by dance movements that were dictated by a specific tempo and style of drumming. Singing on the part of the spectators was another common feature.

The IBO of Nigeria, for example, traditionally incorporated many symbolic rituals into their yam festival, which marked the beginning of a new year. The festival, which dates back to antiquity, is still held yearly. In preparation, the homes of the Ibo are cleaned and painted in the traditional colors of white, yellow, and green, while the remnants of former harvests are discarded. One of the primary objectives of the festival is to honor the earth goddess Asase Yaa as well as the ancestors of specific clan lineages. As a result, the event begins with the sacrifice of the new yams to the regional deities and ancestors. This is followed by a feast that includes palm wine and the popular regional dish known as yam foo-foo.

Among the other societies with a long history of harvest festivals are the Akamba and Gikuyu of KENYA, the Shilluk of the SUDAN, the Shona of ZIMBABWE, and the Sonjo of Tanzania.

Another type of festival was historically held in the ancient city of ILE-IFE, where special priestesses held a time-honored festival that stretched over several weeks. Dominated by women, the celebration began with the decoration of a special shrine to the *orisha* of sickness and disease, Babaluaye. The painters of the shrine were women, and the special colors of the deity—red, black, and white—were applied. In addition, all objects within the shrine were thoroughly cleansed. The women then chanted, danced, sang, and painted in a sacred performance known among the YORUBA as *Oro*.

The FANTE of Cape Coast in central Ghana traditionally have held an annual Oguaa-Afahye festival that also is noteworthy. Meaning "the adorning of new clothes," this seventeen-day purification festival involves the ritual sacrifice of a cow to obtain the blessings of the seventy-seven gods of Oguaa (the Cape Coast). Among the rituals is a procession (*durbar*) of the chiefs and major warrior societies.

Among the most important rites of many African festivals are those that honor the ancestors. A long-standing tradition of offering gifts is maintained in many of these celebrations because this is believed to solidify the reciprocal relationship between humans and the spiritual world. In addition, festivals of this type often call for reenactments of origin myths. Some of these festivals, like one celebrated by the EDO people of BENIN, trace the arrival of the first inhabitants into the region. Other festivals, some of which involve animal sacrifice, honor specific deities. The Efutu, in present-day Ghana, have traditionally held a deer hunt as part of their annual festival. Their objective is to honor their most important deity, Penkye Out, who is considered to be the guardian of the people. Similarly, Ntoa, the spirit of Brong Ahafo, an AKAN state of West Africa, is honored at their annual Apoo festival through a special dance involving the use of ritual swords. This dance apparently symbolizes the origin of the nation's female founder, who is believed to have emerged from a cave near the Basuaa River. Other highlights of the festival include verbal dueling competitions between groups ordinarily divided by social rank or economic status.

One of the most important functions of festivals has been the recognition of divine kingship. Among the AKAN, the Akwasidae festival honors the royal ancestors who were traditionally "enstooled," meaning that they were installed in the office of kingship. These stools, which came to embody the essence of the king, have been noted in rites of the *odwira* festival, which traditionally was held by the ASHANTI between August and September. In this festival, all the royal stools are purified, starting with the "First Paramount Stool" and proceeding until every stool, one by one, is purified. Specially inscribed brass bowls called *kuduo*, highly revered by the king, are also part of the festival activities. Believed to have first originated among the Akan during the fifteenth century, the *kuduo* most likely came from the northern Islamic cities as a result of trans-Saharan trade. During the festival they hold water that is sacred and used to symbolically purify the souls of the reigning monarchs.

See also: DIVINE RULE (Vols. I, II); MUSIC (Vol. I); ORISHA (Vol. I); RELIGION, TRADITIONAL (Vol. I); STOOL, ROYAL (Vol. II).

Further reading: Anthony Ephirim-Donker, *African Spirituality: On Becoming Ancestors* (Trenton, N.J.: Africa World Press, 1998); Robert B. Fisher, *West African Religious Traditions* (Maryknoll, N.Y.: Orbis Books, 1998); Mary H. Noote, *Secrecy: African Art that Conceals and Reveals* (New York: Museum for African Art, 1993); Benjamin C. Ray, *African Religions: Symbol, Ritual and Community* (Upper Saddle River, N.J.: Prentice Hall, 1999).

Fetha Nagast (Judgment of Kings) Codified laws developed in ETHIOPIA between the fourteenth and fifteenth centuries.

The Fetha Nagast consisted of a body of laws adapted from the COPTIC CHURCH of EGYPT and modified for civil use during Ethiopia's medieval period. Judges were appointed by the ruling king or emperor and served under the direction of provincial governors. Responsible for cases involving civil suits, land disputes, and money debts, the defendants and their accusers usually sat on either side of the judge with an array of witnesses, jurors, and onlookers.

Local judges were sometimes passed over in favor of a higher court judge known as a *wambar*. These officials were capable of dispensing justice in the form of floggings, imprisonment, or when necessary, the death penalty. In the case of failure to repay debts, money lenders and those who owed them money were chained together and imprisoned until witnesses could be called to verify the facts or for terms of repayment to be arranged.

See also: LAW AND JUSTICE (Vol. II).

Further reading: Harold G. Marcus, *A History of Ethiopia* (Berkeley: University of California Press, 1995).

Fez City in north-central MOROCCO, on the banks of the Wadi Fes; the eastern bank was founded by Idris I c. 789, the western bank, in 809, by Idris II. Idris I used a silver and gold pick axe, called a *fas* in Arabic, to mark the boundaries of the city, hence the city's name. These two parts of the city were merged in the eleventh century under ALMORAVID rule.

Located on the trade routes that connect the countries south of the SAHARA to the Atlantic Ocean, Fez had a busy market, or *souk*, and became an important commercial center.

There are more than 100 mosques in Fez, including the oldest and holiest shrines in northern Africa. Pilgrims traveled long distances to visit the tomb of Idris II. The al-Qarawiyin Mosque, the oldest and one of the largest mosques in northern Africa, is located in the old city. Also in the old city, which sometimes is known as the *Medina*, is the mosque of Mulai Idris, the city's founder, which is considered so sacred that non-Muslims and animals may not even approach its entrance.

Residents during this period enjoyed a rich and varied existence. Scholars, for example, came to Fez to study at al-Qarawiyin University, which was founded in 859. It is one of the oldest institutions of higher learning in the world. A new section of the city, called Fès el-Jedid, was founded by the MARINIDS in the thirteenth century. They also built the Royal Palace and adjacent Great Mosque, known for its distinctive minaret. The Jewish quarter, called the Mellah, south of the Royal Palace, was home to the ancient city's Jewish goldsmiths, silversmiths, and jewelers.

Traditional crafts flourished in Fez, including leather, POTTERY, jewelry, wrought IRON, and carpets. Different districts of the city became known for particular specialties, and professional guilds ensured that the quality of these goods remained first-rate.

Up until modern times, this was the only place in the world to buy one of the most familiar items of Muslim dress in the Middle East: the brimless, round, red felt hat, known as a *fez*.

See also: FEZ (Vol. III); ISLAMIC CENTERS OF LEARNING (Vol. II).

Fezzan (Fezan) Saharan region of LIBYA. Fezzan is among the most scenic areas of the SAHARA desert. Known in ancient times to both the Greeks and Romans, it was conquered in 666 by the ARABS, under whom ISLAM replaced Christianity throughout the region.

Fezzan was on the TRANS-SAHARAN TRADE ROUTES that connected the MEDITERRANEAN SEA with the SUDAN. Caravans carrying GOLD, IVORY, and slaves from the western Sudan to markets on the Mediterranean regularly passed through Fezzan, stopping at the oases along the way.

The Arabs ruled Fezzan until the tenth century, when the region regained its independence under various native Berber dynasties, who were supported by the FATIMID rulers in Egypt. In the thirteenth century, the king of BORNU, an African Muslim state in the Lake CHAD Basin, invaded Fezzan from the south, and the Bornu kingdom maintained control over the important trade routes until the early sixteenth century.

See also: KANEM-BORNU (Vol. I).

Filippos (c. 1314–1341) *Abbot of the early Christian monastery of Asbo in Ethiopia.*

As CHRISTIANITY expanded through ETHIOPIA in the thirteenth and fourteenth centuries, monasteries emerged as the primary vehicles for the expansion. One of the more important monastic groups was the House of Tekla-Haymanot. Tekla-Haymanot (c. 1215–1313) was a Christian reformer who founded a monastic community called Asbo in his hometown of Shoa. Shoa had become an important center of the Christian state, so Asbo was able to win the support of both Egyptian bishops and the Ethiopian emperor, Amda Siyon.

Abba Filippos, the abbot of Asbo in the mid-fourteenth century, led a revolt against two Ethiopian emperors, Amda-Siyon and Sayfa-Ar'ad. Although Christian, the emperors still adhered to the age-old practice of polygamy. Filippos won the support of a large number of Tekla-Haymanot followers, but he was soon captured by the emperors and sent into exile. With their leader in exile, Filippos's followers left Shoa and settled in surrounding areas in the central highlands with little Christian influence. In this way Abba Filippos's rebellion played an important role in the spread of Tekla-Haymanot Christianity throughout Ethiopia.

fishing Fish were caught in the oceans, streams, and rivers throughout the African continent. As African peoples learned agriculture, became more sedentary, and established trading economies, fish became trade products. The MALI EMPIRE, as well as the SONGHAI and YORUBA Empires, and the city-states of the SWAHILI COAST all used fish as a commercial product and as a part of their diet. Along with kola nuts, salt, GOLD, and COPPER, dried fish were traded via the TRANS-SAHARAN TRADE ROUTES.

food The gradual transition from hunting and gathering to hunting and cattle raising and the subsequent sustenance patterns in medieval Africa occurred as a result of several factors. Among these are variations and changes in climate, population growth and resettlement, cultural traditions, caste systems, political structures, and trade, as well as the introduction of IRON tools.

Sorghum (*dhurra*) and millet were the two most popular food CROPS and were found in many regions of Africa. Typically they were grown on small farms and were cultivated using an iron hoe. Due to insufficient growing conditions (either too much or not enough rain) and soil exhaustion, farmers were forced to relocate frequently. Once harvested, the grains were placed in underground pits or in elevated mud vessels to prevent insect infestation. The flour from these grains was often mixed with boiling water and made into porridge. The consistency and amount of spices and garnishes used depended on what time of the day the meal was served. Sorghum and millet were ideal staples because they were easy to cultivate and high in proteins, vitamins, and salts. They were especially important in regions where the population seldom ate meat and were at risk of being undernourished due to crop failure.

Another significant African food staple was the yam. Although yams needed more maintenance and care and a wetter climate than sorghim and millet, they produced more food per acre and therefore were a highly valued crop in those areas that could sustain them, such as East and central Africa and the forest regions in the west. Seed yams were buried in small hills and then covered with grass and weeds for protection. Yam paste was prepared by soaking and mashing the yams and then leaving them to bake in the sun for a day. The paste was used for porridge in the morning and for stew and bread in the evening. Often the bread was rolled into balls and dipped into the stew. Yams, however, did not have the same nutritional value as sorghum and millet. Vegetables and meats, when available, were added to the diet in those areas where yams were the main source of food.

According to ARAB writers, wheat was a main food source in northern Africa, particularly among the Barghawata in MOROCCO between the tenth and eleventh centuries. It was also a source of economic wealth as an export. Nubians ate cattle and made bread and beer from white sorghum.

The countries of East Africa enjoyed a varied diet as a result of the trading ports located along the coast. Not only were they introduced to foods from other parts of Africa like the BANANA, which came from MALAWI and the ZAMBEZI basin, but they were also exposed to international delicacies such as the Asian yam. In addition to sorghum, millet, and yams, they ate a wide variety of vegetables (onions, tomatoes, eggplant, spinach, peppers), fruit (melons, coconut, dried fruit, berries), beans and spices. Those on the southern seaboard lived on turtles, fish, and mollusks. Arab writer AL-IDRISI attests that there was very little if any cattle raising among the East Coast people, and that hunting was not commonly practiced. However, Chinese authors claim that the East African coastal peoples not only ate cattle but also drank their milk and blood.

Plantains (starchy vegetables that appear similar to bananas), vegetables, and yams were grown in the central African forests; however, trapping and gathering still remained an important part of food production in the area. Grains were more popular than meat in the regions infested by the TSETSE-FLY.

In the eastern and lower parts of southern Africa agriculture was commonplace by the third century. The main food crops were sorghum, millet, or finger millet. Nomadic herders occupied the land in the drier western regions, such as BOTSWANA, northern UGANDA, and KENYA. Hunting, gathering, and fishing were not as significant as they were in central Africa. The ninth century saw drastic improvements in cattle raising.

Unlike most other regions of Africa, the SAHARA did not rely on agriculture for its food. Here camel meat and milk, as well as wild plants, were the main food sources. In Nisar and north of GAO people ate snake meat. By the tenth century, diet was determined along class lines. Those in the upper stratum ate wheat, fruit, and meat. The lower castes survived on dhurra from which they made bread and girdle cakes. In the western Sahara and east in Kawar, the people consumed dhurra, rice, fish, and livestock.

Like many African societies early in the common era, the inhabitants of the GHANA EMPIRE in West Africa were still mainly hunters and gatherers. The region provided them with a diverse diet, including wild buffalo, cattle, antelope, turtle, snail, ostrich eggs, and seafood. As IRON-WORKING provided the West African farmers with the means with which to tend their land and crops, they grew a variety of fruits and vegetables as well as yams and rice and, of course, sorghum and millet. Palm and kola trees were also important in this region. The palm tree provided necessary oils that were used in West African cooking. The kola nut, while being a delicious food source, was also a cultural symbol that was used in ceremonial rites, political arenas, and as currency and a symbol of friendship.

See also: AGRICULTURE (Vol. I); ANTELOPE (Vol. I); BUFFALO (Vol. I); CATTLE (Vol. I); COFFEE (Vol. II); DIET (Vol. I); FISHING (Vols. I, II); KOLA NUTS (Vol. I); MILLET (Vol. I); OIL PALM (Vol. III); SORGHUM (Vol. I); YAMS. (Vol. I).

Fouta Djallon (Futa Jalon)

Mountainous region in what is now west-central Guinea, covering an area of more than 30,000 square miles (77,000 sq km), and the site of FULANI migration from the thirteenth to fifteenth centuries.

The terrain of Fouta Djallon is characterized by stepped sandstone plateaus with trenches and gorges. At 5,046 feet (1538 m), its highest point is Mount Loura (Tamgué) near the border with present-day Mali. The central plateau of the Fouta Djallon gives rise to the majority of the rivers of Upper Guinea, including the GAMBIA, the SENEGAL, and the Niger.

The region is named after the YALUNKA (Djallonke) ethnic group, its earliest inhabitants. The nomadic Fulani people, who had been moving south in search of grass and water for their cattle, settled in the region in the thirteenth century. In the fifteenth century, a second wave of Fulani, resisting assimilation into the sedentary peoples with whom they had been living in the GHANA EMPIRE and TEKRUR, began their great migration through the grasslands of the SUDAN, eventually reaching as far east as Adamawa in eastern Nigeria. By the fifteenth century, a large number of Fulani had settled in the Fouta Djallon uplands.

See also: FOUTA DJALLON (Vol. III); GHANA (Vol. I); NIGER RIVER (Vol. I).

Fulani (Fulbe, Peul, Pulo)

West African people who lived throughout West Africa, from Lake CHAD to the Atlantic Ocean. The Fulani were one of the few pastoralist groups of West Africa, and their lives were organized around their herds.

The ethnic group referred to here as the Fulani call themselves *Fulbe*. *Fulani* is the HAUSA name of these people and the name by which they are known generally in English. In FULFULDE, the Fulani language, the singular of *Fulbe* is *Pulo*. Hence, the Fulani are called the *Peul* in French historical literature, which is abundant because of French colonization in West Africa in the nineteenth century.

Until the eleventh century, the Fulani lived primarily on the outskirts of the kingdom of Ghana. When Ghana fell at the end of the eleventh century, part of the Fulbe merged with the settled population of the region who had formed a new Islamic state called TEKRUR. The union of these two groups formed the TUKULOR, who spoke FULFULDE, the Fulani language. However, a segment of the population chose to preserve their pastoral and religious traditions and migrated to the east over the savanna grasslands. By the fifteenth century, after years of migration to the south and east, the Fulani had settled in the FOUTA DJALLON massif, Futa Toro, the Bundu region of present-day Guinea, and Macina in present-day Mali.

At this point the Fulani began intermarrying with the nomads and other herdspeople of the Sahel region of SUDAN under the rule of the MALI EMPIRE. The Fulani remained independent from Mali in terms of their social and political customs, but they were required to pay rent on their grazing lands and to render military services to the local authorities. By the beginning of the sixteenth century the Fulani migration had reached the region of the HAUSALAND and KANEM-BORNU in present-day Nigeria.

The social organization of the Fulani was determined by each autonomous clan, which had a leader or headman. Descent was patrilineal, and these lineage groups formed the basis of social organization. Because the Fulani were nomadic, they lived in small populations throughout the regions of West Africa and were never a dominant population themselves. The Fulani merged with other populations during this migration and gave rise to the many different groups who were all known as Fulani. As a group, the Fulani displayed distinct physical similarities, such as lighter skin, long, straight hair, and aquiline features. They also shared a common moral code known as Pulaaku.

See also: CLAN (Vol. I); FULA (Vol. I); FULANI (Vol. I); FULANI EMPIRE (Vol. III); LINEAGE (Vol. I); PASTORALISM (Vol. I).

Fulfulde

A language spoken throughout West Africa. Speakers of Fulfulde are found in a band stretching across West Africa from CHAD to CAMEROON. FULANI is the HAUSA designation for speakers of Fulfulde, *Fula* is the MANDINKA term, and *Peul* that of the WOLOF.

The Fulani were nomadic cattle herders. Between the tenth and fourteenth centuries, many Fulani migrated eastward from SENEGAL, ultimately traveling as far as Nigeria, Chad, and even the eastern SUDAN. Along the way, many found pasturage for their cattle and stopped, inhabiting sub-Saharan grassland regions of present-day GUINEA, Mali, Burkina Faso, Niger, and CAMEROON.

In the twentieth century, an estimated 5 to 10 million people speak one of the six mutually understandable dialects of this language, making it the most widely spoken language in the West Atlantic branch of the NIGER-CONGO family of languages.

G

Ga Ethnic group situated in the southeastern region of the present-day country of Ghana. The Ga are considered Kwa-speakers, a branch of the NIGER-CONGO language family. Related to the neighboring Adangme by language, the Ga have also been credited as the original founders of the modern city known as ACCRA. Their ancient myths indicate that they arrived during several waves of migration, traveling by land and sea, and occupied various regions around Ghana for many centuries.

Recently, archaeologists have concluded that the Ga began to migrate into the region in the 1200s. Remnants of old settlements and large amounts of POTTERY support claims that the Ga settled in Accra Plains, Gbegbe, Little Accra, and Lolovo prior to 1400. At Ladoku and Shai, the settlements suggest occupation before 1400. Various sources indicate that the Ga organized themselves into seven small states with the capital or controlling town, known as an *akutso*, situated on the coast. Village economy was supported by coastal fishing and the cultivation of root crops such as yams, oil palms, and plantains in the inland regions. Their form of government, music, and oral literature closely compares with those of AKAN groups.

Ga society has always been a reflection of patrilineal kinship ties. Great emphasis was placed on the circumcision of boys, particularly the first born male. In addition, each patrilineal group, known as a *we*, was considered a political group that ranked its members by birth order and generational standing. Ritual authority among the Ga also embodied patrilineal dominance since the village priest and the council of elders represented secondary, but no less important, leadership to the reigning chief. Among their various functions was the responsibility of officiating over village rites of passage such as male initia-

tion and ritual planting of millet, the harvesting of crops, or celebration of a successful year of fishing. One of the most prominent of these public ceremonies was the Homowo Festival, which called for special rites and songs, both known as *kpele*.

Women, who acted as trade intermediaries between the coastal and inland populations, held some rights in Ga society. They were able to succeed to public office and own property based on inheritance. Marriage was traditionally initiated and negotiated by the male's family. After marriage, women lived in their own compounds, which generally belonged to the husband's *we*.

Within the framework of religion, the Ga have always recognized a supreme being, whose omniscient presence has been equated with a natural, unseen life force. A strong belief in life after death has always been an influential factor among the Ga as well, and has traditionally been symbolized in lavish funerary customs, one of the most important rites in their society. Their belief system maintains that, after death, the deceased must successfully cross a river to reach the land of the departed. Reaching this goal is dependent upon the rituals performed by the living.

The Ga also share many aspects of worship with the Akan. For example, the use of a symbolic stool is central to both societies. In addition, male and female mediums are often "called" by the gods to channel divine communications. Suitable candidates were generally isolated from society to the point of dissolving marital ties. While in a trance-like state called spirit possession, Ga mediums have been known to participate in extraordinary feats of endurance that could not be accomplished otherwise.

See also: GA (Vol. III).

Gabon Modern country that lies on the equator along West Africa's Atlantic coast. The area has seen extensive migration by BANTU ethnic groups since the twelfth century. Evidence of earlier inhabitants include spearheads dating back to c. 7000 BCE. Little, however, is known about these early inhabitants.

See also: GABON (Vols. I, III).

Gabr'el-Rufa'el One of eleven underground churches expertly carved out of rock in Lalibela (originally called al-ROHA) in north-central Ethiopia in the early thirteenth century.

See also: LALIBELA, ROCK CHURCHES OF (Vol. II).

Gabu (Kaabu, Quebu) Kingdom of West Africa, founded in the mid-1200s and lasting nearly six centuries, until it fell to FULA attacks in 1867. Gabu was founded by the Mali general Tiramakhan Traore, a subject of the famed MANDINKA emperor SUNDIATA (d. 1255) of the MALI EMPIRE, during a period of Malian expansion into territories that are now part of SENEGAL and Guinea-Bissau. Its first emperor, or *mansa*, was Mansa Sama Coli, who was said to be Traore's son or grandson. Other historians credit Mansa Sama Coli himself, and not Traore, with founding Gabu.

The Mali Empire used Gabu to extend its influence into the SALT, GOLD, and slave trades along the coast. Gabu was well situated for this purpose. Kansala, on the modern Guinea-Bissau–Senegal border, was the capital of the three royal provinces of Gabu. Pachana province bordered the headwaters of the Geba River. Jimara province was on the Gambia River. Both of these rivers flow into the Atlantic Ocean. The third province, Sama, lay in the southern region of what is now Senegal, near the CASAMANCE RIVER.

While Gabu was still a secondary kingdom of the Mali Empire, provincial governors had considerable local authority. Each had his own army and symbolic war drums. If there was no heir to succeed, a new king was chosen from the eldest leaders of these provinces. In time of war, command of these armies could be given over to the king. The *mansa* was considered sacred. Unlike that among people of lesser rank, the royal line of succession was matrilineal, or from a mother's side, rather than patrilineal, or from a father's side.

By 1500, most of the Mali Empire had come under the control of the SONGHAI Empire, which stretched from the Atlantic Ocean to what is now central Nigeria. Despite its powerful neighbor, however, Gabu was able to maintain its independence and even expand.

See also: GABU (Vol. III).

Gama, Vasco da (c. 1460–1524) *Portuguese navigator who founded the colonies of Mozambique and Sofala in Africa and initiated Portuguese rule over the islands of Zanzibar and Kilwa.*

In 1497 da Gama was commissioned by King Manuel of Portugal to sail from Portugal to India by way of the Cape of Good Hope at the southern tip of Africa. The purpose of the expedition was to establish a sea trade route from western Europe to the East. For hundreds of years, caravans from the East had brought the spices and riches of the Orient to the tables and fine houses of Europe, but these caravan routes across Asia were now a monopoly of the Muslims. In a first-of-its-kind voyage by a European, da Gama arrived in Callicut, the most important trading center in southern India, on May 20, 1498. His voyage made the small country of Portugal a major commercial power and initiated a period of extensive European exploration and expansion. Along his route to India, da Gama stopped in MOZAMBIQUE, MOMBASSA, MALINDI, and ZANZIBAR. Unable to establish a trade center in India, da Gama returned to Portugal in 1499.

A second expedition was commissioned in 1502 with the goal of asserting Portuguese authority over parts of East Africa. It was on this journey that da Gama established Mozambique and SOFALA, which the Portuguese ruled until 1729.

After establishing Portuguese sovereignty in East Africa, da Gama continued his commercial efforts in India. In 1524, King John III appointed him the Portuguese viceroy to India. He died three months after assuming his new position.

See also: AGE OF DISCOVERY (Vol. II); PORTUGAL AND AFRICA (Vol. III).

Gambia, The Small country in West Africa. Situated midway between the tropic of Cancer and the equator, Gambia is, with the exception of its eastern coastline, completely surrounded by SENEGAL. One of the smallest countries in modern-day Africa, Gambia consists of a mostly flat, narrow strip of land flanking the banks of the GAMBIA RIVER.

Scholars have long been puzzled by the hundreds of stone circles found in the area. Most of the circles are cylindrical in shape with flat tops, although some are square and taper upwards. The stones, made from a relatively common stone known as laterite, are remarkably uniform in size. Most circles are made up of 10 to 24 stones ranging from between 2 and 8 feet (0.6 and 2.5 m) tall and 1 and 3 feet (0.3 and 1 m) in diameter. The largest stones weigh about 10 tons (10.1 m tons) each.

Studies undertaken at Wassu and N'jai Kunda suggest that the stone circles, which date to somewhere between 640 and 860, most likely were the burial mounds of important chiefs or kings. V-shaped stones, it is thought, indicate that two members of a family died on the same day and were buried together. A small stone standing close to a larger one possibly means that a child was buried with a parent.

See also: GAMBIA (Vol. III); GAMBIA STONE CIRCLES (Vol. II).

Gambia River A 700-mile (1,126-km) long river in West Africa that originates in the highlands of FOUTA DJALLON in GUINEA and flows west to the Atlantic Ocean. It has two large tributaries, the Sandougou and the Sofianiama, and smaller creeks, or *bolons,* that include the Bintang, which joins the river at its southern end. In the middle region of the Gambia River, many small islands have formed, including Elephant and McCarthy Islands.

In the period prior to European colonization, the pastoralist Fulbe people lived near the Gambia River, having migrated to the area bordering the river c. 1000 in search of grazing land for their cattle. In the twelfth or thirteenth century, the WOLOF people, whose language is in the same family as the Fulbe's, migrated as far west as the Atlantic coast following the fall of the GHANA EMPIRE in the eleventh century.

Geologists note that the high saline content of the Gambia's waters have contributed to the formation of 100-foot high mangrove swamps in the lower inland regions of the river. These swamps have long been the home of diverse wildlife including hippopotamuses and crocodiles. Hundreds of wild birds, including the heron, sunbird, and hawk, also live within the swamplands, as does the deadly TSETSE FLY, which breeds in its waters. Some regions that border the Gambia have used its enriched silt, or sediment left by annual flooding, for the cultivation of rice and peanuts. Oil palm trees, an important dietary source and trade item, have also been found growing wild in the valley regions of the river as well.

In 1455, Alvise Ca'da Mosto (1432–1488), a Venetian explorer and trader in the service of Prince HENRY THE NAVIGATOR (1394–1460) of Portugal, was the first European to visit the Gambia River. He sailed 150 miles (241 km) inland but turned back when he found the inhabitants hostile. The second European to visit the Gambia River was Diogo Gomes (d. 1484), a Portuguese-born explorer whom Prince Henry sent in 1456 to explore the coast of West Africa. He sailed as far south as the GEBA RIVER. On his way home, he sailed 200 miles (322 km) up the Gambia until he reached the market town of Cantor (modern Kuntaur), which was under the rule of the SONGHAI Empire. The Portuguese closely guarded the information that Gomes's expedition reported regarding the area.

The Gambia River has long been considered exceptional for its ease of navigation. Unlike many other rivers of the continent that hindered potential navigators with outcroppings, rapids, or waterfalls, the Gambia provided even large sailing vessels with a navigable waterway that allowed entry into the interior of the region. This proved advantageous to the other European traders who arrived in the sixteenth century.

Gambia stone circles Clusters of stone pillars found in the Senegambia region along Africa's western coast. The stone circles of Senegambia, which are located north of the GAMBIA RIVER, are actually a series of sites extending over more than 11,583 square miles (30,000 sq km) from Farafenni in the east toward Tambacounda in Senegal. Generally known as *megaliths,* Greek for "large stones," the circular clusters are most concentrated at Dialloumbere, where fifty-four circles consisting of two or three pillars each were erected. Some pillars measure 26 feet (8 m) across and 3 to 7 feet (1 to 2 m) high. At other sites, they stand nearly 10 feet (3 m) high. Many of the pillars have rounded tops, while others were sculpted with a cup-like shape, possibly created to hold offerings. The different shapes, sizes, and styles of the pillars, and the fact that some stones are *dressed* or worked, are what first led archaeologists to suspect that the megaliths were built by a number of different groups at various times.

Scientists at the University of Dakar in SENEGAL have confirmed this theory by using carbon dating methods to gain an approximate idea of the age of the megaliths. They have determined that the oldest stone pillars were located at Sine and Saloum in Senegal and date back to the fourth century. In the region of N'jai Kunda, in GAMBIA, the stone pillars date back to c. 750, a time when IRON smelting was widespread. Since the stones are made of laterite, scientists have suggested a probable connection to iron making.

Based on archaeological evidence and recovered materials, the earliest burials within the stone circles may have initially been limited to the DYULA population, the most ancient inhabitants of the region, who may have been present when the circles were first created. Most archaeologists agree that the site became an exclusive burial ground for kings, chiefs, and priests at some point in history, with the sizes of the stones corresponding to rank. There is a possibility that some of the groups that built the megaliths to honor their rulers were linked by similar cultural practices regarding royalty. These grounds are believed to hold the remains of kings associated with the WOLOF or MALI EMPIRES, or the smaller coastal kingdoms established at Waalo, Kayor, Baol, Sine, and Saloum. During the eleventh century, when Islamic rulers governed the Senegambia region, they too were reportedly buried in this fashion.

In some ways, the megaliths of Gambia compare with those types found in central Africa and the MAGHRIB. However, as Africa's smallest republic, Gambia is notable for having the greatest number of stone megaliths.

Ganda (Baganda, Luganda, Waganda)

BANTU-speaking people who, today, are the largest ethnic group in UGANDA. The legendary founder of the Ganda is SEK-ABAKA KINTU, a chief of the Bito people, who lived in northwestern Uganda c. 1400. When the Bito moved to the shores of Lake VICTORIA, they founded the kingdom of BUGANDA.

See also: GANDA (Vol. III).

Ganwa

Ruling descendants of TUTSI royalty in Burundi; also known as the ruling princes. Burundi was one of several lake-district kingdoms in the eleventh through the eighteenth centuries that included BUGANDA, BUNYORO-KITARA, RWANDA, Burundi, Buha, and Buzinza. Abundant rainfall and fertile soil led to ample harvests, and trade between the various kingdoms brought in additional wealth. As a result, the region attracted one of the highest population densities of any region south of the SAHARA.

Burundi, Rwanda, and their neighboring areas were originally inhabited by the small-statured TWA, who are believed to have occupied the region for as long as 70,000 years. BANTU-speaking HUTU apparently migrated into the area later, perhaps as early as the fifth and sixth centuries. Although it has not been possible to determine exactly when the Hutu arrived, it is clear that they certainly were in place by the eleventh to fourteenth centuries, at which time the Tutsi also invaded Burundi. Subsequently, the Twa were effectively marginalized by both the Hutu and Tutsi, and the Tutsi gained preeminence over both groups.

Once they had settled in the area, the Tutsi established a well-organized feudal system, within which the Ganwa served as a political arm of the Tutsi royals. The Tutsi maintained social control by demanding cattle as payment for their field labor and agricultural products. This practice, which resulted in a highly complex society, ensured that the Tutsi would not be limited to the single—and socially inferior—role of farmers. Through their participation in this system, many Hutus rose in status to become healers or judges, positions usually held by Tutsi pastoralists. The interchangeable roles of the peoples created a common social identity, known as *kwihutura*, which was based on shared work patterns and religious worship as well as a shared language known as Kirundi. Intermarriage between the two groups also was common.

In spite of these interconnections, however, the wealthiest cattle holders were traditionally Tutsi. The royal title also remained in their hands, and a series of dynastic families developed that were ruled by the *mwami*, or king, and the queen mother.

Under the Tutsi system, the Ganwa received their power directly from the *mwami*, who made them responsible for controlling the land and ruling the provinces. The Ganwa also served as military leaders. Because so much of their authority came directly from the *mwami*, competition among the Ganwa was intense, often leading to fierce power struggles.

See also: BURUNDI (Vol. III); TWA (Vol. I).

Gao (Kawkaw)

Capital city of the SONGHAI Empire, located on the Niger River at the southern tip of the SAHARA Desert, bordering ALGERIA, BURKINA FASO, and TIMBUKTU.

The development of Gao has been difficult to trace, and the historical evolution of the area is not clear. It is believed, however, that the city of Gao was founded as a fishing center in the seventh century. In time, it became one of the first great trading bases in West Africa. By the early eleventh century, Gao had become the capital of the SONGHAI Empire, as well as a thriving center for trans-Saharan trade. The Songhai continued to rule the city for almost 500 years. In 1325, Gao was annexed into the MALI EMPIRE, only to fall back under Songhai rule forty years later. When MOROCCO took control of Gao in 1591, the city permanently disengaged itself from Songhai control and fell into decline soon thereafter.

See also: GAO (Vol. III); NIGER RIVER (Vol. I); TRANS-SAHARAN TRADE ROUTES (Vol. II); SONGHAI (Vol. III).

Geba River

A river situated at Bissau, the coastal city and capital of present-day Guinea-Bissau. The Geba and its tributary, the Colufe River, are notable for having supported agricultural activities by groups such as the FULANI, MANDINKA, and Balanta in the period prior to European colonization. The river fostered the region's development as a center of trade because of its ease of navigation and access to the ocean. Following Portuguese exploration and settlement beginning c. 1450, the river soon became the chief means of transportation for thousands of slaves destined for overseas markets.

See also: GOLD (Vol. II); GUINEA (Vol. III); PORTUGAL AND AFRICA (Vol. III); SLAVERY (Vols. II, III).

Gedi

Walled city-state situated along the coast of KENYA. Africa's eastern coast, also called the SWAHILI COAST, has been an active trading region for centuries. According to the Greek sailing guide, *Periplus of the Erythrean Sea*, written in approximately the second century CE, commercial trade in the region dates back 2,000 years or more. Commerce most likely began with indigenous inhabitants of the coast trading with those of the interior for items ranging from agricultural produce to salt and IRON tools. POTTERY also was apparently traded, and recovered remnants indicate that it was produced prior to the arrival of Arab settlers. Unglazed, with minimal decoration or color, these early forms of pottery have a marked resemblance to those types produced in various regions of central Africa and in ZIMBABWE and MAPUNGUB-WE in SOUTH AFRICA. Cooking pots with distinct fingernail designs have also been recovered at Gedi and may have been an early trade item. Their designs were reportedly similar to those made by the GIRIAMA.

By some time between 500 and 800, trading had become well-established within the interior; seagoing trade, which was associated with MERCHANTS from Arabia, Persia, and India, also was well-established. The latter merchants and traders, who came to refer to the region and its population as al-ZANJ, or "the Blacks," subsequently settled in the region. Glazed earthenware from as far away as China suggests that these people expanded their commercial trading links quite far. To support this expanding trade, hundreds of independent ports flourished along the 3,000-mile coastline that stretched from MOMBASSA, in the north, to SOFALA in the south. Some of these ports, like Gedi, became permanent city-states, but many others lasted only a brief time before being abandoned.

During the golden age between the twelfth and thirteenth centuries, Swahili traders exported a wide range of items that included GOLD, IVORY, ambergris, tortoiseshell, leopard skins, sandalwood, and hard ebony woods. These were traded with merchants from the Middle East, Greece, Asia, and Europe. Enslaved individuals were also part of the trade, destined for the overseas markets of the Arabian Peninsula, Iraq, and India, where their labor was used for agricultural expansion.

A mere ten miles from MALINDI, Gedi developed into a major city under Islamic rule. The cultural mix formed by Arabic and BANTU populations took many forms, including a distinctive language known as KISWAHILI. Although the word *swahili* is Arabic for "the coast," the language was primarily Bantu; however, it had strong Arabic elements, including its alphabet and numerous borrowed words and phrases. Swahili societies formed a class structure that consisted of ruling families of mixed Arabic and African ancestry. Within the main population were transient groups of merchants, buyers, and seamen.

Although largely in ruins today, the architectural style of Gedi was once a testament to a great culture. A large enclosing wall surrounded a former palace with courtyards, a large mosque, and many smaller ones, as well as many large houses and pillars said to be grave markers. These extensive ruins have contributed to the region's current status as a national monument.

Traditional forms of Swahili MUSIC have survived as well. One of the most distinctive forms is *taarab,* described as a poetic song that infuses Arabic and Indian melodies. Played on an *oud,* an Arabic type of lute, and the *darbuk,* a leather topped drum with a pottery bottom, *taarab* was originally performed at such rites of passage as wedding ceremonies, male circumcision rites, and female initiation ceremonies.

After Vasco da GAMA arrived along the coast in 1498, a shift in power led to the Portuguese seizing Mombassa and establishing a monopoly over INDIAN OCEAN TRADE. As part of their conquest of the coastal city-states, they built Fort Jesus at Mombassa along with a customshouse on nearby Pate Island. Although Swahili trade merchants tried to resist Portuguese rule, they were forced to abandon their activities in many of the Swahili port cities for a period. Portuguese attempts to align themselves with the city of Malindi against Mombassa failed, but it was not until the late seventeenth century that Portuguese political dominance was broken, largely by a series of conflicts involving the imam of Oman.

See also: ARAB COASTAL TRADE (Vol. II); CHINESE TRADE (Vol. II); FORT JESUS (Vol. III); INDIAN OCEAN TRADE (Vol. II); PERSIAN TRADERS (Vol. II); PORTUGAL AND AFRICA (Vol. II); SLAVERY (Vols. II, III); SWAHILI COAST (Vol. III).

Further reading: James L. Newman, *The Peopling of Africa: A Geographic Interpretation* (New Haven, Conn.: Yale University Press, 1995).

Ge'ez (Geez) AFRO-ASIATIC language primarily associated with liturgical documents and literature of ETHIOPIA. Ge'ez is still used in liturgical celebrations of the Ethiopian Orthodox Church. Ge'ez, among Africa's earliest written languages, is the source of an extensive body of religious and historical writings. Sometimes identified as *Lessana Ge'ez* ("the language of the free"), Ethiopians consider Ge'ez a classical language because of its antiquity and the fact that it reflects the evolution of culture in the northern highlands. Although Ge'ez may have incorporated some indigenous elements of Kushitic speech patterns, its written forms have largely been attributed to Sabaean or Semetic Arabs who migrated from the southern Arabian Peninsula. Traders and agriculturists, the Sabaeans settled in the highlands during the first millennium BCE.

The early structural form of Ge'ez reportedly differed from other Semitic languages. It is written in a cursive script and is read from left to right. Ancient Ge'ez, like ancient Hebrew, had no letter forms for vowels; instead, it relied on small marks next to consonants to indicate the vowel sound to be used. By the second century CE, this script had developed sufficiently to include letter forms for vowels.

During the fourth century, Ge'ez was largely associated with the Ethiopian Church. The resulting body of religious works emphasized stories of Christian saints, religious poetry, sacred law, and rituals. MONOPHYSITE monks translated the Bible into Ge'ez between the fifth through seventh centuries, and religious scholars note that the apocryphal books of the Bible—the Book of Enoch, Book of Jubilees, and others—were translated into Ge'ez as well. These translations may represent one of the only complete versions of these ancient texts in the world, an important contribution to biblical studies.

The language of Ge'ez also played an important role in the royal kingdom of AKSUM, appearing, for example, on numerous inscriptions, coins, stelae, and monuments created between the fourth and ninth centuries.

Ge'ez ceased to be used as a spoken language by 1200 but it was preserved until the nineteenth century as an official vehicle for religious writings. In addition, its widespread influence has had a direct bearing on the development of many of Ethiopia's modern languages including Tigrinya, TIGRAY, and AMHARIC.

See also: GE'EZ (Vol. I); WRITING (Vols. I, II).

al-Ghaba The non-Muslim section of KUMBI SALEH, capital of the GHANA EMPIRE, and location of the palace of the king. Sometimes referred to as one of the "twin cities" of Kumbi Saleh, al-Ghaba traces its history to c. 700 CE and the arrival in the area of several SONINKE peoples under the leadership of a *kaya maghan* ("lord of the gold"). The twin to al-Ghaba, called Kumbi, was more than 3 miles (4.8 km) away at the time Kumbi Saleh was first established.

Never intended as a commercial center, al-Ghaba boasted no marketplace but instead was comprised of the mud and thatch homes of non-Muslim residents of Kumbi Saleh and the grand timber and stone palace of the king. *al-Ghaba*, a name that means "woods" or "forest," was indeed surrounded by woodlands. According to legend, the area was once prohibited to ordinary people because the forest was the provenance of the snake spirit WAGADU-BIDA. Each year, it was here that sorcerers would sacrifice a young virgin girl in order to appease the god. Al-Ghaba stood also as a symbol of religious tolerance: Although Kumbi Saleh was segregated along religious lines, native Ghanaians and Muslims peacefully coexisted here until c. 1040, when a Muslim leader attempted to convert non-Muslims by force. After a decade of struggle, the Muslims took control of the entire city. According to some scholars, this episode marked the onset of the decline of the Ghana Empire.

ghana, the Official title for the succession of ruling kings of ancient Ghana. Called Wagadu by its people, the GHANA EMPIRE flourished in the seventh through the thirteenth centuries.

Although the origins and use of the title are not definitely known, the term *ghana* was a title of prestige that may have come from the MANDE language in which the word *ghana* means "warrior king." Kingship in ancient Ghana was based on matrilineal descent and traditionally passed to the son of the king's sister. As a result, women were often referred to as "king-makers" because they were in full charge of rearing young children. Successors were installed as kings following a number of prescribed ceremonies held in a specially appointed sacred grove.

Based on the descriptions of Islamic historians, including al-BAKRI (c. eleventh century), as well as early travelers in the region, the *ghana* ruled in sumptuous surroundings that included a domed palace that housed the royal family and members of the court. The king was reportedly adorned with golden bracelets and a gold-decorated cap encased in a turban of the finest cloth. He was guarded by members of the nation's large standing army, whose swords and shields were also trimmed in gold.

Both at court and in his travels the king retained a large entourage of official drummers, dancers, and jesters that served as a source of entertainment and as a means of heralding his appearance when he toured the kingdom. Among the king's many functions was the responsibility of serving as the nation's highest-ranking judge. He also created policy, presided over land disputes and capital cases, and addressed innumerable complaints. When necessary, the *ghana* was also responsible for leading the nation in war.

Rulers in ancient Ghana were entombed within large earthen mounds in the same sacred grove in which they were officially installed. Prior to entombment, however, they apparently lay in state for several days on a large wooden bier lined with special carpets and cushions. One of the most important traditions surrounding the death of the *ghana* was that all of the eating and drinking vessels used by the king during his lifetime were filled with offerings and placed by his side. Along with those were placed innumerable household comforts—including his servants. The traditional belief was that servants and household amenities should be made available to the king during his journey to the beyond.

See also: DIVINE RULE (Vols. I, II).

Ghana Empire (c. 800–1240) Ancient empire of western Africa that thrived, along with the empires of MALI, KANEM-BORNU, and SONGHAI, along the Niger River; its economic prosperity was based on trade in, among other items, IVORY, GOLD, and kola nuts. The word *ghana* means "war chief" and was the title given to the rulers of the original kingdom whose SONINKE name was Wagadu. *Kaya maghan* ("lord of the gold") was another title for these kings.

Ancient Ghana was one of the earliest Sudanic kingdoms of West Africa, with its original geographic borders established within the western part of present-day Mali and the southeastern part of MAURITANIA. The modern country of Ghana, situated 500 miles (805 km) to the southeast, named itself after ancient Ghana.

A great deal of mystery has surrounded the origins of

ancient Ghana. Archaeological findings, oral traditions, and a thorough reassessment of accounts of the empire made by Arabic historians and cartographers have led to the current hypothesis that Ghana emerged as a CITY-STATE as early as the third century. It apparently was founded by the SONINKE peoples as an arm of their extensive trading networks.

Wagadu, Ghana's original name, comes from the name of the ancient god of the Soninke, Wagadu-Bida, who was considered the guardian of the nation. Bida took the form of a snake.

The eleventh-century Moorish chronicler al-BAKRI described the Wagadu snake cult. The prospective leaders of this cult would gather around the snake's cave and wait until the snake chose a man to bite. This man would then chase after the snake and rip as many hairs as he could from the snake's back. The number of hairs he ended up with represented the number of years he would serve as leader.

The Soninke established KUMBI SALEH, which was located at the edge of developing TRANS-SAHARAN TRADE ROUTES, as the area's first capital city. Trade, along with a strong agricultural base, contributed to the early wealth of the empire. A diverse number of ethnic groups existed within the capital, including BERBERS and, later, various Islamic groups. The GA, EWE, and MANDE were also part of early Ghana.

By the eighth century, North African traders had spread word of Ghana's prominence as the "land of gold" across vast international territories. Its reputation continued to grow after c. 990 when the kingdom of Ghana conquered the important SANHAJA BERBER–dominated trading center of AUDAGHOST in the SAHARA and emerged as an empire. Several small kingdoms to the north and south—including TEKRUR, SILLA, DIARA, and KANIAGA—also were conquered and became vassal states. The kings of these states were permitted to continue individual rule over their respective kingdoms, while the ruler of Ghana maintained centralized control over the empire.

At this point, Ghana's wide-ranging trade network, which had been accumulating vast wealth from the cara-

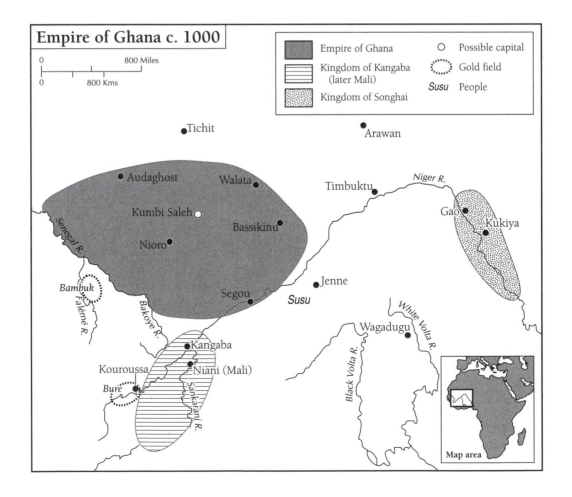

van trade, expanded to include items such as salt, GOLD, COPPER, horses, and slaves, the constant supply of whom was guaranteed by war and conquest. Many of these slaves were put to work in the gold mines that lay to the south. Slaves were also used for agricultural cultivation, which led to even greater quantities of such CROPS as millet, sorghum, and COTTON.

Ghana's proximity to the gold-producing regions of Bambuk, Bure, and WANGARA placed it in the unique position of controlling vast amounts of the gold being transported north by caravan. Although great amounts of gold were transported out of the region, there were also strict policies that helped reserve both gold nuggets for the king as well as a certain amount of gold dust for the regional population. Ghana also controlled the trade into the south, especially the trade in salt, which was a rare and highly prized item in West Africa.

Much of Ghana's wealth came from the taxes that it collected on trade. A donkey- or camel-load of copper, for example, reportedly was taxed at a rate of approximately half an ounce (14 grams) of gold. General merchandise apparently was taxed at the rate of 1 ounce (28 grams) of gold per load. These taxes made it possible for Ghana to maintain a standing army of as many as 200,000 warriors, which was used to provide MERCHANTS with security and safe passage along the trade routes.

By the eleventh century Kumbi Saleh had developed to the point that the state was reportedly divided between traditional Ghanaian rulers and Islamic merchants who were invited to participate in the day-to-day affairs of the royal court. This century also saw the first stages of the crumbling of Ghana's infrastructure as a result of trading rivalries and internal conflicts. There is some speculation that because Ghana never fully embraced ISLAM, religious conflicts also had a role in this social disintegration.

However, most of the causes and details of the final disintegration of Ghana's empire still remain unclear. It appears that Ghana's great wealth attracted competitors bent on loosening the empire's hold on trade. Led by a radically devout Muslim known as ABD ALLA IBN YASIN, Berbers calling themselves ALMORAVIDS attacked Ghana's capital in c. 1076. Some reports claim that the Almoravids destroyed the Ghana Empire, while others assert that the Ghanaians converted to Islam and joined the Almoravid movement in order to spread Islam in Africa. It is not clear whether the Almoravids completely destroyed the capital or gained an appreciable mea-

sure of political and economic control over its inhabitants.

Ancient Ghana was rich in gold and blessed with an abundance of rain. According to Soninke legend, this prosperity was bestowed upon the land by a snake called Wagadu-Bida, and in return for his generosity, a virgin was sacrificed in his honor each year. The days of glory ended under the rule of ancient Ghana's seventh king, when, during the annual ceremony, the lover of the sacrificial virgin slaughtered the snake. In retribution, Wagadu-Bida dried up the land and moved all the gold to Bure on the Upper Niger. With Ghana in ruins, the people were forced to leave their impoverished and barren homeland. Many Soninke clans trace their ancestry to this legend.

A number of feudal states rose in the void left by Ghana's demise, including the SUSU kingdom in the northern part of the former empire and the small KANGABA kingdom in the area that shortly became the Mali Empire. The Susu kingdom launched a second attack against Ghana in c. 1203. It has been reported that the Susu ruler, Sumanguru, successfully captured Kumbi Saleh, thus bringing a violent end to Ghana's economic and military power. Two decades later, about 1240, SUNDIATA (d. 1255), the leader of the Kangaba, launched a successful attack against Sumanguru and gained control of the gold trade. Remnants of the former kingdom of Ghana were then incorporated into the MALI EMPIRE founded by Sundiata.

See also: GHANA, ANCIENT (Vol. I); KINGDOMS AND EMPIRES (Vol. II); KINDOMS AND EMPIRES OF THE WEST AFRICAN SAVANNA (Vol. II); SLAVERY (Vol. II); WANGARA GOLD FIELDS (Vol. II).

Further reading: Claudia Zaslavsky, *Africa Counts: Number and Pattern in African Cultures*, 3rd ed. (Chicago, Ill.: Lawrence Hill Books, 1999).

giraffe The world's tallest mammal. The giraffe's appearance has made it the frequent subject of comment, even among Africa's diverse and unusual animal kingdom. In the thirteenth century, Arab traveler Ibn Khaldun documented the startled reaction of the royal court at TUNIS when a giraffe was presented to the ruling sultan from the king of the KANEM-BORNU Empire. The Chinese admiral Cheng Ho (Zheng He), who led a series of expeditions to the Indian Ocean coast of Africa between 1405 and 1433, returned to China in 1417 with a delegation from MALINDI, who presented the royal court at Beijing with a giraffe.

See also: CHINESE TRADE (Vol. II).

Giriama Ethnic group of the northeast coast of KENYA. Inhabitants of relatively isolated areas, the Giriama reportedly have occupied this region of Kenya since the beginning of the common era. Primarily farmers who supplanted their economy by hunting, FISHING, and raising livestock, they eventually played a prominent role in providing grain to the ships involved in the transatlantic slave trade.

Although this part of the African coast was strongly influenced by ISLAM in the tenth century, the Giriama apparently were less affected by this than were neighboring peoples. They retained many of their own linguistic forms and cultural modes of expression, including their distinctive POTTERY, which was decorated with fingernail designs. The Giriama were also noted for creating grave posts with intricately designed tops.

See also: GIRIAMA (Vol. III); KENYA (Vol. III); MOMBASA (Vols. II, III); SLAVERY (Vols. II, III).

Giyorgis, St. (St. George) Rock-hewn church situated at Lalibela (formerly al-ROHA) in the Lasta Mountains of ETHIOPIA. The architectural splendor of St. Giyorgis Church has been credited to King LALIBELA (c. 1185–1225) of the ZAGWE DYNASTY. Lalibela's rock-hewn churches grew out of the king's religious visions in which he was instructed to build structures that represented a New Jerusalem. He reportedly built two groups of churches, both considered to be monoliths, over a period of twenty-five years.

According to legend, sometime after the completion of these churches, Lalibela had a dream in which St. George, Ethiopia's patron saint, scolded him for not building a church in his name. Lalibela's promise to honor the saint resulted in a monumental structure that sources say was built by workers recruited from EGYPT.

The site where Beta Giyorgis (House of St. George) was built was first hollowed out in what has been described as a perfect cube. The three-tiered church was then sculpted from a rock pedestal within the center and shaped in the form of a religious cross. The church, measuring approximately 39 feet (12 m) high, had an adjoining courtyard surrounded by stone walls. In them, many small caves were sculpted, which, over the centuries, have served as homes to monks and priests as well as tombs for the dead.

See also: ARCHITECTURE (Vol. II); LALIBELA, CHURCHES OF (Vol. II).

Gobir One of the CITY-STATES of HAUSALAND established between the tenth and thirteenth centuries. In the HAUSA-speaking regions of northern Nigeria, several towns came to represent the original Hausa settlements. These sites included Gobir, KANO, ZARIA, and KATSINA. Most historical knowledge concerning these sites has come from the recorded observations of Islamic travelers in the region. According to their descriptions, Gobir and the other sites were part of a feudal system of walled towns called *birnis*. These birnis were regarded as ruling capitals governed by a *sirki*, or local ruler, who controlled a number of armed horsemen. The towns were able to develop as a result of intensive agriculture that took place outside the walls. CROPS reportedly flourished as a result of underground water sources. Within the walled town itself, marketplaces were established. There also were centers in which various CRAFTSPEOPLE—blacksmiths, tanners, weavers, brewers, musicians, and ritual specialists—plied their trades.

The town of Gobir also has been mentioned in relation to the adaptation of Islamic teachings, which first began in the fourteenth to fifteenth centuries. Until that time the walled towns had continued to develop without interference but with a limited export market. By the sixteenth century trade routes established by the TUAREG on the AÏR MASSIF had developed to such a degree that Hausa traders were able to incorporate their COTTON and leather goods into the North African and overseas trade markets. In addition, trading in the SAHARA region led to a political alliance between the Hausa and the Tuareg, who received a tax on trade items. In turn, the Tuareg established a Gobir representative in their territory to serve as the sultan of Agades.

See also: AGADES (Vol. III); GOBIR (Vol. III).

gold A soft and lustrous precious metal that does not tarnish or corrode. Gold was obtained by MINING or panning in several locations throughout Africa from ancient days through precolonial times. Gold was used by kings and traders to buy goods and services from other parts of the known world and was also used locally for adornment.

In Egypt, gold was found in some abundance along streams in NUBIA and Kush. Gold sources in non-Egyptian Africa included the area of the headwaters of the Niger and Senegal Rivers, in what is now Mali and Guinea. In the eighth and ninth centuries, gold was mined in southeast ZIMBABWE by means of excavations in the form of steps, or stopes. The ores were then crushed by pounding stones. Gold became important politically and economically in SUB-SAHARAN AFRICA as a trade item in the seventh century. African kings knew that their fame and wealth depended on precious metals, and they took measures to control the export of gold. Arab travelers and traders were forbidden to enter areas where gold was found lest they divulge the locations of the gold fields.

Located in the western SUDAN, near the great bend of

the Niger River, the ancient kingdom of Ghana became important with the rise of TRANS-SAHARAN TRADE. The kingdom lay north of the region of Wangara, which was rich in gold, and south of the salt mines of Taghaza. Ancient Ghana thus became the intermediary—the place where salt, rare in West Africa, was traded for gold. Salt was sometimes worth its weight in gold.

In Ghana, all gold nuggets belonged to the king, and gold dust belonged to the people. The king carefully controlled the flow of gold. Because the locations of the gold fields were kept secret, merchants from North Africa had to come to designated places on the border and leave their goods. Buyers of goods brought gold and left it beside the goods. The sellers returned, and either took the gold or left it; if the gold was left, the buyers returned and added more gold. The process was repeated until the buyers accepted the amount offered by sellers by taking away the gold.

By about 950, Ghana's ruler was described as the richest in the world. He was known as the *kaya maghan*, or "lord of the gold." A visitor to court wrote that the emperor had a receipt for 42,000 gold dinars, obtained from trade. A dinar was a coin that represented the sovereignty of certain North African rulers. The gold of Ghana was the most prized form of currency in trans-African trade.

The name of Zimbabwe's early rulers, too, was related to gold. The title *mwene matapa* means "master pillager," and refers to the king's ability to amass gold-wealth. The *mwene matapas* used gold to purchase Chinese porcelain, brocades, silks, and other luxuries for their courts. They also purchased fine weapons, which added to their consequence.

Mansa MUSA, the ruler of MALI, used gold to hire architects, writers, and priests. In 1324, he made a pilgrimage to MECCA, taking with him great amounts of gold, which he circulated so freely that the value of the Egyptian dinar was depressed for several years.

The gold of Africa became the lifeblood of trade, which brought new plants to Africa from Asia, such as COTTON, which arrived in the Sudan in the late ninth century. In the fourteenth century, African gold became the basis for Europe's currency.

The Sources of Gold Although gold was produced on a large scale to meet the demands of northern traders and overseas markets from an early period, it played a prominent role in local regions as well.

During the rule of Georgios I (c. 856–915), a Nubian monarch in the Dongola region, foreign trade included gold and IVORY. The gold was extracted from mines situated near Abu Hamed and became the focus of armed conflicts between Georgios's forces and Arab-led armies.

The method of alluvial panning was common in areas where swollen rivers and tributaries would recede, leaving behind gold dust and nuggets. This practice, still in use today, was shrouded in mystery for centuries, and as a result, a number of erroneous myths circulated. There were beliefs that gold represented a type of agricultural product that grew as a result of rainfall. Others believed that the gold traveled underground with the help of ants. One official in the North African city of TUNIS even proposed that wells be dug from MOROCCO to West Africa to extract the gold there. Because mines were always subject to collapse or other dangers, it is thought that many belief systems and rituals developed in response. These rituals may in fact have been the actual mystery that the gold miners sought to preserve from outsiders.

This nineteenth-century Ashanti gold plate is on display in a museum in modern Ghana. The plate gives testimony to the historical importance of gold in the African economy. Gold from the gold fields of Bure and Akan were important in trans-Saharan trade. © *Charles & Josette Lenars/CORBIS*

Among West African gold producers was the kingdom of GHANA, where the metal was panned at the Bambuk and Bure gold fields, situated to the south of

Ghana near the head of the Niger and Senegal Rivers. Based on the written sources of early Arabic traders, gold was produced on a rather large scale during the eighth and ninth centuries. According to these accounts, alluvial panning was optimal between January and May.

Other gold mines in West Africa included Lobi, located in present-day BURKINA FASO. The Lobi gold mine helped to establish JENNE-JENO as a prominent trading depot between the fourteenth and sixteenth centuries. The WANGARA GOLD FIELDS, located south of Mali in a place not yet identified by scholars, was the source of the gold that helped SUNDIATA (d. 1255) extend and enrich his growing empire.

Gold mining also took place within various regions of southern Africa. One of the largest producers of gold was GREAT ZIMBABWE, where the mines and methods of extraction were concealed from outside traders. The resulting myths generated by the Portuguese included the notion that a permanent labor force lived within the mines, including whole families that raised children there. While these accounts were highly exaggerated, entire families apparently carried out panning and working with the ore.

Gold ore was in fact very near the earth's surface in territories stretching from the Mazoe River, in the northeast region of Zimbabwe, to the LIMPOPO RIVER in the southwest. Alluvial gold was found in tributaries of the Zambezi River as well. Men were responsible for digging the gold ores retrieved, in some cases, from more than 100 feet (30 m) below the surface. A method of alternately heating and cooling the ore was then used to split it, at which point women were often responsible for extracting the gold from the ore. Combined techniques were used as well. For example, iron picks could be used to collect ore, which was then crushed with a rock. The crushed rock could then be panned in order to retrieve the gold. Many historians surmise that these mining activities may have represented an alternative, seasonal means of supplementing family earnings.

The African Gold Trade There is little doubt that gold was one of the most highly valued commodities in Africa. Between the eighth and sixteenth centuries, much of Africa's gold was produced in West Africa and was transferred to the ports of North Africa by means of camel CARAVANS. After leaving these northern ports, the gold figured prominently in the economies of India, Arabia, and Asia. Archaeologists' recovery in West Africa of Roman-era weights for gold confirms the prominence of the gold trade to Europe as well and dates it back as far as the fourth century CE. The use of gold within Africa also was significant, especially in the building of the Sudanic empires, such as GHANA, MALI, SONGHAI, and KANEM-BORNU.

Once gold was exchanged for goods, the important task of transporting the gold came next. The develop-ment of a complex set of procedures provided checks and balances for the gold-producing countries as well as northern merchants. One aspect of these procedures involved the use of standardized weights, reportedly introduced to West African regions by Arab traders. The use of gold weights was subsequently adapted and developed by the ASHANTI of Ghana who created highly distinctive figures and symbolic shapes to weigh gold. Significantly, it was also in this century that the Islamic world began to mint gold for currency. It was therefore necessary for men such the tenth-century Arab traveler el-MAS'UDI to make accurate maps of the locations of the gold-bearing regions along with the routes used by MERCHANTS. Two of the better known routes were the road from Taghaza-Timbuktu and the route that passed through Wargla, Takedda, and Gao.

The transportation of gold was often a dangerous proposition. On the trade routes, the transporters were faced with both the possibility of robbery and the very real chance of being stranded without water in the desert. The difficulties associated with transporting gold were underscored by the archaeological discovery of an entire gold caravan that perished in the SAHARA centuries ago. The demise of the transporters was possibly the result of a surprise sandstorm but could have been caused by any number of unknown causes.

There are many conflicting views as to the amount of gold carried by these caravans. On one hand, the archaeological evidence suggests that thirty to forty camels at a time might have been used to carry between 2 and 3 tons of the unrefined gold dust that Islamic traders called *tibr*. On the other hand, many historians maintain that this figure is too low, given the documented significance of the gold trade. To facilitate the transfer of gold received from the inland caravans, the gold was usually converted into ingots, or solid bars, at the trade depots of Timbuktu or SIJILMASA. The gold was then ready for transport to northern ports such as CAIRO. Merchants who purchased the gold in its refined state offered to the northern transporters a return trade of COPPER, brassware, sword blades, and textiles.

The gold trade also effectively linked the eastern or SWAHILI COAST with other parts of southern Africa. For example, the gold trade south of the Zambezi River reached its height between the twelfth and fifteenth centuries. A reported one and a half tons of gold were extracted from the gold-producing regions of Zimbabwe and made its way to KILWA, one of the numerous city-states that formed the trade network of the Swahili coast. By the sixteenth century, the gold trade in the region had shifted to Portuguese traders, who exchanged CLOTH, IVORY, and other items. For reasons that are not entirely clear, the gold trade declined in the area by 1500. It is possible that the mines had been exhausted.

Although it is impossible to determine the exact amounts of gold exported from Africa in the precolonial period, estimates of the gold traded during the first millennium of the common era range from around 7,000 pounds (3,175 kg) up to 18,000 pounds (8,165 kg).

See also: ARAB COASTAL TRADE (Vol. II); CHINESE TRADE (Vol. II); GHANA EMPIRE (Vol. II); GOLD (Vols. I, III); GREAT ZIMBABWE (Vol. II); KUSH (Vol. I); MALI EMPIRE (Vol. II); MINING (Vol. III); SOFALA (Vol. II); WANGARA GOLD FIELDS (Vol. II).

Further reading: Ralph Austin, *Africa in Economic History* (London: James Currey Ltd., 1996).

government, systems of   The various means by which authority is exercised over a social grouping. Contemporary Western-style governments, divided into executive, judicial, and legislative branches, did not exist in the Europe of the day nor in the traditional African societies of the period. Most European governments, including the government of Portugal, the country with the closest links to Africa in the fifteenth century, were monarchies headed by a king or an emperor, sometimes with a judiciary system, but rarely with a legislature of any sort. Islamic government inside and outside Africa was also monarchic, with no formal legislative bodies but a system of religious courts called Shar'ia. In traditional African societies during the period between the fifth and fifteenth centuries, the governing of the kingdom and the maintenance of its systems of LAW AND JUSTICE were combined duties of the chief or king.

Non-Muslim Stateless Societies   Some traditional, non-Islamic African societies were loosely organized or had no defined governing bodies. Sociologists sometimes refer to these types of societies as "stateless." The TWA of central East Africa are an example of a stateless society. Their lack of an organized government made it impossible for them to defend their territory against invading HUTU pastoralists in the fifth through the eleventh centuries. The seminomadic Nuer of the SUDAN are another example of a society that had minimal government. Their constant movement over vast areas and their struggle for subsistence left them very little time to be concerned about a central organizing body.

Such stateless societies were generally organized according to age sets and lineage, whereby the older members of a clan established and maintained the rules of conduct between group members. The clan leaders were responsible for conducting ritual ceremonies, raids, and trade with other groups.

Non-Muslim Monarchies   When advanced IRON tools became widespread in the early part of the first millennium, agriculturalist groups found it possible for the first time to occupy one area or region for an extended period of time. These settled, or sedentary, societies found it necessary to organize themselves in a more structured way than the hunter-gatherers and nomadic pastoralists.

Though they still relied on age sets and lineages, they also organized their groups into levels, or hierarchies, which were led most often by a clan headman.

If the headman became powerful enough, he would assume the title of chief or king (the African title often meant the equivalent of "the head man of the men" in the local tongue) and the society took on the aspects of a kingdom, with a governing monarch. Monarchies were widely distributed throughout Africa, and the societies that were organized as kingdoms are too numerous to list here. Some of the bigger, better known examples include the ASHANTI, GANDA, and KONGO. Smaller kingdoms included the KIKUYU, MBUNDU, and SERER.

Though most African societies were run by kings, some kingdoms were run by very capable queens, whose power was equal to that of a king. Examples of this type of female ruler include ELENI, of ETHIOPIA, and DAHIA AL-KAHINA, of ALGERIA. Other queens acted as regents, rulers who governed the kingdom until the male inheritor of the throne reached a suitable age.

The chief or king always had a number of associates who shared the role of ruling the general population; the bigger the population, the more associates he might have. These aides most often included relatives, respected headmen from other lineages, the primary wife, diviners, healers, and military advisers.

As the leader of his people, the king had certain responsibilities, which included settling disputes, leading the group in the planting and harvesting of crops, controlling the importing and exporting of economic goods (in societies that traded), and, of course, the important task of producing sons to inherit the throne. For this last duty, a king would often take multiple wives, a practice called polygamy.

In the agriculturalist societies of much of SUB-SAHARAN AFRICA, it was the responsibility of the chiefs to distribute food in their villages. As a result, they usually maintained large stores of foodstuffs for themselves, even when food was scarce for the rest of the people. Corpulence, then, became a sign of prestige, and the fatter the chief was, the more powerful an image he was able to project to his people and to foreign visitors.

Under a monarchy based on lineage, a king rarely had to worry about rebellions, or what we today would call coups d'etat, from within his own group. The methods of government in traditional societies did not change quickly. The standard hierarchy of governing monarchs did change, though, when monarchies began to arise whose power was based on military might, rather than lineage. This development caused tension between lineage head men and military leaders, since the military chiefs were a threat to the traditional authority of the patriarchs and clan elders, who relied on the spirits of the ancestors for their right to rule.

Whether military monarchs or lineage headmen, the kings of African societies could generally control the affairs of their kingdoms through the use, or even just the threat, of force. Many kings, even those who did not maintain a military, would surround themselves with loyal armed retainers who ensured his physical safety while at the same time enforcing his rules.

In non-Islamic African societies, there are no examples of kingdoms that were governed according to a written body of laws, or constitution. Instead, the rules of government were based on convention, passed down by village elders.

Islamic Government In Islamic societies of the time, the governments were theocracies rather than monarchies, run by religious leaders rather than kings. (Though non-Islamic kings commonly held their positions by rights of DIVINE RULE, their secular duties kept their kingdoms from being considered theocratic.) For Muslim leaders, the laws of government are to be found in the sacred writings of ISLAM: the KORAN and the Sunna.

The title *caliph* was given to the titular head of the entire Islamic world. Below the caliph were local sovereigns who, from the eleventh century, in Africa as well as in other regions of Islam, generally bore the title *sultan*. Provincial governors and military leaders were given the title *emir*, a designation also sometimes adopted by rulers of independent states. *Sheik* (*sheikh*) is an Arabic title of respect accorded to chiefs, heads of villages, and males in other positions of influence.

The Koran leaves some rules of government open to interpretation, and, in practice, Muslim law is supplemented by regulations derived from local custom. Indeed, within the wider Muslim world, the SUNNI branch of Islam, dominant in North Africa, often differed with the Shiites, over matters of law and governance. These differing viewpoints meant that Muslim governments even in Africa, though based on common principles, were not always consistent, as interpretations of the Koran and the effects of local customs varied greatly.

The North African empires that were governed by Islamic BERBERS—including the ALMORAVIDS and ALMOHADS—were true theocracies. The conflicts among these groups were generally created by their different interpretations of Koranic law.

The Islamic kingdoms of SUB-SAHARAN AFRICA were more diverse that the Saharan empires. Since Islam penetrated these kingdoms along trade routes, it was common for kings to convert to Islam primarily so that their kingdoms could participate in trade with Muslim traders. As a result, kingdoms like ancient GHANA were governed by kings who were avowed Muslims but ruled their subjects according to conventional, or customary, law.

See also: GHANA, THE (Vol. II); ISLAM, INFLUENCE OF (Vol. II); QUEENS AND QUEEN MOTHERS (Vol. II).

Further reading: Peter J. Schraeder, *African Politics and Society: A Mosaic in Transformation* (New York: St. Martin's Press, 1999).

Great Kei River River situated in the eastern Cape Province of SOUTH AFRICA. The Great Kei River originates at the junction formed by the White Kei and Black Kei Rivers southeast of Queenstown. From that point, it flows nearly 140 miles (224 km) toward the southeast, eventually draining into the Indian Ocean. It has several tributary rivers, including the Tsomo.

The river fostered the development of a number of early XHOSA-speaking chiefdoms, including the Gealeka, Thembu, Mpondo, Mpondomise, and others, who are believed to have settled in the region between the fifteenth and sixteenth centuries.

See also: MPONDO (Vol. III); SOUTH AFRICA (Vol. III); XHOSA (Vol. III).

Further reading: James L. Newman, *The Peopling of Africa: A Geographic Interpretation* (New Haven, Conn.: Yale University Press, 1995).

Great Zimbabwe City in the southeastern region of present-day ZIMBABWE on the Zimbabwe Plateau that was the heart of a major trading empire between 1100 and 1450. Population estimates vary, but at its height, the people living in or around Great Zimbabwe numbered between 11,000 and 18,000. By 1450, the region could no longer support its population; the site was abandoned and now lies in ruins. Oral tradition refers to a shortage of salt, but it is thought that the land was no longer suitable for grazing or farming and local sources of wood for cooking and building had dwindled.

Built by the Late Iron Age ancestors of the BANTU-speaking Shona people, Great Zimbabwe is one of some 300 known stone enclosure sites on the Zimbabwe

Plateau. The name *Zimbabwe* in Bantu probably means "stone building," although it has also been taken to mean, very appropriately, "sacred house" or "ritual seat of a king." The ruins cover nearly 1,800 acres (728.5 hectares) and are divided into a hilltop complex and a valley complex. The site of Great Zimbabwe was well chosen to support a large city. The Zimbabwe Plateau offered a wide range of seasonal grazing land for the cattle that were the core of the region's economy. Game, especially elephants for the IVORY trade, was abundant; the soil was fertile and suited to agriculture; and timber, too, was in plentiful supply. From its location at the head of the Sabi River valley, the city could control passage between the gold fields of the western plateau and the trading city of SOFALA on the coast; in the twelfth and thirteenth centuries, taxes levied on the trading CARAVANS

The wall of the Great Enclosure in Great Zimbabwe is 33 feet (10 m) high, 16 feet (5.5 m) thick at its widest point, and more than 800 feet (244 m) in circumference. The tapered wall is broader at the base than at the top. © *Colin Hoskins; Cordaiy Photo Library Ltd./CORBIS*

were a major source of Great Zimbabwe's revenue. Its rulers ate from porcelain made in China and Persia. Its artisans produced fine GOLD and COPPER jewelry and ornaments for the king and royal court and for trade.

When, in the late 1500s, Portuguese traders began to hear rumors of Great Zimbabwe's existence, they thought it was a city of the legendary queen of Sheba or the biblical city of Ophir, from which the queen of Sheba raised gold for the Temple of Solomon in Jerusalem. Unwilling to admit the city's sub-Saharan African origin and arguing that these peoples had no history of building in stone, later visitors to the ruins surmised that Phoenicians, Arabs, Egyptians, or even the fabled Christian king, Prester John, had built Great Zimbabwe. The fact is, however, that unlike other regions of Africa where stone suitable for building is scarce, the Zimbabwe Plateau offers an abundance of stone outcroppings that have weathered into layers easily split into usable building blocks. The fact that Zimbabwean builders used no mortar or bonded joints to join the stone blocks indicates to archaeologists that these builders originated their own techniques for handling stone and are not indebted to Arab or Islamic builders for their methods. Some 200 stone ruins can be found on the Zimbabwe Plateau, a memorial to these builders' craft. Stone was used whenever builders needed to create a structure of considerable size; ordinary dwellings were still made in traditional fashion of dried mud with a pole and thatch roof.

From its perch atop a granite dome, the Hill Complex, started c. 1250, overlooks the rest of Great Zimbabwe. Construction of the Valley Complex began in the early 1300s, about the same time as construction of the outer wall of the Hill Complex.

All significant entrances and exits of the Great Enclosure were designed to ensure that access to and from the complex could be easily monitored. As a further security measure, the long, narrow passage to the Conical Tower allows only single-file movement.

Lying to the south of the Hill Complex, the Great Enclosure is the largest single structure in ancient SUB-SAHARAN AFRICA. The Great Enclosure is made of an outer wall that is 820 feet (250 m) in circumference with a height reaching as much as 80 feet (24 m). An inner wall runs beside the outer wall, forming the narrow, long passage that leads to the Conical Tower. The Conical Tower is 33 feet (10 m) high and 16 feet (9 m) in diameter. Its purpose is unknown, but many experts have theorized that it was a symbolic grain bin.

Researchers theorize that the original structures in the Hill Complex may have been intended for defense, but they point out that the high walls of the later structures offer no access to the top from which to hurl weapons or repel invaders. They may simply have been meant to impress people with the prestige and power of the king. Inside the Valley Complex was the palace of the king, where he and the court lived in luxury. Inside both the Hill Complex and the Valley Complex, archaeologists have found remains of mud-brick structures that may have matched the stone buildings in distinction.

See also: ARCHITECTURE (Vol. II); SALT TRADE (Vol. II); SHONA (Vol. I); SHONA KINGDOMS (Vol. III); ZIMBABWE (Vol. III).

griot Oral historian or "praise singer" trained to recite the history, myths, and cultural beliefs associated with a kingdom, village, or individual lineage. No one has been able to say with any degree of certainty when griots first came into being, but it appears that they were certainly present in many regions of Africa prior to the period of European colonization, perhaps associated with the rise of CITY-STATES.

One of the earliest references made concerning griots occurred in Mali. After traveler IBN BATTUTA visited the royal court of MALI in 1352, he wrote of the man known as Dugha, the king's royal griot. Wearing a symbolic bird mask, Dugha stood before the king and recited the story of his predecessors, their accomplishments, and family history. However, Battuta, a staunch Muslim, was unable to see past appearances or protocol to understand Dugha's actual function, which entailed lengthy recitations. Details concerning births, deaths, members of the royal family, the results of various wars, achievements of the king and his predecessors, and countless myths associated with the original founders of their society were also important aspects woven into the repertoire of the griot.

Counterparts of the griot in West Africa were known in the SUDAN as *wali*. In some North African regions they were called *marabouts*. More often than not, griots were single men who traveled without restraint. Their freedom was often weighed against responsibilities that ranged from simple to extraordinarily complex. For example, some griots were relegated to the category of a public musician-singer and played the *kora*, or small percussive instruments. Their style varied from region to region and sometimes included background singers who also played musical instruments. In other regions such as the GAMBIA, griots performed special chants.

At public events griots often created songs designed to invoke memories and emotions surrounding specific incidents or circumstances from the past. Songs might also relate unfolding experiences of the moment, such as rites of passage that included baptisms, initiation, and funerals.

It should be noted that the griots who performed for the public were often denied recognition beyond their caste. Reasons for this are not fully understood but may have been influenced by the class stratification of West African kingdoms. Within the WOLOF and SERER societies,

griots were among the lowest echelon that also included blacksmiths, butchers, leatherworkers, and other craft workers. These individuals were never able to rise above their occupations, which were positions usually passed on from father to son.

> The range of the griots' artistry often included audience participation, and many historians have likened the call and response between griot and audience to modern day African-American church traditions.

In contrast, griots who were part of the royal kingdoms of West Africa gained recognition, fame, and wealth but had much more complex responsibilities. Among the BAMBARA, griots were known as *dyeli-faama* meaning "royalty." They were also considered custodians or "keepers of words." In addition to the ability to entertain, they served as court historians, teachers, and mediators during disputes and trading transactions. They helped to facilitate political marriages by bringing together not only bride and groom but entire families. They kept history alive for the king, members of the court, and royal descendants by narrating their entire genealogy. Among the AKAN, the griot performed for local inhabitants when a new king was installed. This enabled them to judge the king's abilities and virtues based on the oral recitation given by the griot.

Griots therefore embodied the entire history of a people and, when able to pass their craft on to younger members of the caste, formed a continuous oral tradition that could be preserved for many generations. In many instances, modern griots' presentations have aided archaeologists and historians in significant ways, helping them to interpret the reconstruction of physical remnants of the past or supplying missing aspects about the life and culture of ancient and medieval Africa.

See also: MUSIC (Vol. II); ORAL TRADITIONS (Vol. I).

Further reading: Robert B. Fisher, *West African Religious Traditions* (New York: Orbis Books, 1998).

Gudit (Judith, Yodit, Esato) (d. c. 970) *Ethiopian queen who violently seized the Aksumite throne.*

Very little is known about Queen Gudit beyond scattered references in ancient texts and oral history. It is an accepted fact that she was violently opposed to the Monophysite beliefs of the Ethiopian Christian Church and orchestrated the destruction of the Aksumite kingdom in the late tenth century. Her followers razed churches and killed hundreds of Christian followers. Gudit's origins have been traced to the kingdoms in the country's southern region, specifically to DAMOT. It is believed that she was an AGAW-speaker from the southwest whose reign either ushered in or influenced the rise of the ZAGWE DYNASTY (c. 12th century), who, like her, were originally Agaw-speakers. She may also have been associated with the BETA ISRAEL (Falasha) since rumors persist that she was the daughter of their leader, Gideon.

Following the destruction of AKSUM, Queen Gudit maintained a forty-year rule over a region historians believe may actually have been Aksum. Islamic texts have reported how after claiming the throne, her coruler, known only by the title of Habani, was forced into exile in Shewa where he died in c. 970. Other sources that mention the queen include a letter sent by the last Aksumite king to church officials in Alexandria, EGYPT, that pleaded in vain for their intercession.

See also: MONOPHYSITE (Vol. I); QUEENS AND QUEEN MOTHERS (Vol. II).

Guinea Name used to describe the coast of West Africa south of the western SAHARA. Guinea once included what European traders labeled the Gold Coast (present-day Ghana).

The name *Guinea* is possibly derived from a BERBER word meaning "land of the blacks."

Metal objects, especially iron pieces from perhaps as early as 200 BCE have been found throughout, but it was gold that became the region's most valuable product, especially with the development of TRANS-SAHARAN TRADE ROUTES. Many peoples have dwelled within Guinea's boundaries, the largest groups being the MANDE-speaking MANDINKA and SUSU and the Fulfulde-speaking FULANI.

Geography and Peoples Lower Guinea consists of the alluvial coastal plain that borders the Atlantic Ocean from present-day Ivory Coast, across Ghana, Togo, and Benin to Nigeria. Its earliest inhabitants were reportedly the Baga and the Nalu peoples, who were later displaced by the Susu and the Mandinka. The forest region, nearest to the Sierra Leone and Liberia borders, was inhabited by the Kpelle (Grerz), the Loma (Toma), and the Kissi peoples, who lived in relatively small villages. The forested Guinea highlands, which peak at the Nimba Range, are approximately 5,780 feet (1,752 m) above sea level. The Niger River originates in this dense forest, where the region's heaviest rainfall occurs. Archaeologists believe that yams, oil palms, and other crops were cultivated in

the southeast part of the highlands by 100 BCE. Rice was grown in the swampy areas; elsewhere, kola nuts, mangos, and coffee were grown.

Rising some 3,000 feet (914 m) above the coastal plains at the headwaters of the GAMBIA RIVER, the mountainous FOUTA DJALLON region of Middle Guinea became prominent during the fifteenth and sixteenth centuries. Although the Fulani appear to have been present in this region from an early date, by at least the fifteenth century they were joined by additional Fulani migrants, many of whom were converts to ISLAM from SENEGAL. In the eighteenth century, the Fulani developed what has been described as a theocratic state steeped in Islamic religion and culture.

Upper Guinea, or the northeastern plains, was largely inhabited by the Mandinka. This region's characteristic grasslands supported a number of income-producing trees such as the baobab and the shea. The central area of Upper Guinea gives strong evidence of MILLET cultivation as early as 1000 BCE. To ensure successful harvests, many regional farmers created ancestral stone figures in human and animal likenesses. These figures, known as *nomoli,* were sometimes made of steatite or granite and were associated with fertility rites. They have been recovered by archaeologists in open fields and at sites that may have once been family or community shrines.

Archaeologists have also been able to create a link between early forms of metallurgy and the growth of Guinea's early city-states. Iron-smelting appears to have been actively done from at least 200 BCE to create a wide number of tools and perhaps some ritual objects.

Political Developments Three significant goldtrading empires developed in the West African savanna and controlled much of Guinea: Ghana, Mali, and Songhai. The GHANA EMPIRE (c. 800–1240) dominated the region between the third and eleventh centuries. It was succeeded by the MALI EMPIRE (c. 1250–1600), whose most prominent CITY-STATE in the northeast region was NIANI. A major trading center situated along a tributary of the Niger River, Niani engaged in the gold, salt, and kola nut trade. The SONGHAI Empire (c. 1375–1600) was the third prominent kingdom that arose in the region.

By the fifteenth century, word of Guinea's gold had attracted Portuguese traders. Their caravels—sturdy, oceangoing ships with high sterns and broad bows—enabled the Portuguese to overcome the complex navigational problems associated with the west coast of Africa, and they soon made contact with groups of the interior regions. The Portuguese found Guinea's rich resources and location highly advantageous to trade, and in the sixteenth century, the region supplied them with many captives. In later centuries, the French, English, and Dutch also participated in trade in the area.

H

hajj (hadjdj, hadj) Pilgrimage to the holy city of MECCA located in present-day Saudi Arabia. The hajj is the fifth of the seven pillars, or fundamental duties, of ISLAM; every believer, both male and female, who is physically and financially able is expected to make the hajj at least once in his or her lifetime. The leaders of the Muslim kingdoms in SUB-SAHARAN AFRICA were known to take this religious duty seriously. Mansa MUSA (d. 1332), who ruled the MALI EMPIRE from 1307 to 1332, undertook a famous hajj to Mecca in 1324 that had the further effect of bringing the wealth of Mali to the attention of the Muslim world. Similarly, ASKIA MUHAMMAD TOURÉ (r. 1493–1538), ruler of the SONGHAI EMPIRE, made the hajj in 1495, two years before he ascended the throne.

The pilgrimage to Mecca—the city where the KORAN, the holy book of Islam, was revealed to the prophet MUHAMMAD (570–632)—serves as a unifying force in the Muslim world. Rich and poor, ruler and ruled are expected to perform this holy ritual. The hajj begins on the seventh day of *Dhu al-Huijjah*, the last month of the Islamic year and ends on the twelfth day. According to tradition, the prophet Muhammad himself established the rituals the pilgrims follow.

The first part of the ritual begins when the pilgrim, or *hajjiyy*, is 6 miles (10 m) outside of Mecca. At this point, the pilgrim enters a state of holiness known as *ihram* and puts on an *ihram* garment made of two pieces of seamless white cloth, which will be worn for the rest of the journey. Until the second part of the ritual, pilgrims may not cut their hair or nails and must refrain from sexual activity and any impurity.

Upon entering Mecca, the pilgrims walk around the shrine in the Great Mosque known as Ka'bah seven times,

and then, going inside, proceed to the Black Stone, or the Hajar al-Aswad, which they must kiss or touch. The rituals commemorate Abraham and his son Ishmael's rebuilding of a shrine first erected at the site by Adam, the scriptural father of the human race. (This story suggests the likelihood that the Ka'bah antedates Islam as a site of pilgrimage.) The pilgrims then bend down to pray in the direction of the Magam Ibrahim and the Ka'bah, after which they run seven times between two small hills, Mount Safa and Mount Marwah.

When Muslims face east to pray, it is toward the Ka'bah that they turn. In 622, Muhammad fled from Mecca to Medina in present-day Saudi Arabia to escape persecution. Muslims date the start of the Muslim era from this event, called the *hegira*, Arabic for "flight." Muslim dates are often preceded by the initials AH, which stand for *Anno Hegirae*, Latin for "In the year of the Hegira." Muhammad died, for example, in AH 10, or 632 CE.

When Muhammad returned from Medina and captured Mecca in 628, he had the pagan idols in the building surrounding the Ka'bah destroyed. The building has been a major site of Muslim piety ever since.

The second phase of the ritual begins on the eighth day of the month and ends on the twelfth day. During

Engraved for Middleton's Complete System of Geography. 1779

The March of the GRAND CARAVAN from Cairo to Mecca.

Making the hajj, or pilgrimage to Mecca, located in modern Saudi Arabia, is an important duty of every observant Muslim. Pilgrims on the annual Grand Caravan from Cairo to Mecca, shown here in a woodcut from 1779, often numbered in the thousands. © *Hulton-Deutsch Collection/CORBIS*

this period, the pilgrims visit the shrines of Jabar ar-Rahmah, Mina, and Muzadalifah outside Mecca. On the eighth day, they pass through Mina and Muzadalifah and end their day ascending the mountain named Jabar ar-Rahmah. On the ninth day, the pilgrims perform the ritual of *wuquuf*, or "standing"—the day is spent in prayer; then they go to Muzadalifah and stay the night. On the tenth day, the pilgrims return to Mina, where they gather stones to be used in a later ritual. They sacrifice an animal to commemorate Abraham's sacrifice. The pilgrims' heads are shaved. They then throw the seven stones they have gathered at the pillars of Mina, each of which represents a different devil. Once these rituals have been performed, the hajj is officially over. At this point the pilgrims usually shave their heads, and then they return to Mecca, where they will once again circle the Ka'bah before returning home. A muslim who does the hajj is entitled forever after to add the title *al-hajj* to his name.

Further reading: F. E. Peters, *The Hajj* (Princeton, N.J.: Princeton University Press, 1994).

Hambarketolo City located in the upper inland Niger Delta in the region that is present-day Mali. Based on archaeological evidence, historians believe that Hambarketolo was part of a 100-acre (40.5-hectare) town complex that included JENNE-JENO. Both of these sites show that by the fifth century, the towns had rather developed societies, used cemeteries, used a sophisticated system of agriculture, and traded with other cultures. Excavations have uncovered beads from Rome and COPPER and GOLD imported from distant mines. The region possessed excellent soil for growing rice and access to major river channels.

The excavations at Hambarketolo and Jenne-Jeno are important for the evidence they reveal of complex social structures, urban settlements, and trading economies. It was previously believed that the ARABS brought this type of social organization and trading to the peoples of the Sahel during the seventh and eighth centuries as TRANS-SAHARAN TRADE ROUTES developed.

See also: NIGER DELTA (Vol. I).

Harer (Harar, Harrar) Precolonial capital of ADAL, a Muslim state in ETHIOPIA. The market town of Adal was originally established by Muslim Arab migrants from Hadramawt during the seventh century. Located atop a plateau in the Ch'erch'er Mountains, Harer thrived as the capital of the state until 1577, when it was overthrown by Christian Ethiopians.

See also: ARAB COASTAL TRADE (Vol. II); HARER (VOL. III); ISLAM, INFLUENCES OF (Vol. II).

Hausa Ethnic group that has populated the region known as HAUSALAND, located in present-day Nigeria, since the twelfth century; also, the language they speak.

The origins of the Hausa can be traced through their language, which links them to the Chadic speakers of the western region around Lake CHAD, who have inhabited the area for more than 6,000 years. Hausa, which is infused with many Arabic words due to the influence of ISLAM, is the most widely spoken language of SUB-SAHARAN AFRICA. Chadic speakers eventually migrated south to the region that became known as Hausaland, where they merged with the local populations.

Hausa oral tradition names the descendants of the Muslim prince Bayajida as the probable founders of the settlements that became Hausaland, perhaps in the tenth century. Nevertheless, it is more likely that the settlements had already been established by non-Muslim agricultural peoples centuries before Bayajida's arrival.

See also: HAUSA STATES (Vol. III).

Hausa States (Hausaland) The seven true HAUSA states (*Hausa bakwai*) and the seven satellite, or illegitimate, Hausa states (*banza bakwai*), in what is now northern Nigeria and northwestern Niger.

Scattered Hausa agricultural and pastoral villages in the region can be traced back as far as the fifth and sixth centuries, although it is not until around 1200 that these villages combined into several states ruled by partly divine kings who began to control the region. Hausa legends trace the origin of the kingdoms to Prince Bayajida of Baghdad, but scholars believe that these stories are an attempt on the part of the Hausa, after ISLAM began to filter into the region in the late 1300s, to align themselves with what they perceived to be the mainstream of history.

The Hausa states each played a specialized role based on need and location. RANO and KANO, the "chiefs of indi-

go," grew cotton and produced fine cloth for export to other Hausa states and regions beyond the borders of Hausaland. Kebbi, one of the lesser Hausa states, was the original seat of government. ZARIA, the "chief of slaves," supplied labor. KATSINA and DAURA were the "chiefs of the market" because they were important stops for the CARAVANS that brought SALT from the Sahara and for the CLOTH, leather, and slave traders from the south. GOBIR was the "chief of war," protecting the Hausa states from the aggressive neighboring states of Ghana and BORNU. Each of these cities consisted of a walled city ruled by a king. A considerable rivalry existed among the states over land and control of the trade routes. This lack of unity left them open to periodic attacks from KANEM-BORNU and SONGHAI.

Prince Bayajida journeyed from Baghdad (in what is now Iraq) to the kingdom of Kanem-Bornu, east of Lake Chad, at the request of its king. After a poor welcome, Prince Bayajida left Kanem-Bornu and traveled west until he came upon a city ruled by Queen Daura. Prince Bayajida killed the snake that was terrorizing the city and then took Queen Daura as his bride. Daura bore him a son, Bawogari, whose six sons would become the chiefs of the first six Hausa states—Kano, Daura, Gobir, Zaria, Katsina, and Rano. A son by another wife was the founder of the seventh Hausa state, BIRAM.

Islam entered Hausaland in the 1300s, but its progress was slow and mainly limited to the cities. Rural Hausa people maintained their traditional religion and their belief in a semidivine monarchy.

However, in the 1450s, as a result of increasing desertification in northern Africa, large numbers of FULANI people began migrating into Hausa territory in search of land to support their cattle. The Fulani were mostly Muslims and set up Islamic schools throughout Hausaland. The Fulani ultimately dominated their new land, and by the early 1800s, all power was in their hands.

See also: AGADES (Vol. III); GOBIR (Vol. III);HAUSA STATES (Vol. III); KATSINA (Vol. III);KEBBI (Vol. III); KINGDOMS AND EMPIRES (Vol.I); KWARARAFA (Vol. III); ZAMFARA (Vol. III); ZARIA (Vol. III).

Henry the Navigator, Prince (1394–1460) *Portuguese prince whose sponsorship of voyages of exploration began Europe's Age of Discovery and Portuguese expansion into Africa.*

Portuguese maritime exploration began in 1420 with voyages along the Atlantic coast of MOROCCO and continued, after 1441, with voyages along the West African coast as far south as SIERRA LEONE. Henry himself never set foot in West Africa or sailed on one of the many voyages he sponsored, but he bears the title "navigator" in honor of the developments in SHIPBUILDING, map making, and navigation that took place during his lifetime. The third son of King John, Henry never assumed the throne, mostly because he never wanted to rule. His eldest brother, Duarte, became king in 1433 and ruled until 1438. The voyages that Henry sponsored are often seen as part of a grand scheme to outflank ISLAM, one of the major religious political forces of his day, by establishing contact with lands below Muslim North Africa and establishing direct contact with Asia.

Early Portugal and Africa Modern Portugal, with its capital at Lisbon, is a small country along the Atlantic coast of the Iberian Peninsula, which it shares with Spain. Portugal became an independent monarchy in 1139.

Portuguese contact with Africa began early in its history. The region of the Iberian Peninsula that Portugal now occupies became Christian in the third and fourth centuries. In 406, it was captured by the Vandals, a Germanic people, who were forced out by the Visigoths, another Germanic people, at the instigation of Rome, in 415. They fled to North Africa and established a short-lived Kingdom of the Vandals (428–534). When the Muslims invaded Spain in 711, Berber soldiers occupied central Portugal and Galicia to the north. The UMAYYAD dynasty under Abd ar-Rahman I (flourished 750–788) established its capital at Córboba in Spain in 756. By 1037, following rebellions by local lords against the Córboba caliphate, about three-quarters of the Iberian Peninsula, including Portugal, was divided into ten constantly feuding emirates. By 1142, during the reign of Ali ibn Yusuf (1106–1142), most of the Iberian Peninsula had been annexed by the expansionist ALMORAVID dynasty of Morocco, and the union between Spain and Africa was consolidated. The Almoravids, however, were being pressured on two sides: in the Iberian Peninsula by a period of Christian reconquest that began at Saragossa in 1118 and in North Africa by the revolt of the ALMOHADS in 1125. In 1139, Alphonso I (c. 1109–1185) became the first king of Portugal, winning independence from the kingdom of León in 1139 and capturing the city of Lisbon from the Muslims in 1147. In the rest of Spain, however, Muslim domination persisted. Under ABU YAQUB YUSUF (1163–1184) and his successor, Abu Yaqub Yusuf al-Mansur (1184–1199), Muslim Spain reached the height of its power. Muslim rule in Spain did not end until 1492, after a long period of conflict between Musims and Christians.

The Development of Commercial Interests Direct control of trade was a major concern in the Europe of Prince Henry's day. Most of the goods from the Far East passed through the hands of Muslim traders before they reached western Europe. Marco Polo (c. 1254–1324), a trader, adventurer, and traveler from Venice, Italy, had already traveled overland to China and India in 1271–1295 by way of the caravan routes across Asia. In 1428, Henry read a copy of *Il Milione* ("The million"), known in English as *The Travels of Marco Polo*, that his brother Pedro had brought back from a trip across Europe. By that time, he had already begun his sponsorship of African exploration.

Prince Henry and Africa Henry's personal contact with Africa began in 1415 when, as a young man, he became governor of the city of Ceuta in Morocco after he convinced his father, King John, to attack it as a way for him and his brothers, Pedro and Duarte, to win their spurs as knights. In 1419, he returned home, retired from court, and formed a small princely court of his own at Sagrès, at the southern tip of Portugal, to which he attracted seafarers, shipbuilders, and instrument makers. In 1420, he became Grand Master of the Order of Christ, a secular papal order that had replaced the Knights Templar. Funds made available by the Order of Christ for the conversion of pagan lands provided Henry with the monies he used to finance his expeditions; for this reason, the sails of his ships always bore a red cross. Starting that year, he began to sponsor voyages along the Atlantic coast of Morocco.

By 1434, voyages sponsored by Prince Henry had sailed beyond Cape Bojador on the Atlantic coast of Africa, a point beyond which it had once been thought no ship could ever sail. After 1438, looking for additional sources of funding for his voyages and basing his hopes on information from the Muslims at Ceuta, Henry hoped to find a source of African gold. In 1441, one of his captains returned from West Africa with gold dust and captive Africans. By 1448, his ships had sailed as far south as the GAMBIA RIVER, and trade in the region had increased, whereupon Henry ordered the building of Portugal's first trading outpost, the ARGUIN TRADING FORT, on Arguin Island off the coast of modern-day Mauritania. In 1450, the king of Portugal granted Henry the sole right to send ships and trade with the GUINEA coast. Regardless, so great was Henry's investment in his voyages that he died penniless.

See also: AGE OF DISCOVERY (Vol. II); CEUTA (Vol. III); PORTUGAL AND AFRICA (Vol. III).

Herero BANTU-speaking ethnic group that settled in regions of BOTSWANA, southern ANGOLA, and NAMIBIA. Subgroups of the Herero include the HIMBA, Tijimba, and Mbanderu.

Herero oral tradition indicates that they originated in the Great Rift Valley in East Africa. Cattle-keeping nomads and hunter-gatherers at the time of their migration, the Herero are unique among the peoples of southern Africa in recognizing both patrilineal and matrilineal descent. The roles of chief and priest, however, descended only through the male line. Traditional Herero religion was based on animism and ancestor worship.

See also: ANCESTOR WORSHIP (Vol. I); ANIMISM (Vol. I); BANTU MIGRATIONS (Vol. II); HERERO (Vol. III); PASTORALISM (Vol. I); RIFT VALLEY (Vol. I).

Hima Ruling caste of the NKOLE ethnic group who inhabit a region in the southwestern part of modern-day UGANDA.

The Hima, also known by some groups as the TUTSI, migrated to the Lake VICTORIA region from the north. Traditionally, they were pastoralists who survived almost exclusively on the products of their cattle. By the end of the fifteenth century they had established several kingdoms in the area, which were ruled by *mugabes*, or kings, who were given tribute by local chiefs.

See also: NKOLE (Vol. II); PASTORALISM (Vol. I).

Himba (Ovahimba) BANTU-speaking people who belong to the HERERO ethnic group. By the mid-sixteenth century, the Himba had migrated to the region known today as Kaokoland, in northwestern NAMIBIA.

The Himba are nomadic pastoralists who are dependent upon their cattle. They are a politically decentralized ethnic group that recognizes both patrilineal and matrilineal systems of kinship and descent. The religion of the Himba centers around the god Nyadami (sometimes called Karunga or Huku). They believe that Nyadami is the creator of the world but does not interfere with human activities.

> The Himba also practice the divination of future or past events through the inspection of animal entrails.

The Herero believe in a spiritual force known as *makuru*, which leads the hierarchy of ancestors, who have the ability to make their presence felt in the lives of their descendants. Rituals revolving around sacred fire, which symbolizes the continuity between the dead (ancestors) and the living (descendents), are another important religious practice of the Himba.

See also: ANCESTOR WORSHIP (Vol. I); BANTU MIGRATIONS (Vol. II); DIVINATION (Vol. I); KAOKOLAND (Vol.III); PASTORALISM (Vol. I).

Hombori Mountain range near TIMBUKTU in the southeastern region of present-day Mali; also the name of a city in the Hombori Mountains. The highest point in Mali is Hombori Tondo, which has an altitude of 3,789 feet

(1,155 m). It is a rugged and sparse landscape that gradually slopes westward toward the Niger River valley. To the southeast, the highlands end in steep cliffs.

The Hombori Mountains are home to the DOGON people who moved there sometime between the tenth and fifteenth centuries to preserve their culture and traditions in the face of advancing Muslim invaders. The Dogon cut homes and burial caves out of the cliffs and also constructed small huts at the base of the cliffs using stones topped with straw roofs.

See also: NIGER RIVER (Vol. I).

Husuni Kubwa Palace Immense palace built in KILWA, an Islamic CITY-STATE on the East African coast, in present-day southern Tanzania. At the time of its construction in the late thirteenth or early fourteenth century, the Husuni Kubwa Palace, with more than 100 rooms, was the largest single building in SUB-SAHARAN AFRICA.

Husuni Kubwa Palace was most likely built around the time that the Kilwa throne was taken by the SHIRAZI ARAB leader Abu al-Mawahib. At that time, Kilwa was the most prosperous of the trading centers on the SWAHILI COAST, trading CLOTH and glass, and controlling the GOLD trade with SOFALA on the East African coast. The city's riches were reflected in the splendor of its palace, whose design served as a model for the later dwellings of notables in Kilwa.

The ARCHITECTURE of the building was Arabic and reflected a change in building materials in the thirteenth century from coral and mortar to stone. It had extensive Arabic inscriptions and displayed new architectural features, including columns, cupolas, ornamental bas-reliefs, semicylindrical vaults, and richly carved wooden doors. The rooms in the palace were long, narrow, and parallel and did not have much light, since they lacked windows on the courtyard. There was a space that was probably a pool, and the back corner of the palace had indoor toilets.

See also: ARAB COASTAL TRADE (Vol. II).

Hutu (Bahutu, Wahutu) BANTU-speaking agricultural people who live in RWANDA and Burundi.

The Hutu first came to Rwanda-Burundi during the BANTU MIGRATIONS, which occurred from about 500 BCE to 1000 CE. That they spoke Bantu indicates that they must have come from central or southern Africa. The Hutu, who were farmers, took over the land from the TWA, who were accomplished hunters and potters.

The Hutu's new land was temperate, with a year-round temperature of 70° F (20° C) and above. Their settlements were mostly in the mountains near hills and fertile valleys that were good for growing crops. The only major drawback was that rainfall was uncertain.

The Hutu worshiped clan deities, and their religion also included animism, the belief that natural phenomena had souls.

The social and political structure of the Hutu was kinship-based. Large family clans were ruled by a clan chief, called a *bahinza*. The Hutu formed small kingdoms around a hill or a group of neighboring hills. This system of government worked well for administering work and settling disputes at a local level.

Around 1400, the TUTSI moved south from the Nile River and invaded Hutu lands. The Tutsi, a NILOTIC-speaking people, were warriors and pastoralists who came in search of better grazing land for their cattle. The nonmilitant, agragian Hutu were forced to become vassals to the Tutsi lords, also known as HIMA. The Hutu cared for the Tutsi's cattle and used the manure to fertilize their fields. The Tutsi's military might protected the Hutu. The two cultures gradually became integrated, with the Tutsi adopting the Bantu language of the Hutu. Some historians believe that the Tutsi adopted the clan system of government from the Hutu; others, however, assert that the Tutsi brought this type of government with them and introduced it to the Hutu system. Regardless, the Hutu were ruled by a succession of *mwamis*, or Tutsi kings. The social order was a caste system with the Hima being socially and politically superior and having wealth as well as high status. The Hutu and Twa castes were inferior. By the fifteenth century, larger states began to emerge, some of which eventually grew to include more than 1 million subjects.

See also: HUTU (Vols. I, III).

I

Ibibio An ethnic group located in present-day southeast Nigeria. The Ibibio speak Efik-Ibibio, a language belonging to the Kwa branch of the NIGER-CONGO family of languages. Different subgroups of the Ibibio include the Ibibio proper, Efik, Enyong, Eket, Andonio-Ibeno, and Annang.

The first written records of the Ibibio date from the 1800s, but it is certain that they were present in the area before that time. There is no strong, single tradition of origin among the Ibibio, but Efik oral tradition asserts that the original home of all Ibibio people was the Akwa Akpa, or the western bank of the Cross River; the Andoni-Ibeno claim to have migrated from ancestral homelands in CAMEROON.

The Ibibio believe in an earth deity named Ala, who is celebrated during the Ogbom ceremony, which is performed for eight weeks in the middle of the year. The ceremony is supposed to encourage fertile crops and childbirth.

The Ibibio are primarily agricultural people, cultivating traditional CROPS like yams, cocoyams, and CASSAVA. They were also known as accomplished craftspeople, sculptors, and wood carvers (especially masks). Early Ibibio villages were ruled by village elders known as Ekpo Ndem Isong and the heads of extended family. Rich male members of the village could become members of the Ekpo society, which granted them social status and political power. Ekpo society members acted as messengers of their ancestors

(Ikan) and enforced the decisions of village leaders. The highest rank of Ekpo society, Amama, often controlled most of a village's wealth. Ibibio religion consists mostly of ancestor worship, particularly of those ancestors who achieved high social status during their lives.

See also: IBIBIO (Vol. III).

Ibn Battuta (Shams ad-Din) (1304–c. 1369) *Arab traveler and author of the* Rihlah, *an important historical record of the Muslim world during his time.*

The *Rihlah*, which translates as "Travels" or "Journey," chronicles the visits Ibn Battuta made, over a period of twenty-five to thirty years, to almost every Muslim country of his time as well as to many adjacent non-Muslim territories. Describing his adventures and brushes with death, it also includes details about the social, cultural, and political life of the places he visited, including China, Sumatra, Ceylon, Arabia, Syria, Egypt, East Africa, and TIMBUKTU. Adhering to a self-imposed rule never to travel the same route twice, Ibn Battuta covered approximately 75,000 miles (120,700 km) by land and sea.

Abu Abdullah Ibn Battuta, also known as Shams Ad-Din, was born in TANGIER. His well-educated family included several Muslim judges, and Ibn Battuta received a traditional juristic and literary education in his native town of Tangier. He left there in 1325, at the age of twenty-one, to make his pilgrimage to MECCA and continue his studies there.

Instead of pursuing a career in the law, however, Ibn Battuta decided to see as many parts of the Muslim world as possible. Unlike his contemporaries, who traveled for such practical reasons as trade, pilgrimage, and education, Ibn Battutah traveled for the pleasure of seeing new places, learning about new countries, and meeting new people. He made a living from his scholarly status and later from his increasing fame as a traveler. Thanks to the generosity of the kings, sultans, and princes he met on his travels, at times he lived surrounded by luxury. On more than one occasion, however, he lost everything he owned and had to survive on almost nothing until he could regain the favor of another ruler.

Toward the end of his travels, Ibn Battuta befriended Sultan Muhammad, the ruler of Delhi, who appointed him the *qadi*, or judge, of that city. He held the post for several years before finally returning to his native Morocco in 1353. Toward the end of that year, he dictated his reminiscences at the sultan's request. Ibn Battuta's story was introduced to the Western world in 1829 with a translation of an abridged text of the *Rihlah*.

Further Reading: Noel King, *Ibn Battuta in Black Africa* (Princeton, N.J.: Marcus Weiner Publishers, 1994).

Ibo (Igbo) Largest stateless group of people in ancient Africa. The Ibo probably originated at the junction of the NIGER and BENUE Rivers and then migrated about 100 miles (160 km) south to southeastern NIGERIA, one of the most fertile regions of Africa. Their language, which is also called Ibo, belongs to the KWA branch of the NIGER-CONGO family. There are linguistic connections between the Ibo and nearby groups, including the IGALA, YORUBA, and Idoma, which indicates that the Ibo were once part of a much larger group of Niger-Congo people. The Ibo apparently split off from these other groups around 5,000 to 6,000 years ago. Archaeological evidence indicates that traditional Ibo culture is more than 1,000 years old.

Despite plentiful food, a dense population, and substantial trade, the Ibo did not unite into a single kingdom, as many of their neighbors did. Instead, they lived in small autonomous communities scattered over a wide geographical area. There were five main cultural groups: the Onitsha (northern), the Abakaliki (northeastern), the Cross River (eastern), the Owerri (southern), and the Ika (western). The Ibo language evolved into several distinct versions among these various Ibo communities, some of which were far apart from each other.

The Ibo were independent and democratic, with no centralized government and no dynasties of hereditary lineages. Except for the eastern Ibo, who tended to form larger units, usually referred to as clans, their largest political unit was the village group, a federation of several villages, encompassing on average about 5,000 people. Each village group shared a common market and meeting place. The leadership of each village group was entrusted to a village council made up of lineage heads, elders, and other influential and wealthy men. With no hereditary aristocracy, any Ibo man could become council leader through his own personal success. All Ibo men participated in important decisions that affected the village group. Decisions had to be unanimous, so even the young men in the village group were empowered politically. Women were not included in this political arena, although they played an essential role in the Ibo economy, growing much of the food and participating in the commercial life of the village.

Except for the northeastern groups, most Ibo lived in rain forest country. They were subsistence farmers, and there was a distinct gender-based division of labor in the fields, with the men in charge of yam cultivation, which was the Ibo's staple CROP. The yam harvest was a time for great celebration. The women grew all the other crops, including CASSAVA, taro, melon, okra, pumpkin, beans, and, after the Portuguese introduced it from the Americas, corn (maize) as well. The Ibo also kept some livestock, which was a valued commodity that added to the owners' prestige in the community and was mostly for ritual use in sacrifices.

Land was owned communally by groups of kinsmen and was made available to individuals for farming and building. An Ibo village consisted of a cluster of huts belonging to individual household units, usually of the same patrilineage.

Traditional Ibo religion included belief in a creator god, an earth goddess, and many other deities and spirits. Most Ibo religious practices revolved around ancestor worship. The Ibo believed that their ancestors could protect and help them with everyday life, and they relied on oracles and divination to receive messages from the spirit realm. But if their dead ancestors were angry, the Ibo believed that these restless spirits could cause tremendous trouble in the village. The Ibo had secret men's societies, which were called *mmo* among the northern Ibo. (Other Ibo groups had similar societies, but with different names.) The *mmo* conducted many rituals to appease these spirits and held elaborate funeral ceremonies to show their respect for their more recently departed kinsmen.

See also: IBO (Vols. I, III).

al-Idrisi (Abu Abdallah Muhammad ibn Muhammad ibn Abdallah ibn Idris al-Qurtubi al-Hasani) (c. 1100–1165) *Arab geographer, cartographer, and author of the most important geographical text written in the twelfth century.*

Al-Idrisi was born c. 1100, in Sabtah (present-day Ceuta), MOROCCO, to an aristocratic family that traced its ancestry to the prophet MUHAMMAD. He was educated in Córdoba, in al-ANDALUS (Muslim Spain) and traveled throughout Europe, England, and the Mediterranean. About 1145, al-Idrisi moved to Palermo at the invitation of Roger II of Sicily, himself an amateur geographer. It is believed that al-Idrisi spent the rest of his life in Sicily, working first under the patronage of Roger II and then under that of Roger's son, William I. Among al-Idrisi's accomplishments were the making of a world map that divided the earth into seven horizontal climate zones and the construction of a planisphere made of silver and engraved with a detailed map of the world. His master-work, though, was the *Kitab nuzhat al-mushtaq*, also known as *Kita Rujar* ("The book of Roger"). The study was published in 1154, shortly before the death of Roger II.

Al-Idrisi's classic text is a unique combination of Islamic and European scholarship and the results of al-Idrisi's own travels and research. The book offers the era's most comprehensive look at the geography of the world and is especially accomplished in the study of the Mediterranean and central and North Africa. *Kitab nuzhat al-mushtaq* is striking in its detail, derived in part from al-Idrisi's interviews with travelers, sailors, and fellow cartographers. Some scholars fault al-Idrisi for his weak handling of known scientific data and for his less-than-accurate description of the geography of the Baltic area. Despite these reservations, the treatise, with its rich descriptions and dynamic prose, is considered a classic. The world map it contained was used hundreds of years later by Columbus.

In addition to his groundbreaking work in geography, al-Idrisi was interested in the natural sciences, studied medicinal plants, had a familiarity with several languages, and wrote poetry.

See also: ISLAM, INFLUENCE OF (Vol. II); ISLAMIC CENTERS OF LEARNING (Vol. II).

Ifriqiya Early name for the North African region that lies between Tripoli and Barqah (Cyrenaica), south of the MEDITERRANEAN SEA in LIBYA. Muslims invaded the region in the seventh century, calling their newly conquered land Ifriqiya. Over the next centuries, various dynasties ruled Ifriqiya, including the Aghlabites, the FATIMIDS, and the Zeirids.

See also: ARABS (Vol. II); ISLAM, INFLUENCE OF (Vol. II).

Igala A people of present-day Nigeria, related to the YORUBA, who inhabit the left bank of the Niger River where it meets the BENUE RIVER. The Igala speak a Kwa dialect of the NIGER-CONGO family of languages.

The Igala most likely separated from the Yoruba people, who lived across the Niger River, to the west. They were an agricultural people who cultivated CROPS such as yams, maize, cassava, millet, and beans in the fertile triangular region of the Niger-Benue River confluence. Some traditions, though, link the Igala to the IBO, the Jukun, and the ZARIA.

Between the twelfth and fourteenth centuries, nine Igala settlements, known as the Igala Mela, moved toward greater economic and military unity as BENIN began to make advances into their territory. The Igala *ata*, or king,

was considered divine and held absolute power over the kingdom. Traditionally, the Igala also ruled over two other peoples, the Bassa Nge and the Bass Nkome, who are found by the Benue River.

Igala oral tradition tells of Ayagba, or Ajagba, an outsider of royal descent who was raised by a leopard and came to the city of Idah. Upon his arrival, he settled a heated dispute between two men and was immediately proclaimed the new *ata*, or king, of the region. Ayagba subsequently became the chief of the clan that would become the Igala.

The Igala traded along the Niger and Benue Rivers, exchanging items such as IVORY, BEADS AND JEWELRY, and textiles. They fought and lost a territorial war against Benin in 1516, then made attempts to expand into Lokoja, Idoma, and Iboland.

See also: DIVINE RULE (Vol. II); JUKUN (Vol. III); NIGER RIVER (Vol. I); ORAL TRADITION (Vol. I).

Ijebu The name of a people and their kingdom, found in southwest Nigeria. The Ijebu are related to the YORUBA and, like other Yoruba people, are believed to have come from central SUDAN in a series of migrations that began as early as 700. By the sixteenth century, when they first appear in written records, the Ijebu had for centuries dominated the trading routes between the ports of Lagos Lagoon and the area where Ibadan is now located. The Ijebu were renowned for their woven CLOTH, which they traded mostly with other Yoruba peoples.

The capital of the Ijebu kingdom was Ijebu-Ode, located between Benin City and Shagamu. Ijebu-Ode was the home of the *awujale*, the Ijebu spiritual and political leader. In the early sixteenth century a Portuguese sailor named Pereira described Ijebu-Ode as being "very large" and with "a great moat."

See also: ABEOKUTA (Vol. III); IJEBU (Vol. III); NIGERIA (Vol. III).

Ijo (Ijaw) Ethnic group found throughout the Niger River Delta region of Nigeria. The Ijo speak a language that belongs to the NIGER-CONGO family of languages. The Ijo never formed a unified kingdom but rather existed as a number of CITY-STATES, including BRASS (or NEMBE), BONNY, and Old Calabar. The Ijo occupied the forest around the Niger Delta but were widely respected for their mastery of the water. They were very capable boat handlers whose economy was based on fishing and some trade.

The original homeland of the Ijo people varies according to tradition. One claims that they are originally from Ogobiri and, hence, have always lived in the Niger Delta. Another tradition claims that they came from Egypt. A third tradition, that of the Brass, claims that they migrated from BENIN. According to the Brass tradition, a Benin king sent a group of soldiers on an expedition accompanied by the king's son. When the prince was killed, these soldiers were afraid to return and settled in the delta. BRONZE objects found in the area support this claim.

Ijo clans were governed by village assemblies known as the *amagula*, which were led by the oldest member of the village, called the *ama-okosowei*. A younger man known as the *ogulasowei*, or spokesman, usually carried out the decisions of the assembly. Each clan had a high priest known as the *pere* who conducted rituals honoring a local deity. Among the Ijo of the western and central delta, a single common ancestor often unified clans. In the east, clans were linked by a shared language and culture.

Out of small settlements, the Ijo developed a number of city-states, each led by a different king. By around 1500, when the first European written records of the area

This terra-cotta portrait head of an Ile-Ife king dates from the twelfth through the fourteenth century. It is 10 inches (26.7 cm) high. © *Kimbell Art Museum/CORBIS*

appear, these Ijo states were thriving and conducting trade among themselves. Shortly after making contact with Europeans, the Ijo began trading with them as well, exporting products from the Niger Delta, including palm oil, for manufactured goods.

See also: CALABAR (Vol. III); CLANS (Vol. I); IJO (Vol. III); NIGER DELTA (Vol. I); PALM OIL (Vol. III).

Ilebo Town and river port in the central western region of present-day Democratic Republic of Congo, located near the junction of the Kaisai and Sankura Rivers. Prior to 1000, the region to the east of the Kaisai was inhabited by the TWA people. Between c. 1000 and 1500, however, the Bakuba peoples began to migrate into the area from their previous homeland north of the Sankura River. Eventually the Bakuba absorbed the Twa population and transformed their numerous small villages into an empire that would flourish in the seventeenth century. The Bakuba economy around Ilebo was based on fishing and farming, with their major CROPS being maize and millet. Ilebo was also an important trading center for high-quality Bakuba CLOTH, especially raffia cloth, which was greatly valued throughout central Africa.

See also: BAKUBA (Vol. III); MBUTI (Vol. II).

Ile-Ife (Ife) City in southwestern Nigeria that is recognized as the oldest settlement of the YORUBA people. It is thought that Ile-Ife was established around 850.

According to Yoruba tradition, Ile-Ife was founded by a legendary ancestor named ODUDUWA, who subjugated thirteen nearby settlements and established a monarchy. Oduduwa's descendants would later leave the city to form Yoruba's six kingdoms—Ila, Ketu, OYO, Owu, Popo, and Sabe—as well as BENIN.

By the tenth and eleventh centuries, Ile-Ife was a flourishing city, with a lavish court for its ruler, known as the *oni* and considered the spiritual leader of all the Yoruba. Although Benin and Oyo were more powerful cities, Ile-Ife was revered for its religious and cultural importance, especially its art and sculpture. The artists of Ile-Ife were famous for their naturalistic terra-cotta sculptures of human heads, which were used to honor the *oni*, and are said to share traits with Nok sculpture, the work of a West African culture that flourished between 650 BCE and 200 CE. Ile-Ife was also renowned for its BRONZE castings, which were made using the LOST-WAX PROCESS, the same technique used by the ancient Greeks.

According to tradition, Benin's king was overthrown in a revolt and replaced by an Ile-Ife prince named Oranmiyan. Based on this story, a custom emerged whereby the king of Benin would be decapitated after death and buried in Ile-Ife in a sacred enclosure known as the *orun oba ado*. A head sculpted out of brass would be sent to Benin, where it would be placed on the altar of royal ancestors.

Ile-Ife reached the height of its power early in the fourteenth century, but by the fifteenth century, Benin and Oyo had begun to assume much of the commercial and cultural influence that had previously been Ile-Ife's.

See also: CRAFTSPEOPLE (Vol. II); ILE-IFE (Vol. I); NOK CULTURE (Vol. I); OLD OYO (Vol. II); OLORUN (Vol. I); YORUBALAND (Vols. I, III).

Indian Ocean trade   The exchange of goods across the Indian Ocean, the large body of water that borders the East African coast south of Somalia.

Trade on the Indian Ocean allowed contact between the African cities and faraway places like Arabia, southern Persia, and India, whose MERCHANTS sailed on wooden vessels known as dhows. Items of trade included exotic goods such as IVORY, rhinoceros horn, and tortoiseshell, and also more utilitarian goods like tools, glassware, and wheat.

Beginning around 700, ARAB traders arrived on Africa's east coast south of present-day Somalia. They named the land the "Land of al-ZANJ" (*Zanj* was a name given to the region's black inhabitants). In the tenth century, Arab traders also shipped GOLD from SOFALA in MOZAMBIQUE. Excavations conducted in the town of Manda, near LAMU, on the coast of KENYA, revealed that people living there in the ninth century were prosperous and heavily influenced by Persian culture. There may have also been an IRON-smelting industry in Manda.

Indian Ocean trade resulted in human migration. Between the second and tenth centuries, Indonesians settled in MADAGASCAR and brought to Africa BANANAS and a canoe known as the *ngalawa*. Meanwhile, some Arab traders founded communities on the African coast or on nearby islands, bringing ISLAM with them. At ZANZIBAR an inscription describing the construction of a mosque by Sheikh as-Sayyid Abu 'Imran Musa ibn al-Hasan ibn Muhammad indicates the establishment of a large Muslim settlement by c. 1107. During the twelfth century, the Muslim traders intermarried more readily with the local populations, developed the language of KISWAHILI, and founded trading towns that were the centers of power for the Swahili kingdoms.

Other important trading posts along the Indian Ocean included the towns of Rhapta, in present-day Tanzania, MAFIA ISLAND, and MOGADISHU, which is located off the coast of Somalia. By the thirteenth century,

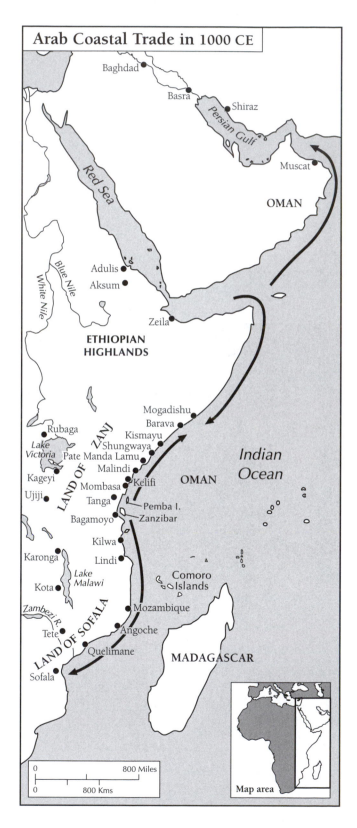

Arab Coastal Trade in 1000 CE

Mogadishu competed for trading dominance with KILWA, which was located in southern Tanzania and ruled by the SHIRAZI ARABS, a powerful trading dynasty who also controlled Zanzibar and PEMBA.

See also: ARAB COASTAL TRADE (Vol. II); CHINESE TRADE (Vol. II); GOLD COAST (Vol. III); INDONESIAN COLONISTS (Vol. III).

Indonesian colonists People who settled the island of MADAGASCAR, off the southern coast of East Africa, during the first millennium. Although linguistic evidence suggests that they may have arrived several centuries earlier, it is clear from archaeological evidence that Indonesian colonists had arrived in Madagascar by the tenth century, at the very latest. How and when they came to the island is still a topic of debate among historians and scholars.

According to one theory, the Indonesian colonists stopped in India, Arabia, and eastern Africa along the way, absorbing local customs and traditions from all of these places. This resulted in a mesh of Indian, Arabian, and African cultures that helped shape the development of Madagascar. Other historians account for this mixture of cultures with the theory that the Indonesian migrations were followed by separate migrations form other regions.

The language spoken by most of the inhabitants is Malagasy, a member of the Malayo-Polynesian family of languages and related to the Ma'anyan language of Borneo. Malagasy contains many loan words from Sanskrit, ARABIC, and BANTU that linguists believe have been part of the language for a long time. Their presence may indicate contact with the speakers of these languages while taking a coastal route from India, along the Indian Ocean, and along Africa, on their voyage to the island. Other researchers posit a direct route from Indonesia. However, the Bantu elements may also have entered the language because of an earlier Bantu presence on the island, perhaps as early as 700. Arab and African influences after the fourteenth century may also account for the presence of Arabic words. In support of the two-route theory is the fact that the people of the interior plateau exhibit many Indonesian genetic traits, whereas the coastal peoples have more African and Arab traits.

See also: BANANAS (Vol. II); MADAGASCAR (Vol. III).

Inland Niger Delta Region in present-day Mali located between the Niger and Bani Rivers. The Inland Niger Delta covers about 11,583 square miles (30,000 sq km) and consists mainly of swamps and standing water, although the territory also crosses areas of savanna grassland and Sahel scrub. The region is flooded for much of the year, but its fertile soil allows for the farming of CROPS such as millet and rice.

Prior to European colonization, the delta was controlled by the GHANA EMPIRE. During much of this time, the main commercial center of the region was JENNE-JENO, which had been founded early in the first millennium CE. ZA, another important trading city in the Inland Niger Delta, was located 62 miles (100 km) west of Jenne-Jeno. Founded by a branch of MANDE speakers known as the Nono, Za was a thriving center of commerce by the tenth and eleventh centuries. It was, in fact, traders originating from Za who are thought to have established JENNE in the thirteenth century.

Jenne eventually came to rival and even supplant Jenne-Jeno as the region's primary commercial power. Trade items included COPPER, GOLD, salt, kola nuts, and IVORY. By the end of the fifteenth century, there was also a thriving trade in dried FISH and cereals. Much of this trade was conducted by BERBER and Sudanese MERCHANTS who used camels and riverboats to transport goods along routes extending northwards to the SAHARA, North Africa, and the MEDITERRANEAN SEA.

See also: NIGER EXPEDITION (Vol. III); NIGER RIVER (Vols. I, III); TRANS-SAHARAN TRADE ROUTES (Vol. II); SALT TRADE (Vol. II).

iron Metal used in the production of tools and weapons. The production of iron implements significantly affected many aspects of African agriculture and trade, as well as its art, culture, and history.

The archaeological discovery of slag heaps, the remnants of iron production, indicates that during the first millennium CE, iron was being used along the IVORY COAST as well as in Bahili in the present-day Republic of CHAD and in Koulikoro in modern-day Mali.

Iron swords and spears were used in West Africa from an early date. It is likely that the SONINKE people, founders of ancient Ghana and the GHANA EMPIRE, may have had the benefit of superior iron-making technology, giving them the superior weaponry they needed to seize better grazing lands from neighboring peoples. By the thirteenth century, Africa had developed a prosperous trade in iron ore, with raw iron being shipped from SOFALA to locations as far away as India. Higher quality Portuguese iron began arriving in Africa by the fifteenth century, however, and the more sophisticated products quickly transformed not only the native Africa iron industry but also the balance of power among many kings and kingdoms.

See also: IRON AGE (Vol. I); IRONWORKING (Vol. II).

ironworking Ironworking was introduced into Africa at various times, beginning, in ancient Egypt and elsewhere, as early as the second millennium BCE. Opinions vary among scholars as to whether ironworking was learned from other cultures or whether African ironworking developed on its own, without outside influence. Archaeologists long held that the smelting of iron spread by process of diffusion from a single point, probably in Turkey. Recent research, however, based on differences in the slag heaps found in Europe and in Africa, indicates that smelting may have occurred independently in Africa.

Generally, the ironworking process began with the mined iron ore being heated to temperatures of 1470° to 1650° F (800° to 900° C). The shape of the actual furnaces varied widely in design and shape. The Chewa of Zambia and the Shona of Zimbabwe both used furnaces shaped like domes. In eastern and central Africa, however, ironworking furnaces generally were made with shafts or with open hearths. Regardless of their shapes, the ironwork often was done near forested areas, since trees were needed to provide the necessary firewood and coal for the flames of the furnaces.

The iron produced frequently needed to be hardened, and this generally was done by means of a complex process of hammering the raw iron and heating it with charcoal. The iron that was produced could then be forged into tools, weapons, or even ornaments by blacksmiths, who, because of the importance of their jobs, held a high place in virtually every iron-producing society.

See also: BARIBA METALURGY (Vol. II); NUMUW (Vol. II); NYAMAKALAW (Vol. II).

Iru Caste of agriculturalists inhabiting the region west of Lake VICTORIA, in the southwestern part of modern-day UGANDA. The BANTU-speaking Iru, who were the descendants of the original inhabitants of the region, were the subjects of the HIMA, or lords, of NKOLE society. They also served the cattle-owning royalty of the BUNYORO-KITARA kingdom, which was dominant over the land of much of modern-day Uganda from the sixteenth century to the nineteenth century. The cattle-owning Hima of Nkole and NYORO were a privileged caste who ruled over the Iru and other agriculturalist peoples of the kingdoms around Lake Victoria. The Iru generally grew millet and lived in settlements of about forty homesteads.

See also: AGRICULTURALIST (Vol. I); BUNYORO-KITARA (Vol. III); NKOLE (Vol. III); UGANDA (Vol. III).

Islam A religion based on the teachings of the seventh-century Arab prophet MUHAMMAD. Originating in Arabia, Islam spread quickly throughout northern and SUB-SAHARAN AFRICA (as well as the Middle East and Asia).

Islamic Theology Islam, Arabic for "submission to God," is one of the world's three major monotheistic religions. Muslims believe in a solitary, omnipotent god (in Arabic, Allah), who created and sustains the universe. Belief in more than one god is rejected. Allah's divinity does not extend to any person and, as a result, in Islamic theology Allah has no equal.

In Islamic belief, Allah plays four primary roles with respect to the universe and humankind: creator, sustainer, guide, and judge. As creator, Allah brought the world into being. As sustainer, Allah is obligated to maintain the world that he created. As guide, Allah teaches humanity proper moral and spiritual conduct. As judge, Allah will punish or reward individuals, communities, and nations on the basis of their actions.

According to Islamic thought, Allah created the universe as an act of mercy. Every element of this creation has been instilled with certain rules that govern its behavior. So while the universe is independent in that everything has its own inherent rules of conduct, it is not self-governing because the behavior has been set and limited by Allah. The universe, therefore, is harmonious and provides the ultimate proof of Allah and his oneness.

Violations in nature have occurred in the form of miracles. Allah, for example, saved Abraham from the fire, Noah from the flood, and Moses from the pharaoh. Islam recognizes these prophets and their miracles. However, Muhammad is considered to be the final and most perfect of the prophets. His miracle is the KORAN.

Although Muslims have developed sects that vary somewhat in their faith and practices, all Muslims adhere to certain central beliefs in addition to the belief in Allah. Most Muslims regard Muhammad as the last (and most perfect) of a line of prophets that includes Adam, Noah, Moses, and Jesus, among others. Muslims hold that God put humans—and especially Muslims—on earth in order to reform it. The struggle to do so, both individually and as a society, is known as JIHAD. Muslims stress the importance of family and fidelity in marriage, and consider it their duty to benefit humanity and improve human society. Muslims also believe in final judgment, a day when God will reward (through admission to the Garden, or Heaven) or punish (by consigning to Hell) individuals according to their deeds during life.

In order to keep central in their minds their obligation to serve Allah throughout their lives on earth, Muslims perform five duties, together known as the Pillars of Islam. A public profession of faith—using the words, "There is no God but Allah and Muhammad is his Prophet"—marks a Muslim's membership in the Islamic community. Every day, Muslims say five prayers (known as *salah*), intoned at different times of day and according to strict observation of ritual (e.g., facing Mecca). Muslims also have a duty to pay ZAKAT to help the poor. (Originally, *zakat* was a tax on the rich used not only to relieve poverty but also to support efforts to gain converts and to wage holy war.) The fourth duty of all Muslims is to fast—and to abstain from drinking, smoking, and sexual intercourse—during the daylight hours throughout Ramadan, the ninth lunar month of the Muslim calendar.

(Anyone who—due to illness, pregnancy, military service, or other unavoidable reasons—cannot fast during Ramadan must do so for a month at the earliest opportunity.) The fifth duty is a pilgrimage (hajj) to Mecca, which must be completed at least once in the lifetime of each Muslim.

Muhammad (c. 570–632), a rich merchant in MECCA (in modern-day Saudi Arabia), believed himself to be chosen by Allah (God) as the Arab prophet of a new religion. Muhammad received revelation of Allah's word through the angel Gabriel. He began preaching in 610 but was scorned and ridiculed by Meccans. In 622, he left for Yathrib (later MEDINA, Saudi Arabia), where he was accepted as a prophet. (The year 622 marks the beginning of the Muslim calendar.) Islam rapidly attracted converts among Arab peoples. Growing in numbers, the Muslims declared war against Mecca, conquering the city in 630. By the time Muhammad died two years later, he had built the foundations for a long-lasting Islamic Arab kingdom.

The Koran and Muslim Law   The Koran, Allah's revelation to Muhammad, lies at the center of Islam. His message was delivered to Muhammad by the angel Gabriel. Since Allah is the author of the Koran, its language is considered perfect. For this reason, believers read and learn the Koran in the original ARABIC. In simple terms, the Koran is a set of rules that governs humankind. As a result, in Islam, there traditionally is no differentiation between church and state; religion and social membership are one and the same. Therefore, Islamic law consists of both legal and moral mandates.

Islamic law is derived from several sources. The primary source, of course, is the Koran. A second source, called the Sunna, consists of rules of conduct set by the prophet Muhammad and complements the Koran. Because the Sunna was transmitted orally and not written down until the ninth century, it is not considered infallible. The values set forth in the Koran and the Sunna, though, are considered to be Allah's will and are to be strictly adhered to in all aspects of a Muslim's life—religious, social, economic, and political.

Stating that humans are the noblest of Allah's creatures, the Koran sees the purpose of humanity in serving Allah and reforming the earth into an ethical social system devoid of evil. However, the Koran also criticizes humans for being proud, petty, closed-minded, and self-centered creatures that will, by their nature, prevent good from spreading to others. The Koran instructs humans to overcome this pettiness, as Allah promises prosperity to those generous to the less fortunate.

Humanity's biggest sin, according to the Koran, is its overwhelming pride. By not recognizing the limitations set for them by Allah, humans become guilty of positioning themselves alongside God. In general, the Koran suggests, humanity only turns to Allah for help when the universe has failed it. This attitude violates the most sacred tenet of Islam, that God is one, with no partner and no equal. Only by transcending this petty behavior, therefore, can people develop *taqwa*, the internal ability to distinguish right from wrong. Humans possess free will, so Islamic practice does not simply involve obeying Allah but rather accepting the deity's mandates, which are transmitted through the prophets who show all creatures the "straight path."

Islam recognizes prophets from the Hebrew scriptures and the New Testament, as well as some extra-biblical characters. As a result, Muhammad is seen as the culmination of a long line of prophecy. He is, however, clearly the most important prophet, as his message from Allah resulted in the Koran. Prophets, even Muhammed, are considered to be human, but they are the most perfect examples of humanity. Holding no place in divinity, each prophet's message is believed to have been sent from the same divine source, Allah. Therefore, one must believe in the message of every prophet because to reject one is to deny the truth of Allah. The messages of the prophets guide individuals in their struggle to follow the will of Allah.

History of Islam   Within a few centuries after Muhammad's death, Islam had spread throughout North Africa, as well as sub-Saharan Africa, Madagascar, and Asia. This expansion, which took place from the seventh through the eleventh centuries, resulted primarily from three factors: Arab military conquests, the migration of Arab traders, and Sufi missionary work.

From the seventh to the tenth century, Muslims from Arabia invaded and conquered lands throughout North Africa. The first Arab invaders conducted military campaigns from a base in EGYPT from 642 to 669. The first Islamic dynasty, the UMAYYADS (661–750), operating from their capital city of Damascus, later recognized the strategic importance of using the Syrian army to establish a Mediterranean presence. The Umayyads established a base in Tunisia in 670 and launched many military expeditions from there. After establishing an alliance with Kusayla, the BERBER leader in ALGERIA and a convert from CHRISTIANITY to Islam, the Umayyads in 682 conquered MOROCCO, where Arabs would remain in power for 150 years. By 711, the Umayyads controlled the entire MAGHRIB (present-day Morocco, ALGERIA, Tunisia, and LIBYA), establishing a new province that they called IFRIQIYA.

By the middle of the eighth century, Arabic Muslims had created a powerful empire that spread as far west as the Atlantic Ocean and into Morocco, MAURITANIA, and SENEGAL. In conquering African lands, the Muslim empire won many converts from both Christianity and indigenous religions, forcing both Islam and the Arabic language upon the vanquished. Arab Muslims treated these African converts to Islam poorly, imposing heavy taxes on all and enslaving some. Oppressed, the Berbers eventually rebelled against Arab rule—but never against Islam. Around 740, Kharijites, an egalitarian sect of Muslims that believed that good works, rather than faith alone, defined Islamic life, led a revolt against the Arabs in the Maghrib. The Kharijites founded a number of short-lived Muslim tribal kingdoms before the Abassids (750–1258), a second dynasty that succeeded the Umayyads, reestablished authority over Ifriqiya. West of Ifriqiya, the central Maghrib was ruled by the Kharijite Rustumid imams from 761 until the early tenth century.

The Spread of Islam throughout Africa In 909, FATIMIDS—leaders of a sect of Muslims called the Ismaili Shiites—conquered most of North Africa, imposing Shiite rule on Egypt and the Maghrib until 1171. The Muslim warrior SALADIN, who deposed the Fatimid caliphs and founded the Ayyubid dynasty in that year, restored the supremacy of the more orthodox Sunni Islam throughout North Africa.

Beyond geographical and political conquest, another factor that helped spread Islamic influence through Africa was the spice trade. The Middle East had long been an important location along the trade routes from Africa to Asia. With the rapid spread of Islam, Muslims eventually controlled the spice trade. Breaking from the previous tradition of buying spices from local merchants and selling them nearby, Muslim traders eliminated the middle man by beginning to travel the whole trade routes themselves. While traveling these routes, Muslim traders also spread the word of God as heard by Muhammad.

In East Africa, traders (as well as settlers and missionaries) from the Arabian Peninsula won many converts. Many Arab merchants married into African families and began converting communities from within. In West Africa, Berber traders from the Maghrib, after converting to Islam, spread the religion south along the trade routes of the SENEGAL RIVER and the Niger River. By the beginning of the eleventh century, they were joined by the SONINKE people of Mauritania, who themselves had converted to Islam and then carried the word farther south and east.

The third influence that helped spread Islam was the movement of Sufi missionaries after the twelfth century. The Sufis—Muslim mystics—won many converts to Islam as they moved westward across North Africa and later through sub-Saharan Africa. Since SUFISM tolerated the preservation of local religious customs and beliefs alongside the adoption of Islam, their vision of Islam seemed less threatening than that of Arab invaders. As a result, Sufism spread quickly, and Africans—especially in

the countryside—revered Sufi holy men, bowing to their moral authority and wise judgment.

The spread of Islam through the combined efforts of military force, trade, and missionaries had a greater impact on North Africa than anywhere else on the continent. By the mid-eleventh century, the Maghrib had been ruled by Muslims—either Arabs or Egypt's Fatimid dynasty—for 350 years, and the majority of indigenous North Africans had adopted this new faith. Islam became even more entrenched in North Africa with the rise of two major Muslim dynasties that ruled over a unified Maghrib from the eleventh to the thirteenth century: the ALMORAVIDS (1062–1140) and the ALMOHADS (1140–1269).

A militant Islamic movement, the Almoravids arose from the Saharan Muslims in Mauritania around 1035. The cause of religious reform helped unify the disparate groups. By 1042, Almoravids had launched a jihad against heretics and nonbelievers. The Almoravids invaded Morocco in 1056, founded MARRAKECH as their capital in 1062, crushed the GHANA EMPIRE by 1076, and established an Islamic empire that stretched from Mauritania to Algiers by 1082. Conquests north, east, and south enabled the Almoravids to gain control of the GOLD trade throughout the region and to force Islam upon its neighbors. By 1110, the Almoravids ruled all of Muslim Spain as well. After gaining power, the Almoravids set up a political state that strictly applied the principles of Islam in all judicial and ethical matters.

Yet the narrow and restrictive rule of these applications of Islamic law gave rise to revolutionary movements. The Almohads, Islamic reformers who stressed the unity of God and urged a return to the Koran and the traditions of the prophet Muhammad, began organizing in the Atlas Mountains around 1120. Within five years, Almohads had begun attacking Moroccan cities under Almoravid control. Between 1140 and 1158, the Almohads wrested all power from the Almoravids and conquered Morocco and all of North Africa west of Egypt. Muslim Spain had also fallen under their rule by 1172.

The Almohad dynasty ultimately broke up into factions. By 1269, the Almohads had been ousted from Marrakech, ending the rule of a united Maghrib by a Muslim dynasty. The Maghrib was divided into three separate Muslim states ruled by Berbers: the MARINIDS in Morocco; the Hafsid in Tunisia, eastern Algeria, and Tripolitania; and the Zayyanids in western Algeria. Under these Muslim rulers, who no longer imposed a single dogma on the people, Islamic culture and religion flourished. The rulers erected new mosques and colleges in their capital cities, which quickly became renowned as places to study Islam.

In fact, Muslims have long emphasized the importance of education. Universities in both Africa and the Middle East, originally founded as places to study Islam and train religious leaders, soon became centers for the study of literature, philosophy, mathematics, medicine, and science as well. Al-AZHAR, for example, founded in CAIRO, Egypt, during the tenth century by the Fatimid dynasty, is still one of the most important centers for Islamic studies in the world.

Today, Muslims still make up the vast majority of Arabic-speaking people in North Africa, from Mauritania to Sudan. Islam remains the primary religion of the peoples of Guinea, Senegal, Gambia, Mauritania, Morocco, Mali, Algeria, Tunisia, Niger, Libya, Egypt, Sudan, Djibouti, Somalia, and the island of ZANZIBAR. In addition, a large population of Muslims reside in Ghana, Nigeria, Chad, ERITREA, ETHIOPIA, and Tanzania.

See also: AL-ANDALUS (Vol. II); ISLAM, INFLUENCE OF (Vols. II, III); ISLAMIC CENTERS OF LEARNING (Vol. II).

Further reading: John L. Esposito, ed., *The Oxford History of Islam* (New York: Oxford University Press, 2000).

Islam, influence of

The political, religious, and social prestige of ISLAM on Africa from the seventh through the fifteenth centuries.

After the death of the prophet MUHAMMAD in 632, Islam became highly influential in Africa. The traditions, or Sunna, of the prophet formed the cornerstone of Islam, governing worship, the law, education, and the promotion of a worldwide Islamic community. The mission to spread the truth of Islam began in the seventh century, the century of the *hijira,* or flight from Mecca, by the Prophet. *Dar al-Islam,* or Islamic expansion, became a holy obligation and spread from Arabia to the Atlantic coast of MOROCCO and Spain.

Arab trading communities gathered significant knowledge about the interior regions of Africa. In the territories where the message of Islam was carried, Arab proselytizers encountered ethnic groups with deeply entrenched traditional beliefs and others who were Christians or Jews. The primary reasons given for the widespread appeal of Islam included its simple teachings, identification with the ruling class, and escape from the forced tribute and taxation levied by Islam conquerors. Non-Muslims were forced to pay a *djizya,* or poll tax, which built the newly installed Islamic state treasury. This in turn supported those carrying the word of Islam.

Egypt and Nubia In 642, Egypt became the first African country to convert to Islam. Egypt may have been especially susceptible to conversion because the rule of the Byzantine Empire in Africa was oppressive and corrupt. The Arabs established the capital city of CAIRO near the ruins of the ancient city of Memphis, although not without some resistance from the departing Byzantine government. The resulting influx of Arabic Bedouins into the region led to intermarriage and the dominance of Arabic culture and language. However, small groups of Coptic Christians and Jews have been able to retain their religion up to modern times.

Islam spread from the north into Nubia where, in the eighth century, nomadic Arabs settled between the Nile Valley and the shores of the Red Sea. Attempts to conquer Nubia were militarily rebuffed. The *bakt,* or treaty, of 652 stabilized social and trade relations between Islamic Egypt and the Nubian regions of Noba (Nobatia), Makurra (Makouria), and Alwa (Alodia), collectively known as Christian NUBIA. In the neighboring Bedja region, a stronghold of traditional religion, intermarriage among Arab and Bedja ruling families created powerful lineage networks known as the *hadariba* and *ababda.* Most Bedja were Islamized by the fourteenth century but maintained their traditional practices as well.

North Africa In the MAGHRIB, Arabs met renewed resistance from the Byzantine forces as well as the BERBERS. They entered into extended battles, defeating the Byzantine navy and combating various Berber groups, such as the Jarawa, led by legendary DAHIA AL-KAHINA (575–702). Some Berber peoples along the coast openly adopted Islam but reverted to their original religion many times—a recurring theme in Africa. To solidify the religion among the Berber population, imprisoned young nobles were reportedly freed and encouraged to embrace Islam and join the Arab army. By the eighth century, Islam and Arabic culture was widespread. This Islamized Berber army was reportedly responsible for the Arab conquest of Spain in 711.

However, even when the tenets of Islam were observed, Arab domination did not necessarily follow. The Islamized Berbers in regions including Tripolitania, IFRIQIYA, and Morocco cultivated Kharijite doctrines, which, although Islamic, espoused democracy along with puritanical and fundamentalist practices. The Berber belief in frugality gave religious authority to their opposition to the luxury of the Arabic overlords. By the tenth century, the Islamic FATIMIDS had destroyed many of the Kharijite states and established an empire in Egypt.

Sub-Saharan Africa At approximately the same time, Islam spread to regions south of the SAHARA. Long-distance trade forged commercial contacts between the MERCHANTS of the North and the rulers of kingdoms, towns and cities of the SUDAN and West Africa. After initial exposure to Islam, Africans from these regions often transmitted the teachings of Islam to members of their population. The primary converts at these early urban sites were members of the royal hierarchy as well as traders exposed to the outside world. Other converts were attracted by Islamic rites that seemed similar to their own religious practice, such as belief in divination, use of charms and amulets, and praying to bring rain.

The coexistence of Islam with traditional African religion occurred in the ancient GHANA EMPIRE and its successor empires of MALI and SONGHAI. It had long been thought that the ALMORAVID conquest in 1076 resulted in Ghana's forced adoption of Islam. However, some historians now suggest that Islam was introduced through a social alliance rather than conquest and even then only to the Ghanaian ruler and not the entire population. This view is based on Ghana's long-standing trade contacts with the North and the fact that they were among the first to establish separate quarters for Islamic merchants in their city. It is also believed that the Islam first brought to the Ghana Empire was of the Kharijite type established centuries earlier in the Maghrib. However, these theories throw the large-scale migration and resistance by large groups of SONINKE into question. It is known that the Soninke who embraced Islam were largely from the merchant class known as the Wangara. They spread the religion further into the Sudanic regions by establishing commercial networks in the Sahel and tropical forest regions.

In the MALI EMPIRE, Islam was first practiced among the rulers who descended from SUNDIATA (d. 1255) during the thirteenth century. Sundiata's son Mansa Uli (d. 1270) was the first known member to have journeyed to MECCA and established the pilgrimage as a yearly tradition. The building of mosques and schools proliferated under the fourteenth-century rule of Mansa MUSA (c. 1312–1337) and Mansa SULAYMAN (c. 1341–1360). As a result, the region generated Islamic religious leaders known as the *torodbe*. Other groups to embrace the religion included the DYULA and the HAUSA, who became actively involved in commercial trade and carried the teachings of Islam to the Gold Coast regions.

However, not all African kingdoms south of the Sahara embraced Islam. From the lower SENEGAL region to Lake CHAD, and particularly among the BAMBARA of Mali and the MOSSI states situated in the Niger bend, resistance was strong. After the Mossi, centered in what is now BURKINA FASO, began to expand, they incurred the wrath of ASKIA MUHAMMAD TOURÉ (1493–1528). A Soninke and devout Muslim, Touré made annual pilgrimages to Mecca and used Islam as a unifying force in his widespread kingdom. Already angered by the refusal of the Mossi to convert, he launched an unsuccessful raid against them in about 1497, declaring it a JIHAD, or holy war. The Mossi, however, maintained their traditional practices until the seventeenth century.

See also: ARCHITECTURE (Vol. II); CHRISTIANITY (Vol. II); GOLD TRADE (Vol. II); ISLAM, INFLUENCE OF (Vol. III).

Further reading: Ali A. Mazrui, *The Africans: A Triple Heritage* (Boston: Little, Brown, 1986); Kevin Shillington, *History of Africa* (New York: St. Martin's Press, 1995).

Islamic centers of learning While Europe was emerging from its Dark Ages (400–1000), Muslim culture and scholarship were rising toward their height. The major centers of learning in the Islamic world were at Baghdad in Iraq, CAIRO in Egypt, and at Córdoba and Toledo in Spain. The Moorish kingdom of al-ANDALUS ruled large territories within the Iberian Peninsula from 711 to 1494. (*Moor* is from the Latin word *Maurus*, meaning "inhabitant of Mauretania" or "Moroccan.") There are scholars who believe that the European Renaissance of the fourteenth, fifteenth, and sixteenth centuries had its roots in the Moorish renaissance in Spain. Islamic scholars in Spain and the Middle East made significant contributions to astronomy, medicine, mathematics, and many other secular fields. Islamic scholars in West Africa were more religion-directed and contributed to the development of Islamic law.

The major centers of Islamic learning in Africa were at Cairo in Egypt and at TIMBUKTU, GAO, KANO, and KATSINA in West Africa. Centers of trade often became centers of learning. Funded in the tenth century by the FATIMID dynasty, the *jam'iyyah*, or university, of al-AZHAR, which is attached to the al-Azhar Mosque in Cairo, may be the world's oldest institution of higher learning; it is still in

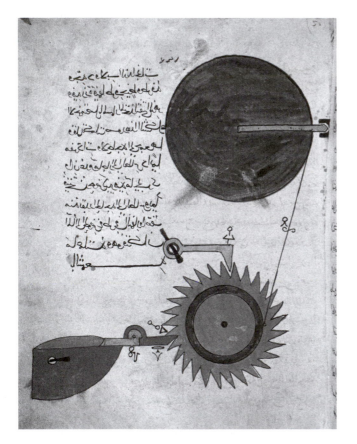

This manuscript illumination of a clock-making system from Al'Dzajari's *Book of Knowledge of Mechanical Processes*, created in 1206, is on display at the Topaki Library in Istanbul, Turkey. It gives evidence of the flourishing of Islamic science after the year 1000 and shows the type of books that would have been available to scholars throughout the Muslim world.
© *Gianni Dagli Orti/CORBIS*

operation today, as it was in the tenth century, as a major Muslim theological school. Al-Azhar first taught Shiite doctrine, but when the Ayyubid dynasty came to power in Egypt in the late twelfth century, al-Azhar became a center of the more traditional SUNNI doctrine, which the vast majority of observant Muslims follow.

The regular subjects of study in the tenth to fifteenth centuries at Al-Azhar University included grammar (*nahw*), literary style and rhetoric (*balaghah*), logic (*mantiq*), and the study of the KORAN. The latter included study of the *Sunna*, the body of traditional Muslim social and legal custom and practice, and *fiqh*, or jurisprudence, considered the most important subject in the curriculum. In classic Islamic thought, the four sources of Islamic law, or *Sharia*, were called the *usul al-fiqh*; these were the Koran, the *Sunna*, *ijma*, or the consensus of scholars, and *qiyas*, or finding analogies with past practices and beliefs as guides to solve a present problem.

Ever since Islam's first appearance in West Africa, the *ulama*, or religious scholars, the leaders of prayer in the mosques, and the reciters of the Koran have been indigenous Africans. Thus, the mosque and the school attached to it, with living quarters for resident and itinerant scholars, was an important feature of a major Islamic African city and a point of contact with the Muslim world outside. The university at the Sankore Mosque in Timbuktu on the Niger River became second only to al-Azhar as the most important center of Islamic learning in Africa. It attracted the sons of the local elite and scholars reputedly from as far as the Arabian Peninsula. Its graduates were widely respected and influential.

As was true of other Muslim universities, Sankore was made up of several independent schools, each run by a single master, or *imam*. Students associated themselves with a single teacher and studied with him in the open courtyard of the mosque or at a private residence. As the number of students increased, topics of study extended beyond the Islamic sciences of Koranic interpretation (*tafsir*), doctrinal theology (*tawid*), jurisprudence (*fiqh*), and the sources of the law (*usul*) to include secular studies also.

At its height, as many as 25,000 students were thought to study at the Sankore Mosque in a ten-year program that covered astronomy, medicine, history, cartography, mathematics, and Islamic sciences. Visiting non-Muslim traders and travelers were encouraged to meet the scholars in residence and were often converted to Islam.

The fortunes of the school depended on political realities. The SONGHAI leader SUNNI ALI (r. 1464–1492), reviled as a tepid Muslim, almost an infidel, by the Muslim clerics of Timbuktu, persecuted the scholars of Sankore when he wrested Timbuktu from the MALI EMPIRE early in his reign. Under his successor, the fervent Muslim ASKIA MUHAMMAD TOURÉ (r. 1493–1538), Sankore once again thrived. When the northern Muslim kingdom of Morocco captured Timbuktu from the Songhai Empire in the early 1590s, however, Sankore's best scholars were deported, and the school never regained its former importance. Around the same time, the Moroccans also took control of Gao, the capital of the Songhai Empire.

Traders brought Islam to Kano, one of the HAUSA STATES, in the fourteenth century, during the reign of Sarki YAJI (r. 1349–1385). A mosque was built and a court established to hand down judgments in religious matters. By the time Sarki RUMFA (1463–1499) came to power, Islam was firmly rooted in Kano. Scholars connected with Sankore are thought to have opened schools in Kano to teach and preach Islam.

The Hausa state of Katsina had become a seat of learning in the 1400s. Both Katsina and Kano were known to have been visited by the famed fifteenth century Muslim theologian al-MAGHILI from Tuat, in present-day ALGERIA, who wrote his influential treatise about Islamic government, *The Obligation of Princes*, during his stay at Sarki Rumfa's court late in the fifteenth century.

Itsekiri Ethnic group and kingdom located in what is today southern Nigeria. Legend states that the kingdom of Itsekiri was founded by a former prince of BENIN named Ginuwa (or Iginua), who moved to the Niger Delta area of WARRI in the fifteenth century after being passed over as a potential oba (king) of Benin. Evidence suggests, however, that the precursors to the Itsekiri peoples were of YORUBA origin and had already established a society based on agriculture and fishing by the eleventh century.

By the time the Portuguese came into contact with Itsekiri in the fifteenth century, the inhabitants were skilled in trading their coastal wares with their inland neighbors. The kingdom thereafter became a significant center for European trade—even surpassing the powerful kingdom of Benin in importance—with commodities such as fish, palm oil, salt, and slaves.

The kingdom of Itsekiri was ruled by the *olu*, or king, who exercised priestly functions and headed a centralized government with a large governing council. The council, which included an *ologbotsere*, or military commander, and an *iyasere*, or prime minister, acted in conjunction with the *olu* to decide important legislative matters. Succession to the throne could be from either the matrilineal or patrilineal side, so long as descent from

Ginuwa could be claimed, therefore ensuring descent from the original oba of Benin as well.

The Itsekiri peoples, who share their origins with other groups such as the Yoruba and EDO, mainly practice a traditional religion based on worship of a creator-god, Ortise, and other lesser gods such as Umale Okun, the god of the sea.

See also: ITSEKIRI (Vol. III); LINEAGE (Vol. I); NIGER DELTA (Vol. I); SALT TRADE (Vol. II); SLAVERY (Vols. II, III).

ivory Dentin harvested from elephant tusks that has long been prized for its color, texture, and durability. Ivory has been an important trade commodity throughout much of African history.

Ivory has been considered a luxury item since ancient Egyptian times, when it was carved into small sculptures, jewelry, and a variety of other decorative items. As Muslim Arabs began settling in northern Africa during the seventh and eighth centuries, the ivory trade continued to flourish. Arab MERCHANTS obtained ivory from sub-Saharan market towns like KUMBI SALEH, the capital city of the GHANA EMPIRE, as well as from TIMBUKTU and GAO. In exchange for this prized luxury item, peoples from south of the Sahara were able to obtain salt, silk, COPPER, and weaponry from Arab traders.

By the twelfth century, a renewed demand for African ivory developed in Europe. Ivory was exported to Europe via North African port towns, and later, along the western coast by Portuguese traders. At the same time, the ivory trade developed along the SWAHILI COAST in eastern Africa. The Swahili received their ivory supply from the continent's interior, particularly from ancient kingdoms in present-day KENYA, Tanzania, and MOZAMBIQUE. The primary recipient of East African ivory was India.

See also: ELEPHANT (Vol. I); INDIAN OCEAN TRADE (Vol. II); IVORY TRADE (Vol. III); SALT TRADE (Vol. II); TRANS-SAHARAN TRADE ROUTES (Vol. II).

Ivory Coast Modern-day country bordered by Mali and BURKINA FASO to the north, the Gulf of Guinea to the south, coastal Ghana to the east, and Liberia and Guinea to the west.

Although reports of North African trade CARAVANS operating in the area of Ivory Coast date to Roman times, little is definitively known of the initial population of the region. According to some scholars, the earliest inhabitants most likely were small-statured peoples who were eventually pushed out or absorbed into subsequent populations. By the second millennium, however, the area had come under the partial control of various Sudanic empires, particularly the MALI EMPIRE, which occupied the northwestern corner of the region during the early fourteenth century. Portuguese explorers began visiting the region, searching for IVORY and African captives, by the fifteenth century.

See also: IVORY COAST (Vols. I, III); PORTUGAL AND AFRICA (Vol. III).

Jenne (Djenné)   Small, thirteenth-century city between modern Mopti and Segu in present-day southern Mali; it replaced the ancient city of JENNE-JENO, slightly less than 2 miles (3 km) to the southeast, as a commercial center when that city went into decline and was abandoned around 1400.

Jenne's location near the Niger and Bani Rivers, directly connecting it by river to the city of TIMBUKTU, made Jenne a successful commercial center that attracted traders from central and western SUDAN and Guinea. It was at the head of the trade routes from the GOLD mines at Bitou in modern-day IVORY COAST and was an important center of the SALT TRADE.

The often-photographed Great Mosque of Jenne, is not the original one. The first Great Mosque was built in the thirteenth century by Koy Konboro, Jenne's first Muslim ruler, who erected the mosque on the site of his former royal palace. This building fell into ruin and was replaced at the beginning of the nineteenth century by the second Great Mosque, a monumental building that dominates the town.

Jenne was captured in either 1468 or 1473 by the SONGHAI emperor SONNI ALI (1464–1492), the ruler who transformed Songhai from a kingdom to an empire. Probably a Muslim city since its foundation, Jenne became an ISLAMIC CENTER OF LEARNING in the 1600s.

See also: JENNE (Vol. III).

Jenne-Jeno   Ancient African city, inhabited from around 200 BCE to 1400 CE, located in the western SUDAN, in what is present-day Mali.

Jenne-Jeno is a mound, located about 2 miles (3 km) from the modern city of JENNE. According to oral tradition, Jenne-Jeno was the original settlement of the town of Jenne. Excavations of the mound in the 1970s and 1980s have provided information about life in Jenne-Jeno.

By around 450, Jenne-Jeno had grown into a settlement that covered about 62 acres (25 hectares). The excavations indicate that the houses of this time were built on foundations of puddled mud, or *tauf*. There were also organized cemeteries, and human remains were buried in urns as well as in simple pits.

Much painted POTTERY was made at Jenne-Jeno from 450 to 850. The population grew during this period, and Jenne-Jeno expanded to cover an area of about 82 acres (33 hectares). This expansion was most likely due to the development of TRADE routes along the border between the dry savanna and the region to the south. The success of both the COPPER and GOLD trades in and around Jenne-Jeno probably led the city to become the center of the government that controlled the surrounding area. One of the neighboring towns, HAMBARKETOLO, was connected to Jenne-Jeno by means of an earthen dike, and the two towns may have functioned as one.

In the ninth century, cylindrical bricks replaced the *tauf* foundations. The cylindrical bricks were also used to construct a city wall 12 feet (3.7 meters) wide and more than a mile (1.6 km) long that surrounded the town.

The presence of rectilinear houses and brass suggest that Jenne-Jeno had contact with North African Muslims in the eleventh and twelfth centuries. It is believed that the people of Jenne-Jeno converted to ISLAM in the thirteenth century. However, urn burial continued into the fourteenth century, suggesting that not all the residents had embraced the Muslim faith.

Excavations of Jenne-Jeno reveal that IRON, COPPER, and BRONZE adornments were produced in the area by middle of the first millennium. The absence of natural iron ore deposits in the INLAND NIGER DELTA region indicates that Jenne-Jeno was involved in long-distance trade long before the arrival of Muslim traders in the eighth century.

In the thirteenth century, the nearby town of Jenne, (modern Djenné) was founded and became a center of trade between central and western Sudan and the tropical forests of Guinea. Jenne became a great center of trade in gold, slaves, and SALT. The city was conquered in 1468 by SONGHAI and later became a center of Muslim learning.

Jenne's development seems to have coincided with Jenne-Jeno's decline. By 1400, Jenne-Jeno was completely deserted. One theory to explain the desertion is that the dry climate started to become even drier around 1200, and there was no longer enough water for CROPS and herds. Another explanation is that people converted to Islam and moved to neighboring Jenne. Whatever the reasons, the decline of Jenne-Jeno was gradual and took place over a period of about 200 years.

See also: JENNE-JENO (Vol. I); TRANS-SAHARAN TRADE ROUTES (Vol. II).

Jeriba Ancient city in the SUDAN region. Jeriba is known to be the original location of the empire of SUNDIATA, the thirteenth-century ruler who established the MALI EMPIRE. Jeriba remained the seat of Sundiata's power until around 1240, when the empire was moved to the city of NIANI (also known as Mali).

jihad (jehad) In Arabic, "fight" or "battle." In Muslim belief, a jihad is a holy war, waged to fulfill a religious duty to spread ISLAM by struggle or conquest. In modern Islam, the word may also refer to an individual's internal struggle against evil. The most famous jihad in Muslim Africa, begun by the Muslim reformer Usman dan Fodio (1754–1817), led to the establishment in 1804 of the Sokoto Caliphate and the FULANI Empire in modern-day northern Nigeria. Earlier, in North Africa, the religious reformer MUHAMMAD IBN TUMART (d. 1130) proclaimed himself the MAHDI, a messianic leader expected to initiate

a period of righteousness, and called for moral reform and a return to fundamental Muslim beliefs. Ibn Tumart then waged a series of military campaigns that led to the fall of the ALMORAVIDS, the ruling dynasty of a BERBER state in MOROCCO and the establishment in c. 1120 of the ALMOHAD dynasty. In earlier years, an Almoravid jihad against nonbelievers in the GHANA EMPIRE across the desert to the south led to the capture in 1076 of Ghana's capital city of KUMBI SALEH. The fall of Kumbi Saleh started the period of Ghana's decline.

The concept of jihad is rooted in the KORAN, the holy book of Islam, and its practice goes back to the earliest days of Islamic conversion and expansion. The laws of the jihad are laid out in the Koran and the *hadith* (sayings), which instruct Muslims to wage war on nonbelievers who refuse to convert to Islam. One of the most important of the laws is that a *shahid*, a Muslim who has perished during combat, is considered a martyr. It is believed that the *shahid* is revered in Paradise for sacrificing his life for Islam. Because the jihad is a religious war, its laws forbid unnecessary pillaging or the slaughter of women, children, religious leaders, the sick, the elderly, and anyone else not directly involved in the war:

After the prophet MUHAMMAD'S death in 632, the first jihad was launched by Muhammad's successor and father-in-law, Caliph ABU BAKR (c. 573–634), also called as-Siddiq, "the Upright." During this period, the major targets of the jihad were polytheists. (Because Jews and Christians were monotheistic and were considered to be people of the book, they were given a certain amount of immunity by early Islam. Instead of being killed, they were allowed to convert or at least submit to Islamic rule and pay a tax, called the *jizya*.) During the next two years, the jihad became a war of conquest. Arab forces under the second caliph, UMAR I (c. 586–644), under whom the Arab Empire, or the Empire of the Caliphate, spread into Mesopotamia and Syria and began the conquest of Iran and Egypt.

See also: FULANI JIHAD (Vol. III); SOKOTO CALIPHATE (Vol. III); USMAN DAN FODIO (Vol. III).

Judaism See JUDAISM (Vol. I); MONOTHEISM (Vol. II).

Juhaynah (Juhayna, Juhaina, Djoheina) A classification of a large group of pastoralist peoples of present-day CHAD and other parts of the eastern SUDAN. The Juhaynah come from the upper portion of the eastern SAHARA, near Aswan. By the 1400s, they had migrated south into the grazing land of the eastern Sudan, introducing ISLAM as they mixed and intermarried with local Nubians. Thereafter, the Juhaynah began to spread around the Nile River to the east and west, converting the local peoples they encountered as they moved.

The northern Juhaynah consider themselves ARABS, since they speak ARABIC, and they practice Islam almost exclusively. Some groups inhabiting the portion of the Sudan further to the south, though, prefer to be called Africans and are either Christian or remain faithful to their traditional African religions.

Primarily nomadic, the Juhaynah are divided into subgroups, including the Kababish, BAGGARA, Kawahla, and Shukriyah, who make their living herding either cattle or camels.

See also: ASWAN (Vol. I); DARFUR (Vols. II, III); NILE RIVER (Vol. I); NUBIA (Vol. I); PASTORALISM (Vol. I).

K

kabaka Title for the king of the GANDA (Baganda) people of BUGANDA. The Ganda trace the origin of their kingdom to the legendary ruler Kintu, who, during the fourteenth century, became the first king, or kabaka, of the Ganda people.

The kabaka held supreme authority within the kingdom. However, the kabaka was not considered divine or sacred, nor was he associated with any gods. He was, instead, simply a monarch who reigned in a feudal-like system of government.

Chiefs appointed by the kabaka ruled over the various regions of the kingdom, and the kabaka had full authority to dismiss, promote, or transfer these chiefs. Chiefs, therefore, tended to remain extremely loyal to the kabaka. However, the kabaka did not rely on this loyalty. Rather, the kabaka appointed another group of officers, the *mutongole*, as lesser chiefs, who were given authority over large estates and their people and who were used by the kabaka to spy on the greater chiefs.

Because the Ganda did nor practice primogeniture, an elder senior counselor selected the kabaka from among men whose father or grandfather had been a kabaka. Once selected, the kabaka ruled for life. The system provided no way to depose him.

See also: GOVERNMENT, SYSTEMS OF (Vol. II).

Kaffa (Kafa, Kefa) African kingdom established in the forested mountain range of southwestern ETHIOPIA. Kaffa, known for its abundant rainfall, lush vegetation, and unusual animal species, is probably the area where COFFEE was first cultivated for export.

It is thought that Arab farmers first cultivated the coffee plant and brewed a beverage called *qahwah,* which became so popular that the plant and its beans quickly became lucrative export items. Other trade items in Kaffa included cattle, horses, musk, and IVORY, along with manufactured CLOTH, IRON spears, and daggers.

> The discovery of coffee's stimulating effects have been explained by a popular Ethiopian legend involving a young goatherd named Kalid. The story tells how Kalid observed the animated behavior of his goats after they consumed the red berries of a plant that grew on the mountain slopes. When the young boy tasted the plant, he also became animated, so he brought the beans to a nearby monastery. The monks there discovered the invigorating properties of a brew made from the roasted beans and felt that it might help them to stay alert during the long hours that they spent praying. One of the monks then took a coffee plant to Lake Tana, where it was cultivated and came into widespread use by local people.

The indigenous people of Kaffa, believed to have been the Minjo, relied on hereditary rule to establish their kings, who took the title *tato*. One of their earliest known rulers was Minjo Tato, who became king in 1390. Crowned rulers in Kaffa were reportedly subject to the control of the Mikrichos, a council of governing priests who controlled succession to the throne. From the capital city situated at Andrachi, the *tato* and council of priests dominated the border states, eventually establishing an empire consisting of the regions of Jimma, Kulo, Konta, Koshya Mocha, and Enareya. These states were populated by ethnic groups that included the SIDAMO and OROMO. Forced to pay tribute to the *tato*, these groups eventually created widespread rebellion in the region. During the fifteenth century, Emperor ZARA YAKOB (r. 1434–1468) promoted CHRISTIANITY in the region, but following his death, the influence of the Christian faith diminished, and traditional religious practices were restored.

See also: ETHIOPIA (Vol. I); KAFFA (Vol. III): OROMO (Vol. III).

Further reading: Harold G. Marcus, *A History of Ethiopia* (Berkeley: University of California Press, 1994).

Kalahari Desert Large, arid region in present-day Botswana, NAMIBIA, and SOUTH AFRICA inhabited by the BANTU and !Kung San peoples since precolonial times. The Kalahari lacks permanent surface water, and the only landforms that rise above the uniformly level plain are occasional outcroppings of old rock that form hills in the northwest, southeast, and southwest regions.

While technically not dry enough to be classified as a desert, the Kalahari is largely unsuitable for any form of agriculture. Its early inhabitants, the Bantu, !Kung, and San, subsisted by hunting, foraging, and limited cattle herding. Due to the severe climate, little has changed in the Kalahari since before the period of European colonization. In the late 1400s and early 1500s, the Kalahari was a barrier to the eastward expansion of the pastoral HERERO people and the agriculturalist OVAMBO people. The increasing competition for arable and grazing land between these peoples would lead to a series of bitter wars between them during the 1800s.

See also: !KUNG (Vol. I); LANGUAGES, MAJOR (Vol. I); SAN (Vol. I).

Kamba East and central African BANTU speakers who have long inhabited the highland regions of KENYA. The Kamba are descendants of the KIKUYU ethnic group, and they trace their ancestral homeland to the plains below Mount Kilimanjaro. In the sixteenth century, the powerful MAASAI people forced the Kamba to flee and settle in their present location.

Traditionally agriculturalists, the Kamba have also maintained substantial herds of cattle, sheep, and goats. They were also shrewd MERCHANTS who later controlled the coastal trade of Kenya for many years because of their access to IVORY from the interior.

Kamba society is patrilineal, with extended families living on large homesteads. Several homesteads form a village. No chieftains dominate Kamba society; rather, individuals are organized into age sets with the eldest members forming village councils. The traditional religion of the Kamba people focuses on the belief in a supreme god and ancestral spirits.

See also: AGE SETS (Vol. I); AGRICULTURALISTS (Vol. I); ANCESTOR WORSHIP (Vol. I); INDIAN OCEAN TRADE (Vol. II); KAMBA (Vol. III); SWAHILI COAST (Vol. III).

Kanajeji (r. c. 1390–1410) *Ruler of the Kano kingdom.*

Kanajeji was *sarki*, or king, of the powerful KANO kingdom from around the end of the fourteenth to the beginning of the fifteenth centuries. Under Kanajeji, the inhabitants of Kano were a mixture of both converts to ISLAM and adherents of the traditional non-Muslim religion. Kanajeji is best known for introducing IRON helmets, chain mail, and *lifidi* (protective armor for horses) to the Kano armies, all of which aided them in their aggressive southward expansion of the kingdom during his reign.

See also: HAUSA STATES (Vol. II).

Kanem-Bornu Trade-reliant empire, centered in the area of Lake CHAD, that lasted from the ninth to the nineteenth centuries.

At various times during their histories, Kanem and BORNU were separate states; at other times they were merged. In general, however, the histories of the countries are so closely aligned that they are usually discussed together.

According to records kept by Arab scholars, the kingdom of Kanem existed well before the ninth century. Its subjects were a pastoral BERBER and Negroid people who settled in the area in the seventh century. Kanem's kings, or *mais* as they were called, ruled with the help of a council of peers, although the people at large apparently considered their kings to be deities. According to one of the more prominent tales of the kingdom's history, the Kanem-Bornu *mais* were descendants of Sayf Ibn Dhu Yazan. This charismatic Arab is believed to have migrated to Lake Chad from the SAHARA and is said to have begun the SEFUWA dynasty that ruled Kanem-Bornu for a millennium.

As the empire expanded, the Sefuwa established control over the KANURI as well as the BULALA, or SAO, people from the Lake Chad area. From the start, however, the empire was based more on trade than on military might. Its capital was NJIMI, northeast of Lake Chad, which made the Kanem Empire a natural location for trade within North Africa, Egypt, the Nile Valley, and SUB-SAHARAN AFRICA.

In the tenth century, ARABS brought ISLAM to the area, and, by the end of the next century, Kanem's Mai UMME (r.

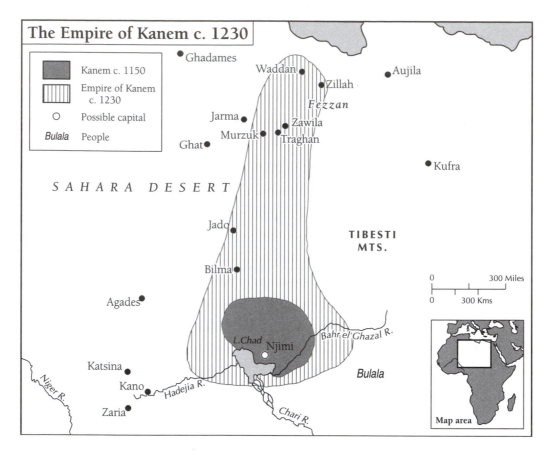

The Empire of Kanem c. 1230

Kanem c. 1150
Empire of Kanem c. 1230
Possible capital
Bulala People

SAHARA DESERT

TIBESTI MTS.

Ghadames
Waddan
Zillah
Aujila
Fezzan
Jarma
Zawila
Murzuk
Traghan
Ghat
Kufra
Jado
Bilma
Agades
L.Chad   Njimi   Bahr el Ghazal R.
Katsina
Kano   Hadejia R.   *Bulala*
Zaria   Chari R.
Niger R.

0   300 Miles
0   300 Kms

Map area

c. 1085–1097) had abandoned his people's traditional religion and converted to Islam. This association with Islam brought Kanem-Bornu into contact with the Arab world and its ideas, but the extent of this influence often was limited, as the populace did not wholeheartedly embrace Islam and refused to forsake their ancient beliefs.

For the next two centuries, Kanem's kings enlarged the kingdom through warfare, using nobles and slaves trained as soldiers to do the fighting. Mai Dunama DIB-BALEMI (r. 1221–1259) oversaw the greatest growth of the Kanem Empire. Dibbalemi's reign marked the beginning of the establishment of diplomatic ties with North African kings; it also saw the establishment of lodgings, in CAIRO, for those traveling to MECCA. Dibbalemi also undertook religious wars against neighboring states.

Eventually Kanem's empire extended as far west as the Niger River, east to Wadai (now part of eastern Chad), and north into the Sahara Desert. This huge area, from Lake Chad to the HAUSA STATES, was directly in the path of those wanting to trade in North Africa, which was of enormous strategic advantage to the Kanem. Another result of this accumulation of land and power was that the Kanem people became increasingly settled, exchanging their nomadic lives for sedentary ones. In time, however, dynastic disputes and other problems caused a decline, and, by the late thirteenth century, the Kanem Empire had begun to lose control of much of its territory.

Dibbalemi's death about 1259 also brought into the open a struggle for control among his sons, which eventually led to armed strife. The most distant peoples of the Kanem Empire saw no reason to continue to pay taxes to a preoccupied and chaotic government, and Kanem's power dissipated.

Once the Kanem Empire began to wane in the late 1300s, the internal struggles escalated. The Bulala people, who had chafed under the control of Kanem, rebelled around 1380. They fought against Kanem aggressively until Kanem and their leader, Mai Umar Idrismi, had no choice but to leave their capital at Njimi and move to the western shore of Lake Chad. The Bulala killed five of the six *mais* between 1376 and 1400, leaving the kingdom in disarray. This period also led to warfare between the armies of the various leaders who hoped to ascend to the throne.

This internal strife was the beginning of the end for Kanem power and the emergence of Bornu as a regional power. For the next several centuries, Bornu dominated the Kanem-Bornu alliance. Bornu rulers, like those of Kanem, were converts to Islam. Also like the Kanem *mais*, the Bornu retained some traditional practices. In the Bornu culture women had significant power; the queen mother, for example, played an important role, advising the sitting king and enjoying chief-like status. Kings, for their part, were elected by a group of elders and given divine status, a traditional system that predated the people's conversion to Islam.

Like Kanem before it, Bornu thrived on trade. Among Bornu's exports were slaves, eunuchs, livestock, saffron-dyed CLOTH, and salt.

The early years of the fifteenth century saw yet more turbulence in the kingdom. Between c. 1400 and 1475 there were fifteen different kings. Mai Ali Dunamami, who took control in 1472, stabilized the Kanem-Bornu kingdom and solidified control of the outlying areas. He also established a new capital in NGAZARGAMU. Located west of Lake Chad, it was the first real capital of Kanem-Bornu since the capture of Njimi.

See also: KANEM-BORNU (Vol. III).

Kangaba Ancient dynasty in the western SUDAN, believed to have been established before 1000; it became the foundation of the great MALI EMPIRE.

The small kingdom of Kangaba on the Upper Niger River was inhabited by the MANDINKA (also called Mandingo), a West African people who spoke a MANDE language and who acted as mediators in the GOLD trade of the area. In the thirteenth century, SUMANGURU (d. c. 1235), the ruler of neighboring KANIAGA, invaded Kangaba. Mandinka oral tradition says that Sumanguru murdered eleven of the twelve royal heirs, sparing only SUNDIATA (d. c. 1255), who could not walk and was not seen as a threat. Sundiata, whose name means "hungry lion," went into exile, where he learned to walk and became an expert hunter and horseman. Sundiata then returned to Kangaba to claim his rightful place on the throne. Aided by a coalition of Mandinka chieftains as well as by the support of his people, Sundiata won the Battle of KIRINA in 1235 and restored Kangaba to its people.

Sundiata and his successors expanded the borders of Kangaba until they included most of present-day SENEGAL, GAMBIA, and Mali. Parts of modern BURKINA-FASO, Guinea, Niger, and MAURITANIA also fell within his empire's borders. This expansion was the beginning of the Empire of Mali, and the name *Mali* succeeded the name *Kangaba*.

The Mali Empire remained strong until it grew too large to be controlled by its military resources. GAO rebelled around 1400, TIMBUKTU was taken by the TUAREGS, and the MOSSI people of Burkina-Faso refused to obey their Mali ruler. As a result, by about 1550, Mali had declined as a political power.

Kaniaga (Diafunu) Kingdom of the SUSU, a sub-group of the MANDE-speaking SONINKE, located in present-day Mali. Kaniaga was a thriving chiefdom by the eighth century, and it remained a major power as the trans-Saharan trade economy reached its peak after the ninth century.

In the thirteenth century, Kaniaga was ruled by SUMANGURU, a despotic leader who lost his kingdom to the MANDINKA warrior chief SUNDIATA. Kaniaga was then incorporated into the MALI EMPIRE.

See also: KANGABA (Vol. II); KIRINA (Vol. II); TRANS-SAHARAN TRADE ROUTES (Vol. II).

Kano Capital of the Kano state in northern Nigeria; historically one of the largest and most powerful of the ancient HAUSA STATES.

The Kano area boasts a rich past dating back hundreds of years. The Kano kingdom was supposedly founded c. 999 by a descendant of a famed Hausa forefather. Growing trade in the area quickly helped Kano become an important commercial center. ISLAM, introduced to Kano by way of the MALI EMPIRE, was adopted in the mid-fourteenth century and has remained the dominant religion.

Kano's prosperity sparked long-lasting rivalries with other Hausa states, particularly with neighboring KATSINA, which was the largest and most politically influential state in Hausaland. As a result, throughout its history Kano was forced to become a tributary state of several rival powers, including BORNU and the SONGHAI Empire.

See also: CITY-STATES (Vol. II); JUKUN (Vol. III); KANO (Vol. III).

Kano Chronicle Document that traces the history of the HAUSA STATE of KANO, an important CITY-STATE and emirate in northern Nigeria. Many historians consider the chronicle to be not only a critical account of Kano itself but also the most important native history of the Hausa people. It is believed to be the oldest written record of the area, and it is said to document the ancient kingdom from about the year 1000 to the early twentieth century.

The chronicle follows the developments of Kano, from its founding as one of the Hausa Bakwai ("Seven True Hausa States") in the year 999 by its first king, BAGAUDA. It traces the growth of the kingdom, its dealings and competition with the other Hausa city-states, and the introduction of ISLAM to the city by fourteenth-century religious scholars from the MALI EMPIRE.

See also: KANO (Vol. III); KANO CHRONICLE (Vol. III).

Kanuri Muslim people who have lived in the region of present-day Niger and Nigeria for about 1,000 years; also the language spoken by this group.

The Kanuri have Muslim roots that date back to the eleventh century, when Mai, or King, KOSSOI converted to ISLAM c. 1010. Kossoi's successor, Mai UMME, converted to Islam in c. 1085.

By 1100, the Kanuri settled in KANEM, replacing a confederation of a variety of ethnic groups. During the thirteenth century, the Kanuri were led by Mai Dunama DIBBALEMI (r. c. 1210–1259). He converted to Islam and declared a JIHAD, or holy war, against his neighbors. His military forces included more than 40,000 horses, and his reign began what has become known as a major period of conquest in Africa.

The commercial traffic that went through northern Africa passed through the Kanuri territory. Seeing much military and commercial growth in Kanem, the Kanuri subsequently abandoned their nomadic lifestyle to adopt a more sedentary one. At the peak of their success, the Kanuri dominated the territory from LIBYA to Lake CHAD to the HAUSA STATES.

During the thirteenth century, civil conflicts in the Kanuri territory began to disable the empire. By the end of that century, Mai Ibrahim Nikale, who had ruled for about twenty-five years, was assassinated after killing one of his sons. In the early fourteenth century, four Kanem rulers were killed, all sons of Mai Abd Allah ibn Kaday. In the final years of that century, four other rulers of Kanem were killed.

The next *mai*, Umar Ibn Idris, found it necessary to move the capital to BORNU, another Kanuri kingdom that lay south and west of Lake Chad. The Kanuri state of Bornu experienced rapid growth after the fall of the SONGHAI. Later, under the reign of Idris Alawma (1575–1610), the Kanuri united the kingdom of Bornu with Kanem, again creating a very large empire, KANEM-BORNU, that lasted until the nineteenth century.

See also: KANEM-BORNU (Vol. III); KANURI (Vol. III).

Karagwe East African chiefdom; during the mid-fourteenth century, it was briefly a part of the powerful KITARA state.

Kitara, founded by the BUGANGAIZI, was an important, albeit short-lived, political force in East Africa, and Karagwe was part of Kitara until the empire's dissolution around 1398. By the beginning of the fifteenth century, the BANTU-speaking Basiita people ruled Karagwe under the leadership of Ruhinda, a wealthy pastoralist chief. Ruhinda governed Karagwe from 1405 until his death in 1447.

See also: BUNYORO-KITARA (Vol. II); KARAGWE (Vol. III).

Karamojong (Bakaramoja, Ikaramojong, Karimojon) East African NILOTIC pastoralists whose lineage can be linked with the Jie, Teso, Dodoth, Labwor, and Turkana peoples. The seminomadic Karamojong are one of the largest ethnic groups in UGANDA. From about 1000 to 1600, their ancestors migrated south from areas in southern ETHIOPIA and the SUDAN. The exact origins of the Karamojong are unknown, but their oral tradition points to either KAFFA or possibly the Omo River valley as

their original homeland. They first moved toward a plateau in western KENYA that they called Moru Apolon and then continued on to locations north of Mount Elgon. The area in which they subsequently settled became known as the Karamoja region.

For centuries the Karamojong have engaged almost exclusively in cattle herding, the traditional form of subsistence. Despite drought and disease, over the centuries the Karamojong have been able to raise substantial herds for their milk, meat, and blood. Their entire culture centers around these prized animals that not only provide nourishment but also serve as a symbol of social status.

See also: KARAMOJONG (Vol. III); PASTORALISM (Vol. I).

Karanga BANTU-speaking people who have lived in the eastern region of modern ZIMBABWE since around 950; the rulers of the great MWENE MATAPA Empire, which flourished from c. 1450 to c. 1650, were Shona peoples, a sugroup of the Karanga.

Beginning about 950, the Karanga inhabited the area long known as the Acropolis, supplanting the indigenous KHOISAN-speaking peoples. In time, the Karanga established extensive trading networks that reached as far as the Indian Ocean. Their most important trade items included GOLD, IVORY, and salt.

The center of the Karanga Empire was located in the valley below the Acropolis known as the Great Enclosure or the GREAT ZIMBABWE, meaning "stone dwelling." This massive compound, which was built about 1200, included a tall, cone-shaped structure, small houses, and a surrounding wall of granite block that measured 32 feet (10 m) high and 800 feet (244 m) long.

About 1420, however, the Karanga abandoned Great Zimbabwe, probably because the city had grown so large that the surrounding land could no longer support it. By the beginning of the sixteenth century, the Karanga Empire had moved north, toward the Zambezi River, and had evolved into the Mwene Matapa state, which would dominate the region for the next 200 years.

See also: CHANGAMIRE (Vol. II); ROZWI KINGS (Vol. III).

Karifa, Mansa (Khalifa, Mansa) (c. thirteenth century) *Minor king who briefly ruled the Mali Empire (c. 1200–1400).*

Mansa Karifa was one of several sons of SUNDIATA, a strong and successful ruler of the MALI EMPIRE. After Sundiata's death (c. 1255), Karifa's brother, Mansa Uli, ruled Mali, increasing the empire's territory during his brief reign (1260–1270). After Mansa Uli's death, Karifa and his brother Wati (also known as Wali) fought for control of the empire. Both had brief, uneventful reigns that jeopardized Mali's strength and influence. Few details are known of Karifa's leadership, but his rule generally is considered a period of disorder and political weakness.

After Karifa's death, the battle for control of Mali continued. First, ABU BAKR (d. c. 1285), a grandson of Sundiata, took the throne. He was then overthrown by SAKURA (d. c. 1300), a former servant who became a general. After Sakura's death, Sundiata's royal line again was restored to power.

Kasonko earthworks Series of ancient ditches along the Katonga River in the grasslands of what is now western UGANDA. The earthworks at Kasonko were dug by the BACHWEZI for unknown reasons. Like the neighboring BIGO and Munsa earthworks, which date from the fifteenth century, the Kasonko ditches measure more than 10 feet (3 m) deep. Due to the absence of archaeological evidence at Kasonko, the purpose of the ditches remains unclear. However, excavations at Bigo and Munsa suggest that the structures there served some sort of agricultural or pastoral function. Some speculate that the earthworks formed a monument around which the Bachwezi would gather to worship hero spirits.

See also: ARCHITECTURE (Vol. II).

Katsina City and emirate in north-central Nigeria near the border with Niger; one of seven major HAUSA STATES, dating back to the eleventh century. For hundreds of years, Katsina played a vital role as a center of trade, culture, politics, and religion.

Katsina's history can be traced to the tenth or eleventh century, when it was founded and named after Kacina, a princess of the kingdom of DAURA, some 50 miles (80 km) to the east. The city began as a walled-in community that, over time, added other walled-in sections for new arrivals. This gave Katsina a unique architectural structure that reflected its growth and diversity.

See also: KATSINA (Vol. III).

Keita clan Traders from the upper Niger Valley who ruled over the West African MALI EMPIRE.

The Keita, originally from lower Niger, were MANDE-speaking traders. In 1235, they defeated the armies of the GHANA EMPIRE and gained control of the newly formed kingdom of Mali. Over the next 200 years, the Keita expanded their empire eastward, conquering the important trans-Saharan trade cities of TIMBUKTU, JENNE, and GAO. At the height of its power, the Keita's empire expanded over much of present-day SENEGAL, GAMBIA, and Mali, as well as parts of MAURITANIA, Niger, BURKINA-FASO, and GUINEA.

One of the clan's best-known members was SUNDIATA Keita (r. 1235–1255). A Malinke warrior known as the "Lion Prince," Sundiata was the founder and first ruler of the Mali Empire. According to legend, Sundiata miraculously overcame a childhood disability that made him unable to walk. He later became one of the most powerful princes in the Keita clan, defeating the empire of Ghana and building a new capital in the city of NIANI (also called Mali).

The Mali Empire flourished under the rule of Sundiata's descendents, who continued the Keita clan's dominance over the kingdom. Mansa MUSA (r. 1312–1337), one of Sundiata's relatives, encouraged the institution of ISLAM as the imperial religion of Mali. Musa was recognized as the Islamic caliph of West Africa and used his power to consolidate Mali's imperial authority. Under Musa's influence, trade flourished. New GOLD reserves were discovered, and Timbuktu became an important center for Islamic education.

By 1430, the Keita's control over Mali began to decline. When the autonomous kingdoms in the Mali confederacy asserted their independence, Mali's armies were unable to retain their power. By the close of the fifteenth century, the kingdom of SONGHAI had captured what remained of the Keita clan and the Mali Empire.

Kenya Modern East African country on the Indian Ocean that is home to more than thirty different peoples. One of the earliest groups to inhabit the region were the KHOIKHOI, who subsisted primarily by hunting and foraging. Other early residents included Kushite agriculturalists and NILOTIC peoples, who migrated to areas in western Kenya from their homelands in the SUDAN. Kenyan chiefdoms prior to the era of European colonization were largely decentralized, with most groups practicing agriculture and animal herding, although both internal and coastal trade played an important role. Food, cattle, salt, IRON tools, and POTTERY were common trade commodities.

Limited commercial activity along the Kenyan coast greatly expanded with the arrival of ARAB traders, beginning in the eleventh century. IVORY, GOLD, beads, CLOTH, rhinoceros horns, tortoiseshell, and slaves were valued export items.

As the Arabs intermarried with coastal Kenyans, a new people, the Swahili, emerged. Beginning in the twelfth century, the Swahili dominated Kenyan coastal trade, and by the fifteenth century, the port town of MOMBASA was one of the most important trading centers along the East African coast.

When the Portuguese arrived in the late fifteenth century, they aligned themselves with the Swahili in an attempt to gain control of coastal trade. However, tension between the Portuguese and Swahili soon developed, and, in 1529, the Portuguese gained autonomous control over the Kenyan coast.

The word *swahili* is derived from the Arabic word *sahel*, meaning "coast." The Swahili, then, were known as the "people of the coast." The same Arabic word is used to name the southern border of the SAHARA, the Sahel.

See also: INDIAN OCEAN TRADE (Vol. II); KENYA (Vol. III); PORTUGAL AND AFRICA (Vol. III); SWAHILI COAST (Vol. II).

Keta Coastal town located on the Gulf of Guinea in present-day Ghana, between the mouth of the VOLTA RIVER and the modern border with Togo. As early as 1475, Keta was an important trade center of the Anlo people, a subgroup of the EWE. When European traders arrived in the latter half of the fifteenth century, Keta, which means "head of the sand" in Ewe, was a prominent Atlantic coast market for the trading of GOLD, silver, IVORY, and spices.

See also: ANLO (Vol. III); KETA (Vol. III).

Kharijite Fundamentalist Muslim sect to which the BERBER peoples of North Africa converted during the eighth century.

Originally, the Kharijites, or Khariji sect, were supporters of Ali (r. 656–661), the fourth caliph and son-in-law of the prophet MUHAMMAD (c. 570–632), during the civil war in Arabia between Ali's supporters and the UMAYYADS over control over the Caliphate, often called the Arab Empire. Unlike Shiites, the Karijites held that anyone, even a servant, rightfully could be elected caliph if he was pious and morally pure. For their fanatical devotion to Ali's cause and puritanical, deeply fundamentalist beliefs, the Kharijites have been called the earliest Islamic sect. The movement was suppressed in its native Iraq during the seventh century but, in more moderate forms, it spread to eastern Arabia, North Africa, and eastern Africa, carried by missionaries and believers, where it survives even today.

Kharijite doctrines appealed to the Berber peoples in North Africa because they seemed to offer alternatives to Arab political domination of the Muslim world and allow rebellion against a ruler when the ruler acted in an unrighteous manner. Berber resentment against the Arabs stemmed in part from the way Berber warriors were treated when they served in the Muslim armies that invaded Spain (al-ANDALUS) in 711. They were treated as *malawi*, or clients, of the Arab states, paid less for their services, not allowed to share in the spoils, all of which went to Arabs, and forced to offer human tribute—slaves, especially female slaves—to the Arab rulers.

In 740, the Berbers rebelled against Arab rule in Tangier. By 742, they had taken all of Algeria. At the same time, all of Tripolitania in North Africa was won over to Kharijite control by the conversion of the Berber peoples who lived in the region.

In 750, the Abassid dynasty (r. 750–1278) overthrew the reigning UMAYYAD caliph in Damascus, moved the capital to Baghdad in present-day Iraq, and turned the focus of the Caliphate eastward, toward Persia. For the first time, the Caliphate did not rule over the entire Muslim world. In Egypt, North Africa, and Spain, local dynasties claimed the status of caliph, or ruler of the Muslim world. In North Africa, four separate Muslim states claimed power, one of which nominally accepted Abassid authority and three of which rejected it outright. The only state in Berber hands was the relatively insignificant state of Banu Midrar in Morocco. Its principal town, SIJILMASSA, was primarily a trading community. Banu Midrar fell to the FATIMIDS in 909.

See also: ISLAM, INFLUENCE OF (Vol. II).

Khoikhoi (Khoe Khoe, Namaqua, Khoi, Hottentots) Khoisan-speaking pastoralists of southern Africa. Seminomadic herders, the Khoikhoi have inhabited present-day NAMIBIA for the majority of the second millennium. Descendants of an ancient Ethiopian people, the Khoikhoi migrated south to Namibia in the fourteenth century, later moving on to the Cape of Good Hope. They subsisted by hunting, gathering, and raising sheep, cattle, and goats. Their handicraft skills included POTTERY, basketry, weaving, and metalworking.

When the Portuguese arrived in 1488, the Khoikhoi responded aggressively, killing dozens of the foreign invaders. The Portuguese slaughtered the Khoikhoi in large numbers several years later. By the mid-seventeenth century, European settlers had forced the Khoikhoi from their Cape homeland.

See also: KHOIKHOI (Vol. III); KHOISAN LANGUAGES (Vol. I); PASTORALISM (Vol. I); PORTUGAL AND AFRICA (Vol. III).

Kigali Capital city of present-day RWANDA, located in the rural highlands along the Ruganwa River. During the late fifteenth century, Kigali served as a major trade center of the TUTSI kingdom.

See also: RWANDA (Vol. III); TUTSI (Vol. III).

Kikuyu Language and people of East Africa living in present-day KENYA. Today numbering 4 million, the Kikuyu make up the largest percentage of Kenya's population. Although a well-defined Kikuyu ethnic group emerged only in the seventeenth century, it is theorized that the clans that made up the Kikuyu people began moving into Kenya from southern Somalia during the great BANTU MIGRATIONS of the first millennium. The merging of multiple cultures produced an eclectic mix of Kikuyu rituals over the centuries. From the Thagicu they adopted ceremonial dances and initiation rites, which became common in Kikuyu culture. Young men and women were fully integrated into the social circles of the village (*itura*) after circumcision and clitoridectomy ceremonies. After the initiation, the males became warriors, and the females' social responsibilities increased beyond the village proper.

According to oral tradition, Ngai, the Kikuyu God, commanded Gikuyu, the forefather of the Kikuyu, to build his home near Mount Kenya. Gikuyu settled in the center of the land. It was full of fig trees, so he named it the Tree of the Building Site (Mukurue wa Gathanga). Ngai sent Gikuyu a wife, Mumbi, who bore Gikuyu nine daughters. Along with one other child, these women became the progenitors of the ten ancestral clans of the Kikuyu.

As early as the eighth century, the proto-Kikuyu groups practiced clearing their woodlands for agriculture. Preparing land to sustain a single family required approximately 150 days of labor, so groups of men joined together to accelerate the process. These small groups (*mbari*) would clear a large plot of land and then divide it among themselves. Once the land was cleared, the *mbaris* served as the political leaders of the area. The revered elders in each *mbari* were given the most power. Subsequent settlers (*ahoi*) could not become members of the ruling *mbari* council.

Famine was always a major problem in East Africa. Kikuyu agriculture suffered from the arid climate, and regular harvest failure affected the local *mbari* communities. Approximately every seventy years, a major catastrophe struck that extended beyond the local *mbari*, and these severe famines resulted in massive death throughout the Kikuyu lands.

From the Thagicu the proto-Kikuyu learned irrigation techniques that became vital to their expanding agricultural economy. Combined with their enterprising spirit, irrigation allowed them to produce enough food to sell to neighboring people, such as the KAMBA and MAASAI. They initially grew BANANAS, yams, millet, and sorghum. (Maize, CASSAVA, and rice became important items in the nineteenth century when the Kikuyu traded with European MERCHANTS.)

See also: KIKUYU (Vol. III).

Kilwa (Kilwa Kisiwani) One-time trading center on the East African coast. ARABS and Iranian MERCHANTS established Kilwa as a trade center in the late tenth century. Spurred by a demand for GOLD and IVORY, Kilwa became the preeminent East Coast trading city by about 1200. Kilwa was able to gain control of the gold exports from SOFALA, a port city south of the Zambezi River, through which MWENE MATAPA gold flowed. By the end of the fifteenth century, a series of internal political struggles greatly weakened the city's economic power. When the Portuguese seized Kilwa around 1505, Swahili traders responded by using other ports; within ten years the city's role as a principal gold-trading center was greatly diminished.

See also: ARAB COASTAL TRADE (Vol. II); HUSUNI KUBWA PALACE (Vol. II); KILWA (Vol. III); PORTUGAL AND AFRICA (Vol. III); SHIRAZI ARABS (Vol. II); SWAHILI COAST (Vols. II, III).

kingdoms and empires Historical records and the archaeological study of the ruins of palaces, mosques, royal cemeteries, and walled enclosures indicate that a substantial number of kingdoms and empires flourished in Africa between the fifth and the fifteenth centuries.

A kingdom is a large territory or political unit that has a monarchical form of government usually headed by a king or queen. An empire, on the other hand, consists of a number of states or territories united by conquest or by diplomatic means and ruled by a central sovereign authority. Before the period of European colonization, Africa had many kingdoms, some large, most small, but usually inhabited by a single people or by a dominant cattle-raising people and a subject agriculturalist people. The major indigenous empires of West Africa encompassed vast territories and many different peoples under a single ruler.

In the lands of North Africa, collectively known as the MAGHRIB ("West" in ARABIC), empires flourished between 534 and 1554: first Byzantium and then, after the rise of ISLAM, the Caliphate, the ALMORAVID Empire, the ALMOHAD Empire, and the Ottoman Empire. In SUB-SAHARAN AFRICA, both kingdoms under local rule and empires under central rule flourished. By the eleventh century, ancient Ghana had transformed itself from a kingdom into an empire and began the process that culminated in 1464 with the rise of SONGHAI, the largest indigenous empire in the history of Africa. The kingdoms and empires of Africa were often highly complex, stratified societies that developed from modest beginnings as obscure villages, as commercial centers or depots established along trade routes, or as agricultural settlements. Although each was governed by its own distinct political, social, and cultural beliefs, interregional trading may have influenced each other's practices.

Dynastic rule was a feature of some African kingdoms. A dynasty is a series of rulers from the same family or a select group that maintains ruling authority over several generations. The royal line of the Christian kingdom of ETHIOPIA offers one such example. Known as the SOLOMONIC DYNASTY, it dates back allegedly to the marriage, c. tenth century BCE, of the Jewish king Solomon and the mythical queen of Sheba. According to Ethiopian legend, the son of this union, Menelik I, was considered the first dynastic ruler of the nation. The rulers of the ZAGWE DYNASTY briefly occupied the region around the eleventh century, but they were violently overthrown by the Solomonic imperial warrior king YEKUNO AMLAK (r. 1270–1285), who restored the dynasty to power.

The Importance of Diversification and Specialization Many kingdoms evolved because, once populations became self-sustaining, areas of specialization could be developed. One segment of the population would serve as an agricultural labor force to raise crops for sustenance and trade while others developed specialized skills and thus generated additional sources of income to bolster the economy. Specialists often included CRAFTSPEOPLE, artists, and ironworkers, who produced articles for trade; specialized skills might include the ability to perform religious rites as a way to reinforce ancient moral codes and religious values. Armies capable of defending the kingdom's resources represented another form of specialization. The kingdoms of ILE-IFE, GREAT ZIMBABWE, and the KONGO show the effect of diversification and specialization on the development of kingdoms.

The twelfth-century YORUBA kingdom of Ife in present-day Nigeria was noted for its agricultural success in producing yams and oil palms and raising livestock. Ife expanded as a result of cooperative work and the joining of villages. It had a central ruler or king and a profoundly important religious focus that fostered many areas of specialization, including the production of artistic metalwork. The layout of Ife, which consisted of a royal compound on the city's interior and the farming community on the outskirts, served as one of several early models for the cosmopolitan city-state.

The kingdom of ZIMBABWE (c. 1200–1450) in southern Africa developed in a way similar to that of Ife, with farming serving as an important base. Although MAPUNGUBWE was the first kingdom in the region, the most notable was GREAT ZIMBABWE, which spread over 2.8 square miles (7.2 sq km) of open woodland and was encircled by hills. Like Ife, the city of Great Zimbabwe was enclosed by a large wall, known as the Great Enclosure, which measured nearly 40 feet (12 m) high and had a circumference of approximately 800 feet (244 m). Equally notable were the odd shaped boulders that marked Great Zimbabwe's Hill Complex as a site of religious activities.

During the fifteenth century, the Kongo Kingdom grew even larger than Zimbabwe. The Kongo Kingdom had landholdings of approximately 200,000 square miles (517,997 sq km) and a population estimated at between 4 and 5 million people. This large region consisted of six small states, each headed by a chief, who in turn was governed by the king, known as the *manikongo*. The Bakongo, the people of the Kongo kingdom, were primarily an agricultural society, but they also developed many diversified specialties that included weaving, ironwork, and the LOST-WAX PROCESS of casting metal that became valuable trade items.

The Importance of Trade The ability to engage in large-scale trade was also a common factor in many self-sustaining nations. The kingdom that began as KANEM, for example, was directly impacted by TRANS-SAHARAN TRADE ROUTES. In the early 1200s, it developed lucrative trade networks that included sending large shipments of salt from Bilma, Agram, and other neighboring regions into the Sahel. Kanem also supplied alum to Egypt and countries in the Maghrib, along with elephant tusks, ostrich feathers, live GIRAFFES, embroidered garments, and IRON weapons.

The most expansive trade links usually developed within regions that were in close proximity to the coast. Trade explains the rise of the SWAHILI COAST, made up of approximately 170 CITY-STATES on Africa's eastern coast, which were founded by Arab traders in the INDIAN OCEAN TRADE in the eighth century and later. These states extended along the coast from the southern region of Somalia to MOZAMBIQUE.

See also: KINGDOMS AND EMPIRES OF EASTERN AFRICA AND THE INTERIOR (Vol. II); KINGDOMS AND EMPIRES OF EQUATORIAL AFRICA (Vol. II); KINGDOMS AND EMPIRES OF THE LOWER GUINEA COAST (Vol. II); KINGDOMS AND EMPIRES OF THE MAGHRIB (Vol. II); KINGDOMS AND EMPIRES OF SENEGAMBIA (Vol. II); KINGDOMS AND EMPIRES OF THE WEST AFRICAN SAVANNA (Vol. II).

Further reading: J. D. Fage, *A History of Africa*, 3rd ed. (London: Routledge, 1995); I. Hrbek, ed., *General History of Africa*, Vol. 3: *Africa from the Seventh to the Eleventh Century* (Paris: UNESCO, 1989); Kevin

Shillington, *History of Africa* (New York: St. Martin's Press, 1995); G. T. Stride and Caroline Ifeka, *Peoples and Empires of West Africa* (New York: Africana Publishing Corporation, 1971).

kingdoms and empires of eastern Africa and the interior

There are two parts to the story of East Africa. One part traces the development of the Swahili trading states along the Indian Ocean coast that developed as a result of pre- and post-Islamic Arab trade. These mercantile CITY-STATES were wholly directed toward the sea and commerce and, until the nineteenth century, had little direct political impact on inland peoples; they were mainly transfer points for IVORY, GOLD, and other trade goods to their final destinations outside Africa. The second part records the rise of the inland kingdoms that resulted from the migration of BANTU-speaking peoples into the region.

Arab Coastal Kingdoms The East African coast was known to Greek and Roman traders of the first centuries CE. Arab traders settled in the region and intermarried with the local peoples, but there is no record of their living anywhere but in existing fishing and trading communities. The rise of Islam in the seventh and eighth centuries helped boost INDIAN OCEAN TRADE and the Arab presence along the coast. In the eighth century, Shiite refugees from the Arabian Peninsula who were fleeing persecution by the dominant Sunni sect settled along the East African coast. They also intermarried with the local peoples, learned their language, and began trading with the rest of the Muslim world. Arab writers of the time called this portion of the coast the "Land of ZANJ." By the thirteenth century, Arabs had also successfully established colonies along the eastern coast, including MOGADISHU, LAMU, MOMBASA, KILWA, PATE, and SOFALA where they traded slaves, ivory, and gold.

African ivory, easier to carve than ivory from India, was especially prized in China and even in India, where it was used to make ceremonial objects and sword hilts.

The city-states along the coasts were commercial rivals but rarely military rivals. One historian notes that until the Portuguese arrived in the fifteenth century, there is little record of piracy. Relations with the inland peoples were generally good as well; it was to the advantage of the commercial states to stay on good terms with the peoples who provided the goods that made their cities prosperous. There were occasional attacks from inland, often in retaliation for cattle raids or slave raids staged by

rulers of the coastal cities, notably the sultans of Kilwa, who got most of their wealth from the gold traded at Sofala far to the south and did not fear jeopardizing a portion of their wealth in the anticipation of more. The leaders of other coastal cities were more cautious.

The Arab coastal cities never developed any kind of central authority or transformed themselves into a united kingdom or trading empire. They maintained their independence until the early 1500s when the Portuguese began a systematic conquest of the East African coast.

Linguistic and archaeological evidence and the oral traditions of the modern peoples of the region provide most of the information available about the kingdoms of the interior before the nineteenth century.

Kingdoms of the East African Interior With some exceptions, the East African interior is the story of peoples rather than kingdoms. Governance was local—by clan or village—rather than by central authority. In northwestern Tanzania, for example, the Bantu-speaking Sukuma and Nyamwezi peoples were governed by chiefs called *ntemi*, whose duties were as much religious as political. This style of governance spread southward to include the Nyamwaga, the Hehe, the Safwa, and other peoples of the region. The other inhabitants of the region were the NILOTIC, or NILO-SAHARAN-speaking, peoples who moved into the northern and northwestern parts of East Africa under pressure from the Kushitic OROMO peoples from the Horn of Africa. They, as well as the Oromo, lacked a tradition of kingship; individual leaders were less important than the elders of the clans. Exceptions occurred where Nilotic peoples established dominance over peoples who may previously have evolved a form of political leadership. Such a kingdom was founded by the LUO people at the end of the fifteenth century, displacing an earlier CHWEZI KINGDOM, which had flourished in the lake region in the middle of the fourteenth century.

The lake region, great lakes region, and interlacustrine ("between the lakes") region are the names given to the area of land between Lakes Albert, Victoria, Tanganyika, Kyoga, and Edward.

The Chwezi are known for their development of several sites, including Mubende, BIGO, Bugoma, Kibengo and Munsa, in what is now west UGANDA. At Bigo are the remains of an extensive earthen and stone channel network more than 6 miles (9.6 km) long that is thought to have encompassed both the capital and an ample grazing pasture for herds of cattle. These ditches also indicate that the Chwezi were sufficiently well-organized to field large teams of laborers to construct such a system.

In the sixteenth century, the southern reaches of Chwezi rule were then taken over by the Hinda peoples and their Hima rulers; the northern reaches of Chwezi rule ended when they were overcome by the Nilotic Bito peoples from present-day Sudan, whose Luo dynasty established the BUNYORO-KITARA kingdom northwest of Lake Victoria in what is now Uganda. A form of local rulership first emerged in the early thirteenth century when the resident Bantu-speaking farmers began to form alliances with migratory Nilotic-speaking cattle herders, who became a higher caste. The fifteenth century saw the new Bito priest-kings mount a series of boundary expansions that began Bunyoro-Kitara's three centuries of prosperity. The empire remained powerful until the nineteenth century when the neighboring kingdom of Buganda rose to prominence.

Further south are the ruins of an extensive city called GREAT ZIMBABWE, after which the modern country of Zimbabwe is named. At its peak in the years 1100 to 1500, Great Zimbabwe supported a population estimated between 10,000 and 20,000 people in the city and the surrounding valley. Built by the Bantu-speaking Shona people and supported by a local economy based on agriculture and cattle, Great Zimbabwe was the center of a flourishing trading empire that sent gold and other trade goods as far east as the Arab trading towns on the Indian Ocean coast. There is some speculation based on the monoliths and sculptures found in the ruins that the city was also a religious center. By c. 1450, however, the balance of trade had shifted to the north, and the city was abandoned. It is thought that local resources, including salt, had dwindled to dangerously low levels.

South of Great Zimbabwe, on the borders of modern-day Zimbabwe, BOTSWANA, and SOUTH AFRICA, lay the city of MAPUNGUBWE, claimed by some to be South Africa's first urban center. Having started as a large village, it rapidly developed into a town of perhaps 10,000 people. Mapungubwe was abandoned during the twelfth century, very possibly because trade routes to the coast shifted northward and became dominated by Great Zimbabwe as it grew into its prime. Both Great Zimbabwe and Mapungubwe, as well as other settlements of the Bantu-speaking peoples, were generally ruled by chiefs who had considerable power but who had to consult the elders on matters of importance. These Bantu-speaking settlements were characterized by relatively strong stratification based on age, wealth, gender, and rank.

Further south, in the Transvaal region of modern-day South Africa, the Bantu speakers called Sotho-Tswana, from their dialect, began to gather into larger settlements in the thirteenth and fourteenth centuries. The Fokeng and the Rolong were two of a number of powerful dynastic chiefdoms that started to emerge in the region. The Fokeng chiefdoms spread southwards; the Rolong chiefdoms spread over lands controlled by peoples of the KALAHARI Desert, who either accepted Rolong rule or moved further west across the Kalahari. The Rolong cities developed as centers of farming, cattle raising, and commerce and featured a strongly hierarchical social structure. At its height in the late sixteenth century, Taung, the capital of the Rolong chiefdoms, had a population of as many as 15,000 to 20,000 people.

The great kingdom of the ZULU peoples, so closely associated with this region in the popular mind, did not rise until the eighteenth century.

See also: KINGDOMS AND EMPIRES (Vol. II); KINGDOMS AND EMPIRES OF EASTERN AFRICA AND THE INTERIOR (Vol. III); SWAHILI COAST (Vols. II, III).

kingdoms and empires of equatorial Africa

During the period prior to European colonization, the kingdoms lying on or near equatorial Africa were of BANTU origin and flourished between the thirteenth and seventeenth centuries. The kingdoms of Loango and KONGO on the Atlantic coast were situated slightly south of the equator. Their governments were generally built on clan structures. Agriculture, cattle-raising, and trade were the important elements in their economies.

The Atlantic coast kingdom of Loango, located north of the Congo River, was settled toward the end of the fifteenth century by the Bantu-speaking Vili people.

To the south of the Congo River was the powerful KONGO KINGDOM, which was founded by Bantu-speaking peoples in the fourteenth century. It occupied an area stretching into what is now Angola and the Democratic Republic of the Congo.

The Kongo Kingdom was ruled by a high king, the *manikongo*, who was elected by a council of the ruling elite and presided over lesser kings and local hereditary governors. The *manikongo* ruled over a network of settlements spread out over a large geographical area. By the fourteenth century, a sophisticated trading system with widely accepted currencies—including raffia CLOTH and shells—gave the various settlements of the Kongo kingdom a sense of unity.

See also: KINGDOMS AND EMPIRES (Vol. II); KONGO KINGDOM (Vol. III).

kingdoms and empires of the Lower Guinea coast

During the period prior to European colonization, the Lower Guinea coast was home to several important kingdoms. Below the Gambia River lived the MANDE, among the last people to settle along the coast. The kingdom of GABU that they founded c. 1250 in what is now Guinea-Bissau was originally a tributary state of the MALI EMPIRE and provided Mali, which controlled the GOLD-producing regions of the upper SENEGAL and upper Niger Rivers, with access to the sea. The later Gabu kingdom held power over various indigenous non-Mande chiefdoms, such as the

Kokoli, the Biafada, the Niumi, and the Badibu, that it conquered and reduced to servitude. Contributing to Gabu's autonomy in the late fifteenth and early sixteenth centuries was the weakening of Mali by attacks from the growing Songhai Empire. The Gabu state survived until the nineteenth century.

Further down the Lower Guinea coast were the kingdoms of BIGO, BONO, BENIN, ILE-IFE, OYO, Nri, Ganeboafo, and AKAN. They evolved from the cultures of coastal peoples such as the Akan, the BRONG, the EDO, the Guan, the GA, the Dangme, and the peoples of YORUBALAND, whose success was intrinsically linked to the development of IRON technology. This technology enabled them to produce more CROPS and the appealing trade goods that brought them prosperity.

The Brong of Akanland developed a preurban site at Bigo between 965 and 1125 in what became modern coastal Ghana. Bigo was a trading center from the eleventh century onwards and reached its peak in the fourteenth century. At its height, 5,000 people lived in the various compounds inside the settlement. Archaeological evidence indicates that the city was divided into five different districts soon after the establishment of the permanent trade route to JENNE in the first half of the fifteenth century. Little else is known about Bigo other than that leadership fell to clan leaders rather than to any central authority. Trade was more important than political life.

Bono, located where the forest and the savanna meet, was a center of trade for the region, especially for the gold and kola nuts (prized as a nonalcoholic stimulant by Muslims) that Mande traders from the north sought out for the Arab trade. Bono quickly dominated nearby settlements. Bigo and Bono gave rise to the Akan kingdoms of the fifteenth century.

The Ga and Dangme settled such sites as Gbegbe, Little Accra, Prampram, and Lolovo before 1400. These settlements supplanted Ladoku and Shai, which had risen to importance in the years 600 to 1400. Life in these newer settlements revolved around pastoralism, fishing, the production of salt, and the cultivation of crops such as corn.

The Yoruba people established both Ife and Oyo. According to tradition, the Ife Kingdom was ruled by ODUDUWA, who founded it in the eleventh century. Ife became one of the first kingdoms south of the Sahel. The sovereign power of the Ife's king was based on common territorial residence, common law, and his authority over the various Yoruba-speaking states. The city-states that made up the kingdom were organized around one city and its surrounding villages. Archaeological evidence suggests that the Ife dynasty was overthrown in the sixteenth century. This evidence includes the disappearance of potsherd floors—found throughout the kingdom from the twelfth to the sixteenth century—that suddenly vanished from the local architecture.

The Oyo kingdom, which is believed to have evolved at approximately the same time that Oduduwa founded Ife, was another major center. There, the Yoruba traded with peoples of the Sahel and the forest region. It became a substantial city by the fourteenth century but did not reach its zenith of imperial power until the seventeenth century.

The other major kingdom, Benin, was located southeast of Ife and became a kingdom in the twelfth century. In the fourteenth century the people of Benin asked the king of Ife to send them a prince. The rule of the prince, who was named Oranyan, was limited by the powers of the local chiefs, known as UZAMAS. It is not clear whether or not the *uzamas* were allies of the king of Ife because the fourth ruler of Oranyan's dynasty battled with the *uzamas* to gain more power. He ultimately succeeded, and upon his victory built a palace in his own honor and established titles as grants rather than birthrights. The *uzamas* did not concede, however, and still exercised their power until the fifteenth century, when an autocracy was installed under the leadership of EWUARE the Great (r. 1440–1480).

Under the oba, or king, Ewuare, the city of Benin was renamed Edo. During his rule, which lasted from 1440 to 1473, the political organization of the empire was created. Three groups of titled chiefs—the *uzamas*, the palace chiefs, and the newly created title of town chiefs—were responsible for Edo's leadership. During this period, Ewuare conquered the eastern and southern territories of the Yoruba, thereby consolidating the neighboring regions into his empire. Ewuare maintained Edo's independence from European control and established a peaceful relationship with the Portuguese upon their arrival to the region in 1472.

By the end of the fifteenth century, at least twelve small kingdoms of coastal peoples—including Afutu and Gomoa—could be counted among the major kingdoms of Benin and Oyo. These major kingdoms held the reins of trade with other states in the region, a factor that made it very easy for the Portuguese to tap into the vast trading network by establishing an economic relationship with a few major kingdoms.

See also: GOLD COAST (Vol. III); GUINEA (Vol. III); GABU (Vol. III); KINGDOMS AND EMPIRES (Vol. II); PORTUGAL AND AFRICA (Vol. III).

kingdoms and empires of the Maghrib The history of North Africa is almost entirely that of empires rather

than kingdoms. From 428 until 534, the kingdom of the Vandals, founded by invading Germanic warriors, supplanted the Western Roman Empire as ruler of the lands bordering the MEDITERRANEAN SEA. In 534, ALGERIA and Tunisia were subsumed into the Byzantine Empire, whose dominion lasted until 675, when all of North Africa fell to Muslim invaders and became part of the Caliphate, or Arab Empire, including the BERBER kingdoms of FEZZAN and LIBYA in central North Africa. In 909, Algeria and Tunisia fell under the power of the FATAMID dynasty, which ruled the region until 1015, and then the Hammadid dynasty, which ruled from 1015 until 1152. The ALMORAVID Empire, centered in Morocco, and the Berber ALMOHAD Empire contended for dominion from 1152 until 1360, when the Almohad Empire gained firm control and united the MAGHRIB for the first time under a single ruler. The region remained under Almohad control until it became part of the Ottoman Empire in 1554.

Throughout the fifth through fourteenth centuries and later, the cities of the Maghrib were the African end points of the vast trans-Saharan networks of trade routes that brought gold, foodstuffs and metalwork from SUB-SAHARAN AFRICA for shipment to Europe, the Middle East, and other lands that ringed the Mediterranean. The African goods were traded for European textiles, copper, beads, jewelry, and other items.

See also: ISLAM, INFLUENCE OF (Vol. II); KINGDOMS AND EMPIRES (Vol. II); OTTOMAN EMPIRE (Vol. III); TRANS-SAHARAN TRADE ROUTES (Vol. II).

kingdoms and empires of Senegambia

Arab historians of the tenth and eleventh century writing about the SENEGAL RIVER mention a number of black African states along its banks, the most important of which were TEKRUR and SILLA, just up river from the salt-exporting coastal town of Awil. It is thought that Tekrur, founded by the ancestors of the TUKULOR people, was established as early as the first century CE. By the tenth and eleventh centuries, it had become an orderly kingdom with a large army and an important commercial center, shipping GOLD and salt to North Africa in exchange for wool, COPPER, and BEADS AND JEWELRY, among other items. The local economy depended on farming, raising cattle, camels, and goats, and weaving the CLOTH that gave Tekrur considerable fame. Tekrur was one of the first kingdoms in Western Africa to accept ISLAM and became for a time the staging area for a JIHAD, or holy war, against elements of the SANHAJA BERBERS, who were persecuting Muslim missionaries.

By the eleventh century, the GHANA EMPIRE, located further inland between the Niger and the Senegal Rivers, was the most important power in West Africa and had incorporated Tekrur as a semi-independent state within its empire. Eventually, Tekrur joined forces with the militant Islamic force later known as the ALMORAVIDS in a war

that led to the conquest in 1076 of Ghana's capital at Kumbi. Ghana's fall, however, did not increase Tekrur's power. The FULANI and WOLOF peoples, among others, carved kingdoms from Tekrur territory and weakened it. The Wolof Empire, originally a confederation of small, independent village-states in Walo, eventually consisted of the states of Kayor, Baol, and Walo and the former SERER states of Sine and Saloum, the rulers of each acknowledging kinship with the Wolof ruler, known as the *burba jolof*.

The Wolof system of government, based on personal wealth and the preservation of personal privilege and power, became one of the most autocratic systems of government in West Africa. Hereditary GRIOTS sang the praises of the divine leader and their aristocratic masters and transmitted the history of the people from generation to generation. A rigid caste system of royalty, nobility, free persons, and a class of forced laborers existed. Military service was an important element in Wolof life. It is reported that in the early sixteenth century the Wolof Empire could field an army of 10,000 cavalry and 100,000 foot soldiers. Islam made almost no inroads in this society, which owed its achievements to few outside influences. The empire began to decline in the sixteenth century when Kayor, one of its constituent states, asserted its independence.

The former Serer states were similar to the Wolof Empire in their deification of the king, or *bur*, and their rigid class structure. At the top was an influential warrior class from which rulers, soldiers, judges, and tax collectors were selected; at the bottom were those bound to domestic and agricultural service. The underclass contibuted to the growth of the Serer states, though, through their advanced farming techniques, which included crop rotation and the swampland cultivation of rice. The Serer states vehemently resisted conversion to Islam.

See also: KINGDOMS AND EMPIRES (Vol. II); SENEGAL (Vol. III); SENEGAMBIA (Vol. III); WOLOF EMPIRE (Vol. III).

kingdoms and empires of the West African savanna

The West African savanna was home to the three great empires of Africa before 1450—GHANA, MALI, and SONGHAI—as well as numerous smaller, often tributary, kingdoms.

Ghana Empire The oldest empire in West Africa, founded according to some scholars as early as 300 CE, ancient Ghana was a powerful GOLD-trading kingdom situated between the Senegal and Niger Rivers, 500 miles (805 km) northwest of the modern coastal state of Ghana. Originally called Wagadu by its SONINKE founders, the kingdom later adopted the name *Ghana*, or "war chief," after the title of the ruler, who enjoyed semidivine status as both king and chief priest of all the traditional cults.

By 1068, Ghana was the largest and wealthiest state in West Africa. The capital, Kumbi, was the most important trading center of the region, where salt, horses, and luxury goods from North Africa were exchanged for GOLD, ostrich feathers, ivory, and other goods. The *ghana* collected customs duties on all these goods. Kumbi was actually two connected towns: Kumbi proper was the Muslim section, with commercial areas, twelve mosques, and many North African merchants and Muslim scholars in residence; al-GHABA, the Soninke section, was where the *ghana's* palace was located. Buildings there were constructed in the traditional mud-and-thatch style, in contrast with the stone buildings of the Muslim quarter. ISLAM was the religion of the commercial class, but, as commonly happened in many African societies, most Soninke practiced their traditional religion.

To govern its empire, which included many non-Soninke peoples, two types of provincial government were used. In Soninke regions, the governor was often a close relative or friend of the *ghana*; in non-Soninke provinces, the governor was the local ruler selected according to local custom and confirmed in office by the *ghana*. In return, after mutual exchanges of honors and expensive gifts, the *ghana* provided protection, the rule of law, and opportunities for trade. An important factor that enabled ancient Ghana to extend its borders was its military forces. In the eleventh century, it could field an army of 200,000 infantry and cavalry. Very likely, the Soninke learned early how to work IRON. Its well-equipped army carried metal swords and hurled iron-tipped spears and arrows at foes armed sometimes only with war clubs and stones.

The rituals of the royal court were both splendid and rigid. The *ghana* held audiences inside a magnificent pavilion of state, which was guarded by armed warriors bearing shields and swords decorated with gold and by the king's constant companions, dogs in collars made from gold and silver. No petitioner was allowed to address the *ghana* directly. Non-Muslim petitioners approached the *ghana* on all fours, with dirt sprinkled on their shoulders. On tours of his kingdom, wild animals were driven into a town in advance of the *ghana's* arrival, to signify his power over man and beast.

Ghana fell in 1076 after a fourteen-year JIHAD, or holy war, led against it by its Muslim fundamentalist neighbors to the north, the SANHAJA BERBERS, who founded the ALMORAVID Empire and were bent on purifying the "pagan" Soninke people of Ghana and gaining control of the gold trade. Although this takeover was temporary and Ghana reasserted control over the empire at the beginning of the twelfth century, Ghana never fully recovered from the Almoravid invasion. Internal discontent, fueled by

rivalries between client states and the desire of local chiefs to stop paying tribute to the central government, may have been contributing factors. By the thirteenth century Ghana had lost its trading power and dispersed into small states. The power vacuum in the region was filled by the rise of the SUSU Kingdom, another warrior state also ruled by a high priest-king. Susu acquired much of the territory of Ghana and existed until it fell in 1240 to the rising power of the KANGABA Kingdom, one of its subject states, which evolved into the empire of Mali.

Mali Empire Mali, founded in the thirteenth century by MANDINKA Prince SUNDIATA (r. 1235), became heir to the Ghana Empire and the largest empire in West Africa up to that time. While Ghana was supreme, the Mandinka lived in scattered settlements between the upper reaches of the Senegal and Niger Rivers. The Mandinka Kingdom of Kangaba was formed in response to the despotic rule of the Susu king SUMANGURU (r. c. 1230), whose tyrannies forced merchants to flee from Kumbi, thereby destroying the former capital of Ghana as a trading center. Under Sundiata's leadership, Kangaba crushed Susu's forces, razed Kumbi, and destroyed all resistance within the kingdom of Susu. He molded the conquered lands into an empire by restoring them to the rule of their rightful kings, not as independent monarchs but as subkings under his authority as the first *mansa* of Mali. Sundiata established his capital at NIANI on the Niger River and built up the region as an agricultural center, with cotton as the prime crop. He captured the WANGARA GOLD FIELDS and diverted the gold trade through Niani, which now attracted merchants from North Africa. The gold trade, plus the reputation he built for LAW AND JUSTICE, made Mali prosper.

A *mansa* of Mali was expected to give expensive presents to his followers. Victorious warriors were given anklets, bracelets, necklaces, and other gifts and ornaments. The most distinguished received an enormous pair of trousers—the wider they were, the more esteemed was the wearer.

Dynastic disputes and power struggles following the death of Sundiata's son Mansa Uli (r. 1255–1270) left the kingdom in disarray until the most important ruler of Mali, Mansa MUSA (1312–1337), came to power. He restored order and, because of his famed pilgrimage, or hajj, to MECCA (1324–1326), he advertised the power and extent of his empire throughout the African and Muslim worlds. Mansa Musa was a strict Muslim who established Islam as the religion of the nobility and commercial class. Under his rule, the city of TIMBUKTU became an important center of trade as well as Muslim scholarship and law, adding further to the renown of Mali. Mansa Musa consolidated his empire with the help of Islam. Although his position as a semidivine priest-king of the Mandinka people might have worked to his disadvantage in the many non-Mandinka areas of Mali, when the rulers of those areas converted to Islam, they had a religious obligation to obey him as long as he acted justly. Thus he achieved unity and extended the greatness of his empire.

Mali's decline was gradual, but by late in the fourteenth century, Mali had suffered substantial blows from which it never recovered, first at the hands of the MOSSI states, which captured TIMBUKTU in the late 1330s, and then from SONGHAI, which rebelled and gained its independence in the 1460s. The BERBERS and TEKRUR nibbled at its western flanks. After 1464, all that remained was the Mandinka homeland. Songhai became the dominant power in the region. The Mali Empire continued its gradual decline until the mid-seventeenth century.

The Mossi States   The Mossi states were located to the southeast of Mali. By the sixteenth century five Mossi states were formed in the region of the upper VOLTA RIVER. These included Wagadugu, YATENGA, Nanumba, MAMPRUSI, and DAGOMBA. Wagadugu became the Mossi capital in c. 1495 when the first king, called the *mogho naba*, reigned. These states managed to maintain their independence until the nineteenth century when they fell to the French.

The Songhai Empire   After Songhai declared its independence from Mali, it rapidly surpassed Mali in size and became the largest indigenous empire of West Africa. The original peoples of the area were the Da, who were farmers; the Gow, who were hunters; and the SORKO, fishermen whose boats gave them great mobility along the Niger. The Sorko established a tyrannical dominance over the Gow and the Da that lasted until sometime between 690 and 850, when nomadic Zaghawa invaders from the Lake CHAD region overran the Sorko, established the Za dynasty, and began the Songhai state. The first important Za ruler was KOSSOI (r. c. 1000), who converted to Islam and moved the capital to the city of Gao, which was closer to the TRANS-SAHARAN TRADE ROUTES. Gao gradually attracted merchants from North Africa and became a major commercial center. The success of Gao made it attractive to Mali, whose army captured the unfortified city during the thirteenth century.

Not yet a military power, Songhai chafed under Malian rule. It gained its independence after the death of Mali's Mansa Musa in c. 1337 but was mainly involved in fending off attacks from neighboring Mandinka, Mossi, and TUAREG peoples. The kingdom expanded slowly until the reigns of the warrior SUNNI ALI (c. 1464–1492) and the statesmanlike ASKIA MUHAMMAD TOURÉ (d. 1538), who usurped the throne in 1493 and ruled until 1538. Under Sunni Ali and Askia Muhammad, the Songhai Empire acquired most of its vast territory.

Sunni Ali was a tepid Muslim, a fact that incurred the wrath of *ulama*, Timbuktu's religious leaders who considered him an infidel. As semidivine king in the minds of traditional believers, Sunni Ali was all-powerful. Sometimes arbitrary, sometimes savagely cruel, he was an outstanding soldier and strategist. His cavalry never lost a battle. His large fleet of war canoes both protected the empire and helped it expand along the Niger. Sunni Ali captured JENNE in 1473, giving Songhai access to the gold resources of the region. In 1483, at the battle of Jiniki To'oi, he shattered the power of the Mossi but never incorporated them into the empire. Perhaps to break Muslim hold on trans-Saharan trade, he opened the empire to the Portuguese by allowing them, before his death in 1492, to set up a trading outpost at Wadan near the Atlantic coast.

The usurper Askia Muhammad, in contrast, was a devout Muslim. To solidify his power, he won the loyalty of his fellow Muslims with royal patronage and attention to their religious needs. To gain the support of the rural Songhai people, he made no attempt to convert them to Islam and allowed the chief priest to hold high office in his government. He reorganized the government, deftly combining decentralization and strong central control, and encouraged trade and education. In 1499, he began to send his armies westward. By 1507, his territorial conquests extended as far as Galam, at Mali's westernmost border, near Tekrur. By 1513, he had marched southeast into the HAUSA STATES and plundered all its major cities except for KANO, which offered fierce resistance. He attacked the sultanate of Aïr (on the AÏR MASSIF) in an attempt to defeat the Tuaregs and control Hausa trade. His success did not last. His allies, especially the Hausa state of KEBBI, rebelled, and the Hausa states once again became free.

Hausaland, located to the southeast of Songhai, was a group of large and small city-states that arose between the tenth and eleventh centuries. Kano, KATSINA, Kebbi, Kwararafa, Nupe, Sokoto, and ZARIA were among the most notable. Although these cities were unified culturally, they never established themselves as a kingdom or empire. When Kebbi broke free from Songhai in 1516, it assumed control over most of Hausaland.

In the last decade of Askia Muhammad's life and for the fifty years that followed, Songhai was shaken by dynastic struggles that affected the stability of the government. By 1591, it was past its peak. That year, the Songhai army was defeated by the firearm-bearing forces of Morocco at the battle of Tondibi, near the Songhai capital of Gao. The collapse of Songhai was immediate. MOROCCO occupied Gao, Timbuktu, and Jenne and established a local government at Timbuktu. The Moroccan victories all but destroyed trans-Saharan trade. Law and order in the region collapsed. The Tuaregs, the Mandinka, the Fulani, and the Mossi raided the lands of their former overlords, and the Moroccans themselves were more interested in taking what gold they found in Songhai cities than in developing large-scale commercial ventures. The fall of Songhai caused the economic collapse of the region.

Kanem-Bornu The empire of KANEM-BORNU (sometimes called the KANURI empire, after its founding people) lay to the east and north of Songhai, the Tuareg sultanate of Aïr, and Hausaland and established its own sphere of influence to the north across the Sahara, far distant from Mali and Songhai. Kanem, founded by the nomadic Kanuri people, emerged separately c. 800 and built its wealth on its domination of the trade routes to FEZZAN and Tripoli on the Mediterranean coast, to CAIRO in Egypt, and to the Arab traders of East Africa. It exported gold, ivory, and other products in exchange for, among other items, salt, COPPER, and horses. By 1150, Kanem had converted to Islam. By 1230 it had expanded its territory as far north as Waddan, more than 1,000 miles (1600 km) from its capital at NJIMI.

Pressed for years by attacks from the nomadic Bulala people of the SAHARA, the people of Kanem fled west, abandoning much of their Saharan conquests, and founded the state of Bornu in 1386. For a time, Bornu and Bulala-dominated Kanem were separate states, but in 1526 Bornu regained control of its former lands and the empire of Kanem-Bornu was born. Kanem-Bornu forged trade links with its neighbors, once again dominated the trade routes to North Africa, and competed with Songhai to expand into the Tuareg sultanate of Aïr and into Hausaland. When Songhai collapsed in 1591, Kanem-Bornu was the most powerful empire in West Africa.

See also: ISLAM, INFLUENCE OF (Vol. II); KINGDOMS AND EMPIRES (Vol. II); KINGDOMS AND EMPIRES OF THE LOWER GUINEA COAST (Vol. II); KINGDOMS AND EMPIRES OF SENEGAMBIA (Vol. II); SALT TRADE (Vol. II); SONGHAI (Vol. III).

Kinshasa Important trading center, located on the Congo River about 320 miles (515 km) from the Atlantic Ocean, in present-day Democratic Republic of the Congo.

Although little is known about the early settlement of Kinshasa, by the fourteenth century it had become one of the most important port cities of the KONGO KINGDOM.

See also: CONGO RIVER (Vol. I); KINSHASA (Vol. III); CONGO (Vol. III).

Kirina Ancient MANDE city in present-day Mali. In the thirteenth century, Kirina was the site of an important battle between the SUSU and Mande. The early Mande

inhabitants of southwestern Mali united under central rule in the twelfth century. In the early thirteenth century, however, Mande clans, including the Camara, Keita, Konate, and Traore peoples, were confronted by Susu invaders. Under the leadership of SUNDIATA, the united Mande defeated the Susu, who were led by SUMANGURU, at the Battle of Kirina. The victory not only became a symbol of ancient Mali's emerging power but, since the Susu leadership had been anti-Muslim, it also enabled ISLAM to spread southward into the SUDAN.

See also: KEITA CLAN (Vol. II); MALI EMPIRE (Vol. II)

Kiswahili Language spoken among the various groups along East Africa's Indian Ocean coast in regions of Somalia, KENYA, Tanzania, UGANDA, MOZAMBIQUE, and the Comoro Islands (collectively known as the SWAHILI COAST).

Though it is difficult to ascertain information on the early development of Kiswahili, language historians believe that a form of proto-Kiswahili may have been spoken by trading communities on Africa's east coast as early as the ninth century.

True Kiswahili did not emerge until the thirteenth century, when extensive coastal trade between ARAB and African MERCHANTS required a common tongue in which to conduct business. Early Kiswahili was a BANTU language that had many borrowed words—up to 50 percent in some poetic forms—from the ARABIC language. The earliest written forms of true Kiswahili—in Arabic script— date from the early seventeenth century and consist of folk tales from East African oral tradition.

Kiswahili stands out among African languages because it appears as a written language a few hundred years prior to the arrival of Europeans.

In many East African coastal communities, Kiswahili served as the main language or, at the very least, as a second language. Today, it is considered one of the twelve major languages of the world.

See also: ARAB COASTAL TRADE (Vol. II); COMORO ISLANDS (Vol. III); INDIAN OCEAN TRADE (Vol. II); KISWAHILI (Vol. III); LANGUAGES (Vol. I); LANGUAGES, MAJOR (Vol. II); SWAHILI COAST (Vol. III).

Kitara Fourteenth-century empire located in the East African lake district. What finally emerged as the Kitara Empire began during the fourth century with the large-scale migration of people originally from the central SUDAN. This was followed by another period of heavy immigration, this time by BANTU-speakers. These people began arriving in the region from their homelands, west of Lake Albert, during the tenth and eleventh centuries. From this migration emerged what is generally known as the Batembuzi period, which lasted until the middle of the fourteenth century. The Batembuzi were succeeded by a new state, the CHWEZI KINGDOM, which established the Kitara Empire.

The greatest ruler of this period was NDAHURA (c. 1344–1371), who seized power in the wake of a rebellion set off when rival chiefs rose up against King Isazza (c. 1301–1328), who was resented by the chiefs for his commoner birth. Ndahura eventually expanded his holdings and transformed them into an empire extending over Bunyoro and TORO, western BUGANDA, NKOLE, Kiziba, KARAGWE, and even into parts of RWANDA. Ndahura, however, had difficulties in maintaining control over his empire. He tried various innovations in government and administration, including the appointment of loyal agents to monitor the important products of salt, cattle, and IRON. Still, he faced unrest and insurrection and eventually was captured in battle. Released, he abandoned his capital at Mwenga and moved westward.

In time, Ndahura was succeeded by his son WAMARA (c. 1371–1398), who endured an equally unstable reign. For Wamara, the biggest obstacle to stability was the massive immigration into his area by Bantu-speaking clans. Striving to appease the Bantu speakers, Wamara gave many high-level administrative posts to representatives of the immigrants. The newcomers were not satisfied, however, and they ultimately rose in rebellion. In the end, the Bantu speakers succeeded in murdering the majority of the BACHWEZI aristocrats. From the resulting turmoil and instability sprouted both the Luo-Babito states of BUNYORO-KITARA and the Bahinda states further south.

Kongo Kingdom BANTU settlement in western central Africa that became a powerful trade kingdom in the fourteenth century. At the height of its influence, the Kongo

This nineteenth-century illustration of Kongo people shows African peoples through European eyes. © *Leonard de Selva/CORBIS*

Kingdom covered much of the area along the Atlantic coast to the south of the Congo River and spread east as far as the Kwango River

In the twelfth century, the area that would become the Kongo Kingdom was settled by agriculturalists. By the fourteenth century, many of the small, loosely organized farming communities had formed a cohesive kingdom. The settlement of Mbanza Kongo, located on the Congo River, became the center of this early kingdom.

The Kongo Kingdom was strategically located at the junction of several West African trade routes. This enabled the Kongo king, known as the *manikongo*, to secure adequate wealth to dominate neighboring peoples. The *manikongo's* means of conquest were generally peaceful, relying more on alliances and intermarriage than on warfare, and he increased his kingdom's wealth by levying taxes on the surrounding provinces.

The economy of the early Kongo Kingdom was based on trade and subsistence farming. Women typically tended the fields, while the men were responsible for more labor-intensive tasks, such as clearing forestland and building homes. The men also tended to the palm tree crops, as they were valuable sources of wine, fruit, oil, and raffia.

The Kongo Kingdom was exposed to European culture around 1483, when Portuguese explorers landed on the coast. The Kongo were surprisingly receptive to the Europeans, and a number of Kongo emissaries even returned to Portugal with the explorers. In 1491, the Portuguese returned to Kongo, but this time with Christian missionaries. Shortly thereafter, the reigning *manikongo*, Nzinga Mbumba, converted to Christianity and assumed the Christian name Afonso I. During Afonso's reign, the Portuguese took advantage of their relationship with the Kongo Kingdom, trading extensively at Kongo markets up and down the Atlantic coast.

By the beginning of the sixteenth century, Portugal had begun pressuring the people of the Kongo Kingdom, known as the Bakongo, into supplying them with captives taken from surrounding villages. In return, the Portuguese brought firearms for trade, and they also assisted the Bakongo in the continuing warfare that stemmed from the raids that they instigated.

See also: AFONSO I (Vol. III); KONGO KINGDOM (Vol. III); PORTUGAL AND AFRICA (Vol. III).

Further reading: Kenny Mann, *Kongo Ndongo: West Central Africa (African Kingdoms of the Past)* (Minneapolis, Minn.: Dillon Press, 1996).

Kono People who have long occupied areas of eastern SIERRA LEONE; their language belongs to the family of NIGER-CONGO LANGUAGES.

Primarily rice farmers, the Kono also have grown palm oil, CASSAVAS, millet, and peanuts, among their subsistence CROPS. For centuries, they have practiced a form of agriculture known as slash-and-burn, or shifting, cultivation. This involves establishing new farms every year between December and March, when hot dry winds blow from the SAHARA Desert. By cutting the brush of their former homesteads and burning it, the Kono create a thin layer of ash that fertilizes the land for future crops. These practices also helped bring the forest environment under their control by scaring off wild animals and, according to Kono belief, placating unseen forces.

Along with farming, raising livestock and producing such traditional handicrafts as woven CLOTH, leatherwork, baskets, and POTTERY supplemented the economy. Age and patrilineal ties have been two important elements of Kono society. Traditionally, only a select number of married men could receive farmland from village elders and rise to a position of social recognition.

See also: FARMING TECHNIQUES (Vol. I); SIERRA LEONE (Vol. III).

Konso Kushitic ethnic group of ETHIOPIA, KENYA, and UGANDA. Related to the OROMO, the Konso are composed of Garati, Takadi, and Turo peoples, who have long inhabited the Ethiopian Highlands. The group's patrilineal society is largely egalitarian. Agriculture has long been the traditional means of subsistence, but they also raise cattle and goats.

Traditional Konso religion centers on Waga, the sky god, who supposedly manifests his authority through village elders. Konso woodworkers are known for their statues, called *waga*, that commemorate the deeds of Konso warrior heroes.

See also: ETHIOPIA (Vol. III); OROMO (Vol. III).

Koran (Qur'an) Sacred book of ISLAM. According to Islamic belief, the Koran was revealed by God to the prophet MUHAMMAD. It is strictly followed by devout Muslims. The Koran is sacred in the same way to Muslims as the Bible is to Christians and Jews.

Allah is the ARABIC name for the Supreme Being, or God. *Koran* in Arabic means "recitation." Muslims, or followers of Islam, believe that the Prophet received the word of Allah through the mediacy of the angel Gabriel and then recited it to the faithful. Islam, which means "submission to the word of God," is the third of the world's great monotheistic religions, Judaism and Christianity being the other two. Devout Muslims believe that Allah sent several prophets, including Moses, Jesus,

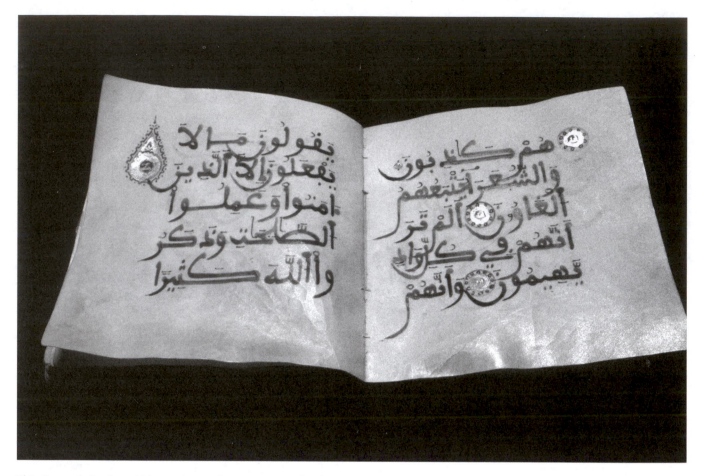

This Koran, dating from 1334 to 1345 and written on gazelle skin, is now on display in Jerusalem, a gift of Sultan Abdulah Ben Abdal Hag of Morocco. © *Bojan Brecelj/CORBIS*

and, last but most important, Muhammad, to save humankind from its sins. The teachings of Muhammad were passed orally among believers until they were recorded in book form after his death in 632 CE. Devout Muslims regard the written text of the Koran to be an earthly copy of a book that exists as an independent and eternal entity of the universe.

The Oral Tradition　The Koran was originally intended to be a spoken text. According to tradition, Muhammad, while in a heavenly trance, received the Koran from the angel Gabriel a few verses at a time over the years 610 through 632, the year Muhammad died. Thus, the teachings of the Koran follow the events of the Prophet's life. Each time Muhammad awoke from his trance, he repeated Allah's revelations in Arabic to his followers. Legend states that scribes recorded the revelations on paper, palm-leaves, stone, or other objects that were on hand. Muhammad's followers then memorized the passages and recited them to other ARABS.

Shortly after Muhammad's death, Muslims grew concerned that the recited passages would be forgotten. In 633, Zayd ibn Thabit, a contemporary of Muhammad, compiled a written record of the revelations. Thabit recorded as many versions of each revelation as he could find. Several other versions of the Koran were compiled at the same time, but only Thabit's text was considered pure. A few years later Uthman, the reigning caliph, asked Thabit to edit his version of the Koran. The official version came about from Thabit's efforts to verify his document against those of oral scribes as well as other versions of the written text. Thus, the Koran is the earliest existing work of Arabic literature.

Reverence for the Koran　Reverence for the Koran is great. Understood to be the authoritative word of Allah, it serves as the code of ethics for Islamic life and the highest authority in Islamic law. Believers firmly adhere to its teachings and treat the book itself with reverence. Muslims never carry it below the waist and always purify their hands before touching it. The Arabic text of the Koran is considered sacred and non-translatable because it is the direct Word of God. Almost all Muslims, even the illiterate, memorize at least portions of the text—and often the complete text. The proper recitation of the Koran is considered an art. The Koran remains the most widely circulated book in its original language. Only since the early 1900s have Muslims begun to translate the Koran into other languages.

The passages in the Koran prescribe a Muslim's religious, social, and commercial commitments. It requires daily prayers, urges the practice of charity and brotherly love, and teaches that Muslims must be humble in spirit, temperate, and just. Upon death, all people face final judgment by Allah. Those who have lived their lives according to the Koran will live in eternal paradise, but those who have sinned will suffer.

The Structure and Language of the Koran The body of the Koran is divided into 114 chapters, or *surahs*. The first chapter is a prayer (*fatihah*). The remaining chapters are revelations from the oral tradition. Chapters vary widely in length and content. Some chapters deal with one subject, while others address several topics. The text follows a rough chronology in that longer chapters corresponding to events that took place late in Muhammad's life are generally found at the end of the book. Each chapter includes a title, which may not be directly related to the subject of the text, and an indication of where the revelations occurred, usually the cities of MECCA and MEDINA. Each chapter also contains a traditional prayer, or *basmalah*. During the holy month of Ramadan, the chapters are rearranged into thirty segments, to correspond with each day of the month. A segment of the Koran is then recited during each day of the month.

The verses, or *ayats*, that make up the chapters are also diverse in their composition. When Allah speaks, the first person plural form (we) is used. Verses that correspond with Muhammad's early life are shorter than those found later. This early writing follows a form reminiscent of the rhymed prose used by ancient soothsayers, or *kahins*. Later chapters contain verses with a more complex sentence structures and embellished style. The verses place greater emphasis on the lessons learned from an event rather than on the narrative aspects of the revelation.

The dialect chosen for the Koran has significantly influenced Arabic linguistic studies. In ancient Iraq, scholars at Basra established grammatical rules for the Arabic language based on the word structures found in the Koran. Scholars in neighboring Kufa also studied linguistic issues in the Koran, although they were more interested in exceptions to grammatical rules. The interest in the structure of the Koran has been an important means of preserving the classic Arabic language over time.

Historical Interpretations of the Koran Several theological disputes have arisen regarding the content of the Koran. Scholarship that focuses on *tafsir*, or interpretation of the Koran, has existed for centuries. The passages themselves and the literature surrounding the life of Muhammad (Hadith) are used to illuminate meaning from the revelations. Historically, orthodox Muslims rejected any interpretations that could not be supported by Hadith literature.

Medieval *tafsir* focused on two important works. The first, written by al-Tabari (839–923), was an encyclopedic volume summarizing the different interpretations of the Koran. The second, and more popular, volume was the *Kashshaf* of Zamakhshari (1075–1143), a liberal scholar from the Mu'tazilite branch of Islam. This work became the standard for traditional *tafsir* scholarship.

The different branches of Muslim thought used *tafsir* scholarship to support their doctrines. The Mu'tazilites challenged the idea that the Koran exists independently from Allah. Relying on logical arguments borrowed from Greek philosophy to support their theory, the Mu'tazilites propounded the belief that Allah in fact created the Koran, arguing that, if the Koran is independent of Allah, then something eternal other than Allah exists and Allah could not be the sole God of eternity. Thus, Allah must have created the Koran, or his power as the single ruler of eternity would be challenged. Orthodox Muslims reject the Mu'tazilite view in favor of the traditional idea that the Koran itself is eternal.

By the nineteenth century, the revival of ancient interpretations of the Koran had replaced the more radical views. The modernists revived ancient texts in a quest to reveal an untainted Islamic faith. They also sought to link modern science with the ancient teachings of the Koran. To that end, some of the passages were loosely interpreted to fit with popular notions of humanity, science, and culture.

See also: GOVERNMENT, SYSTEMS OF (Vol. II); ISLAM, INFLUENCES OF (Vols. II, III); ISLAMIC CENTERS OF LEARNING (Vol. II); LAW AND JUSTICE (Vol. II).

Further reading: Thomas Wyatt, ed., and N. J. Dawood, trans., *The Koran* (New York: Penguin, 1990).

Kossoi (early eleventh century) *Early ruler of the Songhai Empire in West Africa.*

Little is known about Kossoi, the *dia*, or king, of the SONGHAI Empire. He is thought to have converted to ISLAM in 1009 or 1010, becoming the first in a line of Muslim Songhai rulers. Although Dia Kossoi converted, the customs of the royal court remained traditional and therefore non-Muslim. During his reign, Kossoi moved the capital of his empire to GAO. Henceforth, Gao became a very important city for both Muslims and the Songhai people. It became an ISLAMIC CENTER OF LEARNING and a major commercial center, especially for the GOLD and SALT TRADE.

Kotoko Ethnic group of West Africa who are descendants of the SAO ethnic group. The Kotoko are Muslims who traditionally have spoken the Kanuri language. They ruled a large kingdom in present-day CAMEROON and Nigeria until the fifteenth century. After that, they became subjects of the KANURI people who reigned over the kingdom of BORNU.

See also: KANEM-BORNU (Vol. II).

Kukiya (Kukya, Kaw Kaw)

Earliest city of the SONGHAI people. Located on the Niger River, Kukiya eventually became the capital of the Songhai Empire.

Kukiya was located in what is presently Nigeria, down the Niger River from the city of GAO. Kukiya was the Songhai people's first major city, existing well before they acquired more territory and became recognized as an empire. When it became the capital of the Songhai Empire, Kukiya prospered as the rulers acquired more and more territory. Between 1000 and 1100, Songhai's rulers moved the capitol to Gao, but when the MALI EMPIRE conquered Gao, about 1300, the weakened Songhai moved back to Kukiya. They remained there until the 1400s, when the Songhai recaptured Gao after the fall of the Mali Empire.

Arab reports of Kukiya dating back to c. 1000 state that COTTON, millet, and wheat were grown in the area. The land was said to be so fertile near the river that farmers could plant and harvest twice in a growing season. The SORKO fishermen were also known to be significant to the city. GOLD was found in the area around this time as well.

Kumbi Saleh (Koumbi Saleh, Koumbi Salih, Kumbi Salih)

Capital of the GHANA EMPIRE, the first great trading empire in West Africa. Kumbi Saleh was located 200 miles (322 km) north of the modern city of Bamako, Mali.

During the eleventh century, Ghana was widely known as the "land of GOLD," and Kumbi Saleh—sometimes called simply Kumbi—was the empire's capital. The most important desert trading town of the time, Kumbi Saleh became a commercial and intellectual center. Its population grew to between 15,000 and 20,000 people, making Kumbi Saleh perhaps the biggest West African city of its time.

Like other cities of its era, Kumbi Saleh consisted of two towns. One town, called al-Ghana (the word *ghana* being the king's title), was the home of the king. Al-Ghana was fortified with strong walls that enclosed the king's palace. The MANDE-speaking SONINKE people, who founded the Ghana Empire in the sixth century, also lived in al-Ghana.

The second town, which was larger, was home to the Muslim traders and included as many as twelve mosques. About 6 miles (10 km) apart, the two towns were surrounded by farms that provided food for the large population.

Trade was the lifeblood of the city, and GOLD was the empire's principal commodity. Ghana's MERCHANTS brought gold from the southern part of the empire to Kumbi, where it was traded, often for salt, which came from the SAHARA Desert to the north. Caravans traveling along the TRANS-SAHARAN TRADE ROUTES also brought food, which was traded for such locally produced goods as COTTON, CLOTH, metal ornaments, and leather products. Regardless of the commodities involved, however, the king taxed trade, which brought the empire enormous wealth and great quantities of natural resources.

> **With all this wealth, Ghana's rulers could indulge themselves. TUNKA MANIN, for example, who was caliph of Ghana from about 1065, put glass windows in his palace. He even maintained a private zoo stocked with elephants and GIRAFFES.**

Attacks from the ALMORAVIDS, a militant Muslim religious group from MOROCCO, began to weaken the empire during the eleventh century. In order to expand their territories and convert the native peoples to Islam, the Almoravids had declared a JIHAD, or holy war, against their neighbors. Led by ABU BAKR, the Almoravids invaded Ghana, seizing Kumbi in 1076. The Almoravids forced many of the SONINKE to convert to Islam, but the Soninke's military and religious activities disrupted trade, making the Almoravid Empire difficult to control. In 1087, the Soninke regained control of Kumbi. They tried to rebuild their empire, but a number of states had adopted Islam and others were forming separate kingdoms, all of which prevented the empire from being reestablished. By 1203, Kumbi Saleh was under the control of one of these kingdom-states. King SUMANGURU, chief of the KANIAGA peoples called the SUSU, overthrew the Soninke king and ruled Kumbi Saleh for a short time. The city finally was destroyed by the Mande emperor SUNDIATA, in 1240.

Kuranko (Koranko, Kouranko)

West African ethnic group of MANDE descent. The Kuranko, who are related to the MANDINKA, were—and still are—a mixed group in a religious sense, with some converting to ISLAM, and others practicing non-Muslim religions. They were a loosely organized group who had settled in the forests of present-day Guinea. Beginning in the fifteenth century, however, they, along with the neighboring VAI and Kano peoples (not of the Hausa confederation), were driven from their homeland by migrating Malinke traders and warriors; they eventually settled in the forests of present-day SIERRA LEONE.

Kurmina

One of the two provinces, along with DENDI, that comprised the SONGHAI Empire, which flourished in the fifteenth century. Kurmina, the western province of the empire, was considered more important than southeastern province of Dendi. The ruler of Kurmina, called the *kurmina fari* or *kanfari*, was second in power to the Songhai emperor. The *kurmina fari* was generally the crown prince of the region and ruled the territory west of TIMBUKTU. Kurmina was very important because of the many trade routes that crossed it, and its administration required strong leadership. To that end, the *kurmina fari* maintained a powerful army that not only kept peace in the region but also was used to keep the power of the Songhai monarch in check.

See also: SONGHAI (Vol. III).

Kwahu (Akwahu, Kwawu, Quahoe) Ethnic group of modern-day coastal Ghana; also a plateau region in that same area. The Kwahu, a Twi-speaking subgroup of the AKAN people, inhabited Ghana's Kwahu Plateau as early as the eleventh century. Archaeological evidence from the area suggests that these people hunted, fished, and raised some cattle. It is known that most Akan groups were involved in the West African GOLD trade, as well. Archaeologists also have found items that indicate that Kwahu artists were skilled woodcarvers and made elaborate funerary ceramics.

Kyoga, Lake Body of water located in the central part of UGANDA. One of the oldest East African state systems, the KITARA complex, formed in the area between Lakes Albert, Kyoga, and VICTORIA as early as the eighth century.

The groups of people who composed the Kitara complex were the BUNYORO-KITARA, TORO, and portions of the NKOLE and BUGANDA. (The ancestors of these peoples arrived in the region before the BANTU speakers and were believed to have migrated from the SUDAN in the fourth century.) From the twelfth to the fifteenth centuries, various clans, including the Batembuzi, the BACHWEZI, and the BITO, dominated the region of the Kitara complex. The Bito dynasty also dominated portions of the region from Buruli to Bugerere along the southern shores of the lake.

After the fifteenth century, this region was dominated by various Bantu-speaking clans, who had been in the area since the eleventh century after migrating from the area west of Lake Mobutu.

L

Lalibela (c. 1185–1225) *Ethiopian king known for directing the construction of the stone churches at the town that bears his name.*

Lalibela, like famous rulers the world over, is surrounded by legends of all kinds. One such legend tells how Lalibela came to have his name. According to it, a cloud of bees swarmed around the newly born Lalibela. Seeing the bees, the infant cried out: "Lalibela!" which means "the bees know he will rule."

Another legend tells of Lalibela as a youth, at a time when Lalibela's brother was king. Knowing of the legend surrounding Lalibela's name, the king was afraid that the bees' prophecy would come true. So the king poisoned the young prince, sending young Lalibela into a coma that lasted three days. During that time, says the legend, Lalibela was in Heaven, where God told the youngster that he would indeed survive to become king; God also commanded Lalibela to construct a series of unique stone churches. Lalibela survived and eventually came to power. The new ruler immediately started work on the churches, helped, according to the legend, by angels who had been sent by God to make sure that his command was carried out quickly and precisely.

Lalibela was the most famous king of the ZAGWE DYNASTY that ruled in northern ETHIOPIA during the twelfth and thirteenth centuries. His reign was marked by several accomplishments, including the construction of a series of churches carved out of volcanic rock.

The Zagwe were devout Christians and claimed to be descended from biblical ancestors. They identified themselves with Moses, who, according to them, came into Abyssinia and married the king's daughter, an Ethiopian woman.

Under Lalibela's direction, eleven churches were carved out of pink-red rock at the Zagwe capital of al-ROHA, about 435 miles (700 km) from the city of Addis Ababa. Until this time, there had been very little Christian influence on African ARCHITECTURE. Because Jerusalem had fallen under Muslim control, Lalibela made every effort to re-create the Christian Holy Land of Jerusalem, hoping that his new city of churches would become a major place of pilgrimage, since journeys to Jerusalem had become difficult. As part of this, he even gave biblical names to various places in the city: A local hill, for example, was called Calvary, and a stream was renamed Jordan. After Lalibela's death, the city of al-Roha was renamed in his honor.

The churches constructed by Lalibela are called Madhane Alam, Amanu'el, Maryam, GIYORGIS (St. George), Golgotha (in which Lalibela is believed to be entombed), Mika'el, Masqal, Denagel, Marqorwos, Libanos, and Gabr'el.

See also: CHRISTIANITY (Vol. II); LALIBELA, CHURCHES OF (Vol. II).

Lalibela, churches of Group of churches carved out of the rock in the Lasta Mountains of ETHIOPIA, probably during the ZAGWE DYNASTY (c. 1137–1270). Eleven churches have been discovered so far, built over a series of passages and tunnels that form an elaborate maze. Though the exact purpose of the churches and the dates of their construction remain a mystery, Ethiopian tradition asserts that they were built during the reign of King Lalibela, who ruled from his capital, al-ROHA, in the early thirteenth century.

Ethiopian legend says that King Lalibela was magically transported to Jerusalem, where he was instructed to build the churches out of the rocks of the Lasta Mountains. Upon his return to al-Roha, Lalibela instructed his men, aided by the angels who were sent to help, to build the churches.

Lalibela's eleven churches were hewn out of solid rock entirely below ground level. To build these churches, trenches were dug in rectangular shapes, leaving isolated blocks of granite. Carvers worked from the top, carving both inside and outside the rock. There are two main clusters of churches, and they are linked by underground tunnels. One group of churches is surrounded by a trench that

The Church of St. Abba Libanos in Lalibela, Ethopia, and its sister churches nearby are carved from solid rock. © *Roger Wood/CORBIS*

is 35 feet (11 m) deep and includes the House of Emmanuel, House of Mercurios, ABBA LIBANOS, and the House of Gabriel. All of these churches were carved from the same rock hill. Nearby, the House of Medhane Alem has an external colonnade of pillars on all four sides. Medhane Alem is also the largest church, measuring 109 feet (33 m) long, 77 feet (23 m) wide, and 35 feet (11 m) deep. The House of St. GIYORGIS is shaped like a cross, while the House of Golgatha is thought to contain Lalibela's tomb.

Recent archaeological excavations of the site indicate that the style of the construction is very similar to ancient Aksumite architecture, which would date the construction of the buildings to centuries before the Zagwe dynasty. An earlier construction date is also suggested by the architectural anomaly of the churches, which are not facing east, as would have been customary of religious architecture. This detail suggests that the buildings might not have been places of worship at all, and were perhaps palaces or royal residences for people of the Aksumite culture. However, the site was revered as a religious one, so much so that it was referred to as the "New Jerusalem" after Lalibela's death.

See also: ARCHAEOLOGY (Vol. II).

Lalibela, town of See al-ROHA.

Lamu Oldest town in KENYA, as well as a port, island, and archipelago in the same region; known as a distribution center in the GOLD, IVORY, spice, and slave trades. The area was settled by immigrants from Arabia in the late twelfth century.

By the fifteenth century, the islands of the archipelago, particularly PATE, had become centers of trade between Asia and Africa. Portugal, seeing the area's strategic economic value, began to exert influence over the islands. By the end of the fifteenth century, Portugal had a firm grip on commerce in the region and continued its dominance until the seventeenth century.

See also: ARAB COASTAL TRADE (Vol. II); INDIAN OCEAN TRADE (Vol. II); LAMU (Vol. III); PORTUGAL AND AFRICA (Vol. III); SWAHILI COAST (Vol. II).

Lango One of the largest groups of non-BANTU people who settled in what is now UGANDA during the fifteenth century; also the language of these people. Unlike their Bantu-speaking neighbors, the Lango were part of a NILOTIC migration and spoke LUO, a language that evolved into Lango.

Lango society was very decentralized, and conflicts were settled by a council of elders from the various clans. Traditionally, the Lango were governed by nonhereditary chiefs, called *rwot*, who oversaw the hereditary chiefs. Relations between different groups were controlled by kinship, and descent was patrilineal. Typical Lango villages were small, and the villagers practiced pastoralism and also grew millet and sorghum.

Traditional Lango religion revolves around a creator whom they call Jok. They practice ancestor worship and believe that every person has a guardian spirit that must be ritually freed from the body after death. They also believe in a shadow self or soul, which is thought to join the creator after the person dies.

See also: CLAN (Vol. I); GOVERNMENT, SYSTEMS OF (Vol. II); LINEAGE (Vol. I); PASTORALISM (Vol. I); UGANDA (Vol. III).

languages, major The four largest classifications of African languages. Most of the numerous languages spoken on the African continent—estimates vary from 700 to nearly 3,000—can be organized under four major language family categories: Afro-Asiatic, Khoisan, Niger-Congo, and Nilo-Saharan.

Nearly 4,500 years ago, the AFRO-ASIATIC LANGUAGES were spoken throughout North Africa. Although ARABIC, an Afro-Asiatic language, is the original tongue of ISLAM, it did not become as widespread as the religion on the African continent. By c. 1000 CE, the Afro-Asiatic languages were still largely confined to North Africa.

Perhaps the most significant change in the Afro-Asiatic languages during the first millennium of the common era was the development of MALAGASY, the language of the people of the island of MADAGASCAR. Located in the Indian Ocean off the coast of East Africa, Madagascar was largely uninhabited as late as the seventh century, when INDONESIAN COLONISTS arrived by sea. Malagasy, based on the Malay (Indonesian) language of the original settlers, also reflected BANTU, Arabic, and Persian influences from the merchants who frequented the island.

The Niger-Congo family of languages, on the other hand, underwent a remarkable change during the same period, in large part due to the great BANTU MIGRATIONS that took place between c. 1000 BCE and 500 CE. Whereas the NIGER-CONGO LANGUAGES were mostly confined to the southern coastal regions of West Africa in 2500 BCE, by 1000 CE they had spread along a band that stretched from West Africa, through central Africa, all the way to the southern coast of East Africa. During their southeastward migrations, the Bantu-speaking peoples displaced Khoisan speakers, who had inhabited the area for thousands of years. As a result, the KHOISAN LANGUAGES that had been spoken almost exclusively throughout southern Africa and most of coastal East Africa were confined to a pocket in the southwestern corner of the African continent by 1000 CE.

See also: AFRO-ASIATIC (Vol. I); AMHARIC (Vol. I); BANTU (Vol. I); KHOISAN LANGUAGES (Vol. I); LANGUAGES (Vol. I); NIGER-CONGO LANGUAGES (Vol. I); NILO-SAHARAN LANGUAGES (Vols. I, II); KISWAHILI (Vols. II, III).

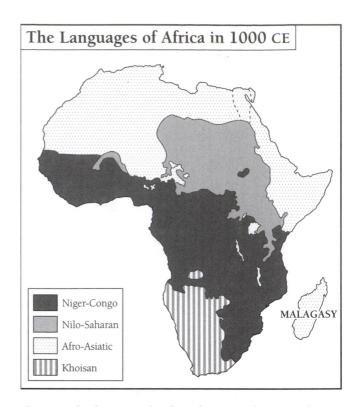

The Languages of Africa in 1000 CE

Niger-Congo
Nilo-Saharan
Afro-Asiatic
Khoisan

MALAGASY

The map, after linguist and anthropologist Joseph H. Greenberg, shows the spread by the year 1000 of the Afro-Asiatic languages, which include Arabic, and the Bantu languages of the Niger-Congo language family. **See also:** The Languages of Africa to 2500 BCE, a map in LANGUAGES (Vol. I).

Lasta Mountains Mountain range located in southern ETHIOPIA that was the site of al-ROHA (Edessa), the capital of the ZAGWE DYNASTY, which ruled in the twelfth and thirteenth centuries. Al-Roha, renamed Lalibela in the thirteenth century to honor the great Zagwe emperor of the same name, is known for its monolithic churches, which were carved out of the rock in the mountains' highlands.

See also: LALIBELA, CHURCHES OF (Vol. II).

law and justice The concepts of law and justice varied greatly from group to group in Africa between the fifth and fifteenth centuries, but all societies had rules that its members thought it right to obey.

Non-Muslim Law and Justice in Traditional Societies In most traditional societies of non-Muslim Africa, the responsibility of maintaining the rules of conduct and the right to exercise judgment in disputes were assumed by the headmen of the social group. Laws were never preserved in written form but were instead incorporated into the social customs through example and practice.

Sometimes, as in the case of the Kuba, an ethnic group of central Africa, the headmen constituted a court of sorts, whose job it was to examine disputes, recall customary law, and then make rulings based on consensus. The IBO, who have inhabited parts of southern Nigeria for more than 1,000 years, have a similar system. The *okpara*, or oldest male member of a lineage group, conferred with other lineage headmen and then exercised the authority of his judgment over younger, lower-ranking individuals.

The KAMBA people of KENYA carried out a judgment called *kingolle*, whereby a member of the society would be condemned to death by the ranking elders who reviewed his case. In most instances, the offending individual was accused of a heinous crime like homicide or incest. However, there are cases of *kingolle* in Kamba lore that tell of a man who failed to pay back his debts, and another of a man who was remiss in his duties as a father and husband. Usually, a close relative of the offender would approve of the *kingolle* judgment and promise not to avenge the death.

Among societies that were large enough to constitute kingdoms, judging disputes was one of the prerogatives of the chief or king. In cases where the king held his power through military might (rather than through lineage ties), he might designate a special judge to help him settle disputes. This judge would usually be a wise, respected elder whose authority was based on his age and experience. Despite his position, though, the judge would not have the power to exercise the punishment he recommended; he would give his opinion, and the ultimate decision was left to the king.

When a dispute developed between two members of the same lineage, the arguing parties would appear before their ranking elders, present their cases, and abide by the ruling that was handed down. If members of two different lineages had a quarrel, the individuals would ask the ranking headman of their lineages to represent them and present their cases, sometimes before the king or chief. In difficult cases, a diviner might be called upon to consult the spirits of the ancestors, who were viewed as the ultimate arbiters of justice.

The most serious offenses that were brought to the judges to be examined included homicide, incest, and adultery. The punishment for these crimes could be the loss of an eye or limb, banishment from the group, or even death. Among some groups, like the MAASAI, death was preferred to the dishonor that came with the crime.

The concept of an organized "police force" to enforce the laws was foreign to most traditional societies. Still,

some chiefs employed armed retainers who kept him safe and maintained peaceful relations in the kingdom. Usually, the mere presence of a chief (or one of his family members or wives) would be enough to keep the peace. For this reason, many chiefs who practiced polygamy would install a child or wife in a village that was in upheaval.

In homicide cases among some pastoralists like the Nuer of the SUDAN, the judgment might be made for compensation to be paid in heads of cattle. Generally, the person who owed the debt did not volunteer the cattle, but when the cattle were taken by the representatives of the offended, the theft would not be contested.

Muslim Law and Justice In many parts of North Africa and the SUDAN, the concept of law and justice was defined by the religious tenets of ISLAM. In these Muslim theocracies, where civil law was exercised by religious leaders, the law was set forth in the KORAN and the Sunna, the books based on the words and deeds of the prophet MUHAMMAD.

These books do not present codified laws specifically, but Muslims believe that their sacred words present the divine will of Allah to humanity. According to the Koran, human actions could be classified under five categories: things commanded, recommended, left legally indifferent, scorned, or absolutely forbidden by Allah. By studying the Koran, then, devout Muslims believed that they could develop *taqwa*, the innate ability to determine right from wrong. *Taqwa* guided Muslims to lead lives that followed the "straight path." However, in many situations regarding questions of law and justice, the words of the Koran were open to vastly different interpretations.

In North Africa, where Islam spread most rapidly and with the most fervor, differing interpretations of the Koran and Sunna led to the division of Islam into its major sects. For members of the MALIKI SUNNI sect of Islam, the most important legal interpretation of the Koran was presented by their founder, MALIK IBN ANAS, a great jurist (legal scholar) and Islamic holy man. Differing interpretations of the Koran also led to the reform movements that created the ALMORAVID and ALMOHAD dynasties of North Africa.

In the West African Muslim states, Islamic law had a different aspect. Often, peoples in these states would nominally convert to Islam, but only to be able to participate more actively in the GOLD and SALT TRADES, which were run mostly by Muslim MERCHANTS and traders, like the DYULA. In the GHANA EMPIRE (c. 800–1240), where traditional, customary law was more fully developed than among the nomadic peoples of North Africa, the Koran tended to be helpful as a guide to legal matters regarding trade but did not represent any absolute authority in other situations. When Koranic law disagreed with customary law—which was often—the customary law usually was followed.

See also: CLAN (Vol. I); DIVINE RULE (Vols. I, II); GOVERNMENT, SYSTEMS OF (Vol. II); ISLAM, INFLUENCE OF (Vol. II); LINEAGE (Vol. I).

Further reading: Hilda Kuper and Leo Kuper, eds., *African Law: Adaptation and Development* (Berkeley: University of California Press, 1965).

Leopard's Kopje See MAPUNGUBWE.

Libya
North African country located on the MEDITER-RANEAN SEA and bordered by present-day Tunisia, ALGERIA, Niger, CHAD, the Republic of the Sudan, and EGYPT. Between the fifth and fifteenth centuries, the strategic geographical location of Libya between the Mediterranean to the north, the SAHARA to the south, and its eastern border with EGYPT, made it an important trade region, as well as a key entry point for the dissemination of ISLAM into SUB-SAHARAN AFRICA.

In the seventh century, ARAB armies brought Islam to North Africa with the objective of conquering the vast continent. By the middle of the century, Arabs controlled Tripolitania, the ancient Roman province on the Mediterranean coast, and proceeded to extend their influence westward into the region they called IFRIQIYA. During this period Libya was controlled first by a Muslim dynasty of emirs called the Aghlabids, and then by the FATIMID dynasty, which ruled from CAIRO. The region of Cyrenaica came under the control of the Arabs at this time as well. Despite the Arab dominance, Cyrenaica maintained its close political and economic ties with Egypt. (The Egyptian influence had begun in the fourth century when Christians in Cyrenaica came under the influence of the Egyptian COPTIC CHURCH.) It was however-er, Bedouin Arab chiefs who maintained real political and economic control over Cyrenaica by taxing the CARAVANS of pilgrims and MERCHANTS on their way to Egypt.

Islam arrived at FEZZAN, located in the interior of the country, twenty years after it had reached Cyrenaica. The peoples of this region lived in oasis communities developed along the TRANS-SAHARAN TRADE ROUTE between the central SUDAN and the MEDITERRANEAN SEA. The Islamic KHARAJITE rulers established an Islamic theocracy at the oasis city of Zawilah, which guaranteed Islamic control of an important arm of the trans-Saharan trading route.

During the eleventh century, a massive influx of Hilalians moved into Tripolitania and Cyrenaica after being forced out of Egypt by drought, famine, and the political turmoil caused by the Fatimids. One Bedouin Arab group,

the Banu Salim, resided in Tripolitania for the next two centuries. These migrations marked a linguistic shift for the BERBERS, who had previously maintained their linguistic and cultural autonomy but now began to adopt the language of the Arab-speaking Muslim elite.

In the thirteenth century, the Muslim Hafsids established a dynasty that would last for three centuries. Under their rule, Tripolitania developed into a thriving Mediterranean trading center. This period of prosperity lasted until Christian and Muslim powers began to compete for control of the important Libyan seaports.

By the fourteenth century, the Fezzan region was the northernmost boundary of the kingdom of KANEM-BORNU, which stretched as far as Wadai in the east. By controlling Zawilah in the Fezzan, Kanem-Bornu was guaranteed an important route to the Mediterranean coast for the salt trade.

See also: CYRENE (Vol. I); LIBYA (Vols. I, III).

Further reading: Ronald B. St, John, *Historical Dictionary of Libya* (Lanham, Md.: Scarecrow Press, 1998).

Limpopo River
A 1,100 mile-long (1,770 km) river located in Southeast Africa that passes through the present-day countries of SOUTH AFRICA, BOTSWANA, ZIMBABWE, and MOZAMBIQUE before emptying into the Indian Ocean. The word *Limpopo* may come from the Sotho word meaning "river of the waterfall." Its main tributary is the Olifants River, which flows into the Limpopo about 130 miles (209 km) from its mouth, just north of Maputo in Mozambique. The upper portion of the river is known as the Crocodile (Krokodil) River. The lower portion waters Mozambique's fertile agricultural region.

As early as the eighth century, the Limpopo was an important artery connecting TRADE routes between the interior of southern Africa and the towns on the SWAHILI COAST. These connections made it possible for peoples of the interior to participate in INDIAN OCEAN TRADE. For instance, Africans brought IVORY, animal skins, and later GOLD and COPPER from the interior and traded these goods for Arab wares. Archaeological finds at interior sites—in Botswana, GREAT ZIMBABWE, and present-day South Africa—attest to the vast circulation of Indian Ocean trade goods.

Before the fifth century, the fertile valley between the Limpopo and the Zambezi Rivers was populated by the KHOIKHOI, whose culture did not reach its zenith until between the eleventh and fifteenth centuries, after they converted to pastoralism from being nomadic hunter-gatherers. Around 1100, BANTU MIGRATIONS influenced the region with the BANTU-speaking Sotho, Chopi, and Tsonga peoples moving into the lower valley of the Limpopo. The Shona, VENDA, and Shaba peoples also populated the region between the middle Zambezi and the Limpopo before the fifteenth century.

At the end of the fifteenth century, in 1498, Portuguese explorer Vasco da GAMA saw the Limpopo River for the first time and renamed it the Espiritu Santo ("Holy Spirit") River.

See also: MAPUTO (Vol. III); MOZAMBIQUE (Vol. III); PORTUGAL AND AFRICA (Vol. III); SHONA KINGDOMS (Vol. III).

lost-wax process Method of hollow metal casting that dates to c. 3000 BCE. Also known by the French term *cire perdue*, this type of casting was used in Africa during the thirteenth and fourteenth centuries, most notably by the YORUBA of present-day Nigeria and the people of BENIN. Art historians consider the BRONZE sculptures to be masterpieces. The strikingly realistic Yoruba and Benin sculptures often portrayed kings and other members of the aristocracy, in whose tombs the objects were placed. Images of nature were also important subjects for the Benin and Yoruba sculptors, as can be seen by their depictions on bronze bowls and pots with elaborate designs.

The lost-wax process, still in use today, begins with a wax mold that is encased between two heat-proof layers. The wax is melted and drained off, and the resulting hollow form is filled with molten metal, which assumes the desired form of the original wax mold. This process is also used to cast bronze sculptures using clay models. In this case a figure or shape is made out of beeswax and then covered in liquid clay and cooked over a fire. The heat of the flames dissolves the wax, and the wax is then replaced by empty space. At this point, tin and copper, which are the alloys used to make bronze, are melted and then poured into the cavity of the hardened clay. Once the object has cooled, the clay is knocked away from the metal and the bronze sculpture is cast.

See also: ART (Vols. I, II, III); CRAFTSPEOPLE (Vol. II); METALLURGY (Vol. I).

Lualaba River Headstream of the Congo River, located entirely in present-day Democratic Republic of the Congo. The river is about 1,100 miles (1,770 km) long.

Archaeological discoveries indicate that several Iron Age groups had settled along the banks of the Lualaba toward the end of the first millennium. Excavation sites at Katoto and SANGA produced evidence of technologically sophisticated cultures that were involved in TRADE and small-scale mining.

The lakes formed by the Lualaba River created an important link for trade between the Shaba peoples of the savanna with peoples of the LUBA and LUNDA Kingdoms, located to the east of the Lualaba. The region between the Lualaba and the Luapula Rivers contained salt mines and COPPER deposits, which were mined, refined, and exported to the coastal regions by the kingdoms.

See also: CONGO RIVER (Vol. I); SALT MINING (Vol. II); ZAÏRE (Vol. III).

Luba (Baluba) Ethnic group of present-day Democratic Republic of the Congo and Zambia. The Luba are regarded as one of the earliest peoples to practice IRONWORKING in central Africa. Their ancestors were farmers who, as early as 400, inhabited the Lake Kisale region in what is now the Katanga province of Congo (Kinshasha).

Oral tradition mentions Luba chiefs in Malawi and Zambia, but very little is known about their early history. The area in which the Luba lived, however, was well-suited to the growth of powerful chiefdoms: The COPPER mines of the Katanga region were nearby, the soil was fertile, and ease of movement through the savannah stimulated trade. The Luba were an agricultural people whose communities slowly grew into small trading and farming chiefdoms. Between 1300 and 1400, they came under the sway of the Nkongolo dynasty, which, in turn, was conquered in the early 1400s by Ilunga Kalala, whom oral tradition describes as a fierce hunter. Ilunga Kalala expanded the kingdom's boundaries and took control of the Katanga copper mines and the trade routes to East Africa.

See also: LUBA EMPIRE (Vol. III); LUNDA EMPIRE (Vol. III); MALAWI (Vol. III); MINING (Vol. III).

Lugbara Ethnic group inhabiting present-day northwestern UGANDA and the adjoining part of the Democratic Republic of the Congo. Isolated by geography, the Lugbara have maintained their traditional ways longer than their neighbors. They and the Madi people, to the east, are the only speakers of Eastern Sudanic languages in the area. They are settled agriculturalists who lack a central political authority. Little is known of Lugbara history prior to 1900.

Lunda kingdom Monarchy established c 1450 or earlier in central Africa in a region on the upper Kasai River that is within the boundaries of modern ANGOLA and the Democratic Republic of the Congo.

Some histories place the foundation of the kingdom of the powerful BANTU-speaking Lunda c. 1450, when members of the LUBA royal family broke off to start their own kingdom in lands to the west. Other histories suspect an even earlier starting date but note that the Lunda kingdom remained a loose confederation and did not develop its hallmark strong centralized government until around 1450. At that time, a chief from Luba territory named Chibunda Ilunga married a Lunda princess named Rweej and then united the disparate clans of Lunda country under his political and religious leadership. As a result, the Lunda kingdom developed into a complex governing structure that united the groups under a common Lunda culture.

The Lunda kingdom practiced "perpetual kingship," whereby a new king assumed the identity of the one he replaced. In essence, the successor to the title became his predecessor. Through perpetual kingship, alliances and agreements could remain in force from generation to generation because they were made by the "same" king.

In the sixteenth century, the Lunda model of government began to spread throughout the savannas of central Africa as several Lunda princes and adventurers left the kingdom with small groups of followers.

See also: LUNDA EMPIRE (Vol. III); PORTUGAL AND AFRICA (Vol. III); SHONA KINGDOMS (Vol. III).

Luo (Lwo, Lwoo, Dholuo, Kavirondo) NILOTIC people of the Great Lakes region of East Africa who migrated there from the southern SUDAN in a steady stream that started in the sixteenth century and ended in the nineteenth century. Their language belongs to the Chari-Nile branch of the family of NILO-SAHARAN LANGUAGES.

Luo society, governed by clan leaders and bound by ties of patrilineal kinship and marriage, has traditionally been decentralized. The people live in scattered homesteads and survive by hunting, FISHING, farming, and cattle herding. Unlike many of their neighbors, they do not practice circumcision or group themselves in age sets. Their traditional religion is animist.

As they moved into UGANDA, the Luo supplanted the TUTSI people, who, according to some theories, had begun migrating there from the north as early as the eleventh century. The Luo reorganized KITARA as the kingdom of BUNYO-RO-KITARA under the Bito dynasty and established a number of kingdoms north and west of Lake VICTORIA, including Buddu, BUGANDA, Buruli, and Busoga, all of which were governed by relatives of the Bito dynasty kings.

See also: AGE SETS (Vol. I); ANIMISM (Vol. I); BUNYORO (Vol. I); BUNYORO-KITARA (Vols. II, III); LUO (Vol. III); NKOLE (Vol. III).

M

Maasai (Masai) Nomadic people of present-day central KENYA and northern Tanzania.

The Maasai ethnic group emerged around 500 BCE along the Nile River; however, it was not until the sixteenth century that they migrated into Kenya and Tanzania. As the Maasai moved through the Great Rift Valley of Kenya, they found the highland region inhabited by numerous pastoral groups. In order to open up pastures for their herds, the Maasai forced the local peoples from their lands. As a result, they became a feared group that ultimately gained control over much of East Africa's grazing lands.

Maasai society was based on age sets, which were established for military purposes. In the system of age sets, children, young adults, and elders each had their own duties and responsibilities. Young boys were given extensive military training because they were expected to serve as soldiers during their young adult years. Their job was to guard the herds and secure grazing lands. The Maasai did not operate under a centralized authority. Instead, they were organized into villages made up of several extended families and governed by a council of elders.

See also: AGE SETS (Vol. I); MAASAI (Vols. I, III); PASTORALISM (Vol. I); RIFT VALLEY (Vol. I).

Madagascar Fourth-largest island in the world, located in the Indian Ocean, 242 miles (390 km) off the southeastern coast of Africa across the Mozambique Channel. The modern country of Madagascar is made up of the island of Madagascar and several much smaller islands that surround it.

Although significantly closer to Africa than to Asia or the islands of the Pacific, the first inhabitants of this mountainous island were probably INDONESIAN COLONISTS, who arrived by sea between 400 and 900. To account for the BANTU influence on the island, anthropologists theorize that en route to Madagascar in the ninth or tenth centuries, a second wave of Indonesian emigrants picked up a number of Bantu-speaking peoples along the East African coast. It is also possible that the country's Bantu influence came with the arrival of Antalaotra traders in the eleventh century. This mixture of Arab, Bantu, and Persian people, known as the MALAGASY, engaged in extensive trade with Arabia and the African coast.

Portuguese traders arrived in 1500, but they were not successful at colonizing the islands. By the middle of the sixteenth century, three Malagasy groups, the Antemoro, Sakalava, and Merina, developed monarchies. None of these groups, however, was able to dominate the greater part of the country until the Merina conquered many of their neighboring kingdoms almost 200 years later.

See also: ANTALAOTRA (Vol. III); ANTEMORO (Vol. III); INDIAN OCEAN TRADE (Vol. II); MADAGASCAR (Vol. III); MERINA (Vol. III).

Madhane Alem The largest of the eleven underground churches carved out of rock in the village of LALIBELA (originally called al-ROHA) in north-central ETHIOPIA in the early thirteenth century.

Mafia Island Island located off of Tanzania on the East African coast, south of ZANZIBAR. For centuries, possibly as long as two millennia, ARABS and Persians traded from the port of Mocha, which is now Yemen, down the

African coast as far as MOZAMBIQUE, and including MADA-GASCAR, Zanzibar, and Mafia Island. Though KILWA was the major port on the Indian Ocean, Mafia Island was an important stop on the trade route.

According to the *Kilwa Chronicle*, the Mwera people lived on the island but were ruled by Muslim settlers from Songo Songo before Arab rule. This chronicle also records that the SHIRAZI ARABS bought the island of Kilwa around 975. The reigning sultan sent his son Bashat to rule Mafia Island. Kua and Kisimani, two ancient towns built c. 1000 that are now in ruins, may have been founded by Bashat. For centuries, the Shirazi were powerful in this area at the same time that ISLAM was being introduced throughout eastern Africa.

As was the case with much of the East African coast, the first Europeans to arrive were the Portuguese, led by explorer Vasco da GAMA, in about 1498. Within seven years, Arab control was put down, and the Portuguese claimed Mafia Island, along with much of the coast, as their own. The Arabic name for the island, *Morfiyeh*, or *Manifiyah*, meaning "archipelago," remained in use. Scholars speculate that the name *Mafia* could also be derived from the Kiswahili words *mahali pa afya*, meaning "healthy dwelling place."

See also: INDIAN OCEAN TRADE (Vol. II); MAFIA ISLAND (Vol. I).

Maghan, Mansa (r. 1337–1341) *Son of Mansa Musa and short-term leader of the Mali Empire.*

Son of the empire-builder Mansa MUSA, Mansa Maghan assumed control of the MALI EMPIRE after his father's death. Little is known about Maghan's rule, but at the time he came to the throne, Mali was a powerful and prosperous nation. Brief references to Maghan by scholars make it clear that he was not able to lead with the same ability as his father, which led to invasions of Mali's territories, including GAO.

al-Maghili (late fifteenth century) *Arab cleric from the Saharan oasis region of Tuat in Algeria, who wrote guidelines for early Muslim leaders striving to uphold the teachings of the Koran.*

As a young man, Muhammad al-Maghili was a North African Muslim scholar known for persecuting Jews. Around 1490, he left Tuat and traveled south to Agades, TAKEDDA, KANO, KATSINA, and GAO, where he converted many people to ISLAM. His primary goal was to get Muslim rulers to apply the teachings of Islam to state rule. He stressed the need for a militant foreign policy, limited or nonexistent taxation, and a good advisory board. During this time, sharifs gained social prominence in Muslim society because al-Maghili adamantly encouraged states to respect them and compensate them gener-

ously. (*Sharif*, an Arabic word meaning "noble" or "high born," is a title of respect given to members of the prestigious Hashim clan, of which the prophet MUHAMMAD was a member.) Al-Maghili's work played an important role in shaping the early HAUSA STATES, particularly the areas from Lake CHAD to the middle Niger.

In his *Obligations of Princes*, al-Maghili outlined his teachings. This work was commissioned by Sarki RUMFA of Kano, one of the first rulers in early Hausaland to accept Islam. Rumfa commissioned al-Maghili to write guidelines for princely behavior so that he could better serve his people. A few years later ASKIA MUHAMMAD TOURÉ, a Muslim leader who took control of the SONGHAI Empire at the end of the fifteenth century, also called upon al-Maghili for guidance. For Askia Muhammad, al-Maghili wrote a treatise called *Answers to the Questions of the Emir al-Hadjdj Abdullah ibn Abu Bakr*. Askia Muhammad commissioned al-Maghili to help him face the challenge of ruling a largely non-Muslim population, although he did not appear to heed much of al-Maghili's advice.

Despite al-Maghili's teachings, Islam did not penetrate more than a handful of small states. It was almost 100 years after his death that al-Maghili's teachings reached the height of their influence.

Further Reading: John O. Hunwick, *Shari'a in Songhay: The Replies of Al-Maghili to the Questions of Askia Al-Hajj Muhammad* (Oakville, Conn.: David Brown Book Company, 1985).

Maghrib (Maghreb) Region of North Africa that covers the stretch of the Mediterranean coast as well as inland areas from LIBYA to the Atlas Mountains, west of Gibraltar. The Maghrib was originally inhabited by BERBERS. However, after the ARABS conquered Egypt in 642, they extended their military campaign west into the Maghrib, which they also referred to as Bilad al-Maghrib, or "Lands of Sunset." The first capital of the Maghrib was Al-Qayrawan (Kairouan), founded just south of Tunis by Uqbah Ibn Nafi (Sidi Okba), who was in charge of the Arab army that occupied Tunisia in 670. Uqbah's successful military campaigns and dramatic death in battle made him the legendary hero of the Muslim conquest of the Maghrib.

The Maghrib became a province of the Arab Muslim empire in 705. ISLAM spread rapidly among the Berbers, and, by the eleventh century, had replaced CHRISTIANITY in almost all of the Maghrib. But the Berbers were not content under Arab rule, which was often oppressive and benefited only the Arab ruling class. The Arabs took Berber captives, especially women, which further infuriated the population.

In the ninth century, the Berbers rebelled against the Arabs, fragmenting the Maghrib into separate Muslim states. The uprising wasn't a total success, however. In the end, only the small principality of SIJILMASA in southern MOROCCO was ruled by Berbers (Banu Midrar). The other states remained under Arab rule and retained most of the political influence.

This changed during the eleventh century, when the ALMORAVIDS came to power. This Muslim Berber dynasty ruled Morocco and Muslim Spain in the eleventh and twelfth centuries and unified the Maghrib for a second time. The Almoravids were succeeded by the ALMOHADS, Zenata Berbers, who declared a jihad, or holy war, against the Almoravids and ended their empire.

Maguzawa Ethnic group that has long inhabited the region south of KANO, one of the HAUSA STATES. Also called the Bamaguje, the Maguzawa probably settled in the area even before the founding of Kano by Sarki, or King, BAGAUDA around 1000. Though the Maguzawa share the HAUSA culture and language, they historically have distinguished themselves from other Hausa people by rejecting ISLAM. In fact, the name Maguzawa most likely evolved from the Arabic word *majus*, meaning "pagan."

Mahdi According to Islamic prophesies dating to c. 680, the Mahdi is a messiah-like deliverer who is to arrive shortly before "the end of time" to restore justice and spread ISLAM throughout the world.

The word *mahdi* means "enlightened" or "one who is divinely guided." The prophet MUHAMMAD is reported to have promised that a descendent from his family would come to earth seven to nine years before the end of the world. This person would bring equity and justice to a world that would, at the time, be filled with neither. While some believe that Muhammad said that the Mahdi would bring people to God through Islam, others dispute this part of the prophecy.

Over the last two millennia, several people have identified themselves as the Mahdi. Ubayd Allah, founder of the FATIMID dynasty, is one of the best-known. During the seventh century, followers of Islam split into two factions, the Sunni and the Shiites. About 900, Shiite Muslims brought the Kutama BERBERS of LIBYA into Islam, which led to war between Shiites and Sunni Muslims in Libya over territory. The victorious Shiites installed Ubayd Allah, also known as Ubaidalla Said, as their political leader and imam. (The imam was the Shiite religious leader, believed to be the successor of the prophet Muhammad.) Berbers asserted that Ubayd Allah was the Mahdi, and the city of Mahdia was so called in his honor.

Later, in the twelfth century, the Shiite MUHAMMAD IBN TUMART (c. 1080–1130) emerged as the leader of the ALMOHAD movement. As a reformer of the established order, ibn Tumart was believed to be the Mahdi by many of his followers.

See also: MALIKI SUNNI DOCTRINE (Vol. II); SHIISM (Vol. II).

Maimonides, Moses (Musa ibn-Maimon)
(1135–1204) *Jewish physician and philosopher.*

Moses Maimonides has been called the most important figure in medieval Judaism. Son of a rabbi, he was born in Córdoba in Muslim Spain in 1135. The full freedom of religion that the people of Córdoba enjoyed was abrogated in 1148 when Córdoba fell to the fundamentalist ALMOHAD rulers of Morocco, who demanded that all nonbelievers submit to Islam or leave the city. For eleven years, Maimonides' family remained in the city, secretly practicing Judaism while living as Muslims, until in 1159 they decided to flee Spain and move to Fez in North Africa. Moses continued his religious studies at Fez and also began to study medicine. Fez, also under Almohad rule, was no more welcoming to Jews than Córdoba was. Thus, Maimonides moved to Palestine in 1165 but soon left for Egypt, where Jews were accorded freedom of religion. Maimonides stayed until his death in 1204.

In Egypt, he was at first the rabbi, or religious leader, of the Jewish community of al-Fustat (now Cairo), the Egyptian capital. In need of money to support himself, he also became court physician to the famous sultan Salah ad-din (c. 1137–1193), known in the west as SALADIN, the Egyptian leader who was victorious over the English monarch Richard the Lion-Hearted (1157–1199) in the Third Crusade (1189–1192). Maimondes also served as physician to Salah ad-din's elder son, Sultan al-Malik al-Afdel (r. 1198–1200).

It is as a writer and philosopher that Maimonides has had his greatest impact. He wrote, in ARABIC, a commentary on Jewish law, the *Kitab al-Siraj*, at the age of 23. In Hebrew, he wrote a major codification of Jewish law, the *Mishne Torah* ("The Torah reviewed"), which he completed in 1178. He also translated many Arabic medical texts into Hebrew, which made them accessible for subsequent translation into Latin. Maimonides' most famous and influential book, written in Arabic and completed in 1191, was his philosophical work, *Dalalat al-Hai'ran*, or *The Guide of the Perplexed*, in which he tried to reconcile logic and faith.

Further Reading: Kenneth Seeskin, *Searching for a Distant God: The Legacy of Maimonides* (New York: Oxford University Press, 2000).

Malagasy Ethnic group of the island of MADAGASCAR and the language that they speak. Malagasy dialects evolved exclusively on Madagascar, beginning with the arrival of the Malayo-Polynesian peoples who first colonized the island, perhaps as early as the first century CE.

By the tenth century, the original INDONESIAN COLONISTS had mixed with BANTU-speaking peoples from the African mainland, and the Malagasy language consequently adopted many Bantu words. The diverse mix of African and Indonesian peoples established several agricultural chiefdoms on the island and also practiced animal husbandry and FISHING.

After the tenth century, Malagasy culture began to reflect the influence of the East African SWAHILI COAST kingdoms that were active in INDIAN OCEAN TRADE. Because of their influence, Malagasy came to have many Arabic words as well. In the early sixteenth century, Portuguese explorers visited Madagascar and came into contact with the Malagasy kingdoms of the Antemore, Antaisaka, and Merina. Fortunately for the Malagasy, the Portuguese were more interested in establishing strongholds on the East African mainland than they were on an offshore island, and, therefore, never conquered or colonized Madagascar.

See also: BETSIMISERAKA (Vols. II, III); PORTUGAL AND AFRICA (Vol. III).

Mali Empire Empire in western Africa that flourished from the mid-thirteenth century through the fifteenth century. At its zenith, Mali commanded not only the entirety of the ancient GHANA EMPIRE but surrounding territories from the coast of the Atlantic Ocean on the west to TAKEDDA on the east.

As the 1,000-year empire of Ghana (c. 300–1240) declined, the once prosperous land became the target of invaders. Among those was the legendary MANDINKA leader SUNDIATA (d. c. 1255), considered the first unifying king of Mali. Tradition holds that Sundiata (which means "the hungering lion") was a sickly boy who grew into a powerful ruler through sheer determination and remarkable skill. In 1230, after wresting control of Mali from SUMANGURU (d. c. 1235), king of the SUSU, Sundiata was declared the undisputed king of Mali. At the time of Sundiata's death in 1255, Mali was a greatly expanded, thriving empire. Sundiata had revived the GOLD trade and the SALT TRADE, started a rich agricultural system, and developed a political infrastructure with provinces and towns attended by royally appointed governors.

Sundiata was succeeded by a series of kings who did little to advance the empire. In 1307 Mansa (or Emperor) MUSA, a descendant of Sundiata, began his extraordinary reign. Mali was at the peak of its political and economic influence when Mansa Musa made the HAJJ, or pilgrimage, to MECCA—a longstanding tradition of the Muslim rulers of Mali. In an impressive display of wealth and power, his journey in 1324 included an entourage of

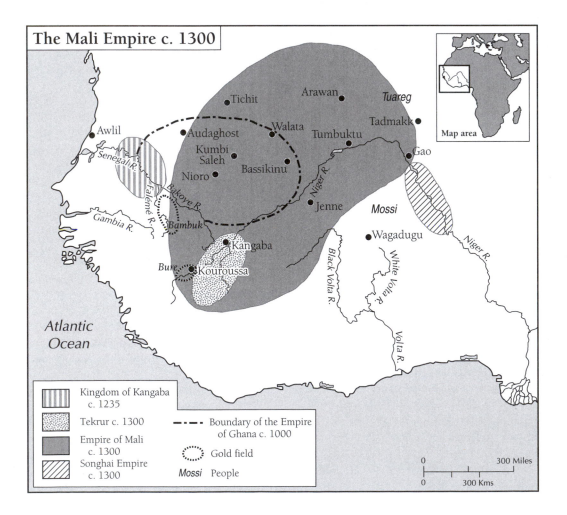

The Mali Empire c. 1300

Awlil

Tichit

Arawan

Tuareg

Tadmakk

Walata

Audaghost

Tumbuktu

Map area

Kumbi Saleh

Gao

Senegal R.

Nioro

Bassikinu

Niger R.

Falemé R.

Bakoye R.

Gambia R.

Bambuk

Jenne

Mossi

Wagadugu

Niger R.

Kangaba

Black Volta R.

White Volta R.

Bure

Kouroussa

Atlantic Ocean

Volta R.

	Kingdom of Kangaba c. 1235
	Tekrur c. 1300
	Empire of Mali c. 1300
	Songhai Empire c. 1300

Boundary of the Empire of Ghana c. 1000

Gold field

Mossi People

0   300 Miles

0   300 Kms

This carved wooden door in in the village of Ogdol in Mali follows an ancient tradition of symbolically decorated doors.
© *Charles & Josette Lenars/CORBIS*

some 60,000 retainers and enough gold to depress the CAIRO gold market. A man of culture and learning, Mansa Musa's renown spread to western Europe, bringing the empire of Mali international fame. Moroccan traveler IBN BATTUTA chronicled his visit through Mali in 1352 and 1353, further enhancing the empire's reputation as a land of plentiful lodgings, bustling markets, safe roads and well-followed rules. Mansa Musa brought Muslim scholars into Mali and made the city of TIMBUKTU a center of learning for all ISLAM.

The golden age of the Mali Empire began to decline after Mansa Musa's death in 1332, although it enjoyed a brief return to glory from 1351 to 1359 during the reign of Mansa SULAYMAN. Gradually, however, the rival SONGHAI Empire supplanted Mali in the lands that it once dominated; the city of GAO in Mali became the center of this new empire.

ASKIA MUHAMMAD TOURÉ, often called Askia the Great, ruled Songhai from 1493 to 1528. During his reign, he seized vast lands from Mali as well as from the HAUSA STATES and the BERBERS. In those years, Timbuktu flourished again as an ISLAMIC CENTER OF LEARNING. Invaders from MOROCCO overran Songhai in 1591.

See also: KINGDOMS AND EMPIRES (Vol. II); KINGDOMS AND EMPIRES OF THE WEST AFRICAN SAVANNA (Vol. II); MALI (Vol. III).

Further reading: N. Levtzion, *Ancient Ghana and Mali* (New York: Holmes and Meier Publishing, 1973).

Malik ibn Anas (Malik ibn Anas ibn Malik ibn Abi 'Amir al-Asbahi) (c. 715–795) *Medina's leading Islamic legal scholar and theologian.*

Malik came from a family dedicated to the study and transmittal of knowledge. His great-grandfather is believed to have been a companion of the prophet Mohammed (c. 570–632).

The *Muwatta* is Malik's most famous work. It is heralded as being the foundation on which Islamic law is built and consists of Malik's interpretation of the doctrines and discussions of Muhammad, his companions and followers, as well as the most respected legal scholars of the city of MEDINA in what is today Saudi Arabia. The word *muwatta* means "the approved," and the work was so named because it was accepted by seventy of Malik's contemporaries in Medina. The title also means "the clear book" in that it can be understood by anyone interested in attaining knowledge. Ash-Shafi'i, Malik's most renowned student, declared that besides the KORAN, the *Muwatta* was the most important book in the world.

Malik was so respected and admired in his time that at the end of the UMAYYAD dynasty (c. 660–750), when the caliph, Abu Jafar al-Mansur, was trying to usurp political control from his rival Muhummad ibn 'Abdallah, the people of Medina sought Malik's advice as to where their loyalties should lie. Malik reasoned that allegiance to Mansur was not binding because it had been given under force. Malik eventually paid for his frankness: after securing power, Mansur executed Muhummad and had Malik beaten for his disloyalty during the rebellion.

In honor of their teacher, Malik's students formed the Maliki sect, which began in Medina but flourished throughout North and West Africa and in much of Arabia. Tradition, reason, and tolerance were the hallmarks of Malik's philosophy and the ideology of those who followed him.

See also: MALIKI SUNNI DOCTRINE (Vol. II).

Further reading: H. Mansour Mansour, *The Maliki School of Law: Spread and Domination in North and West Africa 8th to 14th Centuries C.E.* (Bethesda, Md.: Austin and Winfield Publishers, 1994).

Maliki Sunni doctrine One of the four SUNNI schools of Islamic law. Sunni ISLAM is the mainstream, traditionalist branch of the Muslim faith and also its largest. The Maliki sect is one of the four major orthodox Sunni sects and the one dominant in North and West Africa.

Sunnites, as the follower of Sunni law are called, believe that the rightful successors of the prophet Muhammad (c. 570–632) were the first four caliphs (a title, from the Arabic *kalifah*, meaning "successor," given to the civil and religious head of the Muslim state that came into being following Muhammad's death). These were ABU BAKR (c. 573–634), Muhammad's close companion and adviser, and the three caliphs that immediately followed. According to the Sunni, all caliphs thereafter were required to be descendents of Muhammad, although in practice they accepted the authority of any ruler who maintained order and promoted Islam, whatever his origins. In contrast, the minority Shiite sect of Islam, which followed the tenets of SHIISM, believes that authority belongs solely to Muhammad's son-in-law, the fourth caliph, Ali, and his descendants. Disagreements regarding the source of political, and ultimately spiritual, power outlasted the end of the Caliphate in the thirteenth century.

The Hanafi, the SHAFII, and the Hanbali are the three other orthodox Sunni sects. Each sect acknowledges three sources of Islamic law: the KORAN; the Sunna, or the words and deeds of Muhammad; and *qiyas*, or reasoning by analogy to similar situations at the time when Muhammad lived. The sects differ only in the amount of emphasis they give each legal source. The Maliki school, founded by MALIK IBN ANAS and centered in MEDINA, is the dominant Sunni sect in North and West Africa. Malik, an eighth-century imam, or religious leader, wrote the earliest surviving Muslim book of laws, the *Muwatta*. Malik's writings focus on practicing Islam in accordance with the Sunna of the Holy Prophet. His followers established a school of *figh*, or religious law, called the Maliki Madhhab that is modeled after his teachings.

By the thirteenth century, Islam had spread throughout much of Africa. Shortly thereafter, the ALMOHADS announced a return to the Maliki school of Islam. Maliki remains the most widely practiced sect of Islam in Africa today.

Further reading: H. Mansour Mansour, *The Maliki School of Law: Spread and Domination in North and West Africa 8th to 14th Centuries, C.E.* (Bethesda, Md.: Austin and Winfield Publishers, 1994).

Malindi Settlement on the SWAHILI COAST that was an important source of IRON ore in Africa before the period of European colonization. Like other East African coastal towns, Malindi attracted a large number of Arab, Persian, and Indian MERCHANTS. Although iron ore was the primary export, seashells, pearls, turtle shells, and fish were also traded in Malindi. The goods imported included glass beads, painted ceramic tiles, and POTTERY.

See also: ARAB COASTAL TRADE (Vol. II); MALINDI (Vol. III); PERSIAN TRADERS (Vol. II).

Mamluks Members of an elite military unit made up of captives enslaved by Abbasid or other Islamic rulers to serve in Middle Eastern and North African armies. Mamluk, or Mameluke, from an ARABIC word that means "one who is owned," has been used to describe the young children who were removed from their homelands to serve the Abbasid dynasty caliphs in North Africa from about 750 to 945. Rigorously trained as mounted horsemen and skilled archers, the Mamluks became powerful soldier-kings who enforced the payment of tax revenues to the ruling class. Many Mamluks were converted to Islam and rose to positions of great influence and even

Costume de Roustant Mameluk du Premier Consul
À Paris chez Jean, rue Jean de Beauvais, N.º 3a.

The Mamluk rulers of Egypt (r. 1250–1517) were descended from an elite force of fighters of Turkish, Afghan, Balkan, and Circassian origin whom the Ayabbid sultans of Egypt (r. 1099–1250) bought out of slavery as children, trained, and put into royal service. This nineteenth-century illustration gives a very romantic view of a Mamluk cavalryman. © *Gianni Dagli Orti/CORBIS*

royalty. Although guaranteed their freedom at age eighteen, the Mamluks were still restricted by their enslaved status and were unable to pass their status as soldier-kings or landowners on to their descendants. In the thirteenth century, the Mamluks seized power and established a Mamluk state that encompassed Arabia, Syria, EGYPT, and parts of LIBIA and Nubia.

See also: MAMLUKS (Vol. III).

Mamprusi (Manprusi, Mampruli)

People who inhabit the region between the White VOLTA and Nasia Rivers in present-day Ghana and BURKINA FASO who established a kingdom in West Africa during the fourteenth century. Known as the Dagbamba in ancient times, the Mamprusi changed their name to avoid confusion with the neighboring DAGOMBA.

Traditional Mamprusi society was patrilineal, with a strong emphasis on ancestor worship. Their agricultural economy focused on hoe cultivation to produce millet, corn, and yams. Hunting and FISHING were a secondary means of subsistence. Mamprusi, like most of the kingdoms south of the Niger bend, also participated in exchange along TRANS-SAHARAN TRADE ROUTES.

According to oral tradition, Na Gbewa, the son of a semimythical figure named Kpogonumbo, was the founder of the Mamprusi kingdom. The three youngest sons of Na Gbewa led the three kingdoms of Mamprusi, Nanumba, and Dagomba.

See also: ANCESTOR WORSHIP (Vol. I); MAMPRUSI (Vol. III).

Manan

Pre-Islamic capital of the ancient Kanem Kingdom, located in the Lake CHAD region. Historical evidence suggests that the ancestors of Kanem's SEFUWA people were the Duguwa, who established their capital at Manan as far back as the sixth century. Nearly 100 years later, the Sefuwa seem to have taken control of Kanem and moved the capital to NJIMI.

Sefuwa oral tradition, however, maintains that Manan remained the capital until the thirteenth-century. It is likely that this reflects changes in Sefuwa oral history that took place shortly after their conversion to ISLAM. Most likely, these changes represent an attempt by the Sefuwa to establish a clear hereditary claim to Manan, which was the supposed birthplace of the thirteenth-century Muslim sultanates.

See also: KANEM-BORNU (Vol. II).

Mande (Manding, Mandingo, Mandingue)

Group of West African peoples that includes the BAMBARA, SONINKE, and MANDINKA; also the language that these people speak. The Mande are credited with introducing agriculture, IRONWORKING, and advanced political systems to western Africa. They are divided into two groups, the Mande-tan and the Mande-fu.

The Mande-tan inhabit the region surrounding the upper Niger River. This area, which is the original Mande homeland, includes parts of present-day Guinea, Liberia, Mali, SIERRA LEONE, and SENEGAL. The Mande-tan have traditionally established strict hierarchical class structures, with farmers holding the highest rank in society. In contrast, craftspeople and other artisans were considered to be of lower social rank.

The Mande-fu, who migrated from the Mande homeland, developed more egalitarian societies as they moved to new areas. The majority settled in present-day BURKINA FASO, The GAMBIA, Guinea-Bissau, IVORY COAST, and Senegal.

The Mande were among the first agriculturalists in Africa. They domesticated millet, sorghum, African rice, peanuts, and okra, all of which became staple CROPS of SUB-SAHARAN AFRICA. GOLD mining became the primary source of income for some of the more powerful Mande kingdoms. Both the GHANA EMPIRE, which flourished from around 900 to 1200, and the MALI EMPIRE, active especially from around 1200 to 1400, traded gold for SALT and textiles. Nonetheless, agriculture remained the primary economic activity of most Mande peoples prior to the period of European colonization.

Mande social structures varied from group to group. Most were patrilineal and practiced polygamy. Those that converted to ISLAM (after their early contact with ARAB traders starting in the seventh century) integrated Middle Eastern customs into their own traditions.

See also: MILLET (Vol. I); SORGHUM (Vol. I).

Mandinka (Malinka, Malinke)

West African people who are part of the larger MANDE group; founders and rulers of the great MALI EMPIRE (c. 600–1250); also the name of the language spoken by these people.

Historically, the Mandinka people have made their home in western Africa. As one of the Mande cultures, the Mandinka likely descended from the ancient agriculturalists who invented crop cultivation in western Africa. In addition to agriculture, the Mande were known to be skilled CRAFTSPEOPLE and traders.

One of the most famous, oldest, and largest of the Mande kingdoms was the Mali Empire, which was founded by SUNDIATA (d. 1255), who is credited with unifying the people of his homeland of KANGABA in western Africa. Soon afterwards, Sundiata organized the Mandinka chiefs to fight in a war of independence against the SUSU people

This almost 22-inch (52-cm)-tall mask in the form of a face with comblike horns is of Mandinka origin. The mask is of a type used by the N'Tomo (Ndomo), a secret society that initiates young males into adulthood. © *Bowers Museum of Cultural Art/CORBIS*

The people of the Mali Empire had religious freedom, even though their ruler, Sundiata, was Muslim.

As a male-dominated culture, the oldest man in an extended Mandinka family was considered the head of the whole family. Groups of families with the same name, or clans, lived together in a village, and labor was divided along gender lines, with men tending the farm and women the home.

Traditionally, Mandinka homes were round, made of mud, and covered with a thatched roof. A wall enclosed the groups of homes that form a village.

Music always has been an important part of Mandinka culture, and the influence of the Mandinka has been traced to twentieth-century music. Traditional drum music is used in many rituals, such as the marriage ceremony.

Mapungubwe Capital city of ZIMBABWE from about 1075 to 1220, located above Bambandyanalo, just south of where the Shashe (Sashi) and the LIMPOPO Rivers meet.

Around 1075, a great influx of the Leopard's Kopje people, a BANTU-speaking group, emigrated from their site northwest of Mapungubwe, where they established a sophisticated community that thrived culturally, politically, and economically. Though they were a pastoral and agricultural society, the majority of their wealth came from the local and long-distance trading of GOLD, IRON, COPPER, IVORY, livestock, and BEADS AND JEWELRY. Local CRAFTSPEOPLE produced and traded fabric, ceramics, bone tools, and sculptures. Spindle whorls, which were used as weights for weaving, were first introduced in this part of Africa.

The social structure of Mapungubwe was three-tiered. At the top of the political ladder were the chiefs or kings, who lived in stone houses high up on the hill. The second tier was occupied by their wives and associates, who lived nearby but separate. The third tier, the majority of the population, was made up of the peasants—craftspeople and laborers who were dependent on the elite. This system in which the aristocracy lived isolated from their subjects is one of the earliest found in southern Africa.

Initially, there was much debate about the origin of the Mapungubwe inhabitants. Archaeologists who excavated sites in and around the Mapungubwe region refused to acknowledge the influence that the Leopard's Kopje people had on the area, for they felt that the society they were uncovering was so complex that it must have been heavily influenced by Muslims from the northern parts of Africa. But later discoveries of skeletal and cultural remains ended the dispute, proving beyond a doubt that the people of Mapungubwe were of sub-Saharan African descent.

Sometime between the thirteenth and fourteenth century the people of Mapungubwe headed north to GREAT ZIMBABWE for better trading resources and wealth.

and in the process extended his rule over the ancient GHANA EMPIRE as well. In time, the gold fields of western Africa also became part of the Mali Empire, and GOLD was added to the list of commodities traded by the Mandinka.

Unlike many other Mande peoples, the Mandinka adopted ISLAM. Although most Mandinka retained some of their traditional beliefs and spiritualist leanings, the majority had become Muslim by the thirteenth century.

Marinids BERBER people who conquered the ALMOHADS in the thirteenth century. The Marinids, also called the Banu Marin, ruled MOROCCO and other parts of North Africa until the early fifteenth century.

The Marinids were a nomadic group of the Zanatah people who, during the early part of the thirteenth century, began to migrate into northeastern Morocco from ALGERIA as the Almohad Empire slowly weakened.

In 1248, the Marinid sultan Abu Yahya conquered the Almohad towns of FEZ, Taza, Meknes, Sale, and Rabat. Fez was rebuilt as the Marinid capital. During the reign of Abu Yusuf Yaqub (1258-1286), who was unrelated to the earlier Almohad ruler of the same name, MARRAKECH and the remaining Almohad-ruled lands of the High Atlas region came under Marinid rule. With the capture of Marrakech in 1269, the Almohad dynasty effectively came to an end.

By the beginning of the fifteenth century, the Marinid dynasty was in chaos. After failed attempts under ABU AL-HASAN 'ALI (1297–1351) to conquer Christian Spain and to expand their territory in North Africa, Marinid resources were depleted. In Morocco they were overtaken by a related branch of people known as the Wattasids, who ruled until Fez was captured by the Sa'di sharifs in 1548.

See also: SA'DIDS (Vol. III).

Marka (Marca, Merca) Indian Ocean port city located in present-day Somalia. ARAB traders founded the city in the tenth century, but by the thirteenth century, Somali immigrants had settled extensively throughout the area. Soon, the Somalis became involved in inland TRADE via the CARAVAN routes from the African interior. Although the Indian Ocean coastline of Somalia does not have good harbors, Marka and the nearby towns of Brava and MOGADISHU are suitable ports. For this reason, the stretch of coast where these towns are situated became known as the Benadir coast, from the Persian word *bandar*, meaning "port."

See also: ARAB COASTAL TRADE (Vol. II); INDIAN OCEAN TRADE (Vol. II).

marketplace There is little evidence to suggest that marketplaces were a regular feature of village life in most regions of SUB-SAHARAN AFRICA between the fifth and the eighth centuries. It is thought, however, that it was common for small villages to create marketplaces to facilitate barter between peoples living in close proximity. Later, as villages evolved in all parts of sub-Saharan Africa, peoples like the IBO of Nigeria set up complex systems of organized markets that would be held on a regular basis, perhaps at intervals of four, ten, or twenty days, depending on the season. The commodities usually traded at these village marketplaces were local CROPS and foodstuffs and handmade items like baskets or jewelry. People who had no goods to trade would often barter for items by offering their labor in fair exchange.

Village markets existed primarily to balance the food surpluses and deficits between neighboring villages. Until about the eighth century, these local markets rarely played a role in long-distance TRADE, the exception being the local market that possessed rare items of high value—like beads or shells—or large volumes of less exceptional goods, such as certain grain crops. In these cases, goods might travel through a complex trade network organized by professional merchants. The goods moved along with the professional merchants from village to village before eventually finding their way to a larger regional marketplace.

Village markets were also differentiated by function. In seaside villages such as Yoff in Senegal, for example, a large marketplace traditionally would open when fishermen returned to shore with their catches. Hundreds of women would be involved in buying fish in bulk and then cleaning and preparing them for the village marketplace. In villages that had a mosque, the mosque served as a social center for the men, and the marketplace had the same function for the women. Many villagers visited the market once a day, if not more often, to obtain the goods they needed.

The bigger regional markets typically developed along busy trade routes or near government centers, where, unlike in the villages, there might be laborers for hire and accommodations for the traders and their pack animals.

A public market or market district in North Africa was called a souk, the Arabic word for "marketplace." In the larger cities such as TUNIS, these would also have been places to import and export Mediterranean-region goods. Visitors to the souk in thirteenth-century Fez in Morocco would smell bread being made and sold, see piles of olives, peppers, and spices for sale, and be able to buy goods made from leather produced at the nearby tannery or purchase a variety of silk, cotton, or woolen thread dyed in town, and do all this within sight of the Qarawiyin Mosque and theological school, founded in 859, the oldest university in the world.

See also: BARTER (Vol. I).

Marrakech (Marrakesh) City in west-central MOROCCO, on the fertile Haouz Plain.

Marrakech has long been one of the principal commercial centers of Morocco. The old section of the city, called the medina, was surrounded by a large palm grove and fortified walls that were built in the twelfth century. The medina is also known as the "red city," because its buildings and ramparts, built during the ALMOHAD period, are made from beaten clay of a rusty color. The heart of the medina is the Jema al-Fna (Jemmaa el-Fna) square, a busy souk, or marketplace. Nearby is the twelfth-century Koutoubia Mosque with its 253-foot (77-meter) minaret. Other buildings of historic significance include the sixteenth-century Sa'di Mausoleum, the eighteenth-century Dar el-Beda Palace (now a hospital), and the nineteenth-century Bahia royal residence. Much of the medina is still surrounded by twelfth-century walls.

The city was founded in 1062 by Yusuf ibn Tashfin (r. 1061–1106), the leader of the militant religious Muslim reformers called the ALMORAVIDS. As the Almoravid movement shifted its emphasis from promoting ISLAM to engaging in military conquest, the empire came to include territory as far east as ALGIERS as well as parts of Spain up to the Ebro River. Although it was not an entirely peaceful time for the region, North Africa benefited economically and culturally during the Almoravid period.

In 1147, Marrakech was captured by the Almohads, who between 1152 and 1160 were able to conquer all of the eastern MAGHRIB. Then, in 1269, Marrakech passed into the hands of the MARINIDS, who moved their capital to FEZ, in northern Morocco. New CARAVAN routes began to bypass Marrakech, and the city suffered economically. By the time the Sa'dids seized control of the city in 1522, it was a poor place, largely in ruins. The Sa'dids revitalized Marrakech, making it the new capital of southern Morocco. By the end of the sixteenth century, Marrakech was once again the leading city of Morocco, culturally and economically, with about 60,000 inhabitants.

See also: SA'DIDS (Vol. III).

Masmuda Group of sedentary BERBERS from MOROCCO who established the ALMOHAD dynasty. In the twelfth and thirteenth centuries, the Almohad dynasty stretched from North Africa to Spain. The dynasty's founder, MUHAMMAD IBN TUMART (c. 1080–1130), was recognized by the Masmuda as the messiah-like figure known as the MAHDI, meaning "righteous leader."

The Masmuda lived in the Grand Atlas region of southern Morocco. Unlike nomadic Berbers, the Masmuda had settled in permanent homes, farmed the land, and domesticated animals. The Masmuda were devout Muslims who often spoke both ARABIC and their native Berber dialect.

The Almohad dynasty, like the ALMORAVID dynasty that preceded it, was ruled by the Berber people. Its founder, Muhammad ibn Tumart was a Masmuda leader who sought to reform the excesses of the Almoravids. After studying in cities like Baghdad and MARRAKECH but failing to gain support, ibn Tumart returned to his home, where he gained a personal following among his fellow Masmuda. With their support, ibn Tumart began a rebellion against the ruling Almoravids by attacking their centers in Marrakech and Sus.

After ibn Tumart's death, his successor, ABD AL-MUMIN (c. 1094–1163), expanded the Almohad dynasty to include Spain. Al-Mumin, who did not belong to the Masmuda, changed the Almohad leadership into a traditional monarchy based on heredity. As a result, al-Mumin often fought with Masmuda chiefs for control of the dynasty. Between the pressures of unrest at home and long wars against Christian Crusaders in Spain, the Almohad Empire collapsed in the middle of the thirteenth century.

Further reading: Michael Brett and Elizabeth Fentress, *The Berbers* (Malden, Mass.: Blackwell Publishng, 1997).

Massawa (Metsewwa, Mits'iwa) Vital port city in northern ERITREA, extending from the region's coast to the neighboring islands of the DAHLAK ARCHIPELIGO. During Aksumite rule in the early Christian era, Massawa provided an essential link between merchants of the RED SEA TRADE and the exotic export items they sought in the interior of ETHIOPIA. In the early part of the eighth century, Muslims reportedly captured Massawa and the entire Dahlak Archipelago, subsequently destroying the city of ADULIS in reprisal for raids that the Aksumite rulers had made on southern Arabia.

Arab traders in Ethiopia made it impossible for Aksum to resume its former status in the lucrative Red Sea trade. However, under the ZAGWE DYNASTY (c. 1137-1220) trading briefly flourished, reportedly as a result of mutual cooperation between the Zagwe rulers and the early Muslim settlers in the region. By the time the SOLOMONIC DYNASTY reclaimed the Ethiopian throne about 1270, these Muslim settlements had developed into formidable CITY-STATES that dominated trade in Massawa and other ports along the Ethiopian coast.

Despite the attempts of several Solomonic rulers to restore control over trade, it was not until the mid-fifteenth century that Emperor ZARA YAKOB (r. 1434–1468) was successful in regaining dominance. He accomplished this by ordering military units and keeping a watchful administration on the region.

See also: TRADE (Vol. II).

Further reading: Jean Doresse, *Ethiopia* (New York: Frederick Ungar Publishing Company, 1959); Harold G. Marcus, *A History of Ethiopia* (Berkeley: University of California Press, 1994); Richard Pankhurst, *The Ethiopian Borderlands* (Lawrenceville, N.J.: The Red Sea Press, 1997).

Mas'udi, el (Masudi, Abd al-Hasan Ali ibn al-Husayn, Mas'udi, al-, Mas'udi al-Fustat, Abu al-Husayn 'Ali ibn al-Husayn al-Mas'udi, Masoudi) (888–957) *Arab writer and traveler.*

Mas'udi was born in Baghdad and exhibited a great capacity for learning from a young age. He felt the need to not rely only on books and teachers for his knowledge and chose to wander most of his life, learning about things firsthand and from those he met on his travels. He visited the east coast of Africa, Armenia, the Caspian Sea, China, India and the Indus Valley, Iran, Oman, Russia, Spain, Sri Lanka, and Syria before finally retiring to EGYPT about 947.

Mas'udi was a prolific writer and chronicler of all of the knowledge he gained on his travels. Though the manuscripts no longer exist, it is known that he wrote at least twenty titles, including volumes on Muslim beliefs and even one on poisons. It was his historical works, however, that earned him the title "Herodotus of the Arabs." Covering the breadth of world history, *Akhbar az-zaman* ("The history of time") filled thirty volumes.

As a follow-up to this ambitious work, Mas'udi wrote *Kitab al-awsat*, a companion work most likely covering history from a chronological standpoint. Mas'udi's best-known work, however, was *The Meadows of Gold and the Mines of Gems*; in ARABIC, *Murujadh-dhahab was ma'adin al'jawahir*. This work covered the same material as the previous two books but in far less detail, only 132 pages, thereby making it more accessible and readable. *The Meadows of Gold* began with the creation of the world and covered a wide range of topics, everything Mas'udi deemed intriguing or of use, including reflections on the geography, climate, economies, calendars, religion, literature, customs, and history of the various places he had visited. He described weather conditions, oceans, and the solar system as well.

Mas'udi's final work was *The Book of Notification and Verification*, or *Kitab at-tanbih wa al-ishraf*, written in the year before his death. In it, Mas'udi revised and recapitulated his earlier works.

See also: HERODOTUS (Vol. I); IBN BATTUA (Vol. II).

Matope (d. 1480) *Ruler of the Mwene Matapa kingdom that ruled in Southeast Africa from the fifteenth to the seventeenth century.*

Little is known of the events of Matope's life. He left the throne to his son Mokombo, whose rule became a period of unrest. Finally in 1490, Changa, the governor of the southern and central provinces of the MWENE MATAPA kingdom, rebelled against Makombo, declared the provinces independent, and named them the Rozwi kingdom. Changa added the Arabic title *amir*, "commander," to his name and has became known to historians as CHANGAMIRE. The Rozwi kingdom is often called Changamire, after the Changamire dynasty that Changa's son Changamire II founded. Changamire became the greatest power in central Africa until its fall in 1830.

See also: CHANGAMIRE DYNASTY (Vol. III), ROZWI (Vol. III).

Mauritania Modern country located on the Atlantic seaboard of northwestern Africa. During the third century, BERBERS from North Africa migrated into Mauritania. Many of the native peoples were enslaved, while others were integrated into a feudal system. The Berbers succeeded in monopolizing TRADE in the western SAHARA over the next few centuries. Three dominant Berber clans, the Lemtuna, Messuta, and Djodala, formed an alliance known as the Sanhaja confederation. By the ninth century, the confederation administered all trade between KUMBI SALEH, AUDAGHOST, TIMBUKTU, and the salt mines of the northwestern Sahara.

In the late tenth century, Ghanaian armies captured Audaghost, greatly cutting into the Berber trade monopoly. By the middle of the eleventh century, the ALMORAVIDS, who had organized in the coastal Mauritanian capital of NOUAKCHOTT, conquered most of the Saharan Berbers and converted them to the Maliki Sunni school of ISLAM. The Almoravids also gained control of the Western Sahara trade network established by the Berbers. They ruled Mauritania well into the thirteenth century.

During the mid-thirteenth century, ARABS from North Africa moved west. For nearly four centuries, they fought with the region's established Berber inhabitants, until finally gaining control over them by the middle of the seventeenth century.

See also: ISLAM, INFLUENCES OF (Vol. II); MALIKI SUNNI DOCTRINE (Vol. II); MAURITANIA (Vol. III); SALT MINING (Vol. II); SANHAJA BERBERS (Vol. II).

Mbanza Kongo (Mbanza Congo) Capital city of the KONGO KINGDOM during the early fifteenth century. This West African town, originally inhabited by the BAKONGO, became an important TRADE port for early Portuguese explorers. As early as 1490, Portuguese missionaries arrived at Mbanza Kongo. The Portuguese then imported masons, carpenters, and artisans, enabling them to build a large town in a few years.

In 1491, Nzinga Mbemba, the son of the Kongo king Nzinga Nkuwu, was greatly influenced by the Portuguese missionaries. He converted to CHRISTIANITY and changed his name to Afonso I. Nzinga Mbemba succeeded his father to the throne around 1505 and ruled for nearly forty years as the native Christian king of Mbanza. Portuguese customs were integrated into Kongo society along with the Christian religion. Mbanza Kongo was renamed São Salvador in 1534.

See also: AFONSO I (Vol. III); PORTUGAL AND AFRICA (Vol. III); SÃO SALVADOR (Vol. III).

Mbundu BANTU-speaking ethnic group of ANGOLA in central Africa. They are sometimes called the North Mbundu or Kimbundu to distinguish them from a related Mbundu-speaking group, who call themselves OVIMBUNDU in their own language.

The North Mbundu descended from three distinct Bantu groups who arrived in Angola during the fifteenth century. They introduced several technologies to the region, including IRONWORKING, new agricultural techniques, and superior hunting methods. In the absence of a centralized political system, North Mbundu society was organized around loose clan affiliations. However, toward the end of the fifteenth century, the emergence of the powerful KONGO KINGDOM to the north forced the North Mbundu to centralize their leadership. They aligned themselves with the king of the Ndongo people, who were building an agricultural and trade kingdom at Kubasa.

The North Mbundu capitalized on their location to control the coastal trade routes, which brought them into contact with the Portuguese merchants who arrived on the coast around the same time that the Kongo Kingdom emerged.

See also: MATAMBA (Vol. III); MBUNDU (Vol. III); NDONGO (Vol. III); PORTUGAL AND AFRICA (Vol. III).

Mecca   City in what is now SAUDI ARABIA, located approximately 50 miles (80 km) from the shores of the Red Sea. Because Mecca is the birthplace of the prophet Muhammad (c. 570–632), the city is of central importance to the religion of ISLAM.

In the seventh century, during the lifetime of Muhammad, the city of Mecca was an important commercial center, bustling with trade from the CARAVANS crossing the Arabian Peninsula. Born into the powerful Qaraysh family, Muhammad preached a monotheistic doctrine that sought to reform traditional Arab religious and social life. He quickly gained followers and became a threat to Mecca's established leadership. In 622, he accepted an invitation to go to the city of Yathrib, later known as MEDINA, where he successfully spread his teachings.

In 630, after a series of conflicts between rival sects in the city of Mecca, Muhammad returned to Mecca, accompanied by 10,000 troops. Muhammad quickly consolidated and expanded his power, and by his death in 632, he had become the spiritual and political leader of all Arabia.

By the end of its first century of existence, Islam had expanded its sphere of influence westward into Africa and east and north into Asia. As time passed, however, the focal points of Islamic power moved as well, and, by the ninth century, the major centers of Islamic power were located in EGYPT and India, far from Mecca and Medina.

THE TEMPLE OF MECCA.

In the holy city of Mecca in Saudi Arabia, the Great Mosque, with the Ka'bah at the center, was the focal point of the devout Muslim's hajj. Thousands of the faithful are shown present in this 1854 print. © CORBIS

Muhammad's move from Mecca to Medina in 622 is called the Hegira (Hijra). The year of this move is considered the beginning of the Islamic era and is commemorated by the annual Muslim pilgrimage to Mecca. According to Islamic doctrine, this pilgrimage, or hajj, is the duty of every true Muslim and is to be completed at least once during each believer's lifetime. The hajj takes place between the eighth and the thirteenth days of the last month of the Muslim year, and annually brings more than 2 million pilgrims to the city of Mecca. Among the many rituals and observances that are part of the hajj is each pilgrim's passage around the Ka'bah, the rectangular brick structure that the Muslim faithful believe was built by Abraham and his son, Ishmael.

medicine   The approach of traditional African medicine to restoring good health has been described as a combination of finding both the right cure along with the disease's underlying cause.

In many traditional African societies, illness or premature death was viewed either as part of a larger, hidden problem within the family or community or as something associated with other, unseen forces. These possibilities inform the work of traditional healers, many of whom made extraordinary efforts to heal the ill. The efforts of these healers included everything from divination and intuitive knowledge to special rites and ceremonies. Another source of traditional cures, herbal remedies, were drawn from a vast knowledge of herbs and roots. Some of the ingredients used were gathered in the wild, some were cultivated, and others, such as fats or milk from domesticated animals, were commonly found in the home.

Traditional treatments might consist of healing bath solutions, inhaled or ingested potions, or the fumigation of the sick person's home with special sprays. Someone with a fever might receive cooling substances made of water, plant essence, and ash. Incisions might be made to the skin so that medicine could be applied. Some healers used specially prepared medicine bundles that were intended to work as a type of charm. Beyond this, one of the most potent aspects of healing within many societies was the spoken word, which represented an important part of traditional healing; ritual chants and incantations were often used as part of the regimen.

The art of divination was also essential in the role of medicine and was considered the first step in understanding the underlying cause of illness. The results of the divination process might identify that cause as misdirected anger, envy, or even an act of deliberate harm intentionally inflicted by another member of the community. Divination might also be used to detect the effects of witchcraft, which many societies believed to be a prime cause of illness.

In various regions of SOUTH AFRICA, divining "bones" were used to diagnose and treat illness. These items, which often consisted of an assortment of special stones, shells, nuts, or other sacred objects, were usually thrown on a flat surface. The patterns that formed were then "read."

Once the cause of an ailment or illness was identified, the healing medicine was dispensed. This could be done in a variety of ways. Often, special rites or ceremonies—sometimes including dancing and drumming—might be part of the process. Patients also might be asked to wear amulets containing certain protective medicines. The ASHANTI of modern Ghana, for example, have traditionally worn a personal talisman, called a *nsuma*, that they believe has been made with the assistance of divinities known collectively as the Abosom.

Members of other societies often stored medicine within wooden carvings that appeared at first glance to be works of art. Known as "power objects," these were mainly depictions of human figures. Some of these held medicines that were meant to remain hidden from public view, while others were meant to inflict harm upon unsuspecting members of the community. Other carved forms were made especially for public display. These were filled with or surrounded by medicine and then placed on shrines or used in rituals. For example, medicines were routinely applied to the masks of the Komo Society, a group associated with the BAMBARA of Mali. The mask, in turn, was thought to be able to transmit healing at specially organized rites. The Bamana also used large sacred sculptures known as *boliw* as repositories for potent medicines.

Similarly, many societies of central Africa, particularly the KONGO, used wooden sculpture known as *nkisi* as a part of the healing process. It was believed, for example, that ordinarily benign forms of herbal medicine, known as *bwanga*, when inserted into the head or abdomen of one of these figures, could thus be transformed into more potent forms of medicine known as *mankishi*. Many peoples who used such methods, such as the Songye, claimed that knowledge of this type of medicine was given to the first humans by their supreme being.

One of the more fascinating uses of traditional medicine and healing involves the Haalpulaaren people, an agricultural society who have long lived in the northern region of SENEGAL. Converted to ISLAM during the eleventh century, the Haalpulaaren were organized in lineage groups, each with its own special expertise in a certain craft. These crafts then determined an individual's status as healer. For example, blacksmiths treated external burns and abscesses, while members of the societies who were weavers of cloth were said to use specially tied knots to alleviate the pain of headaches and toothache.

Medicine also played an important role in divine kingship. Inserted into the crown or royal headdress of ruling kings, certain medicines were considered an essential protective agent. YORUBA kings, for example, had medicine sewn into the top portion of their crowns, always hidden beneath beads or a symbolic bird perched at the top. It was generally believed that herbal medicines aligned the king's divine power with the orisha, the pantheon of spiritual deities who embodied the life-force referred to as *ashe*. The Yoruba also buried special medicines, known as *oogun*, under shrines dedicated to specific deities.

See also: DIVINATION (Vol. I); MEDICINE (Vols. I, III); ORISHA (Vol. I); WITCHCRAFT (Vol. I).

Further reading: Rosalind J. Hackett, *Art and Religion in Africa* (London, Eng.: Cassell, 1996); John S. Mbiti, *African Religions and Philosophy* (London, Eng.: Heinemann Educational Publishers, 1999).

Medina Sacred city located in the Hejaz region of western Saudi Arabia, 110 miles (180 km) east of the Red Sea and 200 miles (320 km) north of MECCA. The prophet Muhammad (c. 570–632) fled to the city in 622 but returned in triumph to Mecca in 630. Muhammad's remains are buried in Medina, making it one of the holiest places of Muslim pilgrimage. Originally called Yathrib, the city came to be known as *Madinat an Nami* (the city of the Prophet), which was later shortened to *Medina*, ARABIC for "the city."

Muhammad's monotheistic beliefs met with great opposition in his native city of Mecca. Eventually, in 622, he and his followers were forced to leave the city, and they chose Yathrib to be the administrative center of the new Muslim community. This flight, known as the Hijra (Hegira), marks the beginning of the Islamic calendar.

Despite constant conflict with the Meccans, Muhammad continued his attempts to unify the Arab people, and his teachings attracted a great following. As a result, Mecca began to decline as prominent citizens moved to Yathrib to follow Islam.

In 630, Muhammad and 10,000 of his disciples seized Mecca, and by 632 all of Arabia was united under Islam. While leading the annual pilgrimage to Mecca in 632, however, Muhammad died in Medina on June 8, 632, without specifying an heir; this lack provoked a major crisis among his followers and later led to dynastic disputes that brought schism and civil war. Muhammad was buried in Medina, and a mosque was subsequently built around his grave. His daughter, Fatima, and Omar, the second caliph of the Muslim Empire, are also buried within the mosque.

For nearly thirty years after Muhammad's death, Medina remained the capital of the Islamic community, serving as the administrative, cultural, and intellectual center of the Muslim Empire. Years later it became a primary center for the legal discussions that initiated the codification of Islamic law.

See also: MALIKI SUNNI DOCTRINE (Vol. II); SHIISM (Vol. II); SUNNI (Vol. III.)

Mediterranean Sea Body of water that provided a key link between the African continent and the Middle East.

Prior to the seventh century, northern Africa and the Mediterranean Sea were controlled by the Byzantine Empire. Although a handful of Mediterranean coastal towns were still under Byzantine influence at the beginning of the seventh century, the arrival of Arab Muslims put an end to Byzantine rule. On a quest to spread ISLAM, these Arab immigrants used military force to dominate ancient coastal towns and establish new Muslim cities. Egypt was the first access point of the Arab conquests in the MAGHRIB. As a result, the Mediterranean became an essential factor in the introduction of Islamic culture to Africa.

Equally important was the rapid economic growth in the area sparked by the Arab interest in Mediterranean trade. TRANS-SAHARAN TRADE ROUTES linked the Mediterranean coast with the African interior, where export goods like GOLD and slaves were in high demand. The influx of gold into western Europe enabled countries like Spain, which had previously relied solely on silver, to diversify their currency and increase their financial stability. In addition, the growth of Mediterranean trade encouraged advances in SHIPBUILDING technology and sparked interest in areas as diverse as geography, banking, and astronomy. Partly because of this economic prosperity, Islam was fully incorporated into Mediterranean coastal towns by the eleventh century and gradually began to spread southward along the trans-Saharan trade routes.

For the next several hundred years, the Mediterranean figured prominently in shaping North Africa's history. It was as often the site of power struggles as it was a busy trade center. The Muslim ALMORAVIDS, centered in

Morocco in North Africa, dominated the western Mediterranean in the late eleventh century and supplanted the UMAYYAD dynasty, which had ruled Muslim Spain since 756. (Spain had been invaded and conquered by BERBER Muslim forces in 711.) At the same time, Christian Crusaders attempted to wrest the Holy Land from its Muslim rulers. Control of much of the Mediterranean coastline passed to the ALMOHADS, another Muslim reform group, in the late twelfth century. Over the next 300 years, Christians and Muslims battled for control of Mediterranean trade and coastal dominance. Toward the end of the fifteenth century, the Christians temporarily conquered the Mediterranean under the armies of the Spanish monarchs Ferdinand of Aragón and Isabella of Castile. Important North African port cities under Spanish control included Melilla, Oran, Ténès, Algiers, Bidjaya, and Tripoli.

The Ottoman Empire, which had steadily been growing in size and power since the early fourteenth century, began to seriously threaten Christian dominance of the Mediterranean c. 1500. After conquering key Egyptian cities, the Ottomans allied with the powerful Turkish navy and began raiding Mediterranean commerce vessels. By the middle of the 1500s, the Ottomans controlled the North African coastal towns of TUNIS, Algiers, and Tripoli, thus shifting Mediterranean control to the Turks.

See also: BYZANTINE AFRICA (Vols. I, II); MEDITERRANEAN SEA (Vol. III); OTTOMAN EMPIRE (Vol. III).

Arab and medieval European merchants conduct business.
© Bettmann/CORBIS

merchants A professional merchant class emerged in Africa as TRANS-SAHARAN TRADE ROUTES and INDIAN OCEAN TRADE developed after the rise of ISLAM in the seventh century. The BERBERS of North Africa brought their Islamic faith with them as they crossed the SAHARA and converted many of the merchants who had traditionally dealt with the Arab traders. The conversion of a large percentage of traders brought many benefits to the region. It opened up markets for African trade goods in the Middle East and North Africa. It provided a common language—ARABIC—that both Arab Muslims and black African Muslims spoke. (Until the twentieth century, the KORAN, the holy book of Islam, was read only in Arabic, which most believers learned.) Islam also provided the bond of Islamic law, making it easier to solve disputes under one common legal system.

A powerful and influential merchant class existed in all the major cities of Muslim West Africa—TIMBUKTU, GAO, JENNE, KUMBI SALEH, KANO, KATSINA, and the other HAUSA STATES. By the fourteenth century, clans of DYULA (meaning "itinerant traders"), or Wangara, as the Muslim traders of Mali came to be called, were active throughout West Africa and were known for organizing the large-scale movement of goods from the African interior to the coastal commercial markets and trade depots of the Sahara.

In other parts of Africa, notably the central and southern regions, there were merchants with little or no contact with North African traders or with Arab traders from the Indian Ocean cities. Significant among these in the early fifteenth century were the Mwene Mutapa (Mwene Mutabe), a title borne by a line of kings whose most important trading center was the city of GREAT ZIMBABWE, south of the Zambezi River. Their land is called Mutapa or the Mwene Mutapa Empire. As the Mwene Mutapa expanded their trade routes by military means, they gained access to the Zambezi region's salt, fabrics, and IVORY. They neither had nor sought direct contact with the cities of KILWA, SOFALA, MOMBASA, MALINDI, and others along the East African coast but were instead intermediaries who controlled the inland trade networks that brought Zimbabwean GOLD and goods to the Indian Ocean coast. These goods were carried by foot or by pack oxen to the Arab traders on the coast.

See also: CARAVANS (Vol. II); TRANS-SAHARAN TRADE ROUTES (Vol. II).

metalwork See BARIBA METALLURGY (Vol. II); BRONZE (Vol. II); COPPER (Vol. II); CRAFTSPEOPLE (Vol. II); IRONWORKING (Vol. II).

mining See COPPER (Vols. I, II); GOLD (Vols. I, II); IRON (Vol. II); MINING (Vol. III); SALT MINING (Vol. II).

Mogadishu Port city and present-day capital of Somalia, founded by ARAB traders in the tenth century. Early Mogadishu, also known as Hammawein or Xamar Weyne, was one of the first Arab trading ports on the African mainland. Although originally established and ruled by Arab and Persian families, by the thirteenth century, Mogadishu was governed by both ARABS and Arab-influenced SOMALI clans. Arab customs were integrated into local traditions, and many Somalis converted to ISLAM because of the influence of these ruling families.

The GOLD trade from southern Africa made the city prosperous, but leather, timber, pitch, and civet musk were also shipped abroad. Captives from the interior quickly became an important commodity, along with livestock and IVORY.

The strong influence of Islam was in evidence in the thirteenth century, when Fakhr al-Din established the first sultanate of Mogadishu. As the city's international prominence grew, political power shifted to the Muzaffar dynasty in the fifteenth century. Although the Muzaffar rulers were able to fend off Portuguese invaders, they could not resist the great influx of the Hawaya, a group of indigenous Somali nomads. Cut off from the interior, Mogadishu, along with the port cities of MARKA and Brava to the south, lost much of its trade. By the end of the sixteenth century, Mogadishu was falling into a state of rapid decline.

See also: BENADIR COAST (Vol. III); INDIAN OCEAN TRADE (Vol. II); MOGADISHU (Vol. III); SOMALI (Vol. III).

Mombasa City in modern-day KENYA that is the largest port in East Africa. Established as a trade center by Arab MERCHANTS in the eleventh century, Mombasa quickly became a prominent marketplace for GOLD, IVORY, and slaves. It soon surpassed the coastal city of KILWA in importance, becoming East Africa's premier commercial center by the fifteenth century.

Portuguese explorer Vasco da GAMA visited Mombasa in 1498, and several years later, the Portuguese captured the city in an effort to control INDIAN OCEAN TRADE.

See also: ARAB COASTAL TRADE (Vol. II); KENYA (Vol. III); MOMBASA (Vol. III); SLAVERY (Vols. II, III); PORTUGAL AND AFRICA (Vol. III).

monotheism Belief in one god, as typified by RELIGIONS introduced to Africa like Judaism, CHRISTIANITY, and ISLAM.

Unlike pantheistic religious traditions, which are common throughout SUB-SAHARAN AFRICA, monotheistic religions center on one god, who actively intervenes with humankind. This god typically sets moral standards and is worshiped as the supreme creator. Monotheists often consider other religions intolerable, a fact that has resulted in friction between religious groups throughout much of African history.

The concept of a single god may have originated in Africa during the reign of the pharaoh Akhenaten IV (c. 1379–1364 BCE), known also as Amenhotep. Akhenaten replaced the traditional worship of Amun with rites honoring Aten and the innovation that Aten was to be the only god. The so-called Amarna period that he initiated was a time of religious and political turmoil in Egypt.

The monotheistic religions commonly found in Africa differ in their interpretation of the supreme authority of the one god. The oldest of the three great monotheistic religions, Judaism, centers on the belief in an all-powerful creator sustained and revealed through human action. While early Jews tolerated the existence of other gods, monotheistic principles came to dominate Judaism as it developed. Christianity, which emerged from Judaism, adheres to monotheistic principles as expressed in the Old Testament of the Bible. Catholicism and many Protestant denominations express their belief in a Holy Trinity of three persons in one God: the Father, the Son, and the Holy Spirit, as set forth in the New Testament of the Bible in the Gospel of St. Matthew and St. Paul's Letter to the Corinthians.

In contrast to Judaism and Christianity, Islam is a purely monotheistic religion. Muslims strictly deny the validity of other religions, believing that Allah (the ARABIC word for "God") is eternal and unequaled and is the creator, sustainer, and restorer of the world. Islam views Adam, Noah, Moses, and Jesus Christ, among others, as members of a long line of prophets ending in Muhammad, whose revelations consummate and supercede the work of the prophets who preceded him.

See also: ANIMISM (Vol. 1); PANTHEISM (Vol. I); MONOTHEISM (Vol. I); RELIGION (Vols. I, III).

Morocco Country along the coast of North Africa, with the MEDITERRANEAN SEA to the north, the Atlantic Ocean to the west, the western SAHARA to the south, and ALGERIA to the east; officially known in the present day as the Kingdom of Morocco. The Atlas Mountains in central Morocco separate the fertile coastal plain to the north from the Sahara Desert in the south.

The BERBERS, the native people of Morocco, are an ancient group who were subjected to the invasions of a succession of foreign powers. The Mediterranean coast of Africa was under Roman rule until the area was invaded by the Vandals in 429 and later by Byzantium in 533. Although Christianity spread throughout Morocco during Roman times, only pockets survived the Arab invasion that began in the seventh century.

Muslim Arabs came to Morocco around 685, replacing Christianity with Islam. (A few areas with Jewish populations were allowed to keep their religion.) Arabic influence extended beyond religious reform, eventually including the written language that has remained the primary language of business and culture ever since.

The Berbers did not accept Arab rule, however, and there were many conflicts between the two groups. In 788, Morocco became an independent state under the royal family of the sharif (descendant of the Prophet) Idris ibn Abd Allah, who was invited there by Ishaq ibn Abd al-Hamid, the chief of the Berber Awraba confederation, to lend religious authority to al-Hamid's rule. Arab and Berber dynasties succeeded the Idrisids. The first were the ALMORAVIDS (1062–1147), a Berber Muslim dynasty that united the country through religious reform and military conquests. They were succeeded by the ALMOHADS (1147–1258). Morocco became the center of the Almohad Empire, which included modern-day ALGERIA, Tunisia, LIBYA, and large areas of Spain and Portugal.

The MARANID dynasty (1259–1550) seized control of Morocco from the Almohads, but they could not entirely unify the country. The Berbers and Arabs continued their civil war, and the region was thrown into disorder.

See also: BYZANTINE AFRICA (Vol. II); MOROCCO (Vol. III).

Mossi States (Moshe, Moose, Mohe, Mosi)

Confederation of states located in present-day BURKINA FASO that organized under a single leader around 1500. The Mossi have long spoken the More, or Voltaic, language. Their traditional religious rites involved nature and ancestor worship, and their political system was a hierarchical one headed by a *mogho naba* ("great king") who resided in the capital city of WAGADUGU.

According to tradition, the early ancestors of the Mossi people came to the VOLTA RIVER basin from the east as early as the thirteenth century. Other sources indicate that about 1500, horsemen from northern GHANA rode south and conquered the farming peoples of the area, including the DOGON, Lela, Nuna, and Kurumba. The conquerors and the conquered thus formed the Mossi states, also known as the Mossi Kingdom, with the conquerors adopting the language of the area but retaining their own traditions.

In the early days of the kingdom, Mossi cavalry fought with neighboring MALI and SONGHAI Empires for control of the middle Niger River. The Mossi raids were unsuccessful, and Songhai remained in control of the lake region of the middle Niger.

The Mossi were primarily farmers, raising CROPS both for their own food use and for trade. Leather workers, smiths, and other artisans were common as well. Located along the trade routes between the desert and forest, the Mossi were active in trade between the forest states and cities on the Niger.

Mossi society traditionally was based on a feudal system, headed by a *mogho naba,* or king, who surrounded himself with nobles, officials, bodyguards, and pages. The *mogho naba's* many wives were kept secluded, with the only males in attendance being eunuchs. Division chiefs served as the emperor's advisers, with the next level of government being the village chiefs, who had power over the commoners and slaves.

See also: KINGDOMS AND EMPIRES (Vol. II); MOSSI STATES (Vol III).

Mozambique

Modern country on the southern coast of East Africa. Mozambique borders the present-day countries of SOUTH AFRICA, ZIMBABWE, ZAMBIA, Malawi, and Tanzania. The island country of MADAGASCAR is located in the Indian Ocean off of Mozambique's coast. Because of its abundant natural resources, including GOLD, IVORY, COPPER, and IRON, Mozambique has been an important TRADE region since the middle of the first millennium.

Mozambique originally referred to the site of a coastal settlement that was occupied by BANTU-speaking peoples as early as the third century. Various groups settled also in the highlands west of Mozambique along the Zimbabwe Plateau during the mass BANTU MIGRATIONS from West- central Africa to the south and east. These people brought with them iron technology and knowledge of grain cultivation, which enabled them to sustain an agrarian and pastoral economy in their new home. Among the numerous Bantu settlers, those in the southeast (the Chopi, Tonga, and Tsonga) formed cohesive village units; those who settled along the Zambezi River (the Barue, Maravi, Makua-Lomue, and Shona) did not organize structured political units. Other Bantu peoples, like the Makonde and Yao to the north, lived in virtual isolation.

These Bantu speakers lived as simple farmers and herders until the arrival of Arab traders in the eighth century. The ARABS exchanged Middle Eastern products, including beads, POTTERY, textiles, glass, and salt, for African goods like gold, ivory, and rhinoceros horn. Arab trade was the dominant economic activity along much of the Zambezi River by the fifteenth century.

Early in the fifteenth century, the KARANGA, a subgroup of the Shona, rose to power in the central regions of what is now Mozambique. The dynasty founded by these people, known as the Mwene Matapa, attempted to conquer much of the Zambezi valley, leading to political unrest among the smaller Bantu kingdoms in the region.

In 1498, the Portuguese arrived and became heavily involved in the gold and ivory trades. After securing the coast, the Portuguese headed into the central regions of Mozambique, bringing their Christian missionaries with them. Eventually, they would dominate the region, setting up a feudal political structure and establishing a thriving trade economy.

See also: MAPUTO (Vol. III); MOZAMBIQUE (Vol. III); PORTUGAL AND AFRICA (Vol. III); SHONA (Vol. I).

Muhammad ibn Tumart (1080–1130) *Islamic religious leader and self-proclaimed Mahdi who founded the Almohad dynasty in Morocco in the twelfth century.*

Born in 1080, ibn Tumart was a member of the MASMUDA group of BERBERS in the Atlas Mountain region of southern MOROCCO. After returning from a pilgrimage to MECCA in 1117, he began to preach a doctrine advocating the social and religious reformation of the ALMORAVID dynasty. Ibn Tumart believed in the unity of God and strict adherence to the doctrines of ISLAM.

Declaring himself MAHDI ("righteous leader"), he declared a JIHAD, or holy war, against all Muslims who disagreed with him. His extreme beliefs did not win him friends, however, and his admonitions angered many local Almoravid rulers. At one point he was almost executed after arguing with local scholars in MARRAKECH.

Ibn Tumart returned to the Atlas Mountains in 1122, having failed to gain much support in Marrakech. Once home, he began gaining followers among the Masmuda. Ibn Tumart's supporters began the ALMOHAD rebellion in 1125 with attacks on the centers of Almovarid power, the cities of Sus and Marrakech.

Ibn Tumart died in 1130 and was succeeded by his lieutenant, ABD AL MUMIN (r. 1130–1163), who was able to defeat the Almoravid dynasty. By the end of al-Mumin's reign, the Almohad Empire controlled much of Africa and Spain.

Although ibn Tumart founded and organized the Almohad movement that rejected Almoravid rule, the MUMINID dynasty is named after his successor, Abd al-Mumin, under whose direction the Almohad movement began to flourish in the middle of the twelfth century.

Muhammad the prophet See ISLAM.

Muminid (Mu'minid) Period of ALMOHAD rule in North Africa and Spain under the leadership of ABD AL-MUMIN (r. 1130–1163), a caliph of the BERBER Almohad dynasty, and his successors. Al-Mumin conquered ALMORAVID North Africa and united the Berbers under a single rule.

The Muminid dynasty was founded shortly after the death in 1130 of MUHAMMAD IBN TUMART (c. 1080–1130), the Muslim religious reformer and military leader whose teachings lay the foundation for the Almohad Empire in North Africa and Spain (1130–1269). Without their influential leader, the *Almohads*, whose name, in ARABIC, means "those who affirm the unity of God," fell into a brief period of decline. By 1133, however, a powerful Almohad military commander, Abd al-Mumin, a Qumiya Berber who had been ibn Tumart's trusted lieutenant, had regrouped his people and renewed ibn Tumart's revolt against the ALMORAVID Empire. At that point, the Almoravid Empire, dominated by the SANHAJA BERBERS, controlled Morocco and western ALGERIA as far as Algiers and all of Muslim Spain.

Al-Mumin gained control over key Berber trade routes, greatly increasing Almohad wealth. These new resources enabled al-Mumin to capture the city of MARRAKECH from the Almoravids in 1147 and make it the Almohad capital. Within a few years, al-Mumin dominated all of the MAGHRIB. In 1158–1159, Abd al-Mumin conquered Tunisia and Tripolitania, extending Berber rule to all of North Africa west of Egypt. The Almoravids continued to resist Almohad domination, however, and during a revolt in 1163, Abd al-Mumin was killed.

Al-Mumin's son ABU YAQUB YUSUF (r. 1163–1184) succeeded him. He forced the surrender of Muslim Seville in 1172 and extended Almohad rule across Islamic Spain. However, a series of rebellions during his rule and a failed attempt to conquer the independent Muslim kingdom of Murcia in southwestern Spain stalled Almohad expansion.

Upon Abu Yaqub Yusuf's death in 1184, his son, Abu Yusuf YAQUB AL-MANSUR (r. 1184–1199), inherited the throne. Abu Yusuf Yaqub faced mounting opposition from the Banu Ghaniya, who were the descendants of the Almoravid leader ibn Tashbin, in the central Maghrib. The Almohads eventually lost the eastern half of the Maghrib to the raiding Almoravids.

In 1194, Abu Yusuf Yaqub headed north, across the MEDITERRANEAN SEA, in order to conquer Spain. His Almohad forces captured many Christian territories, earning him the title *al-mansur* ("the victorious").

When Yaqub al-Mansur died in 1199, Almohad power passed to the fourth Muminid leader, Abu Abdallah

Muhammad al-Nasir (r. c. 1205). Al-Nasir staged an offensive against the Banu Ghaniya in the early thirteenth century, soundly defeating them in 1210. At the same time, the Christians embarked to reclaim Spanish territories from the Muslims, forcing the Muminids to withdraw from Spain around 1212. Al-Nasir died shortly thereafter.

Al-Nasir's son, al-Mustansir, took control of the empire c. 1213 and faced increasing resistance from the Christians, the Banu Ghaniya, and the Banu Marin, or MARINIDS. Upon al-Mustansir's death in 1227, the Muminid dynasty fell into disarray. By 1230, the Almohads had lost control of the rest of the Maghrib, and the Muminid dynasty came to an abrupt end.

Musa I, Mansa (r. c. 1307–1337) *Muslim ruler, or* mansa, *of the Mali Empire who became the first West African emperor to embark on a religious pilgrimage to Mecca.*

One of the most important Muslim rulers of the MALI EMPIRE, Mansa Musa I played a key role in the expansion of ISLAM into West Africa. He was also responsible for much of the expansion of the west African GOLD trade to the eastern parts of North Africa and the SUDAN. In addition, although he did not force Islam on his people, he was responsible for the construction of numerous mosques and encouraged the development of Islamic learning throughout his empire. Because of this, during his reign, the city of TIMBUKTU developed into a major ISLAMIC CENTER OF LEARNING.

Mansa Musa I as Ruler Based on evidence presented by Arab scholars, Mansa Musa I was one of the most widely known rulers of ancient Mali and perhaps the most famous person in all of the western Sudan. His rule lasted from roughly 1307 until his death in 1337. During this time, the influence of Mali grew, and its government experienced greater development than it had under any of its former rulers. Mansa Musa I was also the leader who developed Mali's diplomatic relations with EGYPT and MOROCCO, sending ambassadors to both nations and receiving their consuls in return.

Mansa Musa's governance was equally commendable in that he administered justice fairly and impartially. Just as important, because of his strong religious faith, he also insisted on qualities of fairness and equity in his high-ranking subordinates. He traveled extensively throughout his own empire and abroad, most notably in his famous pilgrimage to MECCA, which was conducted in such splendor that it is still discussed today.

The Hajj of Mansa Musa I A devout Muslim, Mansa Musa set out for Mecca to fulfill the Islamic commandment that the faithful must make a pilgrimage, or hajj, to Mecca, the birthplace of their religion. Mansa Musa's journey began in 1324, in the seventeenth year of his reign, with his departure from his capital, NIANI, on the Upper Niger River, and lasted until 1325.

Mansa Musa's entourage for the journey was, according to all accounts, enormous; according to some witnesses he traveled with up to 60,000 courtiers and 12,000 servants. Leading the procession were at least 500 servants, each carrying a staff made from more than 4 pounds (1.8 kg) of gold. Behind them came Mansa Musa himself, on horseback. His chief wife also was part of the procession, and she brought along as many as 500 servants of her own. Beyond this, there were as many as 100 camels—each carrying 300 pounds (136 kg) of gold—as well as thousands of Mansa Musa's subjects.

> Even the slaves and servants were well-dressed for Mansa Musa's pilgrimage. According to most accounts, they were dressed in the finest silks available, and many apparently wore ornate brocaded clothing.

As Mansa Musa traveled to WALATA (in present-day MAURITANIA) and Tuat (now part of ALGERIA), he and his retinue caused a sensation. His dazzling riches—which came from an area that was little known in North Africa—created a surge of interest in both Mansa Musa and his kingdom. The fact that he greeted his hosts both generously and graciously intrigued and pleased people even more.

In CAIRO, Mansa Musa finally met with the MAMLUK sultan al-Malik an-Nasir. (Musa was so devoted to his religious duties that he had been reluctant to take the time to meet with the sultan.) Mali's ruler proved to be an extremely generous guest, heaping gold upon the sultan and his other hosts.

> The amount of gold Mansa Musa bestowed on others—particularly in Cairo—was so great that he depressed the market in the metal and caused a major decrease in the price of gold that lasted for at least a dozen years. According to the Arab historian al 'Umari, the people of Cairo were still telling stories of their mysterious visitor's wealth and generosity when, more than a decade later, al 'Umari visited the city. Mansa Musa's generosity had negative effects on himself, as well as on the gold market. Although he had brought a seemingly vast amount of gold with him on his pilgrimage, it proved insufficient to cover his enormous expenses and largesse. As a result, he was forced to take out loans—at extremely high rates of interest—in order to pay for his own return to Mali.

After Cairo, Mansa Musa continued on to Mecca to complete his hajj. Musa's entourage back to Mali returned with an ARABIC library. It also brought with it many Islamic scholars who went on to help create Muslim schools in the empire. Equally important, Mali's king brought back with him the famous architect al-SAHILI, who set about building mosques in both GAO and TIMBUKTU that influenced generations of builders.

Ultimately, Mansa Musa's pilgrimage changed the way the world thought about Mali—and Africa. In 1339, four years after his return, Mali began appearing on Arabic maps. Indeed, by 1375 at least one cartographer included on a map an illustration of a clearly wealthy king carrying gold. In the wake of Mansa Musa's hajj, trade between Mali and Egypt soared, and as news of the riches and splendor of the king's entourage reached the Middle East and Europe, Mali became an object of fascination. As a result, the curious, the greedy, and the devout all were attracted to Mali, transforming it into a center for everything from Islamic scholarship to trade.

See also: KINGDOMS AND EMPIRES (Vol. II); KINGDOMS AND EMPIRES OF THE WEST AFRICAN SAVANNA (Vol. II).

Further reading: Akbarall Thogbani, *Mansa Musa: The Golden King of Mali* (Dubuque, Iowa: Kendall/Hunt Publishing, 1998).

music Music has long been acknowledged as a major component of daily life in Africa; it is a presence in everything from religious worship and work routines to children's games, funerals, and rites of passage.

Among the qualities that have marked African music as both timeless and yet constantly changing are its adaptability and innovation, traits that have been influenced by the internal growth of kingdoms and CITY-STATES as well as by the impact of TRADE and migration. During Africa's medieval period, greater emphasis appears to have been placed on musical performance and on individual singers, dancers, and storytellers. Along with the praise songs of the GRIOT, classical forms of poetry developed and were accompanied by music. Among the most notable were forms, developed in RWANDA and YORUBALAND, that relied on rhyme, rhythm, and tone to convey their meanings.

Drums and drum music were most commonly found in the woodland areas. One of the most popular drums to emerge was the *dundun*, a drum that came into widespread use among the YORUBA of southwestern Nigeria at some time between the fourteenth and fifteenth centuries. Known as the "talking drum" because of its ability to closely imitate human language, the *dundun*, which had an hourglass shape, was made of a double membrane. It was played with a curved stick, and adjustments to its membrane covering, which was held in place by leather, produced a rise and fall in pitch. The *iya-ilu*,

or mother drum, was another popular drum, and it was often used for recitals and praise songs, as well as a means of announcing visitors to the kingdom. The kings of UGANDA were known to have organized their own drumming ensembles, each of which might have consisted of three to four drummers.

Although the drum held a central place throughout Africa's long history, with the advent of the Iron Age, a wider variety of musical instruments developed. This in turn generated an even wider variation in tone, pitch, and distinctive rhythmic patterns. These patterns, ranging from simple beats to more complex interlocking sound designs, were usually established and maintained by a master drummer. Diversity in instrumentation has been corroborated by the art that has survived from royal palaces, by the writings of Arabic travelers in Africa, as well as by archaeological evidence. Royal plaques from ILE-IFE and BENIN, for example, depict musicians playing instruments—flutes and horns categorized as aerophones—made from the horns of animals. Also pictured are bow lutes that belong to the category of instruments known as chordophones, as well as calabash rattles and iron bells.

Archaeologists have recovered bells of a similar type from western and southern regions of Africa, including single and double iron bells without clappers that are believed to have originated among Kwa-speakers in West Africa. These bells are believed to have been transported into central Africa at a subsequent time by migrating BANTU-speakers. Another bell, the *ogan,* or double bell, was important to musicians in Fon society. Their music was noteworthy for the development of a distinctive time-line pattern, known as *toba,* that has remained an identifiable feature of the region's music for centuries.

Time-line patterns are generally described as a brief single note produced by striking a bell, drum, or calabash or by clapping the hands. They are the basis for creating great variation or improvisation in African music.

The rulers of BUGANDA had a specialized form of improvisational music known as *akadinda.* Similar to the way in which drummers created interlocking rhythms, this form of music was played by an ensemble of groups consisting of two sets of two to three players each.

Other groups with a long tradition of musicality include the MBUTI of central Africa and the SAN of SOUTH AFRICA. (The music of both groups was documented by European observers as early as the fifteenth century.) Known as hocketing, their music involved having each player use flutes or trumpets to play single notes in repeated rotation. Depending on the number of musicians in the ensemble, the music became what musicologists describe as polyphonic, or textured, in pattern. Similar techniques traditionally also have been used in the choral arrangements of the ZULU.

Migration clearly has played an important role in the development of regional music, although that role is still not fully understood. For example, historians of music have pointed out many marked similarities between the vocal chants of the Gogo, from the central region of Tanzania, and the comparable style of the MAASAI in KENYA. Other comparisons include the use of xylophone instruments by both the Makonde of northern MOZAMBIQUE—who play a log xylophone known as the *dimbila*—and the instrument known as the *jomolo*, which is played by the Baule people of IVORY COAST.

See also: ARCHAEOLOGY (Vol. I); DANCE (Vol. I); FESTIVALS (Vol. I); FUNERAL CUSTOMS (Vol. I); MUSIC (Vols. I, III).

Further reading: Robert B. Fisher, *West African Religious Traditions* (Maryknoll, N.Y.: Orbis Books, 1998); Samuel A. Floyd Jr., *The Power of Black Music* (New York: Oxford University Press, 1995).

Muslim law See ISLAM and LAW AND JUSTICE.

Muslims See ISLAM.

Mwene Matapa (Mwene Mutapa, Mwene Mutabe, Monomotapa, Mwenenutapa, Mbire)

Lineage of monarchs who ruled a territory in Southeast Africa from the fifteenth to the seventeenth century; also the kingdom over which they ruled.

The Mwene Matapa, a title that means "master pillager" or "ravager of the land," reigned over a kingdom that extended from the Zambezi River to the LIMPOPO RIVER in ZIMBABWE and MOZAMBIQUE. Legend attributes the founding of the Mwene Matapa dynasty to Mbire, a mythical fourteenth-century ruler from the Lake TANGANYIKA area. (The Mwene Matapa kingdom is sometimes called the Mbire kingdom.) The kingdom proper, however, was formed in the fifteenth century by Nyatsimba, a leader of the Karanga subgroup of the Shona. Nyatsimba was the first ruler to bear the title of *mwene matapa*.

Soon after establishing a kingdom, the Mwene Matapa began to prosper. They maintained an army, which enabled them to secure tribute payments from nearby peoples including the Uteve and Manyika. With their influence growing, they were able to take advantage of their kingdom's position along the trade route between the South African interior and the Indian Ocean. Their territory was rich in GOLD deposits and salt, and by the end of the fifteenth century, the Mwene Matapa were growing rich by trading these commodities with MERCHANTS along the SWAHILI COAST.

See also: INDIAN OCEAN TRADE (Vol. II); GOLD TRADE (Vol. III); MWENE MATAPA (Vol. III); PORTUGAL AND AFRICA (Vol. III); SHONA KINGDOMS (Vol. III).

N

Namibia Modern country located on the southwestern coast of Africa. Although the area is rich in GOLD and gemstones and is today the world's largest source of diamonds, its history has been more influenced by its harsh climate and its two vast deserts—the Namib, along the coast, and the Kalahari, to the east—than by its natural riches.

The nomadic SAN people are the oldest inhabitants of the area, having settled there as early as 8000 BCE. The San later converged with the Khoi peoples to form the ethnic group known as the KHOIKHOI. The great BANTU MIGRATIONS, which took place largely in the first millennium, brought new peoples into the area, including the HERERO and OVAMBO. When these BANTU-speaking peoples reached Namibia, they eventually drove out the Khoikhoi, who found refuge in the KALAHARI DESERT.

As elsewhere in SUB-SAHARAN AFRICA, the Bantu speakers' ability to displace such indigenous populations as the Khoikhoi was most likely due to their knowledge of ironwork, which led to their more sophisticated production of both tools and weapons.

See also: NAMIBIA (Vol. III).

Naod (r. 1494–1508) *Ethiopian emperor.*

The brother of Emperor Eskender (r. 1478–1494), Naod was part of a succession of underaged Ethiopian rulers who came to the throne during a period of great instability in which Christian power declined within the Ethiopian kingdom.

Upon the death of Eskender, the army passed the crown to the late emperor's six-year-old son, Amda-Siyon II, only to have a rival faction within the army elevate Naod to the throne. This created a schism among the administrators of the monarchy that accelerated the decline that had begun during the 1470s. The internal conflict left the empire vulnerable. During the reign of Naod's son, Lebna-Dengel (r. 1508–1540), Muslim invaders occupied much of the empire, bringing about the decline of the once-powerful Ethiopian Christian empire.

See also: ETHIOPIA (Vols. II, III); ETHIOPIAN EMPERORS (Vol. III); LEBNA-DENGEL (Vol. III).

Ndahura (c. 1344–1371) *Founder of the Kitara complex in central Africa and the first of the Bachwezi line of rulers.*

Beginning with a small chiefdom known as BUGANGAIZI, Ndahura eventually created an empire that came to include parts of Bunyoro, TORO, BUGANDA, RWANDA, and other areas within the Great Lakes region of eastern central Africa. He ruled from his capital at Mwenge, in the eastern part of his empire. Lacking any established governmental officials or structure, Ndahura was forced to govern his extensive empire through appointed agents, whose job it was to keep IRON, SALT, and cattle flowing through the kingdom.

Ndahura's system of government did little to quell the unrest that was prevalent in the region at the time, though he did manage to establish the basis of a unified kingdom. The instability that plagued Ndahura's reign continued during the reign of the second BACHWEZI ruler, his son and successor, WAMARA (c. 1371–1398).

See also: BUNYORO-KITARA (Vol. II).

Nema Town located in the southwestern corner of modern MAURITANIA. In the thirteenth and fourteenth centuries, Nema was an active trading center of the MALI EMPIRE. Along with WALATA and TIMBUKTU, Nema was a popular stop for MERCHANTS traveling the TRANS-SAHARAN TRADE ROUTES of the western SUDAN.

By the beginning of the fifteenth century, Mali was in decline. Invading TUAREG nomads were able to wrest control of Nema from the once-great empire. The Tuaregs, who came from the Aïr and Adrar regions of the SAHARA, to the east of Nema, also took control of Walata and Timbuktu during this period, effectively marking the end of the Mali Empire as a power in the region.

Nembe Ethnic group of the southern Niger Delta region. It is thought that the Nembe, who are probably related to the IJO, migrated to the area some time around 1200 and had established a monarchy by about 1400. The Nembe absorbed and adopted the cultural practices of less organized groups in the area, including the ITSEKIRI, whose war god, Ogidiga, became the state god of the Nembe in the late fifteenth century.

See also: NIGER DELTA (Vol. I).

Ngazargamu (Gazargamu) Fifteenth-century capital of the KANEM-BORNU Empire, near Lake CHAD. BORNU, to the west of Lake Chad, and the neighboring kingdom of Kanem, to the northeast, had a shared history that dated back to the thirteenth century, when Bornu was a tributary state of the powerful Kanem Empire. Kanem had established its capital in the city of NJIMI, but the SEFUWA rulers of Kanem chose to move their capital to the town of Kaka, in the better grazing lands of Bornu in the fourteenth century. Around 1475, the Sefuwa *mai*, or king, Ali Dunamami assumed control of Bornu and rebuilt his capital at Ngazargamu. The city remained the capital for Sefuwa rulers for the next three centuries.

See also: NGAZARGAMU (Vol. III).

Niamey Capital city of modern Niger, located on the north bank of the NIGER RIVER in the arid southwest part of the country. Archaeological evidence shows that the area of Niamey was settled by groups from various kingdoms, including both the SONGHAI people of the TAKEDDA Kingdom and the KANURI Empire of BORNU. Niamey began as a small settlement of mostly agriculturalist nomads, including the Maouri, Zerma, and FULANI. By the eleventh century it had become an important TRADE center for agricultural goods.

Niamey's location on the Niger River made it an ideal point from which to conduct commerce between the TRANS-SAHARAN TRADE ROUTES to the north, and the heavily populated areas of present-day Nigeria, further downstream to the south.

Niani Key center of trade and business of the MALI EMPIRE. Niani was located near the confluence of the Niger and Sankarani Rivers. It thrived in an area that not only was near the Bure GOLD mines but that also was good for farming. Rice, beans, yams, onions, grains, and COTTON were among the commonly grown CROPS. The area was densely populated, having at least 100,000 inhabitants in the fourteenth century.

Under SUNDIATA (r. 1230–1255), Niani became the capital of the Mali Empire, and it remained the capital for 300 years. Under the reign of Mansa MUSA I (r. 1307–1332), Niani reached its pinnacle as a key trading center for the western SUDAN. Scribes, judges, guild chiefs, and treasury officials managed their daily affairs in Niani, while gold, salt, and kola nuts were exchanged at the market. The SONGHAI raided Niani early in the fifteenth century and added the city to their expanding empire.

Niger-Congo languages One of the four major African language families. Niger-Congo languages are spoken throughout SUB-SAHARAN AFRICA. The main branches of this family include Bantu-Congo, Kordofanian, MANDE, Voltaic, Kwa, Gur, Ubangi, and Atlantic languages. During the great BANTU MIGRATIONS (c. 1000 BCE–500 CE), speakers of the Niger-Congo languages, especially BANTU-Congo speakers, spread east and south across the African continent from their original homelands in West Africa. By 1500, nearly all of central and southern Africa was inhabited by Bantu-speaking peoples, who had displaced and assimilated the native KHOISAN speakers as they migrated.

See also: LANGUAGES (Vol. I); LANGUAGES, MAJOR (Vol. II); NIGER-CONGO (Vol. I).

Nilo-Saharan languages One of the four major language families of Africa. The Nilo-Saharan languages include the Songhai, Saharan, Chari-Nile, and Fur branches.

See also: FUR (Vol. III); LANGUAGES (Vol. 1); LANGUAGES, MAJOR (Vol. II); NILO-SAHARAN (Vol. I).

Nilotic Word used to describe the peoples originating along the Nile River valley in northeastern Africa; also the name of the languages of these peoples. Nilotic-speakers were primarily cattle herders inhabiting the grasslands and plateaus of the African Great Lakes region in central East Africa. By the eleventh century, the fusion of the Nilotic groups with the neighboring southern Kushites and migrating BANTU-speakers gave rise to the proto-Chaga people, a culture that demonstrated characteristics of all three ethnic groups.

See also: LANGUAGES (Vol. 1); LANGUAGES, MAJOR (Vol. II); NILE VALLEY (Vol. I); NILO-SAHARAN (Vol. I); NILOTES (Vol. 1).

Nine Saints Syrian monks credited with establishing the first monasteries in ETHIOPIA. Towards the end of the fifth century, the Council of Chalcedon expelled the nine men from Syria. At issue was a theological dispute. The saints, whose beliefs were called Monophysite, held that Christ had one divine nature; the council, in contrast, asserted that Christ was both human and divine.

Although there is some dispute over whether or not the saints ever actually traveled to ETHIOPIA, their supposed works in spreading the Christian gospel have been immortalized in numerous folk traditions. According to these traditions, the saints were given shelter by the rulers of AKSUM, after which they were able to practice their Monophysite beliefs. They then followed a path of self-imposed isolation in monasteries they built in the country's northern highlands. Known as *abunas*, the monks were credited with translating Greek scripture into Ethiopia's national language of GE'EZ. Their religious devotion also has been linked to elements of mysticism.

The most noted of the monks was Za Mikael Aragaw, who built the monastery known as Debre Damo. Also of note was ABBA LIBANOS, who lived and practiced his faith for seven years at a site deep in the interior region of Massawa. His monastery, known as DEBRE LIBANOS, was granted significant amounts of land by the Aksumite state and subsequent rulers in the region and has remained an active church for centuries.

See also: CHRISTIANITY (Vol. II); CHRISTIANITY, INFLUENCE OF (Vol. II).

Further reading: Harold G. Marcus, *A History of Ethiopia* (Berkeley: University of California Press, 1994).

Njimi Capital city of the Kanem Empire, located northeast of Lake CHAD. According to legend, a palace was built at the nomad village of Njimi, which became the first capital of Kanem during the mid-ninth century. The tradition goes on to state that the KANURI people of the area, who were of mixed Negroid and BERBER ancestry, constructed the palace of red bricks, a technique they supposedly borrowed from the people of the Nile.

One reason for the establishment of the capital at Njimi may have been its proximity to the FEZZAN, an area of oases on the TRANS-SAHARAN TRADE ROUTES. The Kanem Empire managed to establish dominance over the trade routes and traded GOLD and IVORY for SALT, horses, and metal items.

The Kanuri were ruled by a king, or *mai,* who was considered to be divine. The *mai* was the head of a feudal society of regional governors. In return for the privilege of holding land, local chiefs were loyal to the king and provided him with tribute and soldiers. The area that was governed from Njimi included southern Chad, northern CAMEROON, southern LIBYA, and parts of Nigeria and Niger.

ISLAM came to Njimi via the trade routes and was accepted by Mai UMME in the eleventh century. Umme is believed by some historians to have founded the SEFUWA lineage.

See also: KANEM-BORNU (Vol. III).

Nkole (Ankole, Nkore, Ankore, Nyankole) BANTU-speaking people who inhabit the area west of Lake VICTORIA in southwestern UGANDA; also the name of their kingdom. The Nkole people are made up two ethnic groups who came to share a common language and similar cultures: the pastoral TUTSI and the agricultural HUTU. Nkole society was divided into two castes; the lords, or Hima, were mostly Tutsis, and the underclass, or Iru, consisted of mostly Hutus.

The aristocratic Tutsi migrated from the north around the beginning of the fifteenth century in search of suitable pasture for their cattle. They lived in village communities about a mile apart from one another, surviving almost exclusively on the products of their herds. The Hutu were the descendants of the original Bantu-speaking people who probably moved into the area during the first millennium. They lived in permanent settlements of forty to 100 homesteads, where they cultivated various crops, including millet. Although the Tutsi and the Hutu of Nkole shared a common culture, they were forbidden to intermarry.

See also: CHWEZI (Vols. II, III); NKOLE (Vol. III); TORO (Vol. II).

nobles Members of an aristocratic class whose status is usually determined by lineage. Within many of the KINGDOMS AND EMPIRES of Africa that developed between the years 900 and 1500, a class of hereditary nobles developed who served as counselors to the king, as in the WOLOF and the SERER states, and who were often responsible for choosing the next king, often from among their own number.

In the GHANA EMPIRE (900–1076) and its successor states, the MALI EMPIRE (c. 1200–1500) and the SONGHAI Empire (c. 1464–1591), and to different degrees in other important CITY-STATES and kingdoms such as OYO and BENIN, after his coronation, the king was considered divine or semidivine and often ruled in an autocratic or despotic manner. Local government—in provinces and districts—was often in the hands of the royal or aristocratic families, who enjoyed privileges not available to commoners. In the HAUSA STATES, for example, the nobility was exempt from taxation, thus placing a greater burden on the less privileged.

See also: KINGDOMS AND EMPIRES OF EAST AFRICA (Vol. II); KINGDOMS AND EMPIRES OF WEST AFRICA (Vol. II); KINGDOMS AND EMPIRES OF LOWER GUINEA (Vol. II); KINGDOMS AND EMPIRES OF SENEGAMBIA (Vol. II).

Nouakchott Capital of the present-day country of MAURITANIA in West Africa. In the eleventh century, Nouakchott was the site of the monastery, or place of religious retreat, from which the Muslim fundamentalist ALMORAVIDS set off for their conquest of Africa and Spain and the eventual establishment of the Almoravid Empire (1056–1147).

The monastery, or *ribat*, was built by the eleventh-century theologian ABD ALLA IBN YASIN, who had returned with Yahya ibn Ibrihim, the leader of the SANHAJA BERBERS, when the latter completed his HAJJ to MECCA in 1035. It was the intent of ibn Ibrihim and his followers to establish a place of worship for the members of the former Sanhaja Confederation. (This group, established in the ninth century, wished to practice a more orthodox form of ISLAM than was practiced by other Islamic groups in Mauritania.) In time, Ibn Yasin and his followers—who were called *murabitum*, or "men of the *ribat*"—launched a JIHAD, or holy war, against the former Sanhaja members who failed to practice Islam with the zeal and fervor of ibn Yasin's followers. This holy war has been viewed as the beginning of the Almoravid movement.

Ntusi Site of a large Iron Age town or trading center from c. 1100 to 1400, located in the Masaka district of western UGANDA in the Great Lakes region of East Africa.

The relationship between Ntusi and the archaeological site at BIGO 6 miles (10 km) further south is not yet understood. Bigo is the best-known earthwork complex in western Uganda. It features a system of concentric ditches 6.5 miles (10.4 km) in diameter, some of it hewn from rock, enclosing what is thought to be a large cattle-grazing area on a riverbank. Archaeologists believe that the site is both a royal capital, very likely of the CHWEZI Kingdom, as well as a well-defended cattle enclosure.

Ntusi is important to archaeologists for its large mounds of domestic debris resulting both from grain cultivation and cattle raising. Pottery and bones in two mounds at the site, called the Ntusi male and female mounds, are as much as 13 feet (4 m) deep. Ntusi also features man-made basins, or *bwogoro*, which were probably used to water cattle. Both Bigo and Ntusi suggest that the distinction between pastoralists and agriculturalists, which are typical of this region, began hundreds of years ago.

See also: BACHWEZI (Vol. II).

Nubia, Christian Refers to the land and people of Nubia after the arrival of CHRISTIANITY in approximately 541.

Situated along the Nile River and site of the ancient kingdoms of Kush (1000 BCE–250 CE) and Meroë (600 BCE–300 CE), Nubia had long been a meeting point between Africa and the rest of the Mediterranean region. Little, however, is known about the years between the fall of these kingdoms and the rise of ISLAM in the middle of the sixth century. The region was inhabited by a people called the Nobatae, whose origins are uncertain but whose customs and crafts show links to Meroë. The Nobatae occasionally allied themselves with one of the nomadic peoples of the desert to attack Roman towns in Upper Egypt but were always defeated.

Christian missionaries in the sixth century brought Nubia back into contact with the outside world. At that point, Nubia was divided into three kingdoms, Nobatia (Nobadia), Maqurrah (Makuria), and Alwa ('Alwah), with capitals at Pachoras, Dongola, and Soba. In 543, the Monophysite monk Julian traveled to Nobatia at the request of both the Egyptian Coptic Church and the Empress Theodora of Byzantium. Because Nobatia was relatively close to Christian EGYPT, conversion occurred rapidly. Maqurrah, which was located further from Egypt, between the third and fifth cataracts of the Nile, was converted by monks from Chaldedon in 560. Possibly because it was the furthest from Egyptian influence, the kingdom of Alwa, located above the fifth cataract, was the last of the three kingdoms to convert, in 580. Churches were built and ancient temples rededicated to Christian worship. At this point, Nubia's history again becomes obscure.

After the death of the prophet Muhammad in 632, Arab armies burst forth from Arabia in search of land and converts to Islam. Egypt was invaded in 639. In 652, a Muslim army captured Dongola, capital of the by then combined kingdoms of Maqurrah and Nobatia. Dongola was forced to pay tribute to Egypt. Dongola, however, remained Christian until the fourteenth century and Alwa until the sixteenth century, at which times each succumbed to Turkish or Muslim invaders.

The treaty, called a *bakt*, that ended conflict with Egypt in 652 was without precedent in the Muslim world. It was both a truce between Egypt and Nubia and a nonaggression pact that guaranteed each country safety from attack, allowed the free passage of ARABS through Nubia as travelers but not as settlers, and required each to extradite fugitives from the other. Nubia also pledged the upkeep of a mosque in Dongola for use by visiting Muslims. By the terms of the *bakt*, Nubia sent the governor of Aswan, Egypt, 360 slaves a year, and in turn Nubia would receive specified quantities of foodstuffs and trade goods. This treaty was renegotiated in 835, in an unprecedented meeting between the caliph of Egypt and the head of a subject state—felt to be a diplomatic coup for the Nubians—when Nubia could not afford the demands of the *bakt*. Tribute became payable every third year.

In subsequent centuries, trade with Islamic Egypt brought prosperity to Nubia. The Nubians sent GOLD, IVORY, ebony, ostrich feathers, and slaves and imported textiles, glassware, glazed POTTERY, and other valuable

This twelfth-century wall painting shows Queen Martha of Nubia, the Virgin and Christ Child, and an unnamed martyr. It is in the Christian basilica at Faras, formerly the capital of the Nubian kingdom of Nobatia. This area was flooded when the Aswan Dam was built and Lake Nasser formed. © *Roger Wood/CORBIS*

items. At the same time, the Nubians were making an elaborate pottery of their own, decorated with designs like those found on illuminated manuscripts. Brightly colored murals and paintings on church walls were also a feature of the art of Christian Nubia.

When the MAMLUK sultans came to power in Egypt in 1250, they repudiated the terms of the *bakt* and made

a number of raids into Nubia, none of which led to any long-term conquest. In the two centuries that followed, however, mass migrations of nomadic peoples from Egypt and the Arabian Peninsula changed the population and political balance in the region. The kingdom of Maqurrah was splintered into a series of petty chiefdoms ruled by Arab warlords. Geography preserved

Nobatia to the north; the harshness of its desert location deterred Arab invaders. A small Christian kingdom called Dotawo remained in existence in the region until the end of the fifteenth century, when it, too, disappeared from history.

See also: COPTIC CHRISTIANITY (Vol. II); DONGOLA (Vol. III); KUSH (Vol. I).

numuw Name for the caste of blacksmiths among the Bamana-speaking BAMBARA people, a MANDE subgroup of the upper Niger region of present-day Mali. The Bambara blacksmiths created IRON tools and pieces of ceremonial ART that played an important role in their culture.

Traditionally, the Bambara divided themselves into castes based on occupation; marriage with someone outside one's caste was forbidden. The Bambara recognized two broad castes of farmers and artisans. The artisan caste, which included leather workers, weavers, and poets as well as blacksmiths, was called collectively *nyamakalaw*, or "handlers of power." Although most of their time was taken up in the practice of their craft, they also had to maintain small subsistence plots to grow food for themselves.

The Bambara believed that a life force or spiritual power called NYAMA imbued everything in the universe. *Nyama* was especially strong among blacksmiths, who inherited it from their ancestors (a defense of the caste system) and used it to transform the objects they made at the forge. The blacksmith's activities were surrounded by rituals of prayer, meditation, and sacrifice. The people believed that the blacksmith put *nyama* into the knives, hoes, altar figures, hunting charms, and other objects he made, thus transforming energy into matter. Such power had the blacksmith that it was believed that he could cure infertility in a woman who joined him in prayer and meditation at his forge.

The Bambara blacksmiths also carved a variety of ritual masks and sculptures made from wood. The masks represented gods or ancestors, and only the blacksmith was thought to possess the spiritual power and knowledge to transform the wood for its new purpose. Their animal-head designs were sometimes abstract and sometimes very naturalistic; however, the masks of the Komo Society, the secret society of blacksmiths, were formless shapes of mud, horn, and animal parts applied over a simple frame. The Komo Society supervised the rituals at which new age sets were created and circumcisions performed.

See also: AGE SETS (Vol. I); CASTE SYSTEM (Vol. I); CIRCUMCISION (Vol. I); NIGER RIVER (Vol. I); SECRET SOCIETIES (Vol. 1).

nyama According to BAMBARA belief, the life force or spiritual power that fills everything in the universe. Bambara artisans of the 1200s and later were thought to imbue the practical and ritual objects they made with this power, causing these artisans to be called *nyamakalaw*, or "handlers of power." Blacksmiths, or NUMUW, were thought to be especially powerful *nyamakalaw*.

See also: RELIGION, TRADITIONAL (Vol. I).

nyamakalaw BAMBARA sorcerers, leather workers, bards, and blacksmiths (NUMUW) who formed the artisan caste; they were trained to utilize NYAMA, the life force or spiritual power that Bambara people believe fills everything in the universe. The word *nyamakalaw* means "handlers of *nyama* [power]."

The *nyamakalaw* were trained throughout their lives to control the power of nyama. Everything produced by the *nyamakalaw* was considered art, whether it be the tools of the blacksmith, the spells of the sorcerer, the saddles of the leather worker, or the music of the bard. The Bambara believed that *nyama* shaped all of nature, and, likewise, the *nyamakalaw* had to learn how to shape *nyama*, whether for art or for healing. The *nyamakalaw* married only within their own caste because it was believed that the power to shape *nyama* passed from generation to generation.

See also: RELIGION, TRADITIONAL (Vol. I).

Nyoro (Banyoro, Bunyoro, Kitara) BANTU-speaking people who live east of Lake Mobutu Sese Seko (Lake Albert) in the Great Lakes region of present-day UGANDA. The BUNYORO-KITARA Empire founded in their territory dominated the region from c. 1300 to c. 1900. Elements of a Bunyoro Kingdom persisted until 1966 when the government of Uganda abolished it.

Ancient Bunyoro myth says that their royal ancestors were the children of the founder of humanity, a king named SEKABAKA KINTU. Kintu had three sons, Kairu, Kahuma, and Kakama. To determine who was most deserving of the royal crown, Kintu put his sons through a series of challenges. The youngest, Kakama, won and was thus named king of the Bunyoro and founder of the royal lineage. The middle son, Kahuma, placed second, so he became the progenitor of the middle-class Tutsi pastoralists. Kairu established the Bunyoro peasant class that emerged during the Tutsi migrations.

The early Nyoro people lived in a region in the fertile hills of East-central Africa. Little is known about the ancestors of the Nyoro, though they probably arrived in the region around 700, emigrating from the west. For the next 600 to 700 years, they lived peacefully as farmers, subsisting mainly on millet and sorghum. Small BANANA groves were kept to make beer. Each family tended small plots of farmland and may have raised a small number of cattle. Individual family homes were not organized in structured villages, but the early Nyoro settled within close proximity of one another.

The Nyoro have a complex ancestry that includes the descendents of peoples who moved into the region during the thirteenth and fourteenth centuries and lived among the earlier Bantu-speaking migrants. First to arrive were the TORO people from between Lake Albert and Lake Edward in Uganda. A highly stratified society, the Toro were divided into two classes, the smaller, cattle-owning TUTSI and the agriculturalist Iru, a larger class of subsistence farmers over whom the Tutsi claimed greater privileges. The Tutsi dominated the Iru and the indigenous Nyoro, and Tutsi villages grew into small states. In a shift of power, however, the Tutsi states came under the control of CHWEZI rulers, who dominated western Uganda from their strongholds at BIGO and other sites.

Sometime during the reign of the Chwezi king WAMARA (c. 1371–1398), the BITO clan of the LUO people migrated into Tutsi territory. Although the Chwezi had only recently established their authority over the Tutsi, Chwezi power was already waning in the northern regions. Wamara attempted to integrate the Babito into Chwezi society by giving them positions of authority in the state of KITARA, but the move failed. Political unrest in Kitara was worsened by a severe famine, which eventually sparked a military coup. The Chwezi lost control of Kitara to the Babito; from the remains of this state the Babito founded the Bunyoro Kingdom, which became by 1500 the most powerful kingdom in the region. The Tutsi took control of Ankole and other Chwezi strongholds stretching toward Lake VICTORIA. Chwezi power was broken, and new kingdoms emerged.

See also: BABITO (Vol. II); BUNYORO (Vol. I); BUNY-ORO-KITARA (Vol. III); MILLET (Vol. I); SORGHUM (Vol. I).

O

oba Local chieftain in the OYO KINGDOM. Traditionally, the oba was responsible for all local government in the towns and provinces of the kingdom. Nonlocal issues were handled by the *ALAFIN*, or king, and the ruling council, which was called the OYO MESI.

Oduduwa Semimythical ruler and founder of the ancient Nigerian kingdom of ILE-IFE. YORUBA oral traditions tell how Oduduwa, the son of the supreme god Olorun, founded the kingdom of Ife during the eleventh century. He then supposedly sent his sons (or, as some legends say, grandsons) to rule over BENIN and the kingdoms of OYO, Ila, Popo, Sabe, Owu, and Ketu in YORUBALAND.

Other Yoruba traditions substantiate the claim that Yoruba settlers inhabited the region as early as the ninth century. According to those traditions, Oduduwa is considered the patriarch of Ife but not necessarily the founder of the Yoruba peoples themselves.

See also: OLORUN (Vol. I); RELIGION, TRADITIONAL (Vol. I); YORUBALAND (Vols. I, III).

Ogboni Secret society of the OYO KINGDOM. According to the traditions of Oyo's YORUBA people, the Ogboni rendered judgment in cases of bloodshed and other civil strife. The Ogboni also were responsible for reviewing decisions made by the OYO MESI, or ruling council.

Old Oyo (Katunga) Original site of the OYO KINGDOM in southwestern Nigeria. According to a number of traditional sources, Old Oyo was founded by Prince Oranyan (also called Oranmiyan), the son or grandson of the semi-mythical ruler ODUDUWA. According to these legends, the prince was sent to rule the kingdom of BENIN during the eleventh century and, upon his arrival, placed his capital at the city of Oyo. Other oral legends, however, say that the region's initial settlers were members of the YORUBA clan who came to the area between the eighth and eleventh centuries.

See also: EGBA (Vol. III); OYO EMPIRE (Vol. III).

oni (ooni) of **Ife** Title of the religious and political leader of ILE-IFE, the first capital of the YORUBA Kingdom. The *oni* was believed to be the earthly representative of the Yoruba god Olorun. The position was elective, and the *oni* was chosen from among the aristocracy, which followed patrilineal descent. The *oni* resided in a walled palace located far from his subjects. Throughout his reign, the people of Yoruba did not see the *oni*. Therefore, officials, chiefs, and state leaders were delegated to oversee the lower levels of government.

Much of the sculpture of Ife was a tribute to the *oni* as the position evolved into one of cultural importance. Among the various roles of the *oni* was the responsibility of handing over the traditional sword of justice, called Oranyan's Victory Sword (Ida Ajase or Ida Oranyan), to the new *ALAFIN*, or ruler, of OYO. (Oranyan was the son or grandson of ODUDUWA, the legendary first king.)

According to Ife tradition, all Yoruba kingdoms were subject to the authority of the *oni*, as commanded by Oduduwa upon founding the Ife kingdom, which was called at the time Ile-Ife. Whether or not the *oni* had the absolute power that the people of Ife claim is uncertain.

Eventually, settlements such as the OYO KINGDOM and BENIN broke away and established themselves as autonomous states. Many of these states patterned their governments after the Ife monarchy.

See also: ILE-IFE (Vol. I).

Oromo (Galla) Ethnic group descended from a pastoral people in southern ETHIOPIA, near KENYA; also, the language spoken by these people. The Oromo language belongs to the Eastern Kushitic branch of the AFRO-ASIATIC language group. Early Kushitic speakers migrated to northern Kenya around 1000 and are assumed to be the ancestors of the Oromo and the SOMALI people in this area. Until the sixteenth century, the Oromo, whom the Portuguese later called the Galla, lived a mostly pastoral existence according to their traditional age set system called *gada*, comprised of eleven generational grades in a forty-year cycle.

Starting in the sixteenth century, the Oromo changed from their traditional social patterns and began an extensive expansion into northern regions of Ethiopia. Skirmishes and all-out wars between Muslims and Ethiopian Christians from 1520 to 1543 had left the Ethiopian Plateau open to expansion. By 1600, the Oromo had spread so widely in Ethiopia that the Ethiopian emperor Sarsa Dengel (r. 1563–1597) controlled only ERITREA, TIGRAY, Gondar, and portions of Gojjam, Shewa, and Welo.

See also: AGE GRADES (Vol. I); AGE SETS (Vol. I); ETHIOPIA (Vol. III); GOJJAM (Vol. III); GONDAR (Vol. III); OROMO (Vols. I, III); PASTORALISM (Vol. I); SHEWA (Vol. III); TIGRAY (Vol. I).

Ovambo (Owambo) BANTU-speaking people originally from central Africa, who migrated to regions of modern NAMIBIA and ANGOLA in the fourteenth century. Oshindonga and Oshikwanyama are the two major languages of the seven groups that make up the Ovambo people. These include the Eunda and Ukolonkazi (considered to be one group), the Ondonga, the Ombarantu, the Ukwaluizi, the Ongandjera, the Ukwanyama (Kwanyama), and the Ukwambi.

The Ovambo traditionally lived off the land as herders and farmers, with sorghum and millet their primary CROPS. Although each family worked its own section of land, which could be anywhere from 15 to 50 acres (6 to 20 ha), each family also was part of a larger farming community made up of several hundred people and headed by a king.

Although Ovambo religion involved totem and ancestor worship, it focused primarily on a main god called Ilunga. According to the Ovambo, shortly after creating the world, Ilunga lured the first man and woman out of a ter-

mite hill. The couple was said to have had three children, two sons and a daughter. The Ukwanyama trace their lineage to the eldest son, Kanzi; the Ondonga believed themselves descendents of the second son, Nangombe.

Ovimbundu An ethnolinguistic group that emerged during the sixteenth century in the central highlands of ANGOLA during the time of the precolonial kingdoms in BANTU Africa. The Ovimbundu originally spoke several Bantu languages, though they now speak the Mbundu language. The Ovimbindu are related to the MBUNDU, a neighboring people in Angola, who are often called the North Mbundu or the Kimbundu in order to distinguish the two.

Before the sixteenth century, the Ovimbundu existed in separate sociopolitical subgroups. Of the fourteen distinct Ovimbundu kingdoms that have been identified, Fetu (Feti) is believed to be the earliest settlement. Excavations have radiocarbon-dated this site to late in the first millennium. Later migration among the emerging coastal and interior West African kingdoms created a shared, pastoral Ovimbundu identity during the sixteenth century. Though the Ovimbundu are the largest ethnolinguistic group in modern Angola, historical information on them before the sixteenth century is curiously sparse.

See also: OVIMBUNDU (Vol. III).

Owo YORUBA town located in the present-day state of Ondo in southwestern Nigeria.

Oral tradition states that the semimythical god ODUDUWA had a son named *Owo* (meaning "gentle") who died in the town of Upafa after fighting and conquering the local ruler. Owo's son then established the town at its present-day site and named it in honor of his father.

Legends notwithstanding, archaeological evidence indicates that the town of Owo was inhabited by Yoruba people from the fifteenth century or earlier. The artistic culture of Owo was closely linked to the kingdoms of ILE-IFE and BENIN, and its artisans were known to have created works of art in terra-cotta and IVORY that rivaled the output of those two powerful kingdoms.

A distinctive feature of Owo was its elaborate palace, adorned with silver doors, finely carved veranda posts, beaded silk wall hangings, and royal gables known as *kobi*, said to have been the invention of the fifteenth-century ruler Oluaso. Another distinctive feature of Owo was its walls. A triple wall encircled the town, and an additional wall surrounded the perimeter of the palace.

Oyo Kingdom YORUBA kingdom located in the savannas on the edge of the rain forest in the southwest of modern Nigeria; progenitor of the powerful Oyo Empire of the seventeenth and eighteenth centuries.

Linguistic evidence indicates that Oyo was established some time before the year 1000 during a wave of immigration into the region. The city of OLD OYO, the capital of the kingdom, had a favorable location for TRADE, but the Oyo Kingdom was only a minor power in the region from the time of its founding well into the sixteenth century. In 1550 Oyo fell to the forces of the neighboring kingdoms of Borgu and Nupe and did not rise to become a major state until 1650.

During the fifteenth century and perhaps earlier, goods came into Old Oyo from every direction, carried along the many trails and trade routes that converged at this centrally located town. The local soil was fertile enough to support both herding and farming, and a wide variety of foodstuffs and craft works were traded at Old Oyo. The primary business very possibly was commerce in horses. When the Oyo Empire began to expand in the years after 1650, much of Oyo's military success resulted from its renowned cavalry.

The centralized government of Old Oyo was led by an ALAFIN, or king, who was the spiritual as well as political leader of the kingdom. Considered *ekeji orisa*, or a "companion to the gods," the *alafin* held vast powers. A council, called the OYO MESI, which consisted of chiefs from seven regions and provinces, served to keep the *alafin* in check. It also was responsible for naming successors to the throne.

See also: BORGU (Vol. III); EGBA (Vol. III); NUPE (Vol. III); OYO EMPIRE (Vol. III).

Oyo mesi Ruling council of the OYO KINGDOM, which was a minor state in precolonial YORUBALAND. Traditionally, the Oyo mesi had power over the affairs of state. It also acted to select the next ruler upon the death of the existing king, or ALAFIN. Along with the *basorum*, or prime minister, and the people as a whole, the Oyo mesi also had the power to depose a ruling *alafin* and force him to commit suicide.

P

Pangani Town located on the northern coast of modern Tanzania, at the mouth of the Pangani River. In the eighth century, Pangani became a trading center, specializing in slaves. Muslim Arabs traded their Arabian goods for African captives, then transported them by Indian Ocean and RED SEA TRADE routes to North Africa.

See also: ARAB COASTAL TRADE (Vol. II); INDIAN OCEAN TRADE (Vol. II); SLAVERY (Vol. II); ZANJ (Vol. II).

Pate Trade center located on Pate Island, off the coast of KENYA. Pate was founded c. 1300 as a SWAHILI COAST city-state. Along with the towns of Faza, Siyu, and Shanga, Pate formed an Indian Ocean trading empire that exchanged GOLD, slaves, and IVORY for CLOTH and weapons. The Portuguese gained control of the area in 1498.

See also: INDIAN OCEAN TRADE (Vol. II); PATE ISLAND (Vol. III); PORTUGAL AND AFRICA (Vol. III).

Pemba Small island in the Indian Ocean off the coast of Tanzania just north of ZANZIBAR. Known as Kanbalu in the period prior to European colonization, Pemba was originally inhabited by the ZANJ, the ARABIC name for the BANTU-speaking peoples who inhabited coastal East Africa. By 1100, Muslim MERCHANTS had begun settling in the area, and although their lineage is unclear, these migrants probably were descended from Arabo-Persian and Benadir coastal peoples. They eventually intermarried with the local Zanj, adopting elements of their culture at the same time that they introduced ISLAM to the island.

Persian traders Merchants who made up the dominant sea trade empire after the fall of the Roman Empire, around the fifth century. Like the ARABS, the Persians were among the first settlers of the African coast, having claimed EGYPT as part of their empire as early as the sixth century BCE.

Persia, a vast empire to the northeast of the Arabian Peninsula, sent traders to Africa via the MEDITERRANEAN SEA as well as the Red Sea. They exchanged CLOTH, incense, and spices for African captives, GOLD, IVORY, IRON, rhinoceros horns, and animal skins. Evidence suggests that African captives were present in Persia in the seventh century. By that time, Persia had extended its territory to Iraq and Arabia, allowing it to dominate sea trade.

Persian merchants traded heavily with the BANTU-speaking ZANJ, as they called indigenous East Africans, along Red Sea and Indian Ocean trade routes. As early as the tenth century, SHIRAZI ARABS, originally from Persia, were intermarrying with the local African traders. By the twelfth century, this mix of people was thriving as the SWAHILI COAST culture, which would come to dominate Africa's east coast by the fifteenth century.

See also: INDIAN OCEAN TRADE (Vol. II); PEMBA (Vol. III); PERSIAN CONQUEST (Vol. I); RED SEA TRADE (Vol. II).

Pokomo BANTU-speaking ethnic group that inhabited parts of KENYA and present-day Tanzania in the period of

African history prior to European colonization. Pokomo oral tradition claims that their ancestors originated in the African interior and moved to a land along the East African coast, probably Shungwaya in present-day southern Somalia. After conflicts with the OROMO, their Kushitic neighbors, the Pokomo moved further south to the Tana River basin in Kenya and coastal areas of Tanzania. The Pokomo are related to the Mijikenda and the Taita, and several KISWAHILI-speaking coastal groups.

See also: MIJIKENDA (Vol. III); POKOMO (Vol. III); SHUNGWAYE (Vol. III).

Popo (Peda, Xwla) West African people, related to the EWE, who have long inhabited present-day Togo along the Mono River. Most Popo are farmers who live in small villages and cultivate corn and yams.

The Peda, as they called themselves, were named "Popo" by Portuguese explorers who arrived in the latter half of the fifteenth century, and that is how they are widely known today. The Portuguese found the Popo engaged in small-scale trade of their handcrafted goods including CLOTH, POTTERY, and IRON items.

See also: POPO (Vol. III); PORTUGAL AND AFRICA (Vol. III); TOGO (Vol. III).

pottery Handmade glazed or unglazed clay vessels that were used for cooking, mixing, measuring, and storing food, water, oils, and numerous other items. Broken pottery was used as tiles, weights, and gaming chips. The Fon of DAHOMEY, the ASHANTI of modern coastal Ghana, the IBO of Nigeria, the Bamun and Baya of modern CAMEROON, and the NYORO of modern UGANDA are known for especially fine examples of the potter's art. Terra-cotta, or clay, is the most common substance used, though the Nuba people of Sudan make their pottery from dried dung, which they shape and paint.

Gender roles often determined who made a particular kind of pottery. In most African societies, women, often the wives of the village NUMUW, or blacksmith, manufactured functional vessels, whereas the men shaped decorative vessels in the form of animals and humans. Many cultures believed that women could become infertile if they sculpted animals or humans. The purpose and status of specific pottery types varied among cultures. A container used in one culture as a sacred fertility vessel might be used in another culture as simply a drinking cup; the shape of the vessel alone did not make it sacred or commonplace. It was not uncommon for everyday ware to become a sacred container when the need arose.

Excavations in YORUBALAND in southwestern Nigeria have uncovered examples of naturalistic sculpture, possibly of Yoruba royalty, created in brass and pottery, that date from between 1100 and 1450 CE. Authorities believe

This fine example of Bambara pottery is on display at the Museum of Jos in Nigeria. The intersection of flat rectangles is a common feature of traditional Bambara design. © *Paul Almasy/CORBIS*

that this style of pottery was influenced by Yoruba's neighboring state of ILE-IFE, whose products show a similar naturalism. Both Yoruba and Ife figures feature bulging eyes and stylized lips and ears.

Domestic pottery is made by molding, ring building, modeling on a board, and, more recently, on a potter's wheel. The earliest potter's wheels, dating to c. 3000 BCE, were simply turned by hand. Later models use flywheels to maintain a constant rotation. Just as the texture of kente CLOTH was influenced by the texture of a woven basket, pottery forms even more obviously have been influenced by the shape of baskets and wood carvings and also by the shapes of such natural objects as the calabash and other gourds. Pots not made on a wheel are baked in an open hearth or oven and are decorated with incised lines or colored with various dyes.

> **Gourds provided convenient vessels to tie onto a camel and send off by CARAVAN. Pottery in SUB-SAHARAN AFRICA was often made in the shape of a gourd for this same purpose.**

North Africa also developed a pottery-making tradition, especially in the creation of fine pottery and in the more practical production of the two-handled amphora, or jug, that was often used for transporting olive oil. The olive oil trade was centered near Carthage, in southern Tunisia, and along the northern slopes of the Aurès and Bou Taleb Mountains. By the fourth century, Africa was exporting olive oil in amphorae to all parts of the Roman Empire. Widespread Mediterranean trade in pottery lasted until the Islamic invasion of North Africa in the eighth century, at which time pottery making became once again a mainly local craft.

> During this same time period, North African pottery was also making its way into sub-Saharan Africa, due in part to the introduction of the camel, which made long-distance trade more feasible. North African-made pottery that dates back as far as the third century CE has been found in the Niger Valley.

Some art historians find evidence of classic Greek and Roman shapes in the pottery of the BERBER people, whose two-handled jugs resemble classical amphorae. Making pottery for domestic use was women's work in Berber society and often followed a prescribed ritual for the completion of each stage, from determining a favorable day to choose and knead the clay to the final firing and decorating.

Islamic Pottery   The Islamic cultures of the Middle East, especially the cities of Damascus in Persia (Iran) and Baghdad in Iraq, are well-regarded for their sophisticated forms of pottery. Most of the major innovations in Islamic pottery originated there and not in Africa. A key exception, however, was the rediscovery in ninth-century Egypt and Iraq of a tin glaze that had once been used in ancient Egypt but had been lost for centuries. The rediscovery of this glaze, which creates a grayish white opaque surface, was motivated by the growing popularity in the late eighth and early ninth century of imported Chinese porcelain, which was created by a process that Chinese potters kept secret. Egyptian and Iraqi potters used a fine white clay and the new tin glaze to create a close replica of the Chinese original.

> The tin glaze technique spread from Egypt to Europe by way of al-ANDALUS (Muslim Spain) in the thirteenth century and is the basis for the fine Italian maiolica, French faience, and Dutch delftware of the fifteenth to eighteenth centuries.

Luster painting of pottery also originated in Egypt toward the end of the ninth or early in the tenth century. This decorative technique, first used by Egyptian glassblowers in pre-Islamic times, uses silver and COPPER oxides and a second firing to lay down a very thin, shiny surface, more often than not colored ruby red. Many examples of this luster-painted pottery have been found in excavations at Bahnasa/Oxyrhynchus in Egypt and also at Samarra, near Baghdad. By the middle of the tenth century, this technique added colors that ranged from yellowish green to golden green and added birds, animals, and even human figures to the design. Luster painting became even more refined and sophisticated during the FATIMID period in Egypt (969–1171) and spread into Syria and North Africa from Egypt and Iraq.

Other Imports   Chinese ceramics and glass beads from about 1050 to 1200 have been found at MAPUNGUBWE, the predecessor of GREAT ZIMBABWE in southern Africa. According to written records from the time, these goods entered Africa as part of INDIAN OCEAN TRADE. The Arabs were also the main intermediaries between China and Europe in the ceramic trade until the sixteenth century. They had sole control over the shipping routes along the Mediterranean coast of Egypt and to Persia, India, Southwest Asia, and China. The transshipment port was Cairo. The Portuguese would not discover these sea routes until the 1600s, when they began to take over the porcelain trade.

Western and Eastern Africa   Authorities believe that West African pottery traditions that began in the Early Iron Age persisted into the Late Iron Age and even into the nineteenth century. In eastern Zambia, however, there appears to be a break in tradition, possibly associated with the migration of BANTU-speaking peoples across the continent. Pottery produced in the Lungwebungu and Luanga traditions (so-called from the rivers of the same names) often take the form of necked pots and shallow bowls, often with tapered rims instead of the thicker rims and beveled lips of earlier pottery. In another break with tradition, these vessels were apparently crafted by women instead of men.

Pottery remnants unearthed at Gokomere Mission near GREAT ZIMBABWE indicate the development of another pottery tradition made up of stamped and grooved ware. Pottery in the Gokomere tradition has been found as far south as the LIMPOPO RIVER and dates from the third through the ninth centuries. Pottery found in an original dig site in Zimbabwe, called Leopard's Kopje I, contains examples of the Gokomere tradition. However, pottery in a Leopard's Kopje II site contains little in the Gokomere tradition and instead shows stylus-made designs. Undecorated beakers represent a new pottery. Figurines of women, domestic animals, and cattle made from white clay figure prominently at this site, whose contents date to the tenth and eleventh centuries.

Enlarged buttocks and other features of the female fig-urines suggest a KHOIHKOI influence.

The Shona people, the expert builders in stone who founded GREAT ZIMBABWE, have a long tradition of producing decorative pottery, which may represent a fusion of Bantu and San techniques. However, the discovery at Great Zimbabwe of Ming dynasty (1368–1644) pottery from China also indicates that Great Zimbabwe had extensive trade.

See also: POTTERY (Vol. I); SCULPTURE (Vol. I); ART (Vols. I, II, III).

Q

queens and queen mothers Female rulers of a chiefdom, kingdom, or empire. The words *queen* and *queen mother* do not always reflect the many characteristics and responsibilities of the African woman who held a prominent place in the court of a king.

Queens As in European culture, the queen was usually the wife of the king. (In many polygamous African cultures, the title was given only to the first, or primary, wife of the king. The primary wife was the one who would bear the future king.) But she might also be the mother of the king, the sister of the king, or even a regent—an individual who manages a kingdom's affairs until a young inheritor of the throne is old enough to rule. Since African kingdoms usually developed in patrilineal societies, where the older men held the positions of leadership, it was unusual for women to assume positions of power equal to that of a king. Still, throughout Africa there are numerous examples of women who became powerful rulers in their own right.

Queen GUDIT, of ETHIOPIA, is one of the more remarkable female figures in African history. Although the details of her reign are sketchy, it is known that she was a capable military commander who led her warriors to victory over the Christian kingdom of AKSUM.

In such cultures as the AKAN and ASHANTI of West Africa, the Loango of central Africa, and the NYORO of UGANDA, the women related to the sitting king traditionally were given the status of chiefs, with all of the attendant responsibilities and respect associated with such a position.

Queen Mothers The most important female in a kingdom was sometimes called the queen mother. This title, however, did not always fit the true nature of her relationship to the king. In some kingdoms, the woman holding the title of queen mother may have been the king's sister, grandmother, or a respected female elder such as the former king's chief wife (who was not always the reigning king's biological mother). Whatever her actual relationship to the king, the queen mother nevertheless represented a strong link to the king's royal line and therefore was often regarded as both a sacred entity and a keeper of genealogical history.

Queen mothers held considerable power and importance as they regularly served their kings and kingdoms as advisers, emissaries, and politicians. Queen mothers figure prominently in the histories and lore of such diverse groups as the Akan peoples of Ghana, the TUAREGS of the arid plains of North-central Africa, and the LUBA of southern central Africa.

In many cases, the histories of queen mothers have relied on oral traditions, some of which have been substantiated by pictorial documentation of women figures in both religious and royal splendor. An eleventh-century drawing depicts a Nubian queen mother named Martha in royal garb, being watched over by the Virgin Mary.

Beyond being highly regarded for their secular wisdom, queen mothers might also have either a religious or mythical importance. They may even hold male rights and authority to confirm their chief-like status. In addition, many kingdoms also provided the queen mother with her own royal palace and entourage, often including a personal army for protection.

One of the roles most commonly performed by a queen mother was that of regent to a young king. A prominent queen mother was Ethiopia's Empress ELENI, who became a powerful and respected queen mother and regent to four successive kings in the late fifteenth and early sixteenth centuries after the death of her husband, Emperor Baeda Maryam (r. 1468–1478). Although she lacked blood ties with all except her grandson, Emperor Lebna Dengel (r. 1508–1540), Eleni routinely advised or acted on behalf of each to further the interests of both Ethiopia and the royal family.

Oral traditions throughout Africa honor the queen mother's presence at the king's court, and a prominent woman's visit to a neighboring kingdom was frequently recorded in royal chronicles.

See also: *KANDAKE* (Vol. I); LOVEDU (Vol. III); MERINA (Vol. III); WOMEN IN ANCIENT AFRICA (Vol. I); WOMEN IN MEDIEVAL AFRICA (Vol. II); WOMEN IN PRECOLONIAL AFRICA (Vol. III).

R

Rano One of the seven independent HAUSA STATES located east of SONGHAI, between the Niger River and Lake CHAD. Other Hausa states, established in the tenth through the thirteenth centuries under the empire of KANEM-BORNU, included BIRAM, DAURA, KATSINA, ZARIA, KANO, and GOBIR.

Rano and Kano were dubbed the "chiefs of indigo" because the great plains of these states were conducive to the mass production of COTTON, which was woven and dyed before being exported to the other Hausa kingdoms, as well as to many lands beyond.

Red Sea trade Arab-dominated transport of captives, salt, GOLD, IVORY, and other goods via the Red Sea to and from Arabia and Asia.

Beginning in the eighth century, Muslim ARABS engaged extensively in Red Sea trade. They arrived in North Africa eager to spread Islamic doctrine and to sell and procure captives for forced labor. Salt, gold, and ivory were also traded, but the demand for captives was substantially greater. Female captives, used as concubines and servants, were the most desirable in Arabia.

Captives were procured from Asia, Europe, the Nile Valley, the Horn of Africa, and the East African coast by local kings who raided neighboring villages and by pirates on the high seas. These captives were then sold to brokers at local market towns in exchange for cotton, spices, perfumes, and horses. From market towns, the captives traveled on foot across the savanna to the coast. Persons kidnapped at sea were brought to trading ports.

When captives arrived at the Red Sea port towns such as ADULIS, they were put up for sale. Purchased or kidnapped persons were shipped across the Red Sea to the Arabian Peninsula and Asia. Red Sea trade reached its height from the twelfth to sixteenth century.

See also: ARAB COASTAL TRADE (Vol. II); INDIAN OCEAN TRADE (Vol. II); PERSIAN TRADERS (Vol. II); SALT TRADE (Vol. II); SLAVERY (Vol. II).

religion See AROCHUKU ORACLE (Vol. II); BABALAWO (Vol. II); CHRISTIANITY (Vols. I, II); CHRISTIANITY, INFLUENCE OF (Vols. II, III); COPTIC CHRISTIANITY (Vol. II); CRUSADES, THE (Vol. II); DIVINE RULE (Vols. I, II); ISLAM, INFLUENCE OF (Vols. II, III); JIHAD (Vol. II); KORAN (Vol. II); MUHAMMAD (Vol. II); NINE SAINTS (Vol. II); RELIGION, PREHISTORIC (Vol. I); RELIGION, TRADITIONAL (Vol. I).

Río de Oro BERBER trade region in the western SAHARA situated between Cape Blanco and Cape Bojador. Due to its unsuitable climate for agriculture, the area developed into a thriving marketplace in which Berber MERCHANTS sold GOLD dust to Portuguese intermediaries. The first Portuguese ships passed Cape Bojador in 1434 and Rio de Oro in 1436.

See also: HENRY THE NAVIGATOR, PRINCE (Vol. II); PORTUGAL AND AFRICA (Vol. III).

Roha, rock churches of See LALIBELA, ROCK CHURCHES OF.

al-Roha (Adefa, Edessa) Ethiopian city that was the capital of the ZAGWE DYNASTY for 300 years. Al-Roha, also called Edessa or Adefa because of its proximity to that nearby city, was later renamed LALIBELA, after the famous thirteenth century Zagwe king who built eleven massive churches carved out of solid stone. These remarkable structures made Roha a religious center and a place of pilgrimage over the centuries.

The Zagwe dynasty (r. c. 1137–1270) consisted of a line of fiercely Christian kings who ruled most of northern and central ETHIOPIA during the twelfth and thirteenth centuries from their capital city, al-Roha, which is nestled safely in the LASTA MOUNTAINS. The Zagwe were descended from the AGAW people and led nomadic military lives. Their strong belief in CHRISTIANITY led them to erect many churches and monasteries. An early Zagwe king, Yemrahana Krestos, built one of the finest cave churches of Lasta. But of all their buildings, the monolithic churches of Lalibela in al-Roha remain the most impressive.

The Zagwe dynasty ended by the close of the thirteenth century. They were replaced by the SOLOMONIC DYNASTY, a line of rulers who claimed to be descendants of King Solomon of Israel and the queen of Sheba. The stone churches of Lalibela, as al-Roha is now known, stand today as reminders of the Zagwe dynasty.

See also: LALIBELA, CHURCHES OF (Vol. II).

Further reading: Harold G. Marcus, *A History of Ethiopia* (Berkeley: University of California Press, 1994).

Rumfa, Sarki (Muhammad Rumfa) (r. 1463–1499)
Ruler of the Hausa state of Kano.

During his long reign, Sarki Rumfa made ISLAM the official religion of KANO, one of the seven HAUSA states. Islam had already been practiced in Kano before Muhammad Rumfa became *sarki*, or local ruler, in about 1463, but under his rule, Muslim scholars became part of the government, ARABIC writing was again practiced, and, sometimes, force was used to ensure that the laws of Islam were followed. Even though Sarki Rumfa was a devout Muslim, he may have practiced some traditional rituals. This type of Islam, in which some traditional rituals were still practiced along with orthodox Muslim prac-

tices, was typical throughout HAUSALAND and other areas of Africa at this time. Compromise in religious matters was often necessary to maintain the *sarki*'s power and keep nonbelievers from rebelling. To strengthen his authority, Sarki Rumfa made marriage alliances with influential non-Muslim subjects.

Sarki Rumfa considered himself caliph, a title that proclaimed him both the political and the Muslim spiritual leader of Kano. The most famous of scholars that Sarki Rumfa embraced in his kingdom was the fiery al-MAGHILI, adviser to several rulers in the SUDAN. This Muslim reformer set about to firmly establish Islamic practices and law in Kano, and he established Muslim courts and suggested Muslim judges for appointment. Sarki Rumfa's request that al-Maghili write about Islamic government prompted the famous book, *Obligation of the Princes*. Al-Maghili was a believer in JIHAD, or holy war, even against other Muslims if they practiced Islam half-heartedly.

Sarki Rumfa has been called one of the most important rulers of Kano. Trade flourished under his rule, and to ensure that Kano would continue in trans-Saharan trade, Muhammad Rumfa began a war with the competing kingdom, KATSINA. He also established the Kurmi market.

Rwanda
Densely populated central African country dominated by the TUTSI in precolonial times.

Although the TWA people were the earliest inhabitants of present-day Rwanda, they were largely displaced by BANTU-speaking migrants who arrived in the area during the first millennium BCE. As the Bantu speakers intermarried with local people, a new group, the HUTU, emerged. By the fourteenth century, Hutu settlements had been infiltrated by the Tutsi. Although they probably arrived peacefully, within a few years, the Tutsi minority dominated the Hutu majority. The Tutsi's higher position in the social hierarchy was based on their ownership of cattle and their prowess as warriors. Rwanda did not emerge as a cohesive kingdom until several centuries after these events.

See also: RWANDA (Vol. III).

S

Sabbatarians In ETHIOPIA, a dissident group of four-teenth-century monks whose ideology challenged the imperial authority of church and state. Headed by Abba, or Father, Ewostatewos (Eustathis) (c. 1273–1352), the monks adopted a critical stand against the moral attitudes of state rulers and church officials. Chief among their grievances was the enslavement and sale of men, women, and children to Arabian, Sudanese, and Egyptian traders. They also advocated a return to the tenets of the Bible, insisting on observing Saturday as the traditional day of Sabbath.

The Sabattarians' refusal to accept financial offerings or to pay tribute to the state incurred the wrath of officials from both church and state. Ewostatewos and his followers were subsequently barred from church and state positions, and eventually they were driven from their homes and towns. Isolated in the northeastern region encompassing the highlands of ERITREA, they created numerous communities in which they practiced their principles through missionary work. They built their own churches and won many converts among the population. The best-known of their monasteries was Debre Bizen. Ewostatewos, who reportedly traveled to the Middle East, achieved sainthood upon his death, which occurred in Armenia in 1352.

The strength and prosperity of the Sabbatarian movement attracted the attention of state officials again in 1400. Brought to court by Emperor Dawit I (1380–1412), their new leader, Abba FILIPPOS, voiced the group's refusal to conform to state dictates. Despite imprisonment, they clung to their beliefs, which were subsequently adapted by large segments of the population. Forced by popular demand to release the dissidents in 1403, Dawit's decree allowed them to return to their beliefs and activities until his successor took office.

Sahara World's largest desert. Parts of the Sahara, such as the Libyan and the Arabian Deserts, have separate names, and the northern rim of the desert that centers on modern MOROCCO, ALGERIA, Tunisia, and sometimes LIBYA, is often called the MAGHRIB (in ARABIC, "the West"). The Maghrib encompassed much of Roman Africa besides EGYPT and was the first region of Africa to accept ISLAM during the seventh century. *Sahel*, meaning "border," is the Arabic-derived name for the semiarid fringe of the Sahara that stretches from MAURITANIA in the west to CHAD in the east. Between 450 and 1450, the Sahel saw the growth of the African empires of GHANA, MALI, and SONGHAI. The inhabitants of the Sahel have sometimes been called the Sudanese, from the Arabic word meaning "black."

At the start of the first millennium, the Sahara, from the Arabic word for "desert," was a wilderness of sand sparsely populated by nomads and isolated farmers who were confined to oases on the desert's fringe. Despite the unforgiving terrain, farmers developed agricultural techniques well-suited to the Sahara's arid conditions. Oasis gardens were tended by hand hoe and irrigated with spring water or water brought to the surface with primitive wells. Water made possible the cultivation at the larger oases of fruits and vegetables and an array of grains, including wheat, barley, and millet. Fig trees and grapevines blossomed in the hard conditions, and date palms grew at nearly every oasis.

The Fifth Through the Fifteenth Centuries In the fifth century, the main inhabitants of the western Sahara were BERBERS, whose descendants are the Berber-speaking Tekna people. Originally agriculturalists before they entered the desert, the Berbers became nomadic to protect themselves from the anarchy and strife that resulted from the fall of Roman Africa to the Vandals in 430. By the ninth century, the Berbers had developed a warlike reputation for their frequent raids on CARAVANS and their ongoing feuds with rival groups. In the fourteenth century, Arab peoples, who had swept across North Africa from Egypt after the rise of ISLAM, began to settle in the Sahara. From 1400 to 1700, the Arabs and the Berbers formed alliances and intermarried. The Arabic dialect all but replaced the Berber language, and most Berber peoples were converted to Islam. By the eighteenth century, all former Berbers claimed Arab descent.

The TUAREGS were the largest group of Berber speakers in the desert. They roamed the region from the Niger bend to the Azben highlands in what is now Niger.

Not until the European nations carved up Africa in the nineteenth century did the western Sahara come the control of any central authority. The rule of the Roman Empire, which ended in the fifth century, never extended into the desert. Only the south Moroccan Berber ALMORAVID dynasty (1061–1147), which originated as a religious movement that preached Islamic puritanism, ever held power over the region. The Almoravids conquered the western Maghrib and al-ANDALUS (southern Spain) in the eleventh century and ruled them for a century.

In the eastern Sahara, the primary inhabitants were the TEDA people, who are closely related in language and culture to the Daza people, who live south of the Sahara. The Teda inhabited the Kufra Oasis in Libya and were also strong in the FEZZAN. They also inhabited the Tibesti and the Ennedi Mountains in the desert proper.

The sub-Saharan kingdoms of ancient Ghana and the nomadic Zaghawa people of Chad probably had an early strong presence in the desert. In the east, during the thirteenth century, the KANEM-BORNU Empire ruled the central Sahara as well as the Fezzan until 1591, when the sultan of Morocco captured TIMBUKTU. The kingdom of BORNU controlled the central desert and its trade routes until the seventeenth century when it fell under Tuareg domination.

Pastoralism and Trade The two pillars of the economy in the desert were pastoralism and TRADE. The primary animals raised were sheep, goats, and camels, the latter of which, when introduced into the desert in the first centuries of the common era, made regular trade possible. Unlike most other pack animals, camels could work efficiently for several days without water or nourishment. Most oasis settlements were connected with the trade routes and with the local pastoral population.

The major trade item was salt, and the Tuareg SALT TRADE continues even to the present day. Large slabs of salt could be extracted from the mines at Taghaza (between Mali and Morocco) and transported by camel to the south, where it was exchanged for millet or other foodstuffs. The main products carried north along the caravan routes were GOLD, spices, and leather; weapons, HORSES, CLOTH, and paper were transported south. The

oases through which the caravans passed either provided MARKETPLACES for these foreign traders or collected tolls and tribute. The monies passed into and supported the local economy.

See also: MAGHRIB (Vol. III); SAHARA (Vol. I); SUB-SAHARAN AFRICA (Vol. II); TRANS-SAHARAN TRADE ROUTES (Vol. II).

al-Sahili (Abu Ishaq as-Sahili Tuwajjin, Abu Ishaq al-Sahili, Abu-Ishaq Ibrahim-es-Saheli)
(early fourteenth century) *Architect and poet employed by Mansa Musa I.*

Originally from Granada in al-ANDALUS (southern Spain), al-Sahili was brought to the MALI EMPIRE in the year 1324 by Mansa MUSA I, who was returning from a pilgrimage to MECCA. Al-Sahili designed a mosque in the city of GAO and built another mosque and a palace in TIMBUKTU. His buildings in Mali represented an early northern, or Andalusian, influence on African design and architecture that became apparent in the style of later Arabic structures from areas as diverse as MOROCCO and the SWAHILI COAST.

Saho (Shaho, Afar-Saho) An Eastern Kushitic dialect
and the collective name used for a number of pastoral groups living in the desert region bordered by the Red Sea, the Massawa escarpment, and the southern highlands of ETHIOPIA.

Saho speakers comprise a diverse number of groups that include the Irob people in northeastern TIGRAY, nomadic groups such as the Asa'orta and Hadu, and peoples of Arabic origin. Before the spread of ISLAM in the eighth century, little was known about the character of Saho society except for its warlike reputation. They reportedly launched numerous attacks on the Christian societies of the highlands. It has also been noted that they followed an ancient tradition of electing their rulers based on an age-grades system.

After Islamic penetration into the Horn of Africa, the prevalence of rock salt, a much coveted TRADE item, attracted Muslim MERCHANTS to the Saho region. Saho inhabitants reportedly used camels to bring the salt up from the coastal region to the highlands near Massawa, where Arab merchants used these animals for the internal and export trade markets.

The Arab merchants eventually intermarried with members of the Saho population, converting them to the Muslim faith. However, it appears that many Saho converts chose to practice SUFISM, an Islamic form of mysticism. An even smaller number of Saho, such as the Minifere in the southern region of ERITREA, were converted to CHRISTIANITY by the Amhara.

See also: ARAB COASTAL TRADE (Vol. II); SALT TRADE (Vol. II).

Sakura (r. 1285–1300) *Mali ruler, or mansa, who usurped the throne from Abu Bakr and restored glory to the empire.*

In 1285, Sakura, a person of royal ancestry who had once been held in bondage and later became a general of SUNDIATA (d. 1255), the legendary founder of the MALI EMPIRE, wrested control of the empire from ABU BAKR (r. 1274–1285), Sundiata's grandson, temporarily interrupting the succession of the KEITA CLAN. During his reign as *mansa*, or ruler, Sakura was able to restore glory to the Mali Empire, which had been left in near ruin by the weak rule of his predecessor. Sakura's greatest feat was his capture of the prominent commercial city of GAO, a victory that made Mali a center for MERCHANTS and traders from as far away as the MAGHRIB and the SUDAN.

After securing control of Mali around 1300, Sakura set off on a HAJJ, or pilgrimage, to MECCA, where he paid a visit to the sultan of CAIRO, al-Malik al-Nasir ibn Qula'un. While returning from his pilgrimage, Sakura was killed by nomadic thieves at Tajura, near Tripoli. Leadership of Mali then reverted back to Keita control.

Despite his abrupt seizure of power and his status as someone who once had been held in bondage, Sakura is considered one of Mali's greatest leaders. Historians suggest that by usurping power from Abu Bakr, Sakura did more to restore the Keita dynasty than destabilize it. Proof of the acceptance of Sakura's rule can be ascertained from his pilgrimage to Mecca, a journey that took more than a year to complete and that crossed areas of the Maghrib, the SAHARA, and EGYPT. A journey of such great distance and duration could be taken only by a *mansa* whose hold on power was secure.

Much of what is known about Sakura and the Keita dynasty is known only through the chronicles of the fourteenth century Arab ibn Khaldun (1331–1382), considered the prominent historian of the western Sudan from the ninth to the fourteenth century. His emphasis on both written records *and* oral tradition separates him from his more traditional Arab counterparts. In his travels, Khaldun met people with first- or secondhand knowledge of the events that he chronicled, and he was then able to fill many of the gaps in the written perspective.

Saladin (1137–1193) was sultan of Egypt and Syria and a friend to the Coptic Church of Ethiopia, to which he granted control of a chapel in the Church of the Holy Sepulchre in Jerusalem. Undated woodcut. © *Bettmann/CORBIS*

Saladin (Salah ad-Din -Yusuf ibn Ayyub, Al-Malik an-Nasir Salah ad-Din Yusuf I) (c. 1137 –1193) *Renowned sultan of Egypt (as well as Yemen, Syria, and Palestine), founder of the Ayyubid dynasty (1174–1250), and respected adversary of the Christian crusaders.*

As sultan, Saladin earned a reputation for firmness tempered with generosity and virtue; as a warrior, he became the greatest military hero of the Muslims in their battles against the crusaders. Saladin was born in Mesopotamia, near present-day Tikrit, Iraq, to a powerful Kurdish family. His father served in the court of the Turkish governor of northern Syria. At the age of fourteen, Saladin followed in his father's footsteps, serving in the Damascus court of Syrian emir Nur al-Din (1118–1174).

Saladin helped his uncle, Asad al-Din Shirkuh, a commander of Nur al-Din's armies, in three separate military campaigns (1164, 1167, 1168) that succeeded in keeping the Christian crusaders from overtaking Egypt, which was then ruled by the weak FATIMID caliphates. By 1169, Saladin had risen to second in command of the Syrian army under Shirkuh, who had become the vizier (senior minister) of the Fatimid caliph. When his uncle died that year, Saladin took his place, both as vizier and as commander of the Syrian troops in Egypt.

As vizier, Saladin quickly placed fellow Kurds in positions of power and reorganized Egypt's military forces. By 1171, he had seized power in Egypt from the Fatimid caliphate in the name of the emir. When Nur al-Din died in 1174, Saladin claimed the throne of Egypt for himself.

As sultan, Saladin founded the Ayyubid dynasty, using his military forces to seize control of Syria (left rudderless at the death of Nur al-Din), conquer Yemen, and expand his empire westward as far as modern-day Tunisia. He used both diplomacy and military strength in an attempt to unite all Muslim territories in Egypt, Palestine, Syria, and northern Mesopotamia.

An ardent student of SUNNI Muslim theology in his younger days, Saladin (whose full name means "righteousness of the faith, Joseph, son of Job") restored the supremacy of the Sunni faith throughout his realm. Devoted to the cause of spreading and strengthening Sunni Islam, Saladin waged a JIHAD, or holy war, against the Christian crusaders who had invaded and conquered parts of the Holy Land.

Saladin set out to capture the Latin Kingdom of Jerusalem, which had been occupied by Frankish (Latin-Christian) crusaders since 1099, and to drive the crusaders from Africa. To accomplish this end, Saladin first seized Aleppo, Syria, in 1183 and Mosul, Iraq, in 1186. He then consolidated his growing kingdom by capturing many cities from Muslim rivals.

On July 4, 1187, Saladin led Muslim forces in crushing an army of Christian crusaders in a furious battle at Hattin, in northern Palestine. By year's end, he had also retaken the city of Jerusalem—which Muslims, who call it Bayt Quds (the House of Holiness) regarded as holy because Muhammad stopped there on his journey to Heaven—as well as most of the cities of the Latin Kingdom of Jerusalem. His failure to recapture the coastal fortress of Tyre, however, gave the crusaders both a refuge and a base from which to launch the Third Crusade (1189–1192).

In 1189, King Richard I (the Lion-Hearted) of England led the Christian armies in their attempt to recapture Jerusalem from the Muslims (whom the Europeans called Saracens). The two opposing leaders admired each other for their gallantry and mercy as well as their skill in battle and mastery of their troops. Saladin's armies prevailed, however, limiting Richard's crusaders to the conquest of the fortress of Acre in 1191. A year later, Saladin negotiated an end to the battles. The armistice agreement, known as the Peace of Ramla, conceded to the Christians only a small strip of land on the coast between Tyre and Jaffa. The Muslims retained control of the Holy City of Jerusalem.

His battles won, Saladin returned to Damascus, where he died less than six months later. With his death, the Ayyubid dynasty became fractured and factionalized, yet continued to rule Egypt until 1250.

See also: ISLAM, INFLUENCE OF (Vol. II).

salt mining Process of excavating salt from the earth or collecting it from surface deposits. As far back as the beginning of the tenth century, the mining of salt was a major factor in the African economy. The earliest known salt mine was at Idjil in MAURITANIA, which was worked from the tenth to the fifteenth centuries. Another heavily productive mine was at TAGHAZA in the SAHARA Desert near MOROCCO. Taghaza served as the main source of salt in western Africa from before the fifteenth century until it was destroyed in the sixteenth century and replaced by the mines at nearby Taghza al Ghizlan. Other important salt-mining areas in Africa were the Kisama region of ANGOLA in southern Africa and the AFAR region of Somalia in the Horn of Africa.

In Taghaza, salt was prepared for the market by cutting it into large 200-pound (90.7 kg) blocks which were stored 10 to 15 feet (3 to 4.5 m) below the surface until they were shipped. Blocks were then taken from the mine, packed two per camel, and sent to TIMBUKTU or some other major trade and distribution center. Once there, the salt was dispersed throughout western Africa.

The conditions for the workers in Taghaza were terrible by any standard. As reported by Arab traveler IBN BATTUTA in 1353, the mine was controlled by the *farba musa*, or king, of the BERBER Massufa people and it was worked solely by people who labored only for his profit. Local food supplies were scarce, and provisions such as camel meat, millet, and dates all were brought from elsewhere. In contrast to food, salt was so abundant that both the local mosque and the workers' living quarters were made from rock salt.

By the end of the fifteenth century, after being the main source of salt in the trans-Saharan economy for nearly 500 years, the salt of Taghaza was virtually depleted. The size of the bars and the quality of the salt they contained had diminished. Salt was being shipped in bars half the weight of those 150 years before, and they were thin and prone to falling apart.

Kisamo, in northern Angola, was the major salt mine in southern Africa. In the fifteenth century, Europeans commented on how the miners excavated the salt and then carefully packed it into 23-inch (60-cm) wide blocks. From there, the blocks were taken up the Kwanza River, where they were sold or distributed throughout the CONGO BASIN.

In Somalia, the Afar region became the dominant center of salt production in northeastern Africa. A volcanic eruption 2,000 years earlier had cut off a section of the ocean, turning it into a saltwater lake. This area, which eventually became the Danakil Salt Pans, spanned more than 100 miles (161 km) and lay 37 feet (60 m) below the sea. Every year, the pans filled with rainwater. Miners would then break and mold the deposits into bars 7 inches (18 cm) in length. Other deposits were mined in shallow ditches.

The Uvinza salt pans in what is today Tanzania were a major source of salt in eastern Africa for 1,500 years. Ugogo, in central Tanzania, was another source of salt, but its products were inferior to those of Uvinza.

See also: SALT (Vol. I); SALT TRADE (Vol. II); SLAVERY (Vol. II).

salt trade Significant component of precolonial African economies. Salt, along with GOLD, slaves, and horses, was a major commodity in trans-Saharan and intra-African trade. The main sources of salt in western Africa were the mines at Idjil in MAURITANIA and at TAGHAZA in the SAHARA Desert near the Moroccan border. In southern Africa, in what is now ANGOLA, the salt market at Kabaso, which was adjacent to the salt mines at Kisama, grew into a major commercial center. A fourth major center, with profits going to the local Aksumite rulers as early as the twelfth century, was the Danakil salt pans in the AFAR region of Somalia in the Horn of Africa.

Salt was valued for health reasons (the body must replace the salt it loses in perspiration) and needed to flavor and preserve food. The salt trade existed on both local and long-distance levels. Farmers obtained the salt they needed locally, but this salt was often of poor quality. Better-quality salt, if locally available, was transported to nearby markets, where it was bartered for other products. The best-quality salt, desired by the wealthy, was the rock salt mined at the larger production centers, such as Idjil and Taghaza; bars of this salt were strong enough to be transported by CARAVANS across long distances. By contrast, sea salt obtained by solar evaporation in places along the Atlantic coast did not travel well in the humid climate of West Africa.

The Arab traveler Leo Africanus (1485–1554) reported that the best salt was often bought for its equivalent weight in gold.

By 1000, four major TRANS-SAHARAN TRADE ROUTES had been established. The first two trade routes were in western Africa and were monopolies under the control of the rulers of the GHANA Empire and its successor states, the MALI EMPIRE and the SONGHAI Empire. Both trade routes began in SIJILMASA in MOROCCO. One led to Taghaza and then to AUDAGHOST; the other went south to TIMBUKTU and GAO. Another heavily traveled trade route was through the FEZZAN, connecting TUNIS and Tripoli with the HAUSA STATES and BORNU. A less-frequented route linked West and central Africa to the Nile Valley. In return for salt, the kingdoms of West Africa sent malaguetta pepper, acacia gum, kola nuts (prized for their caffeine content), leather goods and CLOTH from Hausaland, and slaves destined for the Mediterranean and Arabian markets. Cargoes were taxed en route and at both ends of the journey. Still, despite the cost of transport and the risk of the loss of caravans to bandits, the trade was immensely profitable, with a value estimated at several hundred thousand ounces of gold annually.

Rock salt from Kisama in northern Angola was widely distributed throughout the Zaïre basin, with traders journeying nearly a month to obtain it. The salt was carried overland and by canoe from the Kisama mines to the town of Kabaso along the Kwanza River on its route to market. The land along this river was traditionally ruled by the MBUNDU people.

Salt from Uvinza in modern day Tanzania was traded within an area extending from the southern end of Lake Nyanza to the southern end of Lake Tanganyika and from the eastern Congo to the Ruaha Valley.

See also: KISAMA (Vol. III); SALT MINING (Vol. II).

Sanga Town in central Africa located along the LUALABA RIVER in Congo (Kinshasa) in central Africa. It is significant for its necropolis, or burial ground, built by an Early Iron Age Sanga civilization, otherwise unknown, that thrived there from c. 800 to 1000.

Excavations at Sanga suggest that the people who inhabited the area practiced hunting, FISHING, and farming. Agriculture flourished due to the richness of the land and climatic conditions that were ideal for the cultivation of sorghum, millet, oil palms, and even BANANAS. The people had established IRON smelting by around 1000, and this development had a profound impact on agricultural practices. In turn, surplus crop production enabled the people of Sanga to seek profit through TRADE. The CRAFTSPEOPLE of Sanga were accomplished ironsmiths, creating items like needles, bells, and tools, but their greatest advances were made in coppersmithing. COPPER was purchased from local traders in exchange for grains, fish, salt, palm oil, and other regional products. Also, after the farming season was over, Sanga craftspeople themselves would set out with large contingents of workers to seek copper ore. Much of what they brought back to Sanga was used to beautify and honor the bodies of the deceased; corpses were adorned with bracelets and anklets fashioned from fibrous copper wiring, and necklaces were fashioned from beads and thicker wiring. Rings, pendants, and shells were also common funerary items. Recent excavations at Sanga unearthed vast accumulations of copper buried alongside the tombs, which suggests that the metal was collected for commercial means as well as for funeral practices.

See also: IRON AGE (Vol. I).

Sanhaja Berbers Nomadic peoples of western North Africa. During the eighth and ninth centuries, Arabs referred to the inhabitants of the western Sahara as Anbiya, but that title was changed in the tenth century to Sanhaja. The Sanhaja were known to wear veils over their faces and loose-fitting, flowing garments. They produced no crops, choosing to live on wild dates and various camel products, moving frequently and becoming masters of the western Sahara's harsh environment.

Though the Sanhaja were not traders, they became powerful by controlling TRANS-SAHARAN TRADE ROUTES and commercial centers, collecting taxes and tributes, and acting as paid guides and sentinels. During the tenth century, the chiefs of the Sanhaja Berbers became one of the most powerful Saharan rulers. His title was "Sanhaja of the AUDAGHOST," but there is little evidence to indicate that he was ever a permanent resident of the Sudanic trade center. It is more likely that he governed the region from a desert camp north of Audaghost proper.

Sanhaja chiefs maintained diplomatic and trade relations with the rulers of the GHANA EMPIRE. Because he controlled the SALT TRADE, the Sanhaja ruler held the upper hand in these relationships. His power was recognized broadly, and virtually all the leaders of the SUDAN paid heavy taxes to him.

> The Sanhaja rulers were so influential that they could determine the balance of power in the western Sudan. According to one story, a Sanhajan chief helped decide the outcome of a dispute between two Ghanaian provinces, Masin and Awgham. The chief supplied Masin with more than 50,000 camels, allowing the Masin to overwhelm the unsuspecting Awgham.

By the middle of the tenth century, the Sanhaja maintained a heavy political and military presence in Ghana. Despite their influence, though, the people of Audaghost favored the ruler of the Ghana Empire, indicating, perhaps, a shift in regional power. Details regarding this period remain uncertain and highly debated.

The Sanhaja Berbers were comprised of two powerful groups, the Juddala and the Lamtuna. The two formed a union, possibly through intermarriage, that eventually split when the Juddala fell out with the teachings of the Muslim cleric ibn Yasin. Following a period of 120 years of infighting and discord between the Juddala and the Lamtuna groups, a new leader, Muhammad Tarashna al-Lamtuna, emerged. When he died, his in-law (*sihr*), Yahya ibn Ibrahim of the Juddala, became the new Sanhaja leader.

> The history of the Sanhaja in the western Sudan is rather incomplete. The Arab historian AL-BAKRI (c. 1094), who documented many of the events in the region during the tenth and eleventh centuries, had few details of the situation regarding Audaghost's shift in favor of the Ghana Empire as opposed to the Sanhaja Berbers. In the fourteenth century, the Arab historian ibn Abi Zar collaborated with ibn Khaldun on a history of the western Sahara during the eighth through the eleventh centuries. Their history was considered the definitive version until recently, but modern scholars now dismiss Abi Zar's history as revisionist.

Prior to the close of the ninth century, there was no evidence of either ISLAM or law being practiced by the Sanhaja. Muslim traders in the MAGHRIB brought Islam to the region in the mid-tenth century. The Sanhajan chief Muhammad Tarashna was probably the first to convert, and became known as an *emir*, the name for a Muslim ruler, rather than simply a chief.

Muhammad Tarashna was highly regarded for his participation in a holy war, or JIHAD, and for carrying out a HAJJ, or pilgrimage, to Mecca. A succession of devout Sanhajan emirs, including 'Umar, his son Yahya ibn 'Umar, and ABU BAKR all followed the example of Muhammad Tarashna.

Yahya ibn 'Umar was the emir who brought the devout Islamic holy man ABD ALLA IBN YASIN to the Sanhaja. Ibn Yasin's teaching was popular among many of the Sanhaja Berbers, but his extremist approach toward purity and conversion caused conflict with Juddala elders. Consequently, ibn Yasin retreated to a Muslim monastery, where he founded the ALMORAVID movement. When ibn Yasin returned to secular society, he found sympathizers among the Lamtuna. With the help of Yahya ibn 'Umar and Yahya's brother Abu Bakr, the Almoravids gained control of the Sanhaja confederation by c. 1056. The new movement was founded in the Moroccan city of MARRAKECH, north of the Atlas Mountains, which was an indication that the Almoravids were no longer interested in controlling the western Sudan, and would concentrate instead on areas in North Africa.

The Almoravids eventually controlled much of western North Africa and southern Spain, also known as al-ANDALUS, until c. 1147. At that time, the Zenata and Masmuda Berbers, rivals of the Sanhaja, unified themselves against the Almoravids. Their resistance became known as the ALMOHAD movement. By 1172, the Almohads had taken control of much of the former Sanhaja Almoravid territories, including all of al-Andalus.

Further reading: Michael Brett and Elizabeth Fentress, *The Berbers* (Malden, Mass.: Blackwell Publishing, 1997).

Santolo City in the HAUSA STATES in northern NIGERIA. Santolo was located in a fertile area and benefited from migration from nearby areas beset by famine, as well as from trade with MERCHANTS from the SUDAN and the SAHARA. One of the walled cities of Hausaland, Santolo managed to keep its sovereignty, unlike many cities in the area that fell to neighboring kings. As a result, when ISLAM began spreading in the area in the late fourteenth century, the city became a prime target for attack by MUSLIM converts. Sarki YAJI, from the city of KANO, southeast of Santolo, fought alongside Muslim WANGARAWA to subdue Santolo. Muslim accounts of the battle depict the encounter as a holy war. Santolo's traditional religion was vanquished with the hope that Islam would replace the ancient religion as part of the victorious sweep of Islam through Hausaland. Yaji's soldiers and their Muslim reinforcements were successful in destroying Santolo, but Islam was not as firmly established in the region as its adherents had hoped.

Sao (So) Sudanic people who settled south of Lake CHAD as early as c. 500 CE. The Sao were the original inhabitants of the region that became part of the kingdom of BORNU around 850. According to Sao legend, their ancestors were successful elephant hunters and trans-Saharan traders. It is believed that the Sao introduced coppersmithing to the central SUDAN. Due in part to their knowledge of metallurgy, the Sao civilization flourished from the ninth through the fifteenth centuries.

After the founding of Bornu (c. 850), the Sao maintained close trading ties with the neighboring KANURI-speaking SEFUWA people of Kanem. Despite the fact that they spoke different languages and practiced different religions, the two groups coexisted relatively peacefully. Early in the thirteenth century, however, under the leadership of Mai Dunama DIBBALEMI, the Sefuwa declared a JIHAD, or Islamic holy war, against the Sao. During their raids, the Sefuwa took Sao captives, forcing them into

servitude or trading them for horses and other goods from North Africa. By the end of the fifteenth century, the Sao had been supplanted by the KOTOKO people, leaving an incomplete history that is informed mostly by archaeological evidence and oral tradition.

The discovery of forge remnants and artifacts, including ornaments made of BRONZE, an alloy of copper and tin, indicates that the Sao were accomplished metalsmiths. Archaeological evidence also suggests that they used COPPER as currency in the fourteenth century, in addition to GOLD and cowrie shells.

See also: KINGDOMS AND EMPIRES (Vol. II); KINGDOMS AND EMPIRES OF THE WEST AFRICAN SAVANNA (Vol. II).

sarki Name given to the leaders of the CITY-STATES of Hausaland. *Sarki* is a term similar in meaning to the Bornu *mai* and the Songhai *askia*. According to the *sarki* system of leadership, kings were determined by heredity. The *sarki* was considered a sacred person who was responsible for the overall welfare of his people. He possessed absolute power but generally shared it with a select group of officials and advisers to whom he was usually related. The *sarki* was at the top of the social pyramid of influence, with the village chief (*sarkin gari*) below him and the family clan (*gida*) at the base.

See also: ABDULLAHI BURJA (Vol. II); DAUDA, SARKI (Vol. II); RUMFA, SARKI (Vol. II); YAJI, SARKI (Vol. II).

Saylac See ZEILA.

science Some scientific knowledge is theoretical. In traditional societies, however, scientific knowledge is often practical and applied and is achieved by trial and error; it does not necessarily require a full understanding of basic principles in order to reach a desired result. An herbal healer, for instance, can effect a cure without understanding the pharmaceutical properties of the botanical items in a poultice or a rub.

In the fifth through the fifteenth centuries, there were two types of science in Africa: one based on the work of Arab and Muslim physicians and scientists in the cosmopolitan world of Islamic culture, the other a more traditional, applied science in SUB-SAHARAN AFRICA.

North Africa and Egypt The ISLAMIC CENTERS OF LEARNING in the MAGHRIB and in such cities as TIMBUKTU and GAO in West Africa tended to focus their academic attention on Islamic theology and law. The major advances in physics, chemistry, medicine, astronomy, mathematics, and other areas of investigation that have given Muslim science its deserved reputation for accomplishment tended to be made in other parts of the Arab world, notably at Damascus in modern Syria, at Baghdad in modern Iraq, at Córdoba and Toledo in modern Spain, and, to a lesser extent, at CAIRO in EGYPT. These cities were the sites of extensive libraries. Modern Western science is highly indebted to the work of Arab and Muslim scientists, who both preserved the ancient Greek, Persian, and Hindu texts by translating them into ARABIC and adding to them extensive new discoveries. The common use of Arabic throughout Islamic lands made those writings and discoveries accessible to a broad base of peoples.

Many ancient Greek scientific works were preserved by Monophysite monasteries in Egypt and Syria, where the Greek texts had been translated into Syriac in the fourth century. These texts fell into Arab hands in the seventh century.

Islamic scientific study sometimes had religious purposes. The KORAN praised medicine as being close to God, and the movement of the stars and planets was believed to indicate God's will for humans. Astronomy could also help determine the direction of prayer (devout Muslims face east to MECCA when they pray) and the correct date and time on which Ramadan, the most sacred month in the Muslim calendar, should begin. Mathematics was needed to solve problems related to the Islamic law of inheritance. The expansion of science led, in Africa, to the founding of important hospitals, among them, in 832, the Qayrawan hospital in Tunisia, in which female nurses from West Africa worked, reportedly, for the first time in Arabic history; in 872, the al-Fusta hospital in Cairo; in 1190, the Marrakech hospital in Morocco, with aqueducts that brought in water; and in 1284, the al-Mansuri hospital, also in Cairo, that reportedly served 4000 patients a day and was open to rich and poor alike.

Not all who wrote in Arabic were Muslims. One of the most important scientists in tenth-century Africa was the Jewish physician Ishaq al-Isra'ili, or Isaac Judaeus (c. 832–932), who was born in Egypt and worked in TUNIS. His treatises on fevers, simple drugs and nutrients, and urine were later translated into Latin and influenced European medicine.

In the first half of the eleventh century lived Ibn Yunis of Cairo, considered by some the greatest astronomer and trigonometrician of his time. Working in Cairo at the same time was Ibn al-Haitham, the most important physicist that Islamic science produced. He did important work measuring the specific gravity of objects and calculating the speed of light. He also did research in optics. Masawaih al-Mardini, or Mesue the Younger (915–1015), first worked in Baghdad and then moved to Cairo, where he died at the age of ninety. He wrote extensively on purgatives and emetics, and his textbook on pharmacy became, in Latin translation, the standard text on pharmacy in the West. Arguably the most significant figure in African Islamic science was Ibn el Nafis (1208–1288), head of al-Mansuri Hospital in Cairo and the dean of the School of Medicine there. He made important discoveries regarding the physiology of the human circulatory system.

After the twelfth century, Islamic science in the West began to stagnate and decline; in the East, it remained vigorous into the fifteenth century. The reasons given for the decline include a religious reaction to trends perceived in the writings of such scientists as al-Razi (1149–1209) or in the works of Ibn Rushd (1126–1198). Known in the West as Averroës, this highly influential religious philosopher from Marrakech tried to reconcile Islamic thought with Greek philosophy and stressed reason over faith. However, Islam is faith-based and sees itself as being in contact with the eternal. In this view, nature contains signs of God's will; unearthing those signs brings a believer closer to God. A science that is not anchored in faith seemed worthless, if not dangerous, to pursue.

The class A star Sirius, or the Dog Star, in the constellation Canis Major, figures strongly in Dogon myths because its position in the sky customarily regulated their agriculture. It is the only star to which Dogon tradition gave a name. Although their myths contain astronomical data about Sirius (the existence of an invisible companion star, Sirius-B) that they could not have gathered by naked-eye observation, various explanations have been offered to account for this fact. The most cogent is that the Dogon, with a talent shared by many other traditional peoples, seamlessly absorbed modern data about Sirius, in the form of interesting new stories, into their traditional myths because of the star's importance to their people.

Sub-Saharan Africa As in most traditional regions of the world, scientific study in sub-Saharan Africa may have begun with simple applications, such as the processing and preservation of foods or the brewing of palm wine and grain based beers. The clearly visible stars, comets, and movement of planets helped to regulate agriculture and led to the widespread development of solar-based calendars among a diverse number of people, including the DOGON, the AKAN, and the early CITY-STATES of Hausaland and BORNU. These calendars included lunar cycles, mathematical formulas detailing the best times for planting, the direction of seasonal winds, and necessary periods of seed germination.

A great deal of information concerning scientific knowledge in West Africa has come from firsthand accounts by Arabic travelers. The use of an astrolabe (a primitive sextant in wide use in the Islamic world) and compass in nautical expeditions by Arabian navigators was prominently mentioned. Records indicate that Chinese navigators were using a magnetic compass c. 1000 CE, European navigators by 1187, and the Arabs by 1220. It is unknown whether use of the compass developed simultaneously in these places or whether it was introduced by one culture and transmitted to the others.

Other navigation systems were also in use. The MANDINKA, for example, navigated the far reaches of the desert by using the rising and setting of the Sun, the stars, and a compass as a guide. The art of navigation along with surgery and astronomy were all taught at Timbuktu in ancient MALI, financed by the fourteenth emperor Abubakari II (1307–1311). Descriptions of his magnificent palace include mention of numerous doctors and other learned people within the royal court. A high value was apparently placed on books transported to the court from the Barbary Coast as well.

See also: AGRICULTURE (Vol. I); CALENDARS (Vol. I); FOOD (Vol. II); SCIENCE (Vols. I, III).

Further Reading: J. Ki-Zerbo and D. T. Niane, eds., *General History of Africa: Africa from the 12th to the 16th Century* (Paris: UNESCO, 1997); Ivan Van Sertima, *They Came Before Columbus* (New York: Random House, 1976); Claudia Zaslavsky, *Africa Counts: Number and Pattern in African Cultures,* 3rd ed. (Chicago: Lawrence Hill Books, 1999).

Sefuwa African dynasty of kings, known as *mais,* who ruled the region surrounding Lake CHAD during the KANEM-BORNU Empire (c. ninth through nineteenth centuries); also known as Sayfawa or Saifawa.

Renowned for their great trading exploits, the Sefuwa dominated parts of what are now southern CHAD and LIBYA, northern Nigeria and CAMEROON, and eastern NIGER. The Sefuwa's roots can be traced to the Kanembu people who set up their capital at NJIMI. At the close of the eleventh century, ISLAM was adopted as the state religion by Mai UMME. After a series of invasions by the BULALA people, King Umar al-IDRISI moved the Kanembu to Bornu, in 1396, where they and the Bornu, after years

of integration and intermarriage, created a new tribe, the Kanuri. Almost a century later, King Ali Dunamami chose NGAZARGAMU as his capital city and eventually conquered the Bulala and reclaimed Njimi for the Sefuwa. The most notable of the Sefuwa kings was King Idris Aluma or Alooma (r. 1571–1603). It was during his reign that the dynasty reached the height of its military power and economic prosperity.

See also: SEFUWA (Vol. III); IDRIS ALOOMA (Vol. III).

Sekabaka Kintu (Kebaka Kintu, Kintu) Mythical founder of the BANTU-speaking Kintu clans of BUGANDA. The Kintu clans migrated to the area around Lake VICTORIA between c.1100 and 1400. They settled in the area to the south of Lake KYOGA and established several small kingdoms, including Buganda. It is uncertain whether a man named Kintu actually existed, but tradition holds that he was the only inhabitant of Buganda until Ggulu, or God, sent his daughter, Nnambi, to marry Kintu and populate the region.

Kintu means "first man" in the Buganda Bantu language.

Semitic Group of languages spoken in northern Africa and in the Middle East that makes up one of the branches of the AFRO-ASIATIC family of languages. The other branches of the Afro-Asiatic language family are Kushitic, Berber, Egyptian, and Chadic. The groups of this language family that are spoken in Africa are the South Central group, which includes Arabic; the Southern Peripheral group, which includes the languages of northern Ethiopia, including GE'EZ; and the North Central group, which includes Punic, spoken in Carthage in North Africa. This group also includes Hebrew and Aramaic. The KORAN, the sacred book of ISLAM, is written in ARABIC. During the spread of Islam following the seventh century, converts generally learned Arabic because it was the language of prayer and the scriptures, which even illiterate believers often committed to memory.

Senegal Present-day West African country bordering the Atlantic Ocean. The SENEGAL RIVER separates it from modern MAURITANIA on the north and northeast; to the south it borders Guinea-Bissau and Guinea; to the east it borders present-day Mali.

As early as the ninth century, the pastoralist FULANI and TUKULOR peoples of the TEKRUR kingdom inhabited the Senegal River valley. During the tenth, eleventh, and twelfth centuries, the Tukulor, who converted to ISLAM in the eleventh century, became prosperous trans-Saharan traders and broke away from the declining GHANA EMPIRE. By the end of the thirteenth century, though, the Tekrur state fell within the sphere of influence of the larger, more powerful MALI EMPIRE.

During the 1300s, the WOLOF Empire supplanted Tekrur. The empire consisted of five coastal kingdoms—the Wolof states of Walo, Kayor, and Baol, and the SERER kingdoms of Sine and Saloum.

The Portuguese reached Cape Verde in 1444 and explored the Senegalese coast in 1445, but no formal European settlement was built in Senegal until the French opened a trading post at the mouth of the Senegal River in 1638. The rise of the Atlantic slave trade toward the end of the fifteenth century provided a viable alternative to trans-Saharan trade. Coastal communities, like those in Senegal, received the greatest benefits, as they were able to free themselves from the economic constraints of the inland empires that had long ruled over them.

See also: SENEGAL (Vol. III).

Senegal River River in modern SENEGAL that empties into the Atlantic Ocean. In the period before European colonization, the Senegal River served as a source of water for farming and as an avenue for TRADE with the interior. As early as the eleventh century, according to Arab accounts, the river was used to transport salt from Ganjor on the coast to be exchanged for GOLD from the kingdoms upriver. Ganjor's salt mines provided the WOLOF Empire of Kayor with a consistent source of wealth.

See also: SALT TRADE (Vol. II); SENEGAL RIVER (Vol. I).

Serer Ethnic group that inhabited regions of modern SENEGAL; also the language that these people speak. During the eleventh century, the Serer migrated to their present territory between the lower Senegal and the lower Gambia Rivers.

Serer legends indicate that they once lived as far north as the valley of the SENEGAL RIVER.

The Serer were agriculturalists. Resisting mounting pressures from their more powerful neighbors, the Muslim TUKULOR, WOLOF, and MANDE to convert to ISLAM, they formed the small kingdom of Sine in the twelfth or thirteenth century and the kingdom of Saloum by the end of the fifteenth century. Both Serer states were absorbed

into the Wolof Empire, which dominated the region in the fourteenth and fifteenth centuries.

The Serer were known for their adherence to a traditional animist religion and, even today, only a few people among them have converted to either Islam or CHRISTIANITY.

See also: ANIMISM (Vol. I).

Shafii Sunni doctrine One of four schools of Islamic law. Muslim law, or *sharia*, deals with matters of faith and morals, behavior and manners, and practical daily matters. As sources of guidance and rulings, it includes the KORAN, the Sunna, or the sayings of the prophet Muhammad, and *qiyas*, or reasoning by analogy to similar situations during the Prophet's lifetime. The Arabic word *fiqh* ("knowledge," "understanding") refers to the legal rulings of Muslim scholars, based on *sharia* and is the third source of guidance rulings for an observant Muslim. The science of *fiqh* developed when an expanding Islam had to face and resolve issues not explicitly covered in the Koran or the Sunna. The rulings of Islamic law categorize actions in one of five ways: prescribed, recommended, permissible, disliked and unlawful. Further distinctions exist within each category.

Two Sunni schools of law have been dominant in Africa: the Shafii school, dominant in East Africa and the neighboring Arabian Peninsula, and the MALIKI SUNNI DOCTRINE in North and West Africa. The Shafii school of law is named for its founder, Muhammad ibn Idris al-Shafii (767–819), who was a pupil of MALIK IBN ANAS (c. 713–c. 795), the founder of the Maliki school. However, Shafii began to believe in the overriding authority of the traditions from the life of the Prophet and gave them equal authority with the Sunna.

See also: ISLAM, INFLUENCE OF (Vols. II, III).

Shiism Smaller of the two major branches of ISLAM; its adherents are called Shiites and today represent about a tenth of all believers. The majority of Muslims are members of the SUNNI branch. Shiism is the majority faith in modern Iran and Iraq and has followers in East Africa as well as in the Middle East, India, and Pakistan.

Shiites and Sunnis differ on various religious practices but most especially in their belief regarding the identity of the proper successors of the prophet MUHAMMAD. Historically, the Shiites were the *shi'ah*, or "partisans," of Ali, Muhammad's son-in-law, whose descendants, Shiites believed, were the only ones qualified to be caliph, the temporal and spiritual ruler of the growing Muslim Empire. The Sunnis, on the other hand, were willing to accept as caliph anyone who would rule according to the precepts of Islamic law, regardless of lineage. The crisis of succession became a major cleft in the Muslim world as early as c. 660. Another major difference between the two groups is that

Shiites believe that the KORAN was created by humans and that it is not eternal, whereas orthodox Sunnis believe that the Koran was created by God and thus is eternal.

A subgroup within the Shiites is called the "Twelvers." They believe that, including Ali, twelve rightful descendants of Muhammad existed as religious leaders, or imams, of the people and that the twelfth imam, the Hidden Imam, did not die but still exists on a metaphysical plane and will return at the end of the world to begin a new era for humankind. Belief in the Hidden Imam has evolved into belief in the MAHDI, a leader who Muslims believe will rise and usher in a reign of righteousness. Self-styled Mahdis have often been proclaimed in Muslim communities; most important among them in precolonial Africa were Ubayd Allah, founder of the FATIMID dynasty in Egypt in 909, and MUHAMMAD IBN TUMART (c. 1080–1130), founder of the ALMOHAD movement in MOROCCO.

shipbuilding

The construction of oceangoing and river-borne vessels used for TRADE, transport, and war.

Sub-Saharan Africa The ancient Africans of SUB-SAHARAN AFRICA did not go to sea. Coastal trade, both on the Atlantic coast in the west and the Indian Ocean coast to the east was in the hands of Arab traders, as was most of the shipping on the MEDITERRANEAN SEA to the north. Very little is known about the kinds of vessels that the African people used on the rivers that transverse Africa south of the SAHARA. The rivers were used for FISHING as well as for transportation, local trade, and war. The SONG-HAI Empire had both a standing army and a navy; SUNNI ALI (d. 1492), its first emperor and a major expansionist, captured the TUAREG-held trading city of TIMBUKTU on the Niger River in 1468 and then used his fleet of war canoes to expand Songhai along the Niger. ASKIA MUHAMMAD TOURÉ (d. 1538), Sunni Ali's great successor as emperor of Songhai, also relied on his navy as an instrument of conquest and control. With the help of its fleet, Songhai became the most extensive pre-European empire in West Africa. The size and appearance of the vessels in the Songhai fleet has not been recorded. If they followed a pattern used by the Bidyogo people of what is now Guinea-Bissau, the prows, or fronts, of the vessels may have been carved into the shapes of traditional masks. The Bidyogo used a wild bull.

Chinese Oceangoing Ships The largest vessels to have visited Africa before 1500 were not from Europe but from China during the time of the Ming dynasty (1368–1644). The Emperor Yongle (r. 1403–1424) sent seven expeditions to Southeast Asia, the Persian Gulf, the Indian Ocean, and the east coast of Africa between 1405 and 1433. All were headed by Admiral Cheng-Ho (1371–1433), whose name is also rendered as Zheng-He, who commanded a fleet of merchant ships and warships that were in some cases 500 feet (152 m) long and

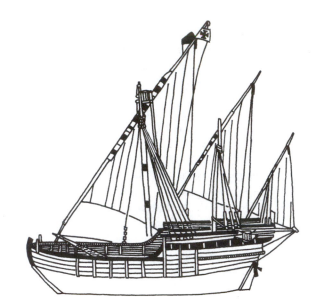

1. Caravel
Portuguese development of the caravel, with its lateen sail and center-mounted rudder, made long voyages of exploration possible. Some caravels also mounted a square sail, which enabled them to take advantage of tailwinds.

2. Junk and caravel
Chinese ships in the years 1200 to 1500 far surpassed what European shipbuilders constructed. The treasure ships of Admiral Cheng-Ho, who visited the Indian Ocean coast of Africa as far south as Kilwa between 1405 and 1533, weighed 1,500 tons (1,515 metric tons) or more; in comparison, a Portuguese caravel was a third or less its size.

weighed 1,500 tons (1,515 metric tons). By comparison, the oceangoing European ships of the time were 100 feet (30.5 m) long and weighed perhaps 500 tons (505 metric tons). Cheng-Ho's ships had up to four masts, a feature found on Chinese ships for centuries, and were divided into as many as thirteen watertight compartments. By comparison, Portuguese shipbuilders introduced a second mast for the first time when they produced the caravel, the oceangoing ship that became Portugal's standard vessel for exploration and trade in the late 1300s. Watertight compartments were not a feature of European-built ships until the nineteenth century.

By the sixteenth century, advances in European shipbuilding methods made European ships equal or better than their Chinese counterparts. In addition, not long after Cheng-Ho's voyages, the Chinese dismantled their fleet and entered a period of isolationism, shunning all foreign contact.

Arab and European Advances It is impossible to separate the arts of navigation, naval architecture, and sail technology; each plays an important role in the design and use of a ship. The earliest sailors stayed within sight of land. Without maps and charts or the ability to determine the direction of sail, mariners felt safer hugging the coast. The Chinese discovered the magnetized needle in the eighth century. By the twelfth century, a form of the mariner's floating compass was in use, developed either by the Arabs or by the Europeans. In the fourteenth century both Arab and Portuguese navigators had developed devices to help in celestial navigation, or navigation by the stars; these were the cross-staff and, later, the astrolabe, which were used to determine latitude based on a known star's altitude above the horizon. With these devices and the astronomical information gathered by Islamic astronomers and mathematicians—knowledge that was accessible to Europeans as well—ship captains were better equipped to find their way across oceans, out of sight of land.

Another important advance in sailing technology was the development of the sternpost rudder, placed amidships, which made it easier to steer a large ship in bad weather than the traditional steering oar that extended from the starboard (the right or *steor*, "steering paddle") side of the vessel. The Chinese had used sternpost rudders since the first century; this rudder style did not appear in Europe until the fourteenth century.

The type and positioning of sails is also important. Going out to sea in a ship totally dependent on oars is dangerous. Galleys powered only by rowers were a feature of the Mediterranean region but not in the coastal trade. Venturing out of sight of land required sails, and the best sails were the ones that maximized maneuverability and let the ship sail into the wind. The early European ships, a good example of which is the oceangoing Viking long ship, had a single square sail mounted on a mast. Such a sail needed to have the wind behind it to propel a ship forward. A major Arab contribution to sailing technology was the development of the triangular, or lateen, sail, which is used even today on oceangoing and lake-borne dhows. The lateen sail allowed the ship to travel along any course, no matter the direction of the wind. The Arab ships that followed the monsoon winds and associated currents from Africa and southern Arabia to India used this style of sail well before the sixth century. Arab traders are known to have traveled as far south as Sofala in modern-day MOZAMBIQUE in pursuit of goods. The rise of ISLAM in the seventh century gave impetus to the introduction of the lateen sail into Mediterranean waters, where it became used on larger, more powerful ships constructed by Syrian and Greek shipbuilding techniques. The Arabs to the south lacked the money and the supplies of wood to adopt the Mediterranean methods of hull construction, and their fleets fell into decline in the thirteenth century.

Portuguese Vessels The earliest Portuguese vessels of exploration were fishing vessels. Most European ships up to that time were clinker-built; that is, their hulls were constructed of overlapping boards. If sail-powered, they had square sails mounted on a single mast. The galleys used in the Mediterranean by Genoa, Venice, and the Turks had limited carrying space for provisions and cargo and were unsuited for oceangoing exploration.

In the fifteenth century, a new type of ship of 50 to 60 tons (50.1 to 60.1 metric tons), the caravel, was introduced. Its smooth hull was made of fitted boards. Its lateen sails, mounted on two, three, or sometimes four masts (the fourth mast carrying a square sail), enabled it to sail into the wind and made it capable of great speed. The caravel's broad beamed hull had substantial space for cargo and provisions, and its tall forecastle and stern castle enabled the this ship to withstand heavy seas. The caravel is the ship that opened Africa to the Portuguese. Almost all of Portugal's voyages of exploration in the fifteenth century were made aboard caravels.

The *Niña* and the *Pinta*, two of Christopher Columbus's ships, on his voyage to the New World in 1492, were caravels.

When longer voyages of exploration began, such as Vasco da GAMA's voyage to Callicut, a seaport in southwest India, in 1498, voyagers used a rounder, heavier ship, the three-masted, square-rigged carrack. (A square-rigged ship has its main sails set at right angles to the masts, in the fashion of most later European ships.) These carracks were armed with cannons, very likely swivel mounted or breech-loading deck guns located in the raised stern castles and forecastles of the ships. Shipboard artillery gave the Portuguese, and later the Spanish and French explorers, a strong advantage over their Muslim foes in the East.

See also: AGE OF DISCOVERY (Vol. II); ARAB COASTAL TRADE (Vol. II); INDIAN OCEAN TRADE (Vol. II); KINGDOMS AND EMPIRES: WEST AFRICA (Vol. II); SHIPBUILDING (Vol. I).

Shirazi Arabs Group of immigrants believed to have originated in Persia and settled the East African coast during the twelfth to fifteenth centuries. The Shirazi Arabs were traders who had come from the Iranian town of Shiraz. Small numbers of Shirazi traders are believed to have visited the East African coast as early as the tenth century, but in the twelfth century, larger groups began to immigrate to Africa.

Beginning in the second half of the twelfth century, the Shirazi settlers made their way to eastern Africa, particularly to the towns of MOGADISHU and KILWA, as well as to PEMBA, MAFIA ISLAND, and the Comoro and LAMU Islands. The Shirazi soon formed a powerful dynasty that controlled much of the important trade in the northwestern area of the Indian Ocean. By the fifteenth century the Shirazi had extended their rule to MOMBASA and ZANZIBAR, where they ruled, primarily, through an organization of independent CITY-STATES. At the same time, other large groups of Shirazi Arabs came to the Comoro Islands, where they introduced the Islamic faith and turned the islands into an important center of trade.

See also: INDIAN OCEAN TRADE (Vol. II); KISWAHILI (Vols. II, III); SHIRAZI DYNASTY (Vol. III); SWAHILI COAST (Vols. II, III).

Sidamo People and region of southern ETHIOPIA. It is assumed that the Sidamo are one of the patriarchal groups that migrated from central Ethiopia between the tenth and fifteenth centuries. There is little written or recorded information about their culture during the period of their migration. However, anthropologists and archaeologists have been able to cull some information from the thousands of massive stelae (large vertical stones or pillars with inscriptions or patterns serving as commemoratives or shrines), which they left behind.

The Sidamo cultivated several CROPS, including *ensete,* or "false banana," and some grains, vegetables, and spices. Researchers believe that the harvest was an important part of Sidamo culture, with many traditions and rituals built around it.

As early as the middle of the ninth century, ISLAM had penetrated the Horn of Africa. The Sidamo, along with other groups located between the Gulf of ADEN and the Blue Nile, were converted in large numbers. (Traditional Sidamo religious belief was animistic.) Soon thereafter,

Islamic culture became the center of both spiritual and economic life in southern Ethiopia.

During the twelfth and thirteenth centuries, ISLAM was at its height in the Sidamo region. Conflict erupted, though, when ruling Muslim sultans began to encroach on Christian Ethiopia, which was under the rule of the ZAGWE DYNASTY. Fighting lasted twenty years, from 1320 to 1340, and eventually the Muslim states were defeated by the Ethiopian Christian empire. As a result of this history, the Sidamo population came to represent the different influences of all three belief systems: traditional animism, Islam, and CHRISTIANITY.

See also: ANIMISM (Vol. I); CHRISTIANITY, INFLUENCE OF (Vol. II); SIDAMO (Vol. III).

Sierra Leone West African country situated on the Atlantic coast and bounded by present-day Guinea on the north and east and by Liberia on the south.

The comparatively small country of Sierra Leone was occupied by fishing and agrarian peoples as early as 2500 BCE, and its later inhabitants, possibly ancestors of the Limba people, were known to be working IRON by the seventh century. The main precolonial inhabitants of the Sierra Leone were the Temne, the Bullom (or Sherbro), and the Limba, who fished, herded cattle, or grew such CROPS as rice and yams. Palm oil and salt were also sought after for household uses and as trading commodities.

These groups, as well as sporadic bands of MANDE-speaking peoples who migrated to Sierra Leone from inland in the fifteenth and sixteenth centuries, generally tended to form small independent kingdoms ruled by a chief and a council of subchiefs. Religious authority was held by secret societies, such as the women's Sande or Bundu and the men's Poro Society, which were responsible for marriage preparation, curing the sick, and military training and education of the village's young people.

Muslim traders introduced ISLAM into the northern part of Sierra Leone; it soon spread through the rest of the region.

In 1460, Pedro da Sinta, the first Portuguese sailor to visit the region, named it *Serra Lyoa* (later corrupted to *Sierra Leone*), after the rugged "lion mountains" he saw around the fine natural harbor. From the fifteenth century on, European traders came together on the Sierra Leone coast to exchange their manufactured goods for African products, including ivory. The area in which they conducted their markets would later become Freetown, the modern capital.

See also: PORTUGAL AND AFRICA (Vol. III); SECRET SOCIETIES (Vol. I); SIERRA LEONE (Vol. III).

Sijilmasa City in southeast MOROCCO, important for its location along ancient TRANS-SAHARAN TRADE ROUTES. From the tenth to the fourteenth centuries, Sijilmasa, which ancient scholars and writers called the "city of GOLD," was a city of great power and wealth.

Sijilmasa was originally established as a city of agriculture and trade during the eighth century. Founded in an oasis near the SAHARA Desert, Sijilmasa was located between the Muslim, Mediterranean, and West African worlds, which made it a strategic point for economic and political control along the trans-Saharan gold trade routes. This was especially true for the routes that connected Sijilmasa to the GHANA EMPIRE, Tuat, GAO, and TIMBUKTU.

In its early history, Sijilmasa was an independent city-state ruled first by the Banu Wasul and then by the Banu Midrar. The city quickly benefited from its strategic location, particularly through the trade route to AUDAGHOST. In the eleventh century, several groups fought for control of Sijilmasa, and around 1054 the ALMORAVIDS (c. 1056–1147), BERBERS from the western Sahara, took hold of the city. The Almoravids, as well as their successors the ALMOHADS (c. 1130–1269), used Sijilmasa's wealth and importance to spread the Islamic religion and build an empire that controlled much of what is now Morocco, ALGERIA, and Spain.

Under the Almoravids and during subsequent periods of Berber control, Sijilmasa became an even greater city. Capital of the empire, it was the center of a vast economic system. It was at this time, during the first half of the fourteenth century, which is generally considered the height of Sijilmasa's power and glory, that Arab writers described the city as one of the most impressive and famous in the world.

After the Berber leadership came to an end in the late fourteenth century, there was another period of civil strife, during which various MARINID leaders fought for control of Sijilmasa. A civil war in 1393 led to the destruction of the city's walls and many of its architectural achievements. At this time, many of the people living in the city moved out into smaller villages in the surrounding countryside. After this time, Sijilmasa is still mentioned in various writings, but it was no longer the center that it had once been.

See also: SIJILURASA (Vol. III).

Silla Trading kingdom of the western Sudan. The agricultural kingdom of Silla, which came into existence about the eleventh century, was located in the vicinity of the Senegal valley near the GHANA EMPIRE. Like the kingdom of TEKRUR, Silla was inhabited by the pastoral FULANI peoples. According to the Arab writer al-BAKRI, Silla's main agricultural crops during this period were COTTON and sorghum. In addition, Silla, along with Tekrur, held sway over the SENEGAL RIVER trade routes, where they were known mostly for commerce in GOLD.

See also: SLAVERY (Vols. II, III).

slavery The state of being or holding an individual in bondage. Scholars have long debated the extent of slavery in Africa prior to the coming of Europeans in the fifteenth century. Some have argued that it was practically nonexistent, while others have claimed that certain societies consisted almost entirely of enslaved individuals. The truth probably lies somewhere between these two extremes. Although Arabic travelers and writers have provided a glimpse of the Saharan and Red Sea slave trades, sub-Saharan Africa offers a major challenge. This has generally been attributed to a lack of written records and reliance instead on oral traditions. However, one fact that is generally accepted by scholars of African history is that slavery within the continent had very little in common with the massive kidnapping and subjugation that characterized the transatlantic slave trade.

Slavery in Africa, sometimes referred to as "domestic slavery," was a well-regulated social institution. The rights of the enslaved were defined and governed by tradition. The enslaved were often procured through purchase or as captives in land disputes or regional wars. Also, individuals could be reduced to bondage for failure to settle a debt (debt bondage) or for violation of some cultural taboo. Technically, these forms of bondage cannot be called slavery, mainly because debt bondage had a fixed termination point and did not necessarily involve the progeny of the bondsperson. There existed many other forms of bondage throughout Africa that have inaccurately been lumped under the general category of slavery. Thus, the number of slaves in Africa during any period of time is impossible to estimate with any degree of accuracy.

The North African slave trade was not a one-way phenomenon, as slaves were transported across the Sahara in both directions. Europeans and Asians who were enslaved found themselves in North Africa as well as sub-Saharan Africa.

While slaves were at the bottom of the social ladder, they were not chattel (i.e., they could not be sold indiscriminately and they could not be separated from their families). Slaves could not be punished with impunity, and masters suffered severe penalties if it was found that they mistreated them. Slaves could, and did, rise above their station by industry and diligence with or without the approval of their masters. Slaves often married into their masters' families and many became rich and powerful. In many cases it was impossible to know if a person was a slave by simple observation. Their dress, duties, demeanor, and speech were the same as the free persons' with whom they were associated.

Two examples include the IBO, mainly a patrilineal society that consisted of nobles, peasants, and those who were either semi- or fully enslaved. Usually the semienslaved were individuals given to creditors as collateral. Those who were fully enslaved were more likely to be strangers to the village. Referred to as *Ohu* or *Oru*, they were were used to perform domestic tasks. Senegambian societies, also patrilineal, were structured in a slightly different way. They consisted of a free population and two groups that were outside mainstream society but which nonetheless cultivated their own wealth and power. The first were caste groups that included blacksmiths, griots, woodworkers, and potters, and the second group consisted of slaves who were sub-stratified. Many individuals from this class took on the skills of those who held them in bondage. It was not unusual for individuals of both the caste and enslaved groups to accumulate greater wealth than those who were technically free but poor because of their status as herders.

In the western SUDAN, slavery was often tied to economic expansion. Some scholars argue that in this region, women were preferred to men and sometimes purchased for as much as one- to two-thirds more. Generally they were valued for their reproductive capabilities and their role as concubines among the elite, including the households of Islamic marabouts and merchants. Enslaved women also produced agricultural products for use by the armies as well as wealthy households, thereby freeing noble women from agricultural and domestic tasks.

See also: SLAVERY (Vols. I, III).

Further reading: John W. Blassingame, *The Slave Community: Plantation Life in the Antebellum South* (New York: Oxford University Press, 1979); Iris Bloom and E. Frances White, *Women in Sub-Saharan Africa* (Bloomington: Indiana University Press, 1999); D. Chu and E. Skinner, *A Glorious Age in Africa: The Story of Three Great Empires* (Garden City, N.Y.: Doubleday, 1965); Stephen Clissold, *The Barbary Slaves* (London: Rowman & Littlefield, 1977); Davidson, Basil, *A Guide to African History: A General Survey of the African Past from Earliest Times to the Present* (Garden City, N.Y.: Doubleday, 1965); Elizabeth Donnan, *Documents Illustrative of the History of the Slave Trade to America* (New York: Octagon Books, 1965); S. Miers, and I. Kopytoff, *Slavery in Africa: Historical and Anthropological Perspectives* (Madison: University of Wisconsin Press, 1977); Page, Willie F., *The Dutch Triangle: The Netherlands and the Atlantic Slave Trade, 1621–1664* (New York: Garland Publishing, 1997).

social structure The anthropologists who study class and social arrangement in Africa c. 500 to 1500 generally map ways in which power was organized within the three main sociopolitical structures that existed at the time: clans, kingdoms, and empires. Within these three social structures, a system of rank, or hierarchy, generally existed that divided the members into four divisions: elders, freepersons, slaves, and nobles.

The role of elder served as a hierarchical structure primarily in clan societies, but it did so without creating strictly defined classes. The clan was mainly a biologically linked group that occupied a more or less clearly defined territory. The clan itself was dedicated to fulfilling its dietary needs through hunting or agriculture.

Within a clan, the system of hierarchy usually was based on precedence, antecedence, or a combination of these. A group might establish precedence, for example, by clearing an unoccupied territory and establishing their homes and fields there. This traditionally was accomplished in accordance with a particular ceremony between the clan and the land's tutelary spirits.

Once this precedence was established, all groups coming into the area were obligated to acknowledge the original group's primacy in order to maintain peaceful relations. To accomplish this, new families sent representatives to meet in council with the original families. (The first families generally presided over these councils.) This council then delegated various duties among the families, including divination, rituals, or even warfare.

Antecedence, the other principle upon which clan hierarchies were based, passed power through a hierarchy based on kinship. The elders of the clan, who possessed the most power, passed that power down to their junior relatives. (Upon entrance into the clan, each new member was invested with the powers of an elder.) However, final authority always belonged to the elders, who, in turn, were subject to the ancestors, who had negotiated for the clan's land with its tutelary spirits. The role of elder was the provenance of the oldest males; however, elder females were in many societies allowed to participate in a debate.

Warfare and the demand for laborers established slaves, or more accurately, a servile class, as part of the social structure in such kingdoms as MALI, Kongo, and the kingdoms of the western and central SUDAN. Kingdoms or empires like these usually were an amalgamation of clans in which the central figure, the king, governed with the help of a council. The king was often the religious head as well, although various clans were allowed to retain particular customs.

Kingdoms such as Mali that grew into empires generally had an aristocracy. Rank among the nobility was determined by the king, and a hereditary aristocracy was a common feature of such societies.

See also: CLANS (Vol. I); LINEAGE (Vol. I); SLAVERY (Vols. II, III).

Sofala Ancient East African harbor and trading city-state in what is now MOZAMBIQUE; first inhabited by BANTU-speaking people in about 400 CE. The city and seaport of Sofala, located south of present-day Beira, at the end of the Great Rift Valley, became one of the first harbors in southern Africa on the Mozambique Channel. Though the harbor is no longer usable and the ancient town is gone, the port was once large enough to accommodate approximately 100 trading ships.

After the arrival of Bantu-speaking people, the area prospered. From about 915 on, ARABS traded salt, metal wares, CLOTH, and other goods for GOLD, IVORY, and other African commodities. Sofala was one of several cities on the Mozambique coast using the KISWAHILI language to facilitate trade in and around Africa. Starting in about the year 1000, Muslims from Persia moved into Sofala and introduced ISLAM into this area. Trade between East Africa, Arabia, and India prospered, as did trade between African states. With the spread of Islam throughout Africa, the Muslim sultanate of KILWA rose to prominence in what is now Tanzania. In the years 1300 to 1500, Sofala became one of Kilwa's important southern outposts.

The Portuguese first arrived in roughly 1480, when Pero da Covilha, passed through Sofala and proved to his Portuguese king that the Indian Ocean does indeed flow into the Atlantic Ocean at the Cape of Good Hope. About 1505, Portuguese settlement began with the building of a fort. In a few short years, by the early sixteenth century, the Portuguese had seized control of the city as well as the lucrative gold trade. Sofala remained a port for three to four more centuries, though its importance declined. The great harbor eventually became obstructed by a sandbar as the harbor filled with silt.

A Portuguese who traveled with Vasco da GAMA in the early 1500s wrote a narrative about Sofala and, believing Sofala to be the legendary land of Ophir, as described by the biblical Solomon, he claimed that the queen of Sheba had lived there. Scholars now know that Sofala was not Ophir and not the home of the queen of Sheba.

Once one of the most important seaports on the Indian Ocean, the old city of Sofala is gone, but today, Nova Sofala on the Mozambique Channel is a reminder of the once-great harbor. At one time, the coastal area around the seaport city of Sofala was also called Sofala; in Mozambique today, the province of Sofala includes this coastal area.

See also: INDIAN OCEAN TRADE (Vol. II); SOFALA (Vol. III); SWAHILI COAST (Vols. II, III).

Soga Peoples of present-day UGANDA; also known as the Busoga. The Soga peoples have inhabited the lake region of Uganda since about the fourteenth century. Oral traditions, however, push their arrival back further, possibly to as early as the thirteenth century. According to these traditions, the Soga originated with a central figure named SEKABAKA KINTU, who traveled into the area with BANANAS, grain, and cattle and founded the Soga clans.

Known as an agricultural people, the Soga speak a dialect of the BANTU language. They have traditionally operated in smaller divisions of clans, called *nda*, who claim descent to a particular ancestor through their paternal line. The traditional religion of the Soga peoples was based on the worship of both ancestral spirits and spirits of the earth, such as trees, rivers, and hills.

Prior to the period of European colonization, the Soga were organized into independent states rather than into a system ruled by one main source of political power. Succession to power in these states was generally patrilineal. Since the eligible princes often held some of the same power as the state ruler, the common classes of the Soga were often instrumental in choosing the particular prince they saw fit to raise to supreme leadership. There was also a hierarchy of tribal members—some royalty and some commoners—who were given chiefly authority by the state ruler and performed such functions as collecting tribute, organizing the armies in times of war, and acting as an administrative council.

See also: CLANS (Vol. I).

Solomonic dynasty Line of rulers that governed ETHIOPIA from 1270 until the 1700s; traditionally accepted as descended from Menelik I, the son of King Solomon of Israel, and Queen Makeda (commonly known as the queen of Sheba). Tradition holds that the dynasty had virtually unbroken rule throughout Ethiopian history. Historians, however, believe that the dynasty actually began in 1270 with the emperor YEKUNO AMLAK, who, with the support of the Ethiopian Church, overthrew the ZAGWE DYNASTY. The latter had ruled Ethiopia from 1137 to 1270.

The legend of the Ethiopian rulers' descent from the biblical King Solomon is part of the rich tapestry of Ethiopian history. In the fourteenth century, the Ethiopian text known as the *Kebra Nagast*, or *Glory of Kings*, legitimized the claim with a retelling of the famous biblical story of King Solomon and Queen Makeda. According to the legend, Queen Makeda traveled from Ethiopia to Jerusalem to meet with and learn from the famously wise King Solomon. While there, she and Solomon became lovers, and, when she returned to Ethiopia, she bore their son, who eventually became King Menelik I.

Beginning with Yekuno Amlak in 1270, the Solomonic kings formed a strong alliance with the Orthodox Church, and, after several successful campaigns, gained control over what had for some time been Muslim territory. The struggle with the Muslims proved to be a back-and-forth affair, however. In the sixteenth century, a Muslim JIHAD, or holy war, ultimately took territory back from the Christian forces.

The link to King Solomon provided a strong foundation for Ethiopian national unity. In fact, despite the fact that the dynasty officially ended in 1769 with Emperor Iyaos, Ethiopian rulers continued to trace their connection to the famous dynastic line right up to the last twentieth-century emperor, Haile Selasse.

See also: MAKEDA, QUEEN OF SHEBA (Vol. I); MENELIK I (Vol. I).

Somali Nomadic East African pastoralists who lived in what is now Somalia and parts of northwestern KENYA, DJIBOUTI, and the Ogaden region of southern ETHIOPIA.

While there is the question as to whether the ancestors of the Somali originated in the Arabian Peninsula or possibly the highlands of Ethiopia, the Kushitic-speaking Somali peoples had immigrated and settled in modern-day Somalia by or around the tenth century.

The Somali were converted to ISLAM by the 1300s, probably by ARABS from across the Red Sea. Oral traditions among the Somali trace their Arab connection back to the tenth century, when, it is said, two Arab sheiks, Darod Isma'il and Ishaq, married two women of the ancient Dir ethnic group from the Gulf of Aden and became the forebears of two of the major subgroups of Somali peoples, the Darod and the Ishaq.

Somali *rer*, or clans, are self-contained groups of families that claim descent from a common ancestor. A Somali owes allegiance both to his clan and to the loosely knit group of clans that his *rer* belongs to. In the thirteenth century, a system known as *diya* ("blood compensation"), based on Islamic law, was instituted to make reparations and resolve blood feuds without resorting to more violence. The basis of this payment system is still practiced.

By the fourteenth century the traditionally nomadic Somali were located in parts of Ethiopia; in the fifteenth century their migrations continued into the arid region of the Ogaden, causing the displacement of the resident pastoral OROMO peoples. In a common pattern found throughout Africa, Islam took hold in a highly orthodox way in the larger urban centers along the coast, but in the countryside, orthodox and traditional beliefs were intermingled.

The Somalis' advantageous location on the Horn of Africa along the Indian Ocean made them the intermediaries between Arab coastal traders and the peoples of the interior. The centuries prior to the colonial era saw a marked increase in trading activities, notably Somali involvement in INDIAN OCEAN TRADE.

See also: ARAB COASTAL TRADE (Vol. I); CLANS (Vol. I); RED SEA TRADE (Vol. II); SOMALIA (Vols. I, III); ZANJ (Vol. II).

Songhai (Songhay, Songhray) West African empire and peoples located mostly in eastern Mali and western Niger that flourished between c. 1400 and 1591. Songhai was the largest empire ever created in the western and central Sudan, stretching at the height of its expansion in the early sixteenth century west to the border of modern SENEGAL, north beyond the salt-mining city of TAGHAZA in the Sahara, east to include the HAUSA STATES and the sultanate of Aïr, and south to BORNU and the MOSSI states, the boundary of the old MALI EMPIRE (1200–c. 1400), which it replaced.

Conflicting models exist about the origins of Songhai, making the history of the empire's first centuries obscure. According to one model, in roughly 1000 CE, the ZA people, Malian in origin, ruled the city of GAO on the north bank of the Niger River. In 1080, it is thought, the ZAGHE, a dynasty of ALMORAVID Berber traders, from their stronghold in nearby Gao-Sané, seized control of Gao with little violence and intermarried extensively with the MANDE-speaking Za population. Their assimilation was so great that by the middle of the thirteenth century, the Zaghe considered themselves Za and adopted the name as their own. By the 1300s the region was firmly under Mali Empire rule. In the early 1400s, the Za were invaded by large groups of SORKO warriors who, according to this interpretation, were the original Songhai, from Kebbi to the southeast. These attacks led to Mali's loss of Gao and the rise to power of SUNNI ALI (d. 1492), the founder of the Songhai Empire.

The conflicting model places the hunter-fisher Sorko (by language a Songhai people) in the region as early as the seventh century. Their settlement at Gao was on the other side of the Niger from the trade routes and was thus protected from attack by BERBER raiders. The Sorko had ties with the nearby town of Kukiya, a settlement of the Za, by language also a Songhai people, who began to dominate the right, or southern, bank of the Niger on which Gao was built.

The location of Gao near the CARAVAN routes, however, led to the development of trading relationships with the now Islamized Berber MERCHANTS and the establishment of the Berber settlement of Gao-Sané on the opposite bank of the Niger from Gao to promote trade in salt, slaves, grain, and CLOTH. By the beginning of the eleventh century, King KOSSOI (r. c. 1000) and the Gao court had converted to Islam and even shared a common place of prayer with their Berber allies. The kingdom began to gain importance as a trading center. Late in the eleventh century, Almoravid Berbers seized control of Gao-Sané but soon became assimilated into the existing Berber population or drifted off into the desert. By the twelfth century, Gao and Gao-Sané had become united in what later became known as old Gao. By 1300, the Za had fallen and Mali ruled Gao. The vacuum left by Mali's decline allowed the descendants of the Za from Kukiya to rise to

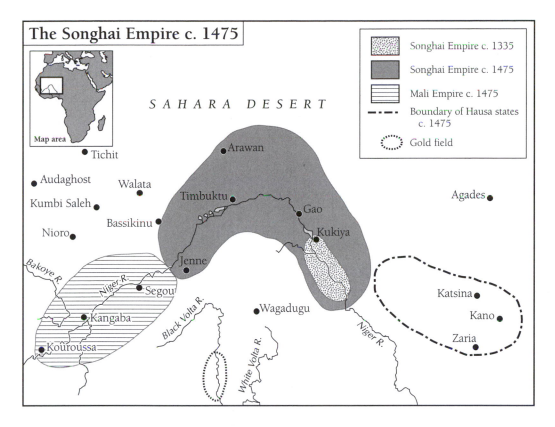

The Songhai Empire c. 1475

SAHARA DESERT

Map area

Legend:
- Songhai Empire c. 1335
- Songhai Empire c. 1475
- Mali Empire c. 1475
- Boundary of Hausa states c. 1475
- Gold field

Tichit • Arawan • Audaghost • Walata • Timbuktu • Agades • Kumbi Saleh • Gao • Bassikinu • Kukiya • Nioro • Jenne • Katsina • Bakoye R. • Niger R. • Segou • Kano • Kangaba • Black Volta R. • Wagadugu • Zaria • Kouroussa • White Volta R. • Niger R.

power in Gao by the middle of the fifteenth century. By warring against such other peoples as the Mossi and MANDINKA, Songhai began to expand its territories.

The Songhai Empire truly flourished during the reign of Sunni (or Sonni) Ali, who ruled from 1464 to 1492. Known as a powerful but ruthless ruler, Ali conquered the trading centers of TIMBUKTU and JENNE, increasing the size of the Songhai Empire to include much of Mali and parts of what is now Niger and Nigeria. He relied on his highly mobile cavalry and naval control of the Niger River to build his empire.

At that time, Islam was still the religion of the city dwellers and had not gained many rural converts. Sunni Ali incurred the wrath of Muslim clerics, or *ulama*, for tolerating paganism, which was how the clerics regarded the people's traditional beliefs, and for not supporting a theocratic form of government, which would have placed Songhai directly and fully under Muslim law and *ulama* authority. Although his government, unlike Mali's, was highly centralized, Sonni Ali favored a more traditional balance of power in which the interests of Muslim and non-Muslims were heeded.

Upon Sunni Ali's death, in 1492, Songhai was taken over by the Muslim general ASKIA MUHAMMAD TOURÉ (1493–1528), who created a centralized government, continued the expansion of the kingdom, and increased the importance of some of its major cities as trading, religious and educational centers. The Songhai Empire remained

powerful under a succession of Askia Muhammad Touré's descendants until the late sixteenth century.

See also: KINGDOMS AND EMPIRES (Vol. II); KINGDOMS AND EMPIRES OF THE WEST AFRICAN SAVANNA (Vol. II); SALT TRADE (Vol. II); SONGHAI (Vol. III); TRANS-SAHARAN TRADE ROUTES (Vol. II).

Further reading: Caroline Ifeka and G.T. Stride, *Peoples and Empires of West Africa* (New York: Africana Publishing Company, 1971).

Soninke (Sarakole, Serahuli, Marka, Wakore)

Northern MANDE peoples (in contrast to the southern Mande, or Malinke) who founded many of the cities and kingdoms that comprised the ancient empire of GHANA (originally Wagadu).

Early Soninke peoples developed IRON tools that allowed them to establish thriving farming communities. The founding of ancient Ghana, perhaps as early as 200 CE, may in fact have been a response by the Soninke farming communities to the threat of raids by BERBER nomads of the western SAHARA.

Originally, the Soninke were not converts to ISLAM but had established close, generally peaceful trading contacts with Muslim GOLD traders as early as the eighth century. The trans-Saharan gold trade was extremely lucrative, and through time, Muslims came to possess prestigious administrative positions in the Ghanaian high court. The majority of the Soninke population practiced a traditional polytheism, but the ascension of Muslims in the ruling structure of the kingdom encouraged many to convert.

By the middle of the eleventh century, the kingdom of Ghana was at its height of power, and the Soninke controlled an area that stretched from the SENEGAL RIVER in the west to the Niger River in the east, and from JENNE in the south to the important trans-Saharan trade outpost of AUDAGHOST to the north.

It is speculated that *Soninke*, a name that the founders of Ghana would not have called themselves, comes from "Sonni." The Sonni were a people who became a ruling dynasty of the SONGHAI kingdom of GAO in the fourteenth century. In the late fifteenth century, the Sonni were chased from Gao by ASKIA MUHAMMAD TOURÉ, and the name *Soninke* may have been used to designate the "fugitive Sonni."

In 1055, Audaghost was raided by the ALMORAVIDS, a SANHAJA Berber dynasty led by ABU BAKR, an act that led to a period of unrest. The conflict came to a head in 1076 when the Almoravids conquered the Ghanaian capital of KUMBI SALEH and began a large-scale conversion of the Soninke people to ISLAM.

From the time of the Almoravid conquest of Ghana to the middle of the twelfth century, the Soninke lost their control over the Ghanian gold trade and began to be torn by internal dissent and civil war. Many of the Soninke groups that rejected Islam migrated south and west, away from Kumbi Saleh, and east to the fertile lands along the Niger valley.

By the beginning of the thirteenth century, a large percentage of the Soninke who had remained in Ghana were Muslims, but their kingdom had weakened to the point that they were defenseless against an invasion from the south by the SUSU people, led by their vehemently anti-Muslim leader SUMANGURU.

See also: SONINKE (vol. III).

Sorko SONGHAI fishermen who lived and worked in the Niger River valley during the time of the Songhai Empire, providing transportation to traders on the river.

The Sorko were among the inhabitants of one of the largest African empires of precolonial times, the Songhai Empire, located in what is presently Mali. As one of the groups of Songhai, the Sorko may have been descended from the people of the ZA kingdom, which ruled the area

from around 800 to 1300. They subsisted by FISHING in the Niger River and lived in small communities in the river valley. The Songhai Empire became a trading power, and the Sorko capitalized on the GOLD and SALT TRADE by controlling transportation on the Niger River during this time. Though ISLAM was introduced in the Songhai Empire, perhaps as early as the latter half of the eleventh century, most Sorko people did not convert.

South Africa Region covering 471,442 square miles (1,221,037 sq km) in the southern part of Africa that, since 1992, has been known as the Republic of South Africa. Its borders are the Atlantic Ocean on the west, the Indian Ocean on the east and south, the modern countries of BOTSWANA and ZIMBABWE on the north, NAMIBIA on the northwest, and MOZAMBIQUE and Swaziland on the northeast. The oldest native people in the region that is now South Africa are the San, who occupied the region while South Africa was still in the midst of the last Ice Age, some 20,000 years ago. They lived in fluid bands of twenty to fifty members, with no hereditary leaders, whose numbers would vary as food was plentiful or scarce. Remnants of the San still live in the KALAHARI DESERT.

About 2,000 years ago, the cattle-raising KHOIKHOI people migrated southward, perhaps from Botswana, and settled mainly in the southern coastal region. This Khoikhoi migration put pressure on the hunter-gatherer San. Some San made their peace with the Khoikhoi, intermarrying and becoming full members of the Khoikhoi community; other San fled to less hospitable desert or mountainous areas; still others turned to brigandage and raided the herds of the intruders.

As BANTU-speaking peoples migrated into their lands starting during the fifth to eighth centuries, the Khoikhoi engaged in extensive TRADE, bartering their fat-tailed sheep and cattle for the IRON and COPPER they used to make tools, weapons, and bodily adornments. Sources record that the Khoikhoi even traded with the coastal peoples of present-day Mozambique to obtain *dagga* (cannabis), which they grew and used for trade. Although they were pastoralists, Khoikhoi settlements often numbered several hundred people and featured a more hierarchical style of leadership than San settlements, which had one chief elder governing in consultation with other elders. Groups, however, responded flexibly to new circumstances; as the Khoikhoi moved in search of better pastureland, patrilineal bands often broke away to start their own communities.

The southward migration, perhaps from the CONGO BASIN, of a cluster of Bantu-speaking peoples called the Nguni started as early as the fifth century. This second influx of peoples is best regarded not as a sudden invasion but as the slow, southward movement of farmers in search of new farmland and grazing land. In a common pattern, the Bantu speakers sometimes shared resources and sometimes warred for resources with the people they encountered, and intermarriage was common. At times even the Bantu languages commingled with the local tongues. Unique to the Nguni branch of the Bantu language family are imploded clicking sounds, which became part of the Nguni tongue through intermarriage with the Khoikhoi, whose language is a click language.

The Bantu-speaking peoples who moved into South Africa in the Early Iron Age first settled low-lying areas, such as river valleys and the coastal plain, which responded well to slash-and-burn agriculture. From the eleventh century, they began to settle the grasslands north of the Drakensberg Mountains and on the interior plateau, where they began to build villages of stone and assume a more settled lifestyle. Cattle-raising increased in social and economic importance at this time. Cattle grew to be a concrete and highly visible sign of wealth; they were used as a source of milk and hides but rarely as a source of meat and were generally killed only at ceremonial occasions. The most important uses of cattle were as bridewealth, or *lobola*, paid to the family of a man's new wife, and as tribute paid as the result of war.

The Bantu-speaking people were also very successful farmers, a factor that allowed their settlements to grow larger and more numerous than any among their San or Khoikhoi neighbors. Hunting and domesticated herds of sheep and goats provided meat; those who lived on the coast fished and gathered shellfish. Their farms supplied beans, sorghum, millet, and melons, along with other produce. In this way, the Bantu-speaking peoples managed to maintain an ongoing supply of food despite the threat of drought, crop failure, and famine.

Some Bantu speakers' settlements were quite large. Archaeologists have found evidence of seventh-century villages of several thousand people each. One, at Toutswe in present-day Botswana, consisted of cultivated lands and cattle pastures. Evidence suggests that the inhabitants worked iron and traded with peoples as far distant as the Indian Ocean coast.

Starting in c. 800, Arab traders in search of IVORY and other exotic products established small trading towns on the coast of modern-day Tanzania and Mozambique. The beads they offered in trade have been found in villages in the interior. The LIMPOPO RIVER, which separates the northern province of modern South Africa from Botswana and Zimbabwe, became a conduit for trade between the coast and the interior. A number of large Bantu-speaking communities arose in c. 1000 just south of the Limpopo River. The most important of these were the CITY-STATES of Bambandyanalo and MAPUNGUBWE. In addition to extensive farming and cattle raising, the residents of these states produced fine GOLD and copper work and engaged in considerable long-distance trade.

Mapungubwe has been called South Africa's first urban center. It was founded in about the year 1000, most likely as a trading town, and was abandoned c. 1200 when GREAT ZIMBABWE to the north began to dominate local trade. At its height, the population of Mapungubwe reached 10,000. The rich, as happens in many cities, lived up the hill at the center of the city, and the less wealthy lived in the valley below. Archaeologists have unearthed lavish burial goods, including a gold rhinoceros, from the graves of the wealthy.

Generally speaking, those peoples who settled inland tended to cluster around trading towns near sources of water. Those who settled the coastal plains lived in smaller, more scattered towns and moved often to find new grazing land. By 1600, all of present-day South Africa had been settled. The coast was inhabited by Nguni, one of whose most famous clans became the mighty Zulu people, the largest ethnic group in contemporary South Africa; the north, west, and south had been settled by other Bantu-speaking peoples, the Sotho and their westerly branch, the Tswana. The west and southwest was populated by Khoikhoi-speaking peoples. Portuguese travelers and shipwrecked sailors reported encountering large towns and relative prosperity.

See also: ARAB COASTAL TRADE (Vol. II); BANTU MIGRATIONS (Vols. I, II); BRIDEWEALTH (Vol. I); CATTLE (Vol. I); NGUNI (Vol. III); SAN (Vols. I, III); SOUTH AFRICA (Vol. III); ZIMBABWE (Vol. III); ZULU (Vol. III).

stool, royal Symbol of the power of a chief or king; thought by some traditional believers to be the repository of the king's spirit or soul. In other cultures, the stool would be the equivalent of a crown. Only royalty and other figures of high social stature have the right to sit during rituals or other court ceremony.

Many of the peoples of West Africa, including the powerful empires of ancient GHANA, MALI, and SONGHAI, as well as smaller kingdoms such as TEKRUR and those of YORUBALAND, believed that their kings were divine and possessed both secular and religious authority over their subjects. The royal stool was a reminder that members of the royal family once sat on the backs of subjects during their highly ritualized court ceremonies.

Among the AKAN people of modern coastal Ghana, a new king carved a stool for himself as part of his coronation ceremony. The stool was the symbol of his authority while he was alive; on his death, his stool was blackened and kept at the shrine of his ancestral spirit. Each lineage group had an ancestor shrine containing blackened stools.

Use of a royal stool and a war stool among the GA of the Gold Coast of West Africa has been traced to 1610. The Portuguese explorer Diogo Cão noted in 1487 the use of an IVORY royal stool by the king of the Mweni-Congo at his capital at Mbanza.

Among the LUBA and Songye peoples of present-day Democratic Republic of the Congo, who share a common ancestry that dates back to the 1500s, the stool was traditionally designed so that the ruler's feet never touched the ground, thereby protecting him from illness. The stool itself was carved with a human figure holding up the seat, a sign that the ruler has power over his people. If a usurper stole the king's stool, he could claim the authority that went with it. Accordingly, royal stools were always safeguarded by trusted officials and rarely used in public.

See also: DIVINE RULE (Vols. I, II); GOLDEN STOOL (Vol. III).

sub-Saharan Africa Term used to describe the large part of the African continent that lies south of the great Sahara Desert. Sub-Saharan Africa begins where the southern edge of the Sahara meets the SUDAN (between approximately 15° and 18° N latitude) and stretches to the southern tip of SOUTH AFRICA.

Sudan, the An inexact term for the geographical area just south of the Sahel, or southern borderland of the SAHARA Desert; not to be confused with the modern country, the Republic of the Sudan.

Arab geographers and historians from the eighth century describe a land south of the Sahara as BILAD AL-SUDAN, or "place of the Blacks." Originally, Bilad al-Sudan referred to the active trade region that contained the southern ends of TRANS-SAHARAN TRADE ROUTES; northern ends were controlled by Arab traders. Early trade items in the Sudan included shells, IVORY, beads, salt, CLOTH, GOLD, slaves, and kola nuts.

The Sudan is often broken into three areas: the western Sudan, the central Sudan, and the eastern, or NILOTIC, Sudan. The western Sudan includes the coastal region around the mouth of the SENEGAL RIVER to west of the Niger bend. Important kingdoms of western Sudan included the GHANA EMPIRE; the MALI EMPIRE, with its important trade center at TIMBUKTU; the SONGHAI Empire, with its capital at GAO; and the MOSSI Kingdom.

The central Sudan includes the region west and north of Lake CHAD. Kingdoms of the central Sudan included KANEM-BORNU and the HAUSA STATES. The FULANI, a pastoralist people who also settled in parts of the western Sudan, ruled over areas from Lake Chad to the Atlantic Ocean.

The eastern Sudan begins around the hills near ENNEDI and extends eastward to include DARFUR and the expanse of land around the White Nile and Blue Nile Rivers. Some geographers and historians stretch the eastern Sudan all the way to the Red Sea, which would make the coastal trading kingdom of AKSUM, near the Red Sea, an eastern Sudanic kingdom.

See also: DYULA (Vol. II); ISLAM (Vol. II); KINGDOMS AND EMPIRES OF THE WEST AFRICAN SAVANNA (Vol. II); SAHARA (Vol. I); SAHEL (Vol. I); TAKEDDA (Vol. II); *TA'RIKH AL-SUDAN* (Vol. III).

Sufism The ascetic and mystical movements, collectively, within ISLAM. Two central concepts in Sufism are *tawakkul* and *dhikr*, which refer to the believer's need for total reliance on God and perpetual remembrance of God. The Sufi's desire is to achieve a direct personal experience of God by creating feelings of divine intoxication and restoration during prayer. The rise of the Sufi movement is explained by some authorities as an organized attempt among pious Muslims to add a spiritual dimension to what believers felt was a growing secularism among Muslims during the early UMAYYAD dynasty, which ruled the empire of the Caliphate, or Arab Empire, from 661 to 750 from its capital in Damascus, Syria.

The Sufi *Rifa'iyya* order, named after its founder, Ali al-Rifai (1106–1182), was extremely widespread, with adherents in Egypt, Syria, Palestine, and elsewhere in the Near East. Members of this order became famous for their extreme practices, such as eating live snakes and handling fire. The Shadhiliyya order, named after its founder, Abu el-Hasan Ali al-Shadhili (1196–1258), became popular in North Africa, Arabia, and Syria because of its tolerance of syncretism, or a combination of new and old beliefs, among converts.

Through the efforts of Sufi missionaries, Islam was extended into SUB-SAHARAN AFRICA; they met with success because they were more willing than the strictly dogmatic adherents of Islam to integrate aspects of traditional indigenous religions into their religious practices.

See also: SUFISM (Vol III).

Sulayman, Mansa (Sulayman Nar) (r. 1341–1360) *Muslim ruler of the ancient Mali Empire.*

According to tradition, Sulayman should have become ruler of the MALI EMPIRE when his brother, Mansa MUSA I, died in 1337. Mansa Musa broke with tradition, however, and left the kingdom to his son. As a result, Sulayman had to wait four years to take the throne.

During Mansa Sulayman's reign, Mali was at its safest and most powerful, able to expand its trade and to convert many neighboring people to ISLAM. Both Mansa Musa and Mansa Sulayman increased the scope of Islam in the empire by encouraging the development of Islamic learning and by supporting the building of mosques.

Medieval traveler IBN BATTUTA called Sulayman "a miserly king" because he failed to greet the arriving traveler with a customary hospitality gift in a timely manner. However, Sulayman apparently was not miserly in other areas, since Ibn Battuta also described one of Sulayman's opulent palaces as a "most elegant" building.

Elsewhere, Ibn Battuta noted a ceremony involving Sulayman that included hundreds of people, music, and much fanfare. It was further noted that no common person was allowed to speak to Sulayman. Instead, the commoner spoke to an interpreter, who in turn spoke to another, who was then allowed to address the ruler.

Sulayman died in 1360. The civil war that was fought to determine his successor ultimately was won by Mari-Djata II, a ruler whose reign nearly ruined the kingdom. Sulayman's death, therefore, is often considered to mark the beginning of the decline of the empire of Mali.

Sumanguru (Sumanguru Kante, Sumaoro Kante) (d. c. 1235) *Ruler of the kingdom of Kaniaga in what is now southwestern Mali.*

Sumanguru conquered several small SUSU states that had once paid tribute to the GHANA EMPIRE, then in decline, and molded them into a single kingdom called KANIAGA. Finally, around 1203, he captured KUMBI SALEH, Ghana's capital. It is thought that the ambitious Sumanguru hoped to gain control over the profitable trade routes to Muslim-controlled North Africa.

According to many accounts, Sumanguru was a cruel and tyrannical ruler. His inability to maintain order, however, caused discontent among the SONINKE people, who began to leave the region. In addition, Sumanguru's strict adherence to traditional Susu religious practices alienated the Muslim traders, who soon abandoned Kumbi and established JENNE and WALATA as important trading centers.

Around 1235, the kingdom of KANGABA, led by the MANDINKA king SUNDIATA (d. 1255), challenged and defeated Sumanguru in the Battle of KIRINA in the present-day Republic of Mali. This victory led to the foundation of the vast MALI EMPIRE, which began a period of rapid expansion under Sundiata's leadership.

Sundiata (Mari Diata, Mari Jata) (d. 1255) *Conqueror of the Ghana Empire and founder of the Mali Empire.*

In 1203, the small SUSU kingdom of KANIAGA, under the leadership of its king, SAMANGURU (d. c. 1235), successfully invaded and conquered KUMBI SALEH, the weakened capital of the once powerful GHANA EMPIRE. However, Sumanguru's greed ultimately led to Kaniaga's downfall. As king, he overtaxed commerce and caused most of the traders to leave the territory and migrate about 100 miles (161 km) north to WALATA.

After occupying Ghana, Sumanguru turned his armies against the nearby small kingdom of Mali, located to the east of Ghana. According to traditional tales and legends, Sumanguru killed nine of the princes of Mali, sparing only one, the handicapped Sundiata. During a period of intense training and study, Sundiata overcame his disability and organized an army of his own, which consisted mostly of hunters whose respect he had earned by his bravery and skill.

Sundiata ultimately embarked on a campaign of conquest and seized several small nations near Mali, including Wangara, Labe, and BAMBARA. With each conquest he annexed the conquered army to his own, thus building a sizable military force within a relatively short time. By 1234, he was ready to challenge the Susu for primacy in the western SUDAN. He returned home in triumph and was immediately viewed as a threat by Sumanguru, who, in 1235, led an army that invaded Mali. Sumanguru was killed at the decisive battle of KARINA (near modern Koulikoro). In 1240 Sundiata seized and razed the city of Kumbi and conquered all of what remained of the Ghana Empire.

While Sundiata did not lead another expedition of conquest after 1240, he proved to be an able leader. Indeed, through the wise utilization of his army and generals, Sundiata directed the kingdom of Mali to become the MALI EMPIRE. This successful period of growth lasted until his death about 1255.

See also: KINGDOMS AND EMPIRES (Vol. II); KINGDOMS AND EMPIRES OF THE WEST AFRICAN SAVANNA (Vol. II).

Sunni See MALIKI SUNNI DOCTRINE.

Sunni Ali (Sunni Ali Ber, Ali the Great, Sonni Ali, Sunni Ali Kolon) (r. c. 1464–1492) *Ruler who built the kingdom of Gao into the powerful Songhai Empire during the second half of the fifteenth century.*

Sunni Ali's place in life began as a matter of chance. Two of the wives of his father, Za Yasiboi, gave birth on the same night. As was custom, the infants were not bathed until the light of the next day. Sunni Ali was the first infant to be washed, thereby gaining the rights of the eldest child. At some point in his youth, he was taken to the MALI EMPIRE, apparently as a hostage. He returned to the SONGHAI Empire in 1464 as its ruler, initiating a period of great expansion for the kingdom.

A member of the Muslim Sunni ruling dynasty of the kingdom of GAO, in the SUDAN, Sunni Ali was a good administrator. Backed by a strong CAVALRY and an organized fleet of ships to take control of the Niger River, he began to expand his native kingdom, filling the power vacuum left by the declining MALI EMPIRE.

A great conqueror with a brilliant military mind, Sunni Ali also was a ruthless despot. His reign was primarily a series of military campaigns as he expanded the Songhai Empire and united the western Sudan. In the meantime, he also fended off incursions by the neighboring MOSSI, FULANI, and TUAREG peoples. He repulsed the Mossi in large part because of his strategic cavalry maneuvers. The Dendi region of the Fulani also fell to him.

In 1468, people of the prosperous Sudanese trading center of TIMBUKTU asked for Sunni Ali's help in overthrowing the oppressive Tuareg chief Akil. Ali took advantage of the opportunity to add Timbuktu to his growing empire. The city's residents found out too late that Ali's rule would prove to be even more oppressive than Akil's. In the process of liberating the city, Sunni Ali displayed a tyrannical nature, killing many of the Muslim residents who failed to fully support his efforts against the Tuaregs.

In 1473, Sunni Ali took the important merchant city of JENNE, located at the junction of the Bani and Niger Rivers, after a protracted battle that, according to Arab histories of the region, lasted more than seven years. In the following decade, Sunni Ali continued to expand and strengthen his empire, failing only in his attempts to subjugate the Mossi people to the south of his capital at Gao. In 1492, Sunni Ali died, apparently by drowning, under uncertain circumstances. At the time of his death, the Songhai Empire was the largest in West Africa and perhaps the most powerful on the African continent.

The Muslim scholars and historians of the Sudan never forgave Sunni Ali for the devastation he wrought on Timbuktu or his treatment of the city's Muslim clergy. As a result, many of the surviving accounts of Sunni Ali cast him as an unjust and capricious despot, and an impious and unworthy Muslim. In contrast, the Songhai viewed him as a nearly mythical warrior-king. They praised him for being both an inspiring leader on the battlefield and a strong political administrator.

Sunni Ali's importance in history was downplayed by the scholars and historians of the time. One of the reasons may have been that the Muslim scholars most likely did not look favorably upon a king who, although he professed to follow the ways of Islam, still clung to some traditional African ways, even incorporating elements of traditional Songhai religion with Muslim rituals.

According to the *Tarikh al-Sudan*, an Arab chronicle of the history of Sudan, Ali once demanded thirty virgin concubines from the port city of Kabara to be brought to him. The women were making the journey on foot, and, because they stopped to rest, Sunni Ali ordered that they all be executed.

See also: AKIL, CHIEF (Vol. II); KINGDOMS AND EMPIRES (Vol. II); KINGDOMS AND EMPIRES OF THE WEST AFRICAN SAVANNA (Vol. II).

Susu (Soso, Soussou, Soosoo)

MANDE-speaking ethnic group that dominated the GHANA EMPIRE for a brief period in the twelfth and thirteenth centuries. The Susu settled throughout parts of modern Guinea, SIERRA LEONE, and SENEGAL.

The Susu were animists who resisted conversion to ISLAM, even as the Muslims began to maintain a strong presence in the Soninke provinces. Sumanguru proved to be an especially cruel emperor, beheading as many as nine of the Muslim kings who opposed his rule. Ironically, about 85 percent of the Susu in Africa today are devout Muslims, having been converted by the FULANI in the eighteenth century.

As Ghana's regional power disintegrated toward the end of the twelfth century, the Susu, operating from their capital at Susu, north of BAMAKO, began to dominate the SONINKE peoples who populated the southern provinces of the declining empire. According to Susu oral tradition, a Susu king named Kemoko united his people with the people of KANIAGA, creating a union that ruled the region for nearly fifty years. Kemoko's son, SUMANGURU (r. c. 1203–1235) continued the conquest of the regions once controlled by Ghana, eventually conquering every kingdom but Mande.

The Susu reign was short-lived, as the MANDINKA king SUNDIATA triumphed over Sumanguru's forces around 1235. By 1240, Sundiata (d. 1255) had conquered the territory that had been controlled by the Susu just a few decades prior.

See also: SUSU (Vol. III).

The triangular lateen sail of the dhow, a common sight up and down the Swahili coast, enabled the ship to steer into the wind. Arab traders used ships of this type to pursue Indian Ocean trade. © *David G. Houser/CORBIS*

Swahili coast Area along the East African shoreline on the Indian Ocean that developed an interconnected trading society between the eighth and fifteenth centuries.

The Swahili coast extends, at a width varying from 12.4 to 124 miles (20 to 200 km) over a distance of 1,864 miles (3,000 km), from 1° N, in southern Somalia, to 25° S, at the mouth of the Limpopo River, which is, roughly, from MOGADISHU, in Somalia, to Cape Delgado, in MOZAMBIQUE.

The major communities were Shanga and Manda, as well as the island communities of Pate, Siyu, Faza, and Lamu, which represented the northern reaches of the region. South of these, near the Tamu River, were the mainland communities of Shaka and Urgwana, with Malindi, Mombasa, Vumba, and Utondwe occupying the central coast. Further to the south, representing the other end of the area, lay Kilwa and Zanzibar.

The history and culture of the Swahili coast always have been interrelated with its geography and ecology. For one reason, this is because the land has never been more than marginally arable, and even the narrow strip of land that can be used for agriculture produces satisfactory yields only at the expense of intense labor. Over the centuries, the basic regional crop has been rice, with the region's poor relying more on millet, sorghum, cassava, and maize. As a result of these conditions, the people of the coast always have tended to be small-time farmers or even just gardeners rather than full agriculturalists. Fishing and trade have been the mainstay of the regional economy.

Beyond this, the topography effectively divides the region into two distinct but related areas. The first is the seacoast proper, which has been the location of the various merchant communities for which the Swahili coast is famous. These towns, built primarily of one form of stone or another, have long been inhabited by a mixed population that has looked to the sea for its livelihood. Beyond this, between the coast and the vast interior, was what have long been known as the hinterlands. These lands served as a buffer between the coast and the interior, and its peoples not only helped protect the coast communities from hostile attacks from inland populations but also served as intermediaries in the active trade that went on between the interior and the coast.

Language, People, and Culture The name *Swahili* derives from the Arabic word *sahel*, meaning "coast"; hence, Swahili means "people of the coast." Swahili represents a collection of diverse and widely scattered peoples who share a common history and religion but who are especially closely related because of their shared language, Kiswahili. Swahili culture and the Kiswahili language spread throughout the region through trade and migration.

The people of the Swahili coast have been, for centuries, the product of a mixture of ethnic groups and cultures. The original population probably was made up of hunter-gatherers. They were followed, long before the beginning of the common era, by pre-BANTU Kushitic pastoralists, the people who most likely constructed the first permanent settlements in the region. After them, most likely during the first or second century, came Bantu-speaking groups who originated in the northwestern Congo.

Early Swahili communities around the ninth century generally consisted of villages located along the coast or on small islands just off the coast. Farming, including the cultivation of crops like sorghum, millet, BANANAS, and sugarcane, and fishing were the main means of subsistence. There was also some small-scale trade of pottery and iron tools between neighboring villages. Despite their proximity to the coast, these villages were not yet able to conduct extensive overseas trade. Commercial activity was generally restricted to exchanges of goods within the local complex of villages.

Another early model of Swahili culture is the culture of the Shirazi Arabs of the northeastern African coast. They dominated coastal trade along the Indian Ocean from the eighth to eleventh century. Their proximity to the ocean also allowed them to gradually develop an international maritime economy that separated them from their inland counterparts. Upon their arrival in KILWA off the coast of ZANZIBAR, the Shirazi offered gifts to, and began trading with, the original Bantu-speaking mainland inhabitants, whom earlier Arab traders had called Zanj, or "Blacks," and enslaved.

Glass beads unearthed in Botswana, on the Zimbabwe Plateau, and at various sites in South Africa give proof that trade with the interior started as early as the eighth century.

During the first half of the second millennium, Swahili trade rapidly expanded to include captives, gold, ivory, and leopard skins, which were exchanged for Arab glass, pottery, and gold. Later, Swahili trade expanded further to include African hardwoods like sandalwood and ebony. Trade routes at this time extended as far east as China and India. As a result, a select few Swahili groups became wealthy, claiming royal titles and authority.

Although little evidence exists of the widespread penetration of Islam among the Shirazi, the group was known to invoke forms of Islamic ritual and magic to prevent the previous landowners from reclaiming their land. These practices and rituals became models for future Swahili groups in their dealings with existing landowners.

The development of Swahili culture was subject to tension between village and town life. Early Swahili communities were homogeneous and agrarian, with most members either related or familiar enough that disputes could generally be resolved through informal discussions by elders. However, as maritime trade developed, once-small coastal farming communities were steadily replaced or absorbed by larger towns. These communities became diverse urban centers, attracting migrants from a variety of ethnic and occupational backgrounds. Local and egalitarian ideals gave way to class and status-based institutions, which led to conflict between old and new inhabitants. Yet, these competing groups were mutually bound by the framework of the Swahili culture and language.

This mixture of diverse groups began to emerge as a recognizable entity—the Swahili—about 1100, with the general acceptance of ISLAM and the appearance of Kiswahili, the modern Swahili language. The various groups within the Swahili mix are diverse socially, politically, and economically. But they have, over time, been amalgamated quite successfully, primarily through marriage, patronage, and conversion to Islam.

Islam was widely adopted by the culture around the turn of the twelfth century, especially along the SOMALI coast. Its influence was widespread and transcended local governing bodies. Though several important Swahili commercial city-states, including Kilwa, Sofala, Malindi, and Mogadishu, became rich and powerful trading centers, there is no indication that any of these cities ever aspired to become an empire or possess unilateral authority.

Political Organization The many towns up and down the Swahili coast never really united into a single state. Instead, they formed a network of independent communities, each with its own government, trade relationships, and so on. Except for Lamu, which was governed by a type of oligarchy, each town was ruled by its own king or queen. These monarchs had limited powers, which involved trade and economic affairs as well as government and justice. It frequently fell upon the monarchs, for example, to bring together the various parties involved in both single business deals and long-term trade agreements. These kings and queens were so involved in their community's economic life, in fact, that they often housed—within the ground floors of their palaces—goods that were being warehoused before or after shipment.

Like the monarch, those holding other positions of authority often obtained these positions through heredity. However, they were awarded in ways that would help maintain the balance of the various ethnic groups within the community.

Trade The backbone of the Swahili coast's economy was long based on trade. Swahili traders mastered a mercantile network that stretched from the African interior to Arabia, India, and beyond, dealing in everything from gold, ivory, and slaves to textiles, ironwork, and even Chinese porcelain. Throughout the centuries, however, the Swahili functioned primarily as brokers and intermediaries, as facilitators rather than as primaries in the countless dealings with which they were involved.

The trading system maintained by the Swahili was based, essentially, on personal rather than market or corporate relationships. As a general rule, each merchant established a relationship with an "opposite number," someone, like himself, who had wealth, social position, honor, and even the trust and respect of his fellow citizens. Helping them do this, of course, was the fact that they tended to share a great deal with their various trading partners—a common religion and culture (Islam), common values, and even common business practices—

regardless of where each particular partner might be. In addition, many of these relationships were long-lasting, frequently being cemented with marriage and family ties.

One of the more interesting facets of Swahili culture was its ironwork, which included both carbon steel and cast iron as well as more familiar ironwork. Dating back to at least the tenth century, Swahili ironwork was described in detail by several Arab geographers and scientists. Swahili smiths carried out the smelting process in bowl furnaces, where the raw ore was melted and refined. Then, using small crucibles, the smiths heated the "bloom," as it was called, until it was liquefied.

The refined iron was then cooled and, often, transported elsewhere for finishing. There, in other towns and villages, it was forged into the desired shapes. As it did elsewhere, the creation of iron remained, among the Swahili, a specialized activity, often shrouded in mystery. But, given the commercial orientation of Swahili culture, it is not surprising that their sophisticated ironwork gave rise to a prosperous trade.

The trade carried out by the Swahili was complex, ranging from simple coastal voyages and exchanges to trips taking them to India, Southeast Asia, and beyond. To begin with, Swahili trade had to be organized on the basis of the prevailing monsoon winds. The northeast monsoon, which runs from approximately November to March, leads to hot, dry, rainless weather. This provided the perfect weather and winds needed to carry ships from India and Arabia to the shores of East Africa. This season was followed by a period of heavy rainfall, lasting from April to June. During this period, only limited coastal sailing was possible. Finally, there was the season of the southeast monsoon. Lasting from July to September, it was the time when ships could make the voyage north and east, carrying African goods to far away markets in Arabia and Asia.

In truth, however, even with this seasonal pattern, sailing was never easy. The dates for the different monsoons varied from year to year. As a result, timely and reliable shipping required careful planning, as well as experience. Otherwise, cargoes could rot on board a becalmed ship. Or, equally ruinous, ships could get stranded, leaving cargoes unable to be delivered at one end of the voyage and unable to be picked up at the other.

The actual sailing done by the Swahili captains and merchants was equally complex. But the Swahili solved their problems with skill and knowledge rather than with machinery and technology, maneuvering their simple lateen-sailed ships across remarkable distances. They navigated the coast of East Africa the same way, using experience rather than compasses and other instruments as their guide.

See also: SWAHILI COAST (Vol. III).

T

Tabora (Kazeh) Capital of the Nyamwezi people; located in the west-central part of what is now Tanzania. Prior to the eighteenth century, Tabora was an important part of the trade linking the CONGO BASIN with the SWAHILI COAST of East Africa. This trade represented an important supplement to the primarily agricultural economy of the BANTU-speaking Nyamwezi, who were also known as the Banyamwezi.

See also: NYAMWEZI (Vol. III); SWAHILI COAST (Vol. III).

Taghaza Important salt-mining village in the central SAHARA close to the Moroccan border. Because salt was an important trade commodity, Taghaza became a major point in the GOLD and SALT TRADE as early as 500 CE.

Originally, the Taghaza region was controlled by the BERBER Massufa people. In the early fourteenth century, under the reign of Mansa MUSA I (r. 1307–1337), the MALI EMPIRE took control of the Taghaza region and the trade routes leading to the mines from the south.

Around 1352, IBN BATTUTA, the famous Muslim traveler, visited Taghaza. He described the village as an unattractive, desolate place of sand, with salty water and no trees. He reported that houses were built from blocks of rock salt, with roofs of camel skins. The salt was mined almost exclusively by slaves, whose work was dangerous and exhausting.

In the fifteenth and sixteenth centuries, the SONGHAI Empire, which displaced the Mali Empire as the major power in the region, extended its dominance into the desert and appointed a governor in Taghaza. Rule later would pass to MOROCCO when the Songhai Empire was destroyed in 1591.

See also: SALT MINING (Vol. II); SLAVERY (Vol. II).

Takedda (Tadmekka, Tigidda) Beginning in the seventh century, Takedda was a major trading center in the western SUDAN; With the expansion of the MALI EMPIRE during the fourteenth century Takedda also became a major site for the mining of red COPPER, which was exported from Takedda throughout West Africa.

During the ninth century, Takedda was a center for Muslim missionaries from North African who were seeking to convert the native peoples of the Sudan to ISLAM. Takedda was also a trading center at the start of an important TRANS-SAHARAN TRADE ROUTE that originated in Takedda and continued to Wargla in the north, linking the MAGHRIB with the SUDAN. Along it, GOLD was brought to Takedda from the WANGARA GOLD FIELDS of the GHANA EMPIRE. Once the gold reached Takedda, like various other products from the Maghrib, it was available for trade.

In the tenth century, Takedda was ruled by kings of the SANHAJA BERBERS. Unlike their Sanhaja masters, however, the ordinary inhabitants of the city were of TUAREG descent and were followers of Islam.

Later, Takedda came under the dominance of the Mali Empire, located just to the west. Indeed, it was Mali's famous ruler Mansa MUSA I (r. 1307–1337) who apparently realized the vast income potential of Takedda's copper resources. Sold to various peoples to the south, the city's red copper added to Mansa Musa's already considerable fortune and helped to finance his architectural endeavors and other projects.

Takedda's strategic location along the trans-Saharan trading route between GAO on the Niger River south of the Sahara, Ghadames (in LIBYA), and Tripoli on the coast of the MEDITERRANEAN SEA helped the city maintain its importance while it was subject to the Mali Empire. Trade

CARAVANS traveled from east to west and from north to south along the various routes that crossed the Sahara, passing through Takedda on their way and generating enormous wealth for the Mali Empire.

Meanwhile, Takedda also was where gold was shaped into bars and sold at wholesale prices. Copper also was a familiar commodity, sold at rates based upon the weight of gold. The buyers came from a vast area. In parts of the Sudan, for example, small pieces of Takedda copper were used as currency. Elsewhere, there is evidence that copper from Takedda reached peoples as far south as the YORUBA and the IBO, the latter of whom used the copper to make BRONZE statues. Takedda copper also reached as far east as EGYPT, where it was exchanged for CLOTH.

See also: MINING (Vol. III).

Tanga Port city in present-day Tanzania, located on the Indian Ocean's Pemba Channel. Although archaeological evidence suggests settlements in the area dating back to the Early Iron Age (c. 1000 BCE), Tanga proper was not established until the fourteenth century, when it was founded by PERSIAN TRADERS. Along with the other ports along the SWAHILI COAST, Tanga was part of an extensive trading link between the interior of East Africa and lands as far away as China. Evidence of the extensive nature of this trade includes the elaborate GOLD decorations in the homes of local MERCHANTS and the presence of Chinese porcelain.

See also: CHINESE TRADE (Vol. II); INDIAN OCEAN TRADE (Vol. II); SWAHILI COAST (Vol. III); TANZANIA (Vol. III).

Tanganyika, Lake Freshwater lake located on the border between present-day Congo and Tanzania. Various nomadic clans of BANTU-speaking hunter-gatherers lived on the eastern shores of Lake Tanganyika before the fifteenth century. Archaeological evidence suggests that the ancestors of the Lega people lived on the eastern shores of the lake during this period, as well as on the shores of Lake Kivu, to the north. These peoples lived in sociopolitical structures known as *bwami*, which constituted a collective moral and political authority that later gave rise to concepts of kingship.

See also: GREAT LAKES REGION (Vol. III); RIFT VALLEY (Vol. I); TANGANYIKA, LAKE (Vol. 1); TANZANIA (Vol. III).

Teda (Toda, Todaga, Todga, Tuda, Tudaga) Ethnic group of the Tibesti Massif in modern-day northern CHAD. The Teda live a solitary existence in the mountainous plateaus of the remote Tibesti, close to the TRANS-SAHARAN TRADE ROUTES. They are divided into a number of clans with no central authority.

Historically the Teda were nomadic pastoralists who also raised CROPS such as dates and grains. However, before the period of European colonization, they extracted payment from the CARAVANS that crossed their isolated lands and served as a conduit for captives being exported to Egypt, the MAGHRIB, and IFRIQIYA in Tunisia. A seventh-century Arab chronicle mentions the region, but sources do not mention the Teda people living there until the thirteenth century. It is speculated that the Teda migrated into what is now Chad from desert oases in LIBYA and further west in the SUDAN. The Teda are devout Muslims whose conversion occurred during the early days of ISLAM.

See also: PASTORALISM (Vol. I); SLAVERY (Vol. II); TIBESTI (Vol. III).

Tekrur (Takrur) Kingdom and empire (c. 900–1700) established by the TUKULOR people in the valley of the SENEGAL RIVER.

Though the Tukulor established a powerful Islamic kingdom in western Africa, the state was controlled first by the GHANA EMPIRE and then by the MALI EMPIRE. The Tukulor people first inhabited the Senegal River valley c. 800, supplanting the FULANI, though some Fulani people settled in Tekrur and became Tukulor. In the eleventh century, the Tukulor became the first people of the Senegal River area to convert to ISLAM, and the Tekrur kingdom became known as an Islamic state

Tekrur came under the control of the Ghana Empire after the SONINKE people gained control c. 700. During the decline of the Ghana Empire, c. 1100 to 1200, Tekrur declared its independence, as did other Ghana states. After the fall of the Ghana Empire, Tekrur was conquered by the Mali Empire, c. 1300, when the rulers who succeeded SUNDIATA (d. 1255) followed his practice of expanding the kingdom. The power of the Tekrur state declined by the fifteenth century, when the WOLOF and SERER peoples, who had inhabited SENEGAL since c. 500, created several states, including the Wolof Kingdom.

See also: KINGDOMS AND EMPIRES (Vol. II); KINGDOMS AND EMPIRES OF THE WEST AFRICAN SAVANNA (Vol. II); WOLOF EMPIRE (Vol. III).

Thulamela Archaeological site that lies within the boundaries of the modern Kruger National Park in SOUTH AFRICA. Important skeletal remains and other artifacts have been found at Thulamela, which takes its name from the VENDA language and means "place of birth." The first occupants apparently came to the site during the thirteenth century, and it was populated, at times densely, until the mid-1600s.

Among the early discoveries at Thulamela were a GOLD bracelet and beads dating from 1240 to 1630. Later, two skeletons were uncovered. The first belonged to a female who was approximately forty-three to fifty years of age and in apparently good health when she died. The other was of a man, possibly a ruler. It is thought that his body, following Venda custom, was allowed to decompose in another area before being moved to this site.

One of the more important finds at the site was a small gong. Made from two metal triangles, it is similar to a gong found at GREAT ZIMBABWE. This, in addition to various POTTERY and gold objects found at Thulamela, has led scholars to suggest that, as early as the thirteenth century, sub-Saharan trade links had become so extensive that they connected areas as far apart as southern and western Africa.

thumb piano Musical instrument found all over Africa that is also known variously as the *mbira*, *sanza*, *likembe*, and *timbrh*.

The thumb piano apparently was invented by the KHOIKHOI about 1,000 years ago. Since then it has spread to most of SUB-SAHARAN AFRICA. It is especially important to the Shona peoples of present-day ZIMBABWE.

A thumb piano is made by fastening five to twenty-eight metal or wooden strips to a wooden soundboard. During performances it is often placed inside a gourd, or *geze*, which acts as an amplifier. It can be played on its own, but during some celebrations as many as twenty are played at once—all delivering different overlapping melodies. The wooden board is held with both hands and, as the name suggests, played with the thumbs.

Thumb piano songs have neither an end nor a beginning. The musician, usually a man, starts when he hears the melody. If there is more than one musician, each does the same, waiting for the melody to take him over and one by one starting when each feels it. Usually the melodies are cyclical, and the musician changes the sound slightly each time he plays the melody. In this way the thumb piano player is a lot like a jazz improviser.

Shells and bottle caps are often attached to the thumb piano, creating a vibrating sound that may sound like static to the Western ear. The desired effect, however, is quite the opposite, as the vibrating is supposed to clear the mind of thoughts and worries and allow the music to fill the consciousness of the listener.

There are many ways of tuning a thumb piano, the only rule being that if two musicians are playing together, their instruments must be tuned the same. Pitch can be changed by adjusting the free ends of the strings or by increasing or decreasing their length.

Today the thumb piano serves as an essential part of popular African music. In fact, it is unusual for a *mbira* song—a Zimbabwean genre that takes its name from the instrument—not to have a thumb piano playing throughout. Historically, it is the bridge between human and spiritual worlds and at the center of the Shona religion. The thumb piano is used to bring rain in drought, stop rain in floods, chase away spirits, and cure illnesses. After a

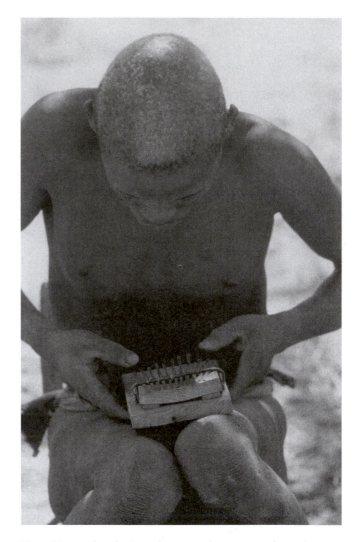

The *mbira*, or thumb piano, has several tongues, or keys, that can vibrate freely. The body of the thumb piano is often a gourd. © *Peter Johnson/CORBIS*

Shona chief's death, the *mbira* is played straight for one week. Ancestors are called by playing their favorite songs, and it is through this tradition that some Shona songs have been popular for as long as 500 years.

See also: SHONA (Vol. III)

Tigray (Tigrai, Tegray) Ethnic group of central ERITREA and northern ETHIOPIA, as well as the name of the historic region of Ethiopia that they occupy. The Tigray, who speak the TIGRINYA language, are often confused with the Tigré ethnic group, who speak the related language Tigré. Descended from SEMITIC immigrants who intermarried with the native Kushitic peoples, the Tigray were directly related to the founders of the ancient kingdom of AKSUM. They traditionally have been sedentary agriculturalists, primarily growing grain CROPS such as wheat, sorghum, and barley. Most Tigray people are Christians, members of the Ethiopian COPTIC CHURCH. Rivalry with the neighboring Christian Amhara people in Ethiopia has often erupted into warfare.

The Tigray region refers to the area, originally inhabited by the Tigrinya-speaking peoples, that lies between Mount Alegua and the Danakil Plain. When Ethiopia was in the throes of Muslim-Christian wars during the 1530s and 1540s, Tigray became one of the states that formed the kingdom of Abyssinia, a much-reduced Ethiopia that consisted mostly of its Christian, Semitic-speaking subjects.

See also: ABYSSINIA (Vol. II); AMHARA (Vols. I, III); TIGRAY (Vol. I); TIGRÉ (Vol. I).

Timbuktu (Timbuctu, Tombouctou) Major trade city located in the central region of present-day Mali, near the Niger River, at the southern edge of the SAHARA Desert. Timbuktu began in the eleventh century as a seasonal camp for TUAREG nomads. The GOLD trade and its growth as a major commercial center helped Timbuktu become an important city by the fourteenth century, when it became part of the MALI EMPIRE. At that time, it served as the beginning and ending point for CARAVANS crossing the Sahara Desert. Timbuktu's location near the Niger River also allowed for trade by water through the port of Kabara, which was linked to the city by a series of canals. In Timbuktu's markets, salt and CLOTH from North Africa were traded for gold and for captives. IVORY, COPPER, horses, and other luxury goods were also traded there.

With the decline of the Mali Empire, the Tuareg regained Timbuktu in 1433. They ruled the city from outposts in the desert rather than within the city itself, demanding excessive tributes and periodically attacking the city for plunder. Tuareg control had little effect on the day-to-day trade and the learning occurring within Timbuktu itself, which continued at a rapid pace. The Tuareg held Timbuktu until 1468, when they were driven from the city by SUNNI ALI, the leader of the SONGHAI Empire.

The Great Mosque, known as Djinguereber, and the Madugu Palace were built by Mansa MUSA I after his great pilgrimage to MECCA in 1324. During the 1400s and 1500s, more mosques were built, and Timbuktu became known as an ISLAMIC CENTER OF LEARNING, with more than 100 schools teaching the Koran. The university at the Sankoré mosque was staffed with well-trained Islamic scholars from as far away as Mecca and EGYPT and had as many as 25,000 students, one-quarter of Timbuktu's population at the time.

Shown is one of Timbuktu's three mosques, the oldest mosques in West Africa, dating back to the fourteenth century. Such mosques were centers of religious study and scholarship as well as houses of prayer. © *Wolfgang Kaehler/CORBIS*

Because of its remoteness and inaccessibility, Timbuktu was an almost mythical place to Europeans, who did not actually see it until 1826. Most of the information Europeans did have about the city came from the account written by el Hasan Ben Muhammad el-Wazzan-Ez-Zayyati, also known as Leo Africanus. A former slave who was freed by Pope Leo X, he was commissioned to write his account of a trip he had taken as a teenager, around the turn of the sixteenth century. He described thatch and clay huts as well as the Great Mosque and Madugu. The wealth of the inhabitants and the abundance of trade goods were points of special emphasis, with details being given on everything from clothing, food, and livestock to the inhabitants' love of music and dancing. El Hasan also outlined the nature of the royal court, writing of its ruler and the vast armies under his control. He also described how enemies—including children—were sold into slavery.

See also: LEO AFRICANUS (Vol. III); TIMBUKTU (Vol. III).

Tlemcen (Tilimsan) City in northwestern ALGERIA. The Islamic history of the city dates back to the eighth century, when newly Islamized BERBERS, who became adherents to the egalitarian, anti-Arab KHARIJITE movement that had spread to North Africa from the Middle East, founded a theocratic kingdom called Agadir, which means "fortress."

In the eleventh century, the ALMORAVIDS led by YUSUF IBN TASHBIN (1062–1106) claimed Agadir as their new capital, calling it Tlemcen. Over the next decade, Tlemcen grew into a center of considerable religious, educational, and cultural importance.

Yusuf ibn Tashbin is credited with commissioning the Great Mosque of Tlemcen, which was begun in 1082 but not finished until 1136. Combining designs from both al-ANDALUS and Iran, this remarkable mosque measures approximately 165 feet (50 m) by 200 feet (60 m).

Throughout its history, Tlemcen was occupied by various North African Berber dynasties who hoped to profit from its location as a center along TRANS-SAHARAN TRADE ROUTES. By the thirteenth century, Tlemcen became the center of a kingdom controlled by the Abd al Wadid, or Zayyanid, dynasty (r. 1236–1550), the Berber dynasty that succeeded the ALMOHAD Empire in northwestern Algeria. In 1299, it was taken by the MARINIDS (r. c. 1300–c. 1500), the Berber dynasty that supplanted the Almohads in MOROCCO. The Marinid leader, Abu Ya'qub (not to be confused with the ALMOHAD caliph of the same name), built a new capital nearby and called it al-Mansura. This town was considered the new center of the Tlemcen kingdom and all trade was redirected through it. However, upon Abu Ya'qub's death in 1307 and the Marinid's subsequent retreat from al-Mansura, the Zayyanids reclaimed their city and demolished the Marinid capital.

The struggle for dominance over Tlemcen continued over the next fifty years until the victorious Marinids once again set their capital at al-Mansura. In the fifteenth century another Berber dynasty, the Hafsids (r. c. 1300–1600) of IFRIQIYA (in Tunisia and eastern Algeria), fought the Marinids for Tlemcen. By the sixteenth century, however, the city was ruled by the Ottoman Turks, who allowed it to fall into ruin.

See also: TLEMCEN (Vol. III).

Toro (Batoro, Tooro) BANTU-speaking ethnic group of the Great Lakes region of East Africa who live in a high plateau between Lake Mobutu and Lake Edward in present-day UGANDA.

The first Bantu-speaking clans appear to have come into the area during the tenth and eleventh centuries from lands west of Lake Mobutu, supplanting a non-Bantu-speaking people who had migrated there from the central SUDAN sometime during the fourth century. It is thought that some of the clans very quickly created small agricultural states. The Toro tradition of a central government, headed by a royal family, dates from this time. They consider themselves descendants of the legendary Tembuzi (Batembuzi) kings, who created the earliest political organization in the area. The Chwezi people overthrew the Tembuzi but were themselves succeeded by the NILOTIC Bito people, to whom the Toro trace their direct ancestry.

Following the tradition of its hierarchical past, Toro society is heavily stratified. It is divided into two classes: the wealthy pastoralist Tutsi and the less privileged agriculturalist Iru.

See also: CHWEZI KINGDOM (Vol. II); CLANS (Vol. I); LINEAGE (Vol. I); PASTORALISM (Vol. I).

Toubou (Tubu) Nomadic pastoralists and agriculturalists of the central SUDAN. The Toubou might be related to the BERBERS, although the fact that the Toubou speak a NILO-SAHARAN LANGUAGE and the Berbers an AFRO-ASIATIC LANGUAGE fails to support this assertion. The Toubou also are related to the TEDA people of the Tibesti Mountains in northern CHAD.

The Toubou came to the central Sudan from the Nile Valley in the seventh century. Upon their arrival they joined with the neighboring Kanembu people to create the kingdom of KANEM. Linguistically, the Toubou are closely related to the Kanembu.

Despite their attempts to maintain control over Kanem and its valuable salt mines, the Toubou lost power during the thirteenth century. After this they continued to battle with their rival TUAREGS and Mobeurs. In later years the Toubou continued their agricultural practices, supplementing their income by levying tariffs on CARAVANS in exchange for safe passage along the TRANS-SAHARAN TRADE ROUTES.

See also: KANEM-BORNU (Vol. II); KINGDOMS AND EMPIRES (Vol. II); KINGDOMS AND EMPIRES OF THE WEST AFRICAN SAVANNA (Vol. II); SALT MINING (Vol. II); SALT TRADE (Vol. II).

towns and cities Although Egypt has historically been depicted as Africa's primary urbanized center, recent scholarship has confirmed that many regions of SUB-SAHARAN AFRICA had comparable degrees of urbanization. Popular misconceptions about these regions have included depictions of vast desert or jungle tracts with isolated villages of simple thatch houses. However, these images do not take into account the impact of import-and-export trading, the influence of religion and culture, or the changing perspectives of African societies. In addition, rather than using size, population, or structure as the defining criteria, modern historians describe a town or city as a centralized site under the jurisdiction of a king or ruler. From these centers, rulers controlled all government policy making, various sociocultural activities, early forms of industry, and even the organization of military units. These centers often depended on the labor of people who resided in the town or, sometimes, in outlying areas. For example, citizens might be responsible for supplying crafts or CROPS for the region's food supply and trade, on which the rulers relied.

One of the earliest and most common ways in which cities and towns developed was through the growth and organization of trade and associated industries. By the eleventh century, for example, KUMBI SALEH had become one of the most prominent capital cities of the ancient GHANA EMPIRE, noted in particular for its production of GOLD. Built in stone, the city stood in the southeastern region of modern-day MAURITANIA and at its peak had a population of more than 15,000 people. The city was described by Arab geographer al-BAKRI as having a main thoroughfare nearly 40 feet (12.2 m) in width, an Islamic center, residences made of stone and acacia wood, and a walled "royal town," some 6 miles (9.7 km) away that consisted of a palace and conical huts.

During the period prior to European colonization, the western SUDAN produced a number of small trading centers that eventually grew into the important towns and cities of TIMBUKTU, GAO, and JENNE. (Archaeological evidence indicates that Jenne was built sometime between the ninth and tenth centuries and that Timbuktu was built slightly before.) These centers showed strong Islamic influence, including educational and religious centers and an architectural style that has been described as box-under-a-dome (a style that became the model for many buildings in West Africa).

Typically, African Islamic towns included mosques with minarets, or towers, that were used for calling the faithful to prayer. There were also embankments for defense and gated walls that led to the outer regions and the city's cemeteries. The densest population clusters were concentrated near rivers, agricultural sites, and trading centers. Unlike some of the river and agricultural communities, a number of these trading towns survived even into modern times, having sustained themselves, after the decline of the trans-Saharan trade in the sixteenth century, through commerce with the outlying farms.

Between 800 and 1500, INDIAN OCEAN TRADE led to the founding of a number of port cities and towns along Africa's eastern coast. From MOZAMBIQUE in the south to Somalia on the Horn of Africa, these cities, which included SOFALA, GEDI, ZANZIBAR, and KILWA, became part of the Swahili culture, a mix of indigenous BANTU, Omani Arabs from the Arabian Peninsula, and SHIRAZI ARABS from Persia. In line with this, villages made of mud bricks, bamboo, and palm leaves gave way to brick and stone buildings built by wealthy Islamic MERCHANTS. Each of these cities had its central ruler, or sultan, who headed an autonomous governmental council of elders culled from the community's wealthiest families. When the noted traveler IBN BATTUTA visited Kilwa in the fourteenth century, he described it as being one the most beautiful and well-constructed towns in the world, elegantly built and inhabited by people noteworthy for their religious devotion and piety.

Walled towns and cities were fairly common in both the western and eastern regions of Africa, the walls having practical as well as political purpose. Walls, for example, provided controlled entryways and gates, which gave inhabitants security from theft and vandalism. Gates also enabled cities to collect tolls from outsiders. Beyond this, walls afforded privacy to the ruling king, his court, and the city's priests, so that governmental and ritual activities might be kept from view by outsiders. Abeokuta and the city of BENIN are two notable examples of cities whose common features included a royal compound, a designated ceremonial site, and a central MARKETPLACE in which trade could be conducted. Elsewhere in Africa, methods other than the construction of walls were used to create many of these same benefits for towns. Deep trenches, surrounding moats, or even thickets were all used to notable effect.

For the most part, African cities and towns—like cities and towns the world over—developed through their ability to extend their influence beyond their borders. For example, radiocarbon testing done at the site of the circular walled city of ILE-IFE (Ife), in modern Nigeria, has confirmed that it existed as far back as the ninth century. Archaeologists maintain that this city began as an extended family compound, from which the early rulers of Ife—and their descendants—created many new kingdoms and dynasties. These expansionist policies were carried out by both conquest and the absorption of smaller villages. Its ethnic lineage and religious cohesion solidified Ife, which was considered highly traditional in its perspective and operation. In this way, shared values and beliefs were the foundations of its growth and influence as well as for its far-reaching reputation for such artistic achievements as the LOST-WAX PROCESS. These artistic skills not only attracted traders and visitors to the city but also continued to serve as strong reminders of Africa's early urban achievements.

See also: ARCHAEOLOGY (Vol II); ARCHITECTURE (Vol. II); FESTIVALS (Vol. II); GREAT ZIMBABWE (Vol. II); SWAHILI COAST (Vols. II, III).

Further reading: Richard W. Hull, *African Cities and Towns before the European Conquest* (New York: Norton, 1976).

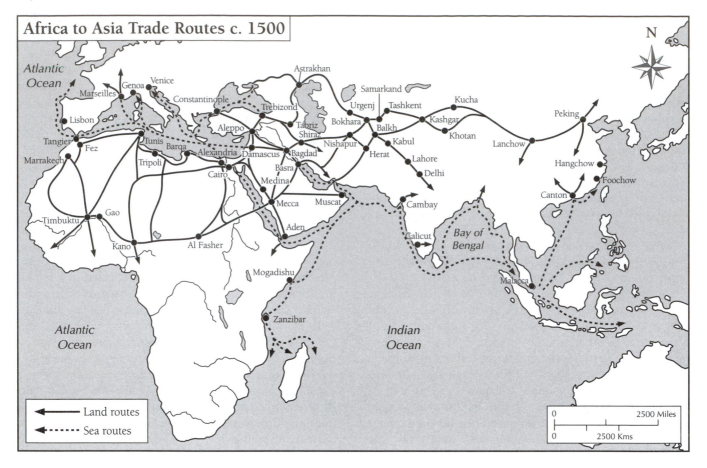

Africa to Asia Trade Routes c. 1500

N

Atlantic Ocean

Atlantic Ocean

Indian Ocean

Bay of Bengal

Genoa · Venice · Marseilles · Constantinople · Astrakhan · Samarkand · Urgenj · Tashkent · Kucha · Peking
Lisbon · Trebizond · Bokhara · Balkh · Kashgar · Khotan · Lanchow · Hangchow
Tangier · Fez · Tunis · Barqa · Aleppo · Tabriz · Shiraz · Nishapur · Kabul · Herat · Lahore · Foochow
Marrakech · Tripoli · Alexandria · Damascus · Bagdad · Basra · Delhi · Canton
Cairo · Medina · Cambay
Timbuktu · Gao · Mecca · Muscat
Kano · Al Fasher · Aden · Calicut · Malacca
Mogadishu
Zanzibar

— Land routes
- - - Sea routes

0 ——— 2500 Miles
0 ——— 2500 Kms

trade See ARAB COASTAL TRADE (Vol. II); ARGUIN TRADING FORT (Vol. II); CARAVANS (Vol. II); CHINESE TRADE (Vol. II); GOLD (Vol. II); INDIAN OCEAN TRADE (Vol. II); IVORY (Vol. II); MARKETPLACES (Vol. II); MEDITERRANEAN SEA (Vol. II); MERCHANTS (Vol. II); PERSIAN TRADERS (Vol. II); RED SEA TRADE (Vol. II); SALT TRADE (Vol. II); SWAHILI COAST (Vol. II); TRADE (Vol. I); TRANS-SAHARAN TRADE ROUTES (Vol. II).

transportation The forms of transportation used in Africa from the fifth through the fifteenth centuries varied depending on the terrain of the region. Throughout Saharan Africa, pack animals were relied upon to transport both goods and people through the harsh desert environment. While evidence suggests that the region's inhabitants were familiar with wheeled transport as early as the last few centuries BCE, there is no doubt that such vehicles often proved ineffective on the sandy terrain.

The camel was introduced to the Saharan trade routes by the fifth century CE. It proved to be the best mode of transport in the desert, as it could travel great distances with little rest or water. In East Africa and other areas, goods such as kola nuts were carried to market by porter, and the ox was the common beast of burden.

In North Africa, the use of horses dates to the seventeenth century BCE. Although the exact date of their appearance in SUB-SAHARAN AFRICA is unknown, horses probably crossed the Sahara as early as 2,500 years ago. According to the tenth-century writer al-Muhallabi, horses were widely used throughout the area of the SUDAN by the late tenth century. Throughout the continent, the horse was a symbol of wealth and prestige. Mounted soldiers greatly contributed to empire building in the twelfth century, as mounted armies, or CAVALRY—like those of the MALI EMPIRE—could more easily conquer neighboring peoples.

Many cultures in Africa relied heavily on water transport, especially those with access to the Niger River, a major north-south transportation route. For centuries, dugout canoes have been used throughout the river settlements of West Africa. A 6,400-year-old canoe, the second-oldest known boat in the world, was found by well diggers at the town of Dujuna in northeastern Nigeria. (The oldest boat was unearthed in the Netherlands.) It is estimated that this 25-foot (8-m)-long canoe could carry five to ten camel loads of salt. Portuguese sailors traveling upriver in the early sixteenth century reported seeing dugout canoes 80 feet (25 m) long carrying passengers and crew that number more than 100. With the invention of the iron saw, even larger vessels were built. It is likely that war canoes similar to the trade canoes the Portuguese saw were used by the SONGHAI Empire to extend its domination over other kingdoms that border the Niger.

Evidence from rock paintings and the writings of the Greek historian Herodotus (c. 484–425 BCE) has been brought forth to support a theory that chariots were used in the desert as early as 2000 BCE. He wrote of how the Garamantes people of LIBYA used chariots to attack their Ethiopian rivals in the desert. The depiction of chariots—generally light, two-wheeled versions with tracks that seem to point to the Niger bend—in rock paintings found in Tassili and southern MOROCCO has led many to believe in the existence of chariot routes across the desert. However, the lightness of the chariots, their relative uselessness for carrying heavy trade items across sandy terrain, and the lack in the Sahara of the skeletal remains of horses contemporaneous to the time of the paintings all serve to disprove the chariot theory.

Along the coast, Arab traders used ships called dhows, whose triangular lateen sails accorded them great maneuverability while sailing into the wind. Such vessels were used in both INDIAN OCEAN TRADE and ARAB COASTAL TRADE in the sixth century and later.

See also: CAMEL (Vol. I); CARAVANS (Vol. I); GARAMANTES (Vol. I); HORSES (Vol. I); LAKES AND RIVERS (Vol. I); SHIPBUILDING (Vols. I, II); TRANS-SAHARAN TRADE ROUTES (Vol. II)

trans-Saharan trade routes   Routes across the SAHARA that trade CARAVANS followed to bring goods from sellers to potential buyers. The major trans-Saharan caravans in the ninth through the twelfth centuries started from KUMBI SALEH in ancient Ghana, from TIMBUKTU and GAO in Mali, and further east, from the HAUSA STATES and KANEM-BORNU. Goods from Kumbi Saleh were carried north across the desert to SIJILMASA in MOROCCO. Goods from Timbuktu often went by way of the salt mines at TAGHAZA to TLEMCEN, near the border of present-day ALGERIA and MOROCCO. A second route from Timbuktu brought goods to FEZ in modern-day Morocco by way of WALATA and Wadan. Caravans from Gao went to TUNIS in present-day Tunisia, to Tripoli in modern LIBYA, and to CAIRO in EGYPT, heading to their destinations either by

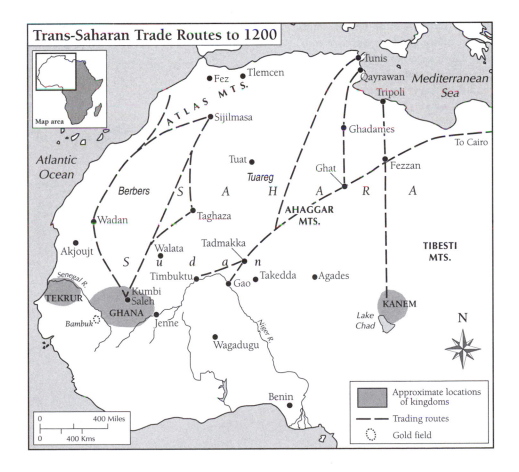

Trans-Saharan Trade Routes to 1200

Map area

Mediterranean Sea

Tunis
Qayrawan
Tripoli
Fez   Tlemcen
ATLAS MTS.
Sijilmasa
Ghadames
To Cairo

Atlantic Ocean

Tuat
Tuareg
Ghat
Fezzan
Berbers   S   A   H   A   R   A
Wadan
Taghaza
AHAGGAR MTS.
Akjoujt
Walata   Tadmakka
TIBESTI MTS.
S   u   d   a   n
Timbuktu   Gao   Takedda   Agades
Senegal R.
TEKRUR   Kumbi Saleh
GHANA   KANEM
Bambuk   Jenne   Lake Chad   N
Niger R.
Wagadugu

Benin

0   400 Miles
0   400 Kms

Approximate locations of kingdoms
Trading routes
Gold field

way of Tuat or the FEZZAN region of what is now south-western Libya. Goods on their way to Gao were often transported by way of Hausaland and Kanem-Bornu to destinations on the lower Nile. JENNE, located south of Kumbi Saleh and Timbuktu, was a major redistribution point for goods from further south.

On the North African side, trans-Saharan trade was the provenance of Berber Arabs. On the sub-Saharan side, the DYULA, SONINKE, MOSSI, HAUSA, and SONGHAI were the peoples who headed trading efforts. Though it existed to some extent in earlier centuries, trans-Saharan trade underwent a dramatic increase at the start of the ninth century. In the typical pattern, GOLD and food-stuffs were carried north in exchange for salt from Taghaza and manufactured goods from the North African coast. By the twelfth century, the trade routes extended as far as the fringes of the modern state of Ghana. In central and southern Africa during this same time period, very little trade with the coast occurred. In West Africa, trading involved and affected very few people directly, although it enriched the traders themselves considerably. Trading here did not create a local market economy where people brought goods to sell directly to the Arab traders.

~~~~~~

Gold, salt, COPPER, and captives were among the most profitable items exchanged along the trans-Saharan trade routes, although there was also commerce in IVORY, fabrics, animal skins, ostrich feathers, and other local goods. The gold fields at Bambuk, Bure, and Galam were so important to the fortunes of the rulers of ancient Ghana that they banned Berber traders from entering them. Gold from there as well as from the VOLTA RIVER region, Lobi lands in modern BURKINO FASO, and the AKAN states also passed through the Sahara to their final destinations in North Africa. Copper, mined at Takkeda in Mali, was traded in local markets, where it became the raw material for local artifacts, but it was also an important part of trade with Egypt, where it was exchanged for fine fabrics and manufactured goods. Arab slave traders also used the trans-Saharan trade routes to transport captives, sometimes as many as hundreds at a time, for use as servants, soldiers, and concubines. From the fifteenth century on, these people were ever more frequently used as field laborers in the Middle East and in the cities of southern Europe.

~~~~~~

See also: DUTCH WEST INDIA COMPANY (Vol. III); ISLAM, INFLUENCE OF (Vol. II); SALT TRADE (Vol. II).

tsetse flies Bloodsucking flies that are found throughout central and coastal West Africa. As a transmitter of the parasite *Trypanosoma*, which causes sleeping sickness (called *nagana* in animals), the tsetse fly has wreaked havoc upon both the human and animal population in Africa. They have also affected the history of the continent. For instance, the ruler Sundiata II (not the founder of the empire), of the MALI EMPIRE, was killed by the sleeping sickness in 1374.

The tsetse fly includes several different species of flies that feed off the blood of both humans and animals. The large flies reach a length of about 1 inch (2.5 cm) and are brown with yellow stripes or spots on their undersides. Sleeping sickness gradually progresses by attacking a person's nervous system, causing an irregular heartbeat, fever, and an enlarged spleen. If untreated, the disease causes mood swings, profound sleepiness, coma, and then death. The disease attacks animals in a similar manner, with death their inevitable end.

Because of Africa's dependence upon agriculture and cattle, the tsetse fly has had a profound impact. Tsetse larvae develop in animal fecal matter, so the presence of tsetse flies leaves farmers unable to use animal dung as fertilizer on their crops. Further, they are unable to plow their fields using livestock, for fear that the animals will contaminate the soil, forcing them to hoe the earth by hand. The large population of tsetse flies in West and central Africa has also limited the areas to which pastoral peoples could migrate in order to feed their livestock. Both factors in turn affected population growth.

See also: DISEASES (Vols. I, II).

This tsetse fly's abdomen is swollen after a meal of human blood. The bite of the tsetse fly is harmful to humans and animals.
© Anthony Bannister; Gallo Images/CORBIS

This 1835 lithograph gives an idealized view of Tuaregs in the Sahara. © *Christel Gerstenberg/CORBIS*

Tuaregs Seminomadic ethnic group that has inhabited the SAHARA and Sahel for centuries; they claim to be descendants of the BERBERS. From the rise of ISLAM until the beginning of the period of European colonization, the Tuaregs exercised a strong influence upon the trans-Saharan trade in the southern Sahara.

After the Arab invasion of North Africa in the seventh century, the Tuaregs, like many other indigenous peoples, were converted to Islam. As a result, their traditional clan system of matrilineal descent switched to a patriarchal system, and their traditional religious practices were replaced by Islam. Despite their conversion, however, the Tuareg maintained many of their own cultural traditions, including their language, written script, and class structure. The latter divided Tuareg society into five ranks, with warriors and religious figures at the top of the hierarchy and slaves and descendants of slaves at the bottom. They also maintained several of their traditional religious practices, most notably a religious ceremony that centered around asking a viper to foretell events. The symbol of the snake remained an important part of Tuareg folklore as a sign of both good and evil.

As the Arab invasion continued, the Tuaregs migrated to the south, moving into the western and central SUDAN. There they organized themselves into political clan structures known as *kels*, each of which was led by a chief. Some of these engaged in frequent raids on other groups, using these raids as an opportunity to acquire slaves and exact tribute. These same *kels*, as well as other Tuareg groups, also continued to carry on their traditional pastoralist activities, combining them with agricultural pursuits and participation in trans-Saharan trade.

Throughout this period, the Tuareg continued to live primarily as nomads, setting up temporary camps that could be easily taken down and transported to their next destination. TIMBUKTU, which was founded by the Tuaregs during the twelfth century, was originally just such a camp settlement that the Tuaregs had used during their travels through the region.

By the fourteenth century, the Tuaregs had gained control over TAKEDDA, an important trading center and COPPER mining area located west of the AÏR MASSIF, on the fringes of the MALI EMPIRE. The acquisition of Takedda gave the Tuaregs far more power in the region. It also gave them increased revenues from TRANS-SAHARAN TRADE ROUTES. By the end of the fourteenth century, though they gained Takedda, the Tuaregs ceded control of Timbuktu to the Mali Empire.

By the fifteenth century, their increased population led the Tuaregs to establish a more complex class system. This new system, which had important similarities to the class system they already had, made distinctions between slaves, the descendants of slaves, peoples who paid tributes to the Tuaregs (usually other ethnic groups they had raided), and the Tuareg noble class. By this time, too, the various *kels* had established vast power in the region, due in large part to their control over portions of the trans-Saharan trade routes. With this increased power the Tuaregs began to establish a kingdom, with several *kel* leaders creating a seat for that kingdom in Agadez, or Agades, in present-day Niger.

Facing competition from the HAUSA STATES as well as the nomadic FULANI of Sokoto, the Tuaregs attempted to consolidate and centralize their increased power over the southern Sahara. This attempt was successful and, in 1433, they recaptured Timbuktu and took control over the trans-Saharan GOLD and SALT TRADE centered in that city. The Tuaregs' power, however, never matched the centralized authority exercised by the kingdoms of KANEM-BORNU and the Hausa. Yet they remained an influential force in the southern Sahara for many years to come.

See also: AGADES (Vol. III); SOKOTO CALIPHATE (Vol. III); TUAREGS (Vols. I, III).

Tukulor (Tukolor, Toucouleur)

West African Muslim people who live in what is now SENEGAL and in adjacent regions in present-day Mali. This region was occupied by the ancient GHANA EMPIRE from the fourth to the eleventh centuries and then by the MALI EMPIRE in the thirteenth century. The Tukulor speak FULFULDE, a FULANI language of the West Atlantic branch of the NIGER-CONGO family, and are related to the SERER and WOLOF peoples.

The Tukulor were converted to ISLAM during the eleventh century, as were other peoples of the SUDAN. When the Ghana Empire fell in 1076, the Tukulor and a group of nomadic Fulani formed a new kingdom called TEKRUR, which lasted into the 1700s. Tekrur was generally governed by non-Tukulor rulers.

The kingdom of Tekrur was rooted strongly in the Islamic beliefs of its people. The social structure was hierarchical, highly stratified, and based upon patrilineal groups. The Tukulor also practiced polygyny. Their economy was based on agriculture, cattle raising, and FISHING.

Tunis

Strategic port located on the MEDITERRANEAN SEA in the modern-day country of Tunisia. The history of Tunis goes back to the first millennium BCE and the Phoenician settlement of North Africa. However, the city did not begin to rise to prominence until the ARAB conquests that began in the seventh century, at which time the city became a vital commercial and military stronghold.

During the eighth century, the Arab leader Hassan ibn Numan used Tunis as the base for his military campaigns against BERBER resistance to the west. The subsequent influx of Arabs to the region helped transform Tunis into a cosmopolitan center that attracted a diverse population of MERCHANTS, scholars, and bureaucrats. As the terminus of the TRANS-SAHARAN TRADE ROUTE, Tunis became a major center for commerce between Africa, the Middle East, and Europe.

Because it was both a point of strategic importance and the origin of Arab attacks on Berber strongholds, Tunis frequently became embroiled in the military campaigns that marked the next centuries of North African history. During the tenth, eleventh, and twelfth centuries, the city was frequently involved in the struggles for control of the western Sahara, or MAGHRIB, between warring factions of the ALMOHADS, the MARINIDS, the Zayyanids, and the Hafsids.

Later, during the thirteenth century, when the Berber Hafsids came into power, Tunis was revitalized as a royal city replete with mosques, palaces, and schools. Under the Hafsids, the city maintained its significant role in the trade between the Mediterranean and the trans-Saharan routes, leading to a period of great prosperity. By the fourteenth century, however, battles between the Hafsids and their rivals, the Zayyanids, erupted, with the main issue being control over Tunis and its trade. Although the Hafsids were able to rule the city until the sixteenth century, control over Tunis ultimately passed first to Spain and then, by the end of that century, to the Ottoman Empire.

See also: ARAB COASTAL TRADE (Vol. II); GRECO-ROMAN PERIOD (Vol. I); OTTOMAN EMPIRE (Vol. III); PHOENICIANS (Vol. I); TUNISIA (Vol. III).

Tunka Manin (r. c. 1063–?) *King of the ancient Ghana Empire.*

Ruling from the capital city of KUMBI SALEH, the SONINKE king Tunka Manin was the most powerful leader of the GHANA EMPIRE during the eleventh century. He assumed kingship upon the death of his maternal uncle, King Basi, in 1063.

Most of what is known about Tunka Manin comes from the written accounts of the Arab scholar al-BAKRI from around 1068. Relying on the reports of Arab traders who had witnessed the grandeur of Ghana's Empire, al-Bakri wrote detailed descriptions of the king, his magnificent court, and the imposing Ghanaian army of more than 200,000 warriors. According to al-Bakri, Tunka Manin was widely respected by both his subjects and foreigners, and Ghana flourished under his rule.

Tunka Manin was able to increase the wealth and power of his empire by controlling trade and levying taxes on the great amounts of salt and GOLD that passed through his territory. His tight grip on power eventually loosened around 1073 when the ALMORAVIDS, invading North African Muslims, began to conquer parts of his kingdom and convert many of his subjects to ISLAM.

See also: SALT TRADE (Vol. II).

Tutsi (Batusi, Batutsi, Tussi, Watusi, Watutsi, Hima)

Ethnic group that lives primarily in BURUNDI and RWANDA, in central Africa. The pastoralist Tutsi—also referred to as Hima, depending on the kingdom—most likely immigrated from ETHIOPIA around 1400, in search of new land on which to raise their cattle.

Though archaeological evidence makes it clear that the Tutsi had not settled in the area prior to the fifteenth century, Tutsi legend puts the founding of Rwanda on a par with the birth of civilization itself. The major Tutsi clans claim to have descended from a mythical ancestor, Gihanga, the founder of several dynasties including the Sindi, Nyakarama, Ega, Shambo, Sita, Ha, Shingo, Kono, and Hondogo.

Partly due to the wealth provided by their vast herds of cattle, the Tutsi rather quickly established dominion over the HUTU and TWA, the original inhabitants of the region. The Tutsi were overwhelmingly superior warriors and, perhaps precisely for that reason, the shift in power from the Hutu to the Tutsi was largely peaceful. Although the Tutsi assumed the language and culture of the Hutu, what eventually developed was a feudal system in which the Tutsi formed an aristocracy and the Hutus took on the role of the peasantry.

Eventually, the Hutu and Twa adopted many aspects of Tutsi culture, most significantly the Tutsi system of government in which the *mwami* (king) was the supreme ruler, wielding both political and religious power. The *mwami*, thought by the Tutsi to be divinely chosen, was usually a Tutsi, but another social group, the GANWA, acted as ruling princes, serving as intermediaries between the *mwami* and the other Tutsis.

Also aiding the Tutsi in their dominion over the Hutu and Twa was their physical stature. Whereas the Hutu are generally small, muscular people and the Twa are especially diminutive, it is not uncommon for a Tutsi male to stand over 7 feet (2.1 m) tall.

Over time, there was much intermarriage between the Tutsi and the other ethnic groups in the region. There also was a change of status as cattle were lost or acquired. So, as a result, it eventually became more difficult to distinguish between Tutsi and Hutu.

See also: TUTSI (Vol. III).

Twa (Batwa, Gwa)

Subgroup of the MBUTI (who are sometimes referred to by the term *Pygmy*), an ethnic group of equatorial Africa. During the fifth through the fifteenth centuries, the Twa inhabited territory around Lake Kivu, in what is now RWANDA, Burundi, and the Democratic Republic of the Congo.

When the Hutu first encountered the Twa, they believed that the diminutive people possessed magical powers. As a result, the Twa received gifts in exchange for their supposed powers, which were used to maintain the rule of the Hutu kings. Twa people functioned as storytellers, mystics, dancers, and musicians in the king's court.

The seminomadic Twa had occupied the Lake Kivu region for thousands of years before the first major influx of HUTU settlers. Though there is evidence of Hutu migration to the area as early as the first century CE, it wasn't until the fifth century that the Hutu began to migrate in great numbers. By the eleventh century, the Twa were being incorporated into Hutu society, and they established a cooperative agricultural relationship. Twa crafts-men also produced excellent POTTERY that was valued by the Hutu.

Despite being included in Hutu society, the Twa were given lower social standing, most likely because of their different appearance and cultural practices. By the fif-teenth century, the TUTSI—an aristocratic, warrior peo-ples—had begun to dominate the region occupied by the Hutu and Twa agriculturalists. Under Tutsi domination, the Twa became even more segregated from larger society than they had been under the Hutu, and this marginaliza-tion continued into the European colonial period, which began toward the end of the sixteenth century.

See also: HUNTER-GATHERERS (Vol. I); HUTU (Vols. I, III); TUTSI (Vol. III); TWA (Vols. I, III).

Twifo   Term that describes the Twi-speaking peoples that populated the forest region of modern coastal Ghana beginning in the fifteenth century. The Twi language is related to the languages of the ASHANTI, AKYEM, Akwamu, Sefwi, Nzima, and FANTE.

The early Twifo, who probably migrated from the area that is now northern Ghana, lived in small clan groups, providing for themselves by means of agriculture and FISH-ING. Eventually, though, they became skilled traders. Because of their strategic location between the coast and the GOLD-producing forest regions, Twifo MERCHANTS were able to participate in the SALT TRADE as well as the gold trade. Other items that moved through Twifo markets included luxury goods like BEADS AND JEWELRY and CLOTH.

The increase in trade had an enormous impact on the Twifo, for in addition to the sudden creation of vast wealth, they also grew in number and developed more complex political structures. Because of this, when the Portuguese arrived in the mid-fifteenth century, they preferred dealing with the Twifo over other cultures in the region. It is through this early Twifo culture that the later AKAN and Ashanti kingdoms traced their ancestry.

See also: PORTUGAL AND AFRICA (Vol. III);

U

Uganda East African country located between present-day KENYA and the Democratic Republic of the Congo, whose southern border runs along Tanzania, RWANDA, and the shores of Lake VICTORIA. BANTU-speaking people migrated from the west into what is now modern Uganda between 1000 BCE and 1000 CE. During the course of this gradual resettlement, the Bantu-speakers perfected the art of food production and IRON technology and at the same time established a sophisticated system of government ruled by clan chiefs. The Bantu speakers were at a disadvantage, militarily and politically, facing the Hima, NILOTIC-speaking cattle herders, who invaded the region and overthrew the Bantu in the tenth century.

Like many herders and agriculturists, there developed between the Bantu and their Hima overlords a two-tiered hierarchy in which the herders secured the region from external aggression and the agriculturists became the laborers. The Hima incorporated some of the Bantu political practices into their own system of government. The first unified state to emerge was the CHWEZI KINGDOM in BUNYORO-KITARA. The Chwezi ruled from 1350 to 1500 and were lead by a *mulama* (king) who delegated palace officials and chiefs to help run the kingdom. By the sixteenth century the Chwezi dynasty was replaced by the BITO kingdom, a dynasty comprised of the LUO people, the second Nilotic group to penetrate the region. At its height between the sixteenth and the nineteenth century, Bunyoro-Kitara controlled several small kingdoms, including Bukoli, Bugwere, Bulamogi, TORO, Bugabula, and Kiziba. Eventually these kingdoms rebelled against the Bito empire, which led to the decline of Bunyoro-Kitara in the 1800s.

See also: UGANDA (Vol. III).

Further reading: Christopher Wrigley, *Kingship and State: The Buganda Dynasty* (New York: Cambridge University Press, 1996)

Umayyad Muslim dynasty, based in Damascus in Syria, that ruled the Arab Empire or Caliphate, whose territory extended from the Arabian Peninsula through Africa and into Spain in the years 661 to 750. The caliph had both religious and secular authority over believers and was seen as the successor to the prophet MUHAMMAD. Bringing an end to the civil war of 656–661 between two factions following the murder of Uthman (r. 644–656), the third caliph, Mu'awiya (c. 602–680) was victorious over Muhammad's son-in-law Ali (r. 656–661), the fourth caliph. Mu'awiya then established the Umayyad dynasty.

During Umayyad rule, ARABIC was made the official language of the Arab Empire, accompanying an extensive Arabization of the financial system and civil administration. The eight governors who ruled over the MAGHRIB from 697 to 740 and promulgated these policies, eventually brought about marked changes in the politics and culture of the region, especially given the brief span of Umayyad rule. Cultural biases led some Arabs, despite the injunctions of the KORAN and the sympathetic actions of many other Arabs toward the BERBERS, to treat the native Berbers as social—or even racial—inferiors. This pattern continued even as more and more Berbers converted to Islam, leading to resentment of the Arabs by the indigenous population.

Umme, Mai (Dunama bin Hummay, Umme-Jimi, Mai Humai) (r. 1085–1097) *Sefuwa king who converted the Kanem-Bornu Empire to Islam.*

The second Sefuwa king, Mai Umme, was a follower of the teachings of Muhammad bin Mani. During the eleventh century, Umme converted the KANEM-BORNU Empire to ISLAM. One of the more important results was that the ZAGHAWA people cut themselves off from the Kanem-Bornu and headed east.

During his lifetime, Umme traveled to MECCA on two occasions, but he perished in EGYPT before completing his third pilgrimage. His son and successor, Dunama I (1092–1150), was with him on his father's and was crowned in Egypt shortly after Umme's death.

See also: ISLAM, INFLUENCE OF (Vol. II).

uzama Hereditary local chief of the EDO-speaking peoples of the kingdom of BENIN, in what is now Nigeria. The *uzamas* reached the zenith of their power in the period from the eleventh to the fourteenth centuries, ruling local villages and serving as members of the royal council that administered the kingdom. Traditionally, the *uzamas* also were responsible for selecting the king of Benin.

The *uzamas* lost power during the reign of EUWARE (r. 1473–1480), who incorporated the *uzamas* into a new, more centralized monarchy. At this time, the power of the *uzamas* was counterbalanced by the creation of a new hierarchy of palace chiefs and town chiefs. Sharing power with these new chiefs created a rift between the *uzama* and the monarchy.

See also: GOVERNMENT, SYSTEMS OF (Vol. II).

V

Vai (Vei) MANDE people living in what is now Liberia and SIERRA LEONE. Called the Gallinas ("chickens") by early Portuguese explorers because of their domesticated fowl, the Vai were farmers, fishers, expert metalworkers, and active traders. Along with their Mande-speaking neighbors, the Vai migrated south from their homelands in present-day Mali and Guinea several thousand years ago. During the fifteenth century, the Vai of the Sierra Leone region merged with the indigenous KONO people.

See also: LIBERIA (Vol. III); SIERRA LEONE (Vol. III); VAI (Vol. III).

Vasco da Gama See GAMA, VASCO DA.

Venda (Bavenda) BANTU-speaking people living in the region between the LIMPOPO and Zambezi Rivers, south of ZIMBABWE, in the eastern half of what is now the Republic of SOUTH AFRICA. They migrated into the area from the Great Lakes region to the north. The Venda's capital city, founded during the thirteenth century by the legendary king Toyandou, is at Dzata, in the Njelele valley of the Zoutpansberg Mountains. The ruins of Dzata are still visible. In the colonial period, the Venda fought off ZULU attempts to conquer them, and they were the last of the peoples in the region to succumb to European domination.

Venda culture was defined by patrilineal inheritance, polygamy, clan totems, and circumcision. They depended on hunting and gathering, trade with neighboring groups, and the mining of COPPER and IRON. The Lembaa are a Venda-speaking Jewish people claiming Falasha descent.

See also: ZULU (Vol. III).

Victoria, Lake Largest lake in Africa, lying on the borders of Tanzania, UGANDA, and KENYA. Lake Victoria is at the center of the Great Lakes region in the interior of East Africa. Numerous peoples have inhabited the lake's coastal regions since the middle of the first millennium, but it seems that the first influential group was a BANTU-speaking population that lived on the northwestern coast of the lake from the twelfth century until they migrated further south by the sixteenth century. There was another Bantu settlement in the twelfth century on the eastern shores of the lake, from Mara in the south to the Kavirondo Gulf in the north. These settlements of Bantu speakers acculturated with the NILOTIC and Kushitic peoples who lived in the region and adopted some of their practices, such as male and female circumcision. The Haya and Zinza peoples inhabited the southwestern shore of the lake during the thirteenth century. Southern Kushitic peoples lived on the eastern and southern shores of the lake during the twelfth century but were replaced by the Sukuma peoples on the southern shore by the sixteenth century.

See also: VICTORIA, LAKE (Vol. 1); BANTU MIGRATIONS (Vol. II).

Volta River Thousand-mile (1600-km) river system in modern Ghana, formed from the confluence of the Black Volta and the White Volta Rivers, along which several powerful precolonial kingdoms emerged. The river's name, given by Portuguese explorers in the fifteenth century, means "turn," after its twisting course.

Beginning around 1260, Diamare people from the east invaded long-established communities along the

Volta. For the next 200 years, intermittent raids occurred throughout the region, and by 1480, because of ease of transport and local TRADE, numerous riverside kingdoms emerged, including the MOSSI STATES of DAGOMBA and MAMPRUSI, founded by fifteenth-century invaders from the HAUSA STATES, and the additional Mossi states of WAGADUGU and YATENGA.

The adjective used to describe the peoples and languages originating in the Volta River region is *Voltaic.*

See also: VOLTA BASIN (Vol. III).

W

Wagadu See GHANA EMPIRE.

Wagadu-Bida (Ouagadou-Bida) A mythical serpent from West African folklore. The legend of Wagadou-Bida describes how the GHANA EMPIRE (c. 800–1200 CE) became rich in GOLD. The story is from the *Epic of the Dausi*, one of several surviving narrative poems composed and recited by traveling storytellers.

As with any oral history, the story of Wagadou-Bida has different versions. For example, sometimes Bida is referred to as a dragon that arose from the desert sands, other times as a serpent or the offspring of a king. But although the details may vary, the allegory is the same.

The first part of the myth describes the origin of the city of Wagadu. As Dinga, the leader of the SONINKE people, lay dying, he sent for his oldest son. But it was the youngest son, Lagarre, who came to his dying father's bed. Dinga told Lagarre to find nine jars of water; the person to wash in them would become king. Next, Dinga asked his son to find the drum Tabele, take it into the northern desert, and strike it. Lagarre carefully followed his father's instructions, and upon striking the drum, a city rose out of the sand of the desert, encircled by the dragon Bida. (Another version of the myth describes the birth of the serpent Bida from the first marriage of King Dinga.)

Lagarre bargained with Bida to gain entrance to the city. He promised that every year, a beautiful young girl would be sacrificed in its honor. In return Bida agreed to scatter gold over the city. This was the city of Wagadu, the beginning of the Ghana Empire.

The tradition of human sacrifice continued for three generations, during which time the people of Ghana enjoyed tremendous prosperity, which they attributed to the spirit serpent Bida. Then, one year, when the time for the annual sacrifice had arrived and a girl had been chosen, the girl's fiancé, a brave, young SONINKE warrior, could not bear to have his beloved die. He hid himself near where the serpent lived and waited. When Bida appeared, the Soninke warrior cut off his head. The severed head flew out of the kingdom to the town of Bambuk, where the people suddenly found their pockets full of GOLD.

The serpent, however, did not die. Its magical powers were so strong that it grew another head. The warrior cut off this second head, and the same thing happened again. Finally, after the warrior had cut off Bida's seventh head, the serpent's powers were exhausted, and it died. The Soninke warrior had saved his fiancée and the two of them rode away together. Soon after, the kingdom suffered a devastating drought. Animals died and crops would not grow. The people knew that without Bida, their good fortune had ended. The people fled with their belongings and became nomads and the empire of Ghana had come to an end.

See also: WANGARA GOLD FIELDS (Vol. II).

Wagadugu (Ouagadougou) Largest and most powerful of the West African MOSSI kingdoms of the Upper VOLTA RIVER region (modern-day BURKINA FASO). Although the town of Wagadugu has existed since c. 1050, it did not become the Mossi capital until the late fifteenth century during the reign of the first *mogho naba* (or "great king," as the supreme leader of the Mossi was called).

The inhabitants of the Mossi states initially came from the Gold Coast. They conquered the southern region of the Upper Volta and assimilated with their Gur or MANDE-speaking subjects. Eventually they formed the Mossi people, with the invaders as chiefs and the conquered as commoners, and created the states of MAMPRUSI, DAGOMBA, Nanumba, Wagadugu, and YATENGA. Wagadugu was captured by the Mossi c. 1328 during a period of conquest in which they destroyed TIMBUKTU and attacked both WALATA and Banko. Like many of the Mossi states, Wagadugu was an agriculturally based society that also participated in both local and international trade.

According to oral tradition, the original Mossi ancestor was Tohajie. It is said that his grandson, Na Gbewa, had three sons who formed the kingdoms of Mamprusi, Dagomba, and Nanumba. Na Gbewa also had a daughter, named Yanenga, who was so esteemed as a combatant that her father refused to allow her to marry. Ignoring her father's orders, Yanenga stole away and married Riale, a MANDINKA prince, with whom she had a son named Wedraogo (or Ouedraogo).

Later, the leaders of the rival Ninisi and Ziri kingdoms tried to win Wedraogo, who was an accomplished warrior, by bestowing upon him a wife. Wedraogo, however, gave the wife to his son Zoungrana, for whom she bore a son named Oubri. Eventually, Oubri conquered the city of Wagadugu and became the first *mogho naba*. In Mossi tradition, Oubri shares the title of founder of Wagadugu with his grandfather Wedraogo, who died before the final conquest of the Mossi capital.

According to Mossi tradition, all those eligible for kingship had to be descended from Wedraogo and Oubri. The Mossi of Wagadugu believed their king, the *mogho naba*, to be superior to all other rulers.

Walata (Oulata)

Major center of trade in the early eleventh century, located on the edge of the SAHARA, in what is presently MAURITANIA.

Walata was an important stop on the TRANS-SAHARAN TRADE ROUTES between the upper Niger River region and MOROCCO. Walata was one of two cities that replaced the Ghanaian imperial capital of KUMBI SALEH as a major trading center of the area. When SUMANGURU, the reportedly cruel founder of the KANIAGA Kingdom, conquered Kumbi, about 1203, traders, MERCHANTS, and even the native SONINKE people began to leave the city. They established new trading settlements at Walata and JENNE.

By about 1230, Walata had become a main center of commerce in this part of Africa. During one period, it was perhaps the best-known CARAVAN stop on the Sahara trade routes. About 1480, SUNNI ALI, ruler of the SONGHAI Empire, took control of Walata, adding this great city to his vast kingdom.

See also: GHANA EMPIRE (Vol. II); WALATA (Vol. III)..

Wamara (Wamara Bwigunda Njojo eyona Rwabwera) (c. 1371–1398) *Second Chwezi king who ruled the Kitara Empire of southern Uganda.*

The KITARA Empire is believed to have existed between 1300 and 1500. However, because much of the information about Kitara and the CHWEZI KINGDOM comes from oral traditions, there is much debate over what is fact and what is mythology.

Many legends are associated with the Chwezi kings and chiefs, who were revered as sons of God and thought to have mystical powers. It was believed, for example, that these individuals wandered without fear and that their eyes were as bright as the Sun.

In spite of these questions, it is generally accepted that there were two Chwezi kings of Hima origin who ruled over Kitara; these are NDAHURA (c.1344–1371) and his son Wamara. Ndahura founded the Chwezi Kingdom but abdicated the throne after he was captured in battle. Convinced that he had disgraced his title and his subjects, Ndahura asked the Chwezi people to elect a successor to the throne from among his children. Although the Chwezi would have gladly welcomed Ndahura back, they respected his decision and chose his eldest son to be their king.

Upon taking the throne, Wamara moved his capital from Mubende to Bwera, where he divided the Kitara Empire among his brothers and chosen associates. Unlike the relative peacefulness that the kingdom had experienced under Ndahura, under Wamara Kitara was faced with constant strife and social unrest. This was mainly due to the influx of immigrants to the region, including the Hima, the Kintu, the Bashombo, and the LUO.

Wamara's growing number of multiethnic subjects proved to be a discontented lot, but Wamara tried various means to appease them. He attempted, for example, to integrate them within the kingdom, giving members of every ethnic group prominent positions in the government. However, the people of Kitara resented the Chwezi kings for expecting too large a share of the country's riches. As a result, Wamara and his brothers eventually lost the respect of their subjects, who no longer considered them divine.

The ruling dynasty met its end with the emergence of the Luo, BITO, and the BAHINDA states. It is uncertain exactly what happened to Wamara and his brothers. Some reports declare that they simply vanished, while other traditions hold that they moved southward. Still others maintain that they drowned. One of the more widely accepted versions declares that, following a famine and an epidemic that struck the region's cattle, one of Wamara's generals staged a coup, during which the Chwezi aristocracy was wiped out.

After their disappearance, however, the Chwezi aristocracy eventually returned to favor. Indeed, the people of Kitrara began worshiping them as gods once again and started praying for their return.

Wangara See DYULA.

Wangara gold fields Regions in western Africa that provided the DYULA, or Wangara, traders with the resources to become the largest commercial brokers in the era between the 1300s and 1500s. Based on the accounts of thirteenth century observers and on recent geological surveys, it is commonly believed that the main Wangara gold fields were located in Bambuk, Bure, and other forested regions of modern Ghana and the IVORY COAST. Bambuk is near the SENEGAL and Faleme Rivers, and Bure lies between the Niger and Tinkisso Rivers, southeast of Bambuk.

Despite the importance of GOLD in the trans-Saharan trading economy, there is limited information about where the gold was mined and the way in which it was processed. To avoid competition, the savvy Dyula managed to keep the location of their gold fields secret. They even went so far as to practice silent trading, a method of commerce in which neither party ever met face to face. The Dyula would place their merchandise at the side of a riverbank and then retreat while the interested parties paid for their goods in gold. A Dyula trader would rather face death than reveal the source of his people's wealth. Even the royalty respected this secrecy. Had they not, they would have suffered the repercussions of the Dyula's withholding trade.

See also: TRANS-SAHARAN TRADE ROUTES (Vol. II).

waqlimi Title that the ZANJ of East Africa gave their king. *Waqlimi*, or *wafalme*, comes from the phrase *Morwa wa ka Limi* and means "Son of the Supreme Lord." Although *al-Zanj*, meaning "blacks," was the term ARABS used to describe all Africans, it came to refer more specifically to the group of people who lived south of the SOMALI region of the Horn of Africa on the East African coast.

In 943, the famous Arab geographer el MAS'UDI, who had sailed as far south as the island of PEMBA (Kanbalu),

described in his book *The Meadows of Gold and Mines of Gems*, the Zanj system of government. They elected the *waqlimi* as a divine representative who was entrusted with leading the kingdom justly.

The Zanj were a spiritual people, although they did not subscribe to an organized religion. Their name for God was *Mkalanjalu*. According to the ninth-century Arab author al-Jahiz, Zanj sermons were delivered before the *waqlimi* by holy men, illustrating the interconnectedness of government and religion in Zanj society.

The idea of justice was extremely important to the Zanj. The *waqlimi*'s role was considerable in this system because he was in charge not only of his own army, which was substantial, but also of all the lesser kings or chiefs within the empire. This was not an easy task considering the Zanj's interests were in GOLD mining and trading—a process that was notoriously rife with corruption in some areas of East Africa. If the Zanj people felt that the *waqlimi* had failed to perform his duty of dispensing justice then he was no longer the "son of God," and they could put him to death and end his line of succession to the throne.

See also: DIVINE RULE (Vol. II); SWAHILI (Vol. II).

Waqwaq People who settled the islands called Kunlun, which were later renamed the land of Waqwaq by Arab sailors in the tenth century. There is some debate as to the exact location of the islands and the origin of the people. One group of Waqwaq is believed to have inhabited a region in Southeast Asia near China. The other appears to have settled along the East African coast prior to the age of intensive Arab exploration in the area starting in the tenth century. This second group of Waqwaq settled primarily in MADAGASCAR, the PEMBA Islands, and throughout the land of SOFALA, near the modern coastal border of KENYA and Tanzania. Arab geographers claimed that the Waqwaqs were of Indonesian descent, but to add further confusion, the name *Waqwaq* is also synonymous in some accounts with KHOISAN.

It is generally accepted that the Waqwaqs came to Africa early in the common era. They prospered in GOLD mining and became ruthless traders. Around 945 they invaded Pemba, called Kanbalu at the time, in an infamous attack that is described in *The Book of the Wonders of India*. The Waqwaqs came in 1,000 ships, and their journey to Kanbalu, they claimed, took almost a year, as they subjugated several coastal towns and villages along the way.

Kanbalu was of interest to the Waqwaqs for two reasons. First, they were after goods that they would later trade with China. These included IVORY, ambergris (perfume made from whales), frankincense, myrrh, panther skins, tortoiseshell, and, most important, the ZANJ people whom they captured and forced into servitude. Second, the Muslims posed a serious threat to the Waqwaqs. Not only did they want to prevent ARABS from infiltrating their gold and IRON mines but they also wanted to hinder the longstanding Muslim dominance of local trade.

Though the Waqwaqs were a powerful force and managed for a time to impede some Muslim activities, they were no match for the Arabs, who had firmly established themselves in the area by the end of the tenth century. As East Africa increasingly converted to ISLAM in the eleventh century, the Waqwaq trading empire eventually collapsed.

See also: ARAB COASTAL TRADE (Vol. II); INDIAN OCEAN TRADE (Vol. II); SLAVERY (Vol. II).

warfare and weapons Although the details of early African warfare are vague, by 1200 distinct military tactics had emerged throughout the continent. The severity of warfare depended largely on the size, government structure, and location of the communities involved.

The earliest known conflicts occurred between loosely organized peoples like those of the DINKA, Nuer, MAASAI, and San. Although their villages, with their elder-dominated social structure, usually lacked a clear hierarchical system, these communities were able to organize into bands during warfare. Bands—groups of related nomadic or foraging peoples—as well as groups of agriculturalists often raided neighboring villages, but they seldom engaged in long battles. Very few people died in these conflicts because of the limited killing power of their weapons, which were generally just modified hunting and farming tools. This early warfare tended to center on domestic disputes, such as conflicts over cattle, land, labor, or social status. Opponents were never really defeated; rather they were simply kept at bay for a period of time.

In the northern parts of SUB-SAHARAN AFRICA, horses were used extensively in the cavalries of the GHANA, MALI. and SONGAI Empires as early as the ninth century because they could survive in the savanna climate. Cavalry forces could be large; Ghana, for example, could field as many as 200,000 armed horsemen. To the west, only smaller horses could survive, so the cavalries were dependent on hand-to-hand combat with sabers and attacks with javelins and bows. Coastal areas of Africa, like Senegambia and the Gold Coast, organized tight armies that used handheld weapons in combination with tactical support from archers. In Angola, loosely organized infantries were composed of highly skilled hand-to-hand

combat soldiers who relied on their ability to dodge weapons rather than utilize shields.

Warri Capital city and port of the ITSEKIRI trading kingdom of southern Nigeria. Founded in the late fifteenth century, Warri was situated just south of the kingdom of BENIN in the western Niger Delta region.

According to oral tradition, a prince of Benin named Ginuwa, or Igunwa, who was proving to be unpopular at home, was sent to Warri by his father, Oba Olua. Once in Warri, Ginuwa established the Itsekiri Kingdom and assumed the name Olu in honor of his father. Ginuwa's was succeeded by his sons, Ijijen and Irame, who led Warri and the Itsekiri Kingdom to great political and economic success.

Itsekiri tradition holds that ghosts, called *imale*, occupied the region before the arrival of Ginuwa.

The Itsekiri traded salt, clay pots, and palm oil with other peoples of the Niger Delta. They also traded large amounts of cassava flour with the Portuguese merchants who began visiting the Delta CITY-STATES in the second half of the fifteenth century. Because of their strong trading economy, the Itsekiri were influential throughout southern Nigeria, and their customs were practiced among both the Liama and Soku communities. The NEMBE people of the Niger Delta adopted the Itsekiri god Ogidiga as their national deity.

After the fifteenth century, the Portuguese attempts to establish Catholic missionaries in the Niger Delta region were more successful in Warri than in any of the other neighboring kingdom.

See also: ITSEKIRI (Vol. III); PORTUGAL AND AFRICA (Vol. III).

weapons See WARFARE AND WEAPONS.

Wolof People, originally of FULANI origin, who migrated to the SENEGAL and GAMBIA region (Senegambia) in the 1300s. The Wolof settled among the Jolof people and gradually began to set up the states that eventually formed the WOLOF EMPIRE. The first of these states to organize was Jolof, and by the fifteenth century, their extensive kingdom included Kayor, Walo, Baol, and the SERER states of Sine and Saloum. Wolof society adhered to a strict class structure that was divided into three major groups: freeborn, low-caste or unfree, and slaves. Each of these groups had its own hierarchical system. Included in the freeborn (*jambur*, in Wolof), in order of importance, were royalty, nobles, clerics, and peasants. The low-caste or unfree (*nyenyo*) were the working class and consisted of laborers (blacksmiths, jewelers, tanners, and cobblers) and CRAFTSPEOPLE (GRIOTS or praise-singers, weavers, and other artisans).

Although the blacksmith and griots were from a lower class, their positions earned them a certain amount of respect. The upper class required the services of the griot, and his was the only position from which a member of the low caste could speak frankly to the freeborn without suffering serious repercussions. The blacksmith was an important member of society because he built instruments of warfare. The slaves (*jam*) were defined as all owned persons, though there was a distinction between those who were born into slavery, those who were bought, and those who were captured. The social position of the slave depended on the position of his owner. For instance, if the slave was owned by a member of the freeborn, he could be given an honorable position that might surpass the low caste. Although moving from caste to caste was possible, it was uncommon. Intermarriages between castes were rare.

In 1455 Cada Mosto, a Venetian writer, described the Wolof system of government. He noted that the leader of all the Wolof states was called the *burba jolof*, and, although each state was given autonomy over its kingdoms, allegiance to the empire concerning economic and security issues was expected.

ISLAM came to the Wolof region between the eleventh and the sixteenth centuries. The lower castes were more willing to convert than were those of the royalty or nobility, but Wolof rulers often would feign conversion to maintain control over their Muslim subjects. The Wolof Empire declined in the sixteenth century when the states began to fragment.

See also: SENEGAMBIA (Vol. III); WOLOF EMPIRE (Vol. III).

Wolof Empire Five states in the West African region of SENEGAL and GAMBIA (Senegambia) that accepted the dominion of the Wolof state of Jolof during the fourteenth through the sixteenth centuries

The first *burba jolof*, or king, of the Wolof Empire is said to have been Ndiadiane Ndiaye of Jolof, who assumed power in the late 1300s. He was able to unite his state with the three other Wolof states in the region—Kayor, Baol, and Walo—and two states of the SERER people—Sine and Saloum—that had a large Wolof minority.

On the face of it, the Wolof Empire was a voluntary confederation rather than a highly centralized kingdom. The rulers of the other states elected the *burba jolof* and voluntarily paid him tribute for the upkeep of his royal dignity. Beyond that, they were free to rule their states independently, although they were expected to cooperate with the *burba jolof* in matters of defense, trade, and taxation.

Heredity was not the important factor in the choice of a ruler; lineage, however, was. The rulers of the individual Wolof states had to be descendants of the founders of their individual states and be born of a noble woman. The *burba jolof* had to be a descendant of Ndiadiane Ndiaye himself in the male line of succession. Once appointed, the *burba jolof* and the lesser kings of the other states underwent elaborate installation rituals that, it was thought, gave them magical powers and made them divine.

Since it was the nobility who elected the *burba jolof*, they saw to it that he ruled as they wanted, or they removed him from the throne. The *burba jolof* was given an army over which he had control, and if his soldiers were powerful enough, they could sometimes prevent the king from being dethroned. The people of the lower stations of society had no political power whatsoever.

The responsibilities of a Wolof leader were spiritual as well as political. He was seen as a divine representative and, as such, was the link between his subjects and their ancestors. Despite the fact that the king could be easily overthrown, he was highly esteemed and treated with the utmost respect by all those under him. The authority of the *burba jolof* and the lesser kings depended on their personal wealth and power. All had private armies and often acted autocratically and in their own best interest because there was often no need to maintain a common front. When rulers appeared in public, they were accompanied by a large retinue of courtiers and warriors.

Starting in 1444, Portuguese merchants began entering the Wolof Empire to develop a profitable trading partnership, and this turn of events led to conflict among the Wolof states. Kayor was the first of the states to break away from the empire, doing so in about 1556. Kayor declared its independence, thereby cutting off the inland Jolof state from access to the sea and European trade. The leader of Kayor, whose name is lost to history, then captured the neighboring Wolof state of Baol, repulsed an invading army from Jolof, and killed the Burba. The other Wolof rulers refused to accept Kayor's dominion and created independent local states.

See also: PORTUGAL AND AFRICA (Vol. III); SENEGAMBIA (Vol. III); WOLOF EMPIRE (Vol. III).

women in medieval Africa The history of women in Africa is elusive at best, and, as a result, researchers frequently have had to rely on nonconventional sources in order to reconstruct it. These sources increasingly have included oral tradition, mythology, and findings associated with archaeological excavations. Because of this, many historians have found it useful to look for certain themes that recur from period to period or from region to region, rather than following a strict chronology.

For example, with the rise of ISLAM and the shift toward more complex CITY-STATES, new divisions along gender lines began to appear in many African societies. Around the same time, many female networks were formed, apparently to meet the needs of female members of society as well as to create autonomous means of income generation. Among the most important of these networks were initiation rites and secret societies, both of which ultimately served to transmit a society's culture and religion.

Religion represented another arena in which women could gain power, although, in many societies, it was only male priests who were able to lead most ceremonies. However, many women were noted for their ability to serve as spirit mediums, which frequently led to greater and more significant responsibilities for women as a whole group. In the Great Lakes region and in ZIMBABWE, for example, the CHWEZI KINGDOM employed priestesses who led a women's ceremony known as *kubandwa*. This rite of passage, which represented a "marriage" between young girls and specific deities, served as an important method for transferring traditions from generation to generation.

The middle centuries also afforded women opportunities to move beyond narrow domestic roles, and, as a result, they often generated wealth through nonagricultural forms of labor. Because trade was already fairly well-established, women generally placed more emphasis on the production of items such as textiles. In what is now SOUTH AFRICA, for example, women of the Inka people earned revenue from their skills as weavers and, like Shona women, also worked in early mining operations. Other women supplemented agricultural work with forms of labor dictated by the length of the lean times between dwindling food supplies and the new harvest. Afikpo women, a subgroup of the IBO of Nigeria, traditionally made pots that were sold in the larger cities of Calabar or the communities bordering the Cross River. Female networks were the basis of women's dominance in the marketplace. Agricultural produce, cooked items, CLOTH, beads, and many other types of crafts were all sold to visiting traders or at the local markets. This source of income not only benefited the women themselves but also figured significantly in the urbanization process of West and central Africa.

The formation of city-states that took place during the medieval and subsequent periods appears to have lessened the influence of matriarchal societies. This has largely been attributed to the influence of ISLAM, with its emphasis on patrilineal descent, especially in the selection of political and religious leaders. Noteworthy in this regard were the women of the early SWAHILI COAST culture, whose activities became more regulated as a result of the gender inequality that accompanied religious conversion and the resulting Arabization.

In spite of the spread of Islam, however, there were many groups that maintained long-standing traditions of powerful female leadership and networks. The MANDE and YORUBA societies of West Africa were prime examples of this. Women leaders among the Yoruba were known as *iyalode,* and one of their primary responsibilities was the protection of market women. Elsewhere, the TUAREG of the SAHARA, who had developed their own tradition of indigenous feudalism and rituals well before their conversion to Islam, also maintained the notion of female independence and matrilineal inheritance.

In royal societies, such as those developed by the AKAN of Ghana, a long line of queen mothers, referred to as the *ohemma,* maintained and exercised power on the basis of their relationship to the king. Considered female kings, their divinity stemmed from their ability to bring forth kings. As such, these women ruled informal networks of family clans that included both men and women. The queen mother's symbol, a knotted cloth tied around a long staff, has been noted among Tuareg women rulers as well. In contrast, queen mothers of the LUBA of southeast Zaïre, for example, although aware of the secrets associated with powerful rule, could not be rulers outright. Instead, as wives and mothers, they remained in the background, serving primarily as counselors to the king.

See also: INITIATION RITES (Vol. I); KANDAKE (Vol. I); ORAL TRADITION (Vol. I); QUEENS AND QUEEN MOTHERS (Vol. II); SECRET SOCIETIES (Vol. I); WOMEN IN PRECOLONIAL AFRICA (Vol. III).

Further reading: Iris Berger and E. Francis White, eds., *Women in Sub-Saharan Africa* (Bloomington: Indiana University Press, 1999); Catherine Coquery-Vidrovitch, *African Women: A Modern History* (Boulder, Colo.: Westview Press, 1997); Elizabeth Isichei, *A History of African Societies to 1870* (New York: Cambridge University Press, 1997); Ivan Van Sertima, ed., *Black Women in Antiquity* (New Brunswick, N.J.: Transaction Publishers, 1997).

writing About a century before the beginning of the common era, the Semitic Sabaean people of southern Arabia introduced a new system of writing. This system, commonly referred to as Sabaean script, evolved into the Ethiopic writing system, Africa's oldest alphabet still in use today. The Ethiopic writing system gave rise to many variations, including GE'EZ, AMHARIC, TIGRAY, and Tigrinya.

The oldest existing examples of Ge'ez writing date back to around the fourth century CE, though the roots of the language date to pre-Christian times. There are translations of the Bible in Ge'ez from between the fifth and seventh centuries. Ge'ez further modified Sabaean script and used different vowel sounds to create syllables. Ge'ez and subsequent Ethiopic writing systems are read exclusively left to right (like English), unlike other SEMITIC languages, which are read right to left. Ge'ez script was in common use until about the seventh century. After that time it was used only for religious purposes, in writings and observances in the Ethiopian Orthodox Church.

Of particular interest are the Nsibidi and Mende styles of African writing. Nsibidi script is the writing system of the Ejagham people of NIGERIA. It is found on tombstones, secret society buildings, costumes, ritual fans, headdresses, and textiles. Mende script, the writing system of the Mende people of modern-day SIERRA LEONE, is considered one of the more artistic examples of written language, with its many curlicues and figures.

The oldest examples of Amharic writing are songs and poems that date back to the fourteenth century. Amharic included additional characters to represent sounds acquired from KUSHITIC languages and further modified the Ethiopic alphabet (which they called *fidel* or *feedel*) to include thirty-three consonant characters. Amharic has seven vowel sounds. Each consonant character can form seven syllables, depending on which vowel sound is used, so Amharic has a total of 231 syllables.

A completely different writing system arrived in Africa with the Muslim invasion, which began around 646 when Arab the Muslims conquered EGYPT. The Muslims were an intensely religious people and their religious texts were written using the ARABIC alphabet. Their influence quickly extended across northern Africa and throughout the continent as the Muslim world expanded through military victories. Until that time, African writing systems were localized. But as ISLAM spread throughout Africa, so did the Arabic language. Literacy increased as more and more Africans converted to Islam. At first, many Africans became bilingual, fluent in both their native language and Arabic. Then, they began using the Arabic alphabet to write their own languages. Now, Arabic script is one of the most common scripts for writing African languages.

See also: EJAGHAM (Vol. III); HIEROGLYPHICS (Vol. I); MENDE (Vol. III); NSIBIDI WRITING (Vol. III); WRITING (Vol. I).

X

Xhosa BANTU-speaking people of present-day SOUTH AFRICA who inhabited the region for several centuries before the arrival of European colonists in the sixteenth century.

The Xhosa, whose roots are traced to a number of eastern Nguni ethnic groups, moved south across the Kei River to establish themselves as the southernmost of the Nguni peoples. Highly retentive of their cultural systems and traditions, they were prosperous and prolific pastoralists.

See also: XHOSA (Vol. III).

Y

Yaji, Sarki (1349–1385) *Ruler of Kano; believed to have been the first Muslim Hausa king.*

Sarki Yaji was one of a series of kings, or *sarkis*, who ruled in Hausaland during the fourteenth century. The king of the important HAUSA kingdom of KANO, Yaji saw the introduction of ISLAM to the region. Evidence suggests that Yaji was helped by pro-Islamic groups in his takeover of Santolo, a "pagan" city to the southeast of Kano. However, even though Yaji captured Santolo, ending its role as a center of traditional worship, the spread of Islam was not very successful overall in the HAUSA STATES at that time because the *sarkis* often allowed subject populations to follow their own local beliefs rather than be fully subject to Islam. It can be argued, however, that the *sarkis* had no choice, reliant as they were on the cooperation of their followers, some of whom refused conversion to the new religion. *Sarkis* were unable to rule with the same undisputed authority as SONGHAI rulers could at the height of their power.

After Yaji's death, his son, KANAJEJI, *sarki* of Kano from 1390 to 1410, restored traditional religious practices after Kano was defeated by another Hausa city-state. It was not until the mid-fifteenth century that Islam again became dominant in the region.

Yalunka (Dialonke, Jallonke) A people of MANDE descent who were among the earliest inhabitants of the FOUTA DJALLON highlands (which bears their name) in what is now the Republic of Guinea. The Yalunka primarily resided in the northern and eastern regions among the Temne, Baga, Daebe (Bari), and FULA, where they hunted and worked the land. Although, more often than not, they coexisted peacefully with these groups, friction sometimes arose between the various clans. The Yalunka became increasingly hostile as more immigrants continued to move into the region. These tensions mounted in the fifteenth century when the immigrants, particularly the newly converted Fula, started bringing their Islamic religion with them.

The Yalunka speak a Mandinka language that is very similar to the SUSU language. In fact, they are so closely related to the Susu, who live in the coastal regions of southern Guinea, that some authorities believe that the Yalunka and the Susu are the same people.

Yaqub al-Mansur (Abu Yusuf Ya'qub Ibn 'abd al-Mu'min al-Mansur, Ya'qub II) (c. 1160–1199) *Third king of the Almohad Muminid dynasty who ruled North Africa and Spain from 1184 to 1199.*

At the age of twenty-four, Ya'qub al-Mansur succeeded his popular father, ABU YAQUB YUSUF (r. 1163–1184), and took the ALMOHAD throne. Unfortunately, Yaqub's reign was not as peaceful as his father's.

> After serving as his father's vizier, Ya'qub seemed the obvious choice as his successor, though this sentiment was not shared by his brother 'Umar, who later betrayed him and was executed for his disloyalty.

Almost immediately upon Yaqub's taking power, internal difficulties arose among his Masmuda clan and rival BERBER clans in the central MAGHRIB and IFRIQIYA. One of these rivals, the Banu Ghaniya, began to take lands in the eastern part of the Almohad Empire, near Tunisia. The Ghaniya rebellion lasted several years and, although the Almohads eventually recovered all the territory they lost, the revolt took its toll on the empire.

In 1194, Yaqub turned his attention to al-ANDALUS—Arab territory in what is now southern Spain—in order to check the advances of the Portuguese and Castilians (Spaniards) on Almohad territories. Castilian king Alfonso VIII had led his troops to take Seville, but what the Castilians didn't expect was that Yaqub and Pedro Fernandez de Castro, a longtime rival of King Alfonso, would join forces. With Fernandez de Castro's backing, the Almohads successfully defended their territory, finally winning a decisive victory at Alarcos in 1195. After this battle, Yaqub was known to the Almohads as *al-Mansur*, which means "one made victorious by God." With renewed confidence, al-Mansur made his way through southern parts of the Iberian Peninsula, conquering Toledo, Madrid, Alcalá, and Cuenca.

Al-Mansur is remembered for his stellar military leadership and for bringing glory to the Almohad Empire. The great caliph was succeeded by his son Muhammad al-Nasir, whom al-Mansur had named his successor upon returning to his capital at MARRAKECH after his victories in al-Andalus.

The strong Almohad interest in artistic and intellectual culture waned during al-Mansur's rule. Instead, he encouraged adherence to strict Islamic doctrine, which, Yaqub felt, had been rather slack during the reigns of both his father, Yusuf I, and grandfather, ABD AL-MUMIN.

Yatenga One of a number of independent West African states, called the MOSSI states, that flourished between c. 1500 and 1895 at the headwaters of the VOLTA RIVER. Named after Naba Yadega (r. 12th century), a WAGADUGU prince and the grandson of Naba Oubri, Yatenga was founded in c. 1170 but did not become one of the Mossi states until c. 1540.

Before King Yadega ruled Yatenga, the region was dominated by Rawa, the son of Wedraogo (Ouedraogo), the progenitor of the Mossi peoples. Rawa successfully took over this area, which included Zandoma, by allowing its people, the Ninsi, religious autonomy. The DOGON, another group in the region, were not so easily pacified and moved north to the Bandiagara cliffs.

Upon the death of Wagadugu's Naba Nyingnemdo, Yadega's younger brother Koudoumie took advantage of the fact that Yadega was engaged in battle elsewhere and claimed the throne. When Yadega discovered this betrayal, he tried to fight for his throne but found Koudoumie's forces too strong. With the help of his sister Pabre, who stole the royal charms of Wagadugu to use on Yadega's behalf, Yadega retreated to Gourcy, where he founded the capital of Yatenga. The royal charms, ownership of which was believed to ensure a successful reign, served Yadega well as Yatenga eventually gained independence from Wagadugu. By the sixteenth century, Yatenga had become an important Mossi state, sending warriors along the Niger bend to plunder the towns of JENNE, Sarafere, TIMBUKTU, and WALATA.

Yekuno Amlak (Yekuno Amlahk, Yekuno Amiak, Yekunno-Amlak) (r. c. 1270–1285) *Solomonic ruler of Ethiopia.*

Yekuno Amlak, a noble from AMHARA, overthrew the ZAGWE DYNASTY in 1270. He received support from the Orthodox Christian Church in Ethiopia, specifically an island monastic school located in Lake Hayq. Yekuno Amlak proclaimed himself king, a right supported by the church since he purported to be a direct descendant of King Solomon and the queen of Sheba (Queen Makeda) through their son Menilek, the first emperor of Ethiopia.

The reign of Yekuno Amlak and his descendants became known as the SOLOMONIC DYNASTY, and they all claimed Solomonic descendancy even though the union itself is most likely a legend. During the fifteen years Yekuno Amlak ruled, his empire widened in influence, continuing the spread of CHRISTIANITY southward and reaching out for contact with Europe and the Middle East. He solidified control of his empire, primarily by keeping his court mobile—traveling to areas in need of overseeing rather than establishing a permanent capital. He also successfully defended it against surrounding pagan and Muslim groups. One of his greatest triumphs was against the Muslim state of Ifat, the defeat of which was important to controlling trade routes.

Yitbarek (d.1270) *Last emperor of the Zagwe dynasty of Ethiopia.*

Yitbarek was a descendant of King LALIBELA (r. c. 1185–1225), the most famous king of the ZAGWE DYNASTY and the monarch responsible for the carving of eleven churches from solid rock at the Zagwe capital of al-ROHA. Despite King Lalibela's shows of devotion, the church, especially the monastic leaders, continued to favor the previous SOLOMONIC DYNASTY of AKSUM, both during Lalibela's life and after his death.

Yitbarek's reign lasted between twenty and forty years until he was driven out and killed by a usurper named YEKUNO AMLAK, a prince of the Amhara kingdom of Shewa in the central highlands of Ethiopia. Amlak's claim to legitimacy was based on his descent from the Solomonic dynasty. One theory about Yitbarek's death and the resulting fall of the Zagwe dynasty holds that Yitbarek succumbed without a fight because the church backed Amlak's claim of descent from King Solomon and the queen of Sheba. Another version suggests that a monk named Yasus Moa encouraged Amlak to believe that he had an ancestral right to the throne. According to legend, Yitbarek retreated to Gaynt, where he sought refuge at the church of Qirqos. He was quickly discovered by Amlak and was assassinated at the altar. Yitbarek's grave is just east of the church.

See also: AKSUM (Vol. I).

Yoruba General term used to describe the language, peoples, and kingdoms of Yorubaland. The Yoruba inhabit parts of present-day Nigeria, BENIN, parts of Ghana, SIERRE LEONE, and Togo. They speak a common Yoruba language (in the Kwa group of the NIGER-CONGO LANGUAGES), and share a common culture but never became a single, unified political group in the same way as, for instance, the MANDINKA founders of the MALI EMPIRE did.

The Yoruba were a highly urbanized people in precolonial times, forming numerous kingdoms of varying sizes in YORUBALAND ruled by a king who bore the hereditary title oba and was considered the descendant of the founding oba. He was assisted by a council of chiefs, usually six, whose positions were also hereditary. The oba lived in a palace at the center of the town with the compounds of the various family groups surrounding it. Farmland surrounded these urban centers.

The most important precolonial Yoruba state was the OYO KINGDOM, which did not expand to become an empire until after 1550 and, as one of the largest states of West Africa, dominated the neighboring states of BENIN and Dahomey. The city of ILE-IFE (Ife) in Yoruba tradition, the birthplace of humanity, remained an important religious center. The kings of Ife still traditionally bear the title ONI (ooni), meaning "this one," the person whom the gods have chosen as ruler.

According to Yoruba tradition, the Yoruba people have their origins with the earth itself. The supreme being, Olorun, sent a lesser god named Obatala to create land upon the water. Olorun instructed him to place some pieces of IRON upon the water and then empty a snail shell full of soil onto them. Oblata was then to release a rooster with five toes to scratch the soil and make it become land. There are two versions of the myth. In one, Obatala does as instructed. In the other version, he becomes drunk, and the task must be finished by ODUDUWA. Oduduwa plants on the land a seed that grows into a huge palm tree with sixteen branches. These branches are said to symbolize the original kingdoms of the Yoruba. The place where creation is purported to

This bronze head of an unnamed Ife king from Yorubaland is of a style that goes back to before the fourteenth century.
© *Paul Almasy/CORBIS*

have taken place is called Ife and has remained a sacred city for the Yoruba.

Probably closer to actual events is a second myth about Yoruba beginnings in which an invading group led by Oduduwa defeats the people already living at Ile-Ife, who are led by Obatala. Either way, Oduduwa claims the role of the founder of the Yoruba.

Agriculture was the predominant way of life, growing such CROPS as cocoa, yams, corn, millet, CASSAVA, cotton, plantains, peanuts, peas, and beans on a rotating basis. The market economy was mainly controlled by women, and their status was determined by their place within this system. This complex economy eventually allowed for an arts culture to develop, and the Yoruba became well-known CRAFTSPEOPLE. Craft work included metalsmithing, most notably BRONZE casting; sculpture in IVORY, wood, brass, and terra-cotta; weaving; beadwork; glassmaking; leather working; and cotton spinning. The brass and bronze that Yoruba craftspeople used was an important trade item; its constituent metals, COPPER tin, and zinc, were imported from North Africa or from mines in the SAHARA and in West Africa.

The Yoruba also developed the literary arts, constructing short stories, proverbs, poetry and myths—many about the 401 deities and spirits that make up the pantheon of their traditional religion. The Supreme Being is named Olorun. Others are Sango, the god of thunder; Ogun, the god of iron; and Eshu, the trickster.

Moremi is one of the celebrated deities of the Yoruba. She earned her place through loyalty to her people and her own unselfishness. According to legend, the Yoruba were being beset by IBO raiders. The Ibo, dressed in frightful costumes, wanted to drive off the inhabitants of Ile-Ife and then burn and sack the city. With the people helpless against the enemy, Moremi turned to the spirit, or orisha, of the Esinminrin River for help. Following its advice, Moremi allowed herself to be taken captive by the Ibo in order to learn their ways. She found that the raiders were merely people dressed in palm leaves. When she escaped, she passed this information on to the Yoruba, who were then able to defeat their enemy easily. Of course, advice from an orisha has its price. Moremi was forced to sacrifice her only son, Oluorogbo, but through this sacrifice, she gained immortality for herself.

See also: DIVINATION (Vol. I); ESHU (Vol. I); OLORUN (Vol. I); ORISHA (Vol. I); RELIGION , TRADITIONAL (Vol. I); SANGO (Vol. I); DAHOMEY (Vol. III); OYO (Vol. III); YORUBA (Vol. I); YORUBALAND (Vol. III).

Yorubaland   Region in present-day southwestern Nigeria in which, during the eleventh through the seventeenth centuries, several CITY-STATES flourished. The most notable of these states were ILE-FE, the OYO KINGDOM, and IJEBU. Ife was the first YORUBA capital and, according to oral tradition, the place at which Olodumare, the god of the sky, created humankind. All royal lineage had to be descended from the mythical ODUDUWA, who subsequently founded Ife. Oduduwa's sons and grandsons were believed to have founded the other Yoruba states.

Migration to the area began in c. 700 and increased steadily over the next three centuries. Various clans and peoples assimilated or clashed, and by 1000 several state-like communities began to be established throughout the region. These were primarily agricultural societies, which, in later years, profited from both local and long-distance TRADE, including the trade in slaves.

The EDO-speaking people of Benin, who share many political and religious traditions and an intertwined history with the neighboring Yoruba, began to develop their monarchial system of government around the same time that Ife was developing its own. As in Yoruba tradition, the ruler of BENIN was also called the oba, and also traced his origins back to the god Oduduwa. By the sixteenth century, Benin's area of control expanded eastward to the Niger River and westward to the Lagos Lagoon as well as to areas directly to the north and south.

In the fourteenth century, OLD OYO began to usurp the political dominance of Ife and became an important trading state. However, territorial conflicts with Borgu and the Nupe Kingdom forced the Oyo people into an exile from which they did not recover until the early seventeenth century. However, Oyo eventually became the most powerful of all the Yoruba kingdoms.

Renowned the world over are the Yoruba BRONZE, brass, and COPPER castings that evidence use of the LOST-WAX (cire perdue) PROCESS, and terra-cotta sculptures that often were created as tributes to Ife gods and kings.

See also: OLODUMARE (Vol. I); SLAVERY (Vols. II, III); OYO EMPIRE (Vol. III); YORUBALAND (Vol. III).

Yusuf ibn Tashbin (Yousef ibn Tashbin, Yusuf ibn Tashfin, Yusuf ibn Tashufin)   (r. c. 1061–1106) *Powerful Almoravid ruler who established Marrakech as the capital of Morocco.*

Ruler of the ALMORAVID dynasty from around 1061 to 1106, Yusuf ibn Tashbin was the second successor, after ABU BAKR al-Lamtuni, of ABD ALLAH IBN YASIN, the founder of the Almoravid movement. Ibn Tashbin assumed power in 1062, designating himself *amir al-muslimin* ("commander of the Muslims"). That same year he founded the city of MARRAKECH, which remained the capital of MOROCCO until the year 1147.

Under ibn Tashbin's leadership, the Almoravids were an unstoppable force that extended beyond even Morocco and ALGERIA. In 1086, after the Spanish Muslims solicited his help, ibn Tashbin led his armies into Spain, defeating Alfonso VI of Castile and León at the Battle of al-Zallaqah. Ultimately, ibn Tashbin's forces went on to take control of the rest of Muslim Spain. After his death in 1106, Yusuf ibn Tashbin was succeeded by his son Ali.

Z

Za Line of SONGHAI-speaking rulers, possibly MANDE in origin, whose ancient court was located at the town of KUKIYA on the Niger River; they ruled GAO from about 1100 to 1300. The Za dynasty was originally established at the town of Kukiya, and its influence spread and led to the establishment of the town known as Old Gao on the banks of the Niger River. Old Gao became the site of the new court of the Za and the center of their administration around 1100.

There is historical evidence to suggest that the SORKO people established a camp on the right, or southern, bank of the Niger as early as the eighth century. (The Sorko, whose economy was primarily based on FISHING, were a branch of the Songhai people.) Eventually, this camp became the town of Gao. Later, BERBER merchants established a camp on the river's left, or north, bank from which they traveled to Gao to trade salt from the SAHARA for slaves and grain. Enjoying access to TRANS-SAHARAN TRADE ROUTES, in time this camp became the town of Gao-Sané.

The Za rulers of Kukiya, who had dealings with the Sorko of Gao, prospered from this trade. As they became more powerful, they extended their reign to the surrounding area. The Za eventually moved their base of operations to Gao in order to better control trade with the Berbers. As a result, Gao became an important trading center.

Originally, the Za practiced an animistic religion that involved the worship of natural spirits such as the river, earth, and wild animals. When the Za converted to ISLAM, around 1000, they apparently retained a number of their original beliefs, integrating them into their new religion.

Around 1100, the Za moved across the river to the left bank and established a royal court at what would come to be known as Old Gao. From there, the Za presided over the area's trans-Saharan trade and ruled the economy, which was agriculturally based. The Berbers of Gao-Sané, also known as the ZAGHE and the Sunni, took over Old Gao, intermarrying with the Mande Za and adopting the title of Za.

Around 1300, the MALI EMPIRE conquered Gao, and the Za were forced back to the old Songhai town of Kukiya, where they ruled as the Sunni Empire. The last descendant of the Sunni dynasty, SUNNI ALI, took the throne in 1464, a date which is also considered to be the beginning of the Songhai Empire. Sunni Ali was a capable warrior–king who greatly expanded his territory, and during his time, the Songhai reclaimed Gao, which became the center of a revitalized Songhai state. Thus the descendants of the original Za came to rule Gao again a few centuries later. After the reign of Sunni Ali, his son was ousted by ASKIA MUHAMMAD TOURÉ (r. c. 1493–1528), who made Songhai the largest empire in West Africa.

See also: NIGER RIVER (Vol. I); SALT TRADE (Vol. II).

Zaghe Dynasty descended from BERBER traders, who came to power around 1080 in Old Gao on the left, or north, bank of the Niger River; ancestors of the Sunni who ruled the SONGHAI state.

Trade brought the Berber merchants, who were the ancestors of the Zaghe, to the SORKO fishing camp of GAO on the right, or southern, bank of the Niger River, which is believed to have been established around 700. Trading salt from the SAHARA for grain, slaves, and CLOTH, these merchants eventually settled and established a base of operations on the left, or north, bank of the Niger River. Called Gao-Sané, this location was chosen because it was directly connected to TRANS-SAHARAN TRADE ROUTES.

The Sorko-Za dynasty that ruled Gao also established a new capital on the left bank around 1100, which became the important trading center of Old Gao. The Zaghe of Gao-Sané were Muslim, and some historians believe that the Zaghe worshiped in common with their Za neighbors of Old Gao, who had been converted to ISLAM around 1000.

The Zaghe eventually took over Old Gao in a mostly nonviolent struggle, ultimately intermarrying with the Za. By the thirteenth century, the Zaghe had adopted the title of Za.

When the MALI EMPIRE conquered Gao, around 1300, the Zaghe moved downriver to the old Songhai town of KUKIYA, where they again rose to power as the Sunni dynasty. In the fifteenth century, SUNNI ALI, the last Songhai ruler, reclaimed Gao and made it the center of the expanded Songhai Empire.

Zagwe dynasty Emperors of an Ethiopian kingdom based in the central highland region of Lasta. After the decline and subsequent destruction of AKSUM in the latter half of the tenth century, Zagwe kings rose to power and ruled from approximately 1137 to 1270. Although written sources in this period are scarce, the Zagwes have been portrayed as part of an elite class, the progeny of intermarriage between colonizing Aksumite military officials and indigenous AGAW-speakers.

Part of the Zagwe dynasty's power came from its large army, which helped it spread CHRISTIANITY by colonizing other regions. The building of monasteries concentrated their power and included influential sites such as Debre Bizan and Debre Maryam. In the southern regions of Gojjam and Shewa, populations that included the people of Amhara and TIGRAY received Christian instruction and later became formidable opponents to Zagwe rule.

Much of what is known about the Zagwe period is derived from the surviving ARCHITECTURE of the churches built under Zagwe direction. Yemrahana Krestos, the grandson of Marara, an early Zagwe king, built several important Christian churches. King Harbe, Krestos's cousin and successor, tried to end the age-old practice of acquiring the head of the Ethiopian Church from the Egyptian Church. During negotiations with the Egyptian Church, Ethiopia faced a severe drought that ravaged the country with famine and fire. Harbe interpreted these catastrophes as heavenly signs that he should not break with the Egyptian Church, so the Christian Agaws remained dependent on EGYPT for another seven centuries.

King LALIBELA (r. 1185–1225), known for his Christian piety, expressed his devotion by becoming a prolific builder of numerous rock churches, constructed in the Zagwe capital of al-ROHA. Some historians believe that Lalibela's spiritual goal was to pay tribute to the Holy City of Jerusalem by creating an imitation. Others, however, have commented that the construction of Lalibela's churches was shown to him in a dream. To accomplish his goal, Lalibela recruited local workers as well as others from as far away as Egypt and Jerusalem. Using only hammers and chisels, these workers fashioned eleven churches from volcanic rock. To this day, these buildings, which include St. GIYORGIS and Madhane Alam, rate among the architectural wonders of the world.

Overall, the Zagwe kings were denied recognition as legitimate heirs to the Ethiopian throne and historically have been categorized as usurpers. Despite the controversy surrounding their rule, however, the Zagwes remained in power for more than 100 years, their longevity resulting from their practice of appointing governing officials who were either well-known or directly connected by blood to their own families. These officials were given large tracts of land and allowed to exact tribute from their subjects. The Zagwe reinforced this form of rule by annual visits to various regions of the kingdom.

One of the most significant factors in their rule was the development of lucrative trading routes through the LASTA MOUNTAINS to the Muslim trading ports along the coast. This exclusive resumption of trade and the empowerment it afforded to Muslim settlers outraged Amhara, Tigrean, and Ethiopian Church officials. According to various sources, rebellions against their rule began in the Christian province of Shoa, led by YEKUNO AMLAK (r. 1270–1285). Imprisoned by YITBAREK, a descendant of Lalibela, Amlak escaped, gathered his forces, and successfully diverted trade from the Lasta Mountains. Yekuno Amlak eventually killed Yitbarek, claimed the title of emperor, and won the support of the Ethiopian Church. He then created allies among Christian Tigreans by claiming descent from King Solomon and Queen Makeda, also known as the queen of Sheba. His rule marked the beginning of what is generally referred to as the restoration of the SOLOMONIC DYNASTY.

See also: CHRISTIANITY, INFLUENCE OF (Vol. II); RED SEA TRADE (Vol. II).

Further reading: Harold G. Marcus, *A History of Ethiopia* (Berkeley: University of California, 1994).

Zaïre See KONGO KINGDOM.

zakat Islamic practice of giving alms to the poor. Among the Five Pillars of Faith of ISLAM is the requirement to make an annual contribution to the needy. This may take the form of *sadaqah,* which is a free-will offering, or *zakat,* which requires that Muslims annually contribute two and a half percent of their wealth to the poor.

See also: ISLAM, INFLUENCE OF (Vol. II).

Zambia Modern country in central Africa. Starting around the beginning of the common era, the Late Stone Age inhabitants of Zambia began to be overrun by migrating peoples, most likely BANTU speakers, who were firmly established in the region by about 800. Their way of life involved agriculture and livestock, mining and metalworking, and POTTERY making. The metalworking itself, primarily with IRON, may have enhanced the ability of these people to change to an agrarian society, since iron tools, such as the ax, allowed slash-and-burn agriculture, also known as *chitemene,* to develop forests and woodlands into farmlands. COPPER was also worked by the metalsmiths, most notably into ingots or cross shapes that were used for currency. It was also used for jewelry. There is evidence that copper, along with iron, was a traded commodity—most likely for items, such as salt, which were difficult to get in the area. Around 800, the first traces of political divisions emerged, most likely due to the need to control trade routes and to protect mineral resources. The making of COTTON thread was added to the list of cultural accomplishments around the year 1000. Pipe smoking also appeared at around the same time. Cattle husbandry increased as well on the Batoka Plateau.

By 1300, an even more economically complex society had evolved. Excavations at Ingombe Ilede, at the junction of the Kafue and Zambezi Rivers, have uncovered distinct class differences among burial practices. Some of those buried, presumably the nobles, had elaborate jewelry incorporating GOLD, glass beads, and seashells. These would have had to come through trade from as far away as ZIMBABWE and the east coast of Africa.

Eventually, this trade led to Zambia's first contact with Europeans, and the domination of INDIAN OCEAN TRADE by the Portuguese beginning in the late 1400s would eventually lead to Zambia's colonization by foreign powers.

See also: BANTU MIGRATIONS (Vols. I, II); PORTUGAL AND AFRICA (Vol. III); SALT TRADE (Vol. II); ZAMBIA (Vol. III).

Zanj (Zandj, al-Zanj, al-Zandj) Ancient BANTU people who lived along the Juba and Shebelle Rivers of present-day Somalia. They were a major source of slaves for North African and Arab Empires, even prior to the beginnings of ISLAM in the seventh century.

Little is known about these East African coastal people before they became suppliers of slaves. Arab historians like Ibn al-Fakih and al-IDRISI mention the Zanj as early rulers of the eastern coast. They engaged in INDIAN OCEAN TRADE with the ARABS, Persians, and Indians, prob-

ably trading tortoiseshell and small amounts of GOLD. According to al-Idrisi, early Zanj territory included the settlements of Badhuna, Karkuna, MALINDI, MOMBASA, and al-Banas. It is possible the Zanj were also living somewhere in al-Kumr. These settlements were among the first in Africa to be exposed to ISLAM. Muslim missionaries arrived in the eighth century, but a distinct Islamic kingdom did not emerge until around the fourteenth century with the rise of the SWAHILI COAST culture.

Since pre-Islamic times, the Zanj traded slaves to Arabia, Persia, Mesopotamia, and Iraq. Slaves were usually captured in raids, but sometimes kings would sell citizens who had violated cultural norms. Around 750, the Islamic Empire conquered the Zanj states and began reducing their citizens to a state of servitude. It soon became one of the largest traffickers of the Zanj, who were used as servants, concubines, CRAFTSPEOPLE, soldiers, or hard laborers.

The Zanj slaves revolted in 689. Although small, it was followed by a more substantial uprising in 694. The leader of the Zanj, Riyah ("lion of the Zanj") led a group of revolutionaries in a series of battles that posed a considerable threat to the local Muslim army. One hundred years later, more than 10,000 Zanj were slaughtered by Caliph Abu Abbas al-Saffah's army. In 869, Zanj laborers launched the largest revolt in the history of the Islamic Empire. This fourteen-year rebellion ended in the collapse of the Zanj state. It was led not by a Zanj but by an Arab, Ali ibn Muhammad, also known as *sahib al-Zanj* ("master of the Zanj"). He rallied the Zanj to rebel against their masters, but the revolt soon turned into a political insurrection against the Muslim Caliphate. Those who participated in the revolt included the Zanj proper, the Kharmatiyya, the Nuba, the Furatiyya, and the Shuridjiyya.

Early in the revolution, the Zanj captured and destroyed part of al-Ubulla. They soon conquered Djubba and an important port center, Basra. Proceeding north, they gained control of Wasit, Nu'maniya, and Djardjaraya but were unable to advance further. In 883, their capital, Mukjtara, was captured by an Abassid prince, and the Zanj slaves were again suppressed.

See also: NUBA (Vol. I); SLAVE REBELLIONS (Vol. III).

Zanzibar Island in the Indian Ocean, off the coast of East Africa, that was a major center of trade in precolonial Africa. The relative proximity of Zanzibar to the Middle East and India contributed to its importance as a trading center in this part of the world. Separated from Africa by only 22 miles (35 km) and located off the coast of what is now Tanzania, the island of Zanzibar was conveniently located along popular routes for INDIAN OCEAN TRADE.

With a landmass of around 640 square miles (1660 sq km), this low island has been home to many peoples. The original inhabitants most likely were the BANTU-speaking people whose descendants have long lived on the island.

Persians were the first foreigners to visit and inhabit Zanzibar, perhaps as early as the seventh century. They did not, however, retain a distinct ethnic group of their own but instead blended into the African population. By the tenth century, ARABS established an important presence on the island as well, creating trade settlements, owning land, and dealing in the trade of captives to and from the African mainland for export to Arabia, India, and other eastern regions.

Vasco da GAMA was the first European to visit Zanzibar, in 1499. Within a few short years after his arrival, the Portuguese conquered this territory and subjected it to their rule.

See also: PERSIAN TRADERS (Vol. II); PORTUGAL AND AFRICA (Vol. III); SWAHILI COAST (Vols. II, III); ZANZIBAR (Vol. III).

Zara Yakob (Zar'a Yaeqob)   (r. 1434–1468) *Ethiopian king best known for his military achievements and church reforms.*

Ruler of a tributary state made up of central Ethiopia, Zara Yakob established for himself the title of *bahr negash*, which means "ruler of the lands by the sea." The title referred to jurisdiction over the north, including Hamasen, Seraye, and the peninsula of Bur. As ruler of a Christian state, Zara Yakob felt threatened by the surrounding Islamic states. He warred against them and, in 1445, defeated the sultanate of ADAL and its Muslim allies. This fear of ISLAM may have also spurred his sending Ethiopian monks to the Conciliate of Firenze (1439–1443), thus aligning himself with Rome and initiating Ethiopia's first contact with western Europe.

As emperor, Zara Yakob was the head of Ethiopia's church. He appointed bishops and initiated church reforms. With the aid of an inquisitor and a network of spies, he hunted down and executed the leaders of heretical sects as well as innocents who had been falsely accused. Taking the title "exterminator of the Jews," he tried, unsuccessfully, to wipe out the Jewish group known as the Falasha, or BETA ISRAEL. In 1450, Zara Yakob called a council and settled a schism in the church by accepting the observation of the Sabbath.

During Zara Yakob's mostly peaceful reign, literature and the arts were able to flourish. Zara Yakob contributed to this by writing several books of theology.

See also: BETA ISRAEL (Vol. I); CHRISTIANITY, INFLUENCE OF (Vol. II).

Zaria (Zazzau)   City in northern Nigeria; founded c. 1000 as one of the original Hausa Bakwai, or Seven True HAUSA STATES. Zaria's function as the southernmost of the seven Hausa CITY-STATES was to kidnap neighboring villagers for sale to the other Hausa states, especially for KANO and KATSINA. Kano was famous for its indigo-dyed CLOTH, which it exported to other cities in Hausaland; Katsina was an important stop on the TRANS-SAHARAN TRADE ROUTES. CARAVANS traveled south to Zaria to exchange much-needed salt for slaves, cloth, grain, and other products. Zaria was converted to ISLAM c. 1456, and Muslim Hausa rulers are recorded in the early sixteenth century. As related by Leo Africanus, the Moroccan traveler who chronicled the history of the SONGHAI Empire, ASKIA MUHAMMAD TOURÉ (d. 1538), the expansionist emperor of Songhai, captured Zaria c. 1512 and made it part of his growing empire.

See also: LEO AFRICANUS (Vol. III); SLAVERY (Vol. II).

Zeila (Seylac, Zayla)   A trading port in present-day northwest Somalia, on the Gulf of Aden. Even prior to the spread of ISLAM in the seventh century, ARAB traders from Baghdad referred to the existence of *Zāylā*, citing it as a lucrative marketplace. The port had grown into a town of significant size with a large Muslim population by the twelfth century. Geographer al-IDRISI described it as an international MARKETPLACE that attracted traders from various parts of the world. Zeila's markets offered GOLD, horses, IVORY, musk, and other rare commodities and manufactured items brought from the interior regions of Ethiopia. Men, women, and children destined for servitude in foreign markets were sold at Zeila as well.

See also: ARAB COASTAL TRADE (Vol. II); SOMALI (Vol. II); RED SEA TRADE (Vol. II) SLAVERY (Vol. II); ZEILA (Vol. III).

Zimbabwe   Plateau region bordered by the present-day countries of ZAMBIA, MOZAMBIQUE, SOUTH AFRICA, and BOTSWANA.

Based on archaeological findings and numerous paintings found within caves and rock shelters, Zimbabwe has one of the oldest established records of human settlement in Africa. The earliest known groups to inhabit the region were the KHOIKHOI, who were primarily hunter-gatherers. They were followed by BANTU-speaking Shona pastoralists who migrated to the area between the second and fifth centuries. Their skills in GOLD mining as well as in IRON smelting and other forms of metalwork were well-established by the fourth century. The Shona, in particular, were noted for their ability to build in dry stone, and the name *Zimbabwe* means "stone building" in the Shona language. The name was chosen for the modern country in memory of the ancestral city of GREAT ZIMBABWE and the culture that ruled an empire based there.

Archaeological evidence, including the ruins of stone cattle *kraals* and other enclosures, suggests that cattle were of primary importance to the Shona. In fact, cattle apparently formed the basis not only for individual wealth but also for early forms of class structure.

By the tenth century, the Shona dominated the region, having pushed the Khoikhoi south into present-day South Africa or, if they remained in Zimbabwe, marginalizing them within outlying areas. As a result, the early success of Zimbabwe was primarily the result of Shona trading networks. TRADE was essential to the growth and development of early Shona states. However, it was the monopoly some states held in the gold and IVORY trade that actually led to the centralization of power. The most powerful Shona states traded with merchants associated with both the SWAHILI COAST kingdoms, along the east coast of Africa, and the INDIAN OCEAN TRADE. The prosperity that resulted led to an unusual hierarchy of wealthy kingdoms and empires, as well as smaller confederated chieftancies.

The first Shona city in the region was MAPUNGUBWE, which archaeologists believe rose c. 1075. From its early days, Mapungubwe exhibited aspects of a class structure that ultimately became an essential feature of Zimbabwe culture. Archaeologists have discovered that the royal palace was built at the top of a hill and that the king lived separate from his people. The wealthy's need for goods may have led to artistic specialization in the production of ceramic POTTERY, cotton CLOTH, and jewelry. (Gold served as the most important status symbol of the empire, and gold artifacts have been recovered from numerous graves of the ruling elite.)

Great Zimbabwe, which includes the Hill Complex, CONICAL TOWER, and Great Enclosure, was perhaps the most notable example of Shona wealth and power. Although there are conflicting reports as to when the city first rose to prominence, it appears that Great Zimbabwe may have been built while Mapungubwe still existed. Regardless, Great Zimbabwe was established by the middle of the thirteenth century. However, by the middle of the fifteenth century, it had been abandoned and was falling into ruins.

See also: CATTLE (Vol. I); PASTORALISM (Vol. I); ROCK ART (Vol. I); SHONA KINGDOMS (Vol. III); ZIMBABWE (Vol. III).

Glossary

agriculturalists Sociological term for "farmers."

alafin Yoruba word for "ruler" or "king."

al-Andalus Muslim Spain.

Allah Arabic for "God" or "Supreme Being."

almamy Religious leader of the Fulani in Fouta Djallon.

amoles Salt, in the form of bars to facilitate trade.

ancestor worship Name incorrectly given to the traditional African reverence for the spirits of those now dead who deserve the recognition and gratitude of the living.

animism Belief that inanimate objects have a soul or life force.

apartheid Afrikaans word that means "separateness"; a system and policy of racial segregation and political and economic discrimination against South Africa's nonwhite majority and formally made into law by the Land Act of 1950.

aphrodesiac Food or other agent thought to arouse or increase sexual desire.

askia Arabic word that means "general"; applied to the Songhai kings. Capitalized, the word refers to a dynasty of Songhai rulers.

ata Igala word for "king."

Australopithicus afarensis Species of Dinkanesh (also known as Lucy), the most famous of the hominid *Australopithicus* specimens found by archaeologists thus far.

Australopithicus africanus *Australopithecus* hominid species that branched off into *Homo habilis* and *A. robustus*.

Australopithicus anamensis Second-oldest species of the hominid *Australopithicus*.

Australopithicus ramadus Oldest of the apelike, hominid species of *Australopithicus*.

Australopithicus robustus A sturdy species of *Australopithicus* that came after *A. africanus* and appears to have been an evolutionary dead end. *Australopithecus robustus* roamed the Earth at the same time as *Homo habilis*.

babalawo Yoruba priest; literally "father of mysteries."

bakwai Hausa word for "state."

bey Provincial governor of the Ottoman Empire.

Bilad al-Sudan Arabic for "Land of the Blacks."

Bosjiemen Dutch for "men of the forest"; the base of the English word *Bushmen*.

bride price The payment made by a groom and his family to compensate the bride's father for the loss of her services because of marriage.

burba jolof Wolof phrase for "king of the Wolof."

caliph Arabic word for "successor"; used as a title for the Muslim political and spiritual leaders who are the successors of the prophet Muhammad.

caliphate Political and religious state that arose after the death of the prophet Muhammad and, in the ninth century, extended from Southwest Asia through North Africa and into Spain.

caravel A small, maneuverable ship used by the Portuguese during the Age of Discovery.

caste A division of society based on wealth, privilege, rank, or occupation.

circumcision The cutting of the clitoris (also called clitorectomy or clitoridectomy) or the prepuce of the penis; a rite of passage in many African societies.

cire perdu French for "lost wax," a technique used to cast metals.

citemene Technique used for burning, clearing, and cultivating land.

clan A group that traces it's descent from a common ancestor.

conquistadores Spanish for "conquerors"; term used to describe the Spanish leaders of the conquest of the Americas during the 1500s.

degredados Portuguese criminals who were sent to Africa by the Portuguese king to perform hazardous duties related to exploration and colonization.

dhow Arabic word for a wooden sailing vessel with a triangular sail that was commonly used to transport trade goods.

dia Songhai word for "king."

divination The interpretation of supernatural signs, usually done by a medicine man or priest.

djembe African drum, often called "the healing drum" because of its use in healing ceremonies.

emir An Islamic ruler or commander.

endogamy Marriage within one's ethnic group, as required by custom or law.

ensete Another name for the "false banana" plant (genus *Ensete*), common in Africa.

ergs Rock-strewn plateaus and sand dunes of the Sahara Desert.

ethnolinguistic Word used to describe a group whose individuals share racial characteristics and a common language.

eunuch A man who has been castrated (had his testicles removed), generally so that he might be trusted to watch over a ruler's wife or wives.

fama Bambara word for "king."

Freeburghers Employees of the Dutch East India Company in South Africa granted the right to farm for profit; later, any Africans of Dutch descent.

fufu A gelatinous food made from cassava that is common in West Africa.

Garamantes Greek name for the Fezzan region.

ghana Soninke word for "king."

griot Storyteller, common in West African cultures, who preserves and relates the oral history of his people, often with musical accompaniment.

hadith Arabic for "sayings"; the name of a book of Muslim wisdom, based on oral traditions.

hajj In Islam, a pilgrimage to Mecca.

hajjiyy "Pilgrim" in Arabic.

hegira Arabic for "flight" or "exodus"; generally used to describe the move of the Muslim prophet Muhammad from Mecca to Medina.

hominid Biological term used to describe the various branches of the Hominidae, the family from which modern humans descend according to evolutionary theory.

Homo erectus Name given to an early hominid species. (*Erectus* is Latin for "upright.")

Homo habilis Name given to one of the early hominid species. (*Habilis* is Latin for "handy.")

Homo sapiens Name given to the most recent species of hominid: human beings. (*Sapiens* is Latin for "wise.")

imam A spiritual and political leader of a Muslim state.

imamate The region or state ruled by an imam.

Janissary From the Turkish for "new soldier," a member of an elite Ottoman military corps.

jebel "Mountain" in Arabic.

jihad Islamic "holy war"; also the daily struggle of Muslims to reform society along Islamic laws.

kabaka The word for "king" in Babito and Buganda cultures.

kahina "Priestess" in Arabic.

kels Tuareg political clan structures.

kemet Egyptian for "black earth."

kintu Mande for "first man."

kora Small percussion instrument played by some griots.

Koran Arabic for "recitation," and the name of the book of Muslim sacred writings.

kraal Enclosure for cattle or a group of houses surrounding such an enclosure.

lineage A group whose individuals trace their descent from a common ancestor; usually a subgroup of a larger clan.

Luso-African Word that describes the combined Portuguese and African cultures, especially the offspring of Portuguese settlers and indigenous African women. (The Latin name for the area of the Iberian Peninsula occupied by modern Portugal was *Lusitania*.)

mahdi Arabic word for "enlightened one," or "righteous leader"; specifically, the Muslim savior who, in Islamic belief, is to arrive shortly before the end of time.

mai Sefuwa for "king."

mamluk   Arabic for "one who is owned"; capitalized: member of an elite military unit made up of captives enslaved and used by Islamic rulers to serve in Middle Eastern and North African armies.

manikongo   Kongo word for "king."

mansa   Mande term for "king" or "emperor."

marabout   A mystical Muslim spiritual leader.

massif   A mountainous geological feature.

mastaba   Arabic for an inscribed stone tomb.

matrilineal   Relating to descent on the maternal, or mother's, side.

medina   Arabic word for the old section of a city.

megaliths   Archaeological term meaning "large rocks"; used to describe stelae and such features as cairns and tumuli that mark important places or events for many ancient cultures.

mestizo   Adjective meaning "of mixed blood."

mfecane   Bantu for "the crushing"; used to refer specifically to the forced migration of South African people during the Zulu campaigns of territorial expansion in the early nineteenth century.

microliths   Archaeological term meaning "small rocks"; used to describe sharpened stone blade tools of Stone Age cultures.

Monophysite   Related to the Christian tradition that holds that Jesus Christ had only one (divine) nature.

Moor   An Arab or Berber conqueror of al-Andalus (Muslim Spain).

mugabe   Bantu word for "king," often the title of the kings of Ugandan societies.

mulatto   The offspring of a Negroid (black) person and a Caucasoid (white) person.

mwami   Head of the Tutsi political structure, believed to be of divine lineage.

negusa negast   "King of kings" in Ethiopic; traditional title given to the ruler of Ethiopia.

Nilotic   Relating to peoples of the Nile, or Nile River basin, used especially to describe the languages spoken by these peoples.

Nsibidi   Secret script of the Ekoi people of Nigeria

nyim   Bantu word for "king" in Bakuba

oba   Yoruba king or chieftain.

olu   The Itsekiri word for "king."

omukama   Bunyoro for "king."

pasha   A high-ranking official in the Ottoman Empire.

pashalik   Territory or province of the Ottoman Empire governed by a pasha.

pastoralists   Sociological term for "herders."

patriarch   Male head of a family, organization, or society.

patrilineal   Relating to descent through the paternal, or father's, side.

polygyny   The practice of having more than one wife or female mate at one time.

prazeros   Portuguese settlers in Africa who held *prazos*.

prazos   Similar to feudal estates, parcels of land in Africa that were leased to Portuguese settlers by the Portuguese king.

primogeniture   A hereditary system common in Africa by which the eldest child, or more commonly, the eldest son, receives all of a family's inheritance.

pygmy   Greek for "fist," a unit of measurement; used to describe the short-statured Mbuti people.

qadi   Arabic for "judge."

ras   A title meaning "regional ruler" in Ethiopia.

ribat   Arabic for "monastery" or "retreat."

rondavel   Small, round homes built by many Bantu people.

salaam   Arabic for "peace."

sarki   Hausa word for "king."

scarification   Symbolic markings made by pricking, scraping, or cutting the skin.

secret society   Formal organizations united by an oath of secrecy and constituted for political or religious purposes.

sharia   Muslim law, which governs the civil and religious behavior of believers.

sharif   In Islamic culture, one of noble ancestry.

sheikh (shaykh, sheik)   Arabic word for patrilineal clan leaders.

sirocco   Name given to a certain type of strong wind in the Sahara Desert.

souk   Arabic word for "market."

stelae   Large stone objects, usually phallus-shaped, whose markings generally contain information important to those who produced them.

stratified Arranged into sharply defined classes.

sultan The king or sovereign of a Muslim state.

sultanate The lands or territory ruled by a sultan.

sunna Arabic word for "the words and deeds of Muhammad."

syncretism The combination of different religious beliefs or practices.

tafsir Arabic for "interpretation," especially as regards the Koran.

taqwa In Islam, the internal ability to determine right from wrong.

taro Another name for the cocoyam, an edible tuber common throughout Africa.

tauf Puddled mud that served as the foundation for some homes in sub-Saharan Africa.

vizier A high-ranking officer of a Muslim state.

Suggested Readings

Abir, Mordechai. *Ethiopia: The Era of the Princes: The Challenge of Islam and the Re-unification of the Christian Empire 1769–1855*. London and Harlow: Longmans, Green and Co., 1968.

Aldred, Cyril. *Egyptian Art*. New York: William Morrow, 1981.

Alpern, Stanley B. *Amazons of Black Sparta: The Women Warriors of Dahomey*. New York: New York University Press, 1999.

Anderson, Martha G., and Mullen Kreamer, Christine. *Wild Spirits, Strong Medicine: African Art and the Wilderness*. New York: Basic Civitas Books, 1999.

Andrews, Carol, ed. *The Ancient Egyptian Book of the Dead*. University of Texas Press: Austin, 1990.

Austen, Ralph A. *Africa in Economic History*. London: James Currey, 1996.

Awolalu, Omosade. *Yoruba Beliefs and Sacrificial Rites*. New York: Longman, 1979.

Ball, David. *Empires of Sand*. New York: Bantam Doubleday Dell, 1999.

Bascomb, William R., and Herskovits, Melville J. *Continuity and Change in African Cultures*. Chicago: University of Chicago Press, 1975.

Bates, Daniel G. *Cultural Anthropology*. New York: Simon & Schuster, 1996.

Baur, John. *2000 Years of Christianity in Africa: An African History, 62–1992*. Nairobi, Kenya: Paulines, 1994.

Berens, Penny, Malherbe, Candy, and Smith, Andy. *The Cape Herders: A History of the Khoikhoi of Southern Africa*. Emile Boonzaier, ed. Athens: Ohio University Press, 1998.

Berger, Iris and White, E. Francis, eds. *Women in Sub-Saharan Africa*. Bloomington: Indiana University Press, 1999.

Beyan, Amos J., Burrowes, Carl Patrick, and Dunn, D. Elwood. *Historical Dictionary of Liberia*. Lanham, Md.: Scarecrow Press, 2000.

Bovill, Edward William. *The Golden Trade of the Moors: West African Kingdoms in the 14th Century*. London: Oxford University Press, 1958.

Brett, Michael, and Fentress, Elizabeth. *The Berbers (The People of Africa)*. Malden, Mass.: Blackwell Publishing, 1997.

Brooks, Miguel F., trans. and ed. *Kebra Nagast* [The Glory of Kings]. Lawrenceville, N.J.: Red Sea Press, 1998.

Browder, Anthony T. *Nile Valley Contributions to Civilization*. Washington, D.C.: Institute of Karmic Guidance, 1992.

Budge, E. A. Wallis. *The Gods of the Egyptians: Studies in Egyptian Mythology*. New York: Dover Publications, 1969.

Burr, Sandra and Potkay, Adam, eds. *Black Atlantic Writers of the Eighteenth Century: Living the New Exodus in England and the Americas: Selections from the Writings of Ukawsaw Gronniosaw, John Marrant, Quobna Ottobah Cuguano, and Olaudah Equiano*. Hampshire, Eng.: Palgrave, 1995.

Butt-Thompson, F. W. *West African Secret Societies*. London: H. F. & G. Witherby, 1929.

Buxton, David. *The Abysinnians*. New York: Praeger Publishers, 1970.

Chauveau, Michel. *Egypt in the Age of Cleopatra*. Ithaca, N.Y.: Cornell University Press, 2000.

Clarke, Peter B. *West Africa and Christianity*. London: E. Arnold, 1986.

Clifford, Mary Louise. *From Slavery to Freetown; Black Loyalists After the American Revolution*. Jefferson, N.C.: McFarland & Company, 1999.

Coquery-Vidrovitch, Catherine. *African Women: A Modern History*. Boulder, Colo.: Westview Press, 1997.

Cugoano, Ottobah. *Thoughts and Sentiments on the Evil of Slavery and Other Writings*. Vincent Caretta, ed. New York: Penguin, 1999.

Curtin, Philip D. *African History*. Reading, Mass.: Addison-Wesley, 1995.

Davidson, Basil. *Africa in History*. New York: Touchstone, 1991.

———. *African Civilization Revisited*. Trenton, New Jersey: Africa World Press, 1998.

Decorse, Christopher R. *An Archaeology of Elmina: Africans and Europeans on the Gold Coast, 1400–1900*. Washington, D.C.: Smithsonian Institution Press, 2001.

Diagram Group, The. *Encyclopedia of African Peoples*. New York: Facts On File, 2000.

Duffy, James. *Portuguese Africa*. Cambridge, Mass.:

Harvard University Press, 1959.

Eades, J. S. *The Yoruba Today*. New York: Cambridge University Press, 1980.

Elleh, Nnamdi. *African Architecture: Evolution and Transformation*. New York: McGraw-Hill, 1996.

Ephirim-Donkor, Anthony. *African Spirituality*. Trenton, N.J.: Africa World Press, 1998.

Equiano, Olaudah. *The Interesting Narrative of the Life of Olaudah Equiano, or Gustavus Vassa the African, Written by Himself*. Werner Sollors, ed. New York: Norton, 2000.

Esposito, John L., ed. *The Oxford History of Islam*. New York, Oxford University Press, 2000.

Fagan, Brian M. *World Prehistory: A Brief Introduction*. 3d ed. New York: HarperCollins, 1996.

Fage, J. D. *A History of Africa*. 3d ed. London: Routledge, 1995.

Fisher, Robert B. *West African Religious Traditions*. Maryknoll, New York: Orbis Books, 1998.

Floyd, Samuel A., Jr. *The Power of Black Music*. New York: Oxford University Press, 1995.

Forester, C. S. *The Barbary Pirates*. Mattituck, New York: Amereon House, 1975).

Frobenius, Leo, and Fox, Douglas C. *African Genesis: Folk Tales and Myths of Africa*. New York: Dover Publications, 1999.

Gailey, Harry A., Jr. *A History of the Gambia*. London: Routledge & Kegan Paul, 1964.

_____. *History of Africa from Earliest Times to 1800*. New York: Holt, Rinehart and Winston, 1970.

Gamble, David P. *The Gambia*. Oxford: Clio Press, 1988.

Gardinier, David E. *Historical Dictionary of Gabon*. Lanham, Md.: Scarecrow Press, 1994.

Garrard, Timothy F. *Akan Weights and the Gold Trade*. London: Longmans, 1980.

Gronniosaw, James Albert Ukawsaw. *A Narrative of the Most Remarkable Particulars in the life of James Albert Ukawsaw Gronniosaw, and African Prince, Written By Himself*. Bath, Eng., 1774.

Grove, A. T. *The Changing Geography of Africa*. New York: Oxford University Press, 1993.

Hackett, Rosalind J. *Art and Religion in Africa*. London: Cassell, 1996.

Hair, P. E. H., Jones, Adam, and Law, Robin, eds. *Barbot on Guinea: The Writings of Jean Barbot on West Africa 1678–1712*. London: The Hakluyt Society, 1992.

Handloff, Robert E., ed. *Côte d'Ivoire: A Country Study*. Washington D.C.: Library of Congress, 1991.

Harrison, Babs Suzanne, Rada, Staefan Eduard, et al. *The Lion in the Moon: Two Against the Sahara*. New York: Rainbow Books, 1994.

Hatch, John. *Tanzania: A Profile*. New York: Praeger, 1972).

Hilton, Anne. *The Kingdom of Kongo*. Oxford: Oxford Studies in African Affairs, 1985.

Hinnells, John R., ed. *The Penguin Dictionary of Religions*. London: The Penguin Group, 1995.

Hiskett, Mervyn. *The Course of Islam in Africa*. Edinburgh: Edinburgh University Press, 1994.

_____ *The Sword of Truth: The Life and Times of the Shehu Usuman dan Fodio*. New York: Oxford University Press, 1973.

Hrbek, I., ed. *Africa from the Seventh Century to the Eleventh Century*. Vol. 3, *General History of Africa*. Abridged ed. Paris: UNESCO, 1992.

Hull, Richard W. *African Cities and Towns before the European Conquest*. New York: Norton, 1976.

Idowu, E. Bolaji. *African Traditional Religions: A Definition*. New York: Orbis Books, 1973.

Ifeka, Caroline, and Stride, G. T. *Peoples and Empires of West Africa*. New York: Africana Publishing Company, 1971.

Isichei, Elizabeth A. *A History of African Societies to 1870*. New York: Cambridge University Press, 1997.

_____. *A History of Christianity in Africa: From Antiquity to the Present*. Lawrenceville, N.J.: Africa World Press,1995.

_____. *A History of Nigeria*. London: Longmans, 1983.

Doresse, Jean. *Ethiopia*. New York: Frederick Ungar Publishing, 1959.

Johnson, Douglas H. *Nuer Prophets*. New York: Oxford University Press, 1994.

Kallen, Stuart. *The Lost Kingdoms of Africa: Black Africa Before 1600*. Edina, Minn.: Abdo & Daughters, 1990.

Kasule, Samuel. *The History Atlas of Africa*. New York: Macmillan, 1998.

Kimambo, I. N., and Temu, A. J. *A History of Tanzania*. Nairobi: East African Publishing House, 1969.

Ki-Zerbo, J. *Methodology and African Prehistory*. Vol. 1, *General History of Africa*. Abridged ed. Paris: UNESCO, 1990.

Ki-Zerbo, J., and Niane, D. T., eds. *Africa from the 12th to the 16th Century*. Vol 4, *General History of Africa*. Paris: UNESCO, 1997.

Kopytoff, Igor and Miers, Suzanne, eds. *Slavery in Africa: Historical and Anthropological Perspectives*. Madison: University of Wisconsin Press, 1977.

Kuper, Hilda and Kuper, Leo, eds. *African Law: Adaptation and Development*. Berkeley: University of California Press, 1965.

Kurtz, Laura S. *Historical Dictionary of Tanzania*. Lanham, Md.: Scarecrow Press, 1978.

Kusimba, Chapurukha M. *The Rise and Fall of the Swahili States*. Walnut Creek, Calif.: Altamira Press, 1999.

Laderman, Carol, and Roseman, Marina, eds. *The Performance of Healing*. New York: Routledge, 1996.

Law, Robin. *The Oyo Empire 1600–1836 A West African Imperialism in the Era of the Atlantic Slave Trade*. Oxford: Clarendon Press, 1977.

Levine, Donald N. *Wax and Gold: Tradition and Innovation*

in Ethiopian Culture. Chicago: University of Chicago Press, 1965).

Levtzion, Nehemia. *Ancient Ghana and Mali.* New York: Holmes and Meier Publishing, 1973.

Levtzion, Nehemia and Randall L. Pouwels, eds., *The History of Islam in Africa.* Athens: Ohio University Press, 2000.

Loth, Heinrich. *Women in Ancient Africa.* Trans., Sheila Marnie. Westport, Conn.: Lawrence Hill, 1987.

Mansour, H. Mansour. *The Maliki School of Law: Spread and Domination in North and West Africa 8th to 14th Centuries, C.E.* Bethesda, Md.: Austin and Winfield Publishers, 1994.

Marcus, Harold G. *A History of Ethiopia.* Berkeley: University of California Press, 1994.

Mazrui, Ali A. *The Africans: A Triple Heritage.* London: BBC Publications, 1986.

Mbiti, John. *African Religions and Philosophy.* 2d ed. Oxford: Heinemann Educational Publishers, 1990.

McCarthy, Justin. *The Ottoman Turks: An Introductory History to 1923.* New York: Longman, 1997.

McIntosh, Susan Keech. *Excavations at Jenne-Jeno, Hambarkatolo, and Kanianga: The 1981 Season.* Berkeley: University of California Press, 1995.

Meyer, Laurie. *Art and Craft in Africa.* Paris: Terrail, 1995.

Middleton, John. *The World of the Swahili.* New Haven, Conn.: Yale University Press, 1992.

_____, ed. *Encyclopedia of Africa South of the Sahara.* New Haven, Conn.: Yale University Press, 1998.

Miers, Suzanne, and Kopytoff, Igor, eds. *Slavery in Africa: Historical and Anthropological Perspectives.* Madison: University of Wisconsin Press, 1977.

Mokhtar, G., ed. *Ancient Civilizations of Africa.* Vol. 2, *General History of Africa.* Paris: UNESCO, 1990.

Morell, Virginia. *Ancestral Passions: The Leakey Family and the Quest for Humankind's Beginnings.* New York: Touchstone Books, 1996.

Murray, Jocelyn, ed. *Cultural Atlas of Africa.* New York: Checkmark Books, 1998.

Newman, James L. *The Peopling of Africa: A Geographic Interpretation.* New Haven, Conn.: Yale University Press, 1995.

Noote, Mary H. *Secrecy: African Art that Conceals and Reveals.* New York: Museum for African Art, 1993.

Nurse, Derek, and Heine, Bernd. *African Languages: An Introduction.* New York: Cambridge University Press, 2000.

Ofcansky, Thomas P. *Uganda: Tarnished Pearl of Africa.* New York: Westview Books, 1996).

Ojo, G. J. Afolabi. *Yoruba Culture: A Geographical Analysis.* London: University of London Press, 1966.

Oliver, Roland, and Fagan, Brian. *Africa in the Iron Age.* New York: Cambridge University Press, 1994.

Page, Willie F. *The Dutch Triangle: The Netherlands and the Atlantic Slave Trade, 1621–1664.* New York: Garland Publishing, 1997.

Pankhurst, Richard. *History of Ethiopian Towns from the Middle Ages to the Early Nineteenth Century.* Philadelphia: Coronet Books, 1985.

_____. *The Ethiopian Borderlands.* Lawrenceville, N. J.: The Red Sea Press; 1997.

Park, Mungo. *Travels in the Interior Districts of Africa.* Kate Ferguson Marsters, ed. Durham, N. C.: Duke University Press, 2000.

Parry, J. H. *The Age of Reconnaisance.* Berkeley: University of California Press, 1982.

Pazzanita, Anthony G. and Hodges, Tony. *Historical Dictionary of Western Sahara.* New York: Scarecrow Press, 1994.

Pearson, Michael N. *Port Cities and Intruders: The Swahili Coast, India, and Portugal in the Early Modern Era.* Baltimore, Md.: Johns Hopkins University Press, 1999.

Peters, F. E. *The Hajj.* Princeton, N. J.: Princeton University Press, 1994.

Quarcoopome, T.N.O. *West African Traditional Religion.* Ibadan: African Universities Press, 1987.

Quataert, Donald *The Ottoman Empire, 1700–1922.* Cambridge, Eng.: Cambridge University Press, 2000.

Ray, Benjamin C. *African Religions: Symbol, Ritual, and Community,* 2d ed. Upper Saddle River, N.J.: Prentice Hall, 2000.

Robins, Gay. *Women In Ancient Egypt.* Cambridge, Mass.: Harvard University Press, 1993.

Scarr, Deryck. *Slaving and Slavery in the Indian Ocean.* Hampshire, Eng.: Palgrave, 1998).

Schoffeleers, J. Matthew. *River of Blood: The Genesis of a Martyr Cult in Southern Malawi, c. A.D. 1600.* Madison: University of Wisconsin Press, 1992.

Schraeder, Peter J. *African Politics and Society: A Mosaic in Transformation.* New York: St. Martin's Press, 1999.

Seeskin, Kenneth. *Searching for a Distant God: the Legacy of Maimonides.* New York: Oxford University Press, 2000.

Sheehan, Patricia. *Cultures of the World: Côte d'Ivoire.* Malaysia: Times Media Private Limited, 2000.

Sherman, Richard. *Eritrea: The Unfinished Revolution.* New York: Praeger Publishers, 1980.

Shillington, Kevin. *History of Africa.* New York: St. Martins Press, 1995.

Shorter, Aylward. *Chiefship in Western Tanzania.* Oxford: Clarendon Press, 1972.

Smith, Anthony. *The Great Rift: Africa's Changing Valley.* London: BBC Books, 1988.

Snowden, Frank M., Jr. *Blacks in Antiquity.* Cambridge, Mass.: Belknap, 1970.

St. John, Ronald B. *Historical Dictionary of Libya.* Lanham, Md.: Scarecrow Press, 1998.

Steindorff, George and Seele, Keith C. *When Egypt Ruled the East.* Rev. ed. Chicago: University of Chicago

Press, 1957.

Sugar, H. *Côte d'Ivoire*. Santa Barbara, Calif.: ABC Clio, 1996.

Swantz, Lloyd W. *The Zaramo of Tanzania*. Dar es Salaam: Nordic Tanganyika Project, 1965.

Thogbani, Akbarall. *Mansa Musa: The Golden King of Mali*. Dubuque, Iowa: Kendall/Hunt Publishing, 1998.

Thomas-Emeagwali, Gloria, ed. *Science and Technology in African History with Case Studies from Nigeria, Sierra Leone, Zimbabwe and Zambia*. Lewiston, N.Y.: The Edwin Mellen Press, 1992.

Thompson, Robert Farris. *Flash of the Spirit: African and Afro-American Art and Philosophy*. New York: Random House, 1984.

Van Sertima, Ivan. *They Came Before Columbus: The African Presence in Ancient America*. New York: Random House, 1976.

_____, ed. *Blacks in Science: Ancient and Modern*. New Brunswick, N.J.: Transaction Publishers, 1983.

_____, ed. *Black Women in Antiquity*. New Brunswick, N.J.: Transaction Publishers, 1997.

Vansina, Jan. *Art History in Africa: An Introduction to Method*. New York: Longman, 1984.

Watterson, Barbara. *The Egyptians*. Oxford: Blackwell Publishers, 1998.

Wheatly, Phillis. *Complete Writings*. Vincent Carretta, ed. New York: Penguin, 2001.

Wrigley, Christopher. *Kingship and State: The Buganda Dynasty*. New York: Cambridge University Press, 1996.

Wyatt, Thomas, ed. *The Koran*. Dawood, N.J., trans. New York: Penguin, 1990.

Zaslavsky, Claudia. *Africa Counts: Number and Pattern in African Cultures*, 3d ed. Chicago: Lawrence Hill Books, 1999.

Index

Italic page numbers indicate main entries. Page numbers followed by the letter *f* refer to illustrations; the letter *m* indicates a map; and the letter *t* indicates a table.